1000 CEOs

EDITOR-IN-CHIEF ANDREW DAVIDSON

BUSINESS EDITOR MARJAN BOLMEIJER

INTRODUCTION BY MARSHALL GOLDSMITH

Contents

London, New York,
Munich, Melbourne, and Delhi

First American Edition, 2009
Published in the United States by
DK Publishing, 375 Hudson Street
New York, New York 10014

09 10 11 12 13   10 9 8 7 6 5 4 3 2 1

Published in Great Britain by Dorling Kindersley Ltd.

A catalog record for this book is available from the
Library of Congress.
ISBN 978-0-7566-4170-2

Printed and bound in China by Sheck Wah Tong.

Discover more at
www.dk.com

Andrew Davidson

This book has two aims. Drawing on input from every continent on the globe, we chart the rise to success of the world's most influential business leaders, as well as bosses of charity, arts, and health bodies. And we present their stories in a form that enables readers to draw practical lessons from the narrative of their success—less about theory, and more about the hands-on examples of what it takes to make the tough decisions. Hence our tagline: "Proven Strategies for Success".

Here you'll find it all: rags to riches, rescues, luck, pluck, bloodbaths, feuds, and sheer hard endeavor. The structure is simple: a mix of long and short profiles, analyzing each individual's success and style, set against the sector in which they have excelled, grouped by vital characteristics. The writing aims to be sharp and succinct, and not afraid to criticize when criticism is called for. Key points are broken out, take-away lessons are highlighted. And the profiles are supplemented by a mix of pithy features by different authors, expanding out on the various topics raised.

So how did we choose the names for inclusion? We used a range of measures: size of company or organization; scale of reputation and renown; recommendations from academics and journalists; power-lists produced by media around the world; and more. Most choices are backed by straight data, such as gross revenue or stock market value. Some are pure instinct. We stuck to leaders—no regional heads, no consultants—and broadened the search to include those who are CEO in everything except job title. We made sure our reach was wide enough to gather in many who had excelled outside the business sector, running not-for-profit bodies that can have greater impact than some of the biggest, globalized firms. And we added "iconic" bosses who have long left their posts, including Henry Ford, Walt Disney, Alfred P. Sloan, Jack Welch, and Estée Lauder. They are chosen because of the profound influence they made on the way we structure and run modern organizations today, and the lessons they still have to teach us. And we produced all this in the teeth of the worst global downturn for half a century, so our list has constantly shifted. The effects of the credit crunch, and personal scandal, have already knocked a few big names out of the running. It also tightened the focus on what it takes to build a business that has long-term strength.

The upshot is a book quite unlike any that has been produced before. Here you will find the new corporate elite emerging from China side by side with the wily leviathans of North America; the Russian oligarchs striding out of the East to contrast with the growing strength of Central and South American business; European bosses facing down ever-larger Asian rivals; African vigor competing with Australian resilience. We hope you will find it encyclopedic in its scope, and invaluable as both a work of reference and a how-to guide. And yes, we expect to update it as top names change and new contenders come to the fore.

As I write, the current downturn seems, if anything, to have cemented many business leaders to their posts, with company boards preferring to stick with experience over youthful exuberance. But as the economic situation shifts, that will change. So this is just the start: 1000 CEOs will evolve, a work in progress, but with vital lessons to communicate. Never dull, never "worthy" and always useful —we hope you enjoy reading it, and practicing what it teaches.

Andrew Davidson
Editor-in-chief

Marshall Goldsmith

For three decades I have had the privilege of working with more than 100 CEOs and their management teams. One of the most important lessons I've learned from these CEOs is that business is more than strategy, competency, and return on investment. A large part is about the "soft" issues like relationships, personal growth, and (yes, I'll say it) feelings! Henry Ford may have put it best when he said, "A business that makes nothing but money is a poor business." I would venture to add that a CEO who improves only the bottom line is a poor CEO.

CEOs, perhaps more than any other occupational group, become synonymous with their jobs. They "become the company". Who can think of Apple without thinking of Steve Jobs; Microsoft without thinking of Bill Gates; or Virgin without thinking of Richard Branson? After a while, the job of CEO becomes not just what these CEOs do, it defines to a large extent who they are. This job is far more than the bottom line. It is personal! CEOs, just like the rest of us, are real people. They are human beings with

real stories behind their successes, and their failures. *1000 CEOs* tells the stories of some of these great CEOs, what got them where they are, the critical decisions they made along the way and why. Of personal interest to me is the behavioral side of leadership. In other words, how CEOs guide their organizations with their personalities, their strengths and talents, and even their weaknesses.

Almost everyone I meet, including all the CEOs, is successful because of doing a lot of things right, and in spite of doing some things that aren't. One of the greatest challenges I face in working with successful people is helping them see the difference between "because of" behaviors and "in spite of" behaviors. What I've found, time and again, is that those people who do finally realize the difference, those individuals who recognize and grow past their bad habits, are the leaders who reach the greatest success both personally and professionally. For example, years ago, I coached a man who burned through people and their feelings like wildfire. As CFO, he had led the organization to the very peak of financial success, and still he was about to be fired. The firm's leaders, who had promoted him to board status because of his great success, finally had a chance to bear witness to his horrible behavior. They, like the rest of the organization, were suddenly in a position to feel firsthand the wrath of "Joe". They brought me in and the first thing I told him was, "You're already making millions a year. I can't help you make more money. But, let's talk about your ego. How do you treat people at home?" He attempted to tell me he was sweet and loving at home. I called his wife! She laughed when I told her how Joe thought he was at home. His kids' response was similar. Joe had a wake-up call with that little phone interaction. Not only had his board hired a coach to help him to change; his family also wanted him to change.

Joe decided then and there to change. The reason he decided this wasn't for money; it had nothing to do with the company. It had to do with his sons. He wanted to change because in twenty years, if his sons received similar feedback, he would be ashamed. Within a year, he was treating people much better. Follow-up feedback had him up past the 50th percentile! He successfully changed his behavior. The moral of the story? Anybody can change, but they have to want to change. Great CEOs want to change. They want to learn, grow, and develop, and they want those they lead to do the same. Being a successful CEO is as much about learning as it is about talent and luck—probably more.

In following the path to executive success, aspiring entrepreneurs, managers, and executives alike can learn much from the example of each of the CEOs included in this book. Learn from the lessons identified here and apply them to your own life and career. Like the great CEOs included in this work, you too must keep growing!

Life is good.

Marshall

What It Takes to Be a CEO

Marjan Bolmeijer

Those that aspire to reach the highest echelons of corporate office need to be able to endure immense pressures; not everyone is cut out for the job and not everyone wants to be the boss. For those who believe they have got what it takes, it is possible to prepare for the top job and to acquire many of the skills, personal traits, experiences, and leadership styles needed to excel.

Inevitably, any list of the most important attributes and competencies will depend on numerous variables such as timing, local cultural characteristics, a company's circumstances, and your own position, background, and development. But, while bearing this in mind, here are a few things every CEO needs to think about.

Get your senior team right

CEOs must understand the need and have the skills to work on their senior team. They must not take the attitude that their team is what it is, and cannot be improved upon; nor must they work on the team and then be too easily satisfied by a small amount of improvement. Failing to work on the senior team often means that the CEO is left with a team that is far less efficient or productive than it could be: they may compete against each other; rarely agree with all the elements of the strategic direction or plan; or be great at championing change but bad at changing themselves.

These issues make it much more difficult to get things done. So it makes sense to take the time to focus on getting the senior team dynamic right, whether through training, internal resource allocation, replacements, or managing politics. There are a lot of criteria that feed into the functional dynamic of the senior team and CEOs need to be sensitive to them all. It is tough but it is worth it, as research suggests that a team that works well together, no matter how diverse its make-up, has a beneficial effect on operational performance.

Find failure fast

Look around the organization, find out what is not working, and root out the activities and people likely to have a negative impact on the firm going forward; an economic downturn is a particularly opportune time to do this. There should be zero tolerance of failure. But while CEOs hone their failure-detection skills during a recession, when the good times return it is easy to allow those skills and instincts to grow rusty. It's like a muscle: if you don't keep training it during the good times, it will fail you when you need it most. So CEOs need to put in place processes to spot failure early, and pay attention to those most attuned to the early signals. Get this wrong and it can easily lead to "failure blindness" and a fatal delay to take corrective action.

Align the brands of CEO, senior team, and company

When it comes to conveying the CEO's message, both internally to a company audience and externally to the wider world, it helps to have alignment between the image of the CEO, the leadership brand of the senior team, and the company's leadership strategy.

First there is the persona of the CEO. The way you execute the job is to some extent influenced by who you are. Whether introvert or extrovert, geek or Renaissance scholar, your personality in part sets the stage for how the company is run. Secondly, there is the brand, or image, of the senior team. For example, the senior team might be perceived internally and in the press as being made up of creative, highly intellectual leaders with a global perspective. Or they may be regarded as overpaid deadweights. Once the CEO's personal brand and the brand of the senior team are aligned, you must align these brands with the company's overall leadership strategy.

Look at the organization and determine what leadership approach it needs. There are five basic approaches: Strategic, Change, People, Expert, and Systems. For example, if the company requires a strong "People" leadership strategy —that is, improving operational results through human resource, training, recruitment procedures, and global team-building—but the CEO is perceived as an introvert finance expert, and the senior team as strong strategic leaders, then you have a brand alignment problem.

Manage global emotions

During the global economic downturn, it became even more apparent that managing global emotions, and getting the senior team and PR people to accept this as part of their role and necessary skills, is a major part of a CEO's responsibility. One result of the financial crisis was that fear became endemic within organizations right around the globe. It paralyzed organizational decision-making processes and negatively impacted on performance.

The CEO's role is to articulate what the future will hold. As a leader, he or she needs to be in the right place emotionally, so that the employees in the organization can take their emotional cue from the CEO. Without this cue it will take the senior team much longer to escape from the reigning emotion of the time, and this will allow the emotion to dominate the organization's actions.

To provide the right cue, the CEO must be sensitive to what the appropriate emotional response might be, depending on what the market and organizational circumstances demand. This may not always be fear; it might equally be confidence when times are good.

Communicate

Any top PR guru will tell a CEO to spend a minimum of ten percent of his or her time on communications, both external and internal. For many *Fortune* 500 CEOs the percentage is higher. Communication topics combine to make up your "Reputation Quotient": social responsibility; products and services; positioning; vision and leadership; financial performance; workplace environment; emotional appeal; and so on. Many CEOs think they just don't have the time for good communication. Yet the CEO is a kind of human billboard for the company and communication is a cornerstone of their responsibilities. During difficult times, especially, you can't communicate enough. Communication can help with many of the intangibles, such as alignment with senior management: once the message has been put out externally it becomes "real", and this can greatly reduce internal bickering and firm up people's commitment to the strategy. And when it comes to public speaking, here is a tip: always focus as much on the feeling you want to leave your audience with at the end of your speech, as on the content.

Get involved in talent management

Even in a downturn, the struggle for talent does not disappear. Talent management includes elements such as CEOs participating in the interviews of their chief lieutenants, CEO succession planning, and succession planning for the company as a whole. The CEO succession context has a significant influence on post-succession company performance. Also there is plenty of research to suggest that board and CEO participation in the succession process of top lieutenants greatly affects the outcome, producing better results than, say, hiring a golf buddy, and filtering through to affect the way other processes are scrutinized. After a CEO succession there can either be a lot or very little senior executive turnover. The rate of turnover is a strong indication of the senior team dynamics, the presence of personal favourites, and the adequacy of processes intended to contain the loss of people. Getting it right is the way to ensure a positive CEO legacy.

Stock up on your emotional intelligence

"Emotional Intelligence" (EI) is a combination of personal and social competencies. Personal competencies determine how we manage ourselves and include self-awareness, accurate self-assessment, self-confidence, self-regulation, self-control, motivation, and commitment. Social competencies like empathy, developing others, political awareness, influence, and conflict management, determine how we manage relationships. Working on EI topics is rarely fun for a CEO. Few CEOs really enjoy reflecting on and making changes to themselves. It's more natural for them to focus on something they are good at and that the company wants them to create time for. Yet working on your EI is always a prerequisite for success. You can be successful with a limited amount of EI, but only for so long; it is essential for sustained success, especially under pressure. When companies change, when the economy changes, when the world changes, when somebody's life changes, they need a lot of emotional flexibility, endurance, and adaptability, and that is why mastering the wider range of these skills ahead of time proves so useful.

Avoid the self-destruct button

Perhaps the most important skill of all is not to self-destruct. Self-destruction is a highly individualized concept; for each CEO the trigger or route is different. For some the route is the loss of positional or social power, for others it is net worth. A great degree of self-awareness is required to recognize where the trigger lies. Some people have a high threshold for pain; senior executives are used to disregarding emotional, physical, personal, and intellectual needs in order to get the job done and get their careers moving forward. Many work seven days a week with complete disregard for sleep, food, and many other basic needs that most people require to live a normal life. It should

be no surprise, therefore, that CEOs can develop a skewed view of the world. Consequently, they may fail to realize when they are pushing the boundaries too far, through lack of sleep or an excessive drive for profits, or any number of other critical issues. They must learn to pay attention to the warning signs. Vigilance is key.

This is not intended to be an exhaustive list by any means, merely an insight into those areas that, in 15 years of working with CEOs in companies of all sizes, industries, and cultures, have proved to be of particular importance. Perhaps, if there is one thing that the very best CEOs demonstrate above all, it is a willingness and a desire to learn how to be better than they already are. That is something we can all aspire to.

Marjan Bolmeijer
Business editor

1

The Innovators

William McKnight President & Chairman (1949–66), 3M

THE MINNESOTA Mining and Manufacturing Company was a struggling young enterprise on the verge of bankruptcy when McKnight became general manager in 1914. By the time he retired as chairman in 1966, 3M was a vast conglomerate with operations all over the world and products that were familiar household names to hundreds of millions of consumers. At the heart of this growth was McKnight's talent for encouraging innovation, the influence of which can be seen in modern management practice.

BIOGRAPHY
1887–1978. Born in White, South Dakota. His parents owned a farm claimed under the Homestead Act, which encouraged the settlement of undeveloped land. He attended Duluth Business University in Minnesota.

LEADERSHIP STYLE
Softly spoken but also direct and efficient. McKnight provided strong encouragement and motivation to his employees through his delegating style.

KEY STRENGTH
Giving his people free rein to develop their creativity.

BEST DECISION
Setting up a small laboratory in 1916, ensuring that 3M's future was guided by science.

THE EDGE OF BANKRUPTCY McKnight joined the business that later became known as 3M as an assistant bookkeeper in 1907, when the company, founded only five years earlier, was struggling to recover from a series of initial blunders that nearly sank it. These errors, including misidentifying a crucial mineral deposit, looked likely to make the enterprise a short-lived one, but McKnight's ability turned 3M around and put it on the path to growth.

FREEDOM TO INNOVATE McKnight quickly recognized that making mistakes was an intrinsic part of innovation and that innovation was the key to success. Putting this insight into practice, he made research the heart of 3M's activities, establishing a laboratory. The research and development approach created breakthrough product

after breakthrough product, many of which have remained in use ever since, among them waterproof sandpaper, masking tape, cellophane tape, Scotchgard, reflective sheets for highway markings, and Post-It Notes. McKnight also understood that invention required a looser approach to management that allowed people to follow their ideas through. That meant delegating and allowing employees a far greater degree of autonomy than was standard at the time. He allowed his engineers to spend 15 percent of their time on projects of their own, stimulating creativity. McKnight formulated a series of pioneering management principles based around the importance of delegation and the idea that, although mistakes will be made, they will be less damaging than the mistakes management will make in telling everyone what to do.

LESSONS IN BUSINESS: ENCOURAGING AUTONOMY

Rather than treating them as tools to transmit your directions, trust your people and give them the room to exercise their creativity, even if it means they make mistakes that you could have avoided.

→ Record successes and mistakes and make this information accessible to everyone. That way the organization learns from its mistakes.

→ Encourage people to look at potential risks, estimating the impact and probability of the risk occurring.

→ People are your greatest asset. Make sure that how you look after your people is consistent with your words.

> "If you put fences around people, you get sheep." William McKnight

Steve Jobs Co-founder, Chairman & CEO, Apple

THE ARCHETYPAL business maverick, Jobs is the face of Apple, the creative force behind its success, and a formidable team builder. He is chairman, CEO, and co-founder (with Steve Wozniak in 1976) of the company, founder of Pixar animation studio, and, since Pixar's sale to Disney, Disney's largest individual shareholder with an important foothold in Hollywood. Jobs can claim joint authorship of three of the most significant technologies of the past three decades: the personal computer, the Graphical User Interface, and digital music.

BIOGRAPHY
Born in 1955 in San Francisco, Jobs is the adopted son of Paul and Clara Jobs. His biological parents were Joanne Carole Schieble and Abdulfattah Jandali, the latter a graduate student from Syria who became a political science professor. Jobs failed to graduate from his literature, poetry, and physics course at Oregon's Reed College.

LEADERSHIP STYLE
Visionary, creative, and entrepreneurial. Some say an autocratic micro-manager. He can be charming and engaging, but some have complained about his indelicate language.

KEY STRENGTH
He has an instinctive understanding not only of where technology is going but also what makes people want to buy it.

BEST DECISION
Developing both the software and hardware elements in the iPod/iTunes combination.

HIRING AND FIRING UP One of the keys to Jobs' enduring success has been his skill in hiring the best team and firing them up. As a young Apple chairman Jobs boldly stole the then-president of PepsiCo, John Sculley, to be his chief executive. Yet Jobs' autocratic style has also caused him problems. Fed up with his unwillingness to be a team player, in 1985 the other Apple directors kicked him out. Aged 30, Jobs was out of a job.

AN i FOR THE FUTURE Using the proceeds from the sale of his Apple stocks, Jobs soon broadened the scope of his business interests with an adroit acquisition, purchasing the computer graphics division of Lucasfilms (later Pixar) which gave him a key future foothold in entertainment content. He returned to lead an ailing Apple in 1997. In the next decade the company's share price rose 36-fold, thanks largely to the success of the iPod and iTunes. From the iPhone to MacBook Air, Apple products ooze desirability and continue to define geek chic. Colleagues describe Jobs as brilliant and a great motivator, but he pushes his team to their limits, and some employees have quit shortly after finishing a product. Jobs' vision and relentless eye for detail have given Apple the kind of brand power other CEOs dream of. He has an unerring ability to create instantly desirable, "must-have" products. He starts by asking his team "what do we want?" rather than "what can we produce?". Hardware and software are then invented to produce the dream. Products that fail to excite Jobs himself are dropped or started again from scratch. Apple's strategy focuses on very few products, but these few have become irresistible bestsellers.

LESSONS IN BUSINESS: ROUTINIZING CHARISMA

Jobs' drive, passion, and creative imagination permeate the work environment at Apple, and allow him to devolve work to his team. His biographer Leander Kahney has called this phenomenon the "routinization" of charisma. Think of it as branding the team with your own values.
- → Brand yourself within—and outside of—the company, and articulate your value to others.
- → Do what you love, and integrate your passions with your job tasks.
- → Identify supporters and create a network of relationships that support your personal brand.

"Steve understands desire."
Alan Kay, GUI pioneer and former fellow, Apple Advanced Technology Group

Francisco González Rodríguez CEO, BBVA

FORMER COMPUTER programmer and stockbroker González is now a leading figure in Spanish banking. Between 1996 and 1999, he was head of the Argentaria group, where he led the successful privatization of the formerly government-owned group. As CEO of the newly merged Banco Bilbao Vizcaya Argentaria (BBVA), González stabilized the troubled company, brought in transparency and ethical standards, embraced new technology, and expanded into Latin America. BBVA is now one of the largest banking groups in Spain.

BIOGRAPHY
Born in Chantada, Spain, in 1944. González obtained a degree in economics from Madrid's Complutense University.

LEADERSHIP STYLE
Austere, technologically savvy, and a workaholic, González believes in delegating.

KEY STRENGTH
Integrity. Without it, González would have been hard pressed to withstand the BBVA's banking scandal in 2000.

BEST DECISION
Expanding into Latin America, giving BBVA a total of more than 28 million customers and a foothold in the lucrative US Hispanic market.

FROM COMPUTING TO BANKING González first worked in computing, but left for a career in stockbroking. He started his own company, FG Inversiones Bursátiles, in the late 1980s, building it into one of Spain's largest independent brokerages. In 1996, he sold it to Merrill Lynch for $30 million and moved into banking, as chairman of Argentaria, a company in its final privatization phase, and it was González's job to get it into shape before the sale took place. He restructured management, cut jobs, refinanced assets, and the group was privatized in 1999.

RESTORING CONFIDENCE After the 1999 merger of Argentaria with Banco Bilbao Vizcaya, González became co-CEO of BBVA. Within a year, he faced one of the biggest crises of his career, when details of BBV's illicit activities, including money laundering, slush funds, and bribery, came to light. González was not implicated, but he was left to deal with one of Europe's biggest scandals, which he did swiftly, closing secret accounts, paying taxes on the funds, and reporting all financial dealings to the Bank of Spain. Co-CEO Emilio Ybarra was among many executives forced to resign, and González was left in charge. To restore public confidence, González overhauled the group's governance, appointing newcomers to the board based on expertise rather than personal friendships. He led BBVA's expansion in Latin America, and the franchise today has operations in 15 countries. In 2004, González took the bank into the US with the aim of wooing the Hispanic market, a shrewd diversification which has helped shield it through the financial crisis, by curbing exposure to the sub-prime debacle, and allowing the company to grow in relative safety.

LESSONS IN BUSINESS: TAKING ADVANTAGE OF NEW TECHNOLOGY

González built on his experience in the computer industry to introduce new services in banking based on the latest technology. He saw the internet, electronic payment systems, and mobile phones as a means to cut costs and free up time, improving the efficiency of the bank.

→ Use new technology to increase efficiency and to enhance knowledge of your customers.
→ Don't be put off by new technology—what's daunting now will, in a very short time, be commonplace.
→ Innovative technology is not optional. Your business rivals will be adopting it, so don't get left behind.

"The thing is having a good team. I don't believe in the chairman having to do everything. I prefer people to think for themselves." Francisco González Rodríguez

Jamie Cooper-Hohn President & CEO, CIFF

USING FUNDS generated by her husband Chris Hohn's highly successful hedge-fund business, Cooper-Hohn has created a new type of charitable institution, the Children's Investment Fund Foundation (CIFF). The foundation brings the cold but effective principles of investment to the pressing issue of children's welfare in developing countries. Cooper-Hohn's vision for a fund that approaches its activities with the same eye for a return as the shrewdest investor is proving to be both effective on the ground, and appealing to donors.

BIOGRAPHY
Born in the US in 1965 and brought up in Chicago, the daughter of an engineer and an academic. Cooper-Hohn received a bachelor's degree from Smith College, Massachusetts, and a master's in public administration from the John F. Kennedy School of Government at Harvard.

LEADERSHIP STYLE
Rigorous and meticulous, Cooper-Hohn brings the precise approach of finance to the sometimes-woolly charity sector.

KEY STRENGTH
The ability to make effective connections between first world profits and third world poverty, building a bridge between high ideals and the bottom line.

BEST DECISION
Linking profitable business with charity in the basic structure of an operation, creating a template for "venture philanthropy."

STUDENT LINK Cooper-Hohn's involvement in charity work while at Harvard introduced her to her future husband, who became concerned at the plight of children in the developing world during a stint in the Philippines. After marrying, Hohn worked in th e hedge fund industry while Cooper-Hohn worked as a fundraiser for a children's foundation. After Chris's career moved to London, they began planning an original foundation of their own.

COMMERCIAL CHARITY Convinced of the benefits of marrying commercial finance and the needs of charity, Cooper-Hohn and her husband set up a hedge fund named TCI, The Children's Investment, in 2002. All management fees and Hohn's profits went to charitable foundation the Children's Investment Fund Foundation (CIFF). Hohn's impressive track record appealed to investors, and soon the business was up and running, reaching a fund value of well over £1 billion. While her husband was largely responsible for running the business that provides the bulk of the investment, Cooper-Hohn set about building a new model of charitable giving. Just as with financial investment, donor projects were selected on the basis of the "return"—measured by the impact they have on the lives of children—that they offered on the investment made. Intensive investigation was required to find the most effective projects, and a private-equity strategy was adopted, using a portfolio manager to monitor each project and ensure it continued to provide the best possible results, when compared with other potential targets. This approach has proven so effective that it could point the way for charitable giving in future.

LESSONS IN BUSINESS: BORROWING MODELS FROM OTHER SECTORS

What works in one area may work just as well in another where it's never been considered before. Cooper-Hohn successfully linked the worlds of charity and hard finance by using the same techniques and skills.

→ Remember that research is the key to creating sound opportunities when raising money, whether for the charity sector or for commerce.

→ Never ignore a formula that has worked before. Imitation can save time and money in innovation.

→ Look at any institution for new stategies: the skill of a CEO is to marry two acts together to derive an insight.

"The marriage of business and philanthropy that is at the heart of [CIFF] provides a great tool to effect serious change in the developing world." Bill Clinton

John T. Chambers Chairman & CEO, Cisco Systems

A SUPERB SALESMAN who has put Cisco networking equipment at the heart of the internet, Chambers has turned the firm into an IT giant. So central is Cisco Systems' technology to the internet, he can justifiably be considered one of the most significant figures in the evolution of the new medium. Chambers has demonstrated a rare understanding of the management of corporate acquisitions, acquiring network specialists StrataCom and Cerent among others, and enabling Cisco to weather the bursting of the dotcom bubble.

BIOGRAPHY
Born in Cleveland, Ohio, in 1949. He holds a bachelor's degree in business studies and a law degree from West Virginia University, and an MBA from Indiana University.

LEADERSHIP STYLE
Collegiate. In an industry famous for mavericks who lead by sheer force of vision or personality, Chambers is that great rarity, a relatively hands-off manager. He sets the strategy but lets his people achieve it.

KEY STRENGTH
Hanging on to top creative talent, often difficult people to manage.

BEST DECISION
Sharing investors' pain after the dotcom crash of 2000. Chambers' decision to take a nominal $1 salary while he set about rebuilding the firm not only kept him his job, it also kept shareholders on board.

TECHNOLOGY LEADER Chambers became CEO of Cisco in 1995, after 20 years in IT sales for IBM and Wang Labs. A natural communicator, he soon made his name as an enthusiast who believed the net would change the way the world works, lives, plays, and learns. He made sure that Cisco took a leading role in making that happen, buying up firms like StrataCom and Cerent in order to build a dominant footprint in the online infrastructure market. Chambers also attracted top people to the company and proved himself a natural manager, as interested in people as technology. By the turn of the millennium, Cisco was the most valuable company in the world, with a market capitalization of $550 billion, but when the tech bubble burst, Cisco's value evaporated, dropping to $100 billion. Remarkably, Chambers survived, a testament not only to shareholders' faith in him but also to the way in which he handled the calamity—he openly admitted his mistakes and was therefore allowed to carry on.

FUTURE GROWTH Chairman since 2006, Chambers has continued to grow Cisco by acquiring companies such as Linksys and Scientific Atlanta. Diversifying into new markets such as Voice over Internet Protocol (VoIP), Ethernet switching, social networking, and telepresence, he has successfully kept the company in pole position as the internet evolves. When demand and growth slowed as a result of the global economic downturn, Chambers announced his intention to continue to invest in emerging technologies and markets, even suggesting that an economic slowdown might be just the right time to continue the strategy of further acquisitions.

LESSONS IN BUSINESS: MANAGING THE BEST

Chambers was a successful junior basketball captain, despite not being a gifted player. According to his father, he realized that the only way for him to win was to attract more talented people to play on his team.
- → Hire the best people: they are ambitious and sometimes more difficult to manage but they get results.
- → Channel ambition using aggressive promotion that stretches people and makes them grow into their jobs.
- → Understand that one of the key responsibilities of the CEO is to unleash the talent of people by listening to them and searching for new insights.

"Education and the internet must go hand in hand. …It will serve as one of the great equalizers."
John T. Chambers

Walt Disney Founder & CEO (1923–66), The Walt Disney Company

KNOWN WORLDWIDE for his timeless popular creations as an animator, Disney was also a dogged entrepreneur who created a huge and enduring business empire from scratch. As well as facing the usual concerns of any entrepreneur, Disney had to contend with economic depression, world war, unscrupulous competitors, and ever-changing public tastes. His ability to innovate and his determination to keep his sights on his business goals ensured that his company prospered, and it remains a powerful corporate presence.

BIOGRAPHY
1901–1966. Born in Chicago, Disney and his family settled in Kansas City in 1911 when he was nine. He began drawing for his school newspaper, and as a driver with the Red Cross during World War I he decorated his ambulance with cartoons.

LEADERSHIP STYLE
Sometimes notoriously tough on his employees. Nonetheless, Disney understood the importance of letting other people's creativity flourish for the benefit of the overall project.

KEY STRENGTH
Immense determination and an intuitive understanding of what would entertain families.

BEST DECISION
Pushing on with *Snow White and the Seven Dwarfs*, even though a feature-length animated film had never been made before and he was running out of money.

FALSE STARTS When Disney's first studio providing cartoons to local theaters in Kansas City went bankrupt, the determined young entrepreneur moved to Hollywood to try his chances in the movie industry. He had success with a series called *Oswald the Lucky Rabbit* and hired a team of animators, but when he discovered that he didn't own the rights, nearly all his animators jumped ship, leaving his business in tatters again.

BREAKING NEW GROUND Undeterred by two business failures, Disney began work on a new character based on a mouse he had kept as a pet while working in Kansas. *Mickey Mouse* proved to be an immediate hit, as did a number of other creations, and Disney's studio took off, giving him the confidence to begin work on another innovative idea—the first animated feature-length film in English. After three years, he ran out of money and had to take a rough cut of the film to his bank in the hope of securing further funding. When it was finally released in 1938, *Snow White and the Seven Dwarfs* became the most successful movie of the year, rewarding Disney's innovation and persistence in creating a whole new genre.

During World War II, a combination of labor strikes and the need to produce government propaganda films sent the business into another decline, but it recovered enough after the war for Disney to begin work on a theme park, another groundbreaking concept that was widely derided. The opening of Disneyland and the continuing success of the studio finally set Disney's business on a solid footing, achieving the base for the diversification that has built today's global media giant.

LESSONS IN BUSINESS: BOUNCING BACK

Every time he looked like he was on the road to success, Disney took a hit. But every time he learned the lesson, picked himself up and came back stronger, proving that genuine innovators are never finished until they allow themselves to be.
- → Take risks, even as a middle manager or team leader. Get a reputation for trying new things.
- → Don't allow the entrepreneurial spirit to exist only at the top—look for innovation from everyone.
- → At the end of every event or project discuss and record what went well and what needed improvement.

"All your dreams can come true if you have the courage to pursue them." Walt Disney

Mark Zuckerberg Founder & CEO, Facebook

THE YOUNGEST-EVER dollar billionaire, Zuckerberg has also made his fortune in record time. A Harvard dropout, he founded social networking site Facebook in February 2004, and a little over two years later he is reputed to have received an offer of $1 billion for the business from Yahoo! Lacking neither ambition nor self-confidence, the self-confessed programming geek turned the offer down. In 2007, Microsoft took a 1.6-percent stake in Facebook, valuing the company at an incredible $15 billion.

BIOGRAPHY
Born in White Plains, New York, in 1984. After attending New Hampshire's exclusive Phillips Exeter Academy, Zuckerberg went to Harvard to study Computer Science, but decided to drop out in 2004 to pursue Facebook full time.

LEADERSHIP STYLE
Perfectionist. Zuckerberg's desire to push the boundaries of what is possible online makes Facebook the employer of choice for a whole generation of top techies.

KEY STRENGTH
Combining high-level technical skills with an understanding of the potential of the internet as a social rather than merely transactional medium.

BEST DECISION
Going open source in 2007. This allowed anyone to create applications for Facebook users, providing a much enhanced service to Facebook users.

COLLEGE WHIZ KID The website that would become Facebook was started by Zuckerberg as a place for his Harvard college mates to meet up online. Facebook turned into such a success that he dropped out to pursue the idea commercially. The quiet and thoughtful—if occasionally outspoken—Zuckerberg certainly knows how to impress. His first backer was PayPal founder Peter Thiel, who has since been joined by Hong Kong billionaire Li Ka-shing. Growth has been explosive: with more than 150 million users it is now the top social networking site and the fourth most-visited website in the world.

SEEKING PROFITABILITY A CEO in his early twenties, Zuckerberg lacks experience, but his vision and commitment, and his ability to attract like-minded colleagues to the company,

have guided the business to runaway popularity. What started as a means of staying in touch with college friends has developed into a broader social network, a public and political forum, and even a search engine, as people tap their friends for advice and information. The Facebook site itself is continually being improved, and Zuckerberg even invites users to submit, and profit from, their own software, increasing what Facebook has to offer.

Zuckerberg insists that his key interest is in building the Facebook community rather than chasing money, a claim that his refusal to sell would seem to confirm. Facebook does not publish its financial performance figures, but it is widely thought to be cashflow negative. Zuckerberg's number one challenge for the future is to figure out a way to make money before his investors start to lose patience.

LESSONS IN BUSINESS: PUTTING IN THE TIME

Facebook's meteoric rise is testament to Zuckerberg's vision, drive, and ambition. His commitment to the website has been unwavering, its early success driving him forward. Zuckerberg is, in many ways, the public face of the company, and he has embraced the responsibilities that come with that role.
→ Good ideas are ten a penny; everyone will have thought of them and the opportunities they raise.
→ Single yourself out from the rest with your willingness to put in the hours and make things happen.
→ Think a year ahead. Ask: "What innovation could I be kicking myself about when someone else does it?"

"I'm trying to make the world a more open place."
Mark Zuckerberg

Henry Ford Founder & President (1906–19), Ford Motor Company

AS THE ORIGINATOR of the productive and efficient industrial system that has endured for a century and forms the basis for today's consumer economy, Ford has rightly taken his place in history. However, when he began his career, he was just one among many talented engineers curious about what could be done with the new technologies and materials of the late 19th century. It was his foresight in introducing a series of key innovations, such as the moving assembly line production process, that made him such a towering industrial figure.

BIOGRAPHY
1863–1947. Born in Detroit, Michigan. Ford began tinkering with watches and other machinery from an early age, a passion that led him into engineering. His industrial methods so impressed Adolf Hitler that a photo of Ford adorned the Führer's office.

LEADERSHIP STYLE
Notoriously stubborn and strongly anti-union. Ford kept what many regarded as an intrusive eye on his employees, but he knew the value of good staff and was willing to pay to keep them.

KEY STRENGTH
Seeing the market possibilities in making expensive things cheap.

BEST DECISION
Introducing the moving assembly line to his factory, a key step in bringing about a dramatic rise in cost-effective productivity.

FROM THE WORKSHOP FLOOR After serving an apprenticeship as a machinist in Detroit, Ford worked servicing steam engines for Westinghouse, and then for the Edison Electric Illuminating Company, helping to build generating stations. In his spare time, his experiments with gasoline engines led him to produce a self-propelled vehicle in 1896, and he set up his own business in 1899. After a series of false starts, he leased a factory in 1903 and began work on an affordable motor vehicle.

MASTER COST-CUTTER Between 1903 and 1914, Ford introduced a series of new methods in response to specific production challenges. The combination of these created an industrial model that has remained fundamentally unchanged since. Until then, motor vehicles had been only for the very rich and therefore

the production cost had not been considered an issue. Ford was the first car manufacturer to focus on cost-cutting in materials, labor, and processes, and the changes that he introduced led to the production of the Model T in 1908. His development of the moving assembly belt in 1913 allowed Ford to drive costs and prices even lower, and by 1914 Model T sales had topped 250,000.

At the same time, he strove for complete vertical integration—control of all aspects of the business from the supply of raw materials to the retail outlets. His goal was economic independence, and to this end he built his own steel-making plant. His low cost base also allowed him to deal with the problem of staff turnover by offering employees $5 a day, doubling the pay rate for most of them and protecting his company's skills base.

LESSONS IN BUSINESS: THINK CUSTOMERS

Ford could have made his cars better, or sexier, or more specialized. But instead he realized that by making them cheaper he could reach an entirely new segment of customers, which ultimately built his success.
→ Use technology and economies of scale to reduce prices. Sell off unnecessary stock cheaply.
→ Know your internal or external customers: ask what they would do if prices were lower.
→ Make sure that everyone in the team, no matter what their job, meets with a customer from time to time and understands their price sensitivities.

"A business that makes nothing but money is a poor business." Henry Ford

THE INSPIRED LEADER

by **Marshall Goldsmith**

There is one critical question that repeatedly gets left out when assessing the potential of our future CEOs: how much do they love to lead people? The greatest business leaders working today possess one quality in common. They love leading people.

One such people-focused CEO is **W. James McNerney, Jr.** (p85) of the Boeing Company, celebrated for his inspirational and sensitive approach to his staff. He knows how to get the best out of people, supporting their personal development outside of work as much as their career paths. He is passionate about the company's Learning Together Program that helps fund employees' further education.

Inheriting control of the family firm at the tender age of just 28, **Kumar Mangalam Birla** (p80) revealed himself to be a natural born leader. He has revolutionized the way Indian conglomerate Aditya Birla does business, by making sure the people who run it are themselves happy in their leadership, measuring the satisfaction levels of his managers with something he calls the Organizational Health Survey. Aditya Birla now has a reputation as one of the best employers in Asia ●

> "Every day I remind myself that leadership is not about me. It is about the great people who are working with me."
> ALAN MULALLY

For the Love of Leading

Alan Mulally, former CEO of Boeing Commercial Aircraft—it must be something to do with Boeing—and now CEO of Ford, is undoubtedly a fantastic leader of people. Over the years, Alan has faced challenges that would have made most people simply want to throw in the towel. Through it all, however, he has never got down on himself, his people, or his company. Alan has an enthusiasm that radiates to those around him. He has an almost childlike joy in leading. Alan's love of what he does enables him to work incredible hours, face daunting adversity, and serve with a smile on his face. His personal example says more about leadership than his words can ever convey.

The legendary management consultant Peter Drucker often noted that **Frances Hesselbein**, former CEO of the Girl Scouts of America and now chairman of the Leader to Leader Institute, was the greatest leader he had ever met. Having worked with Frances on a myriad of projects over the past 25 years, there is no doubting Drucker's assessment. When Frances discusses her work as a leader, her eyes sparkle and her face glows. No matter what personal or professional challenges she is facing, she is always positive and inspirational. Frances defines leadership as "circular", with the leader reaching across the organization to colleagues, not down to subordinates. Her motivation has never come from the outside, from money or status. Instead, it has always come from the inside, from her love of service and what she does.

Great leaders are different from great individual achievers. For the latter, achievement is about themselves. For great leaders, achievement is about others. High level leadership may bring status, power, or money, but these benefits come at a cost. Great leaders work extremely hard, take their jobs very personally, are subject to ongoing and often unfair criticism, and pay a price for their success. If you love leading people, leadership will be a joy and service will be a blessing. You can only inspire the people you are leading if you are inspired to lead.

Learning to Lead Better

Make room for improvement— If you are working with and through others to achieve objectives, you are already a leader. But you can always lead better.

Get 360-degree feedback— Ask co-workers that you respect to judge your present level of effectiveness as a leader.

Pick the most important behaviors for change— Work on those that will enhance your effectiveness as a leader, especially listening and making timely decisions.

Periodically ask co-workers for suggestions— Ask them how you can do an even better job in your selected behaviors for change.

Listen to their ideas— Don't promise to change everything but make the changes that you believe will further increase your leadership skills.

Follow-up— Measure your change in effectiveness over time.

Leaders from the Front

Other CEOs who have put their personal stamp on the company they lead include:

Tony Fernandes, AirAsia (Aviation: Malaysia)—*He bought the business for a nominal fee three days after the 9/11 attacks. Since then, the dressed-down, easygoing CEO has grown the business to fly to 61 destinations.*

Dov Charney, American Apparel (Retail: US)—*The flamboyant boss of this clothing manufacturer divides opinion, but in an age of manufacturing on the cheap in developing economies, AA is lauded for its US base and generous employment benefits.*

Kristin Petursdottir, Audur Capital (Finance: Iceland)—*After Iceland's economic collapse, women bosses such as Petursdottir are thriving as their firms adopt a more "female" approach to investment.*

Martin Glenn, Birds Eye (Foodstuffs: UK)—*Glenn didn't think twice about switching from the biggest snack brand in Britain, Walkers, to the frozen food giant, using his marketing skills to reinvigorate an ailing sector.*

John Lau, Husky Energy (Energy: Canada)—*Lau built the oil business up through a hands-on style and has been nominated "most underpaid" CEO for his efforts.*

Andy Cosslett, IHG (Hotels: UK)—*Cosslett has used his previous career in branding to help reposition Intercontinental for the changing nature of travel.*

A. M. Naik, Larsen & Toubro (Diversified: India)—*A devotee of **Jack Welch** (p311), Naik is a workaholic who took his first vacation 22 years after joining the firm as a junior engineer.*

William Hawkins III, Medtronic (Pharmaceuticals: US)—*Hawkins identifies staff as an asset and spends 50 percent of his time dealing with people issues.*

Richard Fain, Royal Caribbean (Travel: Liberia)—*Fain has adopted a collegiate style of leadership, calling on his managers to provide great ideas. This has helped Royal Caribbean recreate the cruise experience for a younger, more active audience.*

Jure Sola, Sanmina SCI (Electronics: US)—*Sola's relentless energy has built the company into a global player, but he says he could walk away if it stopped being fun.*

Muhammad Yunus Founder & Managing Director, Grameen Bank

AS FOUNDER of the micro-financing Bangladeshi Grameen Bank, Yunus is famed for giving the country's poor a hitherto unheard of leg-up into the world of entrepreneurship. Although the idea of micro-financing as an economic model to help the poor was not new, Yunus is lauded as the first to put the idea into action, first offering loans with government support in the late 1970s. In 2006, Grameen Bank and its founder were jointly awarded the Nobel Prize for Peace for their work in the eradication of world poverty.

BIOGRAPHY
Born in Eastern Bengal (now Bangladesh) in 1940, Yunus was the third of nine children. He spent his early years in the village of Bathua but moved to the city of Chittagong in 1947, where his father had a successful jewelry business. He studied economics at Dhaka University and later completed a PhD in economics at the Vanderbilt University in Nashville, Tennessee.

LEADERSHIP STYLE
Trusting and dedicated, Yunus possesses the capability to translate his visionary ideals into practical solutions.

KEY STRENGTH
The determination to overcome the inertia of the traditional banking system.

BEST DECISION
Making the initial micro-loans out of his own pocket.

A SPUR TO CHARITABLE ACTION
In 1972, Yunus left his position as assistant professor in economics at Middle Tennessee State University to return to Bangladesh. He joined the Department of Economics at the University of Chittagong, becoming professor in 1975. Influenced by his mother's charitable actions in his childhood, Yunus took an active interest in the university's rural research programs. During a field trip in 1976, Yunus encountered villagers who were forced to borrow money from loan sharks at exorbitant rates to buy raw materials, which kept their earnings at subsistence level. Appalled, he took $27 from his own pocket and loaned it to 42 village women at low interest. The lower interest rates not only yielded markedly improved profit margins, but also encouraged personal initiative and enterprise.

FROM IDEA TO REALITY
Realizing that very small loans could make a real difference to those living on the edge, Yunus approached traditional banks, but despite offering to act as a personal guarantor, he was met with blank refusal. Undeterred, Yunus secured backing from the country's central bank and, after trial projects met with success, Grameen (meaning "rural" or "village" in Bangla) Bank came into existence as an independent bank in 1983. Founded on the principles of trust and solidarity, the bank now has over seven million borrowers, primarily women, who also own 90 percent of the bank's shares, the rest being owned by the Bangladesh government. The Grameen initiative has diversified into a range of ventures, including the Village Phone project, which has resulted in mobile phone ownership for some 260,000 people in rural areas.

LESSONS IN BUSINESS: TAKING RESPONSIBILITY

Although Grameen loans are unsecured, repayment is 97 percent—higher than any other banking system. Yunas encourages groups of borrowers to co-guarantee loans and support each other's enterprise efforts.
→ Foster solidarity. Ensure contractors and subcontractors are cooperating both financially and technically.
→ Help individual borrowers, suppliers, and customers to realize that a failure to act responsibly will have a knock-on effect on other businesses or individuals.
→ Encourage your people to understand and protect the interests of their suppliers and customers.

"We never had a sub-prime crisis." Muhammad Yunus

Brian Goldner President & CEO, Hasbro, Inc.

TOYMAKING GIANT Hasbro was casting around for ways to make the most of its impressive portfolio of classic brands when Goldner became part of its leadership team. Despite its renowned and familiar assets, the company behind Monopoly, G.I. Joe, and Mr. Potato Head was having trouble making them count in the new world of technology and entertainment. Goldner's move to turn Transformers and G.I. Joe into movies revolutionized the company, its prospects, and the business model for the toy industry worldwide.

BIOGRAPHY
Born in Huntington, New York, in 1964. Goldner graduated in government at Dartmouth College, New Hampshire, where he was also a radio DJ.

LEADERSHIP STYLE
Goldner takes a team-oriented approach, surrounding himself with people who know things that he doesn't.

KEY STRENGTH
The breadth of vision to see the possibilities of regenerating Hasbro's classic and familiar brands in new platforms.

BEST DECISION
Forging contacts with the film industry, which has turned out to be a lucrative business move.

MARKETING TALENT Goldner began his career as a marketing assistant for a health care consulting firm, before moving through jobs at top advertising agencies Leo Burnett and J. Walter Thompson, promoting a broad range of consumer products. By the age of 34, he was a senior partner in JWT's Los Angeles office. One of his tasks was promoting Power Rangers, licensed by Japanese toymaker Bandai, which brought him to the attention of Hasbro.

NEW PLATFORM Goldner moved to Hasbro in 2000, when the venerable US toy and games giant was going through a painful restructure in response to changing leisure habits. Taking charge of the entire US toy division and brands just months into his new job, Goldner returned the company's focus to its own portfolio of toys and games, and began looking for innovative ways to develop them. After spells as president of US Toys and then COO of Hasbro, Inc., he became CEO in 2008, by which time he had laid the foundations of a major comeback. His most inspired move was approaching film producer Lorenzo di Bonaventura in 2003, after reading that he was interested in making a film about military technology. The producer took up Goldner's suggestion of basing the film on the action toy G.I. Joe, and the contact also led to the film *Transformers*, which took more than $700 million and triggered a sequel. Goldner had transformed Hasbro from a toymaker into an intellectual-property-owning powerhouse. As CEO, he has built on this by signing further film deals with Universal Pictures, working with Nintendo on Hasbro-based interactive games, and expanding into emerging markets such as Brazil.

LESSONS IN BUSINESS: MAKING FRESH CONNECTIONS

Bringing an old asset to a new platform and exploiting your intellectual property with another company can bring remarkable results. Since costs will mostly be met by your partner, you can achieve a very high return.
→ Study your current market and think broadly about their wants in the future, however unrelated those wants may seem to your current products.
→ Look for innovative joint ventures with companies working in the same, or related, markets.
→ Study the "width" of your brand—ask yourself how you can expand the types of product the brand sells.

"You can activate the brand across any platform."
Brian Goldner

David Packard Co-founder, Chairman & CEO (1964–68), HP

ONE OF THE PIONEERS of technology, Packard was the co-founder of Hewlett-Packard (HP), an electronics and computer company that started out from a garage in Palo Alto, California, in 1939, and grew into a multibillion-dollar enterprise. With his partner William Hewlett, Packard created a business style and formula for success that became the prototype for Silicon Valley. He entered politics for a short time, serving as US deputy secretary of defense from 1969 until 1971, when he resumed his career at HP as chairman of the board.

BIOGRAPHY
1912–1996. Born in Pueblo, Colorado, Packard showed an early interest in electronics, becoming treasurer of the local radio club at the age of 12. At Stanford University, California, he graduated in 1934 with a bachelor's, followed by a master's degree in electrical engineering in 1939.

LEADERSHIP STYLE
High-tech visionary, candid, no-holds barred. Packard was the architect of an open-door management style that was aimed at encouraging employee innovation.

KEY STRENGTH
Trusting the ability of others and nurturing their creativity.

BEST DECISION
Going public with the company and expanding the manufacturing operation to Europe.

SMALL BEGINNINGS As a student at Stanford, Packard met fellow undergraduate William Hewlett and they made a pact to go into business together. In 1938, with just $538 in capital, he and Hewlett started a business in Packard's garage to market a resistance capacity audio oscillator (a sound equipment tester) that Hewlett had created as a graduate student. Working into the night, they finally developed the product, the HP200A, which they sold to Walt Disney Studios. Disney used the equipment to fine tune the soundtrack of the animated movie *Fantasia*.

GOING INTERNATIONAL The two partners drew on their individual strengths to grow the company, and HP expanded beyond the garage in 1947. Packard was a great administrator and, together with Hewlett, he put into place the management practices that would later earn them recognition as pioneers of Silicon Valley. Their open-door policy and "management by wandering around" was known as "The HP Way" and helped set the standard for modern business management. In 1957, Packard took the company public and established a manufacturing plant in Germany and European headquarters in Switzerland. Packard left in 1969 to serve in the Nixon government; on his return he found HP on the verge of borrowing $100 million to cover a cash-flow crisis. Within six months, Packard turned things around and the company was back in the black. He was less involved in the 1980s, when HP moved into computers and printers, but when earnings dipped nearly 11 percent in 1990, he stepped in to oversee a major restructuring and boost to profits.

LESSONS IN BUSINESS: BELIEVING IN CHANGE

Trusting in his own, his partner's, and his employees' new ideas, Packard allowed them the freedom to create and innovate. This was at the forefront of a move away from traditional business practices.
→ Join the new wave of business thinking by trusting your people.
→ Manage by "wandering around." If you are not getting out and listening to your staff, you are ignoring the people who will take you forward.
→ Make sure your people never compromise on quality. Get them to act as if their name was on the label.

"[Packard] had great faith in people, in finding people and letting them run with their ideas."
John Ford, vice-president of development, Stanford University

Amancio Ortega Gaona Chairman, Inditex

THE RICHEST MAN IN SPAIN and at one time the eighth richest in the world, with a fortune of $20 billion. Ortega is a self-made success. Building the Zara fashion retail chain from nothing, it now has 3,000 branches in 64 countries. His story is one of hard work, opportunism, and skilled market analysis. Ortega has bucked market trends consistently, always doing things differently to give his shops a unique appeal. His company produces a large range of designs in small numbers, which keeps his customers interested and coming back for more.

BIOGRAPHY
Born in 1936 in León, Spain. Ortega dropped out of school, and had no formal higher education.

LEADERSHIP STYLE
Hands-on, low profile, and relaxed. His ego-free style is said to be key to his success. He himself wears jeans and no tie, and he lives modestly in his home city of La Coruña.

KEY STRENGTH
Innovation. Ortega understands how to make his stores constantly interesting, enticing customers to return frequently and promote sales through word of mouth.

BEST DECISION
Resisting the temptation to outsource manufacturing, prizing flexibility and speed above low production costs.

LOOKS SIMILAR, COSTS LESS Living in the center of the Iberian textile industry, La Coruña, Ortega entered the business aged 14 and in his twenties he was making bathrobes and lingerie in his living room. In the 1960s Ortega realized that it was not only wealthy people who appreciated expensive, well-designed clothes, and he came up with the simple idea of using cheaper fabrics to produce similar-looking items at prices that everyone could afford. In the mid 1970s he opened his first Zara store.

FAST FASHION INNOVATOR Zara is still principally known for the same thing—expensive-looking, trendy clothes at reasonable prices—but it is the unique way Ortega has found to deliver this in a highly competitive market that best reflects his talent. Aware that costs mounted and time was lost as garments moved from designers to factories to stores, he saw the importance of delivering direct to customers. The business strategy he has developed involves controlling all aspects of the chain, reducing costs and gaining speed and thereby flexibility. His designers get ideas from fashion shows and respond quickly to trends. Keeping manufacture in Spain, rather than following the trend of outsourcing to countries with lower labor costs, speeds up his operation—the clothes are designed and in-store within weeks. Stores are freshly stocked twice a week, avoiding high inventory costs and clearout sales, and encouraging customers to visit often.

The highly successful flotation of his holding company Inditex—which also owns Massimo Dutti and Pull and Bear—in 2001 has had little effect on his unpretentious lifestyle.

LESSONS IN BUSINESS: LETTING YOUR WORK SPEAK FOR YOU

There is no need to cultivate a celebrity chief executive status when you have a strong product and a good strategy. Ortega has never given an interview and has allowed few pictures of himself to be made public.

➔ Ask yourself if you are seeking publicity to advance your company or to put yourself in the spotlight.

➔ Remember that, with few exceptions, CEOs eventually hit big problems. Don't make them more public than you need.

➔ The top jobs are listening jobs; avoid making yourself the key to the brand and big up your team instead.

"[We seek] to democratize fashion, in contrast to the idea of fashion as privilege." Amancio Ortega Gaona

Andy Grove President, Chairman & CEO (1987–98), Intel Corp.

BORN ANDRAS ISTVAN GROF, Grove fled the Soviet invasion of Hungary in 1956 to become one of corporate America's most successful and best-known CEOs. A gifted and entirely self-taught manager, Grove provided the strategic savvy and business brains to match the technical expertise of his fellow Intel co-founders Gordon Moore and Robert Noyce. Under Grove's stewardship, Intel underwent drastic restructuring to become the first high-tech giant of the silicon era, and for a time the world's most valuable company.

BIOGRAPHY
Born in Budapest in 1936. After the 1956 Soviet invasion of Hungary, Grove left his home and family to emigrate to the US. In 2000, Grove was diagnosed with Parkinson's disease.

LEADERSHIP STYLE
Constructive confrontation. Famous for shouting down ideas he didn't like and for shutting latecomers out of meetings, Grove could also be charming, generous, and supportive.

KEY STRENGTH
Grove had the rare ability to put himself outside the pressures of both the organization and the moment, and to see situations from a dispassionate perspective.

BEST DECISION
Reinventing the company as a manufacturer of microprocessors instead of memory chips.

CORPORATE VISIONARY As part of the founding team, and as president from 1979, Grove helped to create a vastly successful company from Intel's famous memory chips. But with Intel flying high, it was his seminal restructuring of the business that elevated him to the status of genuine business legend. Spotting what he would later call a "strategic inflection point," Grove decided in the early 1980s to abandon the lucrative computer memory chip trade that Intel had dominated for 20 years in favor of the risky new business of microprocessor manufacture. It was an extraordinary and controversial decision, almost as if Coca-Cola were abandoning fizzy drinks or Ford had decided to make bicycles rather than cars, but he was right. Within a few short years, the price of memory had collapsed as Japanese competition boomed, while the success of the IBM PC meant that Intel was sitting on top of yet another vast fortune as the biggest supplier of microprocessors in the world. Grove wrote a best-selling book about the experience, which remains one of the most memorable titles of all business tomes: *Only the Paranoid Survive*.

PRODUCTIVITY POWERHOUSE Famous for his unflinchingly direct approach and love of argument, Grove's Intel may not always have been a fun place to work, but it was extraordinarily productive. He was a pioneer of Management By Objective: measuring, recording, and managing every detail of every employee's personal productivity. He also insisted on forensic dissections of the reasons behind the firm's occasional failures, in order never to make the same mistake twice.

LESSONS IN BUSINESS: KEEPING UP THE PACE

The most successful companies seek constantly to reinvent themselves if they are to keep ahead of the competition. The pace at which Intel operated was punishing, and employee turnover could be high as a consequence, but Grove drove himself and he got results.
→ Promote people who welcome a fast pace of change; given more responsibility they may blossom.
→ Put in systems that give managers the information they need in time to make rapid decisions.
→ Some people do not fit into an environment of continuous change; if they are reluctant move them out.

"Success breeds complacency. Only the paranoid survive." Andy Grove

Ashok Khosla President, International Union for Conservation of Nature

A LEADING EXPERT on the environment and sustainable development, Khosla was appointed head of the world's oldest and largest global environmental network in late 2008. He has been involved in a range of initiatives aimed at understanding and utilizing the connections between economic development and the environment for more than 40 years, and he founded a network in India that, over the last quarter of a century, has initiated a vast array of schemes to promote development among the country's poor, and improve the environment.

BIOGRAPHY
Born in Kashmir in 1940, Khosla is the son of a university professor and a college lecturer. He gained a master's degree in natural sciences from Cambridge University, UK, and a PhD in experimental physics from Harvard University.

LEADERSHIP STYLE
A highly inspiring figure, Khosla motivates those around him by demonstrating commitment, and with his broad-based approach to the issues he deals with.

KEY STRENGTH
Recognizing that sustainability can only come from considering both the economy and the environment.

BEST DECISION
Setting up Development Alternatives Group, which created a ground-breaking model for sustainable development.

HARVARD PIONEER In the early 1960s, Khosla helped to design and teach Harvard's first undergraduate course on the environment, which explored the interactions between the environment and economic systems, human population, and natural resources. After returning to India in 1972, he became founding director of the government's Office of Environmental Planning and Coordination, the first national environmental agency in a developing country, introducing systems to integrate environmental considerations into the development process.

MODEL FOR SUSTAINABILITY In 1983, Khosla founded the sustainable development network Development Alternatives Group. It has come to be widely recognized as a leading innovator in using environmentally friendly technologies to create sustainable livelihoods, and enabling local enterprises to meet the needs of rural and low-income communities. Among its achievements have been the provision of low-cost housing, the creation of more than 300,000 sustainable jobs, the installation of decentralized power stations using renewable fuel, and the reclamation of degraded land through reforestation, watershed management, and ground water restoration.

The broad approach taken by Development Alternatives, and the impact it has had, have turned Khosla into one of the best-regarded and most influential figures in the area of environment and sustainable economics. In 2002, he was awarded the UN Environment Program's Sasakawa Environment Prize for creating sustainable livelihoods for people living below the poverty line.

LESSONS IN BUSINESS: LOOKING AT THE BIGGER PICTURE

Considering the needs of the environment and local people, as well as commercial questions, can be a powerful driver of innovation. Khosla used this message to make energy firms think about their environmental impact.
➔ CSR should be a major factor in your company's operation, not a self-promoting afterthought. Give back to the communities you work with.
➔ Give the issue of environmental care to a designated person or department in your organization.
➔ Inform current and future customers of what you are doing in the area of energy saving.

"Economic growth isn't very meaningful if half the country that you're growing is left behind in dire poverty." Ashok Khosla

Nicholas W. Moore MD & CEO, Macquarie Group Ltd

FINANCIAL VISION and hard-nosed ambition are the hallmarks of Moore's approach to investment banking, which transformed the fortunes of Macquarie Bank, the Australian offshoot of UK investment house Hill Samuel, into a global investment banking and diversified financial services group. His innovations in restructuring business acquisitions helped bring 14 consecutive years of stellar returns to investors, although he has had to learn diplomacy the hard way, after a badly handled run-in with an Australian broadcaster in 2002.

BIOGRAPHY
Born c.1958. Moore attended the Catholic Saint Ignatius' College in Riverview, Australia, before gaining a degree in commerce and law at the University of New South Wales.

LEADERSHIP STYLE
A risk-taker, Moore typifies the aggressive, entrepreneurial investment banker. Dubbed "cold and calculating", he is tough and focused, keeping his eye firmly on the deal.

KEY STRENGTH
Seeing the vast potential of under-exploited infrastructure and working out a way of exploiting it.

BEST DECISION
Turning Macquarie's purchase of assets such as airports, toll roads, and nursing homes into listed trusts, the management of which has brought many years of record profit growth.

THE ART OF THE DEAL Moore's greatest claim to fame was Macquarie's high-profile but unsuccessful bid for the London stock exchange in 2005. Dismissed as ill-considered and quixotic, the bid summed up Moore's expansionist tendencies and the love for deal-making that marked his tenure at the helm of the bank's Macquarie Capital arm. Moore embodied the go-getting financial culture of the 1990s and early 2000s, and the division thrived under his leadership, growing to deliver 60 percent of the group's profits. Macquarie became known as Australia's "Millionaires Factory" for the generous bonuses taken home by staff. Moore himself was most handsomely rewarded of all, becoming the country's second highest paid executive. Moore was the perfect foil for former CEO Allan Moss's cautious risk management approach.

CHALLENGING TIMES Becoming CEO in 2008 after Moss retired, Moore continued to push for growth, acquiring US futures clearing outfit Shatkin Arbor in August of that year. But he took the helm just as times turned tough for leveraged players such as Macquarie, and soon faced the challenge of the global financial crisis. Macquarie announced record full-year profits of AU$1.8 billion in mid-2008, but profits fell significantly over the next six months. Showing faith in the asset-trust business model, Moore set about rationalizing the business and reversing a precipitous fall in its share price by moving away from areas that offered lower returns, and cutting costs and staffing levels. Some observers regretted the departure of his urbane predecessor, but others saw Moore's tough approach and understanding of risk as ideal qualities for leading the bank in times of turmoil.

LESSONS IN BUSINESS: INCENTIVIZING YOUR STAFF

Human capital is at the heart of Macquarie's success, as demonstrated by Moore's strategy of maintaining headcount and offering bonuses for good performance, even when the global economy stutters.
→ Incentivize people but move away from big cash bonuses based on short-term performance, and instead offer longer-term, equity-based incentives.
→ Your bonus plan should emphasize an understanding of risk, so that staff are aware of the consequences.
→ Bonus payouts attract media publicity. Make sure you can justify them by pointing to convincing results.

> "[Moore] is a hard-driven person, very tough in negotiations... [he] understands risk."
> Trevor Rowe, chairman, Rothschild Australia

George W. Merck President & Chairman (1925–57), Merck & Co., Inc.

UNDER THE LEADERSHIP of its founder's son, Merck & Co. embarked on a program of pioneering drug research that helped create the model for the modern pharmaceutical company. George W. Merck's early recognition of the crucial importance of research and keeping the company focused on solving medical problems turned Merck & Co., founded in Germany but set up as an independent business in America after World War I, into an industry leader, that has discovered and developed countless medical breakthroughs along the way.

JUST ANOTHER DRUG COMPANY Merck was obliged by the outbreak of World War I to abandon his plan to study for a doctorate in chemistry. Instead, he began working in the family company in New Jersey. Propelled to the role of president by his father's ill health ten years later, he found himself running a modest company turning out conventional drugs and chemicals in an industry that was regarded by scientific researchers as slightly distasteful.

RESEARCH PIONEER Merck began his tenure by merging his company with a Philadelphia firm, providing access to broader markets and, crucially, an expansion in capital with which to fund his plans to turn Merck into a new kind of company. In 1933, he established a large research laboratory and began recruiting prominent chemists and biologists to engage in intensive research and come up with new pharmaceutical products—a ground-breaking approach that changed the landscape of the industry.

This move coincided with breakthroughs in the creation of vitamins, antibiotics, and hormones, and Merck's laboratory was soon at the forefront of these new areas. His scientists came up with a stream of key developments during the 1930s and 40s. The new products proved hugely popular, and Merck's policy of getting each one onto the market as quickly as possible and lowering the price when production costs allowed, ensured that products reached the maximum number of customers. Merck's strategic vision was also behind the merger of the company with Sharpe & Dohme in 1953, which laid the foundation of today's multinational group.

LESSONS IN BUSINESS: CHANGING THE SHAPE OF THE INDUSTRY

By extending the range of a company's business interests, you can create an integrated organization that will give you a crucial edge by competing in totally new areas of business. Merck always kept in mind the broad aim of the organization—to improve health.

→ Don't be satisfied with your company's role within the industry. Seek to lead or dictate the way ahead.

→ Look for opportunities to grow and diversify in a way that no one in your industry has done before.

→ Don't be afraid to be the first to change the model for how things are done.

"Medicine is for the people. It is not for the profits. The profits follow. And if we have remembered that, they have never failed to appear." George W. Merck

INNOVATE AND THRIVE

In today's fiercely competitive business landscape, "innovate or die" is an apt phrase; innovation drives growth, and helps CEOs gain competitive advantage. Innovation goes beyond products and technologies to new business models and processes. The ability to innovate new technologies and products often requires innovative ways of working to release the thought potential of the workforce.

For example, Nintendo's CEO **Satoru Iwata** (p216), thought outside the box when he gave his creative teams free rein. The Wii console and its motion-sensitive wireless controller were the result. Rather than focusing on creating a more powerful, faster console, as is the games industry norm, they focused on the users' emotional experience, and as a result opened up the console world to an untapped public of non-gamers.

Other CEOs look to encourage and fund technical innovation from outside. At Shell, **Jeroen van der Veer**'s (p273) GameChanger program seeks out people with novel ideas and funds the most promising. One of these innovations, inspired by a foam toy that swelled in water, has enabled the oil industry to stop depleting reservoirs producing more water than oil, increasing oil flow by 600 percent ●

Empowered to Innovate

Innovation takes several forms. Many risk-taking, assumption-challenging CEOs have had direct input into product and service innovation, with some individuals redefining entire industries. For example, **Nicolas Hayek**'s designs made Swatch a global fashion phenomenon and the world's biggest watch manufacturer in the 1980s. Like his father, current Swatch CEO **Nick Hayek, Jr.** has launched various innovative products: from time-saving Swatch Access technology that bypasses lines with scannable pre-loaded admission tickets, to a time piece that downloads news, weather, and stock quotes from the internet.

"The best way to predict the future is to invent it."
ALAN KAY, formerly of HP Labs

Another type of development is process innovation. Kiva Systems CEO, **Mick Mountz**, is revolutionizing things in the warehouse with his innovative robotic packing line. Collaborative mobile robots bring products to "pickers and packers", reducing the number of people involved and increasing output.

Personal collaboration is crucial when innovating. Even lone inventors need sounding boards and creative teams. Southwest Airline's profit-sharing employees are empowered to innovate by CEO **Gary Kelly** (p138). Ticketless travel, online boarding passes, and the first-ever desktop link delivering live deal updates are the result of this forward thinking.

The web has widened the ideas pool as ideas are shared and refined by internet communities. As a result, good ideas need to be produced and marketed quickly, before someone else gets in first. A team-led rapid innovation solution to this is "skunk works": teams that produce innovative solutions to specific challenges in top secret.

The first skunk works team was created by Lockheed in 1943, under **Courtland S. Gross**, to design spy planes. The result was the revolutionary U-2 spy plane, which was developed and test-piloted in just eight months. Many companies followed this example. IBM CEO **Frank Cary** implemented a research group to develop the PC, while **Steve Jobs** (p17) ran Apple's breakthrough Macintosh computer project as a renegade skunk works.

Management Innovation

Peter Drucker transformed corporate management. His study of General Motors in 1945 introduced the idea of simplifying company structure through decentralization, as opposed to command and control. Central to his philosophy was the belief that highly skilled people are a firm's most valuable resource, and that managers should empower workers by allowing them to perform to their best ability. A more recent management innovation includes the performance metric "Economic Value Added", developed by consultants Stern Stewart, pioneered corporately by Coca-Cola CEO **Roberto Goizueta** (p351), and backed today by 3M's **George Buckley** (p228). EVA® establishes how much money each department has made by calculating its cashflow minus expenses, rather than using conventional accounting measures like profit. As such it is a useful metric for shareholders and employers alike, and can show how much more valuable a company has become over time.

Fresh Minds

Other CEOs who have successfully innovated include:

Patrick Kron, ALSTOM (Transport and energy: France)—*Unveiled a new high-speed train prototype, the AGV, a bullet-type train with a cruise speed of up to 360 kmph (224 mph).*
—

Edward J. Ludwig, BECTON DICKINSON (Health sector: US)—*He's working on a cure for diabetes through adult stem-cell research, plus innovative technologies for preventing the spread of hospital-acquired viruses.*
—

William Coley, BRITISH ENERGY GROUP (Energy: UK)—*Hopes to launch a new UK nuclear power station by 2018 to help lower carbon emissions and reduce imported energy reliance.*
—

Michael Capellas, FIRST DATA (Information commerce: US)—*Spearheaded the launch of GO-Tag, a touchless payment method and prospective credit card successor.*
—

Lee Jong-soo, HYUNDAI ENGINEERING & CONSTRUCTION (Engineering: South Korea)—*Recently began construction of the Taean Corporate City, the first in Korea to combine cutting-edge tourism, environmental, and business functions.*
—

Philip Cox, INTERNATIONAL POWER (Energy: UK)—*Is leading the way in renewable energy as one of the top ten wind farm operators with 57 percent of its portfolio "modern efficient gas fired generation".*
—

Makoto Kawamura, KYOCERA CORP. (Diversified: Japan)—*To take the lead in the solar power global market, Kawamura is building a new large-scale solar cell manufacturing facility to double its annual production.*

Harold McGraw III, THE MCGRAW-HILL COMPANIES (Media and information: US)—*When McGraw took over his great-grandfather's firm in 1998, ahead of the curve he generated revenue with BusinessWeek's online presence.*
—

Michael Mack, SYNGENTA (Agribusiness: Switzerland)—*Announced new technology developments to dramatically improve cost efficiency of sugar cane planting in Brazil. Has an annual market potential of $300 million by 2015.*
—

Bill Gates Chairman & CEO (1976–2000), Microsoft Corp.

A GEEKY APPEARANCE and a commitment to large-scale philanthropy may give the impression that Gates is the easygoing type, but you don't become the richest man on earth by being gentle. A confrontational manager and an aggressive business operator, Gates broke the mold of the computer nerd. His ability to play business hardball ensured that his company cashed in from the very beginning of the IT boom, and his demanding managerial presence has kept Microsoft at the heart of the computing world ever since.

BIOGRAPHY

Born in Seattle in 1955. Gates wrote his first program, a version of tic-tac-toe, on a school computer. He enrolled at Harvard in 1973, but left to concentrate on his software business.

LEADERSHIP STYLE

Confrontational, direct, and abrasive. Gates became renowned for his demanding approach. He also ensured that Microsoft was a meritocracy, that it was product-centered, and that it looked after its people.

KEY STRENGTH

Looking for improvement, always and everywhere.

BEST DECISION

Insisting on keeping the copyright to MS-DOS in the 1980 deal with IBM. This was the key to Microsoft's success.

COLLEGE DROP-OUT After selling a computer program to his school at the age of 17, Gates continued developing software during a brief stint at Harvard. Dropping out of college to concentrate on his IT start-up business, he began creating software for a variety of systems, writing code himself, reviewing every piece of code the company produced, and keeping an eye out for growth opportunities. Offered an agreement to provide the operating system for IBM's new PC in 1980, he saw his big chance.

AGGRESSION AND DRIVE Gates's deal with IBM demonstrated his acute business acumen and his taste for tough dealing. As well as providing the operating system for IBM's ubiquitous PCs, Gates insisted that Microsoft retain the copyright to the system, in the hope that he would be able to license it to other hardware manufacturers. This contractual masterstroke spawned an entire industry of PCs that all depended on MS-DOS and put Microsoft at the center of the computing revolution. That one move provided the basis for Microsoft's phenomenal growth. Gates insisted on the creation of new products to consolidate the company's position, and his aggressive management style continued to drive the business forward. He appointed equally tough partners, such as Steve Ballmer, but also generated a motivating corporate spirit that kept the best people coming to Microsoft. He was even harder on the competition, doing whatever it took to defend Microsoft's dominance. Since 2006, Gates has devoted an increasing proportion of his time to the philanthropic The Bill & Melinda Gates Foundation.

LESSONS IN BUSINESS: BECOMING DOMINANT

Gates's determination is legendary. Most senior managers know that they may have to choose between being well liked and less successful or well respected and capable of developing companies with dominant positions.
→ Be prepared to take any steps that will improve your market domination—including litigation.
→ Accept that your true aim is to be as near to a monopoly as you can and the law allows.
→ When you've established a dominant position, pull out all the stops to defend it. Keep pushing or your dominance will crumble.

"Success is a lousy teacher." Bill Gates

Jochen Zeitz CEO, Puma AG

THE YOUNGEST PERSON ever to head a company on the German Stock Exchange, Zeitz was just 29 in 1993 when he became CEO of Puma. Many in the industry gave him little chance of turning around the ailing shoemaker, which was sinking under the weight of an outdated product line and $100 million in debt. Zeitz's combination of hard-headed cost-cutting and a flair for freewheeling innovation not only made Puma one of the world's hottest fashion brands but also created an entirely new market for sport-style leisurewear.

BIOGRAPHY
Born in Mannheim, Germany, in 1963. He graduated from the European Business School with a degree in international marketing and finance in 1986.

LEADERSHIP STYLE
Obsessive and controlling. Zeitz likes to take care of the details. He even operated as his own board-level finance director for much of his time as CEO.

KEY STRENGTH
Having the marketing vision to see how sportswear could be made cool.

BEST DECISION
Hiring top designer Jil Sander to produce a line of fashion shoes in 1998.

A BOLD BET After training as a marketer at Colgate-Palmolive, Zeitz joined Puma as business manager of footwear marketing in 1990. He rose rapidly as the company went through three CEOs in two years, and when the role came up once again, the company took a bold bet in hiring the youthful and dynamic Zeitz in the hope that he could provide the new ideas needed to put an end to eight straight years of losses.

SPORTS MEETS FASHION Zeitz began by applying the classic cost-cutter's medicine. He laid off staff and closed unprofitable production lines and warehouses, and in 1994 produced Puma's first profit since 1986. He continued with the tough treatment for another three years, stripping away bureaucracy, cutting the workforce almost in half, and shifting production to Asia, creating a leaner, more nimble company. He then made the key move of repositioning the brand, acknowledging it would never outstrip giant rivals Adidas and Nike. This was a bold stroke that changed the company's emphasis from sports performance to fashion and lifestyle. Instead of trying to compete directly over the sporting usefulness of its products, Puma emphasized color, line, and style. He brought in a range of high-profile designers to create and promote new products, crafting a cool, rebellious yet retro image that made Puma a hot fashion property. As a direct result of his strategy, the fashion sportswear side became the heart of the resurrected company, bringing high levels of profitability and altering the nature of the sportswear market, as competitors reoriented themselves toward leisurewear too.

LESSONS IN BUSINESS: FINDING A NEW WAY FORWARD

Going head-to-head with stronger competition in your core products isn't always the best way forward. Maybe those core products can be redesigned and re-launched. You might even create a new market.
→ If you are continuously playing catch-up with a competitor, work out how to change the game.
→ Look for brand "width." To which markets would your brand name give you instant access?
→ Try building new markets by experimenting with your existing consumer base; you'll soon find out if you have created a new demand.

"You need to be relevant and innovative; that's what counts." Jochen Zeitz

James Laurence Balsillie Co-CEO, Research In Motion

THE BLEND of Balsillie's business instincts with the technological vision of founder Mike Lazaridis has proved a potent combination at Research In Motion. The pair joined forces in 1992, and since then this unusual partnership has continued to work for Research In Motion, turning the BlackBerry into one of the most remarkable recent cases of innovation, making the company a technological and commercial powerhouse and firmly establishing Balsillie as one of the key business figures of the digital age.

THE RIGHT MATCH When "Jim" Balsillie joined Research In Motion (RIM) as co-CEO in 1992, RIM was a small technology company with fewer than ten employees and some interesting ideas. Mike Lazaridis had the technological vision to drive the company's innovation, but the commercial side needed something different. Balsillie's background as an entrepreneur, accountant, and CFO of another small technology company equipped him perfectly for the task of pushing RIM ahead, and his business instincts proved the ideal match for Lazaridis' technological nous.

COMMERCIAL INNOVATOR Sharing the CEO's responsibilities between two strong figures would be a risky strategy for many companies, particularly a small one trying to take the difficult first steps toward growth. At RIM, however, the partnership unleashed the potential of the business. A key part of Balsillie's contribution to the success of the BlackBerry has been his well-tuned commercial antennae and strong business fundamentals, but he has also made innovations on the commercial side. His strategic decisions appeared risky at the time but later turned out to be highly prescient. Among these were an early focus on business customers, which ensured RIM's reputation for performance and quality by reaching the high standards required by business users. He also made a controversial move to sell through, and share revenue with, wireless carriers. In 2005, he began an aggressive push to expand internationally. Little is certain in the fast-moving technological world, but Balsillie's reputation as one of its most effective players looks secure.

LESSONS IN BUSINESS: BRINGING SKILLS TOGETHER

At RIM new products are the result of synergy between the research and development, marketing, and production departments. Encouraging that synergy is part of the job of the CEO.
➔ Put acute business insights and far-sighted technological vision together in the right way and you can create something outstanding.
➔ Make sure that two minds are working together: one on operations and the other on vision and strategy.
➔ Understand what sort of a manager you are and find someone who can act in the complementary role.

"Business is not an exercise in perfection; it's an exercise of optimization." James Laurence Balsillie

Ma Yun Co-founder & CEO, Alibaba.com Ltd

BIOGRAPHY
Born in Zhejiang Province, China, in 1946. Ma taught himself English and graduated from Hangzhou Teacher's Institute in 1988.

BEST DECISION
Taking Alibaba public in 2008, proving that a mainland Chinese company can be listed on the Hong Kong stock exchange and attract global investor interest.

LESSON IN BUSINESS
Innovate or die—Ma has grown his company by addressing specifically Chinese market issues, rather than copying competitors' strategies.

SELECTED AS ONE OF THE 25 most powerful business people in Asia by *Fortune* magazine in 2005, Ma, CEO and co-founder of Alibaba, the world's largest online B2B marketplace, is regarded as the pioneer of e-commerce in China.

It was when visiting Seattle as an interpreter with a trade delegation that "Jack" Ma was first exposed to the power of the internet. On his return to China, he began creating websites for friends. After a short spell as head of the China International Electronic Commerce Center's Infoshare division, Ma raised $60,000 to set up a business-to-business website, Alibaba, in 1999. Its early years were difficult and Ma was forced to make layoffs when the dotcom bubble burst. In 2003, however, an outbreak of SARS restricted travel in China but raised demand for online transactions—and Alibaba took off. That same year, Ma launched Taobao.com, a consumer-to-consumer auction website similar to eBay, which also incorporated an innovative online payment service, Alipay. In 2005, Ma acquired Yahoo! China, securing $1 billion of investment for Alibaba. Ma remains confident that Alibaba can survive times of economic crisis, and is committed to making Alibaba the world's largest e-commerce company.

Jeff Raikes CEO, The Bill & Melinda Gates Foundation

BIOGRAPHY
Born in Nebraska in 1948. Raikes earned a bachelor of science in Engineering-Economics Systems from Stanford University.

BEST DECISION
Bundling together Microsoft's word processing, spreadsheet, and presentation applications as MS Office, the source of much of the company's profits.

LESSON IN BUSINESS
Give the customers what they want—in this case an "industry-standard" operating system (Microsoft Windows) and business software package (Microsoft Office).

THE UNSUNG HERO of Microsoft, Raikes created Microsoft Office, and made Windows the main profit generator of the most influential company of the past 30 years. Today he leads the Gates's mission to promote global equity.

When Bill Gates, co-founder of Microsoft, decided the world needed an industry-standard operating system, Apple was the best on offer. It was Raikes who wrote to Apple suggesting the companies collaborate. This offer was regarded as a ploy and rejected, leaving Microsoft to develop its own operating system that could work on any non-Mac. While Gates's vision underpinned its success, it was Raikes who made the system work. He asked the difficult questions, then created the software package, Microsoft Office, that would bring in the money. It is because of Raikes that most executives use Powerpoint for their presentations, Excel for their spreadsheets, and Word for their documents. In 2008, after record quarter revenues of $16 billion—largely driven by his Business Division, which still accounts for more than a third of Microsoft profits—Raikes left to become CEO of The Bill & Melinda Gates Foundation. Its asset trust endowment stands at more than $35 billion.

"I hope I can set up a great company, which the Chinese people can be proud of because it's truly home-grown." Ma Yun

Richard D. Fairbank Founder, Chairman & CEO, Capital One

BIOGRAPHY
Born in California in 1950, Fairbank an received an MBA from the Stanford Graduate School of Business.

BEST DECISION
Devloping and using Capital One's "information-based strategy" to customize financial solutions for customers.

LESSON IN BUSINESS
Keep at it—Fairbank has had to overcome suspicion and resistance to his ideas, but his persistence has enabled him to build a *Fortune* 500 company from scratch.

FOCUSED AND TENACIOUS, Fairbank transformed the American credit card industry in the 1990s with innovative ideas such as "teaser rates" and zero-interest balance transfers drawing customers to Capital One.

Richard Fairbank started his career in 1981 as a management consultant with Strategic Planning Associates. He began developing the idea that would become the hallmark of Capital One—namely its "information-based strategy" (IBS), which used a database-marketing approach to bring customized solutions to consumers. Along with fellow SPA consultant, Nigel Morris, Fairbank persuaded Signet Bank to implement the strategy in 1988. By 1994, the bank's credit card business was growing so fast that Signet spun off Capital One Financial Corporation, making Fairbank CEO, and Chairman in 1995. More recently Fairbank has tried to reduce the company's reliance on credit cards with the purchase of Hibernia National Bank and North Fork Bank, allowing Capital One to compete with larger financial institutions. He has since raised $750 million from a stock offering and, in a further move toward diversification, bought Chevy Chase Bank in a $520-million merger.

Jiang Nanchun Founder, Chairman & CEO (2003–08), Focus Media

BIOGRAPHY
Born in Shanghai, China, in 1973. Jiang graduated from Huadong Normal University with a bachelor's degree in Chinese language and literature.

BEST DECISION
Acquiring Allyes Information Technology Company in 2007, allowing Focus Media to enter the world of internet advertising.

LESSON IN BUSINESS
Learn to delegate—although Jiang built the business from scratch, he handed over the day-to-day running of Focus Media in the interests of good management.

DESCRIBED AS CHARISMATIC and visionary by colleagues, Jiang is the founder and former CEO of Focus Media, the biggest digital signage company in China. He is one of China's richest IT entrepreneurs.

In 2003, "Jason" Jiang joined Aiqi Advertising and transformed it into Focus Media, providing outdoor advertising on LCD displays. As chairman and CEO, Jiang designed the first LCD device himself and secured six-month trials on 50 buildings in Shanghai. He sold slots to major firms including Hennessy, FUJIFILM, TAG Heuer, and China Netcom, then secured $500,000 of funding from Softbank China Venture Capital, which in turn attracted a further $42.5 million in venture capital. This enabled Jiang to target buildings in Beijing, Shenzhen, and Guangzhou, as well as installing screens in supermarkets and airport shuttle buses. By late 2005, the company had 35,000 LCD screens in 52 major cities. A successful initial public offering in 2005 enabled Jiang to acquire rivals Frame Media and Target Media. Excellent results in 2007 were followed by a disappointing year in 2008, and Jiang was replaced by Tan Zhi, who in late 2008 oversaw a $1-billion M&A deal with online media company Sina Corp.

> "[Fairbank] eats, sleeps, and breathes Capital One and the information-based strategy."
> James V. Kimsey, co-founder of America Online and director at Capital One.

Craig A. Dubow Chairman, President & CEO, Gannett

BIOGRAPHY
Born in 1954. Dubow graduated from the University of Texas in Austin.

BEST DECISION
Launching a comprehensive strategy to reinvent the old newspaper newsrooms as a system of "information centers."

LESSON IN BUSINESS
Combine the new with the strengths of the old—Dubow's attempt to link new media with his company's traditional strengths indicate that all is not yet lost for newspapers.

TAKING THE HELM of one of the biggest newspaper groups in the US, at a time of major crisis in the industry, Dubow's innovations have led the way in the industry's efforts to deal with a rapidly changing marketplace.

When Dubow, a Gannett veteran of eleven years, took over in 2005, newspapers had already been written off in many quarters as a dying dinosaur of an industry, a lumbering twentieth-century phenomenon destined for destruction at the hands of the fast-moving, user-driven world of the Internet. Newspaper circulations have continued to decline since then, but Dubow has taken on the challenge of transforming a company built for different times into one fit for a world of new media. His key initiative has been to reinvent newsrooms as "information centers," aimed at distributing news and comment through a variety of media, whether newspapers, broadcasting, or online, and offering a flexible, responsive service that can combine the power of a large newspaper company with the immediacy of the internet. Gannett and the newspaper industry still have a long way to go to take on new media and re-assert old formats, but Dubow has at least begun a fightback.

Hans Helmerich President & CEO, Helmerich & Payne

BIOGRAPHY
Born in Tulsa, Oklahoma, in 1958. Helmerich is the third generation of his family to run the company founded by his grandfather in 1920.

BEST DECISION
Developing an innovative, computerized drilling rig that opened up new possibilities for oil and gas companies.

LESSON IN BUSINESS
Look to the future—by focusing on new technology in the tough times, Helmerich positioned his company perfectly for the next growth phase.

THE OIL AND GAS INDUSTRY was going through a tough time when Helmerich took control of the drilling company founded by his grandfather. His focus on new technology has made it the strongest operator in the business.

When Helmerich took over as CEO in 1989, Helmerich & Payne was the only contract drilling company in the world making a profit. The industry had been severely damaged by the collapse of oil prices in the 1980s, but astute management and an expansion into real estate by Helmerich's predecessors had protected the company from the worst effects. He built up the company for the future by focusing on new technology. The result was the FlexRig, a computerized mobile drilling rig that allowed wells to be drilled much more efficiently and with greater safety. It also gave scope for horizontal drilling, enabling companies to access reserves previously out of reach. With diminishing sources of easily accessible oil, FlexRigs, now in their fourth generation, have become an essential part of modern exploration and production, boosting the company's utilization rates and revenues and giving it a secure place in a notoriously tempestuous industry.

> "Talent, skills, and training aren't enough. They must be teamed together with the inner qualities of integrity and trustworthiness." Hans Helmerich

Qiu Bojun Chairman & President, Kingsoft

BIOGRAPHY
Born in 1964 in China. Qiu graduated with a bachelor's degree in information systems from the National University of Defense Technology in Changsha.

BEST DECISION
Exploiting the niche for Chinese-language products. This led to great gains in a market that until then had been dominated by Roman-script software.

LESSON IN BUSINESS
If you believe in something, be prepared to risk everything—Qiu sold his home to raise capital for the WPS97 project.

OFTEN REFERRED TO as the "Bill Gates of China", Qiu is president of the Chinese software company Kingsoft. A Han national, Qiu once turned down a job offer from Microsoft in order to develop the home software industry in China.

In 1989, nine years after first using a computer, 25-year-old Qiu launched WPS, a Chinese-language word-processing program. More user-friendly to Chinese script than imported software, WPS was an instant hit in China. In 1994, Qiu founded Kingsoft, but in 1996, lack of capital to fund the updated WPS97 project forced him to sell his family home. Fortunately, the software program sold better than expected and in 1998, an injection of capital from the Lenovo Group resulted in a restructure, with Qiu Bojun becoming chairman and president. Since then, Qiu has shifted the emphasis from software development to internet-based technology, with three major divisions: WPS, anti-virus programs, and online games. Known for its innovative research and development, Kingsoft is a leading producer of online games in China, and has been trading on the Hong Kong stock exchange since 2007. Qiu is the company's biggest shareholder, with more than 20 percent of the shares.

Jørgen Vig Knudstorp CEO, LEGO

BIOGRAPHY
Born in 1968 in Denmark, a short distance from Billund, the home of Lego. Knudstorp holds a PhD from Aarhus University.

BEST DECISION
Selling 70 percent of the Legoland theme parks to the Blackstone Group in 2005, which dramatically cut costs.

LESSON FOR BUSINESS
Don't be afraid of change—Knudstorp recognized that LEGO had to move with the times. The focus on "nurturing the child" rather than pursuing profit could no longer remain in the cut-throat 21st-century toy market.

FACED WITH RUNNING a cherished national institution, Knudstorp didn't hesitate to make the sweeping changes in staffing, production methods, and product lines necessary to bring the LEGO brand into the 21st century.

Since its inception in the 1930s, the LEGO company has been synonymous with the founding Christiansen family. When former McKinsey consultant Knudstorp took over in 2004, he was only the second CEO from outside the family to run LEGO. Such a privilege might have caused a more prudent man to move slowly but Knudstorp recognized that LEGO needed swift, wholesale restructuring if the company was to survive. LEGO had been hit hard by the move away from traditional children's games to the more hi-tech options offered by consoles and PCs. To offset vast financial losses ($300 million in 2004), Knudstorp implemented drastic job cuts and turned to cheaper factories in Eastern Europe to manufacture the pieces. Within a year of his arrival, LEGO was back in the black. Under Knudstorp, the company has expanded into advanced robotic technology, movie tie-ins such as the Star Wars range, and computer games in order to enhance LEGO's future profitability.

"Greet success with equanimity; face disappointment calmly." Ancient Chinese saying often quoted by Qiu Bojun

Paul Jacobs CEO, Qualcomm, Inc.

BIOGRAPHY
Born c.1962, Jacobs gained bachelor's and master's degrees in electrical engineering and a PhD from the University of California, Berkeley.

BEST DECISION
Resolving the firm's long-standing patent disputes with Nokia, resulting in a 15-year agreement, an upfront payment, and ongoing royalties, plus the ownership of a number of patents.

LESSON IN BUSINESS
Keep on moving—Jacobs is consistently at the forefront of innovations, such as mobile broadcast TV network MediaFLO.

WITH MORE THAN 25 patents under his belt, Jacobs is a leading innovator in the wireless technology field, and the man who has spearheaded Qualcomm's success in wirelesss telecommunications research and development.

Having joined Qualcomm in 1990 as a development engineer leading the cell phone digital-signal processor software team, Jacobs took over from his father as CEO in July 2005. Since then, he has been the primary driver behind Qualcomm's focus on wireless data services. Jacobs is a long-time advocate of 3- and 4G and social networking, and has driven the company's investment in new technology; its patents are an integral part of all 3G mobile networks. Among his many successes are an improved relationship with telecommunications giant Nokia, the BREW effort (a popular software platform for cell phones), and Qualcomm's development of mobile broadcast TV network MediaFLO, which provides live mobile television content via AT&T and Verizon Wireless, the two largest mobile operators in North America. Jacobs' success has been proven by Qualcomm's results, with increases in both licensing and chipset divisions contributing to revenue of more than $11 billion.

Jeff M. Fettig Chairman, President & CEO, Whirlpool Corp.

BIOGRAPHY
Born in Tipton, Indiana, in 1957. Fettig earned a bachelor's in finance and an MBA from Indiana University.

BEST DECISION
Deciding to make new products the main focus of operations.

LESSON FOR BUSINESS
Find a new differentiator —in white goods, cutting prices is the usual way to increase sales. However, Fettig showed that innovation can be just as effective.

WHIRLPOOL HAS EARNED a strong reputation for its emphasis on innovation under Fettig's leadership. In a market often dominated by price, he has created a distinctive platform for growth in a tough industry.

A career man at Whirlpool, Fettig was part of the leadership group in 1999 when former chairman and CEO David Whitwam decided that focusing on innovation was the best way for the company to advance in its tight markets. When Fettig was appointed chairman, president, and CEO in 2004, he intensified this approach, urging all employees to think of themselves as innovators, and increasing the number of new products in development. His intention was to attract consumers by offering products that stood out from the "white goods" crowd. Within a year, the company had trebled the volume of sales from new products, while plans were on target to continue boosting their share of activity to become the main plank of Whirlpool's operations. The success of this approach soon became apparent. Within three years of Fettig's arrival in the top job, the share price had risen by more than 50 percent and Whirlpool had been recognized as one of the most innovative companies in the US.

"Smart business people succeed because they get the advice in advance. They find out what the rules of the game are and structure accordingly." Paul Jacobs

GREEN INNOVATIONS

Green Tech Ventures

As governments invest in green technology in an effort to meet emissions targets to combat climate change, and customers place an ever greater premium on environmentally-friendly products, businesses have discovered fertile ground in the field of green innovation.

The holy grail of green business is to develop products that not only protect the environment but also present a very real practical and cost benefit to the customer. Monsanto CEO **Hugh Grant** (p426) has set his company the task of finding one such product. Since taking the top job at the food biotech company, Grant has introduced a long-term goal of developing drought-tolerant seeds that offer increased yields and reduced environmental impact, while also using a third less fertilizer, energy, and water per unit.

Another industry on the frontline of the environmental challenge is energy production. Here the big players have had to refocus on greening their business to survive, and find themselves playing catch-up with green start-ups that have the potential to replace them as the sturdy oaks of tomorrow. As the energy crisis looms ever larger, executives like "green revolutionary" **Ditlev Engel** (p106), who has built his wind turbine company Vestas into a market leader in sustainable energy, are well placed to make a lot of money out of saving the world ●

Innovative green technologies have appeared in a variety of different sectors, from electronics to cleaning products, funded by "green capital" from banks adding environmental impact to their investment criteria. Where once CEOs in the energy industry were known for their naysaying in the face of climate change, public pressure and fast-depleting reserves of fossil fuels have prompted an industry-wide push toward sustainability. "Cleantech venture capitalist" **Bob Metcalfe**'s tenure as CEO at US alternative fuel supplier GreenFuel saw him push the company's groundbreaking aim of harvesting second-generation biofuels by fertilizing algae farms with captured CO_2. Since handing over to former Dow Chemical executive **Simon Upfill-Brown** in 2008, Metcalfe has moved his focus to solar cell and geothermal technologies

Fueling a Green Economy

With oil supplies running out and greenhouse gases rising, vehicle manufacturers, agribusinesses, and energy companies have turned to biofuels as a sustainable alternative to the petroleum economy. Producers of the cheapest cars to the most expensive are investing: **Ravi Kant**, MD of India's Tata Motors, is looking to apply biofuel technology to the Nano, the world's cheapest car; while Bentley CEO **Franz-Josef Paegen** aims to introduce renewable fuels across the fleet. Converting to biofuels is seen as a great way to green a business, yet CEOs looking to invest in green technology need to tread carefully; what seems "green" today may not prove so in the future. Once seen as a miracle cure, many now argue that first-generation biofuels, particularly agrofuels from specific crops, are a disaster for the environment: their production can be as polluting as regular fuels; some even release a gas 300 times more harmful than CO_2; and the rush to supply biofuel crops has prompted an agricultural land grab, particularly in rainforest areas. However, hopes lie in promising second- and third-generation fuels produced from non-food crops, waste biomass, crop residues, and low-input, high-yield crops such as algae. Two of the top CEOs in the aerospace sector, **Jon Beatty** of German-US firm International Aero Engines and **Robert J. Gillette** of Honeywell Aerospace, are collaborating to develop jet fuel from algae-based oils. Others even hope to do away with fuel altogether. Arguably the greenest CEO on the planet is **Guy Negre** of French company Moteur Development International, who is working with Tata Motors to build a car that runs on air.

as partner of investment company Polaris Ventures. While 3Com Corp., the computer network company he founded, continues to uphold his green principles under CEO **Robert Mao** by providing the most energy-efficient switches on the market; a tiny technological innovation with a big impact on carbon footprints.

By definition, green investors are in it for the long-term and few more so than Edinburgh-based Pelamis Wave Power Ltd, which, after nearly four decades of research, believes it has finally unlocked the concentrated wind energy of wave power, nature's storage cells. CEO **Phil Metcalf** has presided over the development of the Wave Energy Converter, a marine hydroelectric generator of which a single machine can provide annual power for 500 homes. Opening the world's first wave energy farm in 2008, Metcalf believes wave power is a cost-effective option ready to be rolled out across the seas.

"As the technology develops and becomes more affordable… we can continue to expand… to pretty much anywhere where there is an ocean."
PHIL METCALF

Environmental Adventurers

CEOs at the vanguard of green innovation include:

Dov Charney, AMERICAN APPAREL (Retail: US)—*The clothing company sells only vegan-friendly clothes, has plans to use 80 percent organic cotton, and uses scrap fabric in its underwear lines.*
—

Amy Domini, DOMINI SOCIAL INVESTMENTS (Finance: US)—*Has helped to bring ethical investment into the mainstream, by setting social and environmental standards for the funds they work with.*
—

Mark D. Morelli, ECD OVONICS (Energy: US)—*Pioneering innovations in the areas of hydrogen storage and regenerative fuel cells.*
—

Jørgen Philip-Sørensen, ECOVER (Consumer products: Belgium)—*The company's green cleaning products are proving popular across the world.*
—

Aloys Wobben, ENERCON (Energy: Germany)—*Built the first turbine in his back garden in 1985, and has grown Enercon to become the largest turbine manufacturer in Germany.*
—

Kouji Yamamoto, KANSAI PAINT (Manufacturing: Japan)—*Developed corn-based paint which has a lower carbon footprint than traditional paint.*
—

Martin Roscheisen, NANOSOLAR (Energy: US)—*Produces thin-film technology solar panels, and is moving into nano-tech versions.*
—

Yehudit Bronicki, ORMAT TECHNOLOGIES (Energy: US)—*Has led the way in the eco-alchemy of converting waste into energy.*
—

Hans-Otto Schrader, OTTO GROUP (Retail: US)—*Developed PURE WEAR, a textile made from untreated, biologically-cultivated cotton.*
—

Seiichiro Sano, SANYO (Electronics: Japan)—*Under Sano's leadership they are now among the world leaders in rechargeable batteries and solar technology.*
—

Elon Musk, TESLA MOTORS (Automotive: US)—*Created the super-quick Tesla Roadster, which has single-handedly revitalized the image of the electric car.*
—

Edmund Clark, TORONTO DOMINION BANK (Finance: Canada)—*Has set up a foundation to promote a range of environmental initiatives.*
—

Trevor Baylis, TREVOR BAYLIS BRANDS (Electronics: UK)—*Invented the Freeplay wind-up radio, demonstrating how an existing product could be adapted to save energy.*
—

Peter Blom, TRIODOS BANK (Finance: Netherlands)—*Lends only to businesses that meet strict environmental and social criteria.*
—

2

The Start-up Titans

Jeff Bezos Founder & CEO, Amazon.com

THE FOUNDER of Amazon.com had childhood dreams of becoming a cowboy or astronaut. Instead, he unleashed an internet trading phenomenon. In 1994, Bezos read that the internet was growing by 2,300 percent a year and knew he had to find a way in. With money borrowed from friends and family, Bezos built an online retail empire in about five years and revolutionized the way the world shops. As well as books, music, and DVDs, Amazon now sells a vast range of products, and is the world's biggest online retailer.

BIOGRAPHY
Born in in Albuquerque, New Mexico, in 1964. He graduated from Princeton in 1986 with honors in electrical engineering and computer science.

LEADERSHIP STYLE
Pioneering and visionary, with a trademark guffawing laugh. Bezos is a charismatic leader whose innate confidence, enthusiasm, and energy inspire colleagues to do their best.

KEY STRENGTH
Bezos has made a billion-dollar global career out of knowing what customers want before they know it themselves.

BEST DECISION
Introducing on-the-page customer reviews of products, helping would-be buyers to make their choices.

WEB WUNDERKIND Bezos knew there was a huge amount of money to be made on the internet but was initially unsure what type of business would work best. He researched the mail-order industry and decided on books, believing that the millions of titles in print offered enormous potential for sales. On July 6, 1995, Bezos launched Amazon.com, with financial support from family and friends. The company operated out of the garage at his home in suburban Seattle, Washington.

THE POWER OF PASSION The business was a runaway success from day one. "It was obvious that we were onto something much bigger than we ever dared to hope," says Bezos. By the end of 1999, Amazon.com was a multibillion-dollar corporation selling 3.5 million titles via its pioneering website.

Amazon had fundamentally changed shopping and was a role model for a new generation of e-commerce whiz-kids worldwide. Then came the dotcom share crash. Bezos says he went from "internet poster boy to internet piñata." In 2000, Amazon—still investing heavily in infrastructure—lost $1.4 billion. While other online businesses were bankrupted in the crash, Bezos held on by putting in place dramatic cost-cutting measures, including shedding 1,300 staff. By 2001, Amazon was able to post a net profit of $5.1 million.

Bezos is a rare CEO who can claim to have pioneered a completely new industry from scratch. No longer just a bookstore, Amazon has expanded to sell a diverse array of goods from scientific supplies to groceries, and Bezos is positioned to revolutionize books themselves with the Kindle, an "iPod" of reading.

LESSONS IN BUSINESS: GROWING WITH YOUR CUSTOMERS

Customers want three things, according to Bezos: the best selection, the lowest prices, and the cheapest delivery. At Amazon, all decisions flow from these basic principles.
➔ Start with your customers and work backward—what do they want?
➔ Put that customer strategy into simple terms and tell everyone to justify decisions against those criteria.
➔ Align your internet strategy with your customers needs and wants. Make sure that it echoes and develops your other channels.

"Our mission is to be Earth's most customer-centric company." Jeff Bezos

Sunil Mittal Chairman & CEO, Bharti Airtel

A SELF-MADE MAN with an eye for a market and an innate business sense, Mittal has created one of India's most successful companies from scratch. From small beginnings, he has brought modern telecommunications systems to millions of communication-hungry Indians at prices they can afford, and built a business with a market capitalization that has topped $23 billion, a turnover of $5 billion, and more than 50 million customers. Now Mittal is looking to revolutionize the retail sector and the way India goes shopping.

BIOGRAPHY
Born in India's northern state of Punjab in 1957. Sunil was educated at Punjab University in Chandigarh, India.

LEADERSHIP STYLE
Passionate and ambitious, Mittal is a great delegator, believing the fastest route to a successful company is allowing staff to show initiative and take decisions.

KEY STRENGTH
Understanding the needs of the enormous but complex Indian telecommunications market, and tailoring products accordingly.

BEST DECISION
Attracting millions of new customers by introducing a range of pre-paid cell phone cards available through India's millions of independent, non-chain, local "mom and pop" stores.

WHEELER DEALING After graduating, Mittal borrowed $1,500 from his father and set up a bicycle parts business in Ludhiana in his native Punjab. Aware of its limited potential, he moved to Delhi in the 1980s and, spotting a potential market, started selling imported generators, with profit margins of up to 100 percent. As the Indian government began to lift trading restrictions in 1991, Mittal moved into the nascent telecommunications market, supplying handsets. In the 1990s, he moved quickly to capitalize on the new cell phone market in India, in conjunction with the French telecom group Vivendi.

CALCULATED EXPANSION In 1983, Mittal became the first person to introduce the push-button handset phone to India. Even affluent Indians had to wait years to have a phone connection installed by state-run providers, and Mittal spotted a huge potential market for the private supplier. In the mid-1990s, Bharti Airtel, the company he set up, had fewer than 120,000 subscribers, but the next few years saw a period of enormous growth. His strategy was to offer consumers the best technology with the lowest prices. Mittal gained a reputation as a man who could attract funding and alliances; both SingTel and Vodafone have been his partners. Mittal believes the next big change to hit India will be in the retail sector, as shopping habits move away from markets and corner shops into modern air-conditioned supermarkets. The potential worth of the retail sector in India is estimated to be around $200 billion a year. To this end, in 2006 Mittal signed a deal with Wal-Mart to open a chain of stores under the name of BestPrice Modern Wholesale.

LESSONS IN BUSINESS: GROWING THROUGH PARTNERSHIPS

Mittal built his empire through partnerships with a range of overseas companies. While rivals diversified into steel, hotels, and aviation, Bharti Airtel linked up with Vivendi to capture the mobile telecoms market. When growth slowed, he applied the same partnership approach to a new area with great potential—the retail sector.
→ Form partnerships with other suppliers; encourage growth through mutually profitable joint ventures.
→ When a partnership has worked well in one market, exploit your people's skills in another.
→ Include your managers in partnerships and rely on them to deliver in their own particular way.

"Organized retail will change the face of this country."
Sunil Mittal

Michael Dell CEO, Dell Inc.

THE CLASSIC EXAMPLE of turning a personal obsession into an immense business success, Michael Dell has become one of the leading figures in his generation's glittering pantheon of IT stars. From its beginnings in his university dorm room, his company broke the mould in the PC market, and Dell's innovative thinking and easy management style turned Dell Inc. into a world market leader. When the founder stepped down as CEO, the negative effect on the company's fortunes was clear, and three years later he was back.

BIOGRAPHY
Born in 1965 in Houston, Texas. His father was an orthodontist and his mother was a financial consultant and stockbroker. Dell dismantled an Apple computer and rebuilt it at the age of 15.

LEADERSHIP STYLE
"Egoless". Dell has refused to take a reserved parking space or a door on his office. He applies the company's focus on customer service to the way it deals with its employees.

KEY STRENGTH
Going so far beyond conventional thinking as to establish a new business model.

BEST DECISION
Selling his products direct to the consumer, leaving retailers out of the equation.

FROM THE COLLEGE DORM While a student at the University of Texas in 1984, Dell began putting together PCs and selling them, a venture that proved so successful that, with a loan from his grandparents, he soon dropped out of college and set up the company that became one of the biggest players in the PC world. His innovative business grew so quickly that by the age of 27, Dell was the youngest CEO of a *Fortune* 500 company.

GOING DIRECT Dell hit upon one simple idea that had not yet occurred to anyone else in the PC market—cut out the middle man. By selling PCs directly to consumers, he was able to undercut the big guns of the industry, gaining market share rapidly and earning himself and his company a reputation as the consumer's friend. Dell's youthfulness and innovative streak made him a hot media favorite, while his emphasis on customer service increased Dell Inc.'s popularity in the marketplace, and by 2002 the company was bringing in $35 billion in revenue. By 2004 it had become the world's largest PC maker, and the founder, feeling his job was done, made way for Kevin Rollins to become CEO, while remaining chairman. Dell had demonstrated that it is possible to build rapid success by creating a completely new business model. His refusal to conform to the existing structures of his industry took outside-the-box thinking to an extreme and hugely successful conclusion.

In 2007, after the company had suffered a series of setbacks and had lost its number one spot in the market to Hewlett-Packard, Dell returned as CEO, determined to restore the fortunes of the company.

LESSONS IN BUSINESS: INNOVATING FOR SUCCESS

Dell showed that it is possible to be successful—and in a short space of time—working with a brand new business model. His non-conformist attitude has allowed the company to become truly innovative in its business models, with unprecedented results.
→ Always accept that you could do things better than you are doing at the moment.
→ Avoid accepting business practices whose only reason for existing is "we have always done it this way."
→ Keep shaking your organization up until you and your team are working in the best possible way.

"Our business is about technology, yes. But it's also about operations and customer relationships."
Michael Dell

Adrian Gore Founder & CEO, Discovery Holdings Ltd

NOW ONE OF the best known businessmen in South Africa, Gore is the CEO and founder of Discovery Holdings, a major player in the international health and life assurance markets. It encompasses Discovery Health, Vitality, and Discovery Life in South Africa, Prudential Health in the UK, and Destiny Health in the US. Described by some as obsessive, Gore has an ability to think outside the box that has earned Discovery a reputation for innovative products. Under his guidance, membership has grown to nearly 2 million.

BIOGRAPHY
Born in Johannesburg, South Africa, in 1964. Gore graduated from the University of the Witwatersrand, Johannesburg, with a BSc (Hons) in actuarial science. In 1990, he was admitted as a Fellow of the Faculty of Actuaries (Edinburgh, Scotland) and in 1992 as an Associate of the Society of Actuaries (Chicago).

LEADERSHIP STYLE
Astute, competitive, consensual. Renowned for his tenacity and drive, Gore has little patience for laziness or wasted time.

KEY STRENGTH
A brilliant strategist and problem-solver, Gore is the ultimate optimist.

BEST DECISION
Forming his own company at the age of 28.

PICKING A GAP IN THE MARKET Helping out with his father's tobacco and confectionery business convinced Gore that a career in retail was not for him. After a degree in actuarial science, he joined Liberty Life as an actuary and helped develop its Medical Lifestyle product. However, it was a period of economic uncertainty, and as industry costs began to rise, Gore spotted the potential for a medical scheme that offered sustainability. Coupled with the desire to create his own business, Gore founded Discovery Holdings Ltd.

BELIEVING IN INNOVATION Since its inception, Discovery has made innovation its keyword, and Gore believes this is crucial to survival. However, he is disciplined about introducing new products, being careful not to innovate for innovation's sake. After starting out in the healthcare insurance industry, Gore led Discovery to become a pioneer in the life insurance market. In 2001, he launched a product that was 20 percent cheaper than its competitors', by taking out the unnecessary investment part of the insurance. Within months, the rest of the market did the same and life insurance costs declined across the industry. Displaying the strategic vision for which he has become known, Gore turned to preventative health measures, launching the Vitality loyalty and wellness program, for which the company holds a worldwide patent. When rapid growth threatened to affect operational efficiency, Gore restructured the call center, leading to an instant improvement in service. His personality and self-belief have attracted some of South Africa's brightest personnel, giving Discovery a vital edge.

LESSONS IN BUSINESS: ENJOYING SUCCESS

Gore has always believed it is important to have what he calls a "noble cause and purpose" in business. It is better to be motivated by progress, change, and innovation, than money. A CEO does not get up in the morning thinking about money.
→ Join a company whose objectives you identify with and whose success you can enjoy and feel proud of.
→ In a new role, make sure you are seen to be looking at a career rather than today's take-home pay.
→ Define a personal and business vision that makes you look forward to going to work.

"[Gore]… has an obsession with being the best."
Alan Pollard, CEO, Discovery Vitality

Charles Ergen President & CEO, DISH Network & EchoStar

AN INSPIRATIONAL STORY of starting with nothing, spotting a market, and going for broke, while outsmarting major players along the way, has characterized Ergen's career. Co-founding cable box and satellite infrastructure company Echosphere (renamed EchoStar) in 1980, and satellite TV subsidiary DISH Network in 1996, put him in the top 100 richest people in the world, with a net worth of almost $10 billion. DISH Network is now the third largest direct-to-home satellite television company in the US, with some 14 million customers.

BIOGRAPHY
Born in Oak Ridge, Tennessee, in 1953. Ergen graduated from the University of Tennessee with a bachelor's in general business and accounting, and gained an MBA from the Babcock Graduate School of Management at Wake Forest University.

LEADERSHIP STYLE
Aggressive, opportunistic, focused. Ergen is perceived as both down-to-earth and ruthless, though he is also known as a devoted family man.

KEY STRENGTH
Identifying and exploiting market potential to the full.

BEST DECISION
Handing out free satellite dishes to woo customers away from a rival company.

A GAMBLE THAT PAID OFF Ergen's success was built on friendship and an eye for opportunity. Having spotted their first satellite dish in 1980 on a gambling trip to Las Vegas, Ergen and his friend, Jim DeFranco, identified an exciting new market in rural Colorado, where TV reception was poor. Pooling their resources, Ergen, his future wife, and DeFranco started a business called Echosphere, selling dishes off the back of a truck. The business took off, and Ergen's enthusiasm for new technology kept him ahead of his competitors.

AN UNCONVENTIONAL APPROACH Ergen bought into the satellite business and, in 1992, EchoStar was granted its own orbit. The company had launched three satellites, and registered its millionth customer by 1997. Ergen's technological nous is easily equaled by his business instinct. His unconventional approach has seen him fearlessly take on far larger competitors. In one case he famously distributed free satellite dishes to the whole of Boulder, Colorado, to woo customers away from a rival. He was also the first to sell satellite receivers for under $200. In 1998, he sued Rupert Murdoch's redoubtable News Corp. after Murdoch had withdrawn from a planned merger.

Ergen has also suffered his fair share of misfortunes. In 2008, EchoStar lost one satellite on launch, and another through failure. Then Forbes.com reported a 25 percent drop in DISH Network's shares, following its split from EchoStar, and EchoStar paid out $105m in compensation to TiVo, Inc. over a patent breach. Observers believe it is only a question of time before Ergen bounces back.

LESSONS IN BUSINESS: STAYING FOCUSED

Ergen focuses everyone on his core business at all times, especially when deals are being made and broken. In the satellite business, Ergen's goal is simple: to remain the best value at the best price.
→ Make sure that people understand your vision and their part in it. Present it in appropriate terms to everyone involved.
→ Keep your focus simple so that people can explain it quickly and accurately to colleagues and customers.
→ Try not to let a single customer, no matter how important they are, divert you from your strategy.

"I'm playing to win. I don't spend a lot of time thinking about losing." Charles Ergen

Estée Lauder Founder & CEO, Estée Lauder

ANYTHING BUT a typical CEO, Lauder entered the realm of legend long before her death in 2004. In contrast to her working class upbringing in a shabby district of the New York borough of Queens, her cosmetics creations evoked elegance, luxury, and ultra-femininity. By carefully tending that image, Lauder made consumers want to be like her and convinced millions that buying her products was the key. In 1998, she was the only woman on *Time* magazine's list of the 20 most influential business geniuses of the 20th century.

BIOGRAPHY
1906–2004. Born in New York, Josephine Esther Mentzer was the youngest of six children of European immigrants, who lived above their hardware store in Queens. She claimed her family always called her Esty, but when a public school official spelled it Estée, the name stuck.

LEADERSHIP STYLE
Ambitious, lavish, attentive to detail. The ultimate entrepreneur, Lauder did it all herself.

KEY STRENGTH
She combined work and family while growing what she described as "a nice little business."

BEST DECISION
Lacking sufficient advertising budget, she promoted her products by giving away free gifts to purchasers.

HUMBLE BEGINNINGS Lauder began by selling skin-care products made by her Hungarian uncle, John Schotz, during the 1930s. She went on to mix, package, and sell them herself at beauty salons, resorts, and department stores. She was even known to stop women on the street to sell to them. Her breakthrough came in 1948 when she talked Saks Fifth Avenue into giving her counter space for her products. Her husband Joseph Lauter (the family changed their name to Lauder in the late 1930s) and their elder son worked with her in a rented office to meet the sudden increase in demand for her products.

NO ONE OUTSOLD HER When Lauder set up her first office, in 1944, she added lipstick, eye shadow, and face powder to her line of skin creams. She criss-crossed the United States in the 1950s, marketing her products to high-end department stores and, later, training their saleswomen. She created her first fragrance and bath oil in 1953. Throughout the 1950s and 60s, she continued to add products and develop new lines. She also launched the concept of "the Lauder look," the iconic face of the moment. By 1988, the firm accounted for one-third of the prestige cosmetics market in the United States. By 1998, it was doing business in more than 100 countries and the Lauder family's shares were worth $6 billion.

While she exuded an aura of casual luxury, Lauder was a shrewd businesswoman. When the company was floated in 1995, it was done in such a way as to avoid a $95-million tax bill for her family—leading to a revision of the federal tax law two years later. She remained CEO until 1983 and chairman until 1995.

LESSONS IN BUSINESS: BEING DEVOTED TO THE TASK

Obsessed with quality, and a shameless self-promoter, Lauder once explained her philosophy this way: "I have never worked a day in my life without selling. If I believe in something, I sell it, and I sell it hard."
→ Demonstrate the business and personal benefits of your products to customers to make your people passionate about what they do.
→ Inculcate the "We are all salespeople" culture into your whole organization.
→ Every activity starts when someone has sold something to a customer—there is no business without sales.

"Time is not on your side, but I am." Estée Lauder

Terry Tai-ming Gou Founder & CEO, Hon Hai Precision

PUBLICITY-SHY he may be, but Taiwanese businessman Gou cannot hide from the world's media. As founder and CEO of Hon Hai Precision, Gou is the leader of the world's largest contractor of electronics, making products for household names such as Apple, Nintendo, and Motorola. No one has done more to attract electronics production to the Far East, and his company is one of China's key exporters. A notable philanthropist, Gou plans to give away a third of his estimated $5.5 billion personal fortune to charitable causes.

BIOGRAPHY
Born in Taiwan in 1950.

LEADERSHIP STYLE
Charismatic and autocratic, he leads by example. Taking a leaf out of Mao's *Little Red Book*, Gou has issued a number of "Gou's Quotations", which managers are expected to learn by rote.

KEY STRENGTH
Running Hon Hai in the style of a personal fiefdom, Gou is said to inspire great loyalty among his employees.

BEST DECISION
Opening a factory in mainland China, where labor costs were more competitive.

FROM KNOBS TO iPODS Gou's road to riches began in 1974 when his mother loaned him the money to start making channel-changing knobs for televisions. By the early 1980s, the business was doing well enough for him to break into the PC market by supplying connectors. Improved relations between Taiwan and China encouraged Gou to set up his first factory in the city of Shenzhan, China, in 1988. eager to expand, Gou traveled throughout Japan and the US in the 1980s and 1990s, soliciting new customers. It was a meeting in China with Michael Dell, founder of Dell, Inc. that gave a huge boost to his business, and today Hon Hai is one of Dell's biggest suppliers. By 2000, company revenue had reached $3 billion and Hon Hai's workforce topped 30,000. Gou has since expanded his product lines to include cell phones, flat-panel LCD monitors, digital cameras, and iPods, earning a reputation for good quality products at a competitive price.

BUILDING AN EMPIRE Expansion into China has increased the Shenzhan plant's workforce almost tenfold, and nearly half a million workers can be found on sites across the mainland. Gou has also extended operations globally, opening new plants in Europe, Central and South America, and all over Asia. Now too large for Gou to manage alone, Hon Hai still has a very personality-centerd management ethos, with large photos of Gou on display and biographies for sale in every plant. Famous for crusing around his sites late at night in his golf cart to check on production and tend to repairs, Gou often works 16-hour days to keep production output successfully on schedule.

LESSONS IN BUSINESS: LEADING BY EXAMPLE

Gou demands a lot and is somewhat autocratic in style. Though he is sometimes likened to a "medieval warlord" in the manner in which he runs Hon Hai, he never asks more than he himself is willing to give.
- ➔ Be prepared to lead by example and, like Gou, work long days if necessary to keep customer satisfaction levels high.
- ➔ Make an autocratic style work when you need to meet a short-term problem or a long-term strategy.
- ➔ Lace autocratic style with charismatic leadership. The aim is to motivate, not to frighten or rule by fear.

> "A leader must have the decisive courage to be a dictator for the common good." Terry Tai-ming Gou

Mukesh Jagtiani CEO, Landmark Group

STARTING WITH a single baby goods store in Bahrain, Landmark Group founder and CEO Jagtiani has built up one of the largest retail chains in the Middle East, selling clothes, furniture, shoes, and homeware. Now he controls more than 800 stores, which together comprise more than ten million square feet of retail area in countries across the Gulf, as well as Jordan, India, China, Spain, Pakistan, and Egypt. Former college drop-out Jagtiani has come a long way from his humble beginnings and is now a multibillionaire.

BIOGRAPHY
Born in Kuwait c.1951, to Indian parents who had emigrated from Bombay (Mumbai). Jagtiani moved to London to study accounting but dropped out of college.

LEADERSHIP STYLE
Affable, modest, and charming. Jagtiani is a hands-on boss who expects his executives to spend time on the shop floor.

KEY STRENGTH
The intuition to spot a business opportunity. Jagtiani made the move to Dubai which enabled him to catch the Middle East's retail industry boom.

BEST DECISION
Identifying the potential for baby products in the Middle East and focusing on that retail sector.

FAMILY TRAGEDY STRIKES Sent to study accounting in London, "Micky" Jagtiani failed to stay the course. After a spell as a cab driver, Jagtiani swallowed his pride and returned to his family in Kuwait in 1972. Within a year, three close members of his family were dead—brother, father, and mother. At 21 years old, Jagtiani found himself with no family, no education, and no job. Sorely tempted to go to India, his parents' home country, and devote his life to charity, Jagtiani instead decided to have a go at entrepreneurship. Taking his $6,000 inheritance, he flew to Bahrain and took over his late brother's shop. Recognizing that the Gulf had a large population of Asian expats who were traditionally overindulgent when it came to their kids, Jagtiani opened Baby Shop, selling toys and children's clothes and furniture. The business went from strength to strength as wave after wave of Asian and South Asian expats came to work in the region. Jagtiani opened more shops, and by 1992 had six stores and 400 employees.

THE MOVE TO DUBAI In 1992, Jagtiani decided to move his family and company headquarters to Dubai. The timing couldn't have been better. Dubai was undergoing a massive building boom and transformation into a major business and tourist attraction. Despite being advised to turn his attention to the luxury market, Jagtiani stuck with his gut feeling and concentrated on middle-class consumers. Sales rocketed and Jagtiani diversified into home furnishing. More recently, he has branched out into restaurants and leisure. Landmark Group's annual turnover has topped $2.5 billion and continues to grow.

LESSONS IN BUSINESS: RETAILING SUCCESS

Jagtiani enforces the "category killer" concept, making sure that every brand his stores carry is the best in that sector. The stores themselves are based on the US and European models that many of his customers have experienced—spacious, with easy access and a large range of affordable products
➔ Choose the best location in a geographic area with a large consumer market.
➔ Stock as wide a range of products as possible so that consumers have no need to shop elsewhere.
➔ Know your market: price products competitively to maintain customer loyalty.

"Success hasn't changed [Jagtiani] at all in the last ten years. He's still humble and low profile."
Ishwar Chugani, executive director, Giordano Fashion

THE CUSTOMER-CENTERED APPROACH

Customers are key to business survival. Image, R&D, quality control, customer service, branding, advertising, and pricing all play their part in attracting and retaining customers. Seeking customer feedback and sharing their experience is often an integral part of the process and some CEOs play notably personal roles. **Konosuke Matsushita** (p61), founder of what became Panasonic, lined up incognito with visitors outside the Matsushita Pavilion during the Osaka World Exposition in 1970. His experience left him unimpressed and he immediately changed the admissions system. Giving your customers what they want is key. **Ingvar Kamprad** (p316), founder of IKEA, struck gold when he transformed cheap to chic in massive stores that have become mainstays for cash-strapped students, first-time house buyers and everybody else who wants a cheerfully modern household item at a modest price—a formula that has proved irresistible ●

Care, Not Contempt

Competing for customers is not the whole story. Beyond simple feedback, customers can also become an invaluable source of information to aid product or service development. This is the concept at the heart of co-creation. **Jørgen Vig Knudstorp** (p42), CEO of Danish toy manufacturer LEGO, places the customer at the heart of LEGO's product innovation, making them "active users". LEGO taps the views of a permanent user group of around 4,500 families with children, its "kids' inner circle". Customers are invited to contribute their own designs for LEGO models via the company's website.

A different approach was adopted by the late **Akio Morita**, Sony's co-founder and chairman: "Our plan is to lead the public rather than ask them what products they want," he said. "The public does not know what is possible, but we do." Morita invented the Sony Walkman because he was convinced consumers would love it. Colleagues were sceptical but Morita was proved right when the Walkman became one of the most successful consumer products ever.

Whatever the approach, treating customers with due respect is crucial. As **Gerald Ratner**, former CEO of the UK jewelry chain Ratners Group, discovered to his cost when a joke about how Ratners could sell a cheap sherry decanter "because it's total crap" and a further comment that some of the company's earrings were "cheaper than... [a] prawn sandwich but probably wouldn't last as long", led to appalling publicity and plummeting sales. The company's value nose-dived, and Ratner was fired. However, he learned from his mistakes and in 2004 he launched a successful online jewelry business, Geraldsonline. It is now the largest online jewelry store in the UK.

Online trade

The Internet has changed customer relations for ever. Customers can now access a mine of product, pricing, and performance information, and companies can tap feedback about their consumers, aiding product and marketing design. **Jeff Bezos** (p48) of Amazon has led the way in measuring the online behavior of customers, using the information to improve the online retail experience and target recommendations for purchases. There is also an increasing awareness of the risks of negative publicity, which spreads like wildfire through online forums and blogs. Meanwhile, the nominal cost of online distribution has encouraged a new version of the traditional free sample. While information, news, and articles are freely available, **Shantanu Narayen** (p190), CEO of Adobe Systems, Inc., provides free document display software and **J. R. Smith**, CEO of US security software firm AVG, offers a valuable virus scan free of charge.

Consumer-led Executives

Their businesses are varied and their approaches differ but they share the same determined focus on consumer needs:

Joseph M. Hogan, ABB (Manufacturing: Switzerland)— *Develops unique technologies for utility and industry customers to improve performance and competitivity while minimizing environmental impact.*
—

Doug Tough, ANSELL HEALTHCARE (Consumer products: Australia)—*Their award-winning Guardian℠ service is an innovative risk-assessment tool, which customers can use to tailor Ansell's products, such as rubber gloves and condoms, to their particular needs.*
—

David J. West, THE HERSHEY COMPANY, (Foodstuffs: US)— *Developed a green-tea flavored chocolate to appeal to the Chinese market.*
—

William R. Johnson, H.J. HEINZ (Foodstuffs: US)—*Invited consumers to compete to produce a TV ad for Heinz Ketchup.*
—

Kazuyasu Kato, KIRIN HOLDINGS (Beverages: Japan)—*Tastes differ so Kirin's tweaked the recipe and packaging of their black tea for the Chinese market.*
—

Tom Alexander, ORANGE UK (Telecommunications: UK)— *Focused Orange on getting back to basics to differentiate itself on quality, network coverage, service, and brand.*
—

Joe Fulmer, STITCHING POST (Retail: US)—*Created a profitable community of customers through in-store education, charitable events, and advertising.*
—

"There is only one boss. The customer. And he can fire everybody in the company from the chairman on down, simply by spending his money somewhere else."
SAM WALTON

Philip Knight Co-founder, Chairman & CEO (1964–2004), Nike, Inc.

FROM HUMBLE BEGINNINGS selling footwear from the back of a car, Knight created a business that dominated its industry and became a model of successful innovation, turning Nike into one of the greatest corporate success stories of the 20th century. His simple but original business model, ability to break completely new marketing ground, and preparedness to change the way he did things when the need arose, established Nike as one of the most formidable companies and strongest brands in the world.

BIOGRAPHY
Born in 1938 in Portland, Oregon, Knight is the son of a lawyer who later became a newspaper publisher. He received a journalism degree from the University of Oregon, where he was also a middle-distance runner.

LEADERSHIP STYLE
Renowned for being inscrutable and unpredictable, Knight originally ran his business in an easy-going, collegiate manner, but as it grew he shifted to a more traditional managerial style, showing a willingness to change culture and approach as the needs of the market dictated.

KEY STRENGTH
Understanding how the symbolic power and attraction of sport could be used to move products.

BEST DECISION
Signing Michael Jordan to Nike, intimately linking his brand with one of the sporting icons of the time, and setting the model for similar deals in the future.

ONE BIG IDEA After a year of active duty in the army, "Phil" Knight enrolled at Stanford Graduate School of Business. He wrote a paper entitled, "Can Japanese sports shoes do to German sports shoes what Japanese cameras did to German cameras?", which set out the case for making high-quality athletic shoes cheaply in Japan. After receiving his MBA, Knight traveled to Japan to follow up his idea.

BRANDING GENIUS Co-founding Blue Ribbon Sports in 1964 with Bill Bowerman, his former athletics coach from the University of Oregon, Knight began selling Japanese shoes at athletics meetings in the Pacific Northwest, while also working as an accountant. By 1972, as the jogging boom took off, the company was selling more than $3-million-worth of shoes a year. Knight's business model of high-end

products made at low cost proved hugely successful. The company was renamed Nike in 1978 and went public in 1980, passing Adidas to become the industry leader in the US. Knight took another radical step in 1984 when he signed basketball star Michael Jordan to endorse Nike's products, arguably creating the practice of sports-goods marketing through sporting personalities. His innovative approach, instinct for marketing, and free-wheeling, maverick style pushed company growth, and it became the undisputed leader in the sports-shoe industry in the 1980s. When Nike's position was threatened by Reebok, Knight responded by cutting costs, streamlining the company, and reorganizing it along more conventional corporate lines, laying the basis for its continued growth. He stepped down as CEO in 2004 but stayed as chairman, and remains influential within the company.

LESSONS IN BUSINESS: GROWING A BRAND

Knight's ability to make an unbreakable connection between a brand and a sports star, an activity, or even a mood showed that if you find the right vehicle there are no limits to your brand's potential.
➔ Think hard about how you can make people aspire to owning and using your brand.
➔ Use sponsorship to make people believe your products will improve their performance, reputation, or lives.
➔ Mount campaigns that could turn your product into a cultural icon by connecting it to current heroes, whether sporting or otherwise.

"Every six months is a new lifetime." Philip Knight

Larry Ellison Co-founder & CEO, Oracle

A COMBINATION of a keen insight into where the IT industry was heading, and a preparedness to attack competitors without mercy, enabled Ellison to turn Oracle, the company he founded, into one of the world's leading producers of computer programs for business applications, known as "enterprise software". His eye for the next big move, his ability to weather the tough times, and his relentless commercial aggression have made Oracle one of the giants of the software industry, and ensured his place as one of its most prominent figures.

BIOGRAPHY
Born in Manhattan in 1944, Ellison never knew his father, and his unmarried mother, Florence Spellman, left him to be raised by an aunt and an uncle, Lillian and Louis Ellison, who had emigrated from the USSR. Louis Ellison had taken his name from Ellis Island.

LEADERSHIP STYLE
Combative and aggressive. Ellison keeps a tight grip on every aspect of the company and makes it abundantly clear that he runs Oracle.

KEY STRENGTH
An appreciation of the opportunity that the new world of business software offered, combined with the technical savvy to give this new market what it wanted.

BEST DECISION
Moving into the business database software market early, gaining a crucial advantage over the competition.

GOING WEST Ellison began studying physics at the University of Chicago in the 1960s but, seeing more enticing opportunities elsewhere, dropped out and moved to California to work in the emerging computer industry. In the 1970s, he started work on a database project for the CIA, the title of which, "Oracle," became the name for the company he co-founded in 1977 with Robert Miner and Edward Oates.

SERVING A NEW MARKET Ellison's forward-looking development strategy enabled Oracle to grow strongly throughout the 1980s. As the market for business software expanded rapidly, Oracle released a string of highly successful products targeting this new market. By the late 1980s, Oracle was a public company and a seemingly ever-growing name in the blooming IT industry. In 1990, however, the company was faced with a sudden financial loss due to an overstatement of earnings. Ellison demonstrated that he could deal with difficult conditions as well as good, laying off 10 percent of the company's workforce and bringing in key new staff to bolster performance. From then on, showing an ever-aggressive approach to key competitors, he pursued a program of organic growth. Embarking on an ambitious acquisition campaign in 2006, Oracle spent a total of $19 billion in two years in the purchase of 21 firms to move the company into entirely new areas, including retail and business intelligence software, taking the fight directly to its competitors with the aim of squeezing them out of new markets. These strategies sealed Oracle's position as a software giant and confirmed Ellison as one of the leading figures in an industry with no shortage of big names.

LESSONS IN BUSINESS: ATTACKING THE COMPETITION

Hit the opposition hard, and then hit them again—Oracle's success has been largely down to Ellison's taste for going after the competition wherever he can.
- → Create a system for measuring yourself against the competition, and consider your strengths and weaknesses, as well as those of your competition, from the customer's perspective.
- → Choose your competitive battleground and focus on winning key orders, even if profitability is questionable.
- → Don't be afraid to consider removing a competing product from the marketplace by buying the company.

"When you innovate, you've got to be prepared for everyone telling you you're nuts." Larry Ellison

Juan Trippe Founder, Pan American World Airways

AS A CHILD Trippe watched Wilbur Wright's historic flight around the Statue of Liberty, and was smitten. When the 28-year-old Trippe launched Pan American he turned the aviation industry on its head: his was the first airline to fly across the Pacific and Atlantic oceans in the 1930s and the first to offer affordable tourist-class air travel. By the early 1960s, Trippe's fleet was connecting 86 countries on a route network of over 80,000 miles (128,000 kilometers). Unfortunately, Trippe was also largely responsible for the downfall of the company.

BIOGRAPHY

1899–1981. Born in Sea Bright, New Jersey. Trippe's father was a prominent New York banker. Trippe graduated from The Hill School in 1917, and Yale in 1921, where he started the Yale Flying Club. When his father died, Trippe took a job on Wall Street, but his passion was aviation.

LEADERSHIP STYLE

Unorthodox, flamboyant, and visionary, Trippe was no textbook CEO. He didn't delegate and he made deals without consulting his top managers, but he had a vision that took air travel into the jet age.

KEY STRENGTH

Understanding the power of aviation to connect nations and bring people together. A man of tremendous persuasive ability, he forced an entire industry to follow his lead.

BEST DECISION

Bringing air travel within reach of everyone, not just the wealthy. By introducing two classes of air travel and creating the world's first low fare service, Trippe changed the course of aviation history.

TAKE OFF In 1923, along with some of his Yale Flying Club friends, Trippe set up Long Island Airways, running an air-taxi service for the rich and powerful. By 1927, he had bid for the first US international airmail contract, between Florida and Cuba. Later that year, Trippe merged his new company with a rival, Pan American Airways, forming a company with just two airplanes, 24 employees, and the goal of "providing mass air transportation for the average man at rates he can afford to pay."

FLYING HIGH On November 22 ,1935, Pan Am's "China Clipper" completed the first trans-Pacific flight, a six-day journey from San Francisco to Manila. During World War II, Pan Am was a key transporter for the US government, ferrying military personnel and material. After the war, Trippe concentrated on his dream of making flying affordable. In 1952, he launched a low-fare service on flights over the North Atlantic. He cut the usual round-trip fare in half and introduced two fare classes for passengers. In the late 1960s, Trippe pushed Boeing to expand the size of commercial jets, and the company responded with the 747, which was over twice as large as the 707, making air travel even more affordable. In 1968, Trippe spent $600 million on Boeing's first crop of the giant planes, the last big move he made before retiring that year. Unfortunately, these purchases seriously overstretched the company. Air travel suffered in the early 1970s, and Pan Am was stuck with too many planes. By the time of his death in 1981, the company was shedding unprofitable routes, and it would finally go out of business a decade later. Trippe was posthumously awarded the US Medal of Freedom in 1985.

LESSONS IN BUSINESS: STAYING GROUNDED

Combining bold moves and blind ambition, hard work and connections, Trippe stayed true to his vision of what air travel could be. In the end this vision was not compatible with economic success.
→ Idealism is important, as is following your vision, but do not let it compromise your financial future.
→ Companies operate in the midst of hard economic facts and, whatever your passion, they will prevail.
→ Beware of supplier relationships where your influence is high. Avoid supporting such a supplier in a way that harms your company.

"In one fell swoop, we have shrunken the earth."
Juan Trippe, on the introduction of jet aircraft

Konosuke Matsushita Founder & CEO (1918–61), Panasonic

THE CORPORATE GIANT built from scratch by Matsushita was perhaps the greatest success story among the many in Japanese business in the 20th century. Matsushita's pioneering innovations in mass production, marketing, branding, product development, and retailing turned his company into one of the world's leading electrical and electronics manufacturers, and his unique management style and business philosophy led to him being revered and regarded as the model for Japanese business leaders for decades.

BIOGRAPHY
1894–1989. Born in Wakayama Prefecture, Japan. His father was a wealthy landlord, but the collapse of the family's finances when Matsushita was nine forced the young boy to seek employment in Osaka. There he worked as an apprentice to a brazier and in a bicycle shop before landing a job at 16 with the Osaka Electric Light Company.

LEADERSHIP STYLE
Paternalistic. Encouraged and motivated his employees largely by creating the paternal management tradition in Japan, in which staff are viewed as part of a family and are assured of lifelong employment.

KEY STRENGTH
Recognizing the importance of constant innovation.

BEST DECISION
Designing and standardizing his products for mass-production.

STARTING FROM SCRATCH Matsushita began his career as an engineer in an Osaka power company. In 1917, at the age of 23, he came up with an idea for an improved electrical socket and started his own business. The socket proved impossible to produce in bulk and failed to sell, but Matsushita learned the lesson and ensured that his next invention, a new bicycle lamp, was designed for mass production. It took off and so did the business.

MASS MARKETER Technological innovation and mass production became the key principles behind his company, Matsushita, which began making low-cost household electrical goods for Japanese customers. This strategy played a large part in helping Japan become Asia's first consumer economy. Driven by Matsushita's instinct for marketing and his insistence that each succeeding version of a product should be both better and cheaper than its predecessor, the company grew rapidly. It also became a major supplier to the Japanese army during World War II, leading the occupying Allies to restrict the company's activities after the war.

He survived the crisis and became one of the key entrepreneurs credited with leading Japan's post-war economic success. Matsushita formed an alliance with the Dutch company Philips in 1953, and in 1959 he established the company's first sales operation outside Japan, in the US. He then began to flood America and other Western countries with product brands including National, Technics, and Panasonic (which became the company name in 2006). He left his executive role to become chairman in 1961, and his business model continued long after his retirement in 1973.

LESSONS IN BUSINESS: IMPROVING QUALITY AND LOWERING COST

If it can be made, it can be made more cheaply and it can be made better. Striving for improvement and keeping up the pressure to lower costs are an unbeatable mix in gaining market share.
→ Use your competition for your benchmark on quality and cost. If they can make it better and cheaper, then so can you.
→ Guard against product returns—your reputation is damaged with the retailer and the consumer.
→ Make sure that no customer for your products feels they require a goods inward quality check.

"Every single person you meet is a customer."
Konosuke Matsushita

Mike Lazaridis President & Co-CEO, Research In Motion

A DEEP FASCINATION with the possibilities of science and a well-tuned alertness to the desires of customers have proven a powerful combination for Lazaridis. His company's development of the BlackBerry answered a central need in the corporate market for mobile email, and his ability to guide his product's progress through changing customer demands, technical glitches, and ever-intensifying competition have ensured that its position at the heart of business communications, and more widely, is secure.

BIOGRAPHY
Born in Istanbul in 1961. He was five when his parents emigrated, via Germany, to Windsor, Ontario, Canada. He studied electrical engineering at the University of Waterloo, Ontario, before leaving to pursue his business career.

LEADERSHIP STYLE
Infectiously enthusiastic. Lazaridis's total commitment to his field plays a crucial part in motivating his staff.

KEY STRENGTH
Listening to customers every step of the way.

BEST DECISION
Combining computing and wireless technology, an idea that came from his science teacher John Micsinszki.

ENGINEERING DROP-OUT Lazaridis's confidence in the business potential of emerging technology prompted him to ditch his electrical engineering degree before he had finished in 1984 and to set up in business with an old friend. By the early 1990s, they had come up with a forerunner of the BlackBerry, and in 1997 their years of development and technical innovation paid off with the production of the first small, efficient version, setting off the product's rapid rise to essential business tool.

SHREWD INNOVATOR A compulsive and relentless innovator, Lazaridis has personally overseen every detail in the development of the BlackBerry since the idea first emerged. In the early days of the product he worked tirelessly to optimize its network performance, driven by his own passion for excellence and a deep understanding of science and technology. Under his leadership, Research in Motion is committed to consulting customers at every step of the development process, ensuring that any changes reflect real demand in the marketplace. Lazaridis is determined to avoid the pitfall of letting marketing dumb down innovation to make products simpler.

His attention to customers' needs ensured not only that BlackBerry quickly established itself as the accessory of choice for business professionals, but that it was made available to a much wider market through cheaper price plans and new ranges of handsets and designs. Firmly established as the leader in the field, BlackBerry is now facing some big company competitors keen to grab a larger market share, but with Lazaridis's finger on that market's pulse, rivals are in for a tough fight.

LESSONS IN BUSINESS: ASKING THE CUSTOMERS

However deep your fascination for your product, however convinced you are that it will be the next big thing, keep asking the customers what they want. They are the ones who will make the final decision.
→ Use well-designed and professionally executed market research to ensure the results are not misleading.
→ Use focus groups to get qualitative feedback on a product. Make sure the moderator is skilled in getting everyone's honest opinion.
→ Use the internet for researching a clearly identified market. Send emails to people who fit that niche.

"Our culture is to double-check, check twice, and ask customers before we undertake changes."
Mike Lazaridis

Bob Simpson Chairman & CEO, XTO Energy

IN JUST 15 YEARS, Simpson took XTO Energy from nowhere to being one of the largest independent energy companies in the US. A bold new approach to gas and oil exploitation enabled the company to increase its proven reserves rapidly, at a time when even the oil majors were having trouble pushing theirs upward. Simpson's ability to find reserves in apparently worn-out fields and extract resources at a much lower cost than his competitors has established XTO as a key energy player with an assured future.

BIOGRAPHY
Born in 1949, Simpson grew up in Cisco, Texas. He was naturally entrepreneurial and by age four had his own egg round. He won a scholarship to Baylor University, Waco, to study accountancy, followed by an MBA.

LEADERSHIP STYLE
Swashbuckling and exacting. He admires those with a close eye for detail who can see potential others might overlook, but he leads from the front, often challenging accepted practice.

KEY STRENGTH
A true talent for seeing unappreciated potential in the energy industry.

BEST DECISION
Targeting acquisitions at half-capacity oil wells and gas fields being sold off cheaply.

A NEW ENERGY MODEL Simpson founded XTO in 1986 with two other energy industry colleagues, beginning with a staff of six and no gas and oil reserves at all. He built an entirely new model for the industry, one that would take over where the majors left off and would rely on carefully selected acquisitions, innovative use of new technology, and a determination to drive down costs. Simpson's skill on all three levels soon became apparent.

MONEY FROM OLD WELLS XTO's strategy involved buying existing US oil wells and gas fields where production had fallen to around half its initial level, a point at which the major energy companies were often prepared to unload the sites relatively cheaply. Simpson's model was based on the belief that, by drilling new wells, using the latest technology, and,

above all, better management, XTO could produce oil and gas for many more years and at lower costs. Central to that strategy was Simpson's ability to make the right acquisitions decisions. While the energy sector as a whole did well, XTO's performance was spectacular, and the wide gap in the levels of growth and value creation between the company and its competitors has confirmed the effectiveness of Simpson's approach. XTO's production grew consistently every year, its share price increased nearly fifty-fold in the years since the company went public in 1993, and its proven reserves grew by more than 30 defense in 2007 alone, when the most the majors could hope for was 5 defense. Buying Hunt Petroleum for $4.2 billion in 2008 showed that Simpson's eye for an acquisition was as astute as ever, and XTO's future seems assured.

LESSONS IN BUSINESS: FINANCING OPPORTUNITY

Simpson's mastery of detail allowed him to spot opportunities overlooked by rivals. This gave him the courage to defy the Wall Street financiers and expand.
→ Financiers are often slow to react to changing industry trends and may not be convinced of the opportunities you perceive.
→ Remember that financial institutions are shareholders, not experienced managers, and can get it wrong.
→ Make your company as independent of the finance people as you can by building cash reserves.

"Our basic strategy is to buy quality and make it better." Bob Simpson

Li Yanhong President & CEO, Baidu

BIOGRAPHY
Born in Shanxi Province, China, in 1968. Li read library information management at Beijing University, and received a master's in computer science from the State University of New York.

BEST DECISION
Taking Baidu public in 2005, which made Li one of China's ten wealthiest IT entrepreneurs.

LESSON IN BUSINESS
Seek out challenges—following his mother's advice, Li advanced himself through study in both China and the US, before returning to his homeland to set up his highly successful company.

ARMED WITH a small amount of venture capital, but big dreams, Li co-founded internet company Baidu in 2000. Listed in 2007 among the CNN Money "50 people who matter now," Li is an influential figure in the industry in China.

Following university, "Robin" Li developed software for the *Wall Street Journal*'s online edition, and then joined Silicon Valley pioneer Infoseek as head of search engine development. In 2000, after raising $1.2 million in venture capital, he returned to China with friend Xu Yong to found Baidu, with Li as chairman and Xu as CEO. Baidu initially offered search engines to other Chinese portals, but Li soon developed Baidu's own search engine. Li became CEO after Xu resigned in 2004, and took Baidu public in 2005 in the biggest opening on Nasdaq since the dotcom peak in 2000. Li's leadership skills have been put to the test under accusations of internet censorship, copyright violations, and advertising discrepancies. Baidu also faces fierce competition from Google and the merger of Yahoo! with Chinese e-commerce firm Alibaba. In late 2008, Li released R&D plans for a new search engine platform, Aladdin, aimed at increasing Baidu's search ability and keeping it China's number one navigation site.

Wang Chuanfu Chairman & CEO, BYD Group

BIOGRAPHY
Born in 1966. Wang earned a bachelor's degree from Central South University and a master's from Beijing General Research Institute of Nonferrous Metals.

BEST DECISION
Beating US and Japanese competitors to market with a no-frills electric vehicle whose low production costs are claimed to level the playing field.

LESSON IN BUSINESS
Keep it simple—Wang's market strategy exploits the simplicity of the electric car compared with the complexity of gasoline-powered vehicles.

ELECTRIFYING the competition, China's cell-phone-battery king Wang challenged auto-manufacturing giants when his BYD Group began selling its electric hybrid car in 2008, a year ahead of US and Japanese competitors.

Bored by his government research job, Wang borrowed venture capital from a cousin in 1995 to found BYD, Build Your Dreams, and began making rechargeable mobile phone batteries. Hiring new engineering graduates, he assembled a formidable research capacity while rapidly growing BYD into the world's second-largest producer of lithium-ion batteries. Wang, who at the time did not drive, saw a synergistic opportunity for deploying his company's battery expertise to develop an inexpensive electric vehicle. His strategy was to design simple electric cars that would be to gas-engined vehicles what mass-market digital timepieces became to precision watches. He set a team of top engineers to work on the project while acquiring a small Chinese auto-maker, with a plan to roll out domestic product first and then launch into Europe and the US by 2011. In 2008, US billionaire Warren Buffett bought 10 percent of BYD, which had built annual revenues of more than $3 billion.

"We believe in local markets... that the search engine is not a pure technology phenomenon, but has close ties with culture and language." Li Yanhong

Charles R. Schwab, Jr. Founder & Chairman, Charles Schwab

BIOGRAPHY
Born in Sacramento, California, in 1937. Schwab has a BA in economics from Stanford University and an MBA from Stanford Graduate School of Business. It was not until he reached the age of 40 that Schwab realized he was dyslexic.

BEST DECISION
Moving into online trading services, which vastly expanded the reach of the company.

LESSON IN BUSINESS
Innovate—Schwab responded quickly and decisively to a rapidly changing market place, yielding a competitive advantage.

SELF-MADE BILLIONAIRE Schwab made his fortune offering discount brokerage to the masses. With more than seven million clients, the Charles Schwab Corp. is one of the world's largest financial services companies.

The Charles Schwab Corp. was founded in 1973 by "Chuck" Schwab, who revolutionized the brokerage industry. By offering the same basic services as other firms, but at a much more affordable price, Schwab attracted a new clientele. By the mid-1990s, Schwab saw that the future of trading lay in online transactions, and in 1995 the company introduced its Equalizer software. This allowed customers to trade stocks through their own computers, though not through the internet initially. This changed in 1996 with the launch of the e.Schwab online trading service: 25,000 customers signed up within two weeks, and 2 million by 1998. In 2003 Schwab handed the reins over to his co-CEO, but he returned as sole CEO within a year due to faltering performance. Cutting costs, reducing fees, and refocusing the business on serving individual investors, he soon brought the company back to financial health, and in 2008 he stepped down again to become executive chairman.

Aubrey K. McClendon Chairman & CEO, Chesapeake Energy

BIOGRAPHY
Born in Oklahoma City in 1959. Aubrey's father worked in marketing for energy company Kerr-McGee. McClendon graduated from Duke University, North Carolina, in 1981.

BEST DECISION
Teaming up with fellow landman Tom Ward to co-found the company in 1989.

LESSON IN BUSINESS
Do what's necessary to survive—McClendon took the hard decision in 2008 to sell almost all his shares, in order to save the company.

TIMES HAVE BEEN TOUGH at Chesapeake Energy, the third largest natural gas producer and the most active driller of new wells in the US, McClendon has the potential to take the company back to its former $50-billion market cap.

Although McClendon once considered a career with accounting firm Arthur Andersen, family connections in the energy industry proved too hard to resist. Shortly after leaving university he began working in the accounting department of his uncle's small oil and gas company, Jaytex. After gaining experience there, McClendon left to become an independent oil worker, or landman. In 1983, he met Tom Ward, a recent graduate in petroleum land management, with whom he worked for the next six years. In 1989, they founded Chesapeake Energy with a capital investment of $50,000. By 2008 it was the largest independent gas company in the US. The company's growth has been primarily through acquisitions and mergers. Although the financial turmoil of 2008 forced McClendon to sell nearly all his 33.5 million shares, he expressed confidence in the company's continuing financial security and his aspiration to rebuild his personal holding.

"The man who does not work for the love of work but only for money, is not likely to make money— nor find much fun—in life." Charles R. Schwab, Jr.

THE POWER OF INSTINCT

Everybody makes instinctive judgments, but many intuitive ideas get discarded as self-doubt and caution take hold of the decision-making process. This is not the case with the majority of CEOs. Indeed, 62 percent of CEOs rated gut feelings as being highly influential in their business decisions*. "Instinct can be just as important as data and spreadsheets when it comes to making a truly innovative decision or taking a business risk", says **Stelios Haji-Ioannou** (p404), founder and CEO of easyGroup. Stelios backed his instinct when he challenged established brands and re-engineered processes to provide lower consumer prices, starting with low-cost air travel and taking off from there. As did Adidas CEO, **Herbert Hainer** (p254), when the German athletic kingpin acquired British rival Reebok to compete against Nike. "I can smell good and bad decisions," says Hainer. "It is in my blood and I feel it in my stomach... When you make decisions every day you can't always draw up a business plan" ●

Instinct Guided by Vision

Leading CEOs are united in their unshakeable clarity of vision. A clear vision enables confident risk-taking by giving focus to gut feelings and instinct.

Crispin Davis, CEO until 2009 of UK and Dutch publisher Reed Elsevier, had a clear vision for the future of the company, giving him the confidence to back his instincts and to make his "most fundamental decision, to focus on four core businesses—science, legal, B2B, and education." His decision, which went against the wisdom of some of his advisors, paid dividends by preserving and strengthening the key sectors of the business and revolutionizing the company.

Collective Intuition

Johnson & Johnson, the US healthcare products and pharmaceuticals company, under the leadership of **CEO William C. Weldon**, broke from conventional wisdom by embracing "collective intuition". This is value-guided group dialogue that seeks to establish an instinctive consensus; it is about sharing, listening, and rethinking opinions to create harmony when making decisions or solving problems, to create a shared and focused intent. Proponents of collective intuition argue that, when a group is guided by their values, by a strong vision, they will build up a feeling of "the right thing to do." J&J used this method to take the risk of focusing on a broad portfolio instead of pursuing a single market for higher margin, as conventional industry wisdom dictated. Their decision created accelerated growth, protected them from market changes, and, according to Weldon, enabled them to focus on "providing breakthrough products that cure disease and save lives".

"Sometimes a leader must be able to endure chaos and appreciate it in order to discover the right thing to do." WILLIAM C. WELDON

* 2006 PRWeek/Burson-Marsteller CEO survey

Entrepreneurial instinct enables CEOs to think beyond the conventional. This was the case with **Andrea Casalini**, CEO of Italian digital entertainment company Buongiorno. His decision to shift the focus of the company from email to the burgeoning mobile content industry, was fundamental in transforming the business from a modest start-up into a market leader. Through mergers and acquisitions the company turned its email subscriber base of 25,000 in 1998 to two billion mobile users a decade later. Despite scepticism from outside the company, Casalini, backed by his chairman Mauro Del Rio, instinctively knew to focus on mobile rather than email content, and on a subscription model over advertising. Buongiorno is now the Italian sector leader and a significant global player.

"You have to ask a lot of questions and listen to people, but eventually, you have to go by your own instincts."
KERKOR KERKORIAN

Masters of Instinct

Some of the world's most successful CEOs have made instinctive judgments that have paid off:

R. David Hoover, BALL CORP. (Packaging: US)—*His instinct convinced him that the company's plan to sell its aerospace division was a mistake. He reversed the decision, and the company enjoyed much stronger growth as a result.*

—

Ma Weihua, CHINA MERCHANTS BANK (Finance: China)—*Backed his instincts by making CMB the first Chinese bank to open in New York and the first to acquire an off-mainland financial institution.*

—

Gary M. Rodkin, CONAGRA FOODS INC. (Foodstuffs: US)—*Convinced that the key to the company's future success is to focus on its core packaged foods business, Rodkin agreed to sell ConAgra's profitable commodity-trading and merchandising operations in 2008.*

—

Lorenzo Pellicioli, DE AGOSTINI (Publishing: Italy)—*Has changed the focus of the company from newspapers to television, based on his feeling that the written press is dying out.*

—

Rajiv L. Gupta, ROHM AND HAAS COMPANY (Chemicals: US)—*Driven by his instincts, he dramatically changed the structure of the organization to take full advantage of emerging markets while investing in joint ventures and acquisitions.*

—

Li Ka-shing Founder & Chairman, Cheung Kong (Holdings) Ltd

BIOGRAPHY
Born in 1928 in China, as a child Li fled with his family to Hong Kong.

BEST DECISION
Buying land in Hong Kong during China's Cultural Revolution, when many were selling up to flee a feared Communist invasion.

LESSON IN BUSINESS
See the bigger picture—Li judged China would not invade Hong Kong, so struck cheap land deals, laying the foundations for his business empire.

RENOWNED AS one of Asia's shrewdest dealmakers and philanthropists, Li's Cheung Kong business interests span property, ports, retail, telecommunications, energy, finance and investments, hotels, media and biotechnology.

As a boy, working in a plastics factory and saving for his own business, Li shaved his head to save on haircuts. He worked 16-hour days and, when he finally launched Cheung Kong Industries in 1950, his prodigious research and innovation gave him the edge in outdoing his rivals. Li managed costs in the same way as he managed his barber's bills, and made a fortune selling overseas. When he needed to buy new premises for his plastics factory, he moved into real estate, and set out to topple Hong Kong Land, the territory's biggest property firm. Li achieved this by buying new sites above Hong Kong's new metro stations. One of his best deals was the 1999 sale of his British mobile phone network, Orange, to Mannesmann for a $14-billion profit just months before Orange's value plunged. Li named Cheung Kong after the Yangtze River, visualizing the synergy created by his company's multiple operations as mirroring that of the countless rivers that combine to form that great Chinese river.

Francisco D'Souza Co-founder, President & CEO, Cognizant

BIOGRAPHY
D'Souza was born c.1970 in Nairobi, Kenya. He has a BA in business administration from the University of East Asia in Macau.

BEST DECISION
Buying marketRx in 2007, which strengthened Cognizant's position in the life sciences industry and in India.

LESSON IN BUSINESS
Be versatile – dealing with whatever life throws at him has helped D'Souza manage Cognizant's presence in multiple industries and 40 centers worldwide.

ONE OF THE YOUNGEST CEOs in the United States, D'Souza co-founded Cognizant in 1994 at the age of just 24. The company provides IT consulting and technology services in North America, Europe, and Asia.

A peripatetic childhood, courtesy of a diplomat father in the Indian Foreign Services, helped give D'Souza the confidence to co-found Cognizant in 1994, which he now runs. CEO and president since January 2007, D'Souza set up the Indian side of the company and has been involved in every major business decision and many of its biggest client wins, always maintaining an emphasis on growth. His strategy has been to acquire companies to create new, or strengthen existing, areas of expertize, whilst also expanding Cognizant geographically. In 2007, D'Souza increased investment in India by $100 million and bolstered the firm's position in the life sciences sector with the acquisition of marketRx, a provider of data analytics and related services. He followed this up by expanding into media and entertainment with management and technology consultancy Strategic Vision Consulting. Revenues have risen steadily, standing at almost $3 billion.

"When you study hard and work hard, your knowledge grows. And it gives you confidence."
Li Ka-shing

Lisa N. Drakeman President & CEO, Genmab

BIOGRAPHY
Born in Boston, Massachusetts, in 1953. Drakeman received degrees from Mount Holyoke College, Rutgers University, and an MA and PhD from Princeton.

BEST DECISION
Pursuing a Dutch scientist whose work she thought showed interesting potential, leading to a loan from a Danish bank and the creation of Genmab.

LESSON IN BUSINESS
There is always room for a maverick outsider—armed with a different approach, Genmab has forged its own path in the established US biotech sector.

WHILE WORKING for pharmaceutical company Medarex, Drakeman spotted an opportunity to start Genmab. She has been notably successful in maintaining investors' confidence, and has already signed one record-breaking deal.

European technology firms are often criticized for not being as ambitious as those in the Silicon Valley, but it would be very hard to level that charge against Genmab. Drakeman has positioned the company as an embryonic global powerhouse with aspirations in all big markets. Drakeman has a determinedly global outlook. She sees the value of the company in the drugs it has in clinical trials, such as cancer drug Ofatumumab, which Drakeman believes has potential for $5 billion in annual sales.

Established players bear out this conviction. In 2006, UK drugs firm GlaxoSmithKline agreed a record-breaking licence deal for Ofatumumab, paying $357 million for a ten percent stake. Genmab went public in 2000 and now has a market value of $2.5 billion, making it one of the world's top biotech firms. It has achieved this despite as yet having no drugs on sale—a testimony to the persuasive powers of Drakeman, her long-term ambitious thinking, and her confidence.

Shi Yuzhu Chairman & CEO, Giant Interactive

BIOGRAPHY
Born in China in 1962. Shi studied at Zhejiang University before completing a master's degree in software at Shenzhen University.

BEST DECISION
Asking influential publication *China Computer World* to accept deferred payment for ads when he had just set up in business and was too poor to pay upfront.

LESSON IN BUSINESS
Look out for the next big thing—Shi made his first fortune in technology but his next in healthcare and real estate before moving into online gaming.

CEO OF GIANT INTERACTIVE, Shi has had a finger in every pie during his long career as a serial entrepreneur, leading him from rags to riches more than once. Today, the legendary businessman boasts the top online game in China.

After graduating, Shi started selling a word-processing system he had developed. He was too poor to pay for advertizing, but a deferred payment deal with a magazine allowed him to win enough business to keep going. He made his first million that year. In 1993, his business, Giant Group, became the second largest privately held technology company in China. Foreign software imports soon impacted on sales, and Shi diversified, launching healthcare product Nao Huangjin, which made a billion yuan in sales revenue. Despite this, 1997 saw Giant Group collapse with debts of 200 million yuan, due to over-ambitious expansion and speculation. Undeterred, Shi launched sleep aid Nao Baijin, another success, and, in 2003, he sold most of the business and used the profit to launch online gaming outfit Giant Interactive, which, in 2007, became China's first such company listed on the New York stock exchange. Giant's multiplayer role-playing game, ZT Online, is now China's most popular online game.

"The more players curse, the more they like our games." Shi Yuzhu

Giorgio Armani Co-founder & CEO, Giorgio Armani

BIOGRAPHY
Born near Milan, Italy, in 1934, Armani attended medical school for two years before dropping out to work in a department store.

BEST DECISION
Extending the Armani brand far beyond clothing into such sectors as cosmetics, confectionery, furniture, and even hotels, which has doubled company profits.

LESSON IN BUSINESS
If you've got it, flaunt it—Armani was one of the first designers to seek out celebrities to sport his creations, a marketing strategy that gave his clothing lines a glamorous and aspirational aura.

RISING TO FASHION STARDOM in the 1980s, Armani was dubbed "the father of Italian fashion." Three decades later the Armani brand was a household name, and the self-made man behind the brand had an estimated net worth of $5 billion.

Armani was hired to design for Nino Cerruti's clothing line in 1964 but went freelance six years later, establishing his own menswear line in 1974. His designs gained international recognition in the 1980s when celebrities such as Richard Gere began sporting chic but casual Armani jackets. Today, the Armani brand is heavily associated with the lifestyles of the rich and famous, and those who aspire to live—or at least look—like them. With more than 2,000 points of sale worldwide, Armani's gross revenues exceed $1 billion annually, with half of the profits coming from Armani apparel, and the rest from other unrelated products and services. Named the most successful Italian designer by Forbes in 2001 and 2006, Armani is a known workaholic whose genius lies in recognizing that customers buy into his brand because it represents casual sophistication. Banking on his name, Armani has branched out into cologne, eyewear, the restaurant industry, and luxury hotels in Milan and Dubai.

S. & G. Hinduja Chairman & President, Hinduja Group

BIOGRAPHY
Srichand Hinduja was born in Shikarpur, India, in 1935. Gopichand was born in Iran in 1940.

BEST DECISION
Re-engaging with the new regime in Iran after the fall of the Shah. The Hindujas became one of Tehran's most trusted partners.

LESSON IN BUSINESS
Liquidity is independence—the Hindujas are principally traders, but acquisitions are self-financed, and all sale proceeds are reinvested in the group.

AT ONCE SPIRITUAL, charitable, and ruthless, the Hindujas seek to follow the Hindu god Lord Rama in turning crisis to advantage. They did just that in 1979, when they fled the Iranian revolution and rebuilt their empire from London.

In 1979, the Hindujas were merchant bankers and traders living in Iran. They became early pioneers of Indian globalization when Srichand and Gopichand began diversifying the group into oil, the motor industry, IT, and armaments. They bought the international rights to the Gulf Oil brand, became one of the first to operate a cell phone network when India liberalized telecommunications, and took a major stake in Hutch, which became one of India's largest mobile service providers. The brothers expanded into India's growing IT-enabled services industry, and bought the truck manufacturer Ashok Leyland, acquiring rivals in the Czech Republic to give them a European base. However, it is their business diplomacy that makes them unique: in early 2008, the Hindujas signed a $20-billion deal, backed by Tehran, to develop Iranian oil and gas fields, and to build a 10,000-megawatt power station in India. The Hinduja family fortune is estimated at more than $12 billion.

"I grew up trading, and in trading you don't need money. You need only ideas, and the ability to know how to put things together." Gopichand Hinduja

Naresh Goyal Founder & Chairman, Jet Airways

BIOGRAPHY
Born in Patiala, Punjab, India in 1949. Goyal moved to Delhi to work in his uncle's travel agency—a modest first step to building a hugely successful business.

BEST DECISION
Pulling out of the deal to buy rival Air Sahara for $500 million in 2006, and clinching it for $340 million in 2007.

LESSON IN BUSINESS
Sell your service—Goyal gambled on Indian air passengers being won over by a formula offering high-quality service, comfort, and reliability.

THE PIONEER OF INDIA'S private airlines, Goyal set up his own air travel agency, Jetair, in 1974. In 1993, he launched Jet Airways, hoping that India would soon liberalize its aviation industry. Today, Jet is India's largest airline.

As an international airline agent, Goyal understood the industry and, as an Indian, he knew the frustration felt by India's middle classes towards the state-owned carriers. Persuading a group of Middle East investors to back him, he launched Jet Airways. It was a big gamble, but Goyal sensed that deregulation was in the air. Sure enough, India's state monopoly over scheduled air transport ended in 1994. Jet has since put its rivals to shame with reliable flights and first-class cabin service, yet it operates on a break-even of 65 percent seat sales—20 percent below that of many rivals. Goyal's ruthless cost control and commitment to high standards was reflected in the company's 2006 IPO (initial public offering), which sold out in ten minutes, raising $260 million. This gave him the confidence to expand in a shrinking market when fuel costs soared. Goyal held his nerve and bought chief rival Sahara at a knock-down price. Jet has now moved to become a global operator.

Leslie H. Wexner Chairman & CEO, Limited Brands

BIOGRAPHY
Born in Dayton, Ohio, in 1937. Wexner graduated from Ohio State University with a degree in business administration.

BEST DECISION
Building the Easton Town Center complex in Columbus, Ohio, in 1999, a pioneering residential, entertainment, and commercial open-air mall.

LESSON IN BUSINESS
Never hesitate to reinvent—since opening his first shop more than forty years ago, Wexner has continuously acquired brands, refocused them, and targeted new audiences.

SELF-MADE BILLIONAIRE Wexner is continually seeking out future trends. Initially built on women's clothing, his Limited Brands empire is now focused on personal health and beauty products, such as lingerie, skin care, and cosmetics.

"Les" Wexner launched The Limited clothing company with a loan of $5,000 and opened his first shop in 1963, selling fashion to suit women's lifestyles. He used the proceeds of a 1969 IPO to finance a massive expansion into shopping malls, and gradually built up a large retail empire including Victoria's Secret, La Senza, Bath & Body Works, and Henri Bendel. Known as an entrepreneur rather than a manager, Wexner's tendency to flit from project to project put The Limited in financial crisis by 1993.

Acting on the advice of Harvard professor Leonard R. Schlesinger, Wexner centralized financial management and marketing, sold off poorly performing brands, and closed down more than 100 shops, changing the name to Limited Brands in 2002 to reflect the change in direction. Profits from clothing sales continued to decline, so Wexner sold his Express and Limited Stores in 2007 in order to focus on his personal health and beauty brands, Victoria's Secret and Bath & Body Works.

"I think temperamentally, I've always lived in my own world, and that world is very much in the future." Leslie H. Wexner

Paul V. Galvin Co-founder & CEO (1928–59), Motorola

MOTOROLA STARTED life as a small, backyard operation but is now one of the world's leading telecommunications giants. Its success story is almost entirely due to the character and foresight of its co-founder, Galvin.

After working for Commonwealth Edison Company (ComEd), the largest electric utility company in Illinois, Galvin enlisted in the US Army, seeing active service in World War I. After the war he went into business, and after his first venture ended in bankruptcy, he launched Galvin Manufacturing Corp. with his brother Joseph in 1928 to manufacture battery eliminators. The stock market crash of 1929 and the subsequent Great Depression tested Galvin's business acumen to the limit, but with a little luck, dogged determination, and great self-belief, he survived. Making the right choices at the right time proved crucial, and Galvin learnt to rely on his intuition. This led him in 1930 to spot a niche for a mass-produced car radio—the Motorola. He went on to develop the Handi-Talkie two-way radio for the army, and to enter the TV market. Galvin was also able to motivate and instil worker loyalty by ensuring that they felt part of Motorola's success, financially and emotionally.

Jen-hsun Huang Co-founder, President & CEO, NVIDIA

A FIRST-GENERATION immigrant from Taiwan, Huang is proof that anyone can live the American Dream. He is the co-founder and CEO of NVIDIA, a world leader in visual computer technology with an annual turnover of over $4 billion.

After finishing college in 1984, Huang joined Advanced Micro Devices, Inc. as a microprocessor designer. From 1985 to 1993, he worked for computer chip manufacturer LSI Logic Corporation. During this time he held a number of positions, including director of Coreware, the business unit responsible for LSI's "system-on-a-chip" strategy. He co-founded NVIDIA in 1993, assuming the position of president and CEO of the new company. NVIDIA quickly established itself as a serious player in the highly lucrative graphics microchip field. Under Huang's leadership, it not only developed highly competitive products but also expanded through astute acquisitions of rival companies and intellectual properties. In each of the last four years, the company has doubled in size, and, with the GeForce product line, it has become the number one manufacturer of the graphics processing units (or GPUs) that are responsible for the hyper-realistic interactive graphics of gaming consoles and PCs.

"Do not fear mistakes. Wisdom is often born of such mistakes." Paul V. Galvin

Chen Tianqiao Co-founder, Chairman & CEO, Shanda Entertainment

BIOGRAPHY
Born in China in 1973, Chen grew up near Shanghai. He attended Shanghai's Fudan University, finishing a four-year degree in economics in three years.

BEST DECISION
Responding to a drop in share price with a new strategy that focused on digital home entertainment, giving Shanda greater exposure to China's domestic advertising market.

LESSON IN BUSINESS
Customer service is paramount —Chen has always provided customers with the back-up they need to play Shanda's games.

AS FOUNDER AND CEO of Shanda Entertainment, China's largest online gaming company, Chen has become an icon to millions of users and a favorite among investors as the Chinese online gaming market becomes big business.

Armed with $60,000 of start-up capital, 26-year old Chen co-founded Shanghai Shanda Network Development Co. Ltd in 1999. Using a simple model of acquiring licences for imported online games and selling access by the hour, Shanda soon gathered a following. To expand, Chen set up servers across China and sold prepaid cards online and at internet cafés. Becoming the sole agent in China for Korean game "Legend" led to rapid growth and, after gaining a NASDAQ listing, Shanda acquired online-game developers Haofang and Bianfeng, mobile-game developer Digital-Red, and literature portal Qidian. In 2005, Chen moved toward making Shanda an all-in-one online media supermarket by taking a 19.5-per-cent stake in China's online news portal Sina. Chen has driven further growth through a partnership with Universal Music Group, allowing Shanda users to stream tunes to their PCs; and a new interactive entertainment box that allows TV viewers to go online, play Shanda's games, and buy music and films.

Charles Zhang Chairman & CEO, Sohu.com

BIOGRAPHY
Born in Xi'an, China, in 1964. Zhang graduated in physics from Beijing, and gained a PhD in experimental physics at MIT in 1993.

BEST DECISION
Moving into mobile telecoms services in 2000. The revenue from services such as SMS helped turn the company round.

LESSON IN BUSINESS
Mood matters—faced with a boardroom revolt after the dotcom crash, Zhang credits his non-confrontational style with defusing the situation and keeping investors onside.

HIGH-PROFILE and eccentric, Zhang is the Richard Branson of Chinese internet business, known as much for stunts such as climbing Everest, as for turning portal operator Sohu.com into a brand-leading web presence in China.

Zhang's initial foray onto the web took off in 1997 after Yahoo! founder Jerry Yang inspired him to revamp his collection of weblinks into a search-based portal. The resulting Sohu.com quickly became China's most popular internet destination, but fierce competition and the slump after the dotcom bubble burst, left Sohu floundering at the beginning of the new decade. Luckily, Zhang had the humility and confidence to reinvent the company, loosening the reins to hand greater responsibility to a seasoned management team, and embracing the need for diversification. This has led Sohu to offer wireless and mobile services, as well as online gaming, community-based content, and a rebuilt search engine that has seen it rise up the user rankings again. Meanwhile, content deals such as its coverage of the 2008 Beijing Olympics have boosted Sohu's profile. Zhang's own approach to management is seen as offbeat, but he is widely acknowledged as one of the world's digital elite.

> "Matters of great concern should be treated lightly."
> Charles Zhang

Anil Agarwal CEO, Vedanta Resources

BIOGRAPHY
Born in Patna in Bihar, India, in 1954. He is the son of Dwarka Prasad Agarwal, a manufacturer of aluminum conductors.

BEST DECISION
Creating a cut-price cable factory in India by importing cheap, second-hand plant from the US. Within four years his firm, Sterlite, was the market leader.

LESSON IN BUSINESS
Don't listen to naysayers—rivals told Agarwal that his foreign plant would never work in India. He negotiated aggressively and made it work. Today he is a multibillionaire.

A LIVING BOLLYWOOD movie hero, Agarwal is a genuine "scrap metal to riches" story. He is also a highly effective CEO. By buying up run-down metals plants and reviving them, he made copper producer Sterlite into a world leader.

When Agarwal arrived in Bombay (Mumbai), aged 19, with a single suitcase and a burning ambition to learn English and make his fortune. Today, he lives in London in a swanky Mayfair townhouse and has a butler. Agarwal began his career by collecting and selling scrap metal in Bihar, one of India's poorest states. He made a profit, persuaded a local bank to give him a loan, and bought a cable manufacturing company, anticipating India's communications would lead to a high demand for cable. In 1986, he spent $2 million setting up a greenfield cable factory, saving $7 million by importing second-hand equipment from Illinois, US. The company grew fast, allowing Agarwal to expand and diversify. Hampered by a copper shortage, he bought a disused copper smelting plant in Australia, set it up in India, and then took the company into mining. Today his holding company, Vedanta Resources, presides over a global metals empire and he has a personal fortune of some $12 billion.

Ma Huateng Chairman & CEO, Tencent Holdings Ltd

BIOGRAPHY
Born in Hainan, China, in 1971. Ma studied at Shenzhen University, receiving a BS in software engineering.

BEST DECISION
Launching his company early to the Chinese internet community, allowing him to build up a strong, loyal customer base.

LESSON IN BUSINESS
Defend your customer base—despite demands to enable inter-operability with other IM providers, Ma has defended his customer base as the company's most important asset. QQ has become a top-rated site as a result.

A RELATIVE UNKNOWN outside his native China, Ma is something of a mystery man. However, his instant-messaging service QQ had more than half-a-billion users in 2007, making it the largest registered IM usergroup on the internet.

"Pony" Ma began his career at China Motion Telecom, moving to Runxun Communications. He quit in 1998 to found Tencent, a paging business for domestic telecoms operators, but few could have foreseen his future success. Inspired by the first internet instant messaging service ICQ, Ma quickly developed OICQ (later renamed QQ), a similar program with a Chinese interface. Unable to get a fair price for it, Ma offered the software as a free download. In late 1999, nine months after release, it already had more than a million registered users. Ma has since launched web and game portals, multi-media blog service Qzone and the QQ coin, a virtual currency accepted as payment by outside sites. Tencent was listed on the Hong Kong stock exchange in 2004, and online advertising has developed strongly in recent years. Few Chinese companies have grown as fast as Tencent, which reported a 47-percent annual increase in net profit in 2007 of $221.9 million.

"When we see an opportunity, we grasp it... We view our challenges not as more pressure, but as roads to success." Ma Huateng

William R. Berkley Founder & CEO, W. R. Berkley Corp.

BIOGRAPHY
Born in the USA in 1946. He graduated from New York University in 1966, and in 1968 completed an MBA at Harvard Business School.

BEST DECISION
Deciding not to "sell out" during the 1990s, instead focusing on speciality insurance markets that other companies wouldn't touch.

LESSON IN BUSINESS
Remain prudent—throughout his long career, Berkley has preferred to make modest profits rather than risking dramatic "boom or bust" investments.

INSURANCE PIONEER Berkley has built his business into one of the largest commercial insurance companies in the US. He has a reputation for making low-risk investments that enable him to survive the vagaries of the stock market.

William Berkley displayed an entrepreneurial talent from an early age. At Harvard Business School he began a $2-million mutual fund with a classmate that became the foundation of Berkley Dean & Co. By the time he graduated, the fund stood at $10 million. Ignoring the criticism of peers, who considered him to be arrogant and boastful, Berkley continued to invest in undervalued stocks during the 1960s and 70s, earning a reputation as an investment genius. In 1973 he took the company public as W.R. Berkley. During the 1980s he branched out into other businesses, including alarm systems, food companies, and market research—although not all of these survived the economic downturn of the 1990s. Then Berkley turned his attention to Europe. He increased the company's stake in Kiln plc, a Lloyd's of London insurance underwriter, and subsequently launched Berkley Medical Excess Underwriters LLC and, in 2003, W. R. Berkley Insurance (Europe).

Jerry Yang Co-founder & CEO (2007–08), Yahoo! Inc.

BIOGRAPHY
Born in Taipei, Taiwan, in 1968. Yang moved with his mother and brother to San José, California, aged 10. He studied electrical engineering at Stanford University, postponing his doctoral studies to launch Yahoo! in 1995

BEST DECISION
Restructuring management and refining technology at Yahoo! to increase advertising revenues.

LESSON IN BUSINESS
Trust your employees—Yang knew that he didn't have all the answers, and realized that his employees' skills were essential to the company's future.

TAIWAN-BORN Yang is co-founder of Yahoo!, the internet company that started life as "Jerry and David's Guide to the World Wide Web". As CEO, Yang aimed to change the company's fortunes with new technologies and business partnerships.

Yang and fellow student David Filo founded Yahoo! while graduate students at Stanford University. Yang (known as "Chief Yahoo") kept out of the spotlight, focusing on big ideas and broad strategy rather than the day-to-day running of the company. He helped to build Yahoo! into one of the world's best-known brands and most widely used search engines. Inspiring tremendous loyalty from employees, he was visibly moved when he announced around 2,000 redundancies in 2000 after the dotcom crash. The company's fortunes continued to slide, losing market share to arch rival Google and, in 2007, Yang took control as CEO. He faced tough times, including severe criticism for the role of Yahoo! in helping the Chinese Government track down dissidents, and repelled a takeover bid from Microsoft. For this, and a later unsuccessful attempt to reopen negotiations, his reputation was dented. Stock prices slumped, and in November 2008 Yang stepped down as CEO, remaining on the board.

"Profit is sanity. Volume is vanity." William R. Berkley

FAMILY MATTERS

Family dynasties are endlessly fascinating; never more so than when linked with a well-known brand or corporation that has its roots in another era. The successful ones adapt and survive with Darwinian dexterity, to retain their place in the corporate marketplace.

Osamu Suzuki (p326), CEO of automotive giant Suzuki Motors, was born Osamu Matsudu, in Japan. His wife was a granddaughter of company founder, Michio Suzuki. Osamu took the family name, as is the custom in Japan when there are no male heirs. As president and CEO he is credited with turning Suzuki into a global force by producing low-cost, fuel-efficient small cars for export to India, China, and Eastern Europe.

Acceding to the CEO role at Anheuser-Busch in 2006, **August A. Busch IV** (p401) is a fifth generation brewing magnate and the great-great grandson of Adolphus Busch, the company's co-founder. A determined takeover bid by InBev in the summer of 2008 saw Busch reluctantly yield his leadership of the company to **Carlos Alves de Brito** (p477), but he maintains the family interest in Anheuser-Busch InBev with a place on the board of directors ●

Generational Values

Research has shown that loyalty and mutual respect among staff is often strong in family-owned companies. These ideals can be attributed to the sense of continuity and personal interest passed down. S. C. Johnson, the family-owned household products firm, is renowned for the fellowship it inspires in its workforce. Johnson Outdoors CEO, and family member, **Helen Johnson-Leopold** states that, "Our focus on our people is a solid business strategy that has created enormous employee loyalty and real bottom-line benefit… I don't think there is any one employee program or benefit that demonstrates how much we value our people; rather, it is the collective goodwill built over 120-plus years, across five generations of Johnson family leadership."

In the 1940s, **Charles R. Walgreen, Sr.**, founder of the American drugstore chain Walgreen Co., made his company one of the first to offer profit-sharing to staff, directing his son to use the proceeds from his life insurance policy to fund it. His values have passed down the generations and resonate still. In 2006, CEO **Dave Bernauer** increased the level of benefits to employees called for active military service. Bernauer said, "We won't hesitate to make life a little easier for them."

"I'm a different person than my father. That doesn't mean I'm any less… effective than he is" AUGUST A. BUSCH IV

Dealing with the Relations

Be tough—Avoid situations where less adept family members occupy sinecures. Business will suffer if positions are not earnt.

Specify roles—Clearly define the positions and decision-making powers of family members. Discourage the appointment of "floating" executives.

Stay focused—Avoid family politics by basing decisions on your own sound and considered business strategy.

Respect the brand—Remember that the family name is often more essential to the company than any one individual, CEO included.

Read up on the history—Understand the motives of those you are dealing with. Get to know the family history and understand the founding ethos.

Ask the family—Take advantage of the expertise of founding family executives. They provide direct access to the secrets of the company's success.

Heads of the Family

Other CEOs who have earned their leadership of family-owned companies include:

Desmond O'Connor, ANTOFAGASTA (Mining: Chile)—*The company is 65 percent owned by the Chilean Luksic family, who bought a major interest in 1980. O'Connor works closely with chairman Jean-Paul Luksic.*

—

James L. Dolan, CABLEVISION SYSTEMS (Telecoms and media: US)—*The son of eponymous company founder Charles, Dolan opposed his father's satellite technology business plans, stepping out of his shadow and showing himself to be a skilled businessman.*

—

Gregory Page, CARGILL, INC. (Commodities: US)—*CEO Page has been with the firm for 30 years. Descendants of founder William Cargill (1784–1860) own about 85 percent of the company.*

—

William T. Dillard II, DILLARD'S (Retail: US)—*The current CEO is a direct descendent of founder William T. Dillard. Many executives and directors are family members.*

—

Yoshiharu Inaba, FANUC LTD (Electronics: Japan)—*The only son of the company founder, Inaba was groomed for leadership from an early age. He became president and CEO of the robotics firm in 2003.*

—

Parker Kennedy, FIRST AMERICAN CORP. (Insurance: US)—*The great-grandson of the company's founder, C. E. Parker, Kennedy has been chairman and CEO since 2003. First American has been a family-owned firm since 1894.*

—

Koo Bon-moo, LG (Diversified: South Korea)—*The Huh and Koo families co-founded the company as Lucky GoldStar in 1947. Their descendants own about 59 percent and Koo family patriarch Bon-moo remains in charge.*

—

3

The Motivators

Kumar Mangalam Birla Chairman, Aditya Birla Group

INHERITING CONTROL of the Aditya Birla Group, one of India's largest conglomerates, in 1995, Birla has since doubled turnover and reinvigorated the group, focusing on employee satisfaction and management training, transforming the company into a genuine world-beater. The group is now the world's largest single-location palm oil producer and Asia's leading aluminum producer. In India, the group dominates the insurance, viscose yarn, and asset management sectors. Birla's net worth now stands at over $10 billion.

BIOGRAPHY
Born in 1967, the son of a wealthy Indian industrialist. He was raised in Calcutta (Kolkata) and Bombay (Mumbai). He has a bachelor's from the University of Bombay and a MBA from the London Business School.

LEADERSHIP STYLE
Dynamic, focused, and eager to nurture talent within the company, he encourages even young managers to have their say. People skills are his forte with an impressive ability to get on with staff from top to bottom.

KEY STRENGTH
Birla has proved himself adept at team-building, with an innate talent for managing change.

BEST DECISION
Abandoning his father's old-fashioned business practices and building a modern corporation with global reach based on delegation and consensus.

THE RISING SON When his industrialist father, Aditya Vikram Birla, died in 1995, few people considered his shy and modest son, still in his twenties, capable of handling a conglomerate with interests spanning textiles, and garments, viscose, as well as cement, aluminum, and fertilizers. However, since taking the top job at Birla, he has more than doubled turnover, mainly by overturning business practices laid down by his father and grandfather. With a stated mission to dominate every business, Birla has built a world-beating company in several sectors and now sits atop a $26-billion empire.

CHANGING FOR GROWTH When Birla took over, many of his companies were experiencing a downturn and facing foreign competition. He let go many of the entrenched vice-presidents and began to recruit more widely. He also began to consult his staff and delegate to them, an unthinkable policy during his father's and grandfather's time, when the word of the chairman was law. As a young leader, he faced opposition to change within the organization but he refused to be diverted from his war on outmoded bureaucracy. Birla also founded the innovative Organizational Health Survey (OHS) to measure the satisfaction levels of all managers across the group. Aditya Birla is now seen as one of the best employers in Asia.

In 2007, Birla made his mark on the global stage when his Hindalco company, India's largest aluminum producer, bought Canadian company Novelis for $6 billion. Along with other major players, Birla sees retail as the next big opportunity in India. He recently announced plans to invest over 80 billion rupees in store expansion over the next few years.

LESSONS IN BUSINESS: INVESTING IN PEOPLE

Birla understood what was needed to take an old-fashioned bureaucratic Indian conglomerate into the modern age. He knows the importance of building a strong team, and nurturing staff to retain them.
→ Avoid killing people's ideas and imagination by acting as if only the word of the top person counts.
→ Spend money on development to build a reputation as the best employer; this attracts the best people.
→ Apply modern human resources techniques no matter where in the world your people are—they will appreciate their special treatment.

"When everyone in a Grand Prix drives a Ferrari, it is clearly the driver… that makes the difference!"
Kumar Mangalam Birla

Marcio Cypriano President, Banco Bradesco

TAKING OVER at a tricky time at Brazilian bank Bradesco, Cypriano was faced with sliding profits and a distant managerial style that threatened to undermine the company's reputation among both customers and investors. Cypriano made a series of key moves to strengthen the bank's position in its markets, but he also dramatically overhauled the old corporate culture, replacing aloofness with a culture of communication that was aimed at fostering innovation and helping to extend the bank's reach.

BIOGRAPHY
Born in Brazil in 1943. Cypriano was encouraged by his father to become a lawyer, receiving a law degree from Mackenzie University, São Paulo. However, at the age of 24 he became a bank clerk at Banco da Bahia, which was later bought by Bradesco, and never left.

LEADERSHIP STYLE
Open and accessible, Cypriano made getting close to the staff across his company a key part of his approach.

KEY STRENGTH
His outgoing personality, which has enabled him to become the face of the bank to both its employees, and the outside world.

BEST DECISION
Opening lines of communication with the media and the markets. If people aren't told what's going on in a business, they can easily think the worst.

COMPANY MAN After a quarter of a century as a loyal bank employee, Cypriano was rewarded with the top job at Bradesco in 1999. He immediately brought much-needed fresh air to the bank, dealing with problems that stemmed from a tradition of remote, uncommunicative management, and conservative business practices. He also prepared Bradesco for the fast-changing, modern banking world by rapidly developing new technology, and making bold acquisitions.

CULTURE CLASH Cypriano's immediate priority was to reinforce Bradesco's core activities in the middle to low end of the retail banking sector. However, he could also see that elements of the company's business model were holding it back, foremost of which was its secretive culture. In contrast with his predecessors, who had avoided the media and investors, Cypriano held more than 200 meetings in his first year alone. He also met managers throughout the company's nationwide network of more than 2,000 branches, promoting the flow of ideas within the business and with its customers, and boosting the bank's profile. Cypriano also turned Bradesco into a pioneer of online banking, which brought benefits for customers, as well as improving organizational efficiency. He made a series of important acquisitions, increasing the company's size, and improving its economies of scale and national reach. He also opened mini-branches for low-income Brazilians, adding to the bank's reputation as a national institution. Cypriano has successfully achieved his aim of broadening the customer base, boosting profits, and consolidating Bradesco's position as a key player in Brazilian banking.

LESSONS IN BUSINESS: MAINTAINING CLEAR LINES OF COMMUNICATION

Opening the channels of communication between the company and its investors, customers, and staff is a key step to releasing new stores of energy and innovation.
→ Remember that confidence from every stakeholder will lead to business success. Never believe that only the people inside the business know what is best for its future.
→ Allow investors to contribute to strategy and success. Secrecy will deny you the value of their insights.
→ Recognize the two main things that investors dislike – feeling left out of proceedings, and sudden surprises.

"If you are locked up in your office, you don't know what is happening out there." Marcio Cypriano

Amadeo Giannini Founder, Bank of America

A RADICAL INNOVATOR, prepared to adopt an entirely new approach to a long-established industry, Giannini revolutionized banking. His willingness to provide banking services to small businesses and working people, and his direct, door-knocking approach to marketing, shocked the US banking world in the early years of the 20th century. His methods were gradually adopted throughout the industry, but by then his innovations had already provided the foundations for one of today's global financial giants.

BIOGRAPHY
1870–1949. Giannini was born in San José, California, the son of immigrant farmers from Genoa, Italy. His father was killed while collecting a $10 debt when Giannini was seven years old.

LEADERSHIP STYLE
Direct, personal and familial. Giannini's intimacy with his customers was reflected in his dealings with his employees.

KEY STRENGTH
The confidence to trust others and to inspire their trust in him.

BEST DECISION
Offering a range of hitherto unthought-of but deeply needed banking services to previously ignored customers.

GOING IT ALONE After a successful early career at his stepfather's fruit company in the 1890s, Giannini joined the board of a San Francisco bank, where he argued that it should be offering loans and deposit facilities to the local Italian immigrant community. This bold step was rejected by the board, so in 1904 he resigned and set up his own bank, The Bank of Italy, across the street, quickly building up a strong base of support and business.

REACHING A NEW MARKET Banking was regarded as strictly for the wealthy before Giannini. By opening up his new bank to small-scale investors and providing loans to ordinary people, Giannini broke the traditional banking mold and transformed the landscape of the industry. Among his innovations were car-purchase loans and mortgages that could be repaid in monthly instalments, both fundamental pillars of retail banking today. Giannini's innovative strategy extended to marketing, as well. When he set up shop, it was widely regarded as unethical for banks to tout for business, but Giannini knew that most of his potential customers either knew little about banks or distrusted them. So he walked the streets and knocked on doors, explaining what banks did and how he could help people.

He was an architect of nationwide banking, opening more branches in California as soon as the state allowed it in 1909 and gradually expanding across the US. In 1929, the Bank of Italy and the Bank of America merged.

Giannini also had vision. His financial support helped the California wine and movie industries to grow, and it was he who financed Walt Disney's *Snow White and the Seven Dwarfs*.

LESSONS IN BUSINESS: LOOKING FOR OPPORTUNITIES

Just because things have always been done one way doesn't mean that's the only way to do them. By looking at the people around him, Giannini discovered an entirely new market that bankers had completely ignored.
→ Review your products and markets regularly to make sure your strategic emphasis is still relevant.
→ Constantly search for new channels to current markets watch what your competitors do in this area.
→ Make sure that sales and production are talking to each other and producing a synergy that takes the company into new products and markets.

"Serving the needs of others is the only legitimate business." Amadeo Giannini

Stephen D. Bechtel, Jr. President & CEO (1960–90), Bechtel

WITH HIS SON Riley, Bechtel Jr. is co-owner of San Francisco-based Bechtel, the largest engineering company in the US. He is the grandson of Warren A. Bechtel, the founder of the worldwide engineering and construction business that began in 1898 as a Western railroad construction firm. As head of the company from 1960, Bechtel Jr. positioned the business as a leader in the fields of mining, power, and civil engineering, focusing Bechtel on the most technically challenging end of the market and winning major contracts.

BIOGRAPHY
Born in 1925, Bechtel Jr. spent the first two years of his life with his parents at a railroad construction camp in the western United States. Bechtel holds a bachelor's degree in civil engineering from Purdue University, Indiana, and an MBA from Stanford University Graduate School of Business.

LEADERSHIP STYLE
Influential, dedicated, keeping a low profile to the point of secrecy, Bechtel Jr. has never been afraid to lead the company into large-scale and challenging projects.

KEY STRENGTH
Meticulous networking at the highest levels. US president Lyndon B. Johnson appointed Bechtel Jr. to his Committee on Urban Housing, and president Gerald Ford asked him to join his Labor-Management Committee.

BEST DECISION
Focusing on highway rather than railroad construction, putting Bechtel at the forefront of some of the major engineering projects of the 20th century.

LEARNING THE TRADE First employed by Bechtel in 1941, Bechtel Jr. worked in the field and at company headquarters before being elected CEO in 1960. With the same penchant for the large-scale project as his father, who took the company into such major works as the Hoover Dam, Bechtel Jr. ramped it up another notch. Moving with the times, and often benefiting from close contacts with political movers and shakers, he involved Bechtel in transportation (rapid transit systems in San Francisco and Washington, highways in Turkey and Croatia), space and defense, and energy. He developed Bechtel's technical strengths, and became an advocate of nuclear power, building both the US's and Canada's first commercial nuclear power stations. In the mid-1970s, Bechtel won the contract to construct Jubail, a self-contained city on the Saudi Arabian coast, complete with the world's largest desalination plant, petrochemical plants, and other industries. Tendering for large international projects is bound to lead to conflicts of interest and, in 1976, the Justice Department charged that Bechtel had gone too far to please Arab clients by blacklisting potential subcontractors who dealt with Israel.

STREAMLINED COMPANY The 1980s saw a slowdown in large-scale projects, especially in the Middle East as a result of lower oil prices. To counter this, Bechtel Jr. oversaw a major restructuring of the company, reducing the workforce considerably and creating smaller subsidiaries such as Bechtel Ltd, which took on the building of the Channel Tunnel between Britain and France. In June 1990, Bechtel Jr.'s son, Riley, succeeded him as CEO.

LESSONS IN BUSINESS: GETTING INVOLVED

In the mid-1950s, Bechtel Sr.'s friend General Lucius Clay, chairman of US president Eisenhower's National Highway Committee, invited him to help develop the concept and general plans for what became the interstate highway system. Bechtel Jr. has maintained strong relationships with officials in many US administrations.
→ Form close relationships with government customers. They, like you, are in it for the long term.
→ Link what you are doing to the government of the day's strategy—sell high and wide.
→ You cannot motivate government customers by an appeal to making profits, so listen hard to their aims.

> "[Teamwork] permits common men to do uncommon things." Stephen D. Bechtel Jr

Bradbury Anderson Chairman & CEO, Best Buy Co., Inc.

CEO OF THE LARGEST electronics retailer in the US, Anderson has worked to develop a highly trained, motivated, and customer-oriented sales force, giving the company a formidable competitive edge. He has made a substantial investment in staff training, while customer profiling has led to communications, stores, and services tailored to specific customer categories. As part of his motivational strategy, Anderson has even redirected some of his own stock options annually into a discretionary award pool for non-executive staff.

BIOGRAPHY
Born in Sheridan, Wyoming, in 1950. The son of a Lutheran pastor, Anderson dropped out of a seminary after a year. He received a bachelor's degree from the University of Denver and launched his career as a stereo equipment salesman offering "ridiculous levels of service" to attract customers.

LEADERSHIP STYLE
Values-driven, customer-focused, and unusually self-effacing. Determined to motivate and get the most out of the company's people through putting them in jobs that play to their strengths, and recognizing and rewarding them for high performance.

KEY STRENGTH
Sales expertise. Using his vast knowledge and experience in this area, Anderson has been able to tailor the company's operations more tightly to customer needs.

BEST DECISION
Training staff in "customer-centric" selling techniques to target particular categories of buyers with specific products..

AN EYE FOR TALENT Anderson's success as a sales manager at Sound of Music, the precursor to Best Buy, brought him to the attention of Best Buy founder Dick Schulze, who made Anderson vice-president in 1981. Anderson became executive vice-president in 1986, COO in 1991, and CEO in 2002. Anderson has a talent for motivating staff and has won plaudits for recognizing and rewarding store staff. This has inspired great staff loyalty while also reflecting sound customer-focused business goals. The same goals are pursued in newer markets in Canada, China, and, most recently, Europe.

CUSTOMER CARE Rigorous staff training underpins Anderson's approach. This entails both product and business training—the latter including financial analysis. The benefits are twofold: salespeople are better equipped to help and advise customers, and they can also feed back more useful information to headquarters. Salespeople also have a better appreciation of their own roles, talents, and value; a supremely motivating factor is the realization that the greater their individual contributions, the higher the potential rewards.

Anderson has used his extensive knowledge of sales to introduce detailed purchase and customer analysis in order to tailor store design to local requirements. Identifying five distinct customer segments, ranging from mothers to techies, Best Buy's marketing approach aims to identify customers' motivation and priorities so that product ranges and services can be tailored appropriately. This "customer-centric" approach was initially tried out in a range of stores before being extended company wide.

LESSONS IN BUSINESS: DEVELOPING YOUR EMPLOYEES

Anderson's talent-nurturing approach to his workforce is considered singularly inspiring and empowering. His own and corporate investments in individuals are clearly paying off. His employees are his greatest asset and his treatment of them shows it.
- ➔ Train your people in both products and business processes. Make everyone's training customer-centric.
- ➔ Recognize, encourage, and reward workforce talent and ensure your managers do likewise.
- ➔ Encourage feedback: a well-trained employee is a valuable source of business ideas.

"The secret today is how you invest in your employees, so that they can deliver superior service to customers." Bradbury Anderson

W. James McNerney, Jr. CEO, The Boeing Company

AFTER SPENDING 19 years with diversified power giant General Electric, and proving himself with an incredibly successful tenure as chairman and CEO at diversified technology company 3M, McNerney now runs Boeing, the largest aircraft manufacturer of commercial jetliners and military aircraft in the world, and one of the largest defense contractors. Under his leadership, Boeing stock had risen 30 percent before the 2008 crash, and McNerney has won praise for his turnaround skills and sensitive handling of the company's 160,000 employees.

BIOGRAPHY
Born in 1949 in Providence, Rhode Island, the eldest of five children. His father, Walter James McNerney Sr., was a professor of health policy and CEO of the Blue Cross and Blue Shield Association. He earned a bachelor's in American studies at Yale and an MBA from Harvard University.

LEADERSHIP STYLE
Inspirational, courageous, and visionary. His peers have commended his integrity, ethical initiative, and effective personal leadership style.

KEY STRENGTH
An ability to get the best out of people. McNerney has encouraged his employees to lower their output rather than cut corners, and has stated his willingness to take a personal hit over such matters.

BEST DECISION
Working for GE in Asia, a formative experience that McNerney cites as the most important in his business development. His success in Asia was essential to GE's global growth.

OVERSEAS PERSPECTIVE McNerney began his professional career in 1975 as a brand manager at Procter & Gamble. In 1982, he started a 19-year tenure with General Electric, initially as vice-president of GE Information Services, going on to hold many other executive posts. In 1992, legendary GE chairman Jack Welch named McNerney president of GE Asia-Pacific and gave him free rein to run the company's Asian interests.

TAKING UP THE CHALLENGE McNerney returned to the US in 1995 as president and CEO of GE Lighting, and in 1997 he was named president and CEO of GE Aircraft Engines. Under his leadership, the division became one of the most profitable in the company. It was widely speculated that McNerney was being groomed to take over

after Welch's retirement but the job went to Jeffrey Immelt, and, in 2001, he left to join 3M as CEO and chairman of the board. The first outsider to run the company, McNerney tackled the job aggressively, cutting costs and reorganizing the structure of the company, particularly in research and development, but also retaining 3M's culture of innovation. In 2004, 3M boasted record sales of $4 billion, with profits of $3 billion.

In 2005, McNerney took charge of Boeing, the first externally sourced CEO since World War II. Under his leadership, the Chicago-based aerospace company has seen stocks rise by 30 percent, and McNerney has done much to fix the bureaucratic and negative corporate culture that was blighting the company, by encouraging cost-cutting and increasing his central leadership over three divisons.

LESSONS IN BUSINESS: GROWING THE PEOPLE

McNerney believes that if the people working in a company grow, then the company's growth will take care of itself. Companies should offer employees opportunities to enhance both career and personal development.
→ Offer people the opportunity to pursue further education. Offer financial support for fees and books.
→ Hire the best-educated people you can; but make room for people with no qualifications who have learned lessons in life.
→ Education and training not only improve peoples' performance but also encourage company loyalty.

"I'm unafraid to expect a fair amount from people. It makes them so much better." W. James McNerney, Jr.

Lawrence Kellner Chairman & CEO, Continental Airlines

FACING AN UNCERTAIN future, in 1995, Continental Airlines approached Kellner, then CFO at American Savings Bank, to tackle the same role at the troubled airline. Within a few years, he helped turned around the ailing, debt-ridden company, putting it on a sound financial footing and winning a string of customer satisfaction awards. He took over as CEO in 2004. Far from just a numbers man, Kellner's ability to communicate with Continental's 45,000 employees and bring them on-board has been instrumental in his success.

TIME IS MONEY In 1994, Continental Airlines ranked bottom of US airlines in punctuality, baggage handling, and complaints. It was also buckling under the strain of $500 million in debt, and was in default on $2.7 billion in loans. In Kellner's own words, Continental was "a lousy company" on the verge of going bust.

Taking over as CFO in 1995, Kellner quickly moved to refinance the company, pioneering a new type of air-fleet-backed bond that allowed Continental to raise money cheaply. After calculating that the airline would save $6 million a month by increasing its on-time ranking to fifth place, he proposed handing out half that amount to staff if they could make the improvement. Within two months, Continental had hit number one and Kellner had set the pace for the next dozen years.

BAD NEWS BEARER Kellner managed to soothe stakeholders as the airline rode out the consecutive crises of 9/11 (which led to 12,000 lay-offs), the SARS epidemic, and the invasion of Iraq. By the time he took over as CEO in 2004, he had managed to squeeze out $1.1 billion in costs but still needed more, so he successfully negotiated staff pay cuts, including a 25 percent reduction himself, and instituted a more sustainable profit-sharing model.

During Kellner's time as CEO, Continental has seen profits rise from a loss of more than $350 million to pre-tax profits of more than $550 million. He has worked hard to forge strategic alliances and establish joint ventures that have expanded Continental's global reach, while the airline's environmental stance has led to a partnership with Boeing to produce aircraft powered by biofuel.

LESSONS IN BUSINESS: BEING FLEXIBLE AND OPEN

Following 9/11, Kellner ripped up the year's strategy and made savage cuts to costs. Although criticized at the time, the move left Continental as one of only two airlines to avoid Chapter 11 bankruptcy reorganization.
→ Have the confidence in your own judgement and expertise as a leader to know when to change the company plan, and drive through its implementation.
→ Treat people with respect and dignity. If a painful change of plan becomes necessary, they will trust you.
→ You may have to ask people to make sacrifices for the company to invest in the future.

"I'm a guy who likes to spend money." Lawrence Kellner

Jean-François Decaux CEO, JCDecaux

MULTILINGUAL FRENCHMAN Decaux has been the driving force behind creating and exporting the Decaux poster site company into new international markets, demonstrating how to turn a local, family firm into a global media operation. Although a "blue sky" innovator, his flights of imagination are married to an attention to detail that starts on the factory floor and finishes with the installation of street furniture to carry advertising, the quality of which has made him the envy of his industry.

BIOGRAPHY
Born in Paris, in 1959. Jean-François is the eldest son of Jean-Claude Decaux, founder of JCDecaux. He enrolled at the Institut Supérieur de Gestion in Paris to study business in 1979, and at the same time took a law degree at the Paris V University.

LEADERSHIP STYLE
Far-sighted, provocative, and empathetic. Described as more of a listener than a talker.

KEY STRENGTH
Keeping ahead of his competitors by relentlessly seeking out new innovations.

BEST DECISION
Setting up a bicycle-rental scheme in Paris in exchange for exclusive rights to the French capital's 1,628 billboards.

PROVING HIS WORTH Along with his two brothers, Jean-François Decaux was brought up in the JCDecaux tradition, in which aspirants to the family firm had to prove their worth. After a brief stint working in the US, the fluent German speaker set up a new business in Germany at the age of 23. Using local architects, such as Peter Lanz in Munich, Decaux managed to beat local firms to many contracts. He moved to the UK operation in 1989 and decided to elevate the design, installation, and maintenance of the firm's "street furniture" to a high art. After commissioning award-winning architects and designers such as Norman Foster, Philippe Starck, Phillip Cox, and Mario Bellini to create innovative and high-quality products, Decaux was justified in describing the company as "the Mercedes-Benz of the street-furniture business".

In a company that relied solely on organic growth, Decaux finally overcame internal opposition to making acquisitions when he oversaw the purchase of the outdoor advertising operations of Havas Media in 1999. This included control of European billboard company Avenir and UK outdoor group Mills & Allen, giving JCDecaux a leading global position in exterior advertising.

GLOBAL SCOUT The innovative Decaux has continued to lead the field, launching the first plasma-based airport screens in 2001, and opening up the lucrative Asian market with street furniture contracts in both Japan and China. A man obsessed by his work, Decaux spends time walking the streets of foreign cities looking for potential billboard sites, meeting mayors, and trying to win new contracts.

LESSONS IN BUSINESS: LEARNING THE BUSINESS

Jean-François Decaux, as passionate as ever about his field, has turned a static business that essentially relied on Paris bus shelters into one that uses cutting-edge designers and ultra-modern technology to advertise to millions around the world.
- → Even in a family business, learn it comprehensively from the bottom up, concentrating on core activities.
- → Never lose that contact with the business on the ground; talk to your people on the front line.
- → Use your intimate knowledge of the business to seek out innovation; make the first lead to the second.

"I knew I had to prove myself to succeed my father who invented all this. The education we received was fight, fight, fight." Jean-François Decaux

MOTIVATE SUCCESS

There is no set route to successful motivation, or a course you can take. But a common motivational theme is that employees appreciate a leader with energy, passion, and commitment. They like to feel that the person in charge is prepared to take on challenges, along with everyone else. People like **Martin Sorrell** (p464), founder and CEO of the communications services group WPP, who leads from the front and creates a sense of kinship with his 65,000 staff by overseeing the day-to-day operations of the company. Similarly, **Om Prakash Bhatt** (p105), CEO of the State Bank of India, has sought to establish close connections with his staff, meeting with them and listening to their concerns in a bid to reverse the ailing bank's fortunes. He has also fostered a culture of shared responsibility, in which every employee understands that their day-to-day performance determines the success of the company ●

Focus and Passion

"You don't die for some grand cause," says Anthony Plath, Professor of Finance at the University of North Carolina at Charlotte. "You die for the guy in the trench next to you."

This is how **John Allison IV**, former CEO of BB&T Corp. in the US, motivated employees. "John makes you feel part of a small team even though you work for a large entity," said Plath. Allison turned BB&T into a mission-driven organization with a clearly defined set of values. It was this focus that gave BB&T's employees such a strong sense of purpose.

When he left the company in December 2008 the value of the business had risen from $5 billion in assets to $137 billion. The creation of a strong team ethic and the driven, almost obsessive, pursuit of shared goals can be a potent combination for getting the best out of people.

At Samsung Life Insurance in South Korea, **Lee Soo-chang** likes to think of his position in sporting terms. "I welcome challenges and constantly try to change myself," he says. "It's like throwing fastballs in baseball to win the game." Saying that he "loves his job", Lee's positive thinking and energetic, can-do attitude, pervades the entire company, and has been a significant factor in Samsung Life achieving record-high company revenues and customer satisfaction levels under Lee's leadership.

Darren Entwistle, CEO of Canadian telecommunications firm Telus, is similarly positive and charismatic. He is also widely admired for his exceptional communication skills, particularly for his ability to speak passionately without losing meaning or falling back on empty rhetoric. He uses words intelligently to communicate concepts to his staff, and his passionate delivery inspires them to achieve.

Freight transport company YRC Worldwide's CEO **William D. Zollars** also instils an inimitable team ethic in

> "Our staff were like Hanuman [the Hindu monkey god]. He had to be told about his strength, and the same logic worked with our staff too." OM PRAKASH BHATT

> "Great bosses are the a█elerator of hi█h-potential em█loyees. B█sses should be █oaches and m█tivators."
> ERIC FOSS

his workforce, and understands that visibility and an ability to admit mistakes are essential tools of motivation in a leader. An engaging boss, Zollars deplores the use of intimidation in attempting to get maximum output from staff, insisting that business is a "team sport", where respect means everything, and fear-based leadership earns nothing.

Maximizing Motivation

Set the right atmosphere— Create a stress-free workplace. Employees spend a good portion of their lives working, so it's important that they enjoy it.

Build a team ethic— Strive to create shared values. Business should be a group activity.

Give feedback— Be quick to praise and slow to criticize.

Receive feedback— Ask your staff what they think of the company and act on suggestions.

Hire good communicators— Any manager can master the business, but great motivators are hard to find.

Satisfaction counts— If staff are happy, customers will be happy, and business prospers.

Martin H. Richenhagen, of US agricultural manufacturer AGCO Corp., has an equally personable and optimistic approach to leadership, but with an added European slant, being amazed at American hyper-hierarchical business structures. For him, fostering an inclusive culture at work is key to staff motivation.

Masters of Motivation

Other CEOs known for their motivational skills include:

Charles Edelstenne, Dassault Aviation (Aerospace: France)—*Expanded into the US and fostered a highly loyal and proud engineering employee base.*

Barry Diller, IAC/ Interactivecorp (Media: US)—*Veteran media mover and shaker who has mentored a succession of high-flying executives in the US and pioneered online businesses.*

Naguib Sawiris, Orascom Telecom (Telecommunications: Egypt)—*Has built up the Orascom brand overseas, and also works as a motivational mentor at entrepreneurial NGO Endeavor.*

—

Eric Foss, Pepsi Bottling Group (Beverages: US)—*A renowned motivator of staff, who are encouraged to develop their talents and embrace new ideas.*

—

Paul H. Stebbins, World Fuel Services (Energy: US)—*Cultured, personable communicator who inspires employees through his understanding of the energy business and his strong ethical foundation.*

—

Paul Walsh CEO, Diageo

NOMINATED CEO of Diageo in late 2000, Walsh rapidly made his mark by refocusing and reshaping the alcoholic drinks company, concentrating on marketing and innovation in its premium spirits brands. He became known for his striking sales and promotional campaigns. Walsh's notable purchase of many Seagram brands in 2001, and a raft of other acquisitions and joint ventures, have substantially extended the company's product range and marketing reach, making Diageo the world's leading premium drinks business.

BIOGRAPHY
Born in Lancashire, UK, in 1955. Walsh studied accounting at Manchester Polytechnic, UK.

LEADERSHIP STYLE
Enthusiastic, practical, aggressive, and open, Walsh is known as a hands-on leader and team player.

KEY STRENGTH
Willing to innnovate, especially when it comes to product image.

BEST DECISION
Promoting Diageo's core premium drinks brands, which has built on their position as market leaders and created new directions of growth.

REFOCUSING AND RESHAPING Having risen through the ranks at food-and-drinks firm Grand Metropolitan, Walsh was a member of the board when the company merged with Guinness UDV in 1997 to create Diageo. He was immediately made a member of the board of Diageo, and in early 2000 was nominated COO, subsequently taking over as CEO. Walsh focused on the company's premium alcohol beverage products, buying into Seagram's spirits and wines, and disposing of Diageo's food holdings, Pillsbury and Burger King.

INNOVATIVE BRAND-BUILDING As CEO, Walsh launched an innovative strategy to strengthen the Diageo brands. He aimed to create "adorers" of each brand by marketing them according to the aspirations and social interactions of the consumer. He wasn't afraid to adapt ideas from successful soft-drinks and beer marketing campaigns. The strategy lead to a 23-per-cent rise in sales of the top eight global Diageo brands by the end of 2002. Walsh also introduced a major R&D exercise that led to innovations such as Smirnoff Ice and plastic drinks containers for core brands, making it possible for these to be sold in glass-free venues such as sports stadiums. Walsh has been swift to counter criticism that Diageo's marketing expertise is partly responsible for increasing alcohol abuse among young people. He points to Diageo's own strict guidelines on advertising, and blames rivals. Continuous growth under Walsh, who has masterminded a raft of acquisitions, ventures, and partnerships, has seen Diageo extend its operations worldwide. Today, it trades in more than 175 countries and is the world's largest alcoholic drinks group.

LESSONS IN BUSINESS: LEARNING FROM EXAMPLE

Under Walsh, Diageo gained a reputation for both rapid growth and innovation. He has actively learnt from other sectors of the industry, adopting and adapting ideas used by soft-drink and beer marketers.
→ Learn from winning strategies launched by competitors or other, related industry sectors. Study your competitors constantly.
→ Apply research-based, blue-sky thinking—keeping in mind your customers' profile and aspirations.
→ If you have to take a calculated risk in innovation, do it with a fall-back position in place.

"Strategically, you never want to be in the middle. You either want to be full-scale or you want to be niche." Paul Walsh

Peter Rose Chairman & CEO, Expeditors International

SEATTLE-BASED freight and logistics company Expeditors International has grown into a global world-beater under Rose's stewardship, operating in over 60 countries. Rose began his career working for the Canadian Pacific Railway, followed by a string of other transportation-related jobs, until in 1979, drawing on all his experience, he created a totally new freight business model. Much of the company's impressive growth can be attributed to its CEO's personal principles and he has built a reputation for rigorous ethics.

BIOGRAPHY
Born in 1945 in Montreal, Canada. His strict father was a master of transportation for the Canadian National Railroad. On his father's orders, Rose left school at 15 without finishing high school.

LEADERSHIP STYLE
Ethical, astute, and loyal. Rose is famously blunt, but considered a good listener—if you've done your homework. His company is a leader in IT but Rose refuses to do PowerPoint presentations.

KEY STRENGTH
An awareness of the world's changing freight requirements. Rose has shrewdly positioned himself to capitalize on the growth of Chinese exports into the United States.

BEST DECISION
Renting space from international carriers rather than owning any aircraft or ships.

SHARING SUCCESS Rose believes a corporation is only as good as its staff and that old-fashioned hard work should be rewarded. He has created a dynamic company whose growth is driven by a simple but effective profit share plan. Staff are encouraged to focus on profits, and in return they are rewarded with 20 percent of the net income they generate. The company also annually distributes stock to employees. It is largely this partnership that makes the idea of Expeditors being bought out an anathema to Rose, and he has shrugged off innumerable offers. "This is our baby and you don't sell your baby," he has said.

STAYING LEAN Nearly half of the company's revenue comes from air freight, a third from ocean freight, but Expeditors doesn't own a single ship or plane. This strategy of renting bulk space from other companies has allowed Expeditors to remain lean and profitable and has buffered it from the trials of many other cargo carriers. As Rose says, "You don't have to own these things, just to have your name on it."

The company is intensely driven by the bottom line, but Rose is vociferous in his criticism of what he calls "greed and avarice" in modern corporate culture. Rose himself has drawn the same salary ($110,000) for years. He also doesn't believe in mergers and acquisitions, which, in his view, destroy good companies. He says steady growth has kept Expeditors in good shape. Rose has managed to position his company to reap the rewards of globalization. With over 50 offices in China, Expeditors is now well-placed to capitalize on the eventual growth of exports from the Asian Tiger.

LESSONS IN BUSINESS: GROWING STEADILY FROM WITHIN

If you want your company to remain true to your founding vision and mission, focus on consistent profit, not on fast growth, and on organic expansion rather than on acquisition. Investing early has given Rose a head start in China.

→ Keep your eyes open for markets into which your business can naturally expand.

→ Avoid pursuing short-term profits if that plan in any way threatens the long-term future of the company.

→ No one understands your business like you do; so look for opportunities that exploit that fact.

"Really all you have to do is surround yourself with good employees." Peter Rose

Jeffrey Immelt Chairman & CEO, General Electric

RUNNING A HUGE international conglomerate at a time of difficult markets and international instability takes a certain kind of person. After rising through the ranks at General Electric during the reign of the legendary Jack Welch, Immelt landed the top job just as the corporate and political landscape turned nasty. But his easy management style and his commitment to GE's strong traditions, plus a determination to keep his focus on the long term, have shown him to be an effective manager during difficult times.

BIOGRAPHY
Born in Cincinnati, Ohio, in 1956. His father was a manager of General Electric Aircraft Engines Division. Immelt studied Applied Mathematics and played football at Dartmouth College, New Hampshire, and earned an MBA from Harvard.

LEADERSHIP STYLE
Affable, self-deprecating, and relaxed, Immelt is the polar opposite of his predecessor.

KEY STRENGTH
The ability to think long term to project the company past short and medium-term timeframes and envision future strategies.

BEST DECISION
Abandoning the strategies that worked for Jack Welch and founding his own.

INTO THE FURNACE The moment at which Immelt took over from Welch at the helm of GE in September 2001, after three years as president and CEO of GE Medical Systems, could hardly have been worse. The internet bubble had not long burst, serious corporate scandals were breaking out and, just four days into the job, the 9/11 attacks created a whole new wave of uncertainty. All of these presented a huge challenge to the conglomerate, and to the new CEO who had to guide it.

BUILDING THE LONG TERM Welch's 20 hugely successful years in charge at GE had made his management strategies and style enormously popular and turned him into a role model for CEOs all over the world. When Immelt moved in, his performance was closely watched from day one and initially found to be unworthy of his acclaimed predecessor. However, as time passed it became clear not only that Immelt's gentler style was just as effective as Welch's, but that he was also putting in place long-term changes that were bolstering the company's performance and prospects in troubled times. By moving GE into whole new sets of business, from energy to customized medicine, Immelt was preparing the company for the future.

The company's "ecomagination" initiative, announced in 2005, involving reduction in GE's greenhouse gas emissions and sales of environmentally improved products, was warmly received, and continues to broaden its scope. Immelt's far-sighted approach and the company's reputation for developing its operations and people make it one of the most admired companies in the US.

LESSONS IN BUSINESS: GUARDING AGAINST HUBRIS

Thinking the world revolves around a company of great stature is risky. Immelt's insight has been to look instead at where the world's going and how his company can fit in. Pride often comes before a fall.
➔ Remember: competitors will eventually catch you up and, if you are not careful, they will end up doing what you do only better. Do not rest on your laurels.
➔ If you are top team this year, make sure you know what you have to change to be top again next year.
➔ Never assume that people who bought your old products will buy even more of the new ones.

> "You lead today by building teams and placing others first. It's not about you." Jeffrey Immelt

Galen Weston Sr. Chairman & President, George Weston Ltd

THE WESTONS ARE one of Canada's—and the world's—richest families, and Willard Gordon Galen Weston Sr. is their third-generation patriarch. As well as George Weston Ltd, the bakery firm founded by his grandfather in 1882, the family owns a controlling stake in Loblaws, Canada's largest supermarket chain, and department stores in Canada, Ireland, and the UK. Since the death of his brother in 2002, Galen Sr. has had a seat on the board of the family's UK food business, Associated British Foods.

BIOGRAPHY
Born in Buckinghamshire, UK, in 1940. Weston was raised in Canada where he attended the prestigious Upper Canada College and the University of Western Ontario.

LEADERSHIP STYLE
Inclusive, straightforward, and sociable. Weston is a man of contrasts: a straight talker who likes to have fun, and a friend to plutocrats and royalty who also possesses the common touch. What he looks for in senior managers is similarly unpretentious: work hard, do a good job, and no bulls**t.

KEY STRENGTH
Entrepreneurial flair. He may have inherited money and a taste for the good life, but Weston is no idle playboy. His record of dealmaking is one to make any bootstrapper proud.

BEST DECISION
Selling the US baking business for $2.5 billion to release funds to buy up struggling companies as the recession bites.

A CHIP OFF THE OLD BLOCK Born into a wealthy family, Galen enjoyed the kind of privileged background that Weston empire's founder George—a Cockney with a yearning to be rich—could only dream of, but he shared his grandpa's enterprising zeal. Impatient to get on, Galen left university before graduating. He bought a grocery store in Ireland and turned it into the successful Power chain, then did the same with Brown Thomas, turning it from a moribund drapers into Ireland's premier department store.

AN EYE FOR INTEGRATION Returning to Canada in 1972, he set about improving the family's jaded baking and supermarket interests with the same vigor. Through a series of acquisitions he made Weston's a brand leader in everything from sliced bread to pizza, right across North America and beyond. Weston also grew Loblaws into a chain with the largest market share of any Canadian superstore. Its 1,400 outlets are the shop window for goods produced by the other half of the family empire. Gregarious and outgoing, his relationship with his taciturn elder brother Garry was often fraught; the two ended up more or less estranged, Galen running the family concerns in Canada and Garry those in the UK. After his brother's death, Galen bought top UK department store Selfridge's and took a seat on the Associated British Foods board, moves seen as an attempt to re-unite the family interests.

Galen's nose for a deal remains acute. In late 2008, he sold Weston's US baking business to Grupo Bimbo of Mexico for $2.5 billion, bolstering his war chest to pick up bargains as the recession takes its toll of less resilient rivals.

LESSONS IN BUSINESS: KEEPING IT IN THE FAMILY

It's become fashionable to decry dynastic corporations as old-fashioned, opaque, and prone to emotional upheaval, but as the Weston saga demonstrates, keeping it in the family has powerful benefits, too.
→ Appreciate the advantages of being free from shareholder demands and the fads of the financial sector.
→ Maximize the opportunities afforded by the resilience of the family firm, such as by creating jobs and expanding your business in times of economic hardship.
→ Avoid family feuds by allocating suitable roles and creating space for each family member to thrive.

"In the food business you're constantly dealing with demographics, constantly asking where people are going with their desires and wants." Galen Weston Sr.

Leo Burnett CEO (1935–67), Leo Burnett Worldwide

A CREATIVE GENIUS and advertising icon, Burnett's reputation was founded on his ability to create images that encapsulated a product. Never a typical adman, he created his own agency, not on Madison Avenue, the home of US advertising, but in Chicago. He was inducted into the Copywriters Hall of Fame in 1961, and retired in 1967. Even today, more than 35 years after his death, many of the corporate images he created during a career spanning nearly six decades are still alive and well.

AN EYE FOR IMAGE After many years spent working as a reporter and copywriter at various companies, Burnett moved to advertising agency Ewin, Massey in Chicago, aged 40. He started his own agency five years later, during the Great Depression. His first corporate symbol stemmed from a pessimistic prediction that the agency would fail and Burnett would soon be on the street selling apples. He retorted that he would give them away, and ever since a bowl of red apples has adorned each Leo Burnett receptionist's desk.

BIG IDEAS Throughout his long career, it was Burnett's aptitude for inventing easily recognizable corporate identities, such as the Jolly Green Giant, that earned him his reputation. He was an advocate of consumer research, and pioneered surveys that told him whether his ads were striking the right emotional chords with the public. In the 1950s, his agency won several big advertising contracts, including Kellogg's, for whom Burnett came up with Frosted Flakes' Tony the Tiger, one of the 20th century's top ten icons (along with three other Burnett creations).

By the late 1950s Burnett's agency could take credit for some of the world's most enduring brands, and this continues today. At the time of his death in 1971, the agency's sales exceeded $400 million annually. Today that figure has exceeded $8 billion. Leo Burnett Worldwide is now one of the most successful advertising agencies in the world, with 132 offices in 85 countries. Its very impressive client list includes the household brands McDonald's, Coca-Cola, Walt Disney, Kellogg's, Nintendo, Samsung, and Visa.

LESSONS IN BUSINESS: USING PICTURES

Burnett followed Walter Lippman's philosophy of creating an image around a product. He encouraged staff to concentrate on the visual rather than the narrative, and believed recognition was picture not text based.
→ Make every aspect of your product or service visually appealing. Delivery people in uniform give a much better impression.
→ Once you have decided on a logo for your team or company, stay with it while it gains acceptance.
→ Many people learn more effectively from diagrams and pictures. Bear that in mind when coaching.

"When you reach for the stars you may not quite get one, but you won't come up with a handful of mud either." Leo Burnett

Jean-Paul Agon CEO, L'Oréal

AS THE HEAD of the world's largest cosmetics company, with revenues of over $20 billion, Agon oversees brands such as L'Oréal Paris, L'Oréal Professionnel, Garnier, Lancôme, and Maybelline. Agon is a firm believer in the power of marketing—ads like L'Oréal's "Because I'm Worth It," featuring Penelope Cruz, are known the world over. He believes beauty is "science in a jar" and has adopted a "global or nothing" strategy for all brands, while moving L'Oréal closer to a green and ethical stance.

BIOGRAPHY
Born in 1956 in Paris. He graduated from the Hautes Etudes Commerciales business school in Paris and then joined L'Oréal as a sales rep.

LEADERSHIP STYLE
A people person, charming and charismatic, Agon is a persuasive talker. "It's not just his charm," said Anita Roddick, who sold her Body Shop company to L'Oréal in 2006. "It's that he hasn't got that autocratic, hierarchical attitude that some have. He likes dialog."

KEY STRENGTH
Prepared to take radical decisions and explain why.

BEST DECISION
His 2006 acquisition of Body Shop was a major coup. He persuaded Anita Roddick to get on board and help him make L'Oréal products more "natural."

THE MAKEOVER Agon started out as a sales representative for L'Oréal in the south of France, driving samples around in a Fiat 127. He got his big break in management overseas —overhauling the company's loss-making subsidiary in Greece—only to find the company in such bad shape that five people had refused the job before him. However, Agon was able to use the experience to learn about the business, and subsequently turn the subsidiary around. He cites the event as determinant to his career.

BECAUSE HE'S WORTH IT Under Agon, a newer, more open L'Oréal has emerged, championing more natural products and promising an alternative to animal testing. His predecessor, Lindsay Owen-Jones, credits Agon with "a new sense of dynamism." He earns a very competitve salary, but will certainly be worth it if he can continue to find new avenues for growth in what many regard as an increasingly saturated market. Competition is fierce, with Procter & Gamble moving aggressively onto L'Oréal's patch, but Agon says he is optimistic, given the rapid development of the emerging economies and the aging world population.

He plans to continue the decentralized culture, with each division (consumer, luxury, professional, and active) running its own brands, stocked through a careful strategy of buying local brands and expanding globally. He acquired the Body Shop group in 2006.

The company's research arm is second to none. It is widely believed that if anyone in the industry is going to find ways to end animal testing, it will be L'Oréal under Agon.

LESSONS IN BUSINESS: COMMUNICATING BRILLIANCE

Agon believes that marketing beauty is an art. He wants marketing at L'Oréal to be "a unique combination of intelligence and emotion, rigor and sensitivity, dreams and reality."
➔ Appeal to your customers' needs and they may buy your products; appeal to their "wants" as well and they'll buy in larger quantities.
➔ Even in business-to-business transactions look for the personal benefits to the buyer.
➔ Make sure your marketing messages flatter peoples' intelligence; never talk down to them.

"Individual talent is critical. You need innovation, intuition, sensitivity, and talent." Jean-Paul Agon

Charles E. Merrill Co-founder & Partner (1914–44), Merrill Lynch

REMEMBERED FOR growing a huge client base of ordinary investors and for his shrewd understanding of the markets, Merrill is regarded as one of the most influential and successful American stockbrokers. From a modest background he forged a career on Wall Street, and in 1914 started the firm that became the largest stockbroker in the US. Passionate about the benefits of the capitalist economy, he amassed great personal wealth but was always frustrated that the democratization of the financial markets had not gone far enough.

BIOGRAPHY
1885–1956. Born in Florida. The son of a physician, Merrill studied law at the University of Michigan, but was unable to pay the fees and left after a year.

LEADERSHIP STYLE
Honest and direct. Throughout his career, Merrill made it company policy to give investors clear and truthful information, and he communicated with his staff in the same no-nonsense way.

KEY STRENGTH
Recognizing untapped market potential and finding an efficient way to reach it.

BEST DECISION
Advising his clients, ahead of the Wall Street crash in 1929, that a significant correction in the markets was due and that they should reduce their risk.

MARKET ABILITY Merrill was first and foremost a good market operator. After early days selling common stock and organizing personal investments, his firm made a name for itself underwriting retailers. Much of his wealth derived from an early involvement with S. S. Kresge (which later became Kmart) and Safeway Stores, in which he maintained a large personal stake as the group grew. He was quick to spot the potential of large chain stores to dominate retailing, and investment in the industry became a cornerstone of his success, demonstrating his keen eye for market trends.

SPREADING THE WORD Merrill was able to exploit his skills as an investor and a trend spotter largely because of his ability to communicate with ordinary Americans who, like him, did not come from privileged backgrounds, and to help them become active on the stock market. It was a win-win situation, he found a new and untapped pool of investors, and they found a non-elitist, straight-talking advisor. Berating the industry vogue of persuading investors to go for short-term profit, he encouraged all kinds of people to invest for the long haul and to take informed decisions. He once wrote, "The customer may not always be right but he *has* rights." His firm published vast amounts of popular literature demystifying the markets, and even ran seminars explaining investment and offering child care so that both fathers and mothers could attend. Casting his nets as widely as possible helped to grow his company's client base rapidly.

His capacity for hard work led to a heart condition and in 1944 he retired early, but very rich. He died in 1956.

LESSONS IN BUSINESS: LOOKING FOR NEW MARKETS

Merrill found success by educating people other firms were ignoring, and they became his customers. Other stockbrokers were too set in their traditional, elitist ways to spot the opportunity.
→ Look for unexpected new markets. Read broadly to get insights on where new opportunities may lie.
→ Get your product development and marketing people together to work out what product changes could open up new markets.
→ In a new market, set an end date for the experiment, to avoid losing money by going on for too long.

"Bringing Wall Street to Main Street." Charles E. Merrill's maxim

Alan George Lafley Chairman & CEO, Procter & Gamble

PROCTER & GAMBLE, the world's biggest consumer-products company, was in crisis when "A.G." Lafley took over the top job in 2000. Eighteen months earlier, concern about the need for change had led to the appointment as CEO of Durk Jager, whose attempts at a rapid shake-up left the company in turmoil and triggered a boardroom coup. Lafley was chosen to restore equilibrium, which he did, but he also brought about a quiet revolution in the culture and the marketing strategy of this bastion of corporate conservatism.

BIOGRAPHY
Born in New Hampshire in 1947, the son of a General Electric executive, Lafley graduated from Hamilton College in 1969. He began a doctorate in medieval and renaissance history at the University of Virginia, but left to spend five years in the US Navy. He enrolled in Harvard's MBA program in 1975.

LEADERSHIP STYLE
An expert delegator, Lafley shapes decisions by asking keen questions, and has made nurturing talent one of his highest priorities. He forbids long meetings, hates PowerPoint displays, and encourages executives to discuss rather than just present points of view.

KEY STRENGTH
Using stability and focusing on a considered strategy to create change.

BEST DECISION
Telling his managers to focus on what they did well. This formed the basis for radical change.

COMPANY MAN Procter & Gamble (P&G) is known as an insider's company, and Lafley was the classic company man. He joined in 1977 as a brand assistant for Joy dish detergent. He worked his way up through the ranks to become president of Global Beauty Care and P&G North America. When he was drafted to take over after Jager, it was his reputation as a steady, calming influence that had put him at the top of the list. As it turned out, his enthusiastic, mild-mannered approach proved capable of changing more than any aggression had.

QUIET REVOLUTIONARY Lafley's gentle style masked a firm decisiveness and a long-thought-out set of ideas about how to make P&G relevant in the 21st century, when speed and agility would be far more important than sheer size. In his quiet way, Lafley led the most sweeping transformation of the company since its foundation in 1837. Lafley pushed through the largest acquisitions in its history, at the same time replacing over half of the top tier of executives, more than any P&G boss in memory, and cutting nearly 10,000 jobs. Lafley also moved more women into senior positions.

He nailed firmly into place the central tenet of his vision: that P&G should do what it does best—selling solid, reliable, major brands such as Tide, Pampers, and Crest—and nothing else. He also made it clear that the company's stodgy corporate culture, the very problem that had triggered his predecessor's zealous rush for change, was gone for ever.

Lafley achieved these profound changes by listening, asking, and quietly explaining—proving that, if your ideas are good enough, there's no need to shout.

LESSONS IN BUSINESS: DOING WHAT YOU DO BEST

Instead of always trying to develop the Next Big Thing, focus on what you do best and make sure you keep doing it better. Improving what you do can be more successful than changing everything.
→ If it's not broke don't fix it; stick to your knitting—that is, improve what you do now.
→ Bring out new products when you need to but make sure key customers will welcome them.
→ Introduce new products into existing markets, or take old products into new markets. Beware starting a new market with a new product.

"The consumer is boss." Alan George Lafley

TALKING THE TALK

To be a great leader, a CEO must inspire, motivate, govern, collaborate, and negotiate: no mean feat even with excellent communication skills. However, not everyone is blessed with a silver tongue and, like a pebble dropped into a pool, mistakes at this level can have a ripple effect.

Marjorie Scardino (p218), CEO of media group Pearson, is acknowledged in her industry for getting internal communication right. She believes that good communication involves a dialogue between senior managers and employees. As far as Scardino is concerned, good communication is not simply a case of disseminating information; it's about listening and a willingness to act upon feedback and suggestions.

For Samsung CEO, **Yun Jong-yong** (p274), effective communication with customers is essential to increase awareness of products, secure purchases, and encourage brand loyalty. Samsung's desire to portray itself as a premium brand not only informs its advertising and marketing strategies, but also decisions on corporate citizenship, which it sees as crucial in communicating a positive image of the company to the public ●

> "Even if you're talking to lots of people, you want them to feel as though you're talking directly to them individually."
> PAOLO CAVALIERI

Effective Communication

Conquering the art of communication ranks highly in the average CEO's to-do list. A 2007 survey* revealed that 85.4 percent believe it is important to be perceived as an influencer in their industry, and it found that speaking at events and communicating with top customers were the most popular profile-building tactics deployed.

When **Marc Bolland** took over as CEO of UK supermarket giant Morrisons, the chain was struggling to compete in a tough retail market. Bolland made sure he was available to whoever wanted to speak to him: "The first thing I did on my first morning was call the top five shareholders, analysts, and journalists. I said, 'If there's anything you would like to know this is my mobile number, give me a call.'" Good communication also turned the retailer into one of the UK's "big four" supermarkets. Bolland used focus groups to find out consumer perceptions of the brand then challenged them by adding products, redesigning others, and refurbishing stores to communicate its strong points better.

Effective communication with staff is essential if a business is to fulfil its potential. Traditionally, openness has been seen as the key to good internal communication, but increasingly CEOs are taking this a stage further by actively making personal contact with staff and encouraging management to solicit their opinions. **Paolo Cavalieri**, CEO of Hollard Insurance Group in South Africa, exemplifies this new approach, believing that face-to-face communication with his staff is the most effective way to spread the company's vision.

While face-to-face communication is invaluable in forging relationships with staff, new technologies have allowed CEOs to communicate their vision to a much wider audience. A number of CEOs have embraced the blog. While many keep their thoughts to the corporate intranet, others, like **Tom Glocer**, CEO of media group Thomson Reuters, use theirs to influence public opinion of themselves and their company.

survey by PR Week and Burson-Marsteller

Learning to Communicate

Get trained up—All staff need to learn how to answer the questions they are likely to be asked, and how to deal with customers effectively, managers included.

Cut to the chase—Get to know the customer and make sure your messages always address their needs and issues.

Keep in touch—Keep staff informed about the future of the company, and any changes that might affect them by providing regular progress updates about the business.

Be available—Meet with staff face-to-face and encourage them to contact you with their concerns and suggestions.

Committed Communicators

Other CEOs renowned for their communication skills include:

Tom Dickson, BLENDTEC (Consumer products: US)—*A comic film posted on YouTube of Dickson trying to blend all manner of objects in one of his company's blenders proved far more effective in communicating with customers than a TV ad. Thanks to the viral effects of YouTube, blender sales quintupled almost overnight.*

—

Steven Davis, BOB EVANS' FARM (Restaurants: US)—*Davis' hugely popular blog, on which he frequently joins in conversations with staff, means that employees feel they know him and are unafraid to approach him when he visits the company's plants and restaurants.*

—

Eizo Kobayashi, ITOCHU CORP. (Diversified: Japan)—*Kobayashi prefers talking face-to-face and believes communication is an important part of time management.*

—

Won Kang-chung, KOOKMIN BANK (Finance: South Korea)—*A fluent English-speaker, Won is also admired for his communication skills in his own language.*

—

Champ Mitchell, NETWORK SOLUTIONS (Internet: US)—*Mitchell banned the use of technical language by his customer service operators, and rewarded them for spending more time talking to customers.*

—

Mark Tucker, PRUDENTIAL (Finance: UK)—*Tucker's communication skills are credited with helping Prudential fight off a takeover bid from Aviva in 2006.*

—

Cai Lixing, TAIWAN SEMICONDUCTOR MANUFACTURING (Electronics: Taiwan)—*A peacekeeper in a tough business, Cai is the voice of calm and a problem solver who inspires long-term customer loyalty.*

—

Alan Meckler, WEBMEDIA BRANDS (Internet: US)—*Meckler uses his popular blog to communicate his thoughts on his company, the industry in which it operates, and wider business issues.*

—

Geoff Dixon CEO (2001–08), Qantas Airways Ltd

A LARGELY SELF-TAUGHT businessman, Dixon led Qantas for eight years. His tenure as CEO of Australia's favorite airline coincided with some of the toughest times the aviation industry has faced, from downturn in demand to rising fuel costs, and Dixon was forced to make hard and often unpopular decisions to ensure the airline's survival. His chief legacy is the low-cost subsidiary airline Jetstar. Although its creation was controversial, the dual-brand strategy has left the airline in good shape for the future.

BIOGRAPHY
Born in Australia in the rural New South Wales town of Wagga Wagga in 1940. Dixon left school without a diploma and went back-packing for two years.

LEADERSHIP STYLE
No-nonsense, tough-as-nails, workaholic, with a reputation for letting fly.

KEY STRENGTH
Never shying away from a fight. Dixon said of himself: "Most people, if they like me or not, they know at least I put it on the line."

BEST DECISION
Setting up a low-cost subsidiary airline to attract a new market sector and prevent Qantas customers from defecting to rival budget airlines.

AVIATION DOWNTURN Before joining Qantas, Dixon was general manager of marketing and corporate affairs for TAA (later Australian Airlines). He moved to Qantas in 1993 and became CEO in March 2001, just six months before the 9/11 attacks and the subsequent bombings in Bali caused a major downturn in the airline industry, along with the SARS outbreak and the Iraq war. He failed twice his attempts to link Qantas with Air New Zealand, fought battles with Australia's powerful trade unions, and saw his airline threatened by aggressive new competitors. To add to his troubles, fuel became increasingly expensive.

MAKING IT THROUGH At a time when many airlines in the US and Europe were filing for bankruptcy, Dixon managed to keep Qantas profitable. He steered his company safely through apparently endless challenges, applying aggressive strategic skills and setting out a clear vision for Qantas on both a global and a local front. He sought alliances and mergers where they fitted his vision, and refused to let a failed takeover bid by the Airline Partners Australia (APA) consortium in 2007 dampen his spirits.

Dixon established Jetstar, a low-cost subsidiary that was designed to attract new business rather than siphon off existing Qantas customers. Unlike the subsidiaries produced by most airlines, Jetstar became a star performer, producing consistently solid earnings through the toughest of times. Dixon's time as CEO could scarcely have been more difficult, but by the time he stepped down in November 2008, his clear vision for Qantas had ensured that the airline came through safely.

LESSONS IN BUSINESS: QUALIFICATIONS AREN'T EVERYTHING

Street-wise and savvy, Dixon fought his way to the top of his profession, despite his lack of academic qualifications. At Qantas, he established a management team of men and woman who were bright and quick thinking, but often without the university degree that is the norm at senior level.
→ Don't let a lack of formal education prevent you from reaching for the top.
→ Go for people who are street-smart—they are probably faster on their feet commercially.
→ Look at resumés for achievements rather than qualifications.

"We are great believers in moving quickly." Geoff Dixon

Mukesh Ambani CEO, Reliance Industries

NO ONE PERSONIFIES the shift of economic power from West to East better than Mukesh Ambani, one of the richest men in the world. His Reliance Industries, India's largest private sector company, has reached a market capitalization of more than $75 billion and ranks among the world's top 200 companies. His steady management of business and political relationships has helped keep Reliance Industries center stage as India opens up its communications, infrastructure, and financial markets to the global economy.

BIOGRAPHY
Born in Bombay (Mumbai) in 1957. Mukesh Ambani is the eldest son of the legendary tycoon Dhirubhai Ambani. A chemical engineering graduate from the University of Bombay, he also has an MBA from Stanford University.

LEADERSHIP STYLE
According to colleagues, his secret lies in delegation, but he also believes in rolling up his sleeves and getting his hands dirty. He retains huge amounts of detail, and at one point he was personally involved in the creation of 60 manufacturing facilities.

KEY STRENGTH
He is known in India as the ultimate project manager, able to realize business dreams in ambitious capital projects few would have the courage to try.

BEST DECISION
Bringing cell phones within the reach of even those earning a few dollars a day. In two and a half years he signed up ten million subscribers, quickly creating his own market.

ACCEPTING THE CHALLENGE Ambani joined Reliance Industries, then a textiles company run by his father, Dhirubhai, in 1981. He helped his father to realize his dream of integrating his polyester fabric company backward into petrochemicals to control the supply of his own raw materials. Mukesh was given a huge challenge—to build one of the world's biggest oil refineries, in Gujarat. He lived on site and oversaw 85,000 staff in the construction of Jamnagar. The project was delivered in two years at two-thirds of the cost of BP's smaller refinery in Malaysia.

INNOVATIVE THINKING In 2002, three years after Jamnagar was commissioned, Ambani repeated the trick when he launched Reliance Infocomm, this time demonstrating that he was a business innovator too. Reliance laid fiber optic cable, bought millions of super-cheap CDMA cell phones from China, and sold 25 million handsets for $12 each to a market no one had noticed—India's low earners, including street hawkers and rickshaw drivers. The death of Ambani Sr. in 2002 led to bitter feuding between Mukesh and his younger brother Anil. The group divided in 2007 and Mukesh lost control of Reliance Infocomm.

Mukesh is particularly proud of his company's discovery of the Krishna-Godavari gas field in the Bay of Bengal, which is expected to produce 250,000 barrels a day, making a significant contribution to India's energy needs. Mukesh's current projects include a chain of supermarkets and two new cities on the outskirts of Mumbai and Delhi, providing much-needed infrastructure and creating up to five million jobs.

LESSONS IN BUSINESS: KNOWING YOUR BUSINESS

Learning a new industry takes time and effort. Ambani spent several nights a week sleeping on site in a steel truck container while he learned the oil business. He watched training videos during his morning workout.
→ Observe footfall. In retail it pays dividends to note who goes past an outlet at different times of day.
→ Spend as much time on competitors' websites as you do on your own. Even when you have an advantage people will catch up.
→ Study your industry. Things change all the time, sometimes dramatically but more often by degrees.

"Our biggest challenge is to grow with globalization."
Mukesh Ambani

Susan M. Ivey Chairman, President & CEO, Reynolds American

A 27-YEAR VETERAN of the tobacco industry, Ivey is the first woman to head a US cigarette company. Reynolds American is the parent of four operating companies, and as a result Ivey is responsible for one in every three cigarettes sold in the US and for approximately 6,500 employees. Company brands include Camel and Pall Mall, of which five are among the top ten bestsellers in the US. She has managed the company through strong competition and high-profile opposition to the product, including public smoking restrictions.

BIOGRAPHY
Born in New York in 1958. Ivey has a bachelor's degree from the University of Florida and a business degree from Bellarmine University, Kentucky.

LEADERSHIP STYLE
Daring, positive, infectious, and dynamic. Reynolds is passionate about the tobacco business.

KEY STRENGTH
Finding ways to appease the anti-smoking lobby.

BEST DECISION
Focusing on premium brands to increase revenue in the wake of enforced tax increases.

IMPRESSIVE START Ivey's first encounter with the tobacco industry came in 1981 when she approached Brown & Williamson Tobacco's (B&W) marketing department to complain that she couldn't find her favorite brand of Barclay Menthol cigarettes. Impressed with her style, the company invited Ivey to join them as a sales representative. She went on to hold a number of managerial positions, and in 1990 Ivey moved to London to become brand director for British American Tobacco (BAT), B&W's parent company.

EVER UPWARD Four years later, she became director of marketing at BAT's Hong Kong office, returning to London in 1996 as manager of international brands. In 1999, Brown & Williamson lured her back to the US by offering her the post of senior vice president of marketing, and just over a year later she was promoted to president and CEO. Ivey was instrumental in the successful merger between BAT and R.J. Reynolds Tobacco Holdings in 2004, and was duly rewarded with the position of president and CEO of the resultant new company, Reynolds American, Inc. Ivey immediately faced challenges on a number of fronts. Not only was she under pressure from competitors, but she also had to deal with the fall-out from highly publicized litigation cases and overcome rising cigarette taxes and increasing restrictions on public smoking. The 2006 acquisition of Conwood Co., the US's second-largest smokeless tobacco manufacturer, saw Ivey broaden the scope of Reynolds American, Inc. beyond cigarettes to a "total tobacco" model, massively strengthening the company's position in the national market.

LESSONS IN BUSINESS: TAKING RESPONSIBILITY

Ivey's response to tobacco litigation and the anti-smoking lobby was quick and decisive. As well as issuing a statement admitting the link between tobacco smoking and damage to health, the company set in place a number of corporate social responsibility initiatives.
→ If your company faces possible lobby or legal action, act responsibly.
→ Be careful with the impact your activities could have on children and take public steps to prevent this.
→ Be quick to volunteer compensation for any harm that your company may be inflicting on third parties.

"To be successful, you have to have a vision and a plan." Susan M. Ivey

Ricardo Semler Majority Owner & CEO, Semco SA

WHEN HE INHERITED the family company, Semler introduced a radical program of democracy that turned conventional management upside-down. Staff hired and fired their managers, salaries and financial details were opened up for everybody to see, and traditional structure was ditched. According to the usual rules, the result should have been disaster, but this workplace revolution turned a small Brazilian pump manufacturer into a highly profitable, diversified industrial conglomerate and opened the door to a whole new way of managing.

BIOGRAPHY
Semler was born in São Paulo, Brazil, in 1959. His father was an Austrian émigré who set up Semco in the 1950s to produce his patented vegetable-oil centrifuge. Ricardo earned a degree from São Paulo State Law School.

LEADERSHIP STYLE
As hands-off as it is possible to be. He has enabled Semco to be a genuinely democratic organization, rotating the CEO position, accepting decisions that he disagrees with, and leaving it entirely to the staff to take the business forward.

KEY STRENGTH
Recognizing that people are at their most creative and productive when they have a say in the running of the company.

BEST DECISION
To introduce the boldest experiment in management ever successfully undertaken.

YOUNG MAN IN A HURRY At the age of 21, Semler took over Semco, paving the way for a dramatic transformation of a company that had been declining along with its main customer, the Brazilian shipping industry. Semler signalled his intention to make big changes by firing 60 percent of the top management in one day.

MANAGEMENT REVOLUTIONARY Semler set out to rebuild growth at Semco with a traditional strategy of hiring tough new managers and making rapid acquisitions. Although successful, this approach strained the organization and built serious tensions among the workforce, and when Semler collapsed from stress he decided a different route was needed. During his convalescence, he met an innovative leadership thinker,

Clovis da Silva Bojikian, and came to share his view that employees who participated in key decisions would be better motivated than those who simply obeyed orders.

This conviction led him to launch a bold experiment in participatory management. Staff chose their own managers and decided their own wages and working times, meetings were voluntary, salaries and all the company's financial information were made public, and the company never looked further than six months ahead. It went against all the rules of conventional management, but the result was phenomenal. Semco has produced double-digit growth every year for 20 years, increasing its turnover from $4 million to $160 million, and has almost abolished staff turnover. It made Semler a new type of international management guru, as well as a very rich man.

LESSONS IN BUSINESS: TRUSTING YOUR PEOPLE

Giving employees power over their working lives provides them with the responsibility and freedom to unleash their full potential for their own benefit and the company's. Giving them only directions frustrates them and puts a cap on their contribution.
→ Recognize that people are not fundamentally lazy, and that gratification through work will produce results.
→ Get the right people and trust them to take the company forward, accepting they may make mistakes.
→ Allow people to push through their plans to completion, even when you think you could do better.

"If we do not let people do things the way they want to do them, we will never know what they are really capable of." Ricardo Semler

Muriel Siebert President & CEO, Siebert Financial Corp.

A LEGEND IN AMERICAN stockbroking circles, Siebert did not acheive her status by setting records for CEO compensation or piloting a multinational corporation. Her claim to fame is based on becoming the first woman to buy a seat on the New York Stock Exchange (gaining the right to trade shares directly) and then holding on to it for 40 years. Her secret, she says, is to "take stands, take risks, take responsibility—and care deeply about how America's big institutions affect the lives of individual people."

BIOGRAPHY
Born in Cleveland, Ohio, in 1932. Siebert attended Western Reserve University, Cleveland, but her father's illness cut short her education and she did not graduate. She has since received numerous awards and honorary degrees recognizing her talents.

LEADERSHIP STYLE
Brash, iconoclastic, and willing to take risks. Such attributes have made Siebert a revolutionary.

KEY STRENGTH
Changing the Rules; forward thinking and controversial, her ethic is also the title of her autobiography.

BEST DECISION
Holding on to her company while attempting to forge a career in politics. Despite its fall into disarray in her absence, Siebert turned down subsequent high-profile job offers to turn the business around.

AGAINST THE ODDS Siebert started as a research trainee at Bache & Co. in 1954, and moved on to other brokerages, rising to partner at three of them. In 1967, she founded Muriel Siebert & Co., specializing in research and analysis for banks and mutual funds. She applied for a seat on the New York Stock Exchange, an unheard-of move at a time when every one of the exchange's members was a man. The NYSE tried to block her entry, but after months of perseverance, she came up with the loans and sponsors she needed and was elected to membership on December 28,1967.

MAKING CHANGES In 1975, when the Securities and Exchange Commission abolished fixed commissions for brokers, Siebert & Co. became the nation's first discount brokerage, breaching the etiquette that only corporate customers gained discounts. Wall Street was not amused, but the move led to lucrative success. In 1977, she was appointed as New York's superintendent of banks. She ran unsuccessfully to be the Republican candidate for a US Senate seat in 1982, then returned to her company, which had fallen into disarray after having been placed in a blind trust and run by employees during her absence. She took the firm public by merging it with a publicly traded but defunct Brooklyn furniture company that was liquidating; a controversial move she defends.

She has donated millions to help women get started in the business world, and has created programs to help young people become financially literate. In 1990, she launched the Siebert Entrepreneurial Philanthropic Plan, which offers buyers of new securities an opportunity to support their communities.

LESSONS IN BUSINESS: MAINTAINING DIVERSITY

Venturing solo into a province reserved exclusively for men, Siebert broke down barriers, enabling many more women to make their way in finance. All it took was intelligence, bravado, and determination.
- → Incredible as it seems, many male business leaders continue to ignore the talent women have to offer. They do so at their peril.
- → Diversity expands talent: aim to recruit people from all age groups, backgrounds, and ethnicities.
- → Men, forwardness in women does not mean bossiness. Would you call yourself bossy, or just assertive?

"American business will find that women executives can be a strong competitive weapon." Muriel Siebert

Om Prakash Bhatt MD & Chairman, State Bank of India

VOTED INDIAN Businessman of the Year 2007, Bhatt is credited with transforming the State Bank of India into a competitive bank. As Bhatt puts it, "the elephant has been made to dance." Appointed Chairman in 2006 for an unprecedented five-year term, Bhatt has proved an innovative and audacious leader, motivating staff and implementing a radical in-house training program. Under his leadership, SBI has expanded in the domestic and international markets, and SBI is now the largest bank in India.

BIOGRAPHY
Born in Dehradun, India, in 1951. Bhatt studied science at DAV College, Dehradun, as a National Science Talent Search Scholar. He also holds a master's degree in English literature from Meerut University, Uttar Pradesh. His first career choice was the Indian Administrative Service but his parents suggested banking.

LEADERSHIP STYLE
Hardworking, innovative, a team-member. Bhatt has a hands-on approach to management and knows how to get the best from his employees.

KEY STRENGTH
Proven ability to show strong leadership in a crisis.

BEST DECISION
Taking his top executives for an offsite motivational meeting to kick start SBI's new staff training program.

A LIFE-LONG COMMITMENT Bhatt joined SBI shortly after his 21st birthday in 1972, as a probationary officer, and has spent his entire career with the bank, holding a variety of domestic and international positions, including a six-year stint in Mumbai developing SBI's computerization project, and a spell as the bank's representative in Washington, DC. Back in India, he demonstrated his talents for innovation and teamwork in several managerial positions across the country, and in early 2006 the Government of India appointed Bhatt as managing director of SBI. Within three months he was also chairman.

BREATHING NEW LIFE It was a challenging period in the bank's history. The liberalization of the banking system had led to aggressive competition from the private sector, causing SBI's market share to decline considerably, and, as customer expectations rose, SBI lost respect among its traditional clientele. At the same time, the rapidly expanding eonomy presented huge opportunities, which Bhatt was quick to exploit, drawing on his understanding of the market, his direct experience of IT, and his proven abilities as a team builder. To restore worker pride in the bank, Bhatt implemented a nationwide management program. With a view toward expanding the bank's market, he recruited technology-savvy young professionals to enhance the bank's IT platform, he began a program of opening new branches (the bank now has more than 10,000 across the country), and he broadened the range of products on offer to include pensions and general insurance. Within two years, SBI's market share and profits were climbing steadily.

LESSONS IN BUSINESS: COMMUNICATING STRATEGY

Bhatt's changes made people responsible for their own performance. After supplying the training to take the business forward, the next step was to involve everyone in the process of planning that way ahead.
→ Create the board's plan first and then encapsulate the strategy into a short set of aims and objectives.
→ Get the front line teams to produce their plans secondly, taking into account the strategy handed down.
→ Take this planning process out to the staff divisions. Plan how you are going to support these new operational initiatives.

"Our staff… were like [the heroic Hindu monkey deity] Hanuman, who never realized the immense strength he had." Om Prakash Bhatt

Ditlev Engel CEO, Vestas Wind Systems

KNOWN AS the "green revolutionary," Engel is well-known in global political circles as an ambassador for both his company and for Denmark, which wants to be at the forefront of the battle against climate change. As CEO of Vestas, his competitive instincts have helped to turn the company into the world's leading wind turbine manufacturer. Engel works with national governments, including those of China and the US, and his passion for the subject has helped to move wind power onto the world's agenda, as well as filling Vestas's order book.

BIOGRAPHY
Born in 1964. Ditlev Engel attended the Copenhagen Business School in Denmark, receiving a diploma in business economics in 1990. He studied management at INSEAD, Fontainebleau, France, in 1997. At one time he rode competitively as an amateur jockey.

LEADERSHIP STYLE
Focused, forward thinking, and passionate. Tending to take the long-term view, he has implemented a corporate structure designed to build trust and ensure collaboration.

KEY STRENGTH
Uniting potential users, his company staff, and politicians in a shared belief in wind power.

BEST DECISION
Supporting China's sustainable development by helping to build a wind energy sector there.

DEALING WITH A CRISIS Engel joined Vestas in May 2005, when the company's share price was at a low point and the firm was facing financial crisis in an increasingly competitive market. Having already gone into receivership, in 1987, after putting too much faith in the California wind boom, Vestas was again looking insecure. Engel, who had previously worked for Hempel A/S (a marine paint maker) had no direct experience of the wind turbine industry, but he had shown the strong leadership skills that Vestas felt could transform the company's fortunes.

RESTORING STABILITY To reassure shareholders, he cut costs by expanding production outside Denmark and setting up manufacturing facilities in China. Recognizing that this period of instability had caused uncertainty among the company's employees, Engel instituted a business unit called People and Culture to promote a shared culture across the group. These initiatives formed part of a strategic plan called "The Will to Win." Other elements included the creation of a business unit for technology, devoted to keeping Vestas at the forefront of technical innovation and protecting its inventions, and a focus on presenting Vestas and wind power as a real and very competitive alternative to oil and gas.

Making himself more accessible to his employees, Engel traveled around the world, using his laptop and mobile phone as his office, presenting his recovery plan and the mission statement "Failure is not an option". His efforts have strengthened the company's international competitiveness and turned it into a truly global concern.

LESSONS IN BUSINESS: WORKING TOGETHER

Engels has unveiled a new corporate structure run by a united Vestas "government." By achieving agreement on key areas and the way forward for the company, he has transformed the culture and ensured that management works collaboratively to achieve results.
➔ Meet with your managers, identify their strengths, and involve them in decision making.
➔ Ensure that channels of communication exist between the bottom and the top of your business.
➔ Create a reward system that emphasizes cooperation rather than competition—build up team work.

"It is not the big who eats the small, it is the fast who eats the slow." Ditlev Engel

Xavier Huillard CEO, Vinci

WITH HIS GALLIC CHARM put to good use, Huillard has enjoyed a successful career in the construction industry. He joined Société Générale d'Entreprises (SGE) in 1996, becoming chairman two years later. In 2000, the group changed its name to Vinci, and later that year Huillard played a key role in the merger with the GTM Group, making Vinci the world's largest construction, public works, and concessions company. After spending time as chairman of Vinci Energies, stimulating its growth in Europe, Huillard was appointed group CEO in 2006.

BIOGRAPHY
Born in France in 1954. Huillard studied at the Ecole Polytechnique and the Ecole Nationale des Ponts et Chaussées, both in Paris.

LEADERSHIP STYLE
Decisive, level headed, fair minded. Huillard has not been afraid to shake things up at Vinci. His pursuit of justice led to the resignation of the chairman, as well as other key board members.

KEY STRENGTH
A focus on stability. Huillard has concentrated on infrastructure projects involving construction and the long-term management of assets, which offer steadier profits in a period of economic fluctuation.

BEST DECISION
Acquiring a 3.3-percent stake in the government-controlled Aéroports de Paris, operator of Charles de Gaulle and Orly airports, in 2008, which positioned Vinci as a contender to take over the airport group should it be privatized.

BOARDROOM TROUBLES Huillard did not have the most auspicious of starts as CEO of Vinci. Right-hand man to chairman Antoine Zacharias, Huillard was appointed to oversee the day-to-day running of the company early in 2006. Just five months later, Zacharias was forced to step down over lavish financial perks that he had awarded himself, including generous stock options, a huge retirement package, and a luxury Paris home.

WINNING STRATEGY Freed from internal troubles, Huillard focused on an ambitious three-year strategy, setting objectives in the company's four core businesses: concessions (toll-operating infrastructure), energy, roads, and construction. A revenue target of €30 billion by 2009 was set, as was the goal of winning €1-billion-worth of new public-private partnerships

(PPP) or concession projects each year. Huillard successfully integrated Autoroutes du Sud de la France to give greater strength to the concessions and construction divisions in 2006, and his "integrated concession-construction" model was soon proven when Vinci won the largest concession contract in the company's history to build a toll motorway in Greece. This was followed by other key motorway concessions in Germany, Cyprus, and the Czech Republic. When billionaire French investor Francois Pinault bought an 8.1 percent stake in Vinci in 2007, Huillard had to dissuade "short-term" investors who were keen to sell off the company's public works and concessions branches. As the European market slowed with the economic downturn, he looked for investment opportunities in emerging markets, such as Brazil, Russian, India, and China.

LESSONS IN BUSINESS: ENCOURAGING INDIVIDUAL SUCCESS

Central to Huillard's business manifesto is the belief that long-term economic success cannot come without individual success, and that the company's "human chemistry" is what gives it its competitive edge.
→ Give priority to people over systems, and do not judge success solely on economic performance. Look for "soft" measures of peoples' talents.
→ Value individual input. Use the reward system and one-off praise to demonstrate their value.
→ Use communications campaigns to ensure staff know the opportunities and threats facing the company.

"Our concessions-construction model has never been as relevant... a short-term financial vision would destroy value." Xavier Huillard

GOOD CITIZENS

Corporate citizenship has become an increasingly important component of business life in recent years. While in the past a company stood or fell on the basis of its business performance, today corporations are also measured by their wider effect on the societies in which they operate, and on the environment. The sharpest CEOs recognize this and ensure that their companies address a range of social issues. **Brian Goldner** (p27), CEO of toy manufacturer Hasbro, has made corporate social responsibility (CSR) a focal point for his company, which cut its greenhouse gas emissions by close to half over seven years, and was among the first in its sector to implement a code of conduct for its suppliers. At HSBC, CEO **Michael Geoghegan** (p446) has kept the group high in the CSR league, backing up their slogan of being the world's "local bank" by taking a proactive stance on environmental issues, educational programs, and engagement with local communities around the world. ●

"Whatever you do in your business, leave the earth better for your children." PETER BAKKER

Ethical Corporations

Ben & Jerry's Homemade, one of the most recognized ice cream brands in the world, founded by **Ben Cohen** and **Jerry Greenfield** in 1978, is famous for its social mission, which was enshrined in the reporting structure when the company was sold to Unilever, where the activist approach continues to be championed by CEO **Walt Freese**. Ben & Jerry's activities encompass commitment to: family farms and sustainable dairy and agriculture; fair trade and other forms of socially and environmentally sustainable sourcing; reducing its carbon footprint and making progress toward becoming carbon neutral globally; and speaking out on behalf of world peace.

At media UK company BSkyB, CEO **Jeremy Darroch** is leading the way in his sector on reducing the environmental impact of the business. BSkyB makes environmentally friendly practices a routine part of its everyday business operations. Every time it constructs a building, puts in a new generator, or changes some of its server farms in IT, a fundamental part of the decision process is making these facilities as energy-efficient as possible.

CEO **Peter Bakker** has helped turn the US express mail and delivery company TNT into a world leader in CSR. As well as actively pursuing ways to reduce the company's carbon dioxide emissions and other environmental impacts, he has engaged it in a close partnership with the UN's World Food Program. This is an area where his company's specific skills can be directly useful, and TNT has improved utilization of the World Food Program's trucks in developing regions, mapped out roads in Darfur, Sudan, gone onsite with volunteers, provided equipment for disaster relief, and funded education programs on food. The company has reached the highest score of all companies in the Dow Jones Sustainability Index for two years in succession.

Being Good by Doing Good

Under CEO James A. Skinner (p293), McDonald's produced a list of ideas for how to implement successful CSR. They include:

Measure your progress—When you do CSR activities you need to be able to chart your performance to show you are walking the walk.

Make real change—If you visibly change purchasing policies based on sustainability decision-making criteria, your CSR policies will have more credibility.

Use external verification—Third-party verification builds trust and helps your company avoid accusations of "greenwashing".

Take a lead—It's better to be proactive than be dragged into doing CSR. Solutions that come from strategic proactive thinking are usually better than those stemming from reactive decision-making.

Exemplary Executives

CEOs who have made CSR a key priority include:

Sam Laidlaw, CENTRICA (Energy: UK)—*Laidlaw has spoken out on behalf of action being taken to cut Britain's carbon emissions in a practical manner. He also supports measures to encourage cutting carbon emissions in homes and businesses.*

Thomas F. Farrell II, DOMINION RESOURCES (Energy: US)—*By 2015, Dominion will have invested $3.5 billion to reduce carbon dioxide emissions by more than 80 percent. Between 2004–2007 it gave $43.4 million to almost 4,500 charitable organizations in the communities in which it operates.*

J. Brian Ferguson, EASTMAN (Manufacturing: US)—*In 2008, Eastman was named one of the five best corporate citizens among US chemical companies, for its community programs.*

John E. Bryson, EDISON INTERNATIONAL (Energy: US)—*His company now generates 16 percent of its power through renewable resources.*

Philip L. Francis, PETSMART (Retail: US)—*Donates space and supplies to animal rescue groups, and raises money for local adoption groups.*

Albert Lord, SLM (Finance: US)—*Named one of America's "100 Best Corporate Citizens" five times.*

John Drosdick, SUNOCO (Oil and gas: US)—*Has been listed as the most environmentally responsible company in the Sierra Club's Updated Environmental Guide to Gasoline.*

Henri Poglio, VEOLIA ENVIRONMENT (Energy and utilities: France)—*Prices its services in Africa at an affordable level, regardless of the impact on company profits, and has given resources to fight AIDS on the continent.*

Brett Godfrey *Co-founder & CEO, Virgin Blue*

FASCINATED BY FLYING, Godfrey has spent 20 years in aviation, all but four of them working for Virgin. After stints at Virgin Atlantic and Virgin Express in the 1990s, he came up with the Virgin Blue brand for the Australian aviation market with Richard Branson in 2000. After moving into the black in its first year, the airline enjoyed eight years of profitability, growing from two aircraft to more than 50. Godfrey has been the architect of its can-do culture, which has driven down costs and increased productivity.

BIOGRAPHY
Born in 1963. Godfrey graduated in business from Victoria University of Technology, Australia. After qualifying as a certified accountant with Touche Ross, he followed his father, who worked at Qantas, into aviation in 1989 as a financial controller at Sherrard/National Jet.

LEADERSHIP STYLE
Passionate and focused, but cool. He eschews hierarchy and tends to mock traditional management structures, describing himself as a "benevolent dictator".

KEY STRENGTH
The confidence to trust that successful corporate culture will come from the bottom up. He invests in staff recruitment and gives them significant autonomy.

BEST DECISION
Repositioning Virgin Blue as an airline for the corporate market, which boosted margins and steered the company away from the brutal no-frills price battle.

CREATING A CULTURE A self-confessed graduate of the trial-and-error school of management, Godfrey has achieved a dedicated, customer-focused corporate culture at Virgin Blue by devolving responsibility to staff in the field. The airline's pitch of high quality at low cost relies on well-resourced, top-notch recruitment, and has won Virgin Blue 30 percent of market share, as rivals such as Ansett, which was put into liquidation in 2002, fell by the wayside. It achieved huge profit growth, including a 93 percent annual increase in 2007.

MOVING UPMARKET Rocketing oil costs in 2008 and a looming recession put a brake on growth, and the airline posted a net loss for the second half of the year. However, Godfrey's three-year strategy to differentiate the airline from its no-frills rivals was to come into its own.

The introduction of dedicated passenger lounges and a frequent flyer program gave Virgin Blue a foothold in the lucrative corporate market, and the company has seen a healthy rise in corporate and government sales in a relatively flat market. Godfrey has also taken a number of more defensive measures, such as cost-cutting, ditching marginal routes, and rescheduling new aircraft purchases, positioning Virgin Blue to ride out what he described as "the most volatile operating environment in the history of commercial aviation." He even hopes to steal a march on Virgin Blue's global counterparts by taking advantage of a softer market to drive a harder bargain on new capacity. Godfrey underlined his confidence in the future of aviation by registering for an early flight on Richard Branson's sub-orbital venture, Virgin Galactic.

LESSONS IN BUSINESS: TRUSTING IN PEOPLE

Never the autocrat, Godfrey instinctively understands the benefits of consensus. His mantra is "no rules, just guidelines," which encourages staff to take the lead in all matters, apart from safety, with his full support.
→ Trust people to make good decisions when the chips are down. The people on the ground are in the best position to deal with a problem quickly.
→ Give your staff space to think for themselves, and they will generate results and enjoy their jobs.
→ Create a culture where people can do it their way, confident of your backing if something goes wrong.

"You can't restructure culture." Brett Godfrey

Martin Winterkorn CEO, Volkswagen AG

TAKING OVER AS CEO of the Volkswagen group in early 2007, Winterkorn was appointed on the strength of his success at the group's Audi division. He made it one of the most profitable operations in the industry, helping the brand to become synonymous with quality, and he soon set about doing the same for the rest of the group. His skill at transforming brands and his supreme confidence in the abilities of the organization have brought Volkswagen a strong sense of direction and a renewed emphasis on quality that is increasingly crucial in the global car market.

BIOGRAPHY
Born in Leonberg, Germany, in 1947, to Hungarian immigrants. Winterkorn gained a degree in metallurgy and metal physics at the University of Stuttgart in 1973, then earned a PhD at the Max Planck Institute for Metals Research in Stuttgart in 1977.

LEADERSHIP STYLE
Hugely self-confident and demanding, Winterkorn is obsessed with detail and drives his managers relentlessly.

KEY STRENGTH
Understanding the importance of quality.

BEST DECISION
Clearly defining the heritage, appeal, and qualities of the different VW car brands and marketing each one toward its niche, which enhanced brand perception thoughout the group.

TURNAROUND AT AUDI Winterkorn spent five years in charge of Audi, placing a strong emphasis on the best possible design, the quality of the models, and raising the level of the brand. His rigorous leadership turned Audi into a highly profitable operation, and Volkswagen's most successful division, and set it on the road to catching up with arch-rivals Mercedes-Benz and BMW. This made him the ideal choice to revive the overall group, which was troubled by shrinking profit margins and by protracted disputes at its German factories.

BACK TO BASICS Of all the company's brands, which include Skoda, Lamborghini, and Bentley, Volkswagen was the most troubled. Winterkorn immediately tackled the problem head-on, throwing out most of the upcoming VW designs, which he believed were overly complicated. He concentrated on keeping each brand true to its heritage, from proletarian for VW to upmarket for Bentley. He also restructured the group, leaving its seven car brands to be run as separate entities.

He set a new objective for the VW brand, using lessons he had learned at Audi to make Volkswagen a leader in quality. The company had received embarrassingly low scores in consumer reports, prompting him to order a thorough review of quality; he established a benchmark largely matching the profile of Toyota, long the industry's quality pace-setter. With a team of seasoned lieutenants from Audi, he began the tough process of cost-cutting in the factories. Profits began to climb as a result of Winterkorn's actions, but initial gains were soon reversed due to the slump in demand for cars after the global financial crisis.

LESSONS IN BUSINESS: FOCUSING ON QUALITY

However strong your brand has been, if you let the quality slip it will eventually turn to dust. When the company's history has already set the benchmark, you can't afford to let standards fall; the public is fickle.
→ Make quality your priority to ensure word-of-mouth—the best route to growth—supports your brand.
→ Make your brand last by keeping to the values that made it successful in the first place.
→ Expand your brand by branching out into related products and services: this means going for brand width as well as depth.

> "The tough competition among German manufacturers makes us fundamentally strong."
> Martin Winterkorn

H. Lee Scott, Jr. President & CEO (2000–09), Wal-Mart Stores

RETAIL GIANT Wal-Mart was on the verge of becoming the world's largest company, in terms of sales, when Scott took over the CEO position in 2000. It was also about to face an unprecedented wave of media and consumer criticism of everything from its size and competitive practices to its treatment of staff and gender pay policies. For Scott, a long-time company man, the attacks provided an unexpected challenge that turned what should have been a business-as-usual job into a serious case of crisis management.

BIOGRAPHY
Born in 1949 in Joplin, Missouri, Scott grew up in Baxter Springs, Kansas. He studied business administration at Pittsburgh State University, Pennsylvania.

LEADERSHIP STYLE
Scott combines a charming, affable, and folksy manner, with a ruthless and clear-cut vision.

KEY STRENGTH
A great talent for organization that allows him to get to grips with the big issues confronting a giant like Wal-Mart.

BEST DECISION
Setting out to confront the wave of public criticism of Wal-Mart before it damaged the company.

TALENT FOR LOGISTICS Scott joined Wal-Mart in 1979 as assistant trucking manager and attracted attention with his flair for organization and stripping out costs. As head of the logistics division, he set up the discount retail industry's first in-house distribution centers, removing a layer of middlemen and ensuring that shelves were replenished quickly and cheaply. Two years later he became head of the merchandising division, where he cut $2 billion in excess inventory, making him CEO material.

FACING THE CRITICS Scott brought to the role a new kind of corporate professionalism, which shaped his assertive response to the attacks the company faced as soon as he took over. Accusations of substandard wages, inadequate health benefits, sexism, over working employees, and detracting from American manufacturing

were leveled. It was also facing robust competition from rival discounters. Scott set out to deal directly with the chorus of disapproval. Appointing a new corporate counsel and hiring an outside law firm to review the company's approach to court cases lowered the number of sanctions and fines against the company, erring on compromise rather than all out defence. He announced a highly ambitious plan to transform Wal-Mart into a company that runs on 100 percent renewable energy and produces no waste, and has become an unlikley environmental hero in the process. Most importantly, Scott made communication the center of his job, expanding health care coverage and addressing issues of worker satisfaction. The company has continued to expand both nationally and internationally, despite continued criticism over market saturation.

LESSONS IN BUSINESS: ADDRESSING THE PUBLIC

The public are your customers, the ones who will make or break your business. You might think you're doing just fine, but if the public don't think so, you're finished. Eventually a bad reputation in any part of the business will damage you.
→ Pay attention to public opinion and treat communication as one of your top priorities.
→ Beware of focusing internally and solving problems within the company with no thought to its image.
→ Treat employees properly. If you do not, either they or public opinion will punish you.

"We can't let our critics define who we are."
H. Lee Scott, Jr.

Katharine Graham CEO (1963–91), Washington Post Company

TURNING HER ROLE as president and then CEO of the Washington Post Company into a position of international significance, Graham could lay claim to being the most powerful woman in publishing in the 1960s and 1970s. She oversaw one of the most significant news stories of the 20th century and steered the *Washington Post* to arguably its finest hour: forcing the resignation of President Richard Nixon. She was a formidable presence in Washington, with heads of states and politicians often meeting at her Georgetown home.

BIOGRAPHY
1917–2001. Born in New York City. Graham (née Meyer) was the daughter of a banker who purchased *The Washington Post* in a bankruptcy sale in 1933 for $825,000. After attending Vassar, New York State, then a women-only arts college, for two years, she graduated from the University of Chicago in 1938.

LEADERSHIP STYLE
Described as a "working publisher", Graham was forceful and courageous, yet quick to grant her editors the trust and autonomy they required.

KEY STRENGTH
Trusting her editors and allowing them to take responsibility for news stories.

BEST DECISION
Running the Watergate story that ultimately lead to President Nixon's resignation.

NO CHOICE AT ALL Graham was interested in publishing from an early age, working on a student newspaper before doing stints at the family-owned *Washington Post* during university holidays. After graduating, she was a reporter on the *San Francisco News*, then joined the *Post* in 1939. After her marriage to Philip Graham, she raised the family while he became publisher, but following her husband's suicide in 1963, she became one of the few female executives in publishing. As she later said, "When my husband died, I had three choices. I could sell the paper. I could find somebody else to run it. Or I could go to work. And that was no choice at all."

HOW SHE MADE IT Despite a break of over 20 years, Graham had never lost interest in the *Washington Post*, which still remained the family business. Determined not to let the quality of the paper suffer, she wasn't afraid to pay for top talent, and was careful to offer strong support to her journalists. The *Post* won the right to publish secret Pentagon papers detailing covert aspects of US military involvement in Vietnam, and its investigation of the Watergate scandal ultimately led to Nixon's resignation in 1974. Despite her privileged background, Graham was keen to be a role model for working women, and as she built up her publishing empire she promoted both gender and racial equality. She turned the title of publisher over to her son in 1979, but retained a tight control on the paper's activities, advising on editorial policy and increasing the company's interests in other newspapers and television stations. Her son succeeded her as CEO, but Graham maintained a keen interest in the paper until her death in 2001.

LESSONS IN BUSINESS: SUCCEEDING AS A WOMAN

Having had difficulty in being taken seriously by many of her male colleagues and employees, Graham always believed that there was no reason a talented woman couldn't do the job of any man.
→ Manage people like a "woman", not like a "man". Women tend to be better at giving praise and understanding their people, qualities that can give them the edge over male colleagues.
→ Be decisive and behave so that eventually no one notices that you are a woman in a man's world.
→ Look for a company with no women on the board. The directors will need at least one—make sure it's you.

"Some questions don't have answers, which is a terribly difficult lesson to learn." Katharine Graham

Angela Braly President & CEO, WellPoint

HER APPOINTMENT AS CEO of the health insurance group WellPoint in 2007, saw Braly become the only female head of a Fortune 50 company. She also found herself at the heart of an increasingly heated debate about the future of health insurance in the US, which was threatening the business model that had enabled WellPoint to develop into one of America's biggest companies. Braly's clear view on the direction of the industry and her experience of tough negotiations left her ideally equipped for the new challenges facing the company.

BIOGRAPHY
Born in Dallas, Texas, in 1962. She studied at Texas Tech University and Southern Methodist University School of Law, Texas. She is considered one of the most powerful women in America.

LEADERSHIP STYLE
Friendly and a good listener, Braly is also a hard-headed negotiator.

KEY STRENGTH
Recognizing that unless it became involved in the debate about healthcare reform in the US, the company was likely to suffer the consequences.

BEST DECISION
Setting out a loud, clear position on the future of America's healthcare system.

DEAL-SAVING LAWYER Trained as a lawyer, Braly first became involved in the health insurance industry in 1995 while working on a settlement between a client company and the state of Missouri. Her success in saving a tough deal was rewarded by a full-time job at the company, which was later bought by WellPoint. She soon became an important part of the WellPoint leadership, and was a key strategist during the company's $6.5-billion acquisition of New York-based WellChoice in 2005.

PUBLIC CAMPAIGN At the time of Braly's appointment, the company had achieved an average annual rise in earnings of 55 percent, and its health plans claimed 30–60 percent of market share and offered the widest networks of doctors and hospitals in the US. However, those results were under threat from a growing wave of public sentiment against health-insurance companies, resulting in rising pressure from government for the industry to change its practices or face direct government intervention. Braly quickly became a leading voice against government intervention, while at the same time putting in place strategies to maintain WellPoint's impressive financial performance. Braly put forward the case for healthcare reform carried out in measured steps primarily by the private sector, minimizing the problem of uninsured families by targeting the higher-income part of that population with new health insurance products while government programs were expanded to deal with the poor and the high-risk. Fixing the healthcare system, fending off government, and raising profits was a tough combination that Braly was happy to take on.

LESSONS IN BUSINESS: ENGAGING IN THE DEBATE

Sometimes it's not enough to just get on with business. There may be debates in the public arena that could seriously damage your organization, and the astute leader gets involved at the earliest opportunity to shape the way those debates go.
→ Use the top level of your customers and suppliers to gain access to political debates about the way ahead.
→ Raise your profile by writing articles or a book. Approach local radio and TV stations.
→ Follow up any exposure. Once one radio or TV commentator has used you as an expert, others will too.

"[Braly] knows how to build coalitions around her."
Kathy Osborn, executive director, St. Louis Regional Business Council

Christina Gold President & CEO, Western Union

RECOGNIZED IN 2007 by *Forbes* magazine as one of the "100 Most Powerful Women," Gold has been President and CEO of Western Union, a $4.9-billion company, since 2006. By changing the company's US-centered culture to give it a more global perspective, and by devolving more power to the regional offices, she has improved and expanded services at Western Union, consolidating the company's position as a worldwide leader in money transfer, bill payment, and prepaid services in over 200 countries and territories.

BIOGRAPHY
Born in the Netherlands in 1947, Gold (née Engelsman) emigrated with her family to Montreal, Canada. She graduated from Carleton University in Ottawa in 1969 with a bachelor's in geography.

LEADERSHIP STYLE
Practical, empathetic, analytical. A great problem solver, Gold believes that nothing is more important than the respect of your colleagues, even when you are their CEO.

KEY STRENGTH
Being a good listener. Paying attention to the needs of customers and the opinions of employees has enabled her to provide the right services in the right way.

BEST DECISION
Launching a $300-million global advertising campaign with the new slogan, "Uniting People with Possibilities".

BUILDING HER CAREER Gold began her career as an accountant before joining Avon Canada. After holding 20 different positions in 19 years and gaining experience in all aspects of management, she was named head of Avon Canada in 1989. She relocated to Avon New York in 1993. Her problem-solving skills helped transform the company's fortunes, and she became the first female president of Avon, North America. Observers were surprised when Gold missed out on becoming Avon's first female CEO.

OPENING NEW MARKETS Gold resigned from Avon in 1998 and, in a change of direction, spent four years at Excel Communications, an e-commerce service provider, before becoming president of Western Union in 2002, and CEO in 2006. After 30 years with a cosmetics company, Gold relished the change and focused on expanding Western's core business of helping people to transfer money to their families from abroad. While Avon had needed revival, Western Union simply needed to send payments to and from more countries than ever before. Renowned as a shrewd marketer and adept communicator, Gold led a multimillion-dollar campaign to promote the company around the world, introducing the slogan "Uniting People with Possibilities." She has steadily achieved her aim of penetrating new markets, and Western Union now has 320,000 agent locations worldwide. Her strategy of giving regional offices more autonomy and encouraging local offices to be in tune with their location helped the company to cope with bank strikes in Brazil, hurricanes in the Caribbean, and the tsunami in Asia.

LESSONS IN BUSINESS: COMMUNICATING CLEARLY

Aged six, Gold's family moved from the Netherlands to Canada. It was a cultural and language shock, but it taught her a lesson that's served her well in a global market: the importance of being understood.

→ Never assume that someone working in their second language has understood what has been said. Use translators where necessary.

→ Summarize every conversation and every meeting to make sure all involved agree on what was decided.

→ Take every opportunity you can to make presentations. Practice will make you improve dramatically.

"I am in a great business with tremendous growth"
Christina Gold

Gail Kelly CEO, Westpac Banking Corporation

AUSTRALIA'S "FIRST LADY" of banking has brought a splash of color into a traditionally gray-suited male sector. The country's highest-paid female executive for several years, her reputation was such that her appointment to the post of CEO at St. George Bank in 2002 prompted an AU$97-million boost to its share value. After nearly doubling its profits during her tenure, she took the top job at Australia's fourth largest bank, Westpac, and immediately set the wheels in motion to move it into second place by acquiring her former employer.

BIOGRAPHY
Born in 1956 in Pretoria, South Africa. Kelly (née Currer) studied Latin and modern history at the University of Cape Town, and later gained an MBA.

LEADERSHIP STYLE
Hyper and energetic, Kelly talks fast and sleeps little. Impatient and results-oriented, she has an eye for the bigger picture and has learned to focus on what matters. Colleagues describe her as generous and hard-working.

KEY STRENGTH
A team player. She can pull together the right people to turn a business around, and has consistently taken trusted lieutenants with her as she has climbed the banking ladder.

BEST DECISION
Jumping ship from St. George to Westpac after delivering a AU$3-billion hike in its market cap. The move paved the way for the two banks to merge, creating Australia's second biggest bank.

BRIGHT SPARK Talent-spotted by senior management when working in an HR role at South Africa's Nedcor Bank in the 1980s, Kelly was given a chance to shine by turning around the bank's unimpressive credit card operation, learning it from scratch and successfully building her own team. Widely regarded as CEO material, it was only unease at the direction of post-apartheid South Africa that led her to emigrate to Australia in 1997, where she joined Commonwealth Bank of Australia in a strategic marketing role and later ran its branch network. After moving to St. George as CEO in 2001, she led the bank to six years of record profits. Her strategy of organic growth, engaging with employees, and customer service, combined with an aggressive pursuit of lending, pushed the former building society up to fifth place in Australia's banking hierarchy.

SHAKE-UP Controversy arose after Kelly joined Westpac as CEO in 2008 and promptly set about acquiring her former employer, just as the credit crisis made it vulnerable to takeover. The merger raised concerns with consumer groups, who feared the threat to market competition would lead to higher fees. The deal went through with government approval, however, and the Westpac that emerged was a diversified, AU$66-billion banking behemoth with a huge customer base and an improved ability to see out tough times. The successful acquisition restored Kelly's reputation. She went on to reshape Westpac with a radical shake-up of its lackluster technology operation, and a restructure of other products and divisions. Kelly's achievements were recognized in August 2008 when *Forbes* magazine ranked her the 11th most powerful woman in the world.

LESSONS IN BUSINESS: MOTIVATING EMPLOYEES

A Latin scholar with a penchant for Ovid is not an obvious choice to lead a multibillion-dollar financial organization, but Kelly's capacity for sheer hard work and ability to motivate have propelled her to the top.
- → Work hard to create a culture where people are not satisfied with "just enough."
- → Insist that people should want to overachieve, and encourage them to love their job.
- → Build employee engagement by encouraging staff on an informal level, such as mixing at employee birthday celebrations and making family small talk.

"I like to achieve—I like to achieve quality outcomes."
Gail Kelly

Josette Sheeran Executive Director, UN World Food Program

THE TWIN PILLARS of Sheeran's career have been communication and access. Her solid background in news media, coupled with experience handling *Fortune* 500 clients at technology consultancy Starpoint Solutions in the 1990s, was integral to her rise to chief of the UN's World Food Program (WFP). Holding the rank of ambassador, she has also represented the US at a high level. Her success at maintaining a high profile has generated solid media coverage for the WFP, and has won plaudits from her predecessor in the role.

BIOGRAPHY
Born in 1954 in the US, Sheeran was inspired to enter public service by her father, a former WWII paratrooper and New Jersey local mayor. She graduated with a bachelor's degree from the University of Colorado in 1976.

LEADERSHIP STYLE
A negotiator and diplomat, Sheeran stresses the value of dialogue in leadership and management.

KEY STRENGTH
Understanding the power of networking in the rarefied atmosphere of top-level global policy making.

BEST DECISION
Following the advice of a *New York Times* reporter, whom she met on a flight to Boulder, Colorado, to go into journalism. She has described it as "an epiphany experience".

TOP LEVEL ACCESS First touted as one of Washington, DC's most powerful women in 1997, Sheeran's access to top-level leadership in business and politics has been crucial to her career. Two decades in journalism gave her experience as a political insider as the White House correspondent for *New York News World*, and TV exposure as a commentator while managing editor of the *Washington Times*. During this time she also interviewed heads of state in Europe, Asia, and the Americas.

POLITICAL ANIMAL Sheeran's first CEO role was at Empower America, a conservative-libertarian think-tank advocating radical tax, regulation reform, and free trade. This led to a government post in the US trade department in 2001, then promotion to ambassador level at the State Department in 2005. She led initiatives such as the USAID Trade Hubs program, successfully concluded the free-trade deal between Australia and the US, and helped negotiate Chinese entry to the World Trade Organization. Although critics allege her elevation to the role of executive director at the WFP in 2007 was political, she has successfully raised the profile of the organization at a time of food-supply uncertainty and distortions in markets caused by a fluctuating oil price. In the battle to combat world hunger, Sheeran is working toward improving the delivery of aid through the development of "smart interventions" that seek to target specific needs using local resources where possible, working in harmony with government and community initiatives. She cites the lack of a concerted political will as the main impediment to solving the world's nutritional needs.

LESSONS IN BUSINESS: WORKING YOUR CONTACTS

Making the right connections has been vital to Sheeran's rise in the NGO world. In an environment where meetings and summits are the lifeblood, her experience and contacts at head-of-state level have proved essential.
→ Allocate time in your schedule for seeking and making contact with new people.
→ Keep your network of contacts active so that old contacts that may seem unnecessary now can be brought back into the network if the need arises later.
→ Stay in touch with front-line staff. Sheeran spends time very visibly with staff and gives credit to their work.

"A woman's inclination to talk things through, rather than fight things through, is often useful." Josette Sheeran

Margaret Chan Director-General, World Health Organization

IN THE LATE 1990s, Chan came to prominence when, as head of the local health department, she ordered the culling of all poultry in Hong Kong to prevent the spread of the avian flu that was racing across east Asia. This decisive move stopped the disease in its tracks and established her reputation as a fearless fighter for public health, which, along with her ability to push her agenda through in a wide variety of circumstances, ultimately led to her appointment as the world's leading health administrator in 2006.

BIOGRAPHY
Born in Hong Kong in 1947, Chan has a bachelor's in home economics and a medical degree from the University of Western Ontario.

LEADERSHIP STYLE
Friendly and inclusive. Chan tries to take as many people with her as she can.

KEY STRENGTH
Her powers of persuasion have ensured that politicians around the globe now place public health concerns high on the list of priorities.

BEST DECISION
Making the assessment of WHO's performance one of her key priorities, believing that member states will give the organization greater support if it can demonstrate the health benefits of its work.

THROUGH THE RANKS Chan began her career in health as a medical officer for the Hong Kong government in 1978. She rose through the ranks of the colony's Department of Health, in 1994 becoming the first female director. Shortly after, Hong Kong became the epicenter of one of the most serious outbreaks of a deadly disease in recent years, putting her at the forefront of global health challenges.

FACING EPIDEMICS When avian flu broke out in Asia in 1997, Chan reacted quickly and decisively, ordering a cull of all 1.6 million poultry in Hong Kong, stopping the disease from spreading and preventing a possible pandemic. She pushed ahead with the cull despite widespread opposition, demonstrating her ability to identify and implement key health objectives. Six year later, the outbreak of SARS in southern China left Chan facing yet another epidemic. In 2003, she joined the World Health Organization (WHO), and in 2005 she was appointed director for communicable disease surveillance and response. Following the sudden death of Lee Jong-wook in 2006, Chan was the favorite to succeed him. As director-general she quickly announced a set of core areas on which she would focus. As well as directly health-related issues, these include education, all-important partnerships with other health organizations, and the performance of WHO itself. Engaging her particular interests in women's health and the state of health in Africa, she has made these the bellwethers of the organization's success. Her diplomatic skills and popularity among colleagues have helped her to advance the public health agenda around the world.

LESSONS IN BUSINESS: TAKING A STAND

By ordering a cull of all poultry in Hong Kong during the avian flu outbreak, Chan not only stopped the disease but established in the public mind the importance of what she does—a good model for any manager.
→ It is often useful to make decisions based on small steps, but when a hard decision is necessary, take it.
→ A radical decision will not be universally welcomed. Convince as many people as you can—then act.
→ All managers are exposed at some point to the unexpected. Listen to the evidence, and do not expect to move along the same path for ever.

"Our work must touch on the lives of everyone, everywhere." Margaret Chan

James Leape Director-General, WWF International

A FORMER environmental lawyer, Leape has globalized the Swiss-based conservation organization WWF International (formerly the World Wildlife Fund), effectively focusing popular attention on the big issues, and pushing for deals with big business. Astute and forward-thinking, he has both the intellect and the idealism to negotiate environmental initiatives with a wide range of objectors, from local landowners to heads of government and corporate chiefs. Under his leadership, WWF is bringing about practical change on the ground.

BIOGRAPHY
Born in 1955 in Boston, Massachusetts. Leape was educated at Harvard College and Harvard Law School.

LEADERSHIP STYLE
Intensely committed, but with a sense of humor. As befits his background as a lawyer, Leape chooses his words carefully.

KEY STRENGTH
Having the diplomatic skills to work with, rather than against, national governments and large corporations on key issues.

BEST DECISION
Instituting the Earth Hour campaign, in which tens of millions of people turn off their lights for an hour to raise awareness of global warming.

COURTROOM BATTLES In his legal career, Leape's notable success stories in the US courts include a lawsuit brought against President Reagan's administration in the 1980s to stop the construction of an oil port on the Bering Sea. After working for the United Nations Environmental Program in Kenya, Leape began to shift his focus to more global issues, recognizing, as he said, "that law in itself is limited as a tool for advancing conservation." Nonetheless, he spent the next three years teaching in law school in Colorado and Utah.

GLOBAL WARRIOR In 1989, Leape joined WWF, where he spent the next decade in the role of executive vice-president working on its conservation programs around the world. Working alongside multinational corporations, Leape pushed through a number of high-

profile projects, notably the setting up of the Marine Stewardship Council (MSC) in 1997 with the help of Unilever (the world's biggest buyer of seafood). Leape moved to the David and Lucile Packard Foundation in 2001, but in 2005 he rejoined WWF as director-general. Under Leape, the WWF has targeted key regions of biodiversity, such as the Amazon, in an effort to bring about large-scale change. He also promotes eco-labeling, helping consumers make choices supporting sustainability and ultimately driving change in the retail industry.

Leape has helped to turn WWF into a global organization capable of shrewd negotiations with concerned parties at all levels, from local to multinational. As Leape acknowledges, "We try to be catalytic. We work with partners like communities and governments. In the long-term, action has to be in their hands."

LESSONS IN BUSINESS: NEGOTIATING A WIN–WIN OUTCOME

The WWF began life as a lobby group for endangered animals, but Leape has helped to turn it into a global organization capable of shrewd, well-informed negotiations at all levels.
→ In negotiating, look for a solution that will benefit all interested parties. Win/lose causes resentment and makes future negotiation more difficult.
→ Make sure there are many minor issues that you can give way on while maintaining what is most important to you.

"If everyone around the world lived as those in America, we would need five planets to support us."
James Leape

PEOPLE POWER

It may be a cliché, but the popular business maxim that "people are our greatest asset" is as true today as it's ever been. A business can only achieve its potential if the people working for it are motivated and their talents are tapped. Some of the best-regarded CEOs are those, such as **Terry Leahy** (p327) at UK supermarket retailer Tesco, who encourage employees to tackle new challenges and develop new skills throughout their working lives. Leahy believes that one of the best ways to motivate staff is to create a culture that rewards ability and hard work. He has been keen to stress that there are only six levels between a shelf stacker and CEO at Tesco, and at any one time ten percent of staff are in training for the next rung up the corporate ladder.

As well as giving staff the chance to rise up the ranks, it's also crucial to create enthusiasm for their role. **William McKnight** (p16), former president and chairman of 3M, took a hands-off approach to managing his staff. He pioneered the practice of management by delegation, and allowed his engineers to spend 15 percent of their time on their own projects. He reasoned that, though mistakes would be made, it's better to encourage creativity and keep people happy in their roles than have management telling everyone to do the wrong thing ●

It's Good to Wander

There are myriad ways to encourage staff to work hard and to strive to improve their performance and productivity, but the fundamental rule in good management is clear, effective communication.

It is vital to connect with employees and engage their imaginations. "You have to get people to truly understand what you're trying to do," says **James O'Brien** at Ashland. The US chemical company boss believes a compelling narrative of what a company is working to achieve, combined with a clear definition of what each employee's role is in achieving that goal, is the stimulus staff are seeking from their managers.

For a CEO, good communication doesn't end with defining goals and roles, it's also about being accessible to staff. The concept of MBWA (Management by Wandering Around), pioneered by Hewlett-Packard co-founder **David Packard** (p28) and which came to prominence in the 1970s and 1980s, involves managers meeting their staff and observing them doing their jobs. MBWA benefits managers and staff alike; managers learn valuable lessons about their business and staff feel appreciated and part of the decision-making process. **Mark Hamister**, CEO and chairman of the healthcare and hotel management business, The Hamister Group, is a staunch advocate of MBWA. Convinced that it would yield results for his business, he introduced his management team to the concept, but, to his surprise, he found that the practice didn't have the desired effect. So Hamister decided to engage in some MBWA himself: "What I found was that our management staff was indeed wandering, but they were forgetting that the other half of the practice was interaction." Hamister concluded that the acronym needed adapting to stress the importance of engaging with staff, and he and his company executives now practice Management by Interacting and Wandering Around. Hamister is keen to stress that this management method has resulted in a range of practical benefits for his business, from efficiency savings to more effective staff training.

"An interesting job, being treated with respect, good training, and career opportunities—these are what motivate people, in every part of the world."
TERRY LEAHY

Managing Your Staff

Be affable — People need to know you are the boss, but you can do this sociably and affably. Friendliness will generate respect.

Maintain open channels of communication — "Walk the floor" or hold open conferences, so that employees can raise issues.

Give notice — Provide timely opportunities for consultation on changes that will affect employees, such as relocations or mergers.

Avoid favoritism — Make sure promotions are objectively made, and seek out talented staff from areas you may not be familiar with.

Create appropriate incentives — Align bonuses with strategy rather than simply using them to make employees feel good.

People Persons

These CEOs work hard to get the best out of their staff:

Wan Feng, CHINA LIFE INSURANCE (Insurance: Hong Kong)—*Met the challenge of difficult economic circumstances by promising not to sack employees or cut salaries.*

Ren Jianxin, CHINA NATIONAL CHEMICAL CORP. (Chemicals: China)—*Has stressed that the key to overcoming challenging economic conditions is to avoid layoffs and salary cuts.*

Larry Nichols, DEVON ENERGY (Energy: US)—*A CEO with a sound business plan who offers large bonuses to high performing employees.*

Frederico Fleury Curado, EMBRAER (Aviation: Brazil)—*Sees "employee satisfaction" as central to the company's future success.*

Myron E. Ullman III, J. C. PENNEY (Retail: US)—*Strives to create a friendly and enjoyable atmosphere in department stores, for staff and customers alike.*

James Rohr, PNC FINANCIAL SERVICES GROUP (Finance: US)—*Turned the company around after the accounting scandals of 2003 and 2004, motivating his staff again by introducing astute incentive schemes.*

Masatoshi Sato, SOMPO JAPAN INSURANCE (Insurance: Japan)—*Has led a mission to "unleash" the full potential of employees, including schemes to encourage staff to act on their own initiative.*

Nadine Chakar Chair, BNY Mellon Asset Servicing B.V.

BIOGRAPHY
Brought up in Boston, Chakar gained a degree in economics and finance from the University of Boston.

BEST DECISION
Offering customers a one-stop shop for their investment needs.

LESSON IN BUSINESS
It is possible to grow aggressively and still retain customers—the company claims to have won 65 percent of all new business for which it bid, while retaining 99 percent of existing clients.

AN EXPERT AT MERGING banking operations, Chakar oversaw the creation of what is now the world's largest investor services firm. During the changes, Chakar has maintained high standards and 99 percent client retention.

In 1989, Chakar joined Mellon Financial Corporation, holding a variety of positions in the US and Europe before being put in charge of a marketing alliance with Dutch bank ABN AMRO in 1996. This offered global custody and related services to institutions outside North America. Despite cultural problems it was a success, and in 2003 it was formalized, creating ABN AMRO Mellon Global Securities Services. Chakar puts the success down to creativity, team spirit, and employees' passion for results. When Mellon merged with the Bank of New York in July 2007, the largest investor services firm in the world was created with $20 trillion in assets under custody. The resulting company, Bank of New York Mellon, acquired ABN AMRO Mellon Global Securities Services the same year. For Chakar, this meant pulling together the two parts, with a clear vision. She stressed the importance of the continuity of and investment in people, products, technology, and service levels to ensure profitability.

Andrew Demetriou CEO, Australian Football League

BIOGRAPHY
Born in Melbourne in 1961. Demetriou is the son of Greek Cypriot immigrants.

BEST DECISION
Negotiating a record television deal worth almost AU$780 million to the league.

LESSON IN BUSINESS
Know your business inside out—Demetriou's experience both as a player and in sports management enabled him to dramatically reshape Australia's iconic football league.

ATTACKING A STRUGGLING professional league's business problems with the enthusiasm he brought to the game as a player, Demetriou transformed the Australian Football League into a marketing behemoth that dominates all others.

Demetriou began his career as a professional Australian-rules footballer, playing wing for North Melbourne & Hawthorn for eight seasons. During this time he became a shareholder in Ruthinium Group, a company importing acrylic teeth. On retirement from active sports in 1989, Demetriou was appointed managing director, subsequently boosting the company's sales by more than 500 percent. In 1996, the Australian subsidiary took control of its Italian parent and emerged as a world leader in manufacture and sales of dental products. Demetriou continued as a director of Ruthinium but in 1998 was also appointed CEO of the AFL Players' Association. He managed over AU$40 million in funds and negotiated a watershed five-year players' contract. In 2003, he was appointed CEO of the 16-club football league. Under Demetriou the league has grown dramatically in attendance and TV ratings. Its championship is the most watched event on Australian TV.

"For me, it is a privilege to do this job." Andrew Demetriou

Kevin W. Sharer President, Chairman & CEO, Amgen Inc.

BIOGRAPHY
Born in Clinton, Iowa, in 1948.
Sharer studied at the US Naval
Academy and gained an MBA
from the University of Pittsburgh.

BEST DECISION
Hiring a handpicked team of
executives to help him manage
Amgen, rather than running the
company as a one-man show.

LESSON IN BUSINESS
Beware of overconfidence—
Sharer hung a picture of General
Custer on his office wall to
remind him of the danger of
overestimating his ability and
underestimating the challenges
that he faced.

KNOWN FOR HIS DRIVING ambition and immense self-belief, Sharer served with the US Navy before moving into the corporate world. CEO of Amgen since 2000, he has helped turn the biotech company into a healthcare giant.

In 1978, lieutenant-commander Sharer's ambition outstripped the confines of the navy and he left to pursue a corporate career. His first job, with AT&T, gave him time to complete his MBA, after which he moved to management consultants McKinsey & Co., then General Electric, before taking a high-profile marketing role at MCI Telecommunications. Sharer joined biotech company Amgen in 1992 as president and COO because he reckoned he stood a reasonable chance of becoming CEO. Upon assuming the role in 2000, he increased the company's salesforce, and put together a team of experts to help him turn Amgen into a major player in the healthcare market. The company acquired the blockbuster drug Enbrel from Immunex Corp. in 2002, which both increased revenues and profit, and improved its reputation and competitiveness. Although jobs were lost in 2007 for the first time since the company was founded in 1980, Amgen had grown to be the world's 11th largest pharmaceutical company.

Richard E. Waugh President & CEO, Bank of Nova Scotia

BIOGRAPHY
Born in Winnipeg, Canada, in
1948. Waugh attended the
University of Manitoba, and
gained an MBA from York
University, Toronto.

BEST DECISION
Focusing on providing high levels
of customer satisfaction, a
strategy that brought in two
million new customers in 2006.

LESSON IN BUSINESS
Success is founded on
people—Waugh has remained
with one company throughout his
career, and believes the success
of the bank owes much to
employees, their ideas, skills, and
worth ethic.

AS CEO OF CANADA'S third largest bank, Waugh has pursued a path of modest international expansion coupled with consolidation of domestic growth since 2003, turning Bank of Nova Scotia into the country's most international bank.

Waugh joined Bank of Nova Scotia (Scotiabank) in 1970 as a trainee in a suburban Winnipeg branch. Moving to Toronto, he worked in investment, corporate, international, and retail banking, before transferring to New York in 1985 as the most senior executive in the USA, playing a pivotal role in the development of Scotiabank's US operations. Returning to Toronto, he was appointed vice-chairman of corporate banking in 1993, and of international banking in 1998. In late 2003, Waugh won a three-way succession battle to become CEO. He made it clear that there would be no immediate change to Scotiabank's strategy of consolidating internal growth, but he continued modest international expansion by strengthening the position in Central and South America with acquisitions in Peru, Chile, Costa Rica, and the Dominican Republic. With the onset of the global financial crisis, Waugh assumed a cautious domestic position, reducing mortgage provision to Canadian customers.

"I really do believe in what we've been calling 'one team—one goal'." Richard E. Waugh

Tony Hayward CEO, BP

BIOGRAPHY
Born in England in 1957. Tony Hayward gained a first class degree in geology from Aston University in Birmingham, before receiving his PhD from Edinburgh University.

BEST DECISION
Streamlining the flow of information and encouraging communication by simplifying the company management structure.

LESSON IN BUSINESS
Find a mentor—Hayward has always had people to turn to for advice and a sense of perspective, both practically and commercially.

STARTING OUT as a geologist, Hayward has risen to become CEO of one of the most successful global oil companies. His cutting-edge experience should stand him in good stead in what remain troubled times for the industry.

Joining the UK-based oil giant, BP, as a rig geologist in 1982, Hayward worked in a number of positions and countries throughout the world before becoming president of BP Group in Venezuela in 1985. When in 2003 he was promoted to CEO of BP's exploration and production operations, Hayward was already being groomed for top management by then CEO John Browne. Hayward was appointed to the position of CEO in 2007. Based on his concerns about communication within the company, one of his first decisions was to pare down bureaucracy and increase operational efficiency by shedding four layers of management and centralizing global resources, such as IT and human resources. Hayward also prioritized safety and people management as key objectives. The company's environmental policies, however, have faced criticism. With rising costs and increasing competition from state-controlled companies in Russia and Saudi Arabia, Hayward is facing tough times ahead.

Ben Verwaayen CEO (2002–08), BT Group

BIOGRAPHY
Born in 1952 in Driebergen, The Netherlands. Verwaayen gained a master's degree in law and international relations from Utrecht University.

BEST DECISION
Pushing BT's broadband services in the UK, which opened up a fast-expanding and lucrative new revenue stream for the company.

LESSON IN BUSINESS
Embrace competition and adapt accordingly—Verwaayen realized that former monopolies must modernize in the face of competition from low-cost rivals.

TURNING AROUND a company in crisis was Verwaayen's priority when he took the reigns at BT, the former UK telecommunications monopoly. He immediately set about trimming debt, pushing broadband, and expanding services overseas.

Faced with near bankruptcy, and forced to sell off its potentially lucrative wireless business, UK telecommunications giant BT went looking for a new CEO in 2002. Verwaayen's success transforming Dutch phone company KPN into a private sector operator made him the ideal candidate. He cut costs by sacking staff and reducing capital spending and, seeing the potential of the fledgling UK internet broadband market, Verwaayen successfully expanded BT's domestic access. In 2002, only 200,000 UK households had broadband, rising to 12.5 million by the time Verwaayen left BT. He took the company back into the black within a year, achieving a $4.2 billion profit in 2003, following a $4.1 billion loss in 2002. He is also credited with pushing BT's overseas activity through a string of acquisitions. Verwaayen left BT in 2008 to become CEO of Alcatel-Lucent, although problems with long-term contracts and cost control at BT's global services division have since tarnished his legacy.

"There is a shelf life for good and effective leadership. If you stay too long, the decision won't be your own." Ben Verwaayen

N. Murray Edwards Vice-Chairman, Canadian Natural Resources

BIOGRAPHY
Born in Regina, Canada, in 1959. Edwards graduated in commerce from the University of Saskatchewan and in law from the University of Toronto.

BEST DECISION
Learning from a dying best friend to follow his passion, Edwards left the legal profession and took over a small oil company with nine employees.

LESSON IN BUSINESS
Don't look for silver bullets—Edwards' dealmaking skills are a good example of the success of a balanced, incremental approach to problem-solving.

ENERGY INDUSTRY attitudes toward the new realities of climate change have been transformed by Edwards. His pragmatic political deals between the petroleum industry and government have led to increased investment and lower emissions.

Edwards rose from humble roots to join a prominent Calgary law firm in 1983. He left in 1988 to found Edco Financial Holdings Ltd, an investment company. Believing that if an asset is worth owning, one should own as much as possible, Edwards acquired Canadian Natural Resources Ltd, a small oil company, and grew it to a $30 billion behemoth that now ranks in the world's top 50. The Calgary billionaire's interests range from Alberta's vast oil sands and energy interests in the North Sea, West Africa, and North America, to oil field services, financial management, aerospace, the Calgary Flames hockey team, and Canada's famous ski resort, Lake Louise. A consensus-builder deeply concerned with ethical business, Edwards persuaded the energy industry to work with government on climate change policy, arguing for an incremental reduction in carbon emissions, while enhancing clean technologies. His company reduced emissions generated during oil production by 75 percent in a decade.

R. Kerry Clark Chairman & CEO, Cardinal Health, Inc.

BIOGRAPHY
Born in Ottawa, Canada, in 1952, Clark is the son of a milk-delivery business owner. He attended Queen's University in Ontario, receiving a bachelor of commerce degree in 1974.

BEST DECISION
Offloading the company's entire drug technology division, the sale of which fetched $3.3 billion and impressed industry analysts.

LESSON IN BUSINESS
Develop leaders from within the company—Clark believes in identifying an individual's potential, and then matching them to their "destination job".

LAID-BACK CANADIAN Clark spent 30 years at Procter & Gamble (P&G) before taking the top slot at Cardinal Health, a leading producer of medical products and services. He has since restructured and streamlined the company.

Clark was appointed vice chairman of P&G's $20 billion global health, baby, and family care business in 2004, but left the company in 2006 to take over as CEO of Cardinal Health. Clark's easy-going attitude and ability to inspire made an immediate and favorable impression on his colleagues. He used a leadership development plan to identify the top hundred managers within the company, creating a new "global leadership team." Clark's hands-on style of leadership restored morale within the company, which had faced several years of problems, including an investigation by the Securities and Exchange Commission into its accounting practices. Drawing on his vast operational, strategic, and management experience at P&G, Clark streamlined and restructured Cardinal's international operations, jettisoning businesses that were surplus to requirements, and acquiring others to strengthen core businesses. Clark is committed to growing the company and turning it into a large, multidimensional corporation.

"Our transition has gone extremely well and the company is thriving under Kerry's leadership"
Robert D. Walter, founder, Cardinal Health, Inc.

Jørgen Buhl Rasmussen President & CEO, Carlsberg A/S

BIOGRAPHY
Born in 1955. Rasmussen gained a bachelor's and MBA in economics and business administration at the Copenhagen School of Economics and Business Administration.

BEST DECISION
Acquiring full control from S&N of their successful joint venture, Russian market-leading BBH, boosting Carlsberg's plans for international growth.

LESSON IN BUSINESS
Persevere—it took Rasmussen months to wrestle his target acquisitions from S&N.

EXTENSIVE INTERNATIONAL experience and a recognized ability to win commitment from employees made Rasmussen the best candidate for the post of CEO of Carlsberg A/S, the fastest growing brewer in the world.

Rasmussen's career has spanned diverse roles, industries, and regions. He has worked in product, marketing, and general management at large international companies including Master Foods, Duracell, and Gillette. Joining Carlsberg as executive vice-president in 2006, Rasmussen's strong people skills and extensive international experience, including his part in the company's development in Eastern Europe, won him the CEO role in 2007. He has since shown himself to be a tenacious strategist and dealmaker. Tapping Russia's strongly developing taste for beer by taking full control of Baltic Beverages Holdings (BBH) from joint-venture partner Scottish & Newcastle (S&N) was a masterful move, despite bitter wranglings with S&N over the deal. He also bought the UK company's operations in France, Greece, China, and Vietnam. Rasmussen is steering Carlsberg toward expansion in Eastern Europe and Asia, while restructuring in mature western European markets.

Leslie Moonves President & CEO, CBS Corp.

BIOGRAPHY
Born in New York City in 1949. Moonves studied Spanish at Bucknell University, Pennsylvania, and acted on stage and screen before entering TV management.

BEST DECISION
Looking to the future with the purchase of CNET, with the objective of ensuring CBS's position as a major player in both traditional and new media distribution channels.

LESSON IN BUSINESS
Look out for new talent—time and time again, Moonves has transformed unknown talent into Hollywood's next hottest star.

ONCE VOTED "Showman of the Year" by the entertainment trade newspaper *Variety* and "Most Powerful Man in Hollywood" by *Entertainment Weekly* magazine, Moonves is one of the highest paid and most effective executives in television.

Getting Americans to watch television seems to come easily to Moonves. As president of Warner Bros Television in the 1990s, he brought the nation shows such as *Friends* and *ER*. Under his tutelage, Warner Bros supplied the greatest number of programs to network television for nine consecutive years, including a record 22 series airing on the 1995–96 network schedules. When Moonves became president of CBS Entertainment in 1995, network viewing figures were poor. As CEO of CBS Television from 1998, and then as CEO of CBS Corp. from 2003, he made it the most watched network in America, thanks to phenomenal successes such as *CSI* and *Survivor*. In 2003, Moonves received the prestigious International Radio and Television Society's Gold Medal Award. His next move was to reach new customers and increase advertising revenue by making CBS material available on the internet and cellphones, acquiring internet media company CNET in 2008.

"[Moonves is] a great leader. He's a showman. He's a competitor. He's everything you would want in a guy to lead your company." Sumner Redstone, Viacom Chairman

Sidney Toledano President & CEO, Christian Dior

BIOGRAPHY
Born in Casablanca, Morocco, in 1951. Toledano is an engineering graduate from the Ecole Centrale in Paris. He also holds a master's degree in mathematics.

BEST DECISION
Marketing the Lady Dior handbag in 1995. This brought worldwide recognition to the fashion label.

LESSON IN BUSINESS
Respect creative talent—recognizing that the rational and the artistic do not always go hand in hand, Toledano gives his designers considerable leeway.

THE MODEST MAN behind the success of fashion icon Christian Dior, Toledano has the reputation of being a great manager. Balancing the egos of creative geniuses like John Galliano with company profits is not easy, but Toledano achieved it.

After working in marketing for Nielsen International, Toledano moved to the fashion world at shoe company Kickers in 1982. He joined French handbag company Lancel in 1983, rising to the position of managing director in 1984. His success improving Lancel's sales and image attracted Dior owner Bernard Arnault, who approached him to revamp the Dior accessory line, and Toledano joined in 1994 as director of the Leather Goods Division. The fashion house was suffering a slump, and its image was tired and dowdy. Within a year, he revitalized the company with the launch of his "Lady Dior bag". Toledano was appointed president and CEO of Christian Dior Couture in 1998. He is reputed to manage Dior's designers with empathy and skill, allowing them the freedom to develop lines and products that have made Christian Dior one of the most sought-after labels in the fashion business. Under Toledano, sales rose from €127 million in 1994 to €787 million in 2007.

Robert W. Lane Chairman & CEO, Deere & Co.

BIOGRAPHY
Born in Washington, DC, in 1949. Lane earned high honours in business administration at Wheaton College, Illinois in 1972, and an MBA from the University of Chicago in 1974.

BEST DECISION
Rewarding Deere & Co. workers for good performance while reducing costs and assets.

LESSON IN BUSINESS
Invest globally—investing in other parts of the world improves the lives of people there and at home. Business can be a win-win proposition.

HIGH ON REPUTATION but low on profits, Deere & Co. was decidedly underperforming when Lane became CEO in 2000. Reducing non-productive assets and encouraging global growth, he has boosted both sales and profits.

Lane joined Deere & Co. in 1982 following a global banking career. He rose through the company's ranks and was elected chairman and CEO of the world's largest farm equipment manufacturer in 2000, in time to steer the 163-year-old business through one of its toughest years. Identifying the company's key strength as being the skills of its employees, Lane successfully brought the workforce with him in the creation of a "performance culture," and he linked annual bonuses to costs and profits.

Seeing the company's mission as being to help the world to feed itself, Lane (who was voted *Industry Week* magazine's CEO of the year in 2005) has invested in production plants and research facilities in Russia, China, India, and other countries. He has also overseen the introduction of a range of technological innovations to improve the productivity of Deere & Co.'s green and yellow forestry and agricultural equipment, and the former family company has been reaping the rewards.

"The goal I have had is to surround myself with people who are smarter than I am... [and have] the very high values that Deere stands for." Robert W. Lane

Fulvio Conti CEO, Enel SpA

BIOGRAPHY
Born in Rome, Italy, in 1947. Conti graduated in economics and commerce from La Sapienza University in Rome.

BEST DECISION
Targeting new markets in Eastern Europe and Russia. Demand for energy will grow rapidly in these regions and prices are expected to rise until they are more in line with those in western countries.

LESSON IN BUSINESS
Embrace corporate responsibility—investors are increasingly looking for ethical conduct.

WITH OVER 35 YEARS' experience in financial management, Conti was a good choice for CEO for the debt-ridden utility company Enel. He has sold off its non-energy businesses and has made a clear move towards sustainable energy.

Prior to joining Enel in 2005, Conti held the role of CFO for a number of private and government-owned bodies in Italy, including Telecom Italia and the state-owned railway system. With his focus now entirely on energy production, Conti has expanded Enel's operations into new areas, particularly Eastern Europe and Russia. He has moved the emphasis away from Enel's traditional energy businesses, namely electric power and natural gas, to other more sustainable forms of energy production, including geothermal, nuclear, and wind. Conti has been instrumental in Enel's move towards adopting an ethical code of conduct designed to ensure corporate social responsibility. According to Conti, not only is it the right thing to do, it also makes good business sense, attracting investors who care about the company's sustainability. Conti's main goal now is to reduce the company's €50-billion debt, beginning with the sell off of assets worth some €8 billion.

Carl-Henric Svanberg President & CEO, LM Ericsson

BIOGRAPHY
Born in Porjus, Sweden, in 1952. Svanberg studied at Uppsala University and Linköping Institute of Technology.

BEST DECISION
Partnering against poverty with Columbia University's Earth Institute. The initiative brings mobile communications to isolated villages in Africa, which alleviates poverty and is good for business.

LESSON IN BUSINESS
Share knowledge to boost productivity—Svanberg encourages dialogue across the company, and has been called a "productivity pioneer".

A CONSUMMATE communicator with a track record of successful acquisitions, Svanberg has brought an inclusive and motivational approach to telecoms giant Ericsson but also showed he is unafraid to make tough decisions.

Svanberg's family moved house frequently when he was a child because of his father's work for the Swedish State Power Board. The social skills Svanberg acquired at that time dovetailed well with his love of a challenge, creating a leader who, while CEO of locking-solutions manufacturer Assa Abloy Group, managed to acquire more than 100 companies, without a single hostile takeover. In his nine-year tenure there, Svanberg saw the company achieve 50 percent annual growth in profits. It is a mark of his reputation that the news of his move to troubled LM Ericsson in February 2003 saw Assa Abloy Group's share price plummet, while Ericsson's spiked. Turning the company around was a tough task, involving the decision to cut 60 percent of the workforce—Svanberg later likened his job during that period to whitewater rafting. However, Ericsson saw a return to healthy profitability, with profit margins holding up despite the global economic downturn.

"You have to share the vision... When you get [people] to march in the same direction, you can really move mountains together." Carl-Henric Svanberg

Zhang Ruimin Chairman & CEO, Haier Group

BIOGRAPHY
Born in Shangdong Province, China, in 1949. Zhang earned an MBA at China Science and Technology University in 1995.

BEST DECISION
Responding to a customer complaint at Qingdao Refrigerator Factory by lining up 76 defective units and, together with those responsible, publicly destroying them with a sledgehammer.

LESSON IN BUSINESS
There's no substitute for quality control—rebranding Haier's products with a zeal for high quality, Zhang led Haier to market dominance.

DRIVING HOME the message that time is money, Zhang turned a small, loss-making refrigerator factory run by a Communist collective into China's leading appliance firm, with global ambitions and more than $16 billion in annual turnover.

Charismatic, challenging, and communist, Zhang has been described by western analysts as the Confucian capitalist. His first job was as a construction worker in 1968, and his rise to prominence, both within the Communist Party and as an innovative businessman, symbolizes China's transformation from rigid, centrally run economy to free-wheeling, fast-growing behemoth. Zhang was the first Chinese businessman to be elected to the Communist Party's Central Committee, and to lecture at Harvard. Famous for motivating workers and organizational planning, "the scholar entrepreneur" was appointed CEO of Haier Group in 2000. Zhang achieved average annual corporate growth of 78 percent, and positioned Haier to launch into European and North American markets. Developing new products, from electric razors to flatscreen TVs, Haier became the world's fourth-largest seller of white goods, displacing American rival Whirlpool to lead the world in refrigerator sales.

David M. Cote Chairman & CEO, Honeywell International

BIOGRAPHY
Born in the US in 1952. Cote has a bachelor's degree in business administration from the Whittemore School of Business, New Hampshire.

BEST DECISION
Placing innovation at the heart of Honeywell's turnaround.

LESSON IN BUSINESS
Culture comes first—building the right corporate psyche was the first and crucial step that underlay all the other moves that returned Honeywell to strength.

TAKING THE HELM of aerospace and materials giant Honeywell, Cote found a company suffering the effects of a series of blows. By focusing on efficiency and innovation, Cote made the stalled company productive again.

The merger of AlliedSignal and Honeywell in 1999, the last-minute failure of an attempted acquisition by General Electric in 2001, an underfunded pension plan, and the slowdown in the aviation market post-9/11 all had a bruising and destabilizing effect on Honeywell. Sales were falling and the company was listless and demoralized when, in 2002, Cote was called in to try to turn things around. His 25 years at General Electric and his time as CEO of automotive products and services provider TRW gave him an in-depth experience of the complex industries in which Honeywell was involved, and Cote noted immediately that the company lacked a growth strategy. He sold units, cut costs, and applied his sharply goal-oriented management philosophy right across Honeywell's broad mix of corporate divisions. By building a new, forward-looking culture that emphasized innovation, productivity, growth, and the elimination of defects, he set the group firmly on the path to recovery.

"The greatest learning occurs when you're outside your own comfort zone." David M. Cote

LEADING THE TEAM

Behind every successful chief executive is a highly effective team, a group of individuals with complementary skills and abilities who communicate well and are working together to achieve a shared goal. Separately they would not achieve the result that the group can when functioning as a cohesive whole. In business, as in sports, great teams are not born, they are made. It is an alchemic mix. A successful team that is inspired and valued will feel a greater connection to the company and more motivated to perform well.

When **Peter Löscher** (p303) joined German electronics and electrical engineering company Siemens as CEO in 2007, he did so in the wake of a series of bribery and corruption scandals. To foster an improved team ethic and to motivate his staff, he has established a culture that gives everyone within the organization the same opportunity to progress, and he has actively encouraged staff at Siemens to take on greater responsibility.

Team leadership requires radical action and atypical approaches on occasion. **Subroto Roy** (p414), of the Indian diversified Sahara Group, acts as a paternalistic guardian to his teams of employees, which has resulted in detractors stating that he runs his company like a religious cult. Despite this, his effective sharing of his vision with Sahara's workforce has been hugely successful. His teambuilding is one of his strongest managerial skills, and his implementation of "collective materialism" in his ranks has increased staff pride and workplace satisfaction, mutual team respect, and ongoing collective growth ●

CEOs spend an average of 30 percent of their time focusing on developing corporate talent. They know that the cost of replacing a key team player can be costly and disruptive to other members of the team.

William Hawkins, CEO of US-based medical technology company Medtronic, estimates that it costs $500,000 to replace a top executive. His leadership program broadens the corporate experience of those who show future promise, allowing individual team members to achieve their full potential. By encouraging personal responsibility and initiative, teamwork improves and succession planning becomes easier.

"…we have a unique opportunity to develop future leaders internally by taking them out of their comfort zone and placing them in different functions, businesses, and geographies." WILLIAM HAWKINS

In emerging economies such as China and India the competition for experienced candidates can be intense. In China, companies will often bid for the best talent, and headhunting is on the increase in India. **Shiv Nadar** of HCL Technologies is a pioneer of modern computing. When India had only a few hundred computers in the 1970s, Nadar led a young team which believed passionately in the potential of the burgeoning IT industry. His vision resulted in the creation of a $5-billion global enterprise. His managers are an attractive target for competitors, so he has introduced financial incentives and stock options as a means to retain staff in a highly competitive and fast growing marketplace.

Building Dynamic Teams

Give employees a reason to work together toward shared goals— Companies that offer incentives and reward achievement are more likely to develop effective teams, retain their high fliers, and ensure that their customers benefit.

Map out objectives clearly and accessibly—Effective teams are well-organized, have clear goals, and are commercially focused.

Make team members feel valued— Foster respect for contribution at all levels. Everyone's role is important.

A team is only as strong as its component parts—Make sure that the team environment allows for personal development, responsibility, and challenge.

Build relationships—A strong team dynamic encourages trust and camaraderie among members.

Focus on communication—Ensure that it is open, respectful and honest.

Team Players

The function of successful teams will vary according to industry, but the key qualities remain the same:

Colin Reed, Gaylord Entertainment (Hotels and media: US)—*Wants the top echelon of management to act as "disciples" for the company's vision, to ensure an excellent service to customers and to enhance work enjoyment.*

Ivan Glasenberg, Glencore International (Industrial equipment: Switzerland)—*Values youth and intelligence as well as experience. Several of the company's directors are in their thirties.*

Richard Reed, **Adam Balon**, *and* **Jon Wright**, Innocent Drinks (Beverages: UK)—*The joint founders and unconventional creators of Innocent are united by a shared passion and ethical principles. They still meet each new member of the team personally.*

Michael Critelli, Pitney Bowes, Inc. (Logistics: US)—*Believes that focus on strong succession planning indicates a strong, forward-thinking company. He put this theory into action when he was succeeded by* **Michael D. Martin** *in 2007.*

Perween Warsi, S&A Foods (Foodstuffs: UK)—*She believes that it is as important to keep her team involved now that she employs 600 people, as it was when she employed only a few.*

James M. Wells III, Suntrust Banks (Finance: US)— *He places great emphasis on the importance of long-term team development and planning.*

Lewis B. Campbell, Textron, Inc. (Diversified: US)—*Created Textron's Transformation Leadership Team (TLT). His vision has inspired employees worldwide.*

Lars Josefsson, Vattenfall AB (Energy: Sweden)—*Uses video-conferencing and emails to communicate across cultures and markets. English is used as the primary language, but translators are provided.*

Carol Scott Founder & CEO (1979–2006), Imperial Car Rental

BIOGRAPHY
Born in 1947 in Farnham, England. South African-national Scott was educated in the UK.

BEST DECISION
Using the slogan "Yours Personally" when launching Imperial Car Rental in 1979, a philosophy the company has followed for nearly thirty years.

LESSON IN BUSINESS
Empowerment leads to development—Scott created a unique all-woman management team, breaking a male stranglehold within the industry.

QUEEN OF THE CAR RENTAL business, Scott made her name as the driving force behind the creation of Imperial Car Rental in Johannesburg, South Africa, in 1979, before taking charge of Imperial Holding's car rental and tourism business.

The highly-ambitious Scott started her business life in sales positions with Rennies Travel and Transvaal Avis. After being turned down for a managerial position with Avis, Scott approached Bill Lynch, CEO of Imperial Group, with her vision for a personalized car-rental service. In 1979, Scott launched the business with only nine cars, aiming to out-perform rivals in every area, such as by providing a 24-hour service. Scott used the lack of airport kiosks to her advantage by having staff personally meet customers at any time of day or night. After four years, Scott had established Imperial as a national presence in South Africa, rivaling competitors Avis, Hertz, and Budget. She was appointed to the board of Imperial Holdings in 1990, and became CEO of its new car rental, leasing, and tourism division in 1992. She and her all-female management team grew Imperial into the largest indigenous car rental firm in South Africa by focusing on high-quality service for business customers. She stepped down as CEO in 2006.

A.C.G. "Connie" Molusi CEO (2003–07), Johnnic Comm.

BIOGRAPHY
Born and raised in South Africa. Molusi has a bachelor's degree Rhodes University and an MA from Notre Dame University, Indiana.

BEST DECISION
Leaving the security of the public sector to carve out a career in the more challenging environment of the media industry.

LESSON IN BUSINESS
Believe in yourself—in an industry largely dominated by white executives, Molusi showed that talent and performance could win out regardless of race.

THE FIRST BLACK executive to lead a major media company in South Africa, Molusi rose above accusations that his appointment was a product of affirmative action and confounded his critics with exceptional performance.

"Connie" Molusi blazed a trail for black business leaders in South Africa. He began his career as a journalist in the late 1980s, and in 1995, he moved to the public sector, becoming adviser to the minister of communications. In 2000, he joined multimedia publishing group Johnnic Communications ("Johncom"), publisher of leading South African papers, including the *Sunday Times* and *Financial Mail*, as director of media. He became CEO of Publishing in 2001, and group CEO in 2003, the first black executive to lead a major media company in South Africa. Picking up the reins of a cost reduction and efficiency drive that soon cut the company's debt by 80 per cent, he also made major organizational changes, creating six company divisions, each with its own CEO. Despite sucessfully acquiring other newspapers and producing impressive results—profits were up eight-fold by the end of 2004—he found himself increasingly at odds with the board and was ousted in 2007.

"They're just not playing the same game."
Carol Scott on her competitors

Ingrid Matthäus-Maier CEO (1999–2008), KfW Bank Group

BIOGRAPHY
Born in Werlte, Aschendorf, Germany in 1945. Matthäus-Maier studied law in Giessen and Münster.

BEST DECISION
Capitalizing on her political experience—Matthäus-Maier's background and contacts were invaluable when she took the reins of KfW.

LESSON IN BUSINESS
Switch horses to win the race—Matthäus-Maier excelled in three male-dominated professions (law, politics, and finance), having changed environments in order to move forward.

THE FIRST WOMAN in Germany to head up a major German bank, Matthäus-Maier's career has led her from courtroom to politics before reaching the higher echelons of finance, by which time she was a notably high-profile contender.

After working briefly as a judge, Matthäus-Maier joined the German Free Democratic Party (FDP) in 1969 and became a member of the Bundestag (national parliament) in 1976. In 1982, she switched parties in protest at changes within the FDP, and joined the Social Democratic Party (SPD), winning re-election to the Bundestag. In 1999, she left politics for finance, joining the board of Kreditanstalt für Wiederaufbau (KfW), the $17-billion, state-owned bank. Founded after World War II to help rebuild Germany's economy, KfW is now Germany's seventh-largest bank. In 2007, Matthäus-Maier became CEO, making her the first woman to become chief executive of a big German bank. In this role, she has spoken out on the importance of micro-lending (small loans to the unemployed and small businesses), and the need to financially empower developing nations. She stepped down for health reasons in 2008, and following criticism of her handling of financial problems facing KfW.

Robert A. Niblock CEO, Lowe's Companies Inc.

BIOGRAPHY
Born in the US in 1963. Niblock graduated from the University of North Carolina at Charlotte with a bachelor's degree in accounting.

BEST DECISION
Giving up job security and a potential partnership with accountancy firm Ernst & Young to move to a more challenging retail environment.

LESSON IN BUSINESS
Integrity is paramount—with CEOs facing increasing scrutiny in their business practices, Niblock recognizes the importance of behaving ethically.

AN APTITUDE for numbers, and ability to relate to people have helped Niblock climb the corporate ladder to become CEO of Lowe's Companies Inc., one of the world's largest home improvement retailers.

Niblock started work for Ernst & Young in 1986, standing out immediately as a high-flier. As a senior tax manager, he worked for a wide range of companies, ranging from the very small to *Fortune 500* giants. After nine years, he accepted a job offer from retailer Lowe's, working his way steadily through the ranks, eventually moving up to CFO. By 1994, the company had embarked on an aggressive expansion plan, engineered by then CEO Robert Tillman. A decade later, Tillman retired and Niblock was seen as the ideal successor. Innovative and driven, he had earned the trust and loyalty of the senior management team, employees, and customers alike. Since his appointment, Niblock has faced challenging times as higher fuel costs and a slowdown in the housing market impacted on the business. Nevertheless, he has maintained expansion. In 2008, the first Lowe's store outside the US opened in Canada, Niblock announced plans to enter the Mexican market, and the aim of market development in China.

"In all sales environments, our goal is to prudently manage expenses and identify opportunities to drive efficiencies." Robert A. Niblock

Luiza Helena Trajano Rodrigues CEO, Magazine Luiza

IN THE YEARS that Rodrigues has been running Magazine Luiza, Brazil's third largest retail chain, she has revolutionized the retail landscape for poorer customers by introducing virtual showrooms and low-interest credit.

Aged 12, Rodrigues started a summer job at Magazina Luiza, the family-run store. In 1991, 27 years later, she was appointed CEO. Her first goal was to improve employee morale by giving power to store managers and sales teams, letting them set their own targets. She also granted low-interest credit and pioneered e-shopping in Brazil, opening "virtual showrooms" in rural areas and poorer urban neighborhoods. Equipped only with high-speed computers on which to view the chain's products, they require just 15 percent of the investment needed to set up a conventional store. With around 80 percent of sales on credit, Rodrigues has faced criticism that her policies exploit the poor. However, customers remain loyal and the default rate of clients is 50 percent lower than the average for Brazil's retailers. Opening around 50 stores in the São Paulo metropolitan area, Rodrigues has brought Magazine Luiza one step closer to displacing Ponto Frio as Brazil's second largest retailer.

Mary Kay Ash Founder & CEO (1963–2001), Mary Kay, Inc.

INSPIRING AND EMPOWERING, Ash is widely regarded as the most successful female entrepreneur in US history. By basing her company around the needs and dreams of women employees, she created a new business model.

When she was overlooked yet again for a top direct sales job in favor of a man she had trained, Ash quit the job. Over the years, she had developed her own theory of sales and marketing, and this became the business plan for Mary Kay Cosmetics, which she launched in 1963 using her $5,000 life savings. Forty-five years later, Mary Kay Inc. had expanded to include 33,000 independent sales directors, and global wholesale sales topped $2.4 billion. Ash achieved this by instigating a new corporate philosophy based not on the bottom line, but on her "Golden Rule" of "praising women to success" and putting "God first, family second, and career third." Her natural flair for public relations—she rewarded top saleswomen with pink Cadillacs—received national coverage. Ash recognized the importance of women's aspirations, and the company philosophy appealed to the sales force and customers alike. After her death in 2001, she was succeeded as CEO by her son Richard Rogers.

"I envisioned a company in which any woman could become just as successful as she wanted to be."
Mary Kay Ash

Steven Ballmer CEO, Microsoft Corp.

BIOGRAPHY
Born in the suburbs of Detroit in 1956, Ballmer graduated from Harvard University with a bachelor's degree in mathematics and economics.

BEST DECISION
Introducing the Xbox and moving Microsoft into the popular console gaming industry

LESSON IN BUSINESS
All businesses, especially software companies, are like sharks—either you keep moving forward, or you die.

WITH FANATICAL LOYALTY and a ruthless management style, Ballmer has commanded the largest software company in the world to record profits since being named Microsoft's CEO in 2000.

Ballmer has worked for Microsoft since becoming its twenty-fourth employee in 1980. A friend of Bill Gates from university, Ballmer headed up several major divisions of Microsoft, including operations, sales, and support, before taking over the reins of the company in 2000. A year later, Microsoft released its popular Xbox gaming console. In 2006, Microsoft announced its largest ever corporate dividend paying out $32 billion to shareholders. Ballmer has himself made billions as a shareholder, and his estimated net worth is $15 billion. While his years of loyalty to Microsoft no doubt paved the way to his leadership position, so did his competitive and monopolistic instincts. Known for his passionate outbursts, after losing a top engineer to Google, Ballmer is reported to have thrown a chair across a room and sworn he would "******* bury Google." This kind of intense competitiveness may just be what Microsoft needs as Google and Apple continue to grow and Microsoft finds its market share shrinking.

Junior John Ngulube CEO, Munich Re of Africa

BIOGRAPHY
Born in Zimbabwe, in 1957. Ngulube studied agriculture at the University of Zimbabwe, Harare.

BEST DECISION
Committing equally to financial performance and affirmative action, demonstrating that integration of the black community has fiscal as well as socio-political benefits.

LESSON IN BUSINESS
Be progressive and help others—Ngulube is noted for his progressive views and belief in maintaining a great empathy with his staff and peers.

FORMER AGRICULTURIST Ngulube is the first black CEO of insurance firm Munich Re of Africa, and has pursued a double strategy of improving financial performance, and boosting the economic integration of the black community.

Before settling in the insurance industry, "JJ" Ngulube grew up wanting to be a tobacco farmer and spent five years working with the Zimbabwean Ministry of Agriculture. However, the responsibilities of family life encouraged him to go into business, and he joined Munich Re as an agronomist in 1987. The firm's then head was Ernest Kahle, a liberal businessman who supported the ANC and was a champion of black economic power at a very troubled point in South Africa's political history. Since taking over as CEO, Ngulube has been successful in both his stated aims, with results for 2007 showing a 25 percent rise in premium income to R3.2 billion, despite the global slowdown. Munich Re has consistently exceeded its government-set targets for affirmative action, with some 50 percent of its middle management comprising black people, 20 percent of them female. Ngulube's firm belief is that developing the skills base of the black South African community is not only good for the company, but for the country too.

"I have never, honestly, thrown a chair in my life."
Steven Ballmer

Sibongile Mkhabela CEO, Nelson Mandela Children's Fund

BIOGRAPHY
Born in 1956. Mkhabela has a degree in social work from the University of Zululand.

BEST DECISION
Broadening the fund's focus to help make use of other organizations to reach its objectives.

LESSON IN BUSINESS
Don't give up—Mkhabela kept pushing for her goals against apparently impossible odds.

GROWING UP under apartheid gave Mkhabela a deep understanding of the problems of children in South Africa. After being imprisoned for her political activities, she made improving the welfare of the country's children her life's work.

Growing up in Soweto in the 1970s, Mkhabela was a leading figure in the students' movement that organized the 1976 protests, crushed by the apartheid government with hundreds of deaths. She was imprisoned for three years for her involvement in the protests. On her release, she formed an association providing legal services to workers, and later became programme director of the Development Resource Center. She served as consultant to the United Nations Development Programme, followed by four years spent working in the office of then-deputy president Thabo Mbeki, co-ordinating the legislative process that led to the establishment of the country's National Development Agency for eradicating povery. Appointed CEO of the Nelson Mandela Children's Fund in 2001, she has been a key figure in increasing the fund's endowment, streamlining its operations to form partnerships with other organizations, and extending its focus beyond the borders of South Africa.

Daniel Vasella Chairman & CEO, Novartis AG

BIOGRAPHY
Born in Fribourg, Switzerland, in 1953. Vasella gained a PhD from the University of Bern.

BEST DECISION
Moving from medicine to management. Vasella rapidly rose through the ranks at Sandoz, arriving at the right place and time to engineer the historic merger that created Novartis.

LESSON IN BUSINESS
Deliver value, but preserve values—Vasella pleased shareholders with Novartis's performance, but showed a softer side with social initiatives to distribute medicines in developing countries.

INITIALLY A PRACTICING doctor, Vasella moved into pharmaceuticals, where he oversaw the alliance between Sandoz and Ciba-Geigy that created Novartis, one of the world's largest and most widely respected pharmaceutical companies.

Vasella became interested in the business side of medicine when working as a doctor. In 1987 he joined Sandoz Pharma in New Jersey as a trainee, making his mark by streamlining the process by which new drugs come to market, enabling the identification of profitable new applications. He returned to Switzerland in 1993 to run Sandoz's marketing and drug-development divisions, and in 1995 he was nominated CEO. In 1996, faced with the huge competitive challenges facing all pharmaceutical companies, Vasella led one of the largest corporate mergers in history when Sandoz and Ciba-Geigy joined forces to form Novartis. Some observers doubted the alliance, but Vasella proved them wrong, using a "top down, bottom up, top down" management style that emphasized clear decision-making and getting the most out of people. Novartis had six consecutive years of growth from 1996 to 2002, and made headlines with initiatives to ensure access to medicines in developing countries.

"No tree can yield its fruits unless shaken."
Sibongile Mkhabela

Daniel R. DiMicco Chairman, President & CEO, Nucor

BIOGRAPHY
Born in the US in 1950. DiMicco has a bachelor of science degree from Brown University and a master of science in metallurgy and materials science from the University of Pennsylvania.

BEST DECISION
Embarking on a timely acquisition spree.

LESSON IN BUSINESS
Change the model—acquisition had never been part of Nucor's model before, but DiMicco showed that new approaches can pay big dividends.

ONE OF THE LARGEST US steel producers, Nucor has had a remarkable period of growth under the leadership of DiMicco. His policy of extensive acquisition broke the mold at the company, but paid off handsomely.

Nucor's use of mini-mills employing electric arc furnaces to recycle scrap steel was a revolutionary approach for the US steel industry. This established the company as a heavy hitter. Prior to DiMicco's appointment as CEO in 2000, growth was achieved by building new plants rather than acquisition. One of the reasons for this was the widespread view that the company's distinctive culture, which includes performance-based pay for line workers and a decentralized hierarchy, would be hard to take to acquired plants. DiMicco disagreed and, when steel prices dropped, he bought more than a dozen plants. As the effect of these purchases flowed through to the bottom line, concerns over a possible culture clash evaporated. In the first six years of DiMicco's tenure, Nucor's revenues rose from $4.6 billion to $14.8 billion, and profits increased from $311 million to $1.8 billion, while the share price outperformed the S&P 500 by more than 500 percent.

Brenda C. Barnes Chairman & CEO, Sara Lee

BIOGRAPHY
Born in Chicago in 1953. Barnes has a degree in economics from Augustana College, Illinois, and an MBA from Loyola University, Chicago.

BEST DECISION
Spinning off Pepsi's restaurant businesses, KFC, Taco Bell, and Pizza Hut, and contracting out bottling operations.

LESSON IN BUSINESS
Focus on your core business—Barnes did this at Pepsi, and she is now repeating the trick at Sara Lee.

A STRONG, BOLD LEADER, Barnes was CEO at Pepsi before becoming CEO at Sara Lee. She left Pepsi to spend more time with her children, but proved it was possible to return to the top position after a break.

Barnes's decision to depart from Pepsi in search of a better work-life balance caused despair within the women's movement, which felt it had lost one of its top business role models to the kitchen sink. But the truth is that Barnes never took her eye off business. She immediately took on a raft of directorships, ranging from Sears, Roebuck and Starwood Hotels and Resorts to *The New York Times*, where her success in refocusing Pepsi on what it did best—selling the taste of a new generation—had not been forgotten. Her experience at Pepsi made her a perfect choice for CEO at Sara Lee when the hot seat fell vacant in 2005. Barnes then took a controversial decision to hive off the company's apparel division, including Playtex and Wonderbra, which cut group revenues by $6 billion—a move that attracted heavy flak. However, she has invested in marketing new food products, and sales are rising across the group, with increased profits predicted.

"I set a high bar for myself and others, and I think I help people get over that bar. That's my job."
Brenda C. Barnes

Gary C. Kelly Chairman, President & CEO, Southwest Airlines

BIOGRAPHY
Born in San Antonio, Texas, in 1955. Kelly changed his mind about becoming an oceanographer to play football at the University of Texas at El Paso. He later transferred to the University of Texas in Austin where he earned a BBA in accounting.

BEST DECISION
Modernizing Southwest's accounting system enabled the company to move forward.

LESSON IN BUSINESS
Nurture your employees—Kelly is known for getting the best possible performance from his workers.

WITH A REPUTATION for honesty and integrity, Kelly fits in well as CEO of Southwest. The cut-price airline is one of the nation's most admired corporations and has coped well with the financial troubles facing the travel industry.

After university, Kelly worked for Arthur Young & Co., Southwest's accountants. In 1983, he moved to work as controller for Systems Center, a computer services company, becoming controller for Southwest in 1986. His intelligence was immediately evident, and John Denison, who hired Kelly, recalls telling Southwest co-founder, Herb Kelleher, that he'd employed his own replacement. In 1989, Kelly replaced Denison as CFO. His first task was to persuade the company to move into the computer age. Management was reluctant to invest in a costly IT system, believing it to be anathema to an airline that prided itself on cost-cutting. Kelly's reasoning that technological investment would bring in revenue must have been sound, because Southwest has celebrated consistent profitability since. Kelly became CEO and vice chairman in 2004, and chairman and president in 2008. Institutional Investor magazine has listed him among the best CEOs in the US.

Peter Sands CEO, Standard Chartered plc

BIOGRAPHY
Born in 1962. Sands grew up in Singapore and Malaysia. He gained a degree at the University of Oxford, and a masters in public administration at Harvard.

BEST DECISION
Maintaining expansion in the emerging financial markets of Asia and Africa, which gave Standard Chartered minimal exposure to the effects of the global liquidity crisis.

LESSON IN BUSINESS
Shape the world for good—Sands recognized that this is as important to big-business success as planning for the bottom line.

SOCIAL-CONSCIENCE banking is the hallmark of Sands, who rapidly made a name for himself, both for boosting growth in traditional and emerging markets, and for his role as UK government adviser during the global banking crisis.

Before joining Standard Chartered as financial director in 2002, Sands worked for the UK Foreign Office and for management consultants McKinsey & Co. Four years later he was made CEO and, working closely with his predecessor, then chairman, Mervyn Davies, Sands continued to expand the company into emerging markets, nearly trebling the workforce. Emerging markets rose to account for 95 percent of operating income, and helped the group steer clear of the US and UK banking crises, in which Sands played a key role advising the British government to recapitalize banks and restructure the financial sector. Sands is also known for deploying corporate resources in humanitarian work. Learning that ten percent of Standard Chartered's workforce in Africa was absent daily due to HIV/AIDS, he launched a major education and awareness program. The company provides cataract operations for employees in Africa, and runs a fund for treating non-employees with cataracts.

"Being a leader is about character ... being straightforward and honest, having integrity, and treating people right." Gary C. Kelly

Richard Templeton Chairman, President & CEO, Texas Instruments

BIOGRAPHY
Born in 1959. Templeton graduated from New York State's Union College with a degree in electrical engineering.

BEST DECISION
Developing the relationship with Nokia that began TI's dominance of the mobile phone chip market.

LESSON IN BUSINESS
Serve any customer—TI embraced what it dubbed a "catalogue" strategy of supplying any customer, no matter how small, in the belief that a single chip sale could be the start of a valuable business partnership.

IN HIS FIRST JOB selling computer chips, Templeton demonstrated the drive and stamina that would enable him to turn Texas Instruments around. As CEO, he has wrenched back market share from Intel, and carved out new technology markets.

Texas Instruments (TI) has been as volatile as the semiconductor industry that it pioneered, and the company has been written off in the past. TI was fortunate to recruit "Rich" Templeton, who joined immediately after graduating in 1980 and rose through the ranks, becoming president of the semiconductor division in 1996. His tenure at the head of the division was key to the company's turnaround, as a result of the close relationship he developed with mobile phone giant Nokia.

This led to the use of TI chips in nearly 60 percent of cell phones by 2004, a dominance that pushed number-one chipmaker Intel out of the mobile market. Since taking the CEO's chair in 2004, Templeton has pushed a green agenda, winning plaudits for environmental stewardship and health and safety performance. He has also invested heavily in R&D, forging links with prestigious universities in the US, India, and China to maintain the company's technological edge.

Jeffrey L. Bewkes President & CEO, Time Warner

BIOGRAPHY
Born in Paterson, New Jersey, in 1952. He received a BA from Yale and an MBA from Stanford Business School.

BEST DECISION
Leaving the phenomenally successful Home Box Office to pursue the opportunity of transforming Time Warner.

LESSON IN BUSINESS
Be prepared to take risks—Bewkes often relied on his instincts when backing projects such as *Band of Brothers* and *The Sopranos*—both of which proved to be money-spinners.

MEDIA MOGUL Bewkes has displayed critical leadership skills throughout his career. After a successful stint at US premium television channel Home Box Office (HBO), he has taken the helm of the world's largest media conglomerate.

After leaving Stanford Business School, Bewkes worked briefly for Citibank before joining HBO as a marketing manager in 1979. There he gained a reputation for getting to the heart of a business. Rising through the ranks from 1995 to 2002 to become HBO's CFO, COO, and then CEO, Bewkes tripled the original programming budget and attracted over 38 million subscribers worldwide. He moved to Time Warner in 2002, overseeing its many entertainment and networks groups. At

the beginning of 2008 he assumed the role of CEO, seven years after a disastrous merger with America Online had resulted in a loss of $125 billion in shareholder equity. Bewkes has now split off Time Warner Cable into a separate distribution company, acquired the social network Bebo, shut down New Line Cinema, and reduced corporate overheads. With a five-year employment contract offering $10.25 million in his first year, it is clear that Bewkes is expected to deliver the goods.

> "[Bewkes] projects an absence of panic and fear."
> David Chase, creator of *The Sopranos*

Frederic M. Poses Chairman & CEO (2000–08), Trane, Inc.

BIOGRAPHY
Born in 1943 in Yonkers, New York. Poses gained a bachelor's degree in business administration from New York University.

BEST DECISION
Steering through the sale of newly renamed Trane to Ingersoll-Rand in a $10.1 billion deal—a move agreed with overwhelmingly by shareholders and approved by the union.

LESSON IN BUSINESS
Guide the workforce through major change—keeping all employees fully informed can maintain motivation; good communication is key.

A TRACK RECORD of enhancing shareowner value saw Poses, former chairman and CEO of Trane, Inc., ranked second on the *Forbes* Executive Pay List in 2008, his compensation totalling over $127 million.

After more than 30 years with AlliedSignal Inc., which he joined as a financial analyst, Poses left in 1999 to take up the role of CEO of American Standard Companies, Inc., provider of kitchen and bathroom products, vehicle control systems and, through its acquisition of Trane, global heating, ventilating, and air conditioning (HVAC) systems. Poses expanded the HVAC division in Mexico and China; undertook a significant joint venture in Japan to stave off low-cost competition from China and South Korea; and developed new air-cleaning products. He also improved labor relations through information sharing. With the sale of all but the air-con division in late 2007, American Standard was renamed Trane, Inc. In 2008, when Trane's sale to Ingersoll Rand was announced, Poses's approach to labor relations bore fruit as the union adopted a positive attitude toward the sale. When Trane Inc. became a wholly owned subsidiary of Ingersoll-Rand, Poses retired.

David Morgan CEO (1999–2006), Westpac Banking Corporation

BIOGRAPHY
Born in Melbourne, Australia, in 1947. Morgan studied at La Trobe University, Australia, the London School of Economics, and Harvard.

BEST DECISION
Steering clear of sub-prime excesses to lay the foundations for Westpac's merger with St George Bank in 2008, which created Australia's largest bank.

LESSON IN BUSINESS
Don't forget culture – Morgan's successes at Westpac were achieved largely by focusing on strong corporate culture, communication, and sustainability.

WITH A BLEND of balanced risk-taking and strong focus on the "softer" side of management, Morgan positioned Westpac to become Australia's biggest bank, while rivals were brought to their knees by the global financial crisis.

Morgan worked at the International Monetary Fund in the 1970s, then the Australian Federal Treasury in the 1980s. He joined Westpac in 1990 as deputy managing director of its Financial Services Group, working his way up before becoming CEO in 1999. Morgan built a strong management team, freeing up his time as CEO to focus on culture and values, as well as execution. He devoted significant time to communicating with the bank's top 2,000 managers, aiming to speak with them in small groups at least twice a year. He also provided childcare and flexible hours to break down gender barriers. He worked to create a "no blame" culture, where experimentation was encouraged. In strategy terms, he foresaw the fate that would befall banks who overstretched themselves, and he largely succeeded in keeping "toxic" loans off Westpac's balance sheet. In late 2006, he announced that he would not seek another term as CEO. Morgan is now a director at mining giant BHP Billiton.

"In my view, the essence of great leadership has always been, and will always be, personal integrity."
David Morgan

Carol A. Bartz CEO, Yahoo! Inc.

BIOGRAPHY
Born in Winona, Minnesota, in 1948. Bartz has a BA in computer science from the University of Wisconsin.

BEST DECISION
Leaving 3M when it became clear that being a woman was a disadvantage there, which led to a highly successful move into the IT industry.

LESSON IN BUSINESS
Meet life's challenges—Bartz has never allowed discrimination or illness to get in the way of her ambition and drive.

WITH A REPUTATION as a disciplined yet inspiring leader, Bartz was picked by Yahoo to succeed Jerry Yang in early 2009. A Silicon Valley veteran, Bartz formerly ran Autodesk, the world's fourth largest PC software company.

After university Bartz went to work for 3M, but her time with the blue-chip company ended abruptly after she was told a transfer to head office was out of the question as "women don't do these jobs". The ambitious Bartz left to work in the computer industry, firstly at DEC and then Sun Microsystems, where she rose to second in command before moving to Autodesk in 1992, becoming the first female CEO of a major software firm. Two days into her new job, Bartz was diagnosed with breast cancer, for which she took just four weeks' leave for treatment. During her 14 years with Autodesk, shares rose by an annual average of nearly 20 percent, sales grew from $300 million to $1.5 billion, and Bartz featured on *Fortune* magazine's list of the 50 Most Powerful Women in Business. In January 2009 she was wooed out of early retirement by Yahoo!, who saw her as the ideal person to lead the company back to recovery following its loss of market share to Google, failed takeover by Microsoft, job cuts, and falling share price.

David C. Novak President & CEO, Yum! Brands Inc.

BIOGRAPHY
Born in 1953 in the US. Novak graduated from the University of Missouri in 1974.

BEST DECISION
Pioneering "multi-branding", with KFC, Pizza Hut, and Taco Bell sharing a food court. Novak launched 2,000 joint stores, notching up $2 billion in sales.

LESSON IN BUSINESS
Build a team mentality—Novak united staff in three distinct restaurant chains and made them feel valued. This boosted customer service.

HYPERCOMPETITIVE and driven, Novak built Yum! Brands from a Pepsi spin-off into the world's largest restaurant company. Pizza Hut, KFC, Taco Bell, Long John Silver, and All American Food generate annual sales of over $10 billion.

Novak's challenge as CEO was to bring together three distinct restaurant chain managements and transform them into one team. He identified "division leaders" and made them responsible for a new co-operative style of management He initiated a new employee recognition scheme that injected a sense of fun and achievement among staff, which resulted in improved customer service that Novak dubbed "Customer Mania". Results followed quickly—in the first five years, sales increased by eight percent. In 2002, following the acquisition of the Long John Silver and All American Food brands, Novak rolled out "multibranded" food courts throughout the US and overseas, bringing all their restaurant chains together under one roof. This, combined with successful franchising, helped the group to overtake McDonald's as the world's biggest restaurant chain. In 2008, Yum! continued its rapid expansion into China, where it opened 450 new restaurants, taking the total toward 3,500.

"[Novak] is one of the most competitive leaders that I have ever sat across the table from..."
John Neal, president, JRN Inc.

THE DIVERSITY DIVIDEND

CEOs embracing a culture of diversity and inclusion are thriving thanks to a whole host of business-building benefits. From reducing recruitment costs, winning more business, and inspiring innovation to improving employee satisfaction and productivity, retaining talent, and gaining the edge over competitors, there are plenty of reasons to put diversity at the top of the CEO "to do" list.

Diversity can best be achieved by employing a diverse workforce and by aiming to choose more suppliers from a pool of businesses led by women and people from minority groups. Hotel and catering firm Marriott has a proud diversity record and even provides financial assistance to the minority suppliers with which it works. The diversity ethos at the company began under founder **J. Willard Marriott, Sr.** (p364) and still thrives under the leadership of his son **J. W. Marriott, Jr.**, who audits the company's supplier-diversity numbers regularly himself. While **Angela Braly** (p114), CEO of WellPoint, the largest health benefits company in the US, sees diversity management as "more than just a strategy; it's a fundamental part of how we do business." ●

Pioneers in People

Ivan G. Seidenberg (p247), CEO of US broadband communications company Verizon, was recently chosen from a list of *Fortune* 100 CEOs to receive an inaugural award for "exemplary leadership in achieving multiracial diversity at Board level." With 59 percent of the workforce being female, and ethnic minorities comprising 35 percent of the global company team (double the national average for businesses in the US), this accolade is hardly surprising. Many hold top management positions for which they are mentored and trained and, as valued employees, performance is propelled and value for the company improved: a win-win situation for both the workforce and the company's more profit-focused share and stakeholders.

A. D. David Mackay, president and CEO of Kellogg Company since 2006, also sees diversity as a key ingredient in the company's successes: "It enables us to attract and retain the most talented employees." he says. The company's commitment began with founder **W. K. Kellogg** in 1906, who was a pioneer in bringing women into the workplace and reaching across cultural boundaries. More than a century later and its current CEO is pushing diversity initiatives by sponsoring an 18-strong Executive Diversity and Inclusion Council to ensure that their diversity strategy is implemented. In addition to employee diversity, Kellogg started its supplier-diversity program more than 20 years ago, in the belief that "partnering with diverse suppliers opens up a pipeline of ideas, solutions and better ways of doing things".

"The most powerful solutions come from the widest range of thoughts and ideas."
IVAN G. SEIDENBERG

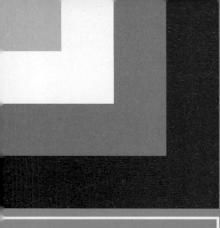

Striving for Diversity

Be accountable—Make executives accountable for promoting diversity, and reward them with performance incentives.

Develop future leaders—Offer mentoring, training, and leadership development opportunities.

Aim to reflect market diversity—"People buy from people", so hire workers who speak the language of your multicultural market.

Encourage employee-affinity—Set up groups for different minorities to enable staff to learn, network, and feel motivated and valued.

Seek out minority suppliers—Spend more procurement on MWBEs (Minority and Women-Owned Business Enterprises).

Shout about it—Audit supplier and workplace diversity numbers, then use these figures to promote your commitment to diversity.

Inclusive Employers

These CEOs are widening the talent pool in their companies with a focus on diversity:

Paul Hermelin, CAPGEMINI (Consultancy: France)—*In support of International Women's Day 2007, Hermelin personally held 300 conference calls with women executives and diversity champions to examine diversity improvements.*

—

Justin King, J SAINSBURY (Retail: UK)—*King has made "Respect for the Individual" one of Sainsbury's core values, promoting diversity through initiatives such as Age Positive and Positive About Disabled People.*

—

Terry J. Lundgren, MACY'S (Retail: US)—*Forty-nine percent of Macy's workforce is Black, Asian, Latino, or Native American. Macy's is number six on Diversity Inc's Top 10 Companies for African-Americans.*

—

Karl-Ludwig Kley, MERCK KGAA (Pharmaceuticals: Germany)—*Has one of the most diverse executive teams in the pharmaceutical industry.*

—

John R. Strangfeld, Jr., PRUDENTIAL FINANCIAL (Insurance: US)—*Strangfeld chairs the diversity council and appoints its members. He also signs off on executive compensation tied to diversity.*

—

Gregory T. Swienton, RYDER SYSTEM (Logistics: US)—*Fortune magazine recognized Ryder for two consecutive years as one of the "50 BestCompanies for Asians, Blacks, and Hispanics".*

—

Gérard Le Fur, SANOFI-AVENTIS (Pharmaceuticals: France)—*CEO of Europe's largest drugs company says, "Diversity gives us the chance to solve health problems." One of South Africa's top gender-empowered organizations.*

—

Ronald L. Sargent, STAPLES (Retail: US)—*In 2005 created a new director level position to manage and grow their Diversity Supplier Program.*

—

Frits van Paasschen, STARWOOD HOTELS & RESORTS (Hotels: US)—*strong mentoring program plus maternity leave and work-site support programs for pregnant women and returning moms, sign-language courses, and floating religious holidays.*

—

G. Kennedy Thompson, WACHOVIA (Finance: US)—*Personally signs off executive bonuses for meeting diversity objectives as well as chairing the diversity council.*

—

John Stumpf, WELLS FARGO (Finance: US)—*Sixty percent of its workforce and 54 percent of managers promoted were women. The company excels in the retention and promotion of its female employees.*

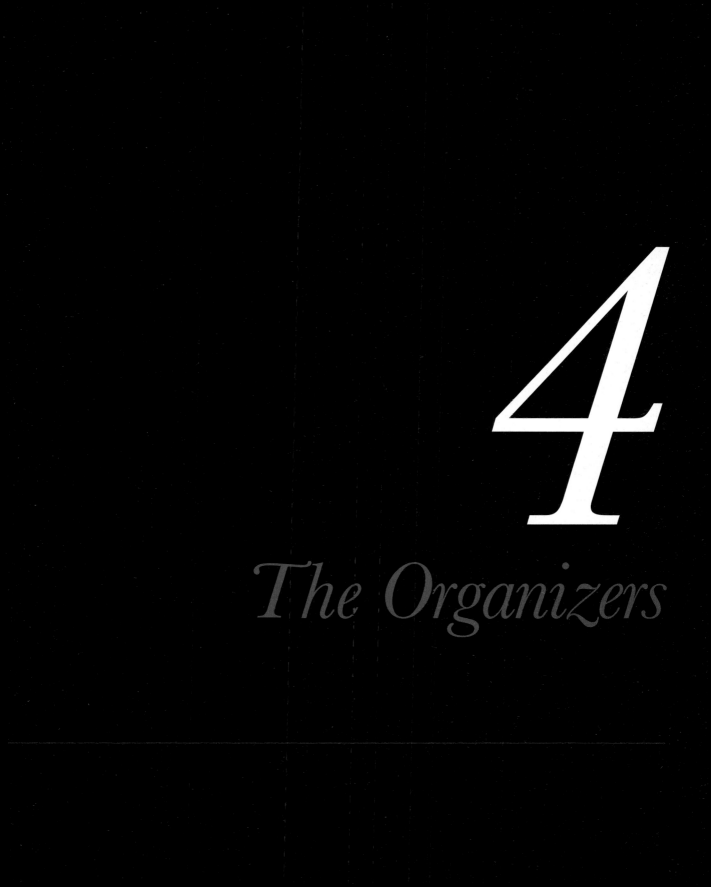

4

The Organizers

Lynn Blodgett President & CEO, Affiliated Computer Services, Inc.

THE SUCCESS of Dallas-based Affiliated Computer Services, Inc. (ACS), a *Fortune* 500 company, is due in large part to Blodgett. He knows the organization inside out, after spending more than a decade as part of the team that built it into one of America's top three business-process outsourcing and IT services companies. Regarded as a sales supremo in the industry, he has also earned world renown for his hobby: he travels the country photographing the homeless to heighten public awareness of their situation.

BIOGRAPHY
Born in Utah in 1955. One of nine children, Blodgett was brought up as a Mormon, and attended the Utah Technical College and Brigham Young University, Utah. He is a world-class photographer, and his first book, *Finding Grace: The Face of America's Homeless*, was published in 2007. He is also a master falconer.

LEADERSHIP STYLE
Persistent, motivational, and responsive, Blodgett encourages good ideas and is always open to suggestions from employees recognizing their contribution through a reward scheme.

KEY STRENGTH
Being in the right place at the right time, enabling him to exploit opportunities for growth.

BEST DECISION
Selling his own company, and thereby becoming part of a global organization.

RISING THROUGH THE RANKS Along with his many siblings, Blodgett learned about the computer business at an early age, watching his parents working from home to build a business from scratch. Inheriting their "work is healthy" attitude, he went on to co-found Unibase Technologies, a data entry company, with two of his brothers in 1985. Jim provided the motivation, while Bill concentrated on the programming side. It was left to Lynn, with his trust-inspiring personality and conversational skills, to bring in the business—a task that he vowed to continue after Jim's death.

RAISING MORALE When ACS bought Unibase in 1996, Blodgett's expertise was seen as critical to its continued success, and he remained with the company, gaining good experience as group president of commercial solutions before becoming COO and finally CEO in 2006. Blodgett's tenure as CEO of ACS has not been without its problems. A second failed attempt to take the company private, boardroom upheavals, and the dismissal of the previous CEO and CFO following an internal investigation into the backdating of stock options all shook the company's public image. With lawsuits still pending, Blodgett had to put these issues to one side and concentrate on driving the company forward. One of his first aims as CEO was to improve morale among employees, which he achieved by traveling the country, running Q&A sessions among the workers. His straight-forward approach has been crucial. Blodgett is committed to continued growth and has set the company ambitious annual targets for doing just that.

LESSONS IN BUSINESS: HANDING OVER RESPONSIBILITY

By motivating his workforce and giving them "ownership" of what they are doing, Blodgett has created an entrepreneurial business environment, which in turn attracts other innovators.
→ Give your employees authority to make decisions, and hold them accountable.
→ Put accountable employees in direct touch with clients to allow quicker decisions and make the company more responsive.
→ Tell everyone you give any new idea careful attention, and the initiator the authority to implement it.

"I really do understand the computer business at the grass roots. And I understand working people."
Lynn Blodgett

Henri de Castries CEO, AXA Group

AFTER THE GROUP pushed through a string of acquisitions and mergers in France and abroad, de Castries cemented AXA's position as a global financial services giant. A one-time civil servant at France's Ministry of Finance, he was still in his thirties when he was tempted into the private sector by the then-head of AXA, Claude Bébéar. He was instrumental in the acquisition of French insurance giant UAP in 1997 and then Guardian Royal Exchange and Dantai Life. As CEO since 2001, he has led a period of international consolidation.

BIOGRAPHY
Born in Bayonne, France, in 1954. De Castries was top of his year at the elite Ecole Nationale d'Administration, from which most graduates go on to illustrious government careers.

LEADERSHIP STYLE
Open, consensual, and outspoken, he is respected by colleagues who admire him for his problem-solving abilities

KEY STRENGTH
Unusually, de Castries combines an outstanding legalistic brain with innate entrepreneurial flair.

BEST DECISION
Pursuing a strategy of global acquisitions, which brought numerous financial services giants around the world under the AXA umbrella.

GOING PRIVATE De Castries was clearly on track for a starry career in government. Perhaps it was his role in the privatization of many French companies that gave him a taste for the private sector. Certainly, when AXA chief Claude Bébéar came calling, de Castries jumped at the chance. He spent two years in the field learning the business and then joined AXA's corporate finance division. In 1997, he became chairman of AXA Financial and took on an increasingly global role.

BOOSTING FROM WITHIN When he took over as CEO in 2001, the insurance industry was hitting a rocky patch. Deregulation had led to what de Castries has called "an entire industrial revolution in financial services". The increased competition coincided with a flood of online activity. In this climate of intense competition, and to continue with his ambitious acquisitions plans, de Castries knew what had to be done: he needed to boost revenues by growing AXA internally and target companies around the world that could be brought into the AXA fold. The sales force was crucial at this time, selling high-margin mutual funds to existing clients, and the company's success in a difficult period was admired.

Pursuing a strategy of bringing "life confidence" to a global customer base, de Castries established AXA's presence in Asia, as well as opening an office in China and setting up joint ventures in India and Korea. He also strengthened the company's position in the Mediterranean. In the US, AXA acquired MONY (Mutual of New York) and brought other subsidiaries under its umbrella. UK partners include Sun Life and PPP.

LESSONS IN BUSINESS: LOOKING TO YOUR STRENGTHS

When times were tough de Castries looked to his core strengths and improved efficiency and profits there. He focused on his most profitable products and markets before adopting an international acquisition strategy.
→ Look to your domestic marketing and sales skills to improve margins and create a base for expansion.
→ Use a profitable domestic base as a springboard to gain shareholder agreement for foreign acquisitions.
→ To build a giant company fast, buy large, well established companies and use your culture to improve their performance.

"I haven't been bored one nanosecond." Henri de Castries

Helene D. Gayle President & CEO, CARE

A RARE MIX of scientific rigor, motivational skills, and organizational and financial expertise has made Dr. Gayle one of the leading figures in the fight against HIV/AIDS, STDs, tuberculosis, and other diseases. Now CEO of CARE (Cooperative for Assistance and Relief Everywhere), which seeks to end poverty by addressing its underlying causes. Her comprehensive grasp of disease, combined with her immense personal energy and drive, has turned her into a central strategist in the quest for solutions to key global health and global poverty.

BIOGRAPHY
Born in Buffalo, New York, in 1955. She studied psychology at Barnard University and medicine at the University of Pennsylvania, where she was one of only eight black women in her class of 160.

LEADERSHIP STYLE
Inspirational, committed, and motivating. Gayle's ability to study detail and to retain a huge amount of information is the key to her effectiveness.

KEY STRENGTH
The ability to communicate at all levels, whether dealing with Government agencies, drug companies, or those directly affected by poverty.

BEST DECISION
Initiating the Gates Foundation's Avahan HIV prevention program in India. Within three years, the project was in regular contact with an estimated 70 percent of high-risk individuals, improving transmission education and health service access.

AIDS EXPLOSION After earning degrees in psychology and medicine, Gayle heard a speech on efforts to eradicate smallpox and decided to devote her abilities to public health. While at the Centers for Disease Control and Prevention in Atlanta she saw the AIDS explosion of the 1980s. Her contributions to the study, control, and prevention of AIDS gained her such renown that she was given charge of a $1.5-billion health portfolio at the Gates Foundation, focusing on HIV, TB, and reproductive health. Her performance there led to the top job at CARE, the international anti-poverty organization, in 2006.

CUTTING THROUGH THE FOG Gayle's personality and her commitment to the objectives of her organizations have enabled her to vault from public-health administrator to inspirational force. Under her leadership, the Gates Foundation expanded its support for HIV and TB prevention, treatment, and research programs and developed a strategy to improve global access to reproductive health. She set in motion "Avahan," a $200-million HIV prevention program in India, which was thought to be on the verge of an epidemic among sex workers and their clients.

CARE's goal is the eradication of poverty, but improving health and education are seen as the key to this. Gayle's strategy toward diseases such as HIV/AIDS has been to look not just at the medical issues but also at the economic, cultural, and social factors that affect them. By fostering coordinated action among various global agencies and addressing the many political obstacles to progress, she has ensured that CARE is a real force for change.

LESSONS IN BUSINESS: KNOWING YOUR STUFF

Gayle's strategy was to become the world expert in her field. Where government bureaucracy would have set up committees, carried out surveys, and written reports, Gayle had the information at her fingertips.
→ Get to know your field as thoroughly as possible, taking in as much data as you can from every possible source, and keep your knowledge up-to-date.
→ Take steps to improve your reading speed. Learn to skim text but still retain and digest the key facts.
→ Gain insights from everyone. A junior member of staff may make the most important observation.

"Politics often get in the way of people's best judgement." Helene D. Gayle

Reto Francioni Chairman & CEO, Deutsche Börse AG

WITH A DISTINGUISHED RECORD in the German stock exchange, Francioni became CEO of Deutsche Börse AG, which runs the Frankfurt stock exchange, in 2005, after Werner Seifert was ousted due to his plan to bid for the London stock exchange (LSE). Francioni mollified critics by returning shareholder cash, cutting costs, and selling assets. A respected academic, he teaches at the University of Basel and at the Zicklin School of Business, New York, and has co-authored two books: *Equity Markets in Action* and *The Equity Trader Course.*

FINANCIAL TRAINING After completing his PhD in 1981, Francioni began his career in banking and financial services, joining the commerce division at UBS. In 1985, he moved on to Credit Suisse, and three years later to Association Tripartite Bourses, where he became deputy CEO in 1991. He joined Deutsche Börse AG as an executive board member in 1993, rising to deputy CEO in 2000. He then moved to Consors AG as co-CEO, before becoming chairman of the supervisory board and president of the exchange association at SWX Group in 2002.

ACTIVIST HEDGE FUND PRESSURES
Francioni was nominated CEO of Deutsche Börse in 2005, partly due to the respect he had won from activist hedge funds Atticus Capital and The Children's Investment Fund (TCI), which owned 19 percent of the Frankfurt exchange and had led a campaign against Seifert. Since 2005, as head of Deutsche Börse, Francioni has overseen not only the Frankfurt stock exchange but also derivatives platform Eurex, and the clearing house Clearstream. In 2007, he was elected chairman of the supervisory boards of Deutsche Börse Systems AG, and Deutsche Börse Dienstleistungs AG, and oversaw a 95 percent rise in the share price. The following year, Francioni gave a positive spin to the turbulence in the financial markets, targeting the growth opportunities that they presented Deutsche Börse. He followed a strategy of pursuing organic growth through carefully judged takeovers, although activist hedge funds opposed his plans, threatening to push for new management to boost shareholder value at the company.

LESSONS IN BUSINESS: PLEASING THE SHAREHOLDERS

Francioni's rise to the top reflected his recognition of the need to keep shareholders happy. Shareholder returns topped more than €700 million, with a consequent rise in share price of more than 90 percent.
- ➔ Commit to a level of dividends and share buybacks whatever the share price, and keep to your promise.
- ➔ Prioritize increasing net profits that improve earnings per share—one of the main measures of performance for shareholders.
- ➔ Aim to increase the annual average return on shareholder equity—the second big shareholder measure.

"Our strategy prioritizes growth over consolidation… we aim for organic growth, complemented by partnerships and selective acquisitions." Reto Francioni

Fred Smith Founder, Chairman, President & CEO, FedEx

AT YALE, Smith wrote a paper for his economics class outlining a radical idea for a company that would guarantee overnight delivery of small, time-sensitive goods, such as banking documents, replacement parts, and medical supplies, to major US cities. His professor was underwhelmed and gave it a "C." That paper was the blueprint for a distribution revolution that we now know as FedEx. The company now operates in over 220 countries, serving over 350 airports worldwide, and delivers over 7.5 million packages every day.

BIOGRAPHY
Born in Marks, Mississippi, in 1944. Smith was educated at Memphis University School and Yale University, where he studied economics before completing two tours in Vietnam.

LEADERSHIP STYLE
Visionary, risk-taking, and tenacious. Smith is considered a hands-on manager who likes to be involved in every aspect of FedEx's strategy.

KEY STRENGTH
He has an instinctive ability to understand and foresee the changing needs of business, and was an early enthusiast for the global economy.

BEST DECISION
Creating an integrated air-ground delivery system, something that had never been done before.

THE "AVERAGE" GENIUS After time in Vietnam, Smith founded Federal Express in 1971, funded by $4 million of his own money—inherited from his industrialist father—and $91 million in venture capital. At first, the economics professor's doubts seemed well-founded; on its first night of business, the company shipped only 186 packages on its 14 Falcon jets, and in its first two years FedEx lost $29 million and faced bankruptcy.

DELIVERING THE FUTURE In the face of odds that would have daunted many, Smith pressed on, firm in his belief that the business world would come round to his way of thinking. It paid off, and by 1976 the company had begun to show a profit, moving everything from Maine lobsters to tractor parts. The idea of a 24-hour delivery service began to seem not only viable but essential, eventually turning FedEx into the world leader in express delivery. His success has come in part from his ability to understand changing business practices, and to appreciate the importance of the internet and internet sales. Smith has always striven for continuous improvement, and has willingly embraced new technology.

Smith runs his company on a simple principle that he calls P-S-P—people, service, profit—with each supporting the others. Smith believes passionately in looking after his employees, providing generous pay and benefits, and his staff respond with extraordinary loyalty. When workers at main competitor UPS went on strike in the 1990s, thousands of FedEx employees worked round the clock to send out the hundreds of thousands of extra parcels that threatened to swamp FedEx.

LESSONS IN BUSINESS: GIVE IT TIME

Risk-taking can take a while to pay off. Be prepared for some lean times, but if you have confidence in your radical business strategy and your original idea has not been superseded, give it time to succeed.
→ Set the strategy that you know will succeed and sit tight and wait for the world to catch up.
→ Watch for how business methods are changing and plan how to take advantage of the next "big idea".
→ Beware of academics: because of their hands-off approach to business, from time to time they can be 180 degrees wrong.

"Being an effective leader is hard and requires you to subordinate your self-interest for the organization." Fred Smith

Alfred P. Sloan CEO (1923–46), General Motors Company

NO STUDY OF ICONIC business leaders would be complete without the name of Alfred Sloan. More than any other single person, Sloan is responsible for the concept and structure of the modern American corporation. In the words of Dr. Edgar Schein at the MIT Sloan School of Management, "His ideas were so clearly correct that we have forgotten that they were an invention." During his three decades of leadership, Sloan transformed General Motors into one of the largest and most profitable corporations the world has ever seen.

BIOGRAPHY
1875–1966. Born in New Haven, Connecticut. Sloan excelled as a student and was the youngest member of his class to graduate from the Massachusetts Institute of Technology (MIT) with a degree in electrical engineering.

LEADERSHIP STYLE
Analytical, innovative, and perceptive. Sloan brought a new concept to management.

KEY STRENGTH
Sloan was the first person to understand that the structure of a company played a vital role in its success.

BEST DECISION
Establishing a pricing hierarchy of different car makes to ensure customer loyalty over time.

A STRONG START After graduating from MIT, Sloan joined the Hyatt Roller Bearing Company of Newark, New Jersey, as a draftsman. His vision and drive ensured that he was made president within a few years, but the company was struggling. Convinced that he could make the company a success, Sloan persuaded his father to buy the firm. He directed production toward the blossoming car industry, a wise decision that eventually led to the company being bought by General Motors, where Sloan took on the role of vice-president in charge of accessories. Determined to challenge Ford's dominant position in car production, Sloan set about revamping GM.

DIVIDE AND PROSPER He decentralized operations by breaking the company into smaller divisions, making each one responsible for its own decision-making, while at the same time retaining a degree of coordinated policy. This allowed for more creativity and less competition within the company and was an entirely new concept at the time.

Sloan also knew how to nurture customer loyalty. By establishing a hierarchy of car makes, from the inexpensive Chevrolet to the costly Cadillac, Sloan ensured that customers would keep coming back to GM as their prosperity increased. As Sloan put it, "a car for every purse and purpose." Sloan's professional approach to management soon brought rich rewards, both for himself and for GM. In 1923, when Sloan became president of GM, Ford had over half of the US car market share and GM less than one-fifth. Within eight years, GM had taken over as the world's leading car manufacturer, a position that it held until 2007.

LESSONS IN BUSINESS: STRUCTURING FOR SUCCESS

Large, fast-growing companies tend to outlive the usefulness of their original structure. Eventually senior managers simply do not have the capacity to micro-manage the organization "hands-on." Sloan recognized this and decentralized to empower people and make them take responsibility for their performance.
➔ Structure your business as a network of small divisions, so that entrepreneurial thinking starts at the top.
➔ Push down profit centers so that managers become aware of their role in making money.
➔ Hand down measurable objectives to reveal any management problems that you can then fix.

"The business of business is business." Alfred P. Sloan

James Wood President & CEO, J. Paul Getty Trust

THE ANNOUNCEMENT that Wood was to take over at the helm of the J. Paul Getty Trust in 2006 was almost universally welcomed. The Trust, an international cultural and philanthropic organization, had been through a period of scandalous turbulence and Wood was widely seen as the man with the experience needed to turn the situation around. Wood has not disappointed, re-establishing both the Trust's reputation and its position in the art world as the third largest foundation in the US, after Gates and Ford.

BIOGRAPHY
Born in 1941. Wood has degrees in Art History from Williams College, Massachusetts and the Institute of Fine Arts in New York. He has also studied in Perugia, Italy.

LEADERSHIP STYLE
Described by colleagues as conciliatory and wise but intensely private, Wood combines a passion for the arts with a capacity for calm leadership.

KEY STRENGTH
Being a stabilizing force in the organizations he has worked for. He is viewed as a man of great integrity, with the respect of colleagues and employees.

BEST DECISION
Focusing on the Trust's core mission of presenting the visual arts while addressing its hefty operating deficit.

EXCELLENCE IN THE ARTS Wood began his career with a series of academic and museum positions, including a post at the Metropolitan Museum of Art, New York. He took over as director of the St Louis Art Museum in 1975, moving on to serve as president and director of the Art Institute of Chicago from 1980 to 2003. In his years at the Art Institute he set standards of excellence that are internationally respected. He oversaw an expansion of the museum's collection, renovations of all the departments, the construction of a new wing, and the initial planning for a second addition.

BACK AT THE HELM When Wood retired from the Art Institute, his reputation for integrity was what the Getty Trust desperately needed and was a key reason for his appointment in 2006. With an endowment of over $4 billion, the Getty Trust is one of the richest arts organizations in the world. Wood is the first person with an arts and museum administration background to serve as president since it was formed in 1982. He replaced Barry Munitz, who resigned amid growing criticism of his leadership and questions about his use of the Trust's money. The Los Angeles-based museum was also in the midst of a scandal over ancient artworks in its collections claimed to have been looted and smuggled from Italian ruins, the gradual return of which Wood has been overseeing.

Aside from repairing the Trust's shattered image through the protracted scandal, Wood has also been steadying the organization in the midst of the global downturn, by streamlining operations and cost-cutting in an attempt to yield a budget increase of 25 percent in core arts programs. Prudence, Wood says, is key.

LESSONS IN BUSINESS: LOVING WHAT YOU DO

When it comes to business, there's no substitute for passion, knowledge, and understanding. Wood's interest covers the entire history of art and this earns him the respect of everyone he works with.
- → Never sacrifice the "functional" side of your business—satisfying customers—to the lure of growth.
- → Remember to consider your customers' particular tastes, as well as their specific practical needs.
- → Approach the business of your company with passion as well as objectivity. Passion motivates people; objectivity avoids mistakes.

"No matter how great your means, focus is absolutely essential." James Wood

Andrew Witty CEO, GlaxoSmithKline

A RADICAL OVERHAUL was needed when Witty became CEO of the world's second-largest pharmaceutical company in 2008. The traditional drug industry model, in which companies made their profits from occasional, huge-selling "blockbuster" products, was falling out of favor. The dwindling number of such blockbusters, demanding regulators, and concern among investors all combined to create a need for a new approach to the industry. Witty took the opportunity to create one.

BIOGRAPHY
Born in Yorkshire, UK, in 1964. Witty earned a bachelor's in economics from the University of Nottingham. From 2000 to 2002, he served as an economic adviser to the governor of China's Guangzhou Province.

LEADERSHIP STYLE
Amiable and open, Witty moved his office next to the staff canteen to make himself more accessible.

KEY STRENGTH
Visualizing how his organization could reshape its activities to meet new conditions.

BEST DECISION
Taking the bold step of meeting his customers to find out what they were prepared to pay for.

SUCCESS IN EUROPE The youngest of the three candidates, Witty was widely regarded as the least likely to succeed Jean-Pierre Garnier as GSK's CEO. However, his dynamism and talent had become apparent when he ran the company's Asian business, and again when he worked in the US. In 2003, he took over the company's European operation, where he combatted a fall in drug prices by increasing sales volumes. His success made him well-placed to take on the big challenges of weakening profits, increased regulation, and the need for restructuring.

BEYOND THE BLOCKBUSTER Witty believed that the obsession with blockbusters left the industry deeply vulnerable to unpleasant surprises, such as lawsuits from generic drugs firms or regulatory crackdowns. He aimed to restructure GSK's research operations to seek more potential drugs, of all sizes, giving the company a more reliable product pipeline. He also wanted to diversify the business beyond prescription sales in the developed world (previously the bulk of its revenue stream) to remove some of the vulnerability inherent in the traditional model. In the past, the company had launched drugs that their largest customers had not always found to be exactly as required. To try to address this problem, Witty met directly with customers such as the UK's National Health Service and America's pharmacy benefit managers, to find out what products they would be willing to pay for. Previously they had refused to pay full price for drugs that they considered provided poor value. It indicated the lengths to which Witty was prepared to go to reshape the drug landscape.

LESSONS IN BUSINESS: RESHAPING THE MODEL

The business model that your industry has always used may seem like common sense to everyone involved. But that doesn't mean it's the right one for the changes ahead
- → Look at your method of meeting customer needs. Search for signs that either product offerings or market requirements are changing.
- → Find a new model to fit the new world even if it means upheaval. Do not let your organization ossify.
- → Instead of examining what products your customers need, look at what they are trying to achieve.

"People who run companies should be visible and accountable." Andrew Witty

THE ANATOMY OF COMPANIES

As well as tactical business genius and the strategic vision of a Bonaparte, a top CEO often relies on a successful corporate framework. General Electric CEO **Jack Welch** (p311) famously stripped out layers of bureaucracy in the 1980s to create a "boundaryless management" structure that powered GE to success, boosting revenues from $26.8 billion to $130 billion during his tenure.

Structure, then, is often seen as the backbone of business, though some could be said to take this analogy too far. Virgin Blue has been likened to a human body, with head **Brett Godfrey** (p110) presiding over an operational leg, a commercial leg, and four arms of IT, HR, corporate affairs, and customer service; though with six limbs perhaps more god than human. More fancifully still, Australian bank Macquarie has been compared to a star, spitting out material that becomes its satellite businesses, with CEO **Nicholas Moore** (p32) acting as the fusion generator at the heart of the process ●

Structure is Destiny

Flat has become popular in the web-enabled world, as devolved, autonomous business units nimbly pursue profits. **Shiro Hiruta** revamped chemicals company Asahi Kasei in the early 2000s to speed up decision-making and improve cashflow. In place of its cumbersome business-unit structure, whose decisions had to be signed off by a 30-strong board, he created a group of independent companies. Oversight is by a slimmed-down board of seven, whose only responsibility is to have a good strategic overview of the company.

For some industries, consolidation is the name of the game. **Larry Weyers**, CEO of energy firm WPS Resources Corp., has been expanding over the US Midwest by acquisitions of, for example,

Understanding the Company Structure

Hierarchy — The traditional top-down chain of command enables consistency of culture and process but can lead to rigidity and market timidity.

Flat — A decentralized structure with few layers of management fosters creativity, the sharing of expertise, and autonomy, but can be difficult to control and puts a brake on decision-making.

Project-based — Management teams tasked with carrying out specific projects allows for a focused execution of strategy. It can be difficult to keep a rein on costs, however, and there is a danger of creating conflicts of interest with the wider organization.

Product-based — This structure is commonly used by innovation-based start-ups where the product is the company, and entails each department taking responsibility for all activity to do with one product. As the company grows, however, it can prompt infighting.

Process-based — In this set-up, resources are directed at perfecting the way in which a business task is carried out, adding value through customer-focus. Business functions can be undermined and standardization becomes a problem.

Function-based — A structure based on organizing employees by job type defines clear career paths and responsibilities but tends to be bureaucratic and create fiefdoms.

Matrix — A matrix design organizes staff by both product and function, combining the best of both for flexibility. The downside is that it can become difficult to manage when power-sharing between interests creates friction.

Network — This is where certain business functions are contracted out to lower costs and boost flexibility, but the increased reputational risk demands close monitoring and oversight of outsourcers.

Peoples Energy Corp. in 2007, to achieve his goal of greater scale and diversity, while cutting costs by $80 million.

In contrast, Mitsubishi Electric, under CEO **Setsuhiro Shimomura**, has made a habit of hiving off parts of its business to lighten the burden of underperforming areas. It spun off the chip-making business into a joint-venture with Hitachi in 2002, then did a similar deal with Toshiba for its automation systems.

Restructuring can go wrong, as **Carly Fiorina** found when she imposed unpopular top-down command at famously decentralized Hewlett-Packard in 1999. Her bid to turn HP into a monolith failed, and the board ousted her in 2005. A miraculous turnaround by replacement CEO **Mark Hurd** (p314), demonstrates how easily a corporate body can revive under emergency surgery.

> "Every company has two organizational structures: the formal one is written on the charts; the other is the everyday relationship of the men and women in the organization."
> HAROLD S. GENEEN, CEO (1959–72), ITT CORP.

Corporate Shapers

Many CEOs like to remake the corporation in their own image:

David Yost, AMERISOURCEBERGEN *(Pharmaceuticals: US)—Merged responsibility for a number of operational areas, including finance, supply chain management, and drug distribution, in a bid to streamline its management structure.*
—

Chang Xiaobing, CHINA UNICOM *(Telecommunications: China)—Used its merger with China Netcom to better embrace the convergence of wireless with fixed-line services.*
—

Parker Kennedy, FIRST AMERICAN CORP. *(Business information: US)— Hived off operations into subsidiary First Advantage to manage multiple brands.*
—

Paul Harris, FIRST RAND *(Finance: South Africa)—Operates distributed profit centers that are able to sniff out and exploit niche opportunities.*
—

Constantinos Gratzios, KED *(Real estate: Greece)—Pioneered public-private partnerships to manage the Greek government's property portfolio.*
—

Lawrence Montgomery, KOHL's *(Retail: US)—Sold its private-label credit card operation to JPMorgan, arguing that a strategic alliance would add marketing and operational clout.*
—

Kwon Young-soo, LG DISPLAY *(Electronics: South Korea)—A 2008 joint-venture with audio-visual manufacturer AmTRAN (CEO, **Alpha Wu**) aimed to expand its customer base and cut the cost of R&D and logistics.*
—

Edmund Kelly, LIBERTY MUTUAL INSURANCE GROUP *(Insurance: US) —Reorganized the group into a holding company owning three separate insurance providers, to make it more competitive.*
—

Kuok Khoon-hong, WILMAR INTERNATIONAL *(Agribusiness: Singapore)—Sought synergies by merging palm-oil refiner Wilmar with plantation PPB Oil Palms in 2007 to create a vast, integrated plantation company worth more than $4 billion.*
—

Mikhail Piotrovsky Director, State Hermitage Museum

SUCCEEDING HIS FATHER who had previously held the role from 1964 until his death in 1990, Piotrovsky became the first post-Soviet director of one of the world's largest museums, the State Hermitage Museum in St. Petersburg, in 1992. He is also a professor at St Petersburg State University, and a member of the Russian Academy of Sciences, the Russian Academy of Art, and the Russian Academy of Humanities. Piotrovsky is the author of over 200 scholarly works. He has also been the head of Russia's largest television channel since 2001.

BIOGRAPHY
Born in Yerevan, Armenia, in 1944, Mikhail Piotrovsky is the son of the eminent archaeologist Boris Borisovich Piotrovsky. He graduated with honors in 1967 from the Faculty of Oriental Studies at Leningrad (St. Petersburg) State University, specializing in Arabic studies. He also attended Cairo University from 1965 to 1966.

LEADERSHIP STYLE
Scholarly, charming, resolute. During the 1990s, he wore a black muffler in protest when the government withheld funding to the museum and heat had to be rationed to keep the galleries, with their three million artworks and 2,000 employees, from freezing.

KEY STRENGTH
Unwavering determination to secure the future of the Hermitage.

BEST DECISION
Opening overseas "branches" of the Hermitage in London, Las Vegas, and Amsterdam.

FROM ARABIC TO ART Piotrovsky first worked as an interpreter in Yemen. Then, at the Faculty of Oriental Studies, he took part in archaeological excavations in the Caucasus, Central Asia, and Yemen. He was invited to join the Hermitage staff as deputy director with responsibility for research work in 1991, before being appointed director by government decree in July 1992. As a child, Mikhail Piotrovsky had virtually learned to walk in the halls of the Hermitage. He recalls his father telling how he had put out flames after rockets hit the museum during World War II, which he viewed as a clash between the forces of culture and anti-culture.

TAKING ART TO THE PEOPLE It was under Piotrovsky's directorship that the Hermitage's links with the rest of the world were developed. Recognizing that the world was entering a period of globalization, he sought to forge links with foreign institutions in an attempt to build on shared cultures and encourage what he perceived as "multicultural globalism." This idea was encouraged by the Kremlin, which realized that cultural exchanges could become a means of establishing diplomatic links. Exchange exhibitions with British, French, and American museums began, often linked to a state visit. In 2000, Piotrovsky opened a London annex, the Hermitage Rooms, in Somerset House; the following year he put Old Masters from the Hermitage on permanent display in Las Vegas in partnership with New York's Guggenheim Museum. Despite calls for his resignation in 2006, after the theft of 200 small but valuable pieces by a museum official, Piotrovsky continues to present the Hermitage's remarkable collection to the world.

LESSONS IN BUSINESS: MAKING ART ACCESSIBLE

Adding an internet café, e-commerce boutique, and computer gallery in St. Petersburg, where young Russians gather to click and play with art, Piotrovsky has demonstrated his belief that tomorrow's museum could become a complex of entertainment and shopping, as well as art appreciation.
→ Young people represent markets of the future and need to be cultivated in business, as much as in art.
→ Remember that a business has a role to play in the overall happiness of the people who support it.
→ A "minority" market can grow to become a mass market if you organize it well and adapt it.

"We have to change from McDonald's to shared cultures—to multicultural globalism." Mikhail Piotrovsky

Takeo Fukui President & CEO (2003–09), Honda Motor Company Ltd

A LIFELONG FAN of Formula One racing, Fukui understands that winning requires good strategy and equipment. After joining Honda in 1969, Fukui helped develop the Honda CVCC engine, making the Honda Civic the first car to meet the US Clean Air Act without a catalytic converter. In the 1980s he led Honda to a string of first-place finishes at the World Grand Prix motorcycle championships, launched the US-produced Acura, and drove the development of the Fit subcompact car. He was made CEO in 2003.

BIOGRAPHY
Born in in Hiroshima, Japan, in 1944. Raised in Tokyo, Fukui graduated from Waseda University with a degree in applied chemistry. He was drawn to Honda because at that time it was the only Japanese car manufacturer involved with Formula One racing.

LEADERSHIP STYLE
Innovative, loyal, and competitive. Fukui's drive to succeed has pushed the company forward.

KEY STRENGTH
His commitment to finding unique technological solutions to problems facing the automotive industry.

BEST DECISION
Placing quality and customer satisfaction above market share, a strategy that has driven sales.

COMPETITIVE DRIVE During Fukui's early days with the company, he was caught applying excessive lubrication to a Honda Civic engine so that it would operate at peak performance during a government-operated fuel-economy test. This legendary competitive streak partly explains why Fukui is now in the driver's seat at Honda. When he became president and CEO in 2003, the company was facing some major challenges: US growth had slowed, and in Japan the company was facing stiff competition from Toyota and Nissan. With his natural drive to succeed, Fukui was the perfect person to get the company out of the pits and back on track.

A NATURAL FIT Fukui understands Honda like few others. He worked as an engineer at the company for 14 years before becoming the director for the Honda Racing Corp. in 1983.

Four years later he was the corporation's president. Since then, he has worked in various management and executive positions within the larger Honda Motor Company, including as the general manager of a factory, head of research and development, and president and director of American manufacturing.

As CEO, he maintained Honda's focus on customer satisfaction. Unlike some other car makers, who build new plants and calculate market share based on increased production capacity, Fukui believed in first stimulating demand through a commitment to quality and performance, enabling a confident strategy of plant expansion. Widely applauded by industry analysts for having placed Honda in a good position to weather the economic crisis, Fukui stepped down from his executive roles in 2009, remaining as a board member and advisor.

LESSONS IN BUSINESS: CHALLENGING TO INSPIRE

Fukui recognized that, to give Honda a competitive edge over its rivals, he had to foster a culture of innovation. He identified the trials that Honda faced and challenged employees to adapt quickly and value teamwork. He concentrated on helping people to welcome and manage change.

➔ Create an environment where all employees can advance their talents, and encourage them to innovate.
➔ No one can be satisfied unless the customer is satisfied: get everyone to focus on that fact.
➔ Achieve the highest quality through continuous improvement, innovation, and helpful technology.

"The truth is, as part of my nature, I don't like to lose."
Takeo Fukui

Juan Manuel Suárez Del Toro Rivero President, IFRC

AGED JUST 19, Suárez Del Toro joined his local youth branch of the Spanish Red Cross in Gran Canaria in the hope of "redressing injustices". As a volunteer, he was motivated by the chance to help people directly, and was inspired by experiences in Senegal and Equatorial Guinea. He rose through the ranks in the Canary Islands and then at the national level in Spain, becoming president of the Spanish Red Cross in June 1994, before taking the reigns of the International Federation of Red Cross and Red Crescent Societies (IFRC) in 2001.

BIOGRAPHY
Born in Las Palmas de Gran Canaria, Canary Islands, Spain, in 1952. He trained as an industrial engineer at the University of Las Palmas.

LEADERSHIP STYLE
Inclusive and optimistic, but determined. His background as a hands-on volunteer gives him authority with Red Cross and Red Crescent volunteers.

KEY STRENGTH
The determination to modernize combined with an approach that builds consensus. These skills have guided the IFRC through some of its most testing times, including its responses to the 2004 tsunami in Asia and the Israel-Palestine conflict.

BEST DECISION
Launching "Our Federation of the Future" campaign, which set out his reforming agenda very clearly but brought the numerous national groups with him in a broad consensus.

REPEATING SUCCESSES While president of the Spanish Red Cross, Suárez Del Toro worked to strengthen cooperation throughout the International Federation of Red Cross and Red Crescent Societies, which lead to him being encouraged to stand for president of the federation. He was duly elected to his first four-year term in 2001. Based in Geneva, Switzerland, the IFRC was founded in 1919 and coordinates the activities of the 186 national Red Cross and Red Crescent societies, organizing relief missions in response to major emergencies.

FEDERATION FOR THE FUTURE Soon after becoming president, Suárez Del Toro launched a consensus-building project titled "Our Federation of the Future", which aimed to modernize and reshape the IFRC to safeguard its future. He also worked to boost the IFRC's profile with governments, encourage more young people to volunteer, and strengthen national Red Cross and Red Crescent societies, particularly those short of resources. In 2004, Suárez Del Toro led the IFRC in its largest mission to date, in response to the South Asian tsunami. More than 40 national societies worked with over 22,000 volunteers to help those left without food or shelter, or at risk of disease. After being re-elected in 2005, he went on to achieve a major coup by successfully restoring the IFRC's financial stability in 2007, which had suffered after some national societies had failed to pay their contributions two years earlier. Suárez Del Toro has also led campaigns to highlight the HIV-AIDS pandemic, and has promoted national awareness programs in the developing world to increase understanding and prevention of the disease.

LESSONS IN BUSINESS: GETTING BUY-IN

Suárez Del Toro heads a massive global organization that could not exist without unpaid volunteers, so his ability to generate commitment from those who aren't obliged to give their full support has been vital.
- → Consult and empower different camps within an organization, so that their commitment to the common cause is a choice, not an obligation.
- → Promote shared values, particularly those shared by opposing sides in a disagreement or conflict.
- → Give respect and explicit thanks, especially in public, to those who work for the vision at all levels.

"It is our duty... to prevent people from suffering, and to work to achieve a world in which everyone enjoys a dignified existence." Juan Manuel Suárez Del Toro Rivero

James E. Burke Chairman & CEO (1976–89), Johnson & Johnson

NAMED BY *Fortune* magazine as one of the ten greatest CEOs of all time, Burke joined healthcare giant Johnson & Johnson in 1953. Rising through the ranks of the company to become chairman and CEO in 1976, he developed it into one of the world's leading manufacturers of consumer healthcare products. He refocused the business on its responsibility to its customers, and is credited with making it one of the most employee-friendly companies in the US. Burke showed great fortitude during the Tylenol crisis.

BIOGRAPHY
Born in 1925 in Rutland, Vermont. James Burke commanded a tank-landing craft in the Pacific during World War II before returning to his college education. After graduating from the College of the Holy Cross, Massachusetts, he completed an MBA at Harvard Business School in 1949.

LEADERSHIP STYLE
Encouraging, incisive, forthright. Burke had strong views but allowed his employees to fight for what they believed in.

KEY STRENGTH
Having the moral fortitude to place principle before profit —and the business sense to make it pay.

BEST DECISION
Recalling Tylenol, thereby returning the company's credo to center stage as the basis for ethical decision-making.

TAKING RISKS Burke joined Johnson & Johnson after three years spent with competitor Procter & Gamble, and was soon leading a new-products division, a role ideally suited to the forward-thinking innovator. However, not all of his initiatives went smoothly. After sustained and unsuccessful attempts to market several new cold-care products for children, he was called to the office of then CEO Robert Wood Johnson II. "I was full of bravado. I thought I was going to get fired," he told *Fortune* magazine. Instead, Johnson said, "I want to congratulate you. Business is about taking risks. Keep doing it."

MANAGING A CRISIS The defining episode in Burke's career as CEO was his confident handling of the Tylenol poisoning crisis in 1982. Following the death of seven people, it was found that some capsules of Johnson & Johnson's Tylenol (the country's best-selling over-the-counter pain reliever at the time) had been laced with cyanide. Placing consumer safety above the immediate cost to the company, Burke launched a nationwide alert through the media, recalled all Tylenol capsules—tens of millions of bottles—and did not resume production of the drug until tamper-proof packaging was perfected. Burke's bold moves may have cost the company as much as $150 million, but they restored consumer confidence. The company even weathered further Tylenol tampering a few years later, and replaced capsules with caplets. Burke's actions reflected the company's credo, that the company's first responsibility was to its customers and then its employees, rather than primarily to its shareholders.

LESSONS IN BUSINESS: EXPLOITING TENSIONS

Having learned much about intellectual discussion from his father, who always encouraged debate among his four children, Burke enjoyed having different viewpoints on board.
➜ Appoint someone in every team to be the critic, monitoring standards and analyzing effectiveness.
➜ As a team leader recognize that anyone, even the most junior person, may come up with the best idea for the way ahead.
➜ Developing talent means allowing people to challenge what you believe is the right course of action.

"He sets high standards for his company, for his people, and for himself."
Robert S. Hatfield, former chairman, Continental Group

Richard T. Clark CEO, Merck & Co., Inc.

A TRUE COMPANY MAN, Clark joined the pharmaceutical giant Merck & Co., Inc. in 1972, and has remained fully committed to it ever since. Appointed CEO in 2005, he took on the task of revitalizing an organization operating in more than 100 countries around the world and employing nearly 60,000 people. The drug manufacturer was facing financial problems related to some of its products, and Clark has drawn on his vast manufacturing experience and knowledge of the company to lead it through a series of major restructurings.

BIOGRAPHY

Born in Johnstown, Pennsylvania, in 1946. After graduating with a BA in liberal arts from Washington & Jefferson College in 1968, he completed an MBA at American University in 1970. He served as a Lieutenant in the US Army from 1970–72.

LEADERSHIP STYLE

Approachable, analytical, and motivational. An exceptional leader who excels at team building to deliver results.

KEY STRENGTH

Identifying the organization's unique strengths and focusing these on building growth.

BEST DECISION

Maximizing operating efficiencies to enable the company to continue to invest heavily in research and development.

WORKING THROUGH THE RANKS Clark joined Merck as a quality control officer and industrial engineer in the manufacturing division after responding to an ad looking for military personnel with an MBA. Gradually working his way through the management hierarchy, he gained experience in production, new products planning, and strategic planning, before becoming CEO of Medco Health (a pharmacy benefits management [PBM] company owned by Merck) in 2002. Identifying and building on the company's strengths, he led it to become one of the largest and most innovative companies in the PBM industry. In his next role, as president of the Merck Manufacturing Division, he demonstrated his operational excellence and his ability to introduce new products. These factors made him the board's first choice to make the

changes needed to keep Merck competitive in a highly dynamic market. Clark's appointment came at a time when the company was already in difficulties. It had experienced a significant drop in profits after the withdrawal of Vioxx, an arthritis painkiller, because of health risks, and it faced expiration of patent protection on its cholesterol-lowering drug, Zocor.

MAKING IMPROVEMENTS To Clark, the priorities were clear—to meet the needs of patients while continuing to build shareholder value. His first task was to reduce the company's costs. Clark implemented a plan to improve efficiency, particularly in the manufacturing and inventory management divisions, with the aim of achieving a $2-billion cost reduction in 2008. This has included major restructuring and significant job losses.

LESSONS IN BUSINESS: SEIZING CAREER OPPORTUNITIES

Clark saw that staying with the same company does not mean standing still. Success can come from within, but you still have to seize opportunities. Potential CEOs need wide knowledge of their companies.
→ Zig-zag your way up the organization, gaining experience in different aspects of the business and geographies around the world.
→ Make sure that the skills you learn are relevant all over the business, departmentally and geographically.
→ Take a job in HR or training when the opportunity occurs: you'll meet a wide range of senior managers.

"I was born and raised in Merck." Richard Clark

Barbara Stocking Director, Oxfam GB

A DISTINGUISHED CAREER in health care management led to Stocking becoming the first female director of international aid agency Oxfam in 2001. She has led Oxfam through a tumultuous period of humanitarian crises and major campaigns, against a backdrop of political, social, and environmental changes. Impassioned and energetic, Stocking has brought a welcome "can-do" approach to Oxfam, annual turnover has reached $300 million, and the charity now has over 6,000 paid staff and 20,000 volunteers in more than 70 countries.

BIOGRAPHY
Born in Cambridge, UK, in 1951, the only child of working-class parents (her father was a postman). She was educated at Rugby Grammar School, where she was head girl, and graduated with a degree in natural sciences from New Hall, Cambridge University, in 1972. Two years later, she obtained a master's in reproductive physiology from the University of Wisconsin.

LEADERSHIP STYLE
Energetic, warm, likeable. Colleagues say she is a good listener, and values the opinions of those who work with her.

KEY STRENGTH
The ability to communicate simply and clearly.

BEST DECISION
Maintaining Oxfam's neutrality by refusing to side with the US-led coalition in the war against Iraq.

HEALTH SERVICE MANAGEMENT After graduating, Stocking worked as a scientific researcher in the US, and then for the World Health Organization in west Africa. She returned to the UK in 1981 as a senior fellow at the London School of Hygiene and Tropical Medicine. In 1983, she joined the King's Fund, a health care charity that trains many top-level staff in Britain's National Health Service (NHS), entering NHS management herself in 1993. Her commitment to patient care was ahead of its time, and she set in place a number of innovative schemes, including programs to aid ethnic minorities. She was promoted to the post of NHS regional director for Anglia and Oxford, then the South East, where she was responsible for the health care management of 8.5 million people, and then to director of the NHS Modernization Agency.

INTERNATIONAL DEVELOPMENT Taking a pay cut of about a third of her NHS salary, Stocking became director of Oxfam GB in 2001. Since then she has been at the forefront of the organization's response to humanitarian crises caused by global wars, as well as natural disasters, such as the 2004 tsunami and the 2005 Pakistan earthquake. Keen to be seen as impartial in the current religious East-West divide that is threatening world peace, Stocking deliberately distanced Oxfam from the Iraq war but was at pains to explain that the organization was opposed to the war on purely humanitarian grounds. She has strengthened the organization's campaigning strategies with the Make Trade Fair and climate change campaigns, and also headed its contribution to Make Poverty History in 2005, increasing commitment to long-term projects in education and health development.

LESSONS IN BUSINESS: PUTTING STAFF AT EASE

Despite a background in academia, Stocking is known for expressing herself simply and clearly, a trait she fine-tuned during her time working at the NHS with a range of people from different backgrounds.
→ Put people at ease by being as affable as possible, and act as a mentor to junior staff whatever your level.
→ Don't confuse your staff by using complicated language and instructions. Think of what you are trying to communicate from their point of view, and phrase your message accordingly.
→ Remember that being friendly does not result in lack of respect from employees. It makes them listen harder.

"We need to change the attitudes of people across the world. No matter how small we are, we can make a change." Barbara Stocking

Frédéric Oudéa CEO, Société Générale

WHEN HE TOOK OVER in 2008 as CEO, Oudéa had been with the historic French bank for 13 years. He had been involved in Société Générale's new business plan as the company tried to mitigate the damage inflicted by the world's worst-ever trading scandal, and had been made deputy CEO as a reward for his role in shoring up the bank's capital reserves through a €5.5-billion emergency share sale. Now Société Générale could see more economic storm clouds looming, and Oudéa was chosen as the man to give the bank the fresh start it needed.

BIOGRAPHY
Born in 1963 in Paris. He was educated at the Louis Le Grand high school and the prestigious Ecole Polytechnique and Ecole Nationale d'Administration.

LEADERSHIP STYLE
Quiet and unassuming. A safe pair of hands.

KEY STRENGTH
Utilizing prudence and applying his influence to help Société Générale recover quickly from one of the worst years in its long history.

BEST DECISION
Moving quickly to calm the nerves of staff, shareholders, and the industry.

QUIETLY IMPRESSIVE In common with many of France's business leaders, Oudéa's early career was spent in the civil service. He joined Société Générale in 1995, and the following year was sent to London to head the bank's corporate operations. He was appointed CFO in 2003, a position in which he impressed industry analysts, becoming the preferred candidate to steer the organization in 2008.

BAPTISM OF FIRE Société Générale was founded in 1864, and now has over 25 million customers. It is one of the largest banks in the Eurozone, and one of France's key financial institutions. In January of 2008, it was hit by scandal when rogue futures trader Jerome Kerviel lost the group almost €5 billion. When Oudéa became CEO, he faced accusations that the bank's top people were out of touch and

had failed to put in place the necessary checks to prevent disaster. At the same time, the sub-prime crisis began to bite, and industry insiders viewed the bank as a potential takeover target, possibly by BNP Paribas. However, the market responded positively to the change of leadership, and Oudéa was quick to apply his steadying influence, responding to criticisms by putting new controls and prudent management in place. The falls in second- and third-quarter profits in 2008 were not as great as some analysts had been predicting, and by fall Oudéa was able to announce—to the amazement of some—that he was ready to embark on an acquisitions program, stating his great confidence in Société Générale's profitability and capital safety. Prudence, as always, has allowed the company to face tough contemporary financial markets with aplomb.

LESSONS IN BUSINESS: HITTING THE GROUND RUNNING

A CEO who takes over in a crisis has to provide balm to his battered staff, customers, and shareholders—and do it fast. Oudéa acknowledged past mistakes but worked hard to make sure they couldn't happen again.
→ Look for quick wins in your plan, however long-term it is. Remember people are motivated by a result.
→ Keep moving forward. Too much introspection and self-analysis can be counterproductive.
→ Avoid being overwhelmed by problems. The job of the CEO is to reassure people that they will drive through all the obstacles.

"Société Générale has shown the resilience of its business model." Frédéric Oudéa

Howard Stringer Chairman & CEO, Sony Corp.

WELSH-BORN Stringer made corporate history in 2005 as the first foreigner to head up one of Japan's commercial flagships. It was a high risk appointment from the normally ultra-traditional firm, indicative of how change was needed for the company that launched the Walkman, Trinitron televisions, and PlayStation. By 2004, it was struggling on all fronts, arriving too late to the flat-screen TV boom and allowing Apple's iPod to win hands down in the personal music player market. Stringer's turnaround promised radical change.

BIOGRAPHY
Born in Cardiff, Wales, in 1942. Now a US citizen, Stringer was awarded an honorary knighthood in 1999.

LEADERSHIP STYLE
Motivational and inclusive. Breaking down walls between Sony's four major divisions is crucial to Stringer's strategy. Regular cross-functional networking, brainstorming, and team-building sessions are now *de rigeur*.

KEY STRENGTH
Communication. Stringer is charming, garrulous, and well-liked. He knows that a simple strategy expertly communicated is more effective than a more complex one that few employees understand.

BEST DECISION
Persuading Lou Gerstner, the man who turned around IBM, to be his exclusive personal coach.

VIETNAM VET TURNED TV MOGUL

Stringer arrived in the US in 1965 and was promptly drafted to fight in Vietnam. On his return he became a documentary TV producer for CBS News, rising to become president of the network and famously poaching comedian David Letterman from rival NBC in 1993. Made president of Sony Corp. of America in 1997, by 2005 he was global CEO.

NEW ENERGY
"Strange people get jobs in strange times," Stringer has said. "I got this job in a crisis." He acted fast to stop the rot, slashing $2 billion in costs and raising a much-needed $4.3 billion for restructuring by selling non-core assets. Like Nissan's Carlos Ghosn, Stringer's key challenges are cultural and organizational. He splits his time between New York, London, and Sony's traditional Japanese base in Tokyo.

Unlike rivals such as Samsung and Toshiba, Sony owns content as well as hardware through its Sony Pictures arm, which has a turnover of over $8 billion. Stringer realized that this could be leveraged into a tremendous competitive strength by building internet connectivity and file-sharing into all its hardware so that games, movies, and music could be downloaded, and paid for, on demand. Before this could happen, however, he would have to attack Sony's infamously rigid silo mentality and turn damaging in-fighting into productive rivalry. Signs for the future are good — Sony's Blu-ray technology beat Toshiba's widely-fancied HD-DVD in the format wars in 2007, largely because of an interdepartmental joint effort. In a suprise new move, Stringer became global president in April 2009, gaining principle control of the company, and moving his focus onto the restructuring of the electronics division.

LESSONS IN BUSINESS: PRIORITIZING COMMUNICATION

Success in the digital age is all about talking. If Sony is to prosper in the networked world of the 21st century, its products need to talk to each other through the internet, and its executives must stay in touch.
→ Tell your investors where the company is headed clearly and frequently by explaining the strategy.
→ Make sure that divisional executives are talking to their opposite numbers in other divisions.
→ Accept the challenge of making all this chatter happen, while simultaneously stimulating the flow of creative and desirable new products.

"My game plan is blindingly obvious. If it weren't, I wouldn't have been able to do it." Howard Stringer

TOWARD A COLLABORATIVE FUTURE

As company figureheads, CEOs rarely work alone. They collaborate with organizations to establish mutually beneficial alliances and forge relationships with their staff to create productive workforces and achieve their vision.

King of collaboration, **Ditlev Engel** (p106), CEO of Vestas Wind Systems in Denmark, sees unity as the key to successful relationships. As such he has created a collaborative culture, uniting staff, customers, and even national governments in a shared vision of global wind power. **Mark Zuckerberg** (p22), CEO of Facebook, opted for a collaborative open source business model enabling anyone to create Facebook applications. This enhanced his existing offering by empowering user relationships, resulting in a swift viral spread and explosive growth that has brought more than 60 million users to the site ●

"Success in the modern world depends on the real connections you have."
REID HOFFMAN

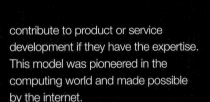

Networking and Open-sourcing

Networking is a successful method of sourcing partnerships, building valuable relationships, and connecting with others. Some CEOs have created entire businesses out of the concept of networking and forging connections. Ecademy is a business social network enabling business people to connect through online networking, one-to-one meetings, and events. "It's not just about transactions," says CEO **Thomas Power**. "It's about connections." **Reid Hoffman**, CEO of Ecademy rival, LinkedIn, says, "LinkedIn is about brokering business relationships... I pay a lot of attention to building relationships." Building a business based on the concept of relationships has led LinkedIn to become the world's largest professional networking website, with over 18 million members. "Our mission is to

make the world's interconnected workforce more productive," adds Hoffman. Indeed, not only have LinkedIn and Ecademy helped companies to connect and build relationships with people to generate revenue, they have become valuable internet businesses in their own right.

Another executive leading the way in leveraging relationships is **Sophie Gasperment**, CEO of ethical beauty products retailer Body Shop, who has continued the work of founder **Anita Roddick** in developing trading relationships with communities in need. As well as supplier relationships, she has focused on building strong connections with store franchisees and the thousands of Body Shop At Home consultants, all of whom have valuable insights into the company's customers.

Push collaboration to its logical conclusion and you get the open source model of collaboration, where anyone can

contribute to product or service development if they have the expertise. This model was pioneered in the computing world and made possible by the internet.

Eschewing the notion of intellectual property as something to be guarded for the profits of the few, a young Finnish student, Linus Torvalds, developed source code for a new computer operating system and published it on the internet so people from around the world could help develop it. Linux became a viable competitor to Microsoft's Windows, revealing the open source model's power.

Many companies have embraced open source collaboration, including: Mozilla (CEO, **John Lilly**) with the Firefox browser and Thunderbird email application, Red Hat (CEO, **Jim Whitehurst**), with its commercial version of Linux, and Openmoko (CEO, **Sean Moss-Plutz**), which offers innovative open source mobile customization.

Building Relationships

Be approachable—Actively listen to people. Find out what makes them tick, what their strengths are, and what they need in order to maximize performance.

Network effectively—Become or find the missing link in network chains. Consider synergies between yourself, people you meet, and people you already know.

Involve managers in decisions—Encourage ownership and create motivated in-house partnerships.

Keep channels of communication open—Encourage teamwork and a collaborative culture between staff.

Close Collaborators

Forging partnerships and cooperating with others can really pay off, as these CEOs have discovered:

John D. Finnegan, CHUBB (Insurance: US)—*Finnegan is known for putting people first and fostering important relationships by implementing inclusive policies and "capitalizing on the skills and experience of its most talented leaders".*

John C. Lechleiter, ELI LILLY (Pharmaceuticals: Japan)—*Opted for a 50/50-owned joint venture with ICOS Corp. (CEO, **Paul Clark**), a Washington-based biotechnology company, to develop and produce impotence drug Cialis, in order to compete with Pfizer's market-leader Viagra.*

R. Richard Fontaine, GAMESTOP (Retail: US)—*Led a merger between video-game retailers Gamestop and EB Games, which helped them enter new markets and compete more effectively by being "able to do more together".*

Jean Francois Cirelli, GAZ DE FRANCE (Energy: France)—*Led a merger between Suez and GDF in 2008 to form a global energy giant and consolidate the European energy market.*

Eric Claus, GREAT ATLANTIC & PACIFIC TEA (Retail: US)—*Spearheaded partnerships with farmers, making it the largest retailer of locally-grown produce in the US north east.*

Ian Cheshire, KINGFISHER (Retail: UK)—*"Our world is one of international collaboration—our retail brands, our employees and our suppliers working together for sustainable long-term growth,"* says Cheshire.

Jeffrey A. Joerres, MANPOWER (Recruitment: US)—*Hosted a live panel discussion on "virtual collaboration" in virtual community Second Life.*

Steve Holliday, NATIONAL GRID (Energy: UK)—*Is calling for greater industry and consumer collaboration to determine a route-map for a low carbon economy to meet government targets.*

Sam K. Duncan, OFFICEMAX (Retail: US)—*Partnered with Safeway, Inc. to offer co-branded office products while also consolidating its headquarters to enhance collaboration.*

Chihiro Kanagawa, SHIN-ETSU CHEMICAL COMPANY LTD (Chemicals: Japan)—*By forging "strong relationships based on trust with users worldwide over several decades", Kanagawa has avoided cutbacks in the face of waning demand.*

Nicholas Serota Director, Tate Gallery

IN HIS 20 YEARS as director of the UK's Tate Gallery, Serota has turned a cash-strapped and under-resourced national arts institution into an international tourist destination and a constant focus of lively discussion in the art world. Dealing with the conflicting opinions and insistent demands of government, the press, the public, and the artists requires a level of management skill at least equal to that involved in running any large corporation. Serota's success also reveals his financial, political, and publicity skills.

BIOGRAPHY
Born in 1946 in Hampstead, London. Serota studied economics at Cambridge University before switching to art history. In 1999 he was awarded a knighthood for services to art.

LEADERSHIP STYLE
Approachable and effective. Communicates his vision clearly.

KEY STRENGTH
Being ready to take big steps when faced with opportunities.

BEST DECISION
Buying the old Bankside power station and developing it into Tate Modern.

ART LESSONS Director of the Whitechapel Gallery for 12 years, Serota knew he was in for a challenge when he applied for the post of director of the Tate in 1988. The entire national collection of British and international modern art was crowded into one cramped museum, government financial support had shrunk, public sector management expectations had changed, and prices in the art market were soaring, limiting the scope for acquisitions.

HANDS-ON ACTIVITY Serota recognized that many areas of the Tate's operations badly needed overhauling and he set about it, taking a close personal interest in every aspect of the improvements. He ensured that neglected rooms were revived and works rotated, and he oversaw the expansion of the Tate to Liverpool and St. Ives. Most importantly, he used the opportunity of National Lottery funding in the mid-1990s to acquire the old Bankside power station across the Thames from St. Paul's Cathedral and convert it into Tate Modern, personally raising the £98-million shortfall from private donations. Serota then organized hugely popular exhibitions and ground-breaking conceptual art displays that established Tate Modern as one of the world's great modern art galleries, with a reputation as "the Cathedral of Cool." Today, Tate Modern is an essential stop on any tourist's London itinerary, while the older gallery, now known as Tate Britain, is revived, refreshed, and pulling in the crowds.

With his huge energy and deep interest in every aspect of the Tate, Serota has shown how one person can reorganize and remotivate even the most complex organization.

LESSONS IN BUSINESS: GETTING STUCK IN

Personal dynamism and driving ambition have been the keys to Serota's success. He has illustrated how one person can unpick, reorganize, and remotivate even the most labyrinthine institution by involving himself in every aspect of the process.

→ Understand every corner of each function in the business, whatever your background.

→ Demonstrate your interest in all aspects of the business by studying them and talking to their operators.

→ Never be afraid to go into detail; you can rely on your people but from time to time you need to delve.

> "When I am most challenged in my own reactions the deepest insights emerge." Nicholas Serota

Ann Veneman Executive Director, UNICEF

HAVING SPENT much of her career dealing with child nutrition and public health, and with a wealth of experience gained at one of the most complex US government departments, Veneman was the ideal candidate to become only the fifth executive director of UNICEF, the United Nations Children's Fund, in its 60-year history. Appointed by UN secretary-general Kofi Annnan in 2005, Veneman has focused the organization on achievable targets, global partnerships, and effective fundraising.

NEW CHALLENGES After a varied career working for law firms and lobbyists, in 2001, Veneman became the first female secretary of the US Department of Agriculture, facing head-on the fallout from foot and mouth disease in Europe, as well as the consequences of 9/11. Under her leadership, USDA received its first clean financial audit. In 2005, she took on a new challenge as executive director of UNICEF, a global agency with about 10,000 staff and an annual budget of $3 billion.

COMMITTED TO IMPROVEMENT Her vision is to ensure that the agency is geared toward achieving the Millennium Development Goals, set by governments around the world, by their 2015 deadline. Although these goals, which emphasize the well-being of children, were formulated before her appointment,

Veneman has been tenacious in their implementation, and instituted a number of initiatives to improve overall business practices within the organization. Since 2005, Veneman has raised UNICEF's profile by traveling extensively and pressing her message of a "culture of continuous improvement" to governments, businesses, foundations, and individuals. She has also worked to promote existing partnerships and build new relationships in the fight against child poverty, malnutrition, and disease.

UNICEF is funded entirely by voluntary contributions, and Veneman has recruited high-profile goodwill ambassadors, such as sports stars David Beckham and Roger Federer, and musician Joel Madden, to highlight the continuing challenges that UNICEF faces and to raise awareness of its work.

LESSONS IN BUSINESS: BELIEVING IN THE FUTURE

Veneman believes education is the key to helping children achieve their potential as adults, particularly schemes that are based on mentoring young people.
→ The next generation is the future of your business, so supporting child welfare is as much a strategic decision as a moral choice.
→ Combine your commercial accumen with a conscience that looks after the community long-term.
→ Convey your social objectives to your people and set them targets and tasks in that area.

"UNICEF… has emerged under [Venerman's] leadership as a crucial protagonist for child survival."

Richard Horton, editor of *The Lancet* medical journal

D. Scott Davis CEO, United Parcel Service

AS CEO of United Parcel Service (UPS), the world's third-largest corporate employer (behind Wal-Mart and McDonald's), Davis finds himself in charge of more than 420,000 employees in some 200 countries. Since he took over the top spot in January 2008, Davis has had to contend with record fuel prices, faltering consumer spending, and a volatile world financial market. He brings his talent for forward planning and a flexible company outlook to maintain UPS's performance. It is now a technology company as well as transportation.

A FINANCIAL BACKGROUND A Certified Public Accountant, Davis started his career with Arthur Andersen, then moved to II Morrow, an Oregon-based technology company, where he held the posts of CFO and then CEO. He joined UPS in 1986 as a result of the company's acquisition of II Morrow. After an overseas assignment as CEO for an affiliated Bermuda reinsurance company, he was made vice president of finance at UPS, then CFO, vice chairman, and in January 2008 he assumed the role of chairman and CEO.

GLOBAL PRESENCE Davis has played a major role in expanding UPS's overseas interests, helping UPS to identify and acquire 30 businesses. Within months of Davis taking over as head of UPS, there was a marked decline in the level of economic activity in North America, and healthy performance in the international market proved vital in helping to offset more sluggish performance at home in the US.

In the boom times, the company resisted the temptation to take on increased debt and increased risk, maintaining a policy of long-term investment as opposed to short-term gain. As Davis says, "At UPS, we don't manage for the next quarter; we manage for the next quarter-century. With the internet, just-in-time techniques, and technology changing constantly, the environment changes quickly."

Davis has made keeping abreast of these changes a priority, seeing flexibility and emerging technologies as the keys to success. To Davis, who has helped UPS to reinvent itself over the years, technological development is now as important to the company as transportation.

LESSONS IN BUSINESS: SEEING YOUR OWN POTENTIAL

As a 22 year-old consultant for Arthur Andersen, Davis often found himself with CEOs and CFOs of large companies. It was this experience that made him first entertain the idea that he was more than capable of running a company himself one day.
→ Look ahead and don't be afraid to think big; people with less talent than you have made it to the top.
→ Create a career plan and stick to it. Let it take you round the company geographically and functionally.
→ Make yourself indispensable and quietly communicate this fact to the powers that be—do not shout.

"You've got to be agile and stay on top of constant change." D. Scott Davis

George David President & CEO (1994–2008), United Technologies

ONCE DESCRIBED as "the philosopher king of manufacturing", David was the cerebral chairman of the multibillion-dollar technology products and services company for almost 15 years. Although neither he nor his company is a household name, you probably encounter its products, which include Pratt & Whitney jet engines, Otis elevators, and Carrier air conditioners, every day. More capably than many of his rivals, David took the best of modern management theory and turned it into the hard currency of cash flow and dividends.

BIOGRAPHY
Born in Pennsylvania in 1942 into a well-off family. His father was one of America's first Rhodes Scholars in 1908, and later became a professor at Bryn Mawr College in Pennsylvania. David took a degree in physical sciences at Harvard University, and then an MBA at the University of Virginia's Darden School of Business Administration before starting work at Boston Consulting Group.

LEADERSHIP STYLE
Cool and deliberative. David thinks before making a decision.

KEY STRENGTH
Understanding that the Japanese passion for excellence and quality could be mixed with American innovation to create a world-beating company.

BEST DECISION
Getting out of supplying the auto industry. He sold UT Automotive for $2.3 billion in 1999, and re-invested the money in aerospace.

AN ACADEMIC START After leaving school, David studied physical sciences at Harvard University, but wasn't inspired to pursue a career in that field. He went to the University of Virginia's Darden School of Business Administration to study for an MBA. He graduated top of his class and then joined the high-powered Boston Consulting Group (BCG). It was a deluxe education in business.

HANDS ON One of David's clients at BCG was the elevator giant Otis. In 1975, David became assistant to its French boss Hubert Faure. When Otis was bought by the aerospace manufacturer UTC, David was sent to run Otis's South American operations, and then to Japan. He brought the businesses under control financially and displayed strong leadership, as well as an amazing grasp of the fine detail of company products and processes. By 1986, David was President of Otis, and eight years later he was chief executive of UTC

From the start, David brought a very intellectual management approach to running UTC, implementing skills acquired at business school and in consultancy. He ran the company by the textbook rather than by instinct. In his first two years he laid off 20,000 workers. Then, through his Achieving Competitive Excellence program, he made sure that in every one of its divisions UTC could deliver technological brilliance as well as low costs. In his first decade, he quadrupled earnings per share, even managing to out-perform its great rival General Electric. David's career highlights the effectiveness that transforming business management into a coherent science can have, with the correct implementation.

LESSONS IN BUSINESS: USING BEST PRACTICE

David brought a cerebral management approach to UTC. Turning management into a science has gone out of fashion in the past few years; but if you get best practice right the results can be spectacular.
➔ Always follow through new management initiatives and processes. Several half-implemented programs lead to cynicism and poor morale.
➔ Use clear words to explain theory and document processes. Jargon puts people off even the best ideas.
➔ Ensure that researching best practice and consolidating your results becomes an action plan—fast.

"What goes down goes up and what goes up goes down, but the trend is up over time." George David

Jean-Bernard Lévy CEO, Vivendi

FRENCH MEDIA GIANT Vivendi was a strange collection of interests when Levy arrived, with a hand in everything from cellular and fixed-line telecom to computer games, record labels, and Hollywood studios. He has sold shrewdly, bought wisely, and kept all corners of the empire working well enough to persuade the corporate vultures to look elsewhere. Today, Lévy can claim credit for strengthening Universal Music, the world's largest record company, while rivals grasp for a new business model in the age of the free download.

BIOGRAPHY
Born in Paris in 1955. Lévy studied in Paris at the Ecole Nationale Supérieure des Télécommunications.

LEADERSHIP STYLE
Respectful, demanding, and charming. He believes in letting expert executives get on with the job while gently raising pressure on them to improve results.

KEY STRENGTH
A natural ability to delegate and a keen eye for a bargain, together these qualities have kept an unlikely group of companies alive and well.

BEST DECISION
Selling an 80 percent stake of Universal to General Electric for $3.8 billion in 2003. The deal swelled Vivendi's coffers and saved the media conglomerate from being broken up and sold.

A DAUNTING TASK By the time Lévy arrived at Vivendi in 2002, he had completed the classic French corporate education, including a stint advising government, but his low-key, discreet style meant little was known about him when he was appointed COO. He was part of a team appointed to save the company after a disastrous series of acquisitions under former CEO Jean-Marie Messier. Vivendi was facing the worst losses in French corporate history of €23 billion. The group has since recovered and recorded profits of nearly €3 billion.

BIG GAME HUNTING Lévy's first task was to help trim down the company to its most promising and profitable divisions and stave off imminent bankruptcy. The sale of an 80 percent stake in Universal was followed by the sale of Vivendi's underperforming NewsWorld International news channel, as well as smaller cellular telephone operations. By 2005, when Lévy was appointed to the position of CEO, Vivendi was ready to expand again. By the end of the year, he had announced the merger of Canal+ with the French pay TV operator TPS, and in December 2007 he revealed his biggest coup, the takeover of the computer games giant Activision, in a deal valued at $18.8 billion. This brought together Vivendi's Blizzard, the makers of *World of Warcraft*, with the owners of the popular *Guitar Hero* and the *Tony Hawk* series. Activision Blizzard now describes itself as "the world's most profitable pure-play online and console game publisher." Lévy has noted that the games business is a bigger earner than the music industry, though his Universal Music Group continues to dominate the record business.

LESSONS IN BUSINESS: PERFORMING TO SURVIVE

Lévy's success in transforming a business on its knees to one standing tall reflects his management style of quietly demanding more of his executives. He knows predators are ready to pick off parts of the business.
- ➜ Drill into your people that only by performing well can they answer those who say a conglomerate should be broken up.
- ➜ Turn round or weed out parts of the business where the biggest financial problems lie.
- ➜ Make sure all divisions are performing well before expanding your—now secure—business.

"I am the enabler." Jean-Bernard Lévy

James J. Schiro CEO, Zurich Financial Services

FOR A LOW-KEY "company man" who spent 34 years with the firm he joined from college, Schiro is today a high-profile global player straddling the worlds of politics and business. He created the world's biggest accountancy firm when he oversaw the merger of Price Waterhouse with Coopers and Lybrand, and is credited with the revival of Zurich Financial Services, which he quickly restructured after being made CEO in 2002. He is also a member of the World Economic Forum's business council.

BIOGRAPHY
Born in Brooklyn, New York, in 1946. Schiro studied at St. John's University, New York, and the Amos Tuck School of Business at Dartmouth, where he took his MBA.

LEADERSHIP STYLE
Inclusive and motivational. Schiro places great emphasis on recruiting—and consulting—top executives, and he believes in developing talent by giving people responsibility.

KEY STRENGTH
The ability to keep his head and think clearly and rationally under intense pressure.

BEST DECISION
Cutting the sprawling and ailing Zurich Financial Services empire back to size, and focusing on its core business.

CHALLENGING TIMES Schiro made his reputation at Price Waterhouse as head of mergers and acquisitions in the early 90s. As deputy chairman, he oversaw the creation of PriceWaterhouseCoopers in 1998. He became CEO of the newly merged colossus just as a report by the Securities Exchange Commission revealed that several PWC directors held stakes in companies for whom they were serving as "independent" auditors. They were also found to be acting as consultants to firms they were auditing. Schiro negotiated rules to prevent conflicts of interest and handled the situation so expertly that he was proposed as successor to SEC chairman Arthur Levitt.

12-MONTH TURNAROUND Having created and then saved the world's biggest professional services company, Schiro went on to a new challenge. In 2002 he was appointed CEO at Zurich Financial Services, which was hemorrhaging cash. Despite having no knowledge of the insurance industry, speaking no German, and inheriting first-half-year losses of $2 billion, Schiro quickly charted a new course. Nine non-core businesses were sold, thousands of jobs were cut, and non-profit making policies worth $800 million were sacrificed. To reduce costs, the company improved its direct services to customers and tightened claims assessments. Within a year he had made a profit of more than $2 billion.

Today Schiro is addressing one of Zurich's remaining weaknesses—that too much of its income is from mature, low-growth markets, such as the US and Europe—by leading an expansion into emerging markets such as Turkey, Hungary, Ukraine, Russia, and China.

LESSONS IN BUSINESS: DEVISING A STRATEGY

Schiro's accountancy expertise gave him the confidence to make the severe cutbacks needed to return Zurich Financial Services to profit: "We're better off giving up market share than losing capital," he said.
→ Always think a few steps ahead and be mindful of the secondary effects of each decision.
→ Avoid over-balancing your strategy by setting an objective that becomes the sole focus.
→ Integrity in the financial services industry is the equivalent of health and safety in a factory. Avoid devising a strategy which might risk the company's reputation.

"I would rather have six people with different perspectives and backgrounds looking at a problem than 60 who have the same." James Schiro

William C. Rhodes III CEO, AutoZone

BIOGRAPHY
Born in Memphis, Tennessee, in 1965. Rhodes studied at the University of Tennessee, and gained an MBA from the University of Memphis.

BEST DECISION
Maintaining AutoZone's unique WITTDTJR policy ("What it takes to do the job right"), which enhances competitiveness.

LESSON IN BUSINESS
Interact with your customers—an in-depth knowledge of the business has enabled Rhodes to see where systems and customer service levels can be improved, giving AutoZone the edge.

BELYING HIS ROLE AS CEO of the giant car-parts retailer AutoZone, Rhodes can frequently be seen working behind the counter of one of his stores, which keeps him in touch with the business at grassroots level.

"Bill" Rhodes spent six years working in Ernst & Young's audit division before joining one of its clients, AutoZone, in 1994. He spent the next ten years in a number of executive roles, then became one of the youngest CEOs of a *Fortune* 500 company when he succeeded in 2005. Annual growth rates were 5–6 percent from 1994 to 2004, but Rhodes could still see potential for growth both in the $36-billion "do-it-yourself" market, and the $53-billion "do-it-for-me" sector that supplies parts and products to chain and independent repair businesses. An excellent analyst, Rhodes oversees the marketing and operational side of the business, and has continued the successful "Get in the Zone" marketing campaign to promote AutoZone's own Duralast brand of batteries, alternators, and brake pads, which have proved popular with money-conscious customers. Although AutoZone has not been immune to economic downturn, Rhodes continues to strive for ongoing growth.

Jürgen Hambrecht Chairman & CEO, BASF

BIOGRAPHY
Born in Germany in 1946. Hambrecht has a doctorate in chemistry from the University of Tübingen.

BEST DECISION
Targeting Asia as both an emerging market and as a location for production.

LESSON IN BUSINESS
Grow in a downturn—by taking over its ailing Korean partners in the late 1990s, BASF was perfectly placed when the Asian economy picked up.

BENEATH HIS COLLEGIATE manner, Hambrecht is a ruthless CEO. He assumed the role in 2003 when BASF profits were falling and the US market was shrinking. To restore health he ordered job cuts and expanded into Asia.

BASF was the world's number one chemical firm when Hambrecht took charge, but the outlook was far from rosy. The company's quarterly profits were in freefall, the European Union was imposing tighter regulations on emissions, and cutbacks in the US were affecting demand. Hambrecht mapped out a strategy to combine the development of better products, improvement of production using new technology, and growth in Asia. While America may have been sneezing, China and India were in rude health, and Hambrecht planned for Asia to account for 20 percent of group sales by 2010. He saved $100 million through efficiencies, and made 1,200 job cuts. In Shanghai, he built the world's largest factory for the production of polytetrahydrofuran, a polymer used in Spandex. Profits rose to €336 million from sales of more than €4 billion, and when the global economic downturn hit, BASF was still making acquisitions while other companies tightened their belts.

"You have to offer returns to secure a company's long-term existence." Jürgen Hambrecht

E. Hunter Harrison President & CEO, Canadian National

BIOGRAPHY
Born in Tennessee in 1944. Harrison studied at Memphis State College.

BEST DECISION
Making the operating ratio (the ratio of expenses to revenue) the central focus of his entire approach to business.

LESSON IN BUSINESS
Cut costs and the rest will follow—Harrison's emphasis on efficiency has been at the heart of his success in the rail industry.

THROUGH AGGRESSIVE cost-cutting and ruthless efficiency, Harrison turned first Illinois Central then Canadian National into the leanest operators in the North American rail industry, confirming his reputation as one of the best in the business.

Harrison began his rail career crawling under boxcars to oil wheel bearings while still a student in 1964. Three decades later, as president and CEO of rail company Illinois Central, Harrison revolutionized the freight train business when he initiated scheduled services for freight shipments. His sharp focus on operational efficiency and asset utilization gave the company the lowest ratio of expenses to revenue in the entire North American rail industry. His achievements made Illinois Central a highly appealing takeover target and, after it was acquired by Canadian National in 1998, his skills were quickly put to use in the new company. Named CEO in 2003, Harrison intensified his efforts to drive his scheduling model even further. He implemented an aggressive operating plan, refined the company's scheduled service, and acquired a number of key Canadian and US rail operators in order to maintain the company's position as one of North America's leading rail operators.

Koichi Fukaya President & CEO (2003–08), Denso Corp.

BIOGRAPHY
Born in 1944, in Japan. Fukaya joined the automotive parts giant Denso in 1966 after graduating in mechanical engineering from the Tokyo Institute of Technology.

BEST DECISION
Dramatically increasing spending on research and facilities. This led to new products, which kick-started expansion in Europe, the US, and Asia.

LESSON IN BUSINESS
Invest in your product—new products and boosted profits helped Denso reduce its reliance on parent company Toyota.

BRINGING NEW DYNAMISM to the Japanese firm Denso, Fukaya has energized sales. When he became CEO, sales stood at $28 billion. By the time he stepped aside in 2008 to become vice-chairman, they were almost $45 billion.

Fukaya's academic and work background as an engineer specializing in thermodynamics and automated control systems gave him an advantage when he was made CEO in 2003. He knew that to increase sales, Denso, which had started its life as a captive of Toyota, had to sell more products to its erstwhile parent company's rivals. To do that, it had to develop new state-of-the-art products, from more fuel-efficient air conditioning to in-car GPS satellite navigation. Fukaya used his contacts from his time as head of Denso's Michigan operation to increase sales to General Motors, and he opened a new air-conditioning plant in the Czech Republic. In his first three years as CEO, Fukaya spent just under $3 billion on new research and facilities. He increased the company's air conditioning sales to Caterpillar and other truck manufacturers, and reopened new auto air-conditioning and satellite navigation plants in Tianjin and Guangzhou in China. Sales went through the roof.

"We will continue to look to the future – anticipating future technology and developing and producing it faster and better than other companies." Koichi Fukaya

Dorothy Thompson CEO, Drax Group

BIOGRAPHY
Born in 1960 in the UK. Dorothy Thompson (née Carrington) studied econometrics and mathematical economics at the London School of Economics.

BEST DECISION
Investing millions in biomass as a fuel for the future, after anticipating the need for new, clean, and efficient technology.

LESSON IN BUSINESS
Know your strengths—aware that her knowledge of power production is limited, Thompson concentrates her efforts on what she knows best: financial and strategic planning.

THE FIRST FEMALE CEO of a FTSE 100 power company, and one of the few in the energy sector with project finance experience, Thompson's economic nous, open managerial style, and tough reputation have revitalized the Drax Group.

Thompson's first exposure to the power sector came at the Commonwealth Development Corp., a UK-government-funded organization financing some of the first independent power stations in Britain's former colonies. This was followed by stints at Powergen, then InterGen NV, where she managed four gas-fired power plants in the UK and Holland. When Thompson joined Drax as CEO in 2005, it was in poor financial shape. The previous year, its US owners, AES Corp., had withdrawn financial support and turned the company over to creditors, and Thompson faced immediate takeover talks with a US-led consortium. Negotiations reached a stalemate and Drax was floated on the stock market. This, coupled with a sharp rise in UK electricity prices, gave Thompson the chance for a major restructure, which led to a swift turnaround in fortunes. She has since overseen investment in projects to reduce greenhouse gas emissions, including plans to build three biomass plants in the UK.

Luis Ubiñas President, Ford Foundation

BIOGRAPHY
Born in the South Bronx, New York City, in 1963. Ubiñas graduated from Harvard University, and has an MBA from Harvard Business School.

BEST DECISION
Gaining experience in business management before starting a career in the not-for-profit sector.

LESSON IN BUSINESS
Use your experiences—Ubiñas' life story echoes the values of the foundation. He has built on his experiences to give him the empathy, insight, and business nous required to make a notable difference.

THE APPOINTMENT of Ubiñas marks a fresh approach at the Ford Foundation. Applying skills honed at McKinsey & Co., he has brought a business ethic to a diversified philanthropic group with nearly $12 billion in assets.

Charitable scholarships enabled Ubiñas to attend top schools in the US, and he was determined to give back to the community. During an 18-year career at the consultants McKinsey, he was an active volunteer for organizations including Leadership Education and Development, which provides educational opportunities to low-income Afro-American and Latino high school students. Within McKinsey, he founded an organization to recruit and mentor individuals from the Latino workforce. His surprise appointment in 2008 to preside over the Ford Foundation reflected his ambitions, and an indicator that Ford intended to adopt a more businesslike approach to its management and grant-making. The economic downturn that started in his first year demanded immediate action to protect Ford's endowment portfolio and safeguard its grant-making budget. Ubiñas rose to the challenge, cutting internal costs, and announcing plans to increase the percentage of Ford's endowment given as grants.

"We didn't want a 'has-been', we wanted a 'will-be'." Gordon Horsfield, former Drax chairman, describing Dorothy Thompson

Jean-Pierre Garnier CEO (2000–08), GlaxoSmithKline

THE COMPANY was in great shape when Garnier stood down from GSK in 2008. Controversies over his pay and refusal to subsidize anti-AIDS drugs notwithstanding, Garnier had enhanced GSK's reputation and increased profits.

Garnier wasted no time when he took over GSK in 2000. He launched a massive cost-cutting exercise that saved more than $500 million, and then addressed GSK's poor reputation for research and development. The problem was a bureaucratic, centrally-controlled system, managing over 14,000 scientists. He decided to decentralize the system, with smaller units focusing on particular diseases, and entrepreneurial unit heads paid according to results. It was a huge gamble that paid off, with the development of several breakthrough medicines, including a "bird-flu" vaccine. The company suffered a number of controversies, including the need to withdraw an antidepressant linked to child suicides. However, by dropping a legal action against the South African government over the use of HIV generics, and by increasing its charitable projects, Garnier has boosted GSK's image among the public and potential scientist recruits. He stood down in 2008.

Clara Furse CEO, London Stock Exchange Group

NOT JUST THE FIRST female CEO of the London Stock Exchange, when Furse took over in 2001 she was also the fourth person in ten years to be appointed to one of the hardest jobs in the City. Since then, she has more than proved herself.

Furse began her career as a broker in 1983, joining Phillips and Drew (now UBS), where she progressed to global head of futures in 1996. She next became group chief executive at Credit Lyonnais Rouse, before joining the London Stock Exchange in 2001. In her early days at the Exchange she was faced with the challenge of having to find her place in an overwhelmingly male environment. Not only has Furse survived, but, more importantly, so has the Exchange. Since becoming CEO, Furse has successfully led the LSE through a very competitive period, seeing off four takeover attempts in the process. Despite interest from Sweden, Germany, Australia, and the US, the LSE has remained in British hands and Furse's detractors have had to credit her with success in this regard. Her reputation for being unclubbable and a rather hard-nosed financier led to some criticism early on, but most now recognize that her style is part of what has helped keep the Exchange independent.

"I don't do intimidated." Clara Furse

THE OVERSIGHT OF THE BOARD

The crucial role of the non-executive board is illustrated by former Intel CEO **Andy Grove** (p30), who decided to shake up his board when he took over as chairman in 1997. As CEO, its passivity had frustrated him during his handling of a crisis over flawed semiconductors a few years before, which had seriously threatened Intel's reputation. He forced members to be more active in the company by reporting back from Intel site visits and condemned a culture of compliance among the board that added nothing to strategic decision-making. Sometimes, however, an active board can take a while to make the right business decision. Urged by Apple CEO **John Sculley** to remove founder **Steve Jobs** (p17) from the company in 1985, the board complied, leaving Apple to drift for 12 years in the wilderness. The board had to work through three CEOs before employing the right man: Jobs finally took the helm in 1997 ●

"Everybody that works needs a boss, especially the CEO."
ANDY GROVE

In the Boardroom

A successful relationship between the CEO and the board requires trust, confidence, and respect, qualities that take time to nurture. **Jim Kilts** took over US consumer products company Gillette in 2001 after the firm had been savaged by Wall Street for several years for under-performance. Analysts condemned his lack of progress, but the board's decision to back him was vindicated when cashflow doubled to $1.7 billion in just two years.

Sometimes shareholders go to extreme measures to ensure that the board and the CEO are in alignment. When they lost confidence in the board of languishing UK marketing and PR company Huntsworth in 2000, a party of shareholders formed their own board, ousted the incumbents, including chief executive **John Holmes**, and installed one of their own as CEO. During his tenure, the highly respected PR figure **Peter Gummer** has taken the company from a £20-million turnover in 1999 to £80.5-million in the first half of 2008 alone, and seen it expand globally.

Not all companies experience such tension, however. Under CEO **Park Hyung-kyu**, Fujitsu Korea has worked hard to bring the board and its executive management together, even going so far as to nurture the relationship at junior levels. Its New Generation Management Conference, which is made up of younger staff, is encouraged to make presentations at board meetings and other decision-making conferences, with the aim of nurturing participation in strategic planning and oversight.

Establishing Good Relations with the Board

Separate powers—Mixing the role of CEO and chairman produces lower shareholder returns

Clear the air—Raise difficult issues during board meetings to ensure tensions don't fester and hamper cooperation.

Embrace diversity—Boards are still often a middle-aged, white, privately-educated male preserve. "If you haven't got women on the board, then you haven't got a proper mix of [...] talent", says co-founder of ReputationInc PR firm, **Nigel Whittaker**.

Seek expertise—When it comes to complex financial issues, such as banking oversight, you must have the relevant heavyweight knowledge available on the board.

Mingle more—Make sure board members and management have a framework to meet and talk.

Shine a light—Create a more transparent compensation mechanism to make it easier to judge performance against pay.

Know your networks—Boards have both formal and informal structures, which affect how they work.

Corporate Cooperators

Success often follows harmonious relations between CEO and board:

Stephen Temares, BED, BATH & BEYOND (Retail: US)—*Took over from founders* **Warren Eisenberg** *and* **Leonard Feinstein** *in 2003. The board's confidence in the former real estate lawyer was repaid by solid earnings growth and a near doubling of stores.*
—

Richard Anderson, DELTA AIR LINES, INC. (Aviation: US)—*The Delta board successfully fast-tracked a merger with rival Northwest in 2008 by bringing in former Northwest airlines CEO Anderson the year before.*
—

Richard Adkerson, FREEPORT MCMORAN COPPER & GOLD, INC. (Mining: US) — *Learned how to pursue negotiations, such as his $26-billion acquisition of larger rival Phelps Dodge, from personal friend and Freeport chairman James Moffett.*
—

Tim Breedon, LEGAL AND GENERAL GROUP (Insurance: UK)—*Continuity was key to Breedon's unanimous appointment by the board in 2006. He rewarded shareholders by returning £1 billion in two years.*
—

Marc Bolland, MORRISONS (Retail: UK)—*The unlikely but effective team of famously cantankerous founder* **Ken Morrison** *and Dutch Heineken executive Bolland has seen profits rise at the supermarket chain.*
—

John Wren, OMNICOM GROUP (Advertising: US)—*Hand-picked protégé of chairman Bruce Crawford has driven global net earnings from $222,415 to $1.3 billion in his decade at the helm by closely following his mentor's philosophy of group autonomy.*
—

John Robinson, SMITH & NEPHEW (Medical: UK)—*Robinson took over from his former boss* **Eric Kinder** *in 1991, with Kinder staying on as chairman. Over the next seven years the pair worked closely together to continue the work Kinder had begun, transforming S&N into a focused and highly specialized tissue repair company.*
—

Robert Dutkowsky, TECH DATA (Information Technology: US)—*Tech Data split the roles of chairman and CEO for the first time when Dutkowsky took over in 2006, a clinching factor that influenced his decision to accept the post.*
—

Hisakazu Imaki President & CEO (2003–08), Mazda Motor Corp.

BIOGRAPHY
Born in 1942. Imaki graduated with BSc in mechanical engineering from the Himeji Institute of Technology in Japan in 1965.

BEST DECISION
Adopting a mixed production line at Mazda which allowed several different models to be built on one production line.

LESSON IN BUSINESS
Tune into the times —Imaki has concentrated on producing fuel-efficient cars in an age of high petroleum prices.

"MR. MANUFACTURER" by nickname, Imaki has spent the majority of his 40-year career with Mazda Motor Corporation in production technology. He is largely responsible for Mazda's current efficient methods of production.

Having joined Mazda (then Toyo Kogyo Co.) in 1965, Imaki has since held a number of executive positions. He became a director and general manager of the Hiroshima plant in 1996, and CEO in 2003. He was named 2006 Person of the Year in Japan by the Automotive Researchers & Journalists Conference of Japan (RJC). In 2008, despite the global slowdown in car manufacturing, production at Mazda's domestic plants was running at full capacity and the auto press warmly embraced the company's "new generation," fuel-efficient compact and mid-sized models. With global sales well on course, Imaki announced that he saw no need to reduce sales targets. In line with his intent to see fuel use drop by 30 percent across the Mazda range by 2015, Imaki also unveiled plans for a hydrogen-based hybrid model. In late 2008, however, in the wake of Ford's decision to sell part of its stake in Mazda, Imaki relinquished his role as president and CEO, becoming chairman.

Paul G. Allen Co-founder, Microsoft Corp.

BIOGRAPHY
Born in Seattle, Washington, in 1953. He began attending Washington State University, but left after two years to work for Honeywell.

BEST DECISION
Leading the deal for Microsoft to buy the QDOS operating system. This formed the basis for the company's contract with IBM.

LESSON IN BUSINESS
Take bold steps—with his friend Bill Gates, Allen set up a business from scratch, made a brave acquisition, and bagged the IBM elephant.

IN 1975, COMPUTER programmer and entrepreneur Allen asked friend Bill Gates to co-found a software company—Micro-Soft as it was first known. It took off, and Allen is considered one of the most influential people on the planet.

Allen's persistence in encouraging schoolmate Bill Gates to leave Harvard and join him in setting up Micro-Soft paid off handsomely for both of them. The company was to become one of the world's biggest businesses. Allen was central to the company's development in its early years, when it gained a crucial contract to supply an operating system to IBM. This contract formed the basis for Microsoft's phenomenal growth. Illness took Allen away from the business in 1983. He never fully returned, resigning from the board in 2000, but remaining a valued adviser. In addition to his ongoing influence at Microsoft, Allen is a committed philanthropist, his significant contributions being notably related to health, sport, science, and technology.

Allen's interests include his investment in SpaceShipOne, which made the first private manned space flight. He also established the Allen Institute for Brain Science, a ground-breaking center for neuroscientific research.

"A snake that does not shed its old skin is doomed."
Hisakazu Imaki

Terunobu Maeda President & CEO, Mizuho Financial Group

BIOGRAPHY
Born in Kumamoto, Japan, in 1945. Maeda grew up in Nakatsu, Oita. He graduated from the University of Tokyo with a degree in law in 1967.

BEST DECISION
Taking a 50 percent pay cut by way of a public apology for his role in Mizuho's IT disaster, when the system crashed on the first day of the operational integration of the new megabank.

LESSON IN BUSINESS
Face your problems head on—throughout a long career, Maeda has always persevered when times have been tough.

A CAREER BANKER with 40 years experience in the industry, Maeda turned around first Fuji Bank and then Mizuho, after both had posted record losses. He is well-placed to steer the megabank through the global financial crisis.

Maeda joined Fuji Bank in 1968, rising up the corporate ladder to become vice-president in 1999, when the bank had just recorded a loss of ¥2.38 trillion. By reducing bad assets and making gains on investments in the Japanese stock market, Maeda returned Fuji to profitability. In 2000, he oversaw the merger of Fuji Bank with Dai-Ichi Kangyo Bank and the Industrial Bank of Japan to form Mizuho Financial Group. By 2002, poor management had led to huge losses and Maeda took over as CEO. To combat Mizuho's falling share price, Maeda reduced top executives' pay, cut 21 percent of the workforce, closed branches worldwide, and sold shares to raise capital. He seemed to have turned things around by 2006, when Mizuho became the first Japanese lender listed on the New York stock exchange since 1989. When Mizuho's exposure to the US sub-prime mortgage market led to significant losses, Maeda worked to stabilize the bank by shoring up its capital base.

Mark G. Parker President & CEO, Nike, Inc.

BIOGRAPHY
Born in Poughkeepsie, New York, in 1956. Parker studied at Penn State University where he also excelled as a runner, adapting his running shoes and socks to make them more comfortable.

BEST DECISION
Pitching to outfit the Chinese Olympic teams for the 2008 Beijing Olympics, resulting in a significant marketing coup.

LESSON IN BUSINESS
Build on your knowledge—Parker's personal experience as a runner and shoe designer has given him an invaluable edge in meeting customer requirements.

FROM DESIGNER TO CEO, Parker has a unique insight into, and experience of, the sportswear market. He has reorganized Nike's divisional spread, encouraging constant innovation, high-profile marketing, and significant international expansion.

Parker joined Nike, the world's largest footwear manufacturer, as a designer in 1979, and rose to CEO in 2006. He reorganized the company, moving away from product lines to dedicated sports divisions, including "sports culture" for people who prefer to dress for, rather than "do", sports. The divisional spread differentiates Nike from its competitors, as does its model for international growth. In China, where the company has opened 3,000 stores, Nike works with people on the ground to respond to local preferences, and Nike products were worn by 22 of the 28 Chinese Olympic teams at the Beijing Olympics. To meet global concerns about waste, in late 2008, Parker announced the launch of a series of "Nike Considered" products, made from recyclable constituents, and more efficiently with less material. The overall goal is to reduce the company's carbon footprint while increasing profit margins. Parker has set targets to ensure all its products eventually meet "Considered" standards.

"[Maeda] is the best of the CEOs of the three megabanks." Japanese analyst

Michio Kariya President & CEO, Nikon Corp.

BIOGRAPHY
No information available.

BEST DECISION
Delaying the release of the D3 digital SLR until all the bugs were ironed out, which won widespread respect and, crucially, the confidence of professional users.

LESSON IN BUSINESS
Quality is key—Kariya's unswerving emphasis on photographic excellence has ensured 90-year-old Nikon's premium brand reputation in a competitive market.

A NIKON MAN through and through, Kariya has worked in the optics and imaging company since 1967. He knows Nikon's products and market like no other, an invaluable advantage in a global company with a reputation for quality.

Kariya's 40-year career at Nikon culminated in his appointment as CEO in 2007, which reflected his major contribution to Nikon's image as a premium-brand producer of digital cameras and precision lenses. Kariya recognised that Nikon's professional customers demand perfection and, in delaying the launch of the D3 digital SLR until November 2007, illustrated that the company is determined to offer optimum quality rather than rush to market. Nikon's principal competitor is Canon and, in the battle for market share, Kariya announced his intention to overtake the company's rival and achieve 40 percent of worldwide digital-SLR sales. He is also focusing Nikon's future development on growing the company's photolithography division and its sought-after Nikon ArF immersion scanner, which is used in the manufacture of integrated circuits for computer processors and memory chips. Kariya has expanded production facilities in two locations to meet demand for its key product.

Heliane Canepa CEO (2001–07), Nobel Biocare

BIOGRAPHY
Born in 1948 in Austria. Canepa studied at the business school in Dornbirn, Austria, as well as West London College, and Sorbonne University, Paris. She later completed the Foreign Executive Development Program at Princeton University, New Jersey.

BEST DECISION
Getting face-to-face feedback from clients. Her motto was: "We provide, but they decide."

LESSON IN BUSINESS
Be passionate and have plenty of stamina—Canepa sets a personal goal and stays focused until it is achieved.

ONE OF THE MOST powerful executives in the medical industry, Canepa turned Nobel Biocare into the world's foremost manufacturer of dental implants. She has twice been named Entrepreneur of the Year by the Swiss financial press.

Canepa's career is a prime example of the rewards of genuine commitment and sheer hard work. Her rise to power began at the age of 31 with a lowly "Girl Friday" position at medical technology company Schneider, a small, seven-person set-up. Fast-forward 18 years and Canepa had risen to CEO of a corporation worth CHF 3 billion. Canepa left Schneider for the Nobel Biocare Group in 2001 after the company was taken over by Boston Scientific, though not before finding new jobs for every one of Schneider's 550 employees at the Swiss plant in Bülach, earning her the nickname of the Madonna of Bülach. During her time at Biocare, Canepa transformed the company into the world's leading maker of dental implants, and doubled turnover, increasing operating margin by more than 20 percent and market capitalization six-fold. Ranked sixth in the *Financial Times*' Top 25 European Women in Business in 2005, Canepa left Biocare in 2007 after six very successful years at the helm.

"If you always stay focused then you go to the top —it's as simple as that." Heliane Canepa

Ray R. Irani Chairman, President & CEO, Occidental Petroleum

BIOGRAPHY
Born in Lebanon in 1935. Irani studied at the American University of Beirut and the University of Southern California.

BEST DECISION
Correctly predicting that domestic oil would deliver big profits for Occidental in the early 2000s, at a time when rivals were focusing overseas.

LESSON IN BUSINESS
Be your own person—Irani's pragmatic hierarchical management style contrasted sharply with the impulsive style of his predecessor, but it was exactly what Occidental needed.

SURVIVING AS PRESIDENT where many had fallen before him, Irani succeeded charismatic CEO Armand Hammer at Occidental Petroleum, and engineered a steady, decade-long turnaround in the company's fortunes.

Following spells with Monsanto, Shamrock, and chemicals company Olin, where he became president and COO, Irani joined Occidental Petroleum (Oxy) in 1983, impressing CEO Armand Hammer by turning around the struggling chemicals division. Irani was made a director and promoted to president in 1984 and, against outsider expectations, succeeded Hammer as CEO after his death in 1990. Irani began stabilizing and streamlining Oxy through divestments, downsizing, and reduced dividends. He also gently steered it into new fields, such as petrochemicals, through carefully selected acquisitions. His changes took many years to come to fruition, with the company and its stock languishing for much of the 1990s. However, by 2003 Irani was being hailed as a gifted strategist. The rewards he has reaped for his success have raised eyebrows: in 2006, for example, rising oil prices and the stellar performance of Oxy stock saw him take home a total of $460 million.

Jesús F. Reyes Heroles CEO, PEMEX (Petróleos Mexicanos)

BIOGRAPHY
Born in Mexico City in 1952, the son of a prestigious lawyer and politician. Heroles gained a bachelor's from the Autonomous Technical Institute of Mexico and a PhD from the Massachusetts Institute of Technology.

BEST DECISION
Pushing to ease PEMEX's rigid constitution, which gave the company freedom to operate.

LESSON IN BUSINESS
Use political nous—Heroles's high profile and contacts mean he is well placed to exert pressure on government.

A FORMER AMBASSADOR to the US with a formidable track record in both public and private sectors, Heroles became CEO of PEMEX in 2006. He faced the challenge of turning around the cash-strapped, state-owned enterprise.

Heroles has had diverse experience across both government and industry. He served at the Mexican treasury, foreign office, and as secretary of energy under president Zedillo, presiding over energy companies PEMEX, CFE and LyFC. He was also CEO of BANOBRAS bank, co-founded GEA (Grupo de Economistas y Asociados), Mexico's first independent political and economic analysis consultancy, and was Mexico's ambassador to the US from 1997 to 2000. In December 2006, he was nominated CEO of PEMEX, the world's sixth largest oil producer, and Latin America's largest company. Heroles has reduced the constraints of PEMEX's state ownership, which had starved the company of the resources needed to identify and tap new oilfields to offset collapsing reserves. In 2008, his reforms were supported by president Felipe Calderón, and measures were introduced to allow PERMEX to keep more of its revenue, and to hire outside service contractors.

> "We have to make clear that for PEMEX, this reform is a matter of survival." Jesús F. Reyes Heroles

José Sergio Gabrielli de Azevedo President & CEO, Petrobrás

BIOGRAPHY
Born in Salvador, Brazil, in 1949. Gabrielli studied economics, took a doctorate at Boston University, and held a series of academic posts before joining Petrobrás in 2003.

BEST DECISION
Increasing transparency and lengthening Petrobrás's debt profile, which enhanced its reputation.

LESSON IN BUSINESS
Experience isn't everything—until he became Petrobrás's CFO, Gabrielli was an academic. In 12 months, he boosted both profits and Petrobrás's reputation.

REFLECTIVE AND ANALYTICAL, Gabrielli was an unlikely candidate to take the helm at South America's largest oil company. Yet, in his first year as CEO, Petrobrás announced record profits of $11.2 billion.

Until he was transferred from the Federal University of Bahia in Brazil to be CFO of Petrobrás, Gabrielli had focused on regional development and labor issues, and had led a largely academic life. But, in 2003, his world changed completely when he was appointed Petrobrás's CFO. Gabrielli set to work cleaning up corporate governance and debt schedules to raise the company's international reputation. Today Petrobrás is listed by *Transparency International* as one of the world's most transparent companies. Made president and CEO in 2005, Gabrielli prioritized exploration and production in Latin America, rather than foreign acquisitions, and his strategy struck black gold. In 2007 Petrobrás announced what is believed to be the world's largest oil discovery in more than 30 years—the Tupi field, located off the coast of Brazil. This is expected to yield up to 8 billion barrels of oil, and Gabrielli is bringing home engineers from abroad to exploit its vast potential.

William H. Swanson Chairman & CEO, Raytheon Company

BIOGRAPHY
Born in 1949. Swanson gained a degree in industrial engineering from California Polytechnic State University.

BEST DECISION
Pushing for the acquisition of the defence operations of Texas Instruments and Hughes, which beefed up Raytheon's Electronic Systems arm ready for the new hi-tech war on terror.

LESSON IN BUSINESS
Ethics matter—Swanson's principled drive for employee diversity is also a hard-nosed recognition of the need to adjust to demographic change.

A RAYTHEON LIFER, Swanson has been widely credited with enabling the defense-focused electronics group to take full advantage of the hi-tech boom in military spending that followed the events of 9/11.

Swanson joined Raytheon in 1972 and became its CEO in 2003. Leadership and ethics lie at the core of his approach to management. One Raytheon executive has described him as "the most honorable leader I have ever worked for". This helps explain why the company has received diversity awards from organizations including the Human Rights Campaign. However, Swanson is also recognized as a tough leader in a tough industry. This quality allowed him, while under fire from employees and US Congress, to manage the difficult absorption of Texas Instruments and Hughes acquisitions, and to gain the respect of military leaders. The only cloud in his career has been an accusation of plagiarism, which he denied, over a book of management homilies. While this has damaged the reputation of a man who has compared unethical behavior with unpatriotic behavior, it perhaps chimes with his view that if someone doesn't make any mistakes, they are not working hard enough.

"Business ethics isn't something you can just put on like a raincoat when the weather gets a bit stormy." William H. Swanson

Risa Lavizzo-Mourey CEO, Robert Wood Johnson Foundation

BIOGRAPHY
Born in Seattle, Washington, in 1954. She received a medical degree from Harvard Medical School and an MBA in health-care administration from Wharton, University of Pennsylvania.

BEST DECISION
Pledging $500 million over five years from 2007 to combat childhood obesity, rightly identifying it as an urgent crisis.

LESSON IN BUSINESS
Know your field—few areas are as difficult to navigate as health care, and Lavizzo-Mourey has inside knowledge of its components.

THE FIRST WOMAN to head the Robert Wood Johnson Foundation, the largest philanthropic health-care foundation in the US, Lavizzo-Mourey has brought a rare mix of medical, administrative, and business expertise to the position.

Lavizzo-Mourey was recruited to work on health in the US administration of Bush Sr. in 1992. She remained in her position under Clinton, serving on the Task Force on Health Care Reform, the attempt to create a national US health-care system. When that plan was rejected in 1994, Lavizzo-Mourey returned to the University of Pennsylvania, aware that health care can be an intensely political issue. She was on the Institute of Medicine committee that produced a report on health care for ethnic minorities in the US, which found that they tend to receive lower-quality care than white people, even when insurance status, income, and age are comparable. In 2001, Lavizzo-Mourey began working for the Robert Wood Johnson Foundation, and 18 months later was appointed president and CEO. She has focused on the needs of elderly patients, increased programs on obesity, and introduced measures to eliminate unequal treatment in health care due to ethnicity.

Josh Silverman CEO, Skype

BIOGRAPHY
Born in the USA in 1969, Silverman grew up in Michigan. He studied public policy at Brown University, and later received an MBA from Stanford Graduate School of Business.

BEST DECISION
Making the move from politics to IT. Silverman felt he could make more impact within the internet industry.

LESSON IN BUSINESS
Listen and learn but be prepared to take risks—throughout his career Silverman has made instinctive decisions that have changed his path in life.

ONE OF THE RISING STARS of the media industry, Silverman spent several years running consumer internet companies before landing the role as CEO of Skype, the Voice over Internet Protocol (VoIP) company, in 2008.

After two years working as a welfare policy writer for US Senator Bill Bradley, Silverman switched to IT, holding management positions at ADAC Labs and Booz Allen Hamilton before co-founding website Evite. He joined eBay in 2003 and led the launch of its highly successful European Classified business. He then became CEO at price-comparison website shopping.com, before taking the CEO's seat at Skype in early 2008. To get a true feel for the company, Silverman spent his first three months in Tallinn, Estonia, where Skype was founded and had its software development unit. He later focused on dealing with the fallout from eBay's $2.5 billion purchase of Skype in 2005, which was later deemed a gross overpayment. With rivals such as Rebtel snapping at Skype's heels, Silverman has kept the company in profit and ahead of the game by moving into cell phones, producing Skype-enabled phones for mobile provider 3, and Skype software for LG, Motorola, Nokia, Samsung, and Sony Ericsson.

"Foundations need collaborators, strategic thinkers, problem solvers, and innovative leaders." Risa Lavizzo-Mourey

Richard L. George President & CEO, Suncor Energy

BIOGRAPHY
Born in Brush, Colorado, in 1950. George joined Suncor, the Canadian energy supplier, in 1981, serving the company in Britain before returning to Canada to become CEO.

BEST DECISION
Taking time over his 1993 strategy review to expand the company while keeping the costs low.

LESSON IN BUSINESS
Plan for expansion—it won't happen by accident. George axed jobs and costs so that he could invest in boosting the company's oil production.

DYNAMIC AND TOUGH, when he took over as CEO in 1991, George could see that energy supplier Suncor lacked direction. He pared down costs and drew executives into a review to identify low-cost, high-growth strategies.

Arriving back in Canada from a stint in the UK as managing director of Sun Oil Britain Ltd, the new Suncor CEO took quick action. George fired 500 workers and narrowed down the corporate focus to increasing production from the company's oil sands fields in northern Alberta and from its conventional oil business in western Canada. He also sharpened up its Ontario refining business. In 1993, after Suncor's parent company sold its 55-percent stake, George launched a three-year restructuring process, investing heavily in production and distribution. Costs were slashed, oil production increased, and profits rose. A swap deal with Ultramar gave Suncor 88 gas stations in Ontario and complete control of a distribution terminal. George signed a $236-million deal to operate a pipeline to carry crude oil from Fort McMurray, and also poured $1.6 billion into increasing production there. Within ten years, production from the oil sands had risen ten-fold.

Marijn Dekkers President & CEO, Thermo Fisher Scientific, Inc.

BIOGRAPHY
Born in Tilburg, Netherlands, in 1957. Dekkers received a BS in chemistry from the University of Nijmegen and an MS and PhD in chemical engineering from the University of Eindhoven.

BEST DECISION
Unifying the disparate companies of Thermo Electron to prepare it for expansion.

LESSON IN BUSINESS
Do what you enjoy—throughout his career, Dekkers has followed his interests, pursuing the sciences at school and university, working in research, and then moving into management.

BIOTECHNOLOGY changes rapidly, yet Dekkers has guided Thermo Fisher Scientific to exploit new opportunities, launching cutting-edge medical technology and applications from lab equipment to new diagnostic methods.

Dekkers worked in research and development and management for General Electric, and later Honeywell, before becoming president and COO of the biotechnology company Thermo Electron in 2000. He was made CEO in 2002. Until Dekkers took charge, shedding some holdings and unifying the rest as a single company, investors had difficulty understanding the loose, inefficient network of companies. In 2006, Thermo Electron spent $10.6 billion buying Fisher Scientific International, creating Thermo Fisher Scientific, one of the world's largest suppliers of lab equipment, software, chemicals and services for health care, scientific research, safety, and education. Thermo Fisher Scientific earns some $10 billion in annual revenues and has 30,000 employees worldwide. The company increasingly supplies life sciences research in various fields. Dekkers sees Thermo Fisher Scientific as ideally placed to develop reliable, non-invasive diagnostic methods.

"...if you are going to get an organization to really change with you, you have to be able to articulate your objectives clearly." Richard L. George

Carol Meyrowitz President & CEO, The TJX Companies, Inc.

BIOGRAPHY
Born in 1954. For such a prominent business figure, she keeps her background and personal life well under wraps.

BEST DECISION
Expanding areas of the stores where consumers were showing increased interest in low-price options.

LESSON FOR BUSINESS
Making economy stylish—low price doesn't have to mean low quality, and astute marketing can overcome snobbery and open whole new markets.

DESPITE BEING FACED by a crisis the moment she took over as CEO in 2007, Meyrowitz used her understanding of TJX's brands and customers' wishes to steer the company to increased sales and a stronger share price.

After more than 20 years with TJX, Meyrowitz's appointment as CEO came at a difficult time for the company. A major payment card security breach had been revealed, opening up countless possible lawsuits and, equally worryingly, the global economic downturn had just commenced.

Meyrowitz rose to the situation, and with her strong skills in merchandising and inventory management she was quick to position the group to maximize its potential. She placed renewed emphasis on ensuring that the group's brands, TJ Maxx, Marshalls, and HomeGoods, expanded jewelry, shoes, and accessories counters to represent style and quality as well as value, and hired more buyers on the west coast of the US to increase the company's fashionable element. TJX stores soon showed increased sales while other retail chains reported falls as the downturn intensified. Meyrowitz's impact was also felt in the share price, in an otherwise depressed retail sector, producing a 20 percent rise in TJX shares in her first two years.

Philippe P. Dauman President & CEO, Viacom

BIOGRAPHY
Born in New York in 1952. Dauman has a BA from Yale and a Juris doctorate from Columbia University School of Law.

BEST DECISION
Splitting Viacom's online developments from its core programming business.

LESSON IN BUSINESS
Keep things clear—rapid developments such as fast-moving digital technologies in entertainment can easily cloud the sense of what's important. Dauman ensured that such developments were kept separate to maintain clarity.

AN ENCOUNTER WITH Sumner Redstone led high-flying lawyer Dauman to ditch law for a leading role at Viacom entertainment group. A few years later he was out, but he returned in 2006 to guide the company through changing times.

While working as a corporate lawyer in New York, Dauman found himself acting on behalf of Redstone. Dauman so impressed the Viacom chairman that he was given a seat on the board in 1987, before moving full-time to Viacom, becoming the company's general counsel, and ultimately taking a key managerial role. Ejected in 2000 as part of Viacom's acquisition of CBS, he was invited back as CEO in 2006, at a time when the entire entertainment industry faced big challenges.

The speed of developments in digital media presented the industry both with problems and with opportunities, creating great management difficulties. Ratings for some key Viacom products had slipped as managers focused on coping with these changes.

Dauman has been credited with restoring financial and operational discipline to Viacom by setting priorities for his lieutenants, assigning some to work on online efforts, and others on core programming.

"I enjoy competition. I really like to win." Philippe P. Dauman

TAKING TIME OUT

The role of CEO does not necessarily lend itself to living a well-rounded life. However, those who learn to balance a high-powered job with life outside work gain not just an immediate sense of perspective and wellbeing, but also greater and longer-lasting success.

Probably the most noteworthy example of how "raising a family and a business together" can pay off in every area, is **Estée Lauder** (p53). From its beginnings at the kitchen table to the multinational giant we know today, most of Lauder's family worked for the business, and she made her office a "beautiful home from home."

Michael Dell (p50), founder of Dell, Inc. is another CEO who works actively to keep his life in balance. He achieves this not by bringing the family into the business, as Lauder did, but by flexibly working around his family, something that has only really become possible in the last decade with the rise in home-based broadband. Dell gets home by 6.30 pm for dinner and family time, helping with homework and putting the children to bed, before returning to his home office desk for a few more hours. As he puts it: "It's a great time to work, really. It's quiet. And everyone else seems to be working" ●

The Right Balance

On average, today's CEOs are 20 years younger than they were two decades ago, and this means they are more likely to be balancing a young family with a heavy workload. But why should company shareholders care about work/life balance? Because studies have found it reduces staff turnover and increases profitability, creativity, and productivity. **Peter Ellwood**, CEO of Lloyds TSB from 1997 to 2003, knew this. Speaking in 2002, Elwood said: "From the mid-1990s, Lloyds TSB conducted research and feasibility studies. One of the key findings showed that for both men and women, finding the right balance between work and home would be the most critical factor in deciding whether or not to move to a different organization. We introduced our flexible-working scheme in early 1999 [and] this has really given us the edge against our competitors."

Stephen Lennard, CEO of Crown Executive Solutions in Australia, points out that most high-level career failures can be traced to the inability of harried leaders to see things in perspective and make informed judgments. "Burnt-out execs haven't the emotional reserves or the clarity of thought to stay ahead of the challenges," he says. "Bad business

Work/Life Luminaries

These executives acknowledge the importance of spending time away from the office:

Ronald A. Williams, AETNA (Health sector: US)—*Introduced flexible working for company employees.*

—

David Lissy, BRIGHT HORIZONS FAMILY SOLUTIONS (Childcare and consultancy: US)—*Lissy has made Bright Horizons into a world leader in strategic work/life solutions, including employer-sponsored childcare, early education, and work/life consulting services.*

Greg James, CENTRAL RAND GOLD (Metals: South Africa)—*Dedicated to balancing work with fitness. Cycles or runs daily and says it helps him relax and refocus.*

—

Jay Adelson, DIGG.COM (Internet: US)—*Uses technology, such as iChat, to conference with his staff, so he can work from home two-thirds of the time and see more of his family.*

—

Joaquin Galan, GALYPSO INTERNATIONAL (Export-import: US) —*Runs his $13-million export company with his wife, Crystin McCormick-Galan, out of their home in San Antonio, Texas, alongside their two children.*

—

Michael B. McCallister, HUMANA (Health sector: US)—*Humana is defining a new world of health benefits, featuring customer-choice health plans that empower employees to choose and use their health benefits with confidence.*

—

Richard Benison, KPMG (Professional services: Netherlands)—*Has introduced employee programmes like telecommuting from home and flexible working schedules.*

—

decisions and bad personal decisions come from the same myopic place." Spending quality time away from work, whether it is relaxing with one's family or something more active, can help CEOs gain new insights into how they run their businesses. **Laurence Walker**, CEO of global software solutions provider SSP, spent four days trekking, cycling, and rapelling through the vast Namib Desert, competing in the Namibia Desert Insurance Challenge, and says the time he devoted to training for the event has made him a more rounded and confident leader.

"Finding the right balance between work and home [is] the most critical factor in deciding whether or not to move to a different organization."
PETER ELLWOOD

Wheel of Life

Take advice from Frank Chapman (p347), CEO of BG Group, who uses the life-coaching tool "The Wheel of Life" to maintain his work/life balance:

Draw a circle to represent portions of your life—Divide it into the eight sections that make up a balanced life: career, money, health, friends and family, partner/romance, physical environment, fun and recreation, and personal growth.

Shade segments to assess your work/life balance—The center of the wheel is 0 and the outer rim 5. Shade in each segment according to how much time you are currently spending on that area of your life. This gives a graphic representation of how balanced, or otherwise, your life is at this point in time.

5

The Strategists

Shantanu Narayen CEO, Adobe Systems

THE SOFTWARE INDUSTRY was at a crucial stage in its development when Narayen took over as CEO of Adobe at the end of 2007. The emergence of so-called "web 2.0" was in full swing, and the industry's heavy hitters were positioning themselves to maximize their opportunities in this new world of user-generated content, social networks, and "rich internet applications." Focusing on software that blurs the boundaries between web, PC, and phone, Narayen is ensuring a leading role for Adobe in this new web world.

BIOGRAPHY
Born in Hyderabad, India, in 1964. He wanted to be a journalist, but his parents insisted he study electrical engineering at Osmania University in Hyderabad. He moved to the US in 1984 and received a master's degree in computer science from Bowling Green State University, Ohio. He also has a master's degree in business administration from the Haas School of Business, Berkeley, California.

LEADERSHIP STYLE
Low-key and cerebral. Narayen has a deep understanding of his field that can cut through prevailing business wisdom and carry people with him.

KEY STRENGTH
An intimate understanding of the possibilities of technology and a rare ability to see where it will go.

BEST DECISION
Buying Macromedia, which left Adobe ideally placed for the new web environment.

AHEAD OF HIS TIME An engineer at heart, Narayen began working in Silicon Valley in the mid-1980s, with spells at Apple and Silicon Graphics, before using $10 million to found Pictra, a digital-image-sharing company. His initiative turned out to be ahead of its time, and he tried to sell the company to Adobe in the late 1990s. Adobe's then-CEO, Bruce Chizen, decided not to buy, but instead hired Narayen as a senior vice president in product research. Narayen's technological insight and strategic vision soon made him a vital part of the leadership team.

PREPARING FOR THE NEW WORLD While officially still in charge of only engineering, Narayen was involved in key strategic initiatives. In 2002, concerned about the strength of business sales groups at the company's main competitors, he suggested that Adobe commission more new products. The management agreed, and software sales rose by 42 percent the following year, underlining Narayen's importance as a behind-the-scenes influence. Appointed president and chief operating officer at the end of 2005, he initiated the biggest acquisition in Adobe's history, when it paid $3.4 billion for Macromedia, bringing the ubiquitous Flash software into its product portfolio, expanding the company's software platform, and strengthening its presence in key markets.

As CEO, Narayen has overseen the launch of Adobe's "next big thing," AIR (Adobe Integrated Runtime), a platform for running web-based applications on a desktop PC, an essential part of his planned expansion into online services and mobile computing.

LESSONS IN BUSINESS: COMING UP WITH THE PRODUCTS

No matter how popular a product has been in the past, a business should not rely on this success to continue into the future. There will always be someone coming up with new products to compete with your current offerings. A business must continue to innovate if it is to thrive in the long term.
→ Ask your customers about products. This will help to fine-tune existing products and to develop new ones.
→ Instruct innovation teams to be creative. Don't cramp their style with false assumptions of what is possible.
→ Talk to your team about what will make customers stop buying your products.

"Being transparent about our plans enables us to get better feedback." Shantanu Narayen

Klaus Kleinfeld CEO (2005–07), Siemens AG

CREDITED WITH turning Siemens into "a proper company," Kleinfeld took over as CEO in 2005. Kleinfeld disposed of under-performing subsidiaries and told workers to accept longer hours for less pay or lose their jobs. His reforms were opposed by the trade unions and some directors, but their impact was dramatic: sales rose by 16 percent and profits leapt 35 percent to just under $4 billion, while shares soared to a 40-percent increase in just over two years. Leaving Siemens in 2007, he now heads up aluminum giant Alcoa.

BIOGRAPHY
Born in Bremen, Germany, in 1957. Kleinfeld received a PhD in strategic management from the University of Würzburg.

LEADERSHIP STYLE
Tough, independent, and resilient. Kleinfeld took on corporate Germany's consensus-minded establishment to boost profits at Siemens, but he left when his contract was not renewed due to allegations, unrelated to him, of corruption amongst Siemens' top management.

KEY STRENGTH
He has a flair for leadership itself, often saying what needs to be said, and doing what is necessary to improve the company rather than being diplomatic.

BEST DECISION
The launch of Siemens One during his time as the company's chief in the United States. It turned Siemens' vast range of services and subsidiaries into a one-stop shop where customers could share the company's economies of scale. It was later rolled out in 40 countries.

BUILDING A ONE-STOP SHOP Kleinfeld began his career as a management consultant before joining Siemens in 1987, but it was his posting to the US in 2001 as COO that gave him his opportunity to shine. He noticed that the different fiefdoms within the Siemens empire did not work well together and customers were faced with conflicting advice and separate bills from different Siemens divisions. Kleinfeld brought them together on a project-wide basis to make sure customers worked with a single Siemens interface.

A CAN-DO BOSS In the US, Kleinfeld met a new corporate culture, and liked the "can-do" approach that favored customers and shareholders. He took these ideas back to Germany with him when he was made CEO in 2005. They were popular with shareholders, who saw profits and share value rise, but they were resisted by the unions and traditionalists in Germany's corporate power elite. When he sold off the company's under-performing cell telephone handset subsidiary to a Taiwanese firm, he faced widespread criticism.

Kleinfeld later announced a tie-up with Nokia to create the world's second largest business telecommunications equipment manufacturer. The deal revealed a key aspect of Kleinfeld's approach: if you are not the market leader or its closest rival, it is not worth your company being in that business. Scale is everything. Unfortunately, corruption allegations, not related to him, caused a delay in his contract being renewed and he resigned in protest in 2007. In May 2008, he was appointed CEO of the American aluminum company, Alcoa.

LESSONS IN BUSINESS: MAKING GLOBALIZATION WORK

Kleinfeld dragged Germany into globalization asking, "Who is the company for, and how can it compete?" His answer was that to survive, Western workers must be as productive as those in the developing world.
→ Avoid a situation where successful divisions subsidize failure in others—that is not a long-term strategy.
→ Understand that in the new globalized world, there's nowhere to hide poor performance. The competition will find your weaknesses.
→ Be bold and implement lower terms and conditions for people in areas where the competition is global.

"We can only stay a technology leader if we continue to invest in innovation, which we will."
Klaus Kleinfeld

Kenneth Chenault Chairman & CEO, American Express

ONE OF THE FEW African-American CEOs of a *Fortune* 500 company, Chenault is an influential player on Wall Street. Trained as a lawyer, he joined American Express as its director of strategic planning in 1981 and held a number of senior posts before being named CEO and chairman 20 years later. His rise to the top position has been underpinned by a clear vision of how to make the $20-billion charge card company profitable. He has brought focus and direction to the company, and kept a clear sight of what customers want.

BIOGRAPHY
Born in 1951 in Long Island, New York. He graduated from Bowdoin College, Maine, *magna cum laude* with a degree in history in 1973. He received a juris doctorate from Harvard Law School in 1976.

LEADERSHIP STYLE
Open-minded, charismatic, and pragmatic. He is a popular and inclusive decision-maker, sourcing new ideas by leaving his door open and encouraging subordinates to speak their mind.

KEY STRENGTH
Possessing a fierce drive combined with concern for people and employees.

BEST DECISION
Refocusing American Express as a travel and credit card business, and concentrating on the corporate business market.

HEADING UP MERCHANDISING After Harvard, Chenault worked briefly as an associate for the law firm Rogers & Rogers and as a consultant for Bain & Company, a Boston-based consulting firm, before moving to American Express. While it was expected that he would throw himself into the company's charge card business, he also volunteered to head its merchandising operations, which at the time was a neglected department in danger of closure. The results were dramatic and in two years he grew the business from $150 million to $500 million in sales.

ADOPTING A FLEXIBLE APPROACH When Chenault took charge as CEO, AmEx was at a low ebb in its fortunes. The company had virtually invented the charge card business, but soon other cards offered more to customers,

and its high fees meant fewer merchants were willing to accept it. Chenault recognized that the relationship between a credit card customer and where they spent their money was key. He brokered a rewards card deal between American Express and Delta Air Lines.

After 9/11, Chenault again demonstrated his ability to adapt to a changing situation. He reduced company staff worldwide by 16 percent, and under his leadership AmEx adopted an approach that was more flexible to opportunities, so that by the end of 2002 the company was growing again.

With the spin-off of American Express Financial Advisors in 2005, after a series of mis-selling claims, Chenault returned to the core American Express business and broke the last link to an era when AmEx tried to be a "financial supermarket."

LESSONS IN BUSINESS: SHOWING RESPECT

Chenault, who would like to be remembered as the best CEO in the financial business, reminds his employees every day of the importance of showing respect to colleagues, business partners, and even adversaries.
➔ Even in a competitive environment treat people how you yourself would like to be treated. Create a culture of openness.
➔ Avoid internal politics, especially plotting against a colleague behind their back.
➔ Be open and honest with customers: that is the way to avoid giving them unpleasant surprises.

"Ken Chenault is living proof that sometimes nice guys finish first." Adam Aron, CEO, Vail Resorts

Patricia Woertz CEO, Archer Daniels Midland Company

PERSONIFYING THE WAY women are now starting to smash through corporate America's "glass ceiling", Woertz was the first outsider to head Archer Daniels Midland (ADM), the US food, feed, and fuel conglomerate run by the Andreas family since 1970. A consistent achiever on her steady climb up the corporate ladder, she was appointed CEO of ADM in 2006. She inherited a company in good shape, and has brought her skills to bear keeping it that way in a climate of rising commodity prices and a heated energy debate.

BIOGRAPHY
Born in Pittsburgh, Pennsylvania, in 1953. Woertz graduated from Penn State University in 1974 with a degree in accounting, and completed an executive development program at Columbia University in 1994.

LEADERSHIP STYLE
Dynamic, hands-on, consensual. Woertz is very people oriented and, according to racing legend and close friend Mario Andretti, she has an uncanny ability to make whomever she is talking to feel like the most interesting person in the room.

KEY STRENGTH
Applying her accounting experience to bring about cost reductions on a grand scale.

BEST DECISION
Expanding ADM's interest in biofuels while making sure that new plants remain cost effective.

RISING THROUGH THE RANKS Woertz began her career as an accountant with Ernst & Young, but was attracted to the opportunities offered by the energy sector, joining Gulf Oil in 1977. Gaining experience in marketing, planning, and finance, she rose to become president of Chevron Corp. after the merger between Standard Oil and Gulf Oil. After nearly 30 years in the oil industry Woertz was looking for a new challenge. Actively pursuing CEO status, she had no qualms about joining a company in which she would stand out not only as a woman, but also as an outsider.

BUILDING UP TRUST Woertz recognized that one of her first tasks as CEO was to meet as many employees as possible, building up their trust and seeing where improvements could be made. She led the first "all-colleague global Town Hall" in 2006, at which she outlined the company's strategic focus. In 2007 she established the ADM Global Safety Week. Both are now annual events.

Woertz had joined a thriving billion-dollar company, one that historically specialized in food and feed processing but was now diversifying into new areas, including bio-ethanol. She has been keen to grow the biofuel side of the business, at the same time ensuring that new plants are cost competitive and that other aspects of the business remain healthy, given the potentially fluctuating margins of ethanol. She has also taken steps to strengthen ADM's political lobbying position. Responding to the political, environmental, and nutritional issues that face the industry, Woertz is proving she shares the company motto, "Resourceful by Nature".

LESSONS IN BUSINESS: BEING TRUE TO YOURSELF

Don't let convention or other people's stereotyping determine the direction of your career. Woertz has always let her business credentials speak for themselves as she pursued a long-held ambition to become a captain of industry. As she says, "I've always been gender-blind in my career."
→ Be judged by your actions and achievements: do not ask for preference because of gender.
→ Believe that in the current business environment any gender or ethnicity can make it to the top.
→ Be "female" in your people orientation skills and "male" in your competitiveness—whatever your gender.

"I'm outside the company, outside the industry, outside the family, outside the gender expectations."
Patricia Woertz

Warren Buffett Founder, Chairman & CEO, Berkshire Hathaway

NICKNAMED "The Sage of Omaha" for his uncanny ability to predict stock performance, Buffett is the world's most consistently successful professional investor and possibly the greatest market capitalist of all time. By consistently adhering to his common sense investment philosophy, Berkshire Hathaway has outperformed the market for an unprecedented 35 of the last 41 years, with an annual growth rate of 21.4 percent—twice that of the Standard & Poor's 500 index over the same period.

BIOGRAPHY
Born in 1930 in Omaha, Nebraska. Rejected by Harvard Business School, he was a millionaire by 35 and the richest man in the world by 2008 (*Forbes* magazine).

LEADERSHIP STYLE
Unassuming. Despite unshakeable faith in his own ability to get rich, Buffett rejects both the trappings of wealth and the suggestion that he is party to any secret formula. His advice to investors and employees alike is, "There are only two rules. Number one, never lose money. Number two, never forget number one."

KEY STRENGTH
A walking value-for-money calculator, he has an unmatched 50-year record of spotting under-priced stocks with long-term growth potential.

BEST DECISION
Successfully predicting that the dotcom bubble would burst and refusing to invest.

SIMPLE TENETS Buffett's father was a stockbroker who lost everything in the Depression. Despite this unpromising start, Buffett Jr. had an unwavering sense of his own destiny. He told his first wife, Susan, that if she married him she was guaranteed a life of unbelievable wealth. A follower of Value Investing, Buffett's approach essentially involves assessing the underlying value of a business and deciding whether that is reflected accurately in the share price. It's a cautious approach that avoids faddy or high-tech investments—Buffett described the dotcom boom in the 1990s as a "mass hallucination"—in favor of big, well-run companies serving basic needs that make money in bad times as well as good. Typical holdings include large stakes in firms such as Coca-Cola, Gillette, and American Express. His straightforward

manner and fondness for aphorisms such as, "risk comes from not knowing what you are doing" and, "never ask the barber if you need a haircut," have helped him achieve a degree of celebrity rare in financial circles. Private investors flock to Berkshire Hathaway's AGMs, which regularly attract over 20,000 participant eager to learn how he does it.

SIMPLE TASTES Buffett believes that money should be put to work. He supports higher taxes for the super rich and he still lives in the house that he bought for $31,500 in 1957. Equally scornful of inherited wealth, he wants his three children to earn their own keep and intends to leave them only $10,000 each. In 2006 he began to give his fortune away, with $30 billion to the Bill and Melinda Gates foundation, the biggest donation in history.

LESSONS IN BUSINESS: LOOKING AT THE LONG TERM

Buffett is living proof that in the long run, the slow and steady tortoise will always outrun the erratic, mercurial hare. "I don't try to jump over seven foot poles. I look for one foot poles I can step over," he says.
➔ Invest now for the future. Business is a long-term activity and planning your strategy is as important as seizing opportunities.
➔ Make sure you understand the business model of your customers and suppliers as well as your own.
➔ Look for opportunities that others are ignoring—that's the way to find a bargain.

"I was wired at birth to accumulate capital." Warren Buffett

Laurence D. Fink Chairman & CEO, BlackRock, Inc.

PIONEERING the mortgage-backed securities market in the US, Fink joined First Boston in 1976. He became a partner at private equity firm Blackstone Group in 1988, but left with a group of colleagues in 1992 to found BlackRock, an investment management firm. Through astute acquisitions and a disciplined approach to risk management, he has grown the company on a foundation that has proved solid, even in stormy conditions. Fink's success led to the company being bought by PNC Financial Services in 1995, who took it public in 1999.

BIOGRAPHY
Born in 1952, the son of a California shoe salesman. Fink graduated with a degree in political science from the University of California, Los Angeles. He gained his MBA with a specialism in real estate at the UCLA Graduate School of Management in 1976.

LEADERSHIP STYLE
His easy, soft-spoken style disguises an intellectual rigor. In an interview with *Fortune* magazine in March 2006, he described the necessary qualities for all types of asset management as consistency, focus on performance, and rigorous oversight.

KEY STRENGTH
Risk aversion. Once an almost derogatory term in his line of business, it has proved to be a golden quality in stormy economic times.

BEST DECISION
Merging with Merrill Lynch Investment Managers in 2006, which doubled the asset-management portfolio.

TIPPED FOR THE TOP "Larry" Fink's leadership qualities had him singled out for advancement early on. At First Boston, he quickly became one of the first traders in mortgage-backed securities on Wall Street, making his mark within the company, where he quickly moved up the ladder, and outside it too. In 1989, newly arrived at Blackstone Group, he was featured in *The Wall Street Journal Centennial Edition* as one of 28 businessmen under 45 likely to be the business leaders of tomorrow.

LOYAL COMPANY MAN Considered a strong candidate for top financial jobs in companies such as Merrill Lynch and Morgan Stanley, Fink has instead preferred to remain with BlackRock and build up the assets of the company he created. Much of BlackRock's recent growth is due to its 2005 purchase of State Street Research Management, a mutual-fund business previously owned by MetLife. This acquisition added a large equity business to BlackRock's funds, which had previously comprised mostly fixed-income securities. A year later, BlackRock completed its merger with Merrill Lynch Investment Managers (MLIM), giving Merrill Lynch a 49 percent stake in the company and acquiring an asset-management portfolio of $1.3 trillion.

Fink's success has been partly due to lessons learnt in his early days as a bond trader with First Boston, and he has developed a disciplined, regimented way of doing business whether markets are performing strongly or weakly. In recognition of his successful approach, Fink took the top prize in the 2008 *Financial News* European Awards for Excellence in Institutional Asset Management for the third year in a row.

LESSONS IN BUSINESS: GROWING BY ACQUISITION

When Fink engineered a merger with Merrill Lynch, he balanced a loss of personal control of BlackRock against the terrific boost that the merger would give to his business.
→ When looking for potential acquisitions, first identify competitor companies you will be able to run better.
→ Don't just look for companies in exactly the same business—work out how businesses in neighbouring industries might complement your business.
→ Choose carefully: ten percent of a big number is worth more than 50 percent of a much smaller one.

"When there is chaos, those who can understand it a little better... are the investors who can profit the most." Laurence D. Fink

Norbert Reithofer CEO, BMW

THE QUINTESSENTIAL BMW executive, Reithofer knows the company inside out. Joining BMW in 1987 as head of maintenance planning, he soon moved on to research and development. His next steps were overseas, as technical director of BMW South Africa from 1994 to 1997 and president of BMW's US division from 1997 to 2000. Since becoming CEO in 2006, he has led a drive for greater production flexibility and more customization, helping to give the luxury car maker a renewed competitive edge.

BIOGRAPHY
Born in Penzberg, Germany, in 1956. Reithofer studied at the University of Munich, initially choosing to read mechanical engineering but switching to marketing and management.

LEADERSHIP STYLE
Diplomatic, methodical, and precise. Reithofer's management decisions are carefully thought through from the outset.

KEY STRENGTH
Reithofer's forward-looking attitude has pushed BMW toward new targets, new models, and new markets.

BEST DECISION
Moving to cut costs in an organization that was already performing well, successfully positioning BMW to ride out the global economic downturn.

FASTER TO MARKET Returning to the base of operations in Munich in 2000 after a successful spell in South Africa and the US, Reithofer joined the board with responsibilities for production. Working alongside chief of development Burkhard Goeschel, he cut the time required to put the new E90 3 Series into production by half, from six months to three. This coup slashed start-up costs and allowed BMW to capitalize on interest in the new model by getting more cars to market more quickly. To deliver it, Reithofer drew on his proven expertise in forming key alliances at all levels within BMW to assemble a crack team of research and development and production experts. On the back of this performance, Reithofer became CEO in September 2006. In 2007, BMW sold a record 1.5 million cars, taking great strides toward Reithofer's targets of 1.8 million annual sales by 2012 and 2 million by 2020. New models announced included a smaller SUV, the X1, and the forthcoming Progressive Activity Sedan. Profits were solid too, but there were clouds on the horizon in the guise of high prices for raw materials and the weak dollar, which hit export-dependent BMW hard.

WEATHERING THE STORM Reithofer announced that BMW would scale up its car production in the US, UK, and China, while refocusing effort on cutting costs and improving return on capital employed throughout the group. The global financial crisis hit BMW very hard, but Reithofer's focus on lean production was paying off. Unlike rival DaimlerChrysler, the firm has remained profitable.

LESSONS IN BUSINESS: DRIVING EFFICIENCY

A "continuity" candidate for CEO rather than a new broom, Reithofer inherited a company that was already running well, but needed to become even leaner to stay ahead of the pack. He recognized that nothing stays the same forever.
➔ Instill in your managers the culture that they should spend the company's money as if it were their own.
➔ Use financial metrics to check that every division of your company is operating efficiently.
➔ Hedge against currency fluctuation by spreading production and purchasing across different countries.

"Managers have to be role models and work together." Norbert Reithofer

David O'Reilly Chairman & CEO, Chevron Corp.

SINCE 2000, IRISH-BORN O'Reilly has been CEO of the second largest oil company in the US (after ExxonMobil), with interests in over 180 countries, production of nearly 3 million barrels a day, and a daily global refining capacity of more than 2 million barrels of oil. Drawn to the oil industry by its singular combination of technology, economics, and geopolitics, he has kept his finger on the pulse of all three, focusing on more efficient production, lower costs, and the development of new resources.

BIOGRAPHY
Born in Dublin, Ireland, in 1947. O'Reilly has a degree in chemical engineering from University College Dublin.

LEADERSHIP STYLE
An egalitarian, merit-based approach to management (he once told his managers to "lose he ties"). O'Reilly is admired for is down-to-earth attitude: during strike at a Chevron plant in the 980s, O'Reilly is said to have one directly to the workers, aying, "What's up lads?"

KEY STRENGTH
Recognizing that, regardless f the vagaries of fluctuating emand, there is ultimately a market for all the energy Chevron an produce, and working to find ew resources for exploitation.

BEST DECISION
Successfully pulling off the mega-merger with Texaco, reating a formidable force the oil industry.

IRISH MAGIC O'Reilly was recruited by Chevron straight from college, and joined the company in 1968 as a process engineer. In 1976, he went to Chevron Corp. as a foreign operations advisor. In the 1980s, he ran various plants and refineries for the group before becoming senior vice-president in 1991. He was appointed chairman and CEO of the corporation in 2000.

DIGGING DEEP As the head of strategic planning for the company in the 1990s, O'Reilly was already seeking out new oil-production opportunities. Following the collapse of the Soviet Union, O'Reilly led the charge into, among others, Kazakhstan. Within a year of becoming CEO, O'Reilly pulled off a successful merger with Texaco, creating the second-largest integrated oil company in the US, and he became chairman and CEO of the merged company, ChevronTexaco. The deal also solved some of company's distribution headaches when the newly merged company established the $2.6-billion Caspian Pipeline.

In 2002, Chevron suffered a 70 percent plunge in profits, which O'Reilly tackled by focusing on operational excellence and cutting costs. In 2003, net income was almost twice the pre-merger figure. In order to offset declining output from existing wells, O'Reilly has continued to look for new resources to boost production, and has bought into alternative energy sources. The acquisition of Unocal Corp. in 2005 made Chevron the world's largest producer of geothermal energy. O'Reilly has been vocal in his calls for the US government to formulate a policy to tackle energy self-sufficiency and the role of nuclear power.

LESSONS IN BUSINESS: POWERING THE FUTURE

In the oil industry, it pays to think long term. Successful leaders need to be strategists and diplomats. Energy supplies inevitably fluctuate, whether you are pursuing home-grown or nurturing partners in other countries.
→ Constantly seek new ways of operating, from sources of supply to new solutions to customers' needs.
→ Recognize the power and wisdom of the green lobby and stay in the forefront of green progress.
→ Recognize that in long-term planning there are "unknown unknowns" and examine as many future scenarios as is practicable.

> "This is a business in which we take risks every day, but you want to take prudent risks." David O'Reilly

Josef Ackermann CEO, Deutsche Bank

THE FIRST NON-GERMAN to run the Deutsche bank, Swiss-born Ackermann had the courage to take on the leadership of one of Germany's iconic companies and make sweeping changes. Unpopular for cutting thousands of jobs, Ackermann has been perceived as the bogey man of global finance in Germany, but his undisputed role in Deutsche's metamorphosis from a failing German-centric money lender into one of the leading investment banks in the world has silenced the majority of his critics.

BIOGRAPHY
Born in Mels, Switzerland, in 1948. Ackermann holds a doctorate in social sciences and economics from St. Gallen Graduate School of Economics. He was a part-time member of the Swiss army, rising to the rank of colonel.

LEADERSHIP STYLE
Affable and approachable. A hands-on manager, Ackermann takes the time to listen to the views of his employees.

KEY STRENGTH
Having the courage to make radical changes in the face of widespread opposition.

BEST DECISION
Abandoning Deutsche's target of achieving a 60:40 balance between investment banking and retail banking.

A RAPID START After college, Ackermann joined Credit Suisse. He spent time in Credit Suisse's New York and London offices, before returning to Zurich where he was made general director and a member of the board in 1990. Three years later, aged just 45, he became CEO. He quit Credit Suisse in 1996, after falling out with chairman Rainer Gut, and was taken on as managing director by Deutsche Bank. Here Ackermann was given a mandate to develop its investment banking business. Eager to transform Deutsche into a major global player, Ackermann oversaw the development of a powerful London-based trading operation. He also handled the integration of Bankers Trust in 1999, a $9-billion acquisition designed to ensure Deutsche gained a valuable foothold in the US market. When Ackermann became CEO in

2002, Deutsche was suffering the consequences of years of financial mismanagement. Saddled with prohibitively high running costs, the bank was underperforming in all its divisions.

TAKING ON AN ICON One of Ackermann's first moves was to whittle the management board down, with himself as a potent US-style CEO. He also appointed a number of experienced international bankers, including the Indian-born Anshu Jain and American Michael Cohrs. After three years in charge, Ackermann felt confident enough to abandon its previously stated goal of a 60:40 balance between investment and retail banking and move more toward investment. Bank stock rose with this announcement, but the winds of the credit storm forced the bank to seek the relative shelter of the retail sector again.

LESSONS IN BUSINESS: MANAGING AN ICON

It's not easy taking charge of a national icon, but Ackermann has proved that if a much-loved institution needs radical changes to move forward, then changes have to occur, whether or not they are popular.
→ Take a long objective look at the company—never believe underperformance will simply mend itself.
→ Ask yourself, and your colleagues, whether traditional methods of practice are the best ones to use in a modern situation.
→ Don't let fear of personal criticism prevent you from acting decisively.

"I no longer believe in the market's self-healing power." Josef Ackermann

Frank Appel Chairman & CEO, Deutsche Post World Net

THE PRAGMATIC Appel was made CEO of Deutsche Post World Net, the world's leading logistics group comprising Deutsche Post, DHL, and Postbank, in February 2008. His appointment followed the resignation of Klaus Zumwinkel, who left after a tax fraud scandal engulfed the company. Appel has brought stability and an established track record, having served the company for six years at board level. He has introduced an efficiency program and oversaw the takeover of the British logistics company Exel.

BIOGRAPHY
Born in 1961. Appel has an MSc in chemistry from the University of Munich and a PhD in neurobiology from the Swiss Federal Institute of Technology, Zurich.

LEADERSHIP STYLE
Growth-oriented, solution-seeking, and cost-focused. He balances the needs of customers and the company's need for internal continuity.

KEY STRENGTH
Supreme pragmatism. In the face of difficulties, Appel was able to outsource and consolidate to enable growth.

BEST DECISION
Providing Deutsche Postbank with a secure base for further dynamic growth through the sale of shares to Deutsche Bank.

CONTINUITY AND GROWTH Taking over the reins of Deutsche Post World Net from Klaus Zumwinkel, Appel was tasked with bringing stability, promoting continued growth, and quelling rumors about the sale of the unprofitable US DHL unit to FedEx. Appel emphasized growth and continuity in his announcement of the sale of 29.75 percent of Postbank shares to Deutsche Bank. This represented a major consolidation in the German banking sector while guaranteeing job and planning security at Postbank. Deutsche Post, meanwhile, could concentrate on its core business of logistics and express. Appel called the partnership "an agreement purely driven by growth."

Reassuring shareholders, Appel kept Deutsche Post World Net's "Roadmap to Value" program, introduced in November 2007, as a core goal. The program focuses on improving profitability, increasing cash generation, adding value for investors, and improving transparency of reporting.

RESTRUCTURE AND INTEGRATE Appel's pragmatic approach to the ailing US DHL business was to outsource air express services to United Parcel Service Inc (UPS). He also took steps to reduce the costs of DHL's ground infrastructure by closing smaller sorting facilities, and by rationalizing pick-up and delivery routes. Job cuts resulting from these cutbacks were seen as inevitable. Appel stated that, "Taking a pragmatic approach, we will go on to be a smarter player in the challenging US express market." Meanwhile, DHL Express is pursuing other growth markets, increasingly focusing on Asia and particularly China.

LESSONS IN BUSINESS: FINDING SOLUTIONS

Appel has shown a knack for finding innovative solutions to problems. The sale of Postbank shares ensured its continued growth and the outsourcing of air express services to UPS ensured the survival of DHL US.
➔ Seek partnerships where they build on both parties' strengths and aid growth.
➔ Create stability and continuity to benefit from existing profit centers that focus on financial performance.
➔ When jobs the solution is job cuts, make the reason for them clear and explain the risks of inaction to the organization and its people.

> "We have promised to focus on improving financial performance and delivering on our 'Roadmap to Value' program." Frank Appel

STRATEGIES FOR SUCCESS

A century ago, companies shared basic business goals of increasing revenue and decreasing costs. But the strategies and business models they use to achieve them have changed and evolved. Thanks to the internet, CEOs have needed to adapt or create innovative new business models to survive.

Google, under the leadership of CEO **Eric Schmidt** (p443), achieved the latter. Everything Google does for consumers is fabulously free and brilliantly innovative, from Google Search to Gmail. This has attracted millions of daily users and created an internet business worth hundreds of billions, with 98 percent of revenues from advertising. "Today we say our strategy is search, ads, and apps," says Schmidt.

Avon has used the same direct-selling business strategy since selling perfume door to door in 1886. By adapting it, CEO **Andrea Jung** (p258) tripled profits in four years. Avon's policy of using teams of independent self-employed sales reps translated well overseas, and Jung took advantage of this by bolstering online initiatives and expanding into new markets. Consequently two-thirds of Avon's sales now originate outside the US ●

> "The company isn't run for the long-term value of our shareholders but for the long-term value of our end users."
> ERIC SCHMIDT

Rapid Growth Plans

Just as companies need strategies to dictate direction, they also need an audience. CEOs of community-led Web 2.0 companies know this. Their strategies focus on building user numbers above all other variables, even revenue. Data, content, community, and attention are the new currency.

Freemium is a twist on the old bait and hook model. The Luxembourg-based Estonian company Skype uses the freemium model by giving away free computer calls (bait) and selling premium voicemail and landline/mobile calls (hook). After eight years at a telecoms company, Skype co-founder and ex-CEO **Niklas Zennstrom** (now CEO of Joost) was drawn to freemium as an alternative to the telecoms industry "operator business model". Unlike traditional phone companies, Skype had no marketing,

distribution, or customer acquisition costs, because their software spreads virally. As a result, serving customers costs nothing because they are simply using file-sharing software and their own bandwidth. Skype's software has been downloaded by 405 million people with only 12 percent of the total call minutes paid for. Yet, Zennstrom's strategy paid off when eBay acquired Skype for $2.6 billion in 2005.

Marten Mickos, CEO of open source software company MySQL also built a large audience via freemium, using dual-licensing to support its loyal community with a sustainable business model. The software is free to all, but enterprise users pay for support and maintenance. The company was aquired for $800 million by Sun Microsystems.

The right strategy can create rapid growth by differentiating a company from competitors sharing the same business model. Companies operating a distribution

business model usually sell products from a range of manufacturers. However, **Peter Jones**, star of British reality TV show *Dragon's Den* and CEO of Phones International Group, decided to focus solely on one manufacturer. "My company [became] recognized as a specialist in their products," explains Jones in his book, *Tycoon*. Data Select became the manufacturer's preferred added-value partner and Jones replicated the concept with other manufacturers, enabling faster growth than rivals, with first year sales topping £13.9 million.

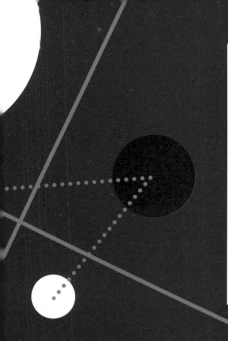

Developing a Strategy

Establish a vision—Have a clear vision, and then effectively communicate what your business stands for and where you are headed.

Model the business plan—Clarify the business model and up-selling plan from the outset.

Identify your revenue streams—Determine which products and services could act as free "bait" and which will be chargeable "hooks".

Be original—Differentiate from competitors and don't be afraid to break the mold.

Invite feedback— Embrace community feedback, which can inspire ideas and improve products.

Strategic Stars

Other CEOs known for their successful strategies include:

Craig Dunn, AMP Ltd (Finance: Australia)—*Continued predecessor's "boring but beautiful" growth strategy that capitalized on business model strengths, including a low-cost business base and resilient brand.*

—

R. David Hoover, Ball Corp. (Packaging: US)—*Likes to share his business model with shareholders and analysts: he wants to make more money than he spends.*

—

Jeremy Darroch, British Sky Broadcasting Group (Media and telecoms: UK) *While retaining the subscription and ad-funded business model, Darroch has transformed Sky from a "dish company" into a major phone and broadband player.*

—

Patrick Daniel, Embridge, Inc. (Oil: Canada)—*CEO of the biggest crude oil provider to the US. Daniel wants Canada to follow other countries in developing a national energy strategy that plans 50 years ahead.*

—

Bruce A. Carbonari, Fortune Brands (Consumer products: US)—*Carbonari helped drive strong organic growth, develop new growth platforms, access and integrate acquisitions, and improve supply chains, thanks to his invaluable blend of strategic and tactical expertise.*

—

André Bergen, KBC Group (Finance: Belgium)—*Bergen's strategy of expanding into Central and Eastern Europe has paid off with wise acquisitions and a strong presence building strong growth.*

—

Felix Miller, Last.FM (Internet: UK) *Miller created a social networking music site based on the freemium model, forming a large community of users and collecting data on listening habits that fueled an advertising model.*

—

Hong Kuok Khoon, Wilmar International (Foodstuffs: Singapore) *Undertook a joint venture strategy to tap into the economic growth of West Africa. This, along with a raw material purchasing strategy and cost advantages from its integrated business model, contributed to record net profits that represented 147 percent growth.*

—

Masahio Inoue, Yahoo! Japan Corp. (Internet: Japan) *Rather than employ a strategy of innovation, Inoue has modeled Yahoo! Japan entirely on Yahoo! US, with immense success: even Google lags behind now in Japan.*

—

Margaret Whitman CEO (1998–2008), eBay

AFTER AN IMPRESSIVE rise through the business world, working for several blue-chip companies, including Procter & Gamble and Walt Disney, it was with some reluctance that Whitman relocated 3,000 miles in 1998 to work for a small outfit that virtually no one had heard of. However, applying her extensive brand-building knowledge and marketing experience, she soon turned eBay into the world's foremost e-commerce consumer site, making the company a household name and transforming the way that people buy and sell over the internet.

BIOGRAPHY
Born in Long Island, New York, in 1956. "Meg" Whitman graduated with a degree in economics in 1977 from Princeton University, where she was also a member of the student organization Business Today. She completed an MBA at Harvard Business School in 1979.

LEADERSHIP STYLE
Dedicated, optimistic, realistic. Whitman avoids taking an authoritative approach toward colleagues, preferring to remain open to advice and criticism.

KEY STRENGTH
A willingness to listen to complaints and criticisms, and to address the issues directly and proactively.

BEST DECISION
Acquiring PayPal, which has become a key element in the eBay experience.

BUILDING UP THE BRAND Launched in 1995 by Pierre Omidyar, a programer from San José, California, auction site eBay was an instant hit. After three years, it needed someone to expand the company and turn it into a major brand. Whitman had transformed Florists Transworld Delivery (FTD), the world's largest floral products company, and overseen management and marketing at toymaker Hasbro, Inc. In 1998 she came in as CEO to head up the small, closely-knit team. She overhauled the website and launched eBay's first national advertising campaign, which immediately increased profits.

FIGHTING OFF THE COMPETITION In part, Whitman's success has stemmed from the instant nature of the business—users could be online to register opinions at any time of day or night. As she said: "The great thing about running this company is that you know immediately what your customers think." If something wasn't working, Whitman took decisive action. When technology problems disrupted proceedings, she worked alongside engineers to solve them. When customers complained of being unable to use PayPal, she bought it up for $1.5 billion.

She broadened eBay's appeal by courting conventional retailers, and purchases of Kruse International and auction house Butterfield & Butterfield moved the company into fine art and cars. After going public, one of her biggest challenges was to increase market share by taking on key competitors, Amazon and Yahoo. A major step was to establish eBay as AOL's exclusive auction site. In 2008, after a decade as CEO, she handed the reins to John Donahoe.

LESSONS IN BUSINESS: REMAINING OPEN TO IDEAS

Don't assume that as CEO you have all the answers. Whitman has never been afraid to listen to the advice of others and knows there are always areas of her knowledge that can be improved.
→ Spend time with people at all levels of the organization—they all have something to add.
→ Use an electronic "suggestion box" to collect and examine people's ideas.
→ Make decisions based on people's suggestions. Reward ones that you implement and, equally, let people know when you are not going ahead with their ideas.

"Every week, there is a different set of issues, a different challenge, something new to think about."
Margaret Whitman

Paolo Scaroni CEO, Eni SpA

A RELATIVE NEWCOMER to the oil industry, Scaroni has clearly impressed his peers, who nominated him Petroleum Executive of the Year in 2008. Since becoming CEO of energy giant Eni SpA, he has confounded sceptics with a series of successes. In 2006, there was a historic agreement between Eni and Russian Gazprom, allowing Gazprom to sell gas direct to Italian consumers. In 2007, Scaroni resolved a dispute with Kazakhstan over the Kashagan oilfield, and in 2008 he signed an agreement with Venezuela to develop resources.

BIOGRAPHY
Born in Vicenza, Italy, in 1946. Scaroni graduated in economics from Bocconi University, Milan, and later gained an MBA from Columbia University, New York.

LEADERSHIP STYLE
Fiercely ambitious, risk-taking, charismatic. Top executives are frequently secretive, but Scaroni does not mind being a figurehead, and is happy to speak frankly about business challenges "He's good at issues, good at picking people and good at leadership," says David Mayhew, chairman of Cazenove.

KEY STRENGTH
A dual focus on efficiency and expansion implemented with a ferocious work ethic.

BEST DECISION
Obtaining exploration and production licences in West Africa on the basis of a "co-operation model" that includes enhancing energy resources in the country and supporting local community initiatives and training projects.

RESCUING PILKINGTON By the time he joined Eni, Scaroni had a significant track record in the glass industry, including six years with Pilkington, where he was CEO. Arriving at the ailing company in 1996, he immediately cut costs, first in Europe and then in the US. He shaved costs by £300 million a year, shed 13,000 workers, and closed two plants. Then, despite concerns about the economy, he launched an international expansion program. The result was Pilkington's transformation into a company perceived to have one of the industry's best cost levels.

SCALE CHANGE Scaroni left Pilkington in 2002 to join Italian electricity company Enel as CEO and general manager, a major step up, since Enel's market value was some €40 billion compared with Pilkington's €2.5 billion.

Scaroni set out to achieve similar performance improvement results, refocusing the energy giant on its electricity and gas core. Three years later, his success led to an approach by the Italian government to head Eni, the huge, part state-owned oil company. Scaroni fitted the bill not only because of his success record but also his nationality, knowledge of the energy sector, and international recognition. Eni needed little in the way of an overhaul, enabling Scaroni to concentrate on overseeing expansion. With a leading international role in the oil and gas, electricity generation and sale, petrochemicals, oilfield services construction and engineering industries, Eni is active in 70 countries. Developments under Scaroni include exploration licences in Gabon and Algeria, projects in the Gulf of Mexico and a new discovery in the North Sea.

LESSONS IN BUSINESS: GETTING THE MESSAGE ACROSS

One of the very few criticisms of Scaroni is that he has a short attention span. However, this has not prevented him from becoming a master of the corporate change-management process, which necessitates taking a "helicopter view" of the situation.
➔ Focus on three or four concepts, then reinforce them so that everyone knows what is needed.
➔ Take change in as small steps as you can, balanced with getting things done in time to be successful.
➔ Be open about what needs to be done and explain how it will benefit staff as well as the organization.

"As long as you work you are a young man. The day you stop you become an old man." Paolo Scaroni

Rex W. Tillerson Chairman & CEO, ExxonMobil

THE OIL INDUSTRY was facing unprecedented challenges when Tillerson took over the leadership of ExxonMobil in 2006. The 1999 merger between Exxon and Mobil, plus a strong rise in the price of oil, had turned the company into the world's largest publicly held corporation. However, growing difficulties in gaining access to international reserves and the problem of climate change pointed to a different future for the industry. Tillerson's proven production skills and his diplomatic style made him the right man for the new oil environment.

BIOGRAPHY
Born in Wichita Falls, Texas, in 1952. Tillerson has a bachelor of science in civil engineering from the University of Texas at Austin.

LEADERSHIP STYLE
Confident and straight-talking, but diplomatic, Tillerson creates an atmosphere of stability and trust around him.

KEY STRENGTH
Being able to wring satisfactory deals from very tough operators.

BEST DECISION
Cultivating international contacts, particularly in Russia, as a means of securing access to future supplies of oil.

GLOBAL DIPLOMAT Having joined Exxon as a production engineer in 1975, Tillerson's effectiveness as head of ExxonMobil's exploration and production side made a crucial contribution to the company's strong growth under his predecessor as CEO, Lee Raymond. His diplomatic skills had enabled the company to do deals in Venezuela, Libya, and Russia, where other oil majors had run into serious problems, and he was an influential figure in Raymond's successful efforts to move into new areas of exploration and future production.

A NEW WORLD FOR OIL Tillerson moved into the hot seat at a challenging time for the oil industry, as easily tapped reserves become increasingly scarce and major Western oil companies face greater difficulties in gaining access to reserves under the control of national governments. With his depth of experience, Tillerson has proved ideally placed to confront these challenges, and his connections with the leaderships of several key nations, particularly Russia, have provided ExxonMobil with a crucial edge. Tillerson's technical skills are also strong, and he has taken steps to keep the company ahead of the pack on the technology front by investing heavily in R&D in the fields of exploration and processing, including spending $100 million on a trial facility to remove impurities, such as carbon dioxide, from natural gas. Tillerson's strategy has placed the company in a strong position, outperforming its rivals. When other big players were pulling in their horns under mounting economic pressures, Tillerson confidently announced that ExxonMobil would be increasing its investments around the world.

LESSONS IN BUSINESS: PERSUADING THE KEY PEOPLE

Companies don't get anywhere by themselves. The good opinion of key outsiders can be crucial in ensuring commercial health. Having the skills to keep those people onside can make all the difference.
➔ Learn the skills of diplomacy when dealing with national governments and powerful individuals with feet in both industry and politics.
➔ Politicians have a totally different decision-making process; make sure you understand their objectives.
➔ Monitor the election timescales of governments and learn how they change their objectives in elections.

"The entrepreneurial spirit will win the race against the regulated spirit every day." Rex W. Tillerson

Didier Lombard CEO, France Telecom

WITH NO TRACK RECORD as a financial leader, Lombard was an unusual choice when he was appointed CEO of France Telecom, France's largest telecommunications company, in 2005. His appointment reflected a desire for continuity with the style of his mentor Thierry Breton, who had left to become French finance minister. In the face of market fears, Lombard quickly cut costs, increased synergies, and lifted sales to achieve unexpected profits of €5.71 billion just months after its share price had fallen dramatically.

BIOGRAPHY

Born in Clermont-Ferrand, France, in 1942. Lombard graduated from the Ecole Polytechnique and Ecole Supérieure des Télécommunications in Paris. Like many French businessmen, he has been involved in government affairs and was director of industrial strategy at the Ministry of the Economy and an advisor on international investment.

LEADERSHIP STYLE

Inspirational, creative, and tough. Lombard has tried to create excitement in the potential for technological development to transform lives, while cutting jobs and costs to reduce large debts.

KEY STRENGTH

His passion for technology and Web 2.0, as well as a vast network of government and business contacts, including Bill Gates.

BEST DECISION

Expanding mobile television services, helping to redefine France Telecom's Orange as a visionary brand focused on the future. It also opened up a new and growing revenue stream.

IMAGE REVIVAL Lombard joined France Telecom in 2003 as director responsible for "technologies, strategic partnerships, and new usages," and it was an inspired move by CEO Thierry Breton. France Telecom had just acquired the Orange mobile brand for $30 billion, and the move had plunged the company into debt. The company needed to revive Orange's image, give it a new direction, and find new sources of income. Lombard came in with a zeal for "Web 2.0", the changing trends and ways in which customers connect with each other over the internet and mobile networks.

A VISION FOR THE FUTURE When Lombard became CEO in early 2005, France Telecom was still weighed down by debts. The Orange mobile brand hadn't really taken off and France Telecom's landline business was under serious threat from voice-communications innovators such as Skype. Lombard's first move was to squeeze costs by bringing together landline, broadband, mobile, and television operations under the Orange banner, improving efficiency and cutting jobs. In his first full year in charge he raised profits by 89 percent, and increased dividends. He published *The Second Life of Networks*, in which he explained how companies like France Telecom must be ready to respond rapidly to an ever-changing communications world, envisioning customers watching real-time television on their cell phones, and homes containing multi-network broadband programming. He expanded mobile television, signed up French soccer onto his network, and has successfully rebranded Orange as a cutting-edge communications innovator.

LESSONS IN BUSINESS: INNOVATING FOR SUCCESS

Some businesses cannot survive in the present without a leader who grasps the future and Lombard is a classic example. He understands how new technology can transform our lives, and has succeeded by refocusing a communications giant around this mission.
→ Think about your customers and how technology can add to their business and personal lives.
→ Use focus groups to understand how people want these changes to be implemented and in what form.
→ Examine every part of your organization to see how innovative technology can improve performance.

"Our environment is changing and we have to change even faster." Didier Lombard

Lloyd Blankfein Chairman & CEO, Goldman Sachs

TAKING OVER the top job at Goldman Sachs when Hank Paulson left to become Secretary of the US Treasury in May 2006, Blankfein has become one of the most powerful and well-paid executives on Wall Street. Under his control, Goldman Sachs handled the sub-prime mortgage crisis that hit the world in 2007 better than most other large investment banks. Although Blankfein was pressured into changing Goldman Sachs' status from an investment bank to a more traditional bank holding company in October 2008, it weathered the storm.

BIOGRAPHY
Born in the Bronx, New York City, in 1954. The son of a postal service clerk, Blankfein was raised in modest circumstances. Supported by scholarships, he studied at Harvard College and Harvard Law School.

LEADERSHIP STYLE
Hands-on and involved. Blankfein pays close attention to the markets, and keeps up direct discussion with his employees.

KEY STRENGTH
Making risk assessment an inherent part of corporate culture, encouraging communication, discussion, and responsibility at all levels within the company.

BEST DECISION
Switching careers, back in 1981, and choosing Wall Street, where he found his métier.

IN THE BACK DOOR Blankfein's route to Goldman Sachs was unconventional. After completing his degree at Harvard Law School, he started as a corporate tax lawyer for the law firm Donovan, Leisure, Newton & Irvine, then tried to move to Wall Street.

Rejected by several of the big hitters, including Goldman Sachs, he joined J. Aron, a small commodities trading house in 1981 as a gold bar and coin salesman. Shortly afterward, J. Aron was acquired by Goldman Sachs, and Blankfein was on the way up.

WHEN THE GOING GETS TOUGH Bringing his considerable intellect to the task of boosting Goldman Sachs' trading arm, Blankfein soon made his mark. In 1988 he was named a partner, by 1994 he was co-head of trading, and in 1997 he became head of the Fixed

Income, Currency, and Commodities (FICC) division. Here he placed a high priority on recruiting the right talent, including top sales people and quantitative analysts, and he worked to foster a successful and co-operative team culture within the organization.

Quick to see its potential, Blankfein took full advantage of Goldman Sachs' rapid adoption of electronic trading technology, and the FICC was soon the firm's most profitable unit.

Rising through a series of more senior posts, Blankfein became Chairman and CEO in June 2006. He showed his mettle in 2007 when, despite the difficult markets, Goldman Sachs was able to report the second-highest revenue figure in the firm's history, demonstrating the company's leading role as an investment bank and its ability to read and profit from the changing world market.

LESSONS IN BUSINESS: ASSESSING RISK

In a tough investment environment, Blankfein has kept a constant eye on the "what if?"—he cited the abundance of credit as a potential cause for concern back in early 2007.
➔ Concentrate on good business cases; make sure they outweigh riskier bets that carry, perhaps, the potential for greater returns.
➔ Try doing risk analysis backward—ask yourself, "Why did we lose money last week?"
➔ Avoid delegating all risk analysis; it's as important as any strategic decision and you should do it yourself.

"We are ever-mindful of the importance of effective risk management." Lloyd Blankfein

Gerd Leipold Executive Director, Greenpeace International

LEADING THE WORLD'S highest-profile environmental organization involves navigating waters that would be a challenge for any CEO. As well as being responsible for 27 national and regional offices, dealing with the logistics of running global campaigns across different regions, and attracting funds and members, the head of Greenpeace has to contend with perennial accusations of being both too radical and not radical enough. Appointed in 2001, Leipold draws on his business experience to chart a course through these turbulent seas.

BIOGRAPHY
Born in Rot, Baden-Württemberg, Germany, in 1951. Leipold studied physics at the University of Munich and meteorology and physical oceanography at Hamburg. He later developed ocean-circulation models for the Max Planck Institute.

LEADERSHIP STYLE
Innovative and imaginative. Leipold has a campaigner's passion that motivates people to reach his objectives.

KEY STRENGTH
An inclusive approach that has helped Greenpeace to engage with industry without diluting the organization's green message.

BEST DECISION
Continuing the dialog with big business that was started by his predecessor, Thilo Bode.

HANDS-ON ACTIVIST Leipold earned his activist stripes at Greenpeace with a period of intense hands-on campaigning in Germany during the 1980s that included flying a hot-air balloon over the Berlin Wall in protest at nuclear weapons testing. As the director of the German office from 1983 to 87, he saw Greenpeace become the biggest environmental organization in the country. Between 1993 and 2001, Leipold developed his business skills as director of a London-based strategy and communication consultancy, before being appointed to the top job at Greenpeace International.

CORPORATE CONTACT Leipold's appointment was regarded anxiously by some observers. His predecessor, Thilo Bode, had turned Greenpeace into a modern, dynamic organization, transforming its financial and management systems, guiding most of its offices toward financial self-sufficiency, and opening a dialog with industry. Leipold's record led to concerns that his appointment would signal a return to radical activism, with the risk of alienating the broader support base. However, Leipold has shown a finely judged ability to combine frontline activism with wider engagement. He has shifted the organization's emphasis from highlighting problems to pushing for achievable solutions, and has congratulated companies for moving in the right direction; for example, Coca-Cola, McDonald's, and Unilever for phasing out the use of greenhouse gases for refrigeration. In doing so, he has extended the effectiveness of Greenpeace by combining on-the-ground campaigns on the environment, climate change, nuclear weapons, and energy, with a deepening engagement with industry.

LESSONS IN BUSINESS: WELCOMING SOLUTIONS

Radical doesn't have to mean isolated. An extreme message or identity on the one hand can be dovetailed with an inclusive approach on the other, broadening your appeal and making the most of all your assets.
→ Work with opponents and look for agreed common ground, as well as putting across your point of view.
→ In debate, take the first opportunity you can to agree with something that has been said, in order to influence.
→ Remember, if in negotiation you make even a small amount of progress toward your main goal, you are succeeding, not failing.

"The environment is an issue for everybody." Gerd Leipold

Carlos Fernández González CEO, Grupo Modelo SA de CV

AN EXCELLENT COMMUNICATOR and determined strategist, as CEO of Mexican brewing giant Modelo, Fernández instituted regular meetings between executives and staff to discuss all aspects of business. He has overseen almost constant growth and his success was highlighted in 2008 with an award from the Palladium Group in recognition of the company's breakthrough performance. Under Fernández, Modelo strengthened its dominance of the Mexican market, and became the leading imported beer in the US.

BIOGRAPHY
Born in Mexico City in 1966, Fernández is a member of one of the five Mexican families that control Modelo. He gained a degree in industrial engineering from Anáhuac University.

LEADERSHIP STYLE
Courteous, strategic, determined. Fernández openly voices his pride in Modelo as a Mexican company and this is shared by staff and reflected in performance.

KEY STRENGTH
A focus on managing and measuring performance. As a result, net sales, share earnings, dividends, and returns rose spectacularly, gaining the company a prestigious performance award.

BEST DECISION
Resigning from the board of Anheuser-Busch to assert his independence and then filing a notice of arbitration against the company to give Modelo leverage in takeover negotiations.

STARTING FROM THE BOTTOM In 1983, aged 17, Fernández joined Modelo, starting with a job hauling sacks of barley and learning about fermentation. During this period, he also saw Modelo introduce modern quality-control and just-in-time systems. Fernández rose rapidly through the ranks and, in 1997, when he was just 31, was made CEO. By then Modelo accounted for 55 percent of all beer sales in Mexico, and Corona Extra was the world's fifth most popular beer.

IDEAS MAN Fernández introduced a number of initiatives to improve sales and profitability: increasing capacity, raising prices in the domestic market, pushing lesser-known brands, and expanding the company's range. He also aggressively pursued export markets, notably the US. In 1997, Corona beer surpassed

Heineken to become the leading imported beer in the US. By then Modelo controlled 80 percent of the export market for Mexican beers and was distributing its brands in 143 countries. Today the company exports five of its twelve brands and is present in more than 155 countries. Modelo is also recognized for its environmental and social responsibility.

Anheuser-Busch has a 50.2 percent non-controlling stake, and Modelo is the exclusive distributor of Anheuser-Busch beers in Mexico. However, in 2008 rival brewer Inbev proposed a $46.4-billion takeover of Anheuser-Busch. Concerned at the implications, Fernández filed a notice of arbitration against Anheuser-Busch to prevent the company from transferring or disposing of any part of its investment without giving controlling shareholders of Grupo Modelo first option.

LESSONS IN BUSINESS: IMPROVING COMMUNICATIONS

Communicating and knowledge-sharing are key to tapping ideas and talents, and making staff feel valued. On becoming CEO, Fernández immediately improved communications throughout the corporate hierarchy.
→ At a high level discuss your market position, mission, and strategy for reaching targets then communicate these down the line.
→ Institute a planning system that all the main teams will use to think about their strengths and weaknesses.
→ Make sure your planning system is not bureaucratic; inundating people with paperwork is unproductive.

"I believe we can succeed because of our intense focus and corporate track record." Carlos Fernández González

Jean-François van Boxmeer Chairman & CEO, Heineken

THE FIRST NON-DUTCH CEO to head the family-controlled Heineken brewing company since its inception in 1863, van Boxmeer was appointed to the top job in 2005. Since then, he has concentrated on boosting sales, primarily through targeting emerging markets in the developing world. He has also worked assiduously to improve the image of the European lager. Once the choice of drunken soccer hooligans, van Boxmeer's Heineken is now marketed as a premium product and promoted by A-list Hollywood movie stars.

WORKING HIS WAY TO THE TOP Van Boxmeer is a veteran of the brewing industry. He joined Heineken in 1984 as a trainee in production, sales, and admin, spending part of his time in Cameroon. This spell in Africa, together with later duties in Rwanda and the Democratic Republic of Congo, gave him vital experience in the developing world and a global perspective on the brewing industry. In 1996, he returned to Europe as president and general manager of Zywiec. In 2000, he moved to Italy to become general manager of Heineken Italy, before being appointed chairman and CEO of Heineken in 2005.

GOING UPMARKET Faced with mounting costs and a stagnating market, van Boxmeer acted fast to shake up the company. Frustrated by Heineken's outmoded style of management, van Boxmeer replaced its old *modus operandi* of consensus building and collective action with a corporate culture based on individual responsibility and innovation. Confident of long-term gain, and always willing to put his head on the block, van Boxmeer took a number of brave decisions. Most notably, in April 2008, he sealed a deal to buy British brewing company Scottish & Newcastle (S&N) for €6 billion, leaving the company with a massive debt. Replacing the UK's standard-strength Heineken lager with the premium-strength brand made in Amsterdam was seen by van Boxmeer as a major step in rebranding the lager as a premium product. Tie-ins with movies *The Bourne Ultimatum* and *Quantum of Solace* helped, as did sponsoring the European Champions League and the Heineken Cup, Europe's premier club rugby competition.

LESSONS IN BUSINESS: PLANNING FOR THE FUTURE

Van Boxmeer is fortunate to work for a company that looks to the future and does not expect instant returns on capital outlay. The global economic downturn has made the S&N acquisition appear inopportune, but van Boxmeer is adamant that the deal will boost Heineken's global presence and bring good future returns.
→ Don't look for instant results, look at long-term prospects—that's the job of the CEO.
→ Make sure that your company is financially secure enough to sit out a long-term investment.
→ Talk to your investors: get them to agree to forego instant payback for long-term success.

"We have to take the long view in this industry."
Jean-François van Boxmeer

Darwin Smith Chairman & CEO (1971–91), Kimberly-Clark

AN ARMY OFFICER once told the young Smith, "You'll never be a leader." When he was appointed CEO of Kimberly-Clark, some of his colleagues were also underwhelmed. But the outwardly shy and modest Smith had a steely resolve, and he spent the next 20 years proving his doubters wrong. Smith's leadership skills turned Kimberly-Clark from the loss-making company he joined in 1958 into the consumer products powerhouse he left 30 years later. His vision helped lead Huggies to the number one brand slot that it holds in America today.

BIOGRAPHY
1926–1995. Born in Indiana. After serving in World War II, he returned to the US and attended Indiana University and Harvard Law School, graduating from both institutions with distinction.

LEADERSHIP STYLE
Considered, forward-thinking, decisive, and a pioneering reformer with the common touch. In an interview, Smith described his management style as: "Eccentric. I am a loner; I am almost anti-social."

KEY STRENGTH
A modest determination to prove himself; in so doing he transformed his company into a world-beating corporation. He is quoted as having always aspired to become better qualified for his job.

BEST DECISION
Selling Kimberly-Clark's paper mills, thereby releasing the funds to allow the company to change direction.

FROM GOOD TO GREAT Smith decided that the only way to turn a good company into a great one was to sell off the paper mills and large areas of prime land in northern California. One Kimberly-Clark director called it the "gutsiest decision I've ever seen a CEO make." Others thought it was downright reckless. Smith saw it in terms related to his own life-threatening brush with cancer: "If you have a cancer in your arm, you've got to have the guts to cut off your arm," he said.

PAPER TIGER With cash reserves of more than $250 million from the sale of mills and land, Smith embarked on a research and development campaign, plowed funds into advertising, and went head-to-head with Procter & Gamble and Scott Paper. Wall Street analysts derided the move, but Smith did not

waver. Smith turned Kimberly-Clark into the leading paper-based consumer products company in the world, notably in the field of disposable diapers, facial tissues, and feminine care products. By the time Smith retired, the company was outperforming companies like Coca-Cola and Hewlett-Packard and giving rivals a major headache. He stepped into the limelight again in the 1980s when he led a multibillion-dollar expansion into Europe.

Smith's humble beginnings gave him an empathy with employees—he believed in helping staff to fulfil their potential. He formed the Educational Opportunities Plan and the Health Management Program. During Smith's stewardship, Kimberly-Clark's net income rose on average 15 percent a year, dividends were increased every year, and the stock price rose an average of 14.2 percent annually.

LESSONS IN BUSINESS: THINKING BEFORE ACTING

An executive must be willing to act boldly, yet boldness is worthless if you're wrong. It's an obvious point, but one routinely ignored by those caught up in the fanfare of big action. Don't let people rush your decision making.
→ Accept that it is better to take your time and get it right than merely to seem decisive.
→ Make a decision, then drive it through remembering that you may face opposition if you are changing a "sacred cow".
→ It's tough and lonely at the top. Back yourself when you know you have a well-worked-out strategy.

"I thought about my job and the company 24 hours a day. Any CEO who doesn't is not a good CEO, in my opinion." Darwin Smith

Alwaleed Al Saud Chairman & CEO, Kingdom Holding Co.

SAUDI PRINCE Alwaleed is chairman and chief executive of KHC, the largest public holding company in Saudi Arabia, dealing in diversified investments. Only 5 percent of the shares are public and the rest are privately owned—93.5 percent of them by Prince Alwaleed. The prince's personal fortune was recently estimated at $29.5 billion by the Arabian Business rich-list. He does not sit on the boards of any companies he invests in, preferring not to have "insider" status. He describes watching his shares go up as "the ultimate kick".

BIOGRAPHY

HRH Prince Alwaleed Bin Talal Bin Abdul Aziz Al Saud was born in Ryadh, Saudi Arabia, in 1955 to Prince Talal Bin Abdul Aziz Al Saud, son of the founder of Saudi Arabia, King Abdul Aziz Al Saud, and to Princess Mona El-Solh, daughter of Riad El-Solh, the first prime minister of Lebanon. He holds a BSc in business administration from Menlo College in California and an MSc in social science from Syracuse University in New York.

LEADERSHIP STYLE

Open-minded, adventurous, straightforward. He is full of energy, sleeping only five hours a night and working 24-hour days when taking business trips in his fleet of three 747s.

KEY STRENGTH

International vision and an eye for a bargain.

BEST DECISION

He buys low. It's a strategy that saw a huge return in profits after Kingdom invested in the then struggling Apple Computer, Inc. in 1997.

HOME START A member of the Saudi royal family, Prince Alwaleed began building his portfolio in 1979. Allegedly mortgaging his house to get himself started with a $400,000 stake, he focused on construction and real estate. The prince's investments grew rapidly and led to the formation of Kingdom Holding Company (KHC) in 1996, which has invested in many industries, in Saudi Arabia and internationally.

INVEST IN THE WEST KHC seeks out companies with strong global brands and good managment, but which have fallen on hard times and can be bought on the cheap. Prince Alwaleed has attracted attention with his investments in the West, especially in hotel properties, buying Fairmont Hotels & Resorts with Colony Capital for $3.5 billion. In 1991, KHC invested $590 million in Citicorp—which became Citigroup in a 1998 merger—and he now holds a 3.9 percent stake, as well as buying into major companies such as Apple, Hewlett-Packard, Kodak, and eBay. He has also rescued Disneyland Paris and Canary Wharf by buying in at their lowest ebb. In July 2005, KHC announced a joint venture with HSBC to invest in growth companies in sub-Saharan Africa. The prince has also invested heavily in Saudi Arabia, where privatizations could generate big profits in the future. Prince Alwaleed is unusual in the Muslim business world in being modern and internationalist, and has made close business connections with the likes of Bill Gates, with whom he co-owns the Four Seasons chain. He has established a diversified philanthropic foundation, and, atypically for a Saudi company, women comprise half the staff of KHC.

LESSONS IN BUSINESS: CRACKING DOWN ON OVERHEADS

The prince is aware of the importance of low overheads. "This is a Buffett-type operation," he says, referring to Warren Buffett, the American investor to whom he is most frequently compared. "We are investors only, a holding company. I have only 60 people here."

→ Overheads go up in steps when you take someone on. They will take time to make their contribution.

→ Avoid potential disasters by making sure all your managers are fully aware of their monthly overheads.

→ Overheads come out of gross margin not sales, so know what your margins are, product by product.

"Once you have $6 billion, the money doesn't matter anymore. What am I going to do, eat fish encrusted with diamonds?" Alwaleed Al Saud

ROUTE TO THE TOP

There's no single route to becoming a CEO. Whatever the sector or industry and whatever the style of the company, the way to the top is as varied as the strategies for success. Some join a company young and work their way up through the ranks. Some start businesses themselves and lead them throughout their careers. Some study for an MBA and are slotted straight into the senior levels, and others make their mark with one great success and are quickly elevated to the highest ranks. **A. G. Lafley** (p97) joined Procter & Gamble as an assistant on a dish detergent brand in 1977 and worked his way through the company for nearly a quarter of a century before arriving in the top job in 2000. **Lloyd Craig Blankfein** (p206), CEO of Goldman Sachs, had a slightly harder time of it. Having trained as a lawyer, Blankfein's initial attempts to move to Wall Street were unsuccessful and he was even rejected by the company he would eventually head. Finally, he joined a small commodities trading house called J. Aron, the company was bought by Goldman Sachs, and the rest, as they say, is history ●

Insiders and Outsiders

The skills required to be a CEO are immensely broad, covering all aspects of business and including mastery of basic attributes such as networking, winning favor, and thwarting your rivals. Despite their best efforts, no academy or company training program can impart the full range of skills. Acquiring them depends largely on the character of the individual, and his or her ability and motivation to seek new skills wherever they can be found, gradually building up the armory needed to challenge for one of the top jobs.

This quest takes different aspiring CEOs in different directions. A large number of CEOs rise through one company's ranks, usually moving around various operations within the company to gain the broadest possible view of how it works and where the problems and possibilities lie, and to build as useful a network of contacts, sources, and supporters as possible. The best starting point for many CEOs is finance, and accounting. Between 20 and 40 percent of CEOs on the UK FTSE 100 have a finance and accounting background. Others follow a completely different route to the top. Take, for example, **Marshall Larsen**, CEO and chairman of the American aerospace company Goodrich. A graduate of the US Military Academy at West Point, Larsen has been described as someone who has made the transition from "good warlike management" to "good business management". It's an unusual path, but good management is good management, and good companies recognize its value, wherever it comes from.

The quickest path to becoming a CEO is to launch your own business. It won't automatically be a success, but if it is, the top job will be yours without the need to claw your way up and engage in politicking. The ranks of founder CEOs include business leaders such as **Paul Foster** at US oil refiner Western Refining, **Mauro Del Rio** at the Italian mobile phone content company Buongiorno, and **Jeffrey Mezger** at the US residential construction company KB Home.

"Think not of yourself as the architect of your career but as the sculptor. Expect to have to do a lot of hard hammering and chiseling and scraping and polishing."
B.C. FORBES, founder, *Forbes* magazine

Breaking the Glass Ceiling

Women are still very much in the minority in the ranks of CEOs, with only 12 ranked among the CEOs of *Fortune* 500 companies. The top job is usually filled by somebody in a senior post so things may be changing in the coming years, as a 2007 report on *Fortune* Global 200 companies revealed women in 11 percent of senior posts. However, the numbers are still far from promising. The same report showed that, of companies with any female representation on the board, nearly half had only one woman at the top table. The route to the CEO's chair is tough for anyone, but still a lot tougher for women than for men. Some of the women who have successfully broken through that glass ceiling include **Marjorie Scardino** (p218) at publisher Pearson, **Andrea Jung** (p258) at cosmetics retailer Avon, and **Meg Whitman** (p202), ten years CEO of eBay.

Successful Pathfinders

A few of the endlessly varied ways CEOs make it to the top:

Gerry McCaughey, CANADIAN IMPERIAL BANK OF COMMERCE (Finance: Canada)— *Not considered for the top job until the 2005 Enron scandal. Untainted by the debacle, McCaughey's knowledge of the business and low profile made him the perfect choice to fix the bank's ailing reputation.*

John D. Johnson, CHS (Agribusiness: US)—*Began his career as a livestock feed salesman in 1974, rising through the ranks to become CEO in 2000.*

Sandy Weill, CITIGROUP (Finance: US)—*Began as a runner for Bear Stearns in 1956, and had a colorful career in finance, becoming co-CEO of Citigroup at its inception in 1998, and sole CEO 2002–08.*

Alexander Frolov, EVRAZ METAL (Metals: Russia)— *Gained a PhD in mathematics and worked as a research fellow at the I.V. Kurchatov Institute for Atomic Energy before joining ErvazMetal in 1994.*

Yasuo Inubushi, KOBE STEEL (Metals: Japan)—*Joined the company in 1967, becoming head 37 years later.*

John Mulcahy, SUNCORP (Finance: Australia)—*Was doing a PhD in reinforced concrete when he decided to change careers.*

Robert T. Huang, SYNNEX (IT: US)—*Sold fruit on the streets of his village in Taiwan at the age of four.*

Franco Bernabe, TELECOM ITALIA (Telecommunications: Italy)—*Began work as a professor in economic politics at Turin University.*

Josue Robles, Jr., UNITED SERVICES AUTOMOBILE ASSOCIATION (Insurance: US)— *Spent 28 years in the US Army before starting in business.*

Eric Daniels CEO, Lloyds TSB plc

AN UNUSUAL CEO in many ways, Daniels' approach to leading UK bank Lloyds TSB has seen him place a strong emphasis on relationship banking and avoiding unnecessary risk—a far cry from the stereotypical pushy American banker. He ruled out mergers and acquisitions between 2004 and 2006, preferring stability over aggressive growth. His careful stance helped Lloyds TSB avoid the worst consequences of the sub-prime fallout and to position itself to swallow rival HBOS during the 2008 financial hurricane.

BIOGRAPHY
Born in Dillon, Montana, in 1951. Daniels studied history at Cornell University and management at the Massachusetts Institute of Technology, before moving to South America.

LEADERSHIP STYLE
Prudent, quiet, and focused. Colleagues value his dry humor and lack of ego. He is known as "the quiet American".

KEY STRENGTH
The courage to be prudent and resist pressure.

BEST DECISION
Steering clear of playing with the high risk securities that poisoned so many banks' balance sheets during the sub-prime crisis.

GLOBETROTTING ACHIEVER Attracted by the promise of travel, Daniels began his banking career in Citibank's Latin American division, working under military juntas in Panama, Argentina, and Chile. Despite the difficult political and economic conditions at the time, he made Citigroup into Chile's second most profitable bank inside just three years. After 25 years at Citigroup, he launched an ill-fated internet start-up in Latin America that quickly fell prey to a regional economic slowdown. Once he had compensated investors, he moved to London, a city he had grown to love during previous travels, and joined Lloyds TSB in 2001 as its head of UK retail banking, quickly rising to become CEO in 2003.

As CEO, Daniels took a careful approach, ensuring that the 240-year old bank did not overreach itself—particularly in the wake of its 1999 acquisition of rival Scottish Widows for £7bn, which some observers claimed left Lloyds with too little capital to fund expansion. Frustrating critics who demanded aggressive growth, he ruled out M&A activity completely between 2004 and 2006, later deciding not to proceed with moves for Northern Rock, Deutsche Postbank, and Dresdner.

CAUTION PAYS When chaos in the financial markets decimated rivals in 2008, Lloyds' profits also fell sharply, but it did not have to go to its shareholders for more funds or cut dividends. This position of relative strength gave Lloyds the opportunity to make a government-approved bid for troubled rival HBOS, helped by an injection of public funds, although some feared that allowing the creation of a UK "superbank" could be anti-competitive.

LESSONS IN BUSINESS: THINKING LONG-TERM

Daniels' determination not to be swept along by financial fads—primarily speculation in derivatives ultimately based on sub-prime mortgages—helped Lloyds TSB to weather the financial storm when it came and expand when others were failing.
→ Ignore people who criticize long-term strategies because they hope for change rather than continuity.
→ Set, and achieve, shorter-term milestones so you can show "quick wins". Build them into every project.
→ Make moves because you should, not because you can. Avoid strategies that simply imitate rivals.

"I don't buy a pair of shoes just because they are cheap." Eric Daniels

Nobuo Kuroyanagi CEO, Mitsubishi UFJ Financial Group

IT IS NO EXAGGERATION to say that Kuroyanagi has played a key role in saving the American banking sector from collapse. As the sub-prime crisis in 2008 sucked down Wall Street's leading investment bankers, including Lehman Brothers and Merrill Lynch, MUFJ stepped in to rescue Morgan Stanley, paying $9 billion for a 21 percent stake. The cash injection steadied the stricken Wall Street giant and transformed it overnight from a bank looking for a saviour to a predator searching for targets.

BIOGRAPHY
Born in 1941 in Japan. Kuroyanagi studied economics at Tokyo University and later completed an MBA at Boston's MIT Sloan business school.

LEADERSHIP STYLE
Forensic, strategic, and, for a Japanese banker, adventurous. Kuroyanagi sets out his aims, bides his time, waiting for the right opportunities, and strikes when they present themselves.

KEY STRENGTH
His international outlook and his understanding of American corporate culture have given him a unique advantage over his Japanese banking rivals.

BEST DECISION
Beating a rival to acquire UFJ Holdings and create Japan's largest bank, and the world's largest according to assets under management.

INTERNATIONAL EXPOSURE Kuroyanagi's exposure to the US, first as an MBA student at MIT Sloan business school, and later as chief executive of Mitsubishi Tokyo Financial Group's American operations from 2000 to 2002, was to influence his development of a more Western financial services model at the bank. In 2005, just a year after becoming overall group CEO, Kuroyagani orchestrated the $29-billion takeover of rival bank UFJ Holdings and became CEO of the newly merged Mitsubishi UFJ Finanical Group (MUFJ).

PUTTING ASSETS TO WORK The merger marked the Japanese banking system's emergence from a crisis similar to the sub-prime debacle. It also created the world's largest bank measured by its assets under management of $1.5 trillion, though a much smaller player by its market capitalization, just $82 billion. Herein lied Kuroyagani's major challenge: how to make assets work harder as investments rather than savings deposits, to generate more income. Kuroyagani set about persuading savers to buy more financial services, and he started to acquire banks in the West that could finance the overseas growth of Japanese companies.

In August 2008, be bought the remaining 35 percent stock of the Union Bank of California as a way to improve earnings from retail banking. Then, as the sub-prime disaster began to cut down major Wall Street investment banks, Kuroyanagi acquired a $9-billion stake in Morgan Stanley in order to generate new fees and premium dividends for MUFJ. Kuroyanagi's goal of making MUFJ one of the world's top five banks seems to be well within hisgrasp.

LESSONS IN BUSINESS: TIMING IS EVERYTHING

Having seen Japan's financial system collapse and then recover, Kuroyanagi knew that timing and preparation are crucial to success. He knew one of the major Wall Street players would become ripe for takeover and he only had to pick his moment.
→ Look for weakness in the competition; predict when they are going to be most vulnerable—then strike.
→ Earn as much from your assets as possible to avoid someone taking over and maximizing return on them.
→ Set a strategy and hunt for organizations that fall behind in competition by studying their performance.

"To become a globally competitive bank, we first have to be a strong local bank." Nobuo Kuroyanagi

Satoru Iwata President & CEO, Nintendo Company Ltd

ONLY THE FOURTH president of a company first established in 1889 to produce handmade playing cards, and the first to be unrelated to the founding Yamauchi family, computer-game designer Iwata has demonstrated that he has the creativity and business skills needed to survive in a rapidly changing environment. Over the past two decades, Iwata has played a key role in the development of some of Nintendo's most important video games and game consoles, including the latest phenomenally successful Wii projects.

BIOGRAPHY
Born in 1959 in Sapporo, Japan. Iwata's interest in computer games was apparent from an early age, when he produced simple games that could be played on electronic calculators with his classmates at high school. He received a degree in computer science from the prestigious Institute of Tokyo in 1982.

LEADERSHIP STYLE
Creative, incisive, original. As a developer-turned-manager, Iwata attributes his ability to prioritize, his decisiveness, and his resolve to be wholehearted, to Yamauchi.

KEY STRENGTH
Creativity combined with market awareness, which has enabled him to target successfully women and middle-aged people, who had previously been completely uninterested in video games.

BEST DECISION
Launching the Nintendo DS and Nintendo Wii, ensuring the company's reputation as a pioneer rather than a follower.

GAME DESIGNER Iwata was a teenager when Nintendo, by then a toy manufacturer, first entered the video game market. He desperately wanted to be part of the new industry, much against his parents' wishes. Recruited by Nintendo-subsidiary HAL Laboratory, Inc., after graduating in 1982, he helped create video games such as EarthBound and Balloon Flight, while continuing to design games on a freelance basis. His input as co-ordinator of software production helped to rescue HAL from the verge of bankruptcy, and he was made president in 1993. Nintendo's president Hiroshi Yamauchi promoted him to head of corporate planning, where he played a key role in shaping company strategy. It was clear to Iwata that profitability for the industry was dropping because games were becoming more complex and more costly to develop.

With a new generation of users in mind, he set out to reduce development time by adding a new and unique twist to existing games. His success within the division was clear as profits rose dramatically, encouraging Yamauchi to name him as his successor in 2002.

LEADING THE NEXT GENERATION Iwata succeeded a man who had reigned for 50 years and had led the company to near-total market domination. He was undaunted by predictions that Nintendo would go downhill without its charismatic leader. As the man behind the phenomenal Nintendo Wii, Nintendo DS, and games such as Brain Age, Iwata revolutionized the industry for the next generation. With his creative skills and understanding of the market, Iwata is guiding Nintendo down its own path, rather than following its competitors.

LESSONS IN BUSINESS: KEEPING IT SIMPLE
As a developer as well as a manager, Iwata has driven the company forward through constant innovation. He uses his knowledge of product design to keep things simple.
→ Introduce new twists so that customers don't tire of sequels and product derivatives.
→ In the entertainment business, simple but highly entertaining is the name of the game. Focus on what your customers want.
→ Avoid over-engineering—over-development can complicate a product and reduce its popularity.

"(Iwata) has the instincts you need to survive in this business." Hiroshi Yamauchi, ex-president, Nintendo Company Ltd

Olli-Pekka Kallasvuo President & CEO, Nokia

TAKING THE HELM at Nokia in 2006, Kallasvuo joined at a time when the cell phone industry was going through substantial change. After a decade and a half of stupendous growth and apparently endless demand, the market had matured, consumers had become more sophisticated, manufacturers were having to compete more intensely on features, and margins had shrunk substantially. Undaunted, Kallasvuo has led from the front, demanding rapid product development and the launching of a range of mobile services.

BIOGRAPHY
Born in Lavia, Finland, in 1953. Kallasvuo holds a master's degree in law from the University of Helsinki.

LEADERSHIP STYLE
Visionary and ethical. At the center of Kallasvuo's approach is his belief in putting values at the heart of the company. If employees adhere to those values, he believes everything works smoothly.

KEY STRENGTH
The ability to adapt quickly and lead with authority in a rapidly changing market.

BEST DECISION
Making it very clear from the beginning that he was prepared to reshape Nokia to meet the changes in the cell market.

RUBBER BOOTS TO CELL PHONES When Kallasvuo joined the company as a lawyer in 1980, Nokia was a manufacturer of general merchandise including cables, paper, and rubber boots. By the time he took over as CEO, it was the world's largest manufacturer of cell phones, with almost 40 percent of the global market. As a member of the executive management "dream team" since 1992, Kallasvuo had already played a key part in this dramatic growth, and a spell as head of the cell phone division had given him a firm grasp of challenges in their core market.

A TRANSFORMED MARKET During the 14-year tenure of Kallasvuo's predecessor, Jorma Ollila, the telecommunications sector experienced an unprecedented revolution that produced a 200-fold increase in the use of cell phones. Kallasvuo, on the other hand, arrived to face a completely different situation. While Ollila's main challenge had been to ensure that the company had the resources to meet the demands of a booming market, Kallasvuo was faced with the job of keeping Nokia's growth on track in a maturing market.

He immediately announced his intention to make Nokia more flexible and responsive, and took steps to speed up the company's product development, ensuring that the timescale for turning out new phones would be months rather than years. Broadening the company's range of products and services, he introduced both more and less expensive handsets, as well as taking Nokia into mobile internet, music, and gaming services. In short order, he has taken bold steps to make Nokia fit for the new environment facing the industry.

LESSONS IN BUSINESS: CHANGING SHAPE

What suits one market won't necessarily suit another: good executives get key changes to their organization in early. Leadership is more than dominance in the marketplace, it is also about shaping debate.

→ Devote resources to innovation. Put it on everyone's job description.

→ Build a culture that combines leadership with bravery, moving first and moving boldly to maintain market share.

→ Get the whole company prepared to change the way they do things quickly, to suit changing conditions.

"Responsibility comes first, then sales and profits."
Olli-Pekka Kallasvuo

Marjorie Scardino CEO, Pearson

THE FIRST WOMAN to become CEO of a FTSE 100 company, Scardino is the highest-paid publishing executive in the United Kingdom. Her appointment as head of Pearson in 1997 signaled the company's openness to a new way forward, and she certainly brought that. She single-mindedly implemented a strategy to streamline a company composed of disparate elements and return its focus to the core activities of business and educational media. In the course of a decade, she has made her mark both professionally and personally.

BIOGRAPHY
Born in 1947 in Flagstaff, Arizona. Scardino (née Morris) grew up in Texas and even did some rodeo riding in her youth. She graduated from Baylor University, Texas, and later took a law degree at the University of San Francisco.

LEADERSHIP STYLE
Open, direct, unpretentious, and low-profile. She sends emails inviting employees to call her about their concerns.

KEY STRENGTH
She trusts her decisions and is willing to give faltering businesses time to turn the corner.

BEST DECISION
Increasing the investment in educational publishing.

ATYPICAL BUSINESSWOMAN Scardino comes from an editorial, rather than a business, background. Working as a desk editor for the Associated Press in Charleston, West Virginia, she got to know a reporter named Albert Scardino, whom she married in 1978. They moved to Georgia, and together started *The Georgia Gazette*, a weekly newspaper that won a Pulitzer Prize in 1984. When the paper folded, they moved to New York, where her husband worked at *The New York Times*. Scardino became chief executive of the North American division of *The Economist*.

DOGGED STRATEGY In her seven years, the US circulation of *The Economist* more than doubled. That captured the attention of her bosses in London, and in 1992 they offered her the post of worldwide CEO of *The Economist*. Global earnings rose 130 percent in the next four years, and her reputation as a skilful businesswoman was sealed. Pearson, the international media conglomerate with a 50 percent stake in *The Economist*, recruited her as CEO in 1997. She soon impressed staff with her open and informal style of management, and investors with her strength of purpose. With the aim of returning Pearson to its primary business of publishing, she sold such non-media assets as Madame Tussaud's wax museum and a stake in Lazard's investment bank, while spending billions to grow Pearson's interests in educational publishing, expand its internet presence, and increase the circulation figures of the *Financial Times*. Her strategy took time to work, giving rise to speculation that she might not stay the course, but it finally paid off, and Scardino saw Pearson's operating profit more than double between 2004 and 2008.

LESSONS IN BUSINESS: STICKING TO YOUR GUNS

Scardino, a novelty when she took the stage at Pearson, failed to achieve her financial goals quickly and the novelty wore off. Rumors abounded that she was on her way out. She held to a strategy she believed in, however, and has seen it pay off.

→ Talk to your major shareholders and warn them that it might take time to deliver your vision.
→ There is bound to be resistance to a new strategy: make sure your key supporters display confidence.
→ Focus on the core skills of the organization. Avoid, or reverse, leaps into non-associated businesses.

"We want Pearson to be known as a company that is brave, imaginative, and decent." Marjorie Scardino

Tom Albanese CEO, Rio Tinto

WITHIN A YEAR of taking over as CEO at Rio Tinto, one of the largest mining groups in the world, American-born Albanese faced a baptism of fire when BHP Billiton declared it wanted to buy its Anglo-Australian rival. So started a lengthy battle in 2008 as both companies sought to persuade shareholders of their case. In the end, Albanese proved the more resilient as the credit crunch rode to his rescue. BHP Billiton backed off, and Rio Tinto, one of the oldest companies on the London exchange, remains under Albanese's control—for now.

BIOGRAPHY
Born in Ohio in 1957, the eldest of five siblings in a third generation Italian-American family. Albanese received a bachelor's degree in mineral economics and a master's degree in mining engineering from the University of Alaska in Fairbanks.

LEADERSHIP STYLE
Albanese has a low-key, friendly approach concealing a steelier core. A geologist and mining engineer by background, his "niceness" was perceived as a weakness in the bid battle with BHP Billiton, but his persuasive powers were vital in the end.

KEY STRENGTH
Albanese adapts fast to change; his ability to learn new skills could determine the future of the entire resources sector.

BEST DECISION
Accepting a job with Rio Tinto in 1993, despite having to take "at least three steps down".

TAKING A STEP BACK Albanese's first year with Rio Tinto, he freely admits, was not the best of his life. Nerco, the company for whom he worked, had just been taken over by the mining multinational in 1993. Just a handful of Nerco's 200 staff were offered jobs and the only way Albanese hung on was by agreeing to a demotion, taking charge of a recently closed gold mine in the wilds of Alaska.

RETURN FROM THE LAST FRONTIER
When Albanese was summoned from the back of beyond to Rio's London headquarters, it was a huge culture shock. He had to ditch his "best Alaska clothes" and head straight for the tailors of Jermyn Street.

Within two months he had pulled off the $38-billion acquisition of Canadian group Alcan, turning Rio overnight into the world's largest producer of aluminum. Then he found himself at the center of a giant takeover battle, fending off a hostile bid from rival BHP Billiton. Albanese launched a campaign to raise the company's profile and rebuff BHP. He hit the road to talk to investors worldwide, hammering home his message that the BHP offer would be bad for investors, with poorer returns than if Rio Tinto pursued its own strategy. He managed to stall the bid and have it referred to European competition regulators.

The company has not been without scandal: for example, the Norwegian government sold its shares in Rio Tinto in 2008, accusing it of "grossly unethical conduct" and causing severe environmental damage at its Grasberg mine in Indonesia. However, Albanese is seen as a calming presence in a sector that is unpopular with environmentalists and politicians alike.

LESSONS IN BUSINESS: TURNING ADVERSITY INTO SUCCESS

Corporate advancement is not always upward. Sometimes you have to take three steps back before making serious progress. You cannot expect every idea to work and this can be true of your career as well.
➜ Be flexible and ready for the twists and turns of business. All plans go at least a little bit wrong during the execution.
➜ The improbable will happen from time to time: all you can do is react with a fit organization.
➜ Make the best of any development in your career, even if it's not in the direction you anticipated.

"The best CEOs take on the ability to manage and develop a range of skills that are not necessarily the ones they start out with." Tom Albanese

Henning Kagermann CEO, SAP AG

GERMAN-BASED SAP AG has grown into one of the world's leading enterprise software companies under Kagermann's leadership. His enthusiasm and analytical approach helped fuel SAP's organic expansion during the tech boom, and his hard-headed instincts guided the company through the technology downturn and safely out the other side. With organizations worldwide gearing up to adopt a new generation of corporate software, SAP has become one of the key global players in the industry.

BIOGRAPHY
Born in 1947, Kagermann studied physics and mathematics at Brunswick and Munich before becoming professor of theoretical physics at the Technical University of Brunswick. He is renowned for his taste for heavy-metal music.

LEADERSHIP STYLE
Cerebral, visionary, and softly spoken.

KEY STRENGTH
A deep passion for his field that drives all his decisions.

BEST DECISION
Rolling out NetWeaver, the integrated technology platform that allows clients to choose different systems and have them run effectively together, rather than having to use just one manufacturer's software.

PHYSICS TEACHER Kagermann's route into business was an unconventional one. He was teaching theoretical physics when, at the age of 35, he left academia behind to pursue a career at SAP. His early work in the development of the company's cost accounting and controlling products gave him a close understanding of its core operations. He was responsible for the development of all SAP's administrative solutions, and his theoretical background and practical abilities made him the natural choice to lead the company.

THE BUBBLE BURSTS Kagermann became joint CEO of SAP in 1998, alongside company founder Hasso Plattner, taking the full role in 2003 when Plattner retired. The early period of his leadership was marked by the sharp downturn in the technology industry that followed the bursting of the dotcom bubble. For many IT companies, used to the rapid and apparently endless expansion of the industry in the 1990s, this sudden change of fortunes proved fatal, but Kagermann demonstrated that he had a tough focus on the bottom line and was prepared to cut jobs when necessary.

As the downturn receded, healthy sales began again and Kagermann was able to devote more time to the company's products, pushing out new ones. The company launched NetWeaver, a software platform that has been hugely popular with large companies, helping them to integrate their programs and compose the business services that suit their needs.

The combination of his boundless interest in the company's products and his firm business hand have enabled Kagermann to maintain SAP's position as a leader in the field.

LESSONS IN BUSINESS: COMBINING PASSION AND TOUGHNESS

Passionate enthusiasm and hardheaded observation of the bottom line are usually separate attributes. Kagermann's achievements show that is possible to encompass both at once, with impressive results.
→ Thoroughly understand the nitty-gritty of the financial and information systems your company uses; consider the financial implication of any decision.
→ Put in place warning lights that are triggered when a financial or other ratio goes out of kilter.
→ Don't let your devotion to the bottom line stop you innovating and taking risks. Obey your passions.

"Our customers expect us to innovate, to lead."
Henning Kagermann

Jeffrey Noddle Chairman & CEO, Supervalu, Inc.

SMALL-SCALE DISTRIBUTOR Supervalu was looking for new ways to grow its grocery business when Noddle joined the firm in 1976. He became CEO a quarter of a century later, by which time the Minnesota-based company had become a nationwide retail giant playing for the highest of stakes. Noddle knew that its future lay either in making a very big take over, or in being taken over itself. In 2006, he made a move that broke the leveraged-buyout record, but it paid off, making Supervalu the third-largest grocery retail company in the US.

BIOGRAPHY
Noddle was born in Omaha, Nebraska, in 1946. He studied business with a minor in marketing at the University of Iowa. Noddle's two older brothers also entered the food retail business, one of whom became the first American to serve on the executive board of the Dutch food retailer Royal Ahold.

LEADERSHIP STYLE
Aggressive when necessary, Noddle is also known for listening to as many people as possible before making a decision.

KEY STRENGTH
An instinct for assessing risks and making the correct judgement call. Cleverly interpreting industry data and doing his research has been key to Noddle's success.

BEST DECISION
Making Supervalu a nationwide grocery retail powerhouse by taking over Albertsons.

OUT OF OMAHA After graduating, Noddle served a brief stint in the Illinois National Guard, took a job in a glass factory in Chicago, then began working in an Omaha grocery chain called Hinky Dinky. His evident talents saw him poached to join Supervalu, a small regional distribution company that was looking to diversify into the retail business, in 1976.

MAKING THE MOVE After overseeing Supervalu's distribution business, Noddle was made vice-president of merchandising and procurement in 1985. In 2000, he became president and COO and, two years later, CEO. His skills were quickly put to the test when he was faced with a potential $2-billion contract to distribute groceries to Kmart stores. He decided the risks were greater than the rewards and pulled out; a difficult decision for a new CEO, but he was proved right when Kmart and the company that had won the contract filed for bankruptcy protection. However, his most audacious move came in 2006, when he led Supervalu into what was at the time the biggest-ever leveraged buyout, paying $17.4 billion for the retail chain Albertsons, more than doubling Supervalu's annual revenue from $19 billion to $44 billion and quadrupling its staff from 50,000 to 200,000. It was a big, bold, and potentially risky move, but Noddle, never known as a rash operator, had done his homework. While many companies struggle to get back to smooth running after a big merger, Supervalu was quickly able to sell the parts of Albertsons it didn't want, and began delivering strong earnings growth and paying down debt from the deal, leaving the company as a mighty presence in the tough world of grocery stores.

LESSONS IN BUSINESS: LANDING THE BIG ONE

Running a good business is one thing, but sometimes making one big deal is the defining moment. Noddle realized that clever interpretation of business data offers an opportunity to see what others do not see.

→ Keep your head up from the operational side of the business as much as you can, and devote the time necessary for planning bold steps.

→ Always examine a take-over opportunity in the context of the resultant company, not just the target business.

→ Follow your instincts, both when they tell you to go ahead, and when they tell you "No".

"There's going to be a battle for consumers, and those who can execute right at the local level are going to ultimately win." Jeffrey Noddle

Atsutoshi Nishida President, Director & CEO, Toshiba Corp.

DESPITE SPENDING almost all of his working life at electronics giant Toshiba, Nishida is not your average company veteran. A polymath who speaks several languages, he considered an academic career before entering business, and his approach is correspondingly studious. He has risen through the ranks to the top job at Toshiba by taking calculated risks, without which, he says, significant growth is impossible. Most famously, in 1983, he pushed for the development of the world's first IBM-compatible laptop computer.

BIOGRAPHY
Born in Mie Prefecture, Japan, in 1943. He has a degree in political science and economics from Waseda University, and a master's degree in law and politics from the University of Tokyo.

LEADERSHIP STYLE
Honest and open, an unusual approach to management in Japan. Nishida demonstrated this in 2008, by discontinuing the Toshiba HD DVD product when content developers opted to use Sony's Blu-ray format instead. The traditional Japanese way would have been to retain company pride by letting it die a slow death.

KEY STRENGTH
A mix of an academic approach with measured excitement. Nishida maintains a great enthusiasm for his business, while still operating with practicality and logic.

BEST DECISION
Pioneering the T1100, the world's first IBM-compatible portable laptop computer.

LAPTOP VISION Nishida's strengths include anticipation of market trends and confidence in his own conclusions. Both were shown with his perseverance over the development of the laptop computer. The company had produced a workable model, the T1100, but was going to abandon the project until Nishida intervened and pressed for continuing development to make the device smaller. In order to convince Toshiba directors, he promised he could sell 10,000 in the first year. With the release in 1985, he kept that promise, and Toshiba went on to become one of the biggest names in a multibillion-dollar market.

GAMBLING MAN A 20-year veteran of Toshiba, Nishida has been CEO since 2005, and he is still prepared to stick his neck out for growth, willing to take risks but never reckless. For example, in 2006, he moved Toshiba into the power industry with the purchase of nuclear plant builder Westinghouse Electric for $4.2 billion. He admitted he was paying more than he wanted to but said he was betting that, with fossil fuels running out, interest in nuclear power generation would grow 50 percent between 2005 and 2020.

Nishida's business philosophy can be seen in his persuasive and innovative management decisions, and it is paying rich dividends for the company that has put him at the helm. Fusing practicality with great enthusiasm, one of his personal mottos is, "Be provocative and clearly communicate your decisions." His future plans for Toshiba include refocusing on the company's strengths: reinforcing a healthy semiconductor business, moving focus back onto the standard DVD format, and establishing computers as living-room entertainment consoles.

LESSONS IN BUSINESS: STANDING YOUR GROUND

If Nishida had been more timid in questioning his bosses, he would never have brought the company the success it has seen. But bear in mind in some countries employees are more deferential to senior people.
- ➔ Find the strength to challenge those above you if you believe you can show their strategy is wrong.
- ➔ In countries with a high level of deference to authority, do not expect middle managers to challenge their superiors.
- ➔ Never blame people for challenging you or prejudice their careers in any way. Encourage debate.

> "Set yourself tough challenges and achieve them."
> Atsutoshi Nishida

Michael Frenzel CEO, TUI AG

ONE OF GERMANY'S most respected businessmen, Frenzel has a reputation for shrewdness and determination, characteristics honed by his legal and banking background. In 1994 he became CEO of Preussag AG, a conglomerate with interests in steel, shipbuilding, and mining. From 1997 he repositioned the company, making a series of key acquisitions. By 2004, the old Preussag AG had been transformed into Europe's leading tourism group, TUI AG, with tourism accounting for almost 75 percent of sales.

LEGAL AND FINANCIAL With a doctorate in law, Frenzel began a career in banking, joining Westdeutsche Landesbank (a shareholder in TUI AG until 2004) in 1981. He brought his analytical skills to the task when, in 1988, he joined Preussag's executive board with responsibility for trading and logistics, and by the time he became CEO in 1994 he was fully aware that the company was in need of a major shake-up.

A NEW FUTURE Steering the group toward the service and leisure industries, Frenzel began his bold acquisition strategy by bringing Preussag into the German tourism market with a stake in Hapag-Lloyd, a company with interests in global container shipping, airlines, travel agencies, and luxury cruises. At the same time, he began selling off the group's industrial businesses. Takeovers of several leading companies followed, including TUI in Germany, Nouvelles Frontières in France, and the British company Thomson Travel, owner of Britannia Airways and Lunn Poly. By the end of 2005, most of the non-core businesses had been offloaded, and TUI AG, as Preussag AG had become, was first in the European tourist industry, serving some 18 million customers throughout Europe, and a major player in the world of container shipping.

In 2008, Frenzel confirmed a new premium cruise partnership with Royal Caribbean International, and also announced the spin-off of TUI's container-shipping unit, Hapag-Lloyd, the proceeds of the sale facilitating further investment in TUI AG's tourism business. Reactions from investors were positive and TUI's share price shot up.

LESSONS IN BUSINESS: FIGHTING BACK

When Frenzel faced sustained attack from an activist shareholder who wanted to oust him, his vision for the future convinced the majority of shareholders that he would be able to develop TUI on the global market.
→ Use your track record for success to stand firm under attack. Get key shareholders actively behind you.
→ Make a strong pitch to shareholders. Think about it from their point of view and explain your business in a way that makes sense to them.
→ Back up words with actions that demonstrate your ability to implement your plan. Look for quick wins.

"We knew the old company had no chance of survival. We had to find another focus, another strategy." Michael Frenzel

Richard Bond President & CEO (2006–09), Tyson Foods

TYSON FOODS' corporate model of protein production in the US has made it the world's leading meat company, but Bond stepped up to the plate at a difficult time in its history. With his long experience of the meat industry, he chose the moment to reduce costs, streamline the company, and redirect it toward new products and new sectors. He also looked outside the domestic market and took steps to extend Tyson's production model onto the global stage, which, if successful, could take the company to a whole new level of growth.

BIOGRAPHY
Born in New Jersey in 1960. Bond earned a degree in business administration from Elizabethtown College, Pennsylvania.

LEADERSHIP STYLE
Easy-going and collegiate. He listens to as many voices with in the organization as he can before making a decision.

KEY STRENGTH
Knowing how to act quickly to deal with bad times and focusing on key strengths for the future.

BEST DECISION
Making acquisitions in fast-growing developing countries.

CEO TWICE OVER Bond worked his way through the management ranks at meat giant IBP to become CEO by the time the company was taken over by Tyson in 2001. He became central to the new operation, appointed president and COO in 2003 and CEO in 2006, when he replaced John Tyson, who remained as chairman, key shareholder, and an important influence on the business. The handover came at a critical time, when the company was in urgent need of surgery.

GOING GLOBAL Bond took over as CEO during one of the company's worst years in memory. A series of problems ranging from the impact of "mad cow" disease in foreign markets to sharp rises in the cost of raw materials had hit Tyson hard, resulting in a fall in sales and the company's first annual loss for over ten years. Bond implemented $200 million of cost cuts by closing plants, shedding jobs, and reshaping operations. He opened a research and development center to accelerate work on new processed products, a faster-growing and higher-margin end of the market than simple meat sales, positioning the company for growth. He also moved into biofuels by signing a joint venture with ConocoPhillips to turn Tyson's huge volumes of waste animal fat into biodiesel. Taking the Tyson integrated meat-production model out into the wider world, Bond began building a base for international expansion, with acquisitions and joint ventures in Brazil, China, and India that placed the company at the heart of the world's most promising markets for new growth. Having taken strategic steps to strengthen the company, Bond stepped down as CEO in January 2009.

LESSONS IN BUSINESS: FOCUSING ON THE FUTURE

When times were tough Bond took radical action quickly. He worked hard putting some problem areas right but never lost his focus on the future, realizing that when times did improve he had to be ready immediately to exploit new opportunities.

➔ Reshape your company in difficult times so it has the best competitive chance when growth returns.
➔ Cut parts of the company that are struggling but expand areas such as research and development.
➔ Go international if you possibly can; it hedges your company against problems in domestic markets.

"It's not just the senior management team, it's the whole team pulling together." Richard Bond

Richard Kovacevich Chairman & CEO (1998–2007), Wells Fargo

A MAVERICK innovator, Kovacevich is widely credited with inventing the modern style of retail banking. As CEO of Norwest and then CEO of Wells Fargo after the two companies were integrated, he introduced ground-breaking innovations in the way banks do business, offering previously specialized services to ordinary customers for the first time. His fresh outlook and power-sharing leadership style not only ensured healthy growth for Wells Fargo but placed the company in a strong position to avoid the worst of the sub-prime mortgage crisis.

BIOGRAPHY
Born in Tacoma, Washington, in 1943, Kovacevich was brought up in the small nearby town of Enumclaw. He was such an outstanding baseball pitcher at high school that the New York Yankees made him an offer, but he turned it down to go to Stanford University, where he earned bachelor's and master's degrees in industrial engineering and an MBA

LEADERSHIP STYLE
Accessible, persuasive, principled. Kovacevich is a committed delegator, believing that true leaders share power with the team and lead by example rather than by pointing fingers.

KEY STRENGTH
The ability to identify what customers want, and delivering their desires.

BEST DECISION
Expanding the products offered by retail banking, transforming the landscape of the industry.

RETAIL BANKING PIONEER Running Citicorp's regional retail operations gave Kovacevich a keen insight into the problems and possibilities of retail banking, and when he took over a similar role at Norwest he launched a series of pioneering initiatives that produced impressive results. Appointed CEO of Norwest in 1993, he drove through the company's acquisition of Wells Fargo five years later, becoming one of the superstars of M&A, and then set about turning the merged organization into a global leader in retail banking.

EXPANDING THE OFFERING Kovacevich ignored the advice of mergers and acquisitions consultants to show quick profits by slashing staff numbers following the merger. Instead, he set out a bold strategy—using the scale of the new organization to transform the offering that retail banking provided to customers. He believed the objective of a merger should not be expense reduction but revenue growth, and he set about achieving that by radically widening the menu of services on offer. Stocks, bonds, and insurance were among the products made available to customers for the first time. These became a key factor in Wells Fargo's growth, backed up by an integrated cross-selling strategy that enabled the company to increase turnover at minimal cost. Kovacevich's formula has become the model for successful retail banking. His innovations were combined with finding the best people and giving them ample scope and responsibility.

He advised California Governor Arnold Schwarzenegger on economic development, and major corporations have sought his expertise as a board member.

LESSONS IN BUSINESS: GROWING, NOT CUTTING

Kovacevich's strategy was to focus on expansion, not on cutting costs. Cost-cutting may save money in the short term, but a successful business is built on finding new combinations to create growth.
- → Look for mergers and acquisitions where you will gain access to a new database of customers.
- → Include cross-selling techniques in any sales or call-center training program. Use role-play to get people comfortable with it.
- → Before you run down a part of the business, explore ways of diverting the resources into a growth area.

"You can't save your way to prosperity." Richard Kovacevich

THE FIRST 100 DAYS

Even the highest-placed executive has faced that first-day-at-school moment, brought in to helm a company in crisis, or ending up as the unexpected choice in an uncertain succession. There is no one way to do it. **Lou Gerstner** (p266) came into IBM guns blazing in 1993, using his outsider status to shake up management and slash costs. And it worked; his new focus on IT services saved Big Blue. **Howard Stringer** (p163) eased his way into his shake-up of Sony in 2006 by sharing a hot spring bath with his new number two, **Ryoji Chubachi**. The lack of any kind of barrier between the two men helped forge a close partnership that slashed costs, sold irrelevant assets, and cut out dead wood. But sharing a bath only takes you so far. Stringer subsequently decided to go it alone at the top to push his digital culture change mission even harder, though Chubachi remains president and is CEO of Sony Electonics, Inc ●

The Shock of the New

Sometimes you need new blood to break a logjam. In the two years before the appointment of former Autodesk chief **Carol Bartz** (p141) at the start of 2009, the reputation of wounded search giant Yahoo! had plummeted, thanks partly to bungled partnership discussions with Microsoft. Her arrival opened the possibility of a rapprochement, bringing famously combative Microsoft CEO **Steve Ballmer** (p135) back to the negotiating table after he had fallen out with former Yahoo! CEO **Jerry Yang** (p75). Tough and decisive, Bartz gained her formidable reputation as a new broom after she succeeded in taming unruly software provider Autodesk, where she licked the anti-managerial culture into shape and boosted revenue from $285 million in 1992 to more than $1.5 billion in 2006. Bartz's first move at Yahoo! was to impose a similar discipline, implementing a more traditional management structure on the existing complex matrix, which lacked clear reporting lines, so enabling faster decision-making and greater customer focus.

Ed Breen had an even more pressing need to wield the knife at the US-based manufacturing firm Tyco when he took over in 2002, after the former CEO, **Dennis Kozlowski**, was sent to jail for defrauding the company. After sacking the board and most of the senior management, he then had to find cash to keep the company afloat after lenders and investors steered a wide berth. After combing through its books, he found Tyco's assets were sound enough for a $4.5-billion bond issue. For its longer term development, he slashed its debt burden and moved Tyco's emphasis away from acquisition and toward organic growth through increased R&D. He also restructured the sprawling conglomerate to improve its flexibility and focus. Tyco's share price tripled and the company returned to profitability, with a net income of $1 billion in 2003. More importantly, Breen's efforts restored a sense of integrity to the disgraced firm.

> "It was decisions like this that started to tell people it was a new day— that we were serious."
> ED BREEN

Making a Fresh Start

Be your own person—Don't try to live up to your predecessor, or, on the other hand, strive too hard to avoid their errors.

Know the players—Understand and win over all the competing factions to stamp your authority on the business.

Wield the knife fast—Don't hesitate to cull underperformers.

Achieve early—An easy win will give your leadership momentum.

But reflect before you act—Understand how the business ticks rather than succumb to a whirlwind of activity.

Get your vision across—Tell it clearly and tell it quickly to avoid misunderstanding.

Reach out—Don't try to seem all-knowing: the best leaders seek out wise counsel.

Dynamic Debutantes

New CEOs who have stepped up to the plate:

Jack Rowe, AETNA (Health sector: US)—*Turned a loss of $266 million into a profit of $2.25 billion in 2004 by cutting 15,000 staff, revamping management, stripping out loss-making businesses and settling a vast number of medical lawsuits.*

Archie Norman, ASDA (Retail: UK)—*Norman did nothing in his first few weeks except listen to the employees. And as evidence that he'd listened he put right lots of little things to win their trust.*

Stephen Hester, BRITISH LAND (Real estate: UK)—*Won over doubters with a radical change agenda that doubled market capitalization and paved the way for its conversion to a tax-efficient trust.*

Tom Nides, BURSON-MARSTELLER (PR: US)—*To inject some vitality, one of the first things Nides did on taking over at the global PR firm was switch around his top executives. "I'm a big believer in moving people out of their comfort zones," he said.*

Cameron Clyne, NATIONAL AUSTRALIA BANK (Finance: Australia)—*Slashed the 40,000 workforce by 10 percent and sidelined operations chief Ahmed Fahour to rebuild shareholder confidence after a share slump.*

Ling Wen, SHENHUA ENERGY COMPANY (Mining: China)—*One of a new breed of communist technocrats, Ling transformed China's largest coal company with a focus on worker safety and environmental standards.*

Lewis B. Campbell, TEXTRON (Diversified: US)—*Began his transformation of the Bell Helicopter owner in his first month as CEO by removing the non-core Avco Financial Services. More restructuring and consolidation followed, leading to a steady rise in the share price from $14 in 2003 to $73 in 2007.*

George W. Buckley Chairman, President & CEO, 3M

BIOGRAPHY
Born in Sheffield, England, in 1947. Buckley gained a BSc in engineering from the University of Huddersfield and a PhD from Huddersfield and Southampton.

BEST DECISION
Acquiring plants close to 3M's developing markets.

LESSON IN BUSINESS
Find hidden value—by altering the supply chain, Buckley unlocked a whole new area of resource.

AN ENGINEER by training, Buckley was brought into US global conglomerate 3M on the strength of his reputation for corporate engineering—just the kind of track record that suited one of America's most innovative companies.

During his five years as chairman and CEO of Brunswick Corp., Buckley sold off various brands, made a range of acquisitions, and carried out a thorough restructuring that boosted revenue and earnings and raised the share price by 30 percent in the last two years of his tenure. He arrived at 3M at the end of 2005 with a similar ambition to find new ways to drive growth. One of his first steps was to remove an intense focus on the Six Sigma management practice, a move welcomed by many employees in 3M's crucial research function. Buckley then began a major strategy of international acquisitions. This was aimed both at providing much-needed capacity, particularly in territories outside the US where 3M generates most of its revenue, and at shortening supply chains and thus freeing up large amounts of capital locked up in the supply system. The results were substantially improved efficiency and a promising new level of growth potential.

Jean-Cyril Spinetta Chairman & CEO, Air France-KLM

BIOGRAPHY
Born in Paris in 1943. Spinetta is a graduate of the Institut d'Etudes Politiques (IEP) and the Ecole Nationale d'Administration (ENA).

BEST DECISION
Buying KLM in 2003, in the first major takeover of a European flag carrier. The deal made Air France-KLM the world's largest airline by revenue.

LESSON IN BUSINESS
In a saturated market, consolidate—Spinetta showed that national airlines could merge across borders, work efficiently, and increase profits.

FORMER CIVIL SERVANT Spinetta took on Air France in 1997, a costly, ailing national airline, but transformed it into a global leader. He quickly saw that it could not compete globally without merging with rivals—which he skillfully achieved.

When Spinetta achieved the merger of Air France and KLM in 2003, many industry analysts doubted that the merged companies could succeed. They questioned how two flag carriers with duplicate routes, operating from two massive, neighbouring hubs—Schiphol in Amsterdam and Charles de Gaulle in Paris—could clear the regulatory hurdles to create a an efficient, global airline capable of meeting the threat of low-cost carriers. However, Spinetta, who has a reputation for quiet, conciliatory, but methodical operating, built confidence by winning the trust of his Dutch counterpart and making improvements to each airline, before linking them more closely. He soothed relations with powerful trade unions, introduced state-of-the-art accounting systems, improved conditions for business travelers at Charles de Gaulle airport, and boosted revenue. Despite soaring fuel costs and an economic downturn, Air France-KLM continues to report profits of more than $1 billion.

"My job is to instill a sense of optimism and a willingness to take risks." George Buckley

Thomas J. Wilson, II Chairman, President & CEO, Allstate Corp.

BIOGRAPHY
Born in Detroit in 1957. Wilson graduated from the University of Michigan and gained an MBA from Northwestern University's J.L. Kellogg Graduate School of Management.

BEST DECISION
Launching Allstate's "reinventing retirement" campaign to counteract the shrinking market for car and house insurance.

LESSON IN BUSINESS
Change is essential—be it new products or a new office design, Wilson has recognized the need to adapt to fluctuating markets in order to grow a business.

AS CEO OF Illinois-based Allstate Corp., the US's largest publicly traded insurer of homes and cars, Wilson has marketed new products aimed at the retirement market during some of the toughest competitive market conditions in history.

While with Sears, Roebuck & Co., Wilson worked on the 1993 public offering of Allstate Insurance Company and the 1995 spin-off of Allstate, subsequently becoming its CFO. One of his first tasks was to sell off non-core assets, which generated $550 million, and refocusing on the core areas of car, home, and life insurance. In 2003 Wilson was nominated COO, becoming CEO in 2007. The following year saw a downturn in the property and car markets, combined with Allstate's over-exposure to areas at risk of hurricanes and tornadoes. Following the success of "Your Choice Auto" car insurance in 2005, Wilson resolved to broaden Allstate's appeal, particularly among middle-income consumers facing a shortfall in retirement funds, and launched the "Your Choice Retirement" savings plan. He faced challenges persuading Allstate's 15,000 independent insurance agents to market unfamiliar products, and to overcome customer scepticism at taking retirement products from a former insurance firm.

Daniel Hajj Aboumrad CEO, América Móvil

BIOGRAPHY
Born in 1966. Hajj Aboumrad has a degree in business administration from Anahuac University, Mexico.

BEST DECISION
Masterminding a campaign of takeovers, licence acquisitions, and expansions in South America to create the world's fourth-largest mobile operator.

LESSON IN BUSINESS
Woo your target market—Aboumrad targeted lower income customers, and now has over 70 million subscribers.

THE SON-IN-LAW of the company boss was never going to struggle, but Hajj Aboumrad proved his own worth by leading wireless services provider América Móvil beyond Mexico to dominate the continent and earn record revenues.

When, in 2000, Hajj Aboumrad took over América Móvil, part of his father-in-law's Grupo Carso, it had nine million subscribers. Hajj Aboumrad began offering subsidized handsets to the country's lower income earners, introduced cheap pre-paid tariffs, bought small start-ups in areas where América Móvil had no presence, and watched his subscriber base soar. Since then it has almost doubled every year. Hajj Aboumrad targeted under-served countries in Latin America with low penetration rates and high growth potential, and invested heavily to offer reliable services. Today the company has a mix of high and low penetration markets. Hajj Aboumrad bought out rivals in Peru, Chile, and Paraguay, and expanded the company by buying new licences in Brazil, Argentina, and Columbia. By 2005, América Móvil's revenues had grown to $17 billion, up more than 41 percent on the previous year. By 2007, revenues had risen to $28.5 billion. Hajj Aboumrad has repaid his father-in-law's faith.

"I like to do things differently, and it's easier to change from a position of strength than a position of weakness." Thomas J. Wilson, II

Sergio Balbinot Co-CEO, Assicurazioni Generali

BIOGRAPHY
Born in Tarvisio, Italy, in 1958. Balbinot graduated in economics and commerce.

BEST DECISION
Moving aggressively into the Chinese market, where Generali stole a march on the competition by signing key sales contracts.

LESSON IN BUSINESS
Keep your nerve—Balbinot persuaded boardroom opponents that the company had to cut jobs and expand overseas. Profits soared.

THE "QUIET DIPLOMAT" took over a company riven with boardroom feuds. He set out a strategy for cost savings, acquisitions, and global expansion. Italy's largest insurance company is now making unprecedented profits.

Balbinot first joined Assicurazioni Generali in the Munich office in 1983. When he was nominated co-CEO in 2002, the company's market capitalization had shrunk to half the previous year's value. The boardroom was plagued by rivalries between shareholders, with directors regularly ousted by influential investors. The company desperately needed stability, and Balbinot set out his vision. He shaved more than 2,000 jobs from the payroll in half the time he'd promised, streamlined the business and, through acquisitions, beefed up its presence in key European markets. More importantly, Balbinot proved his worth by striking deals in China that in 2004 delivered $2.4 billion in premium payments. During this period of expansion, the boardroom battles that had blighted the company before Balbinot took over rumbled on. With continued speculation and activist shareholders circling, uncertainty remains but, whoever wins, Balbinot has delivered a company worth fighting for.

David R. Brennan CEO, AstraZeneca

BIOGRAPHY
Born in 1953 in New York State. Brennan has a business degree from Gettysburg College, Pennsylvania.

BEST DECISION
Making key acquisitions immediately, giving his strategy the best chance of success, and demonstrating to the markets that he had a plan.

LESSON IN BUSINESS
Shake it up—AstraZeneca's weak drug pipeline needed a new approach, and Brennan was the one to provide it.

WITH A BOLD strategy of rapid acquisitions, Brennan took the Anglo-Swedish pharmaceutical group AstraZeneca in an entirely new direction. He sharply improved its prospects in an industry that is constantly seeking the next big thing.

When Brennan took over as CEO of AstraZeneca in early 2006, the company was in need of a change. Its financial performance was strong but its drug pipeline—the long development process for new products—was weaker than those of its peers, spelling bad news for the future. Brennan immediately applied an accelerated policy of acquisition and licencing deals aimed at bolstering the company's position in its difficult markets. He axed a number of unpromising drug developments and initiated a wide-ranging series of acquisitions with the goal of building AstraZeneca's R&D base. These, perhaps most importantly, led the company into the promising and expanding field of biologics —drugs derived from living organisms rather than from specific molecules isolated in laboratories. The pay-off for these investments will not appear for some time, but Brennan's willingness to move boldly into new territory has been welcomed by industry observers.

"As a foreign operator it is not only important to be present but also to arrive among the first movers in order to establish a leadership position." Sergio Balbinot

Michael John Turner CEO (2002–08), BAE Systems

BIOGRAPHY
Born in 1948 in the UK. Turner joined Hawker Siddeley Aviation in 1966 as an undergraduate commercial apprentice while studying at Manchester Polytechnic.

BEST DECISION
Making the unpopular decision to sell BAE's stake in Airbus, a business over which it no longer had operational, management, or strategic control.

LESSON IN BUSINESS
Stand your ground—Turner had to fight his corner on many occasions, not least with the UK Ministry of Defence.

WITH 42 YEARS' SERVICE at BAE Systems and its predecessors, Turner is credited with restoring the fortunes of Britain's biggest aerospace and defense contractor, pushing the company to expand into the lucrative US market.

Rising through the ranks at Hawker Siddeley Aviation and its successor British Aerospace, in 1999 Turner was appointed COO of the newly formed BAE Systems, following a merger with Marconi Electronic Systems. He became CEO in 2002 thanks to his considerable international experience, gained while negotiating the restructuring of Airbus with BAE's European partners. Already precarious, relations between BAE and the UK Ministry of Defence (MoD) came under further strain when two major BAE projects, the Astute class submarine and the Nimrod MRA4, ran years behind schedule and massively over budget. After renegotiating terms of trade with the MoD, Turner brought about a much-improved relationship, which enabled him to concentrate on strengthening BAE financially and strategically. The purchase of Florida-based Armor Holdings for $4.5 billion in 2007 was one of Turner's last major acquisitions before stepping down in 2008, and it made the US the biggest market for BAE.

Mark Thompson Director-general, British Broadcasting Corp. (BBC)

BIOGRAPHY
Born in 1957 in London to an accountant father. Thompson graduated with a degree in English from Oxford University.

BEST DECISION
Leaving the BBC for Channel 4. It helped him see the corporation with fresh eyes and gave him vital commercial experience. It also allowed him to be a clean pair of hands after the fallout of the Hutton public enquiry.

LESSON IN BUSINESS
Be a politician—Thompson thrived under two different director-generals and is regarded as a gifted departmental player.

SKILLED PROGRAMME MAKER and consummate political operator, the highly religious and ambitious Thompson has the vision to take public service broadcasting into the 21st century and is not afraid of the tough choices required.

Thompson took over in 2004 at a traumatic time, after government accusations of bias over the BBC's coverage of the Iraq war, and a public enquiry into the death of an adviser who had been leaking information. As well as restoring the BBC's reputation, he also faced the challenge of adapting to broadcasting's digital future. Fortunately, Thompson is savvy enough to do both. A passionate advocate of public service broadcasting, he was responsible for the development of digital channels BBC Three and BBC Four, and oversaw the launch of the groundbreaking iPlayer web platform. He has also been prepared to get his hands dirty with restructuring that has seen the corporation plan to shed nearly 12 percent of its staff and slash budgets. It is a formula that saw Channel 4 move into profitability during his stint there as CEO and, despite high-profile opposition within the BBC, with luck the affable Thompson will have the departmental experience and creative talent to carry the organization with him.

"Graveyards are full of the bones of economists who predicted the imminent break-up of the BBC."
Mark Thompson

Todd Stitzer CEO, Cadbury Global

BIOGRAPHY
Born in 1952, his father a YMCA director, his mother a nurse. Stitzer is a graduate of Harvard Law School and paid his way through college by working as a tennis pro.

BEST DECISION
Recognizing the need to streamline production, even though it would be unpopular with press and employees.

LESSON IN BUSINESS
Make up your mind and get on with the job—as Stitzer says, "I'm consultative, but not consensual. I don't believe in the tyranny of consensus."

SINCE HIS APPOINTMENT in 2003 as CEO of Cadbury Schweppes, the UK confectionery and soft drinks giant, Stitzer has led the company through a successful demerger with Schweppes, since when international sales have continued to rise.

As an American, and a lawyer who had worked at a large Wall Street firm to boot, Stitzer was not everyone's first choice for the top job at Cadbury Schweppes. Founded by a Quaker family in the early 19th century, the quintessentially English company had been run on paternalistic lines ever since. However, Stitzer had worked for Cadbury Schweppes for more than 20 years, gaining valuable international experience in legal, marketing, sales, and general management roles. Stitzer transformed the company into a more efficient organization, pleasing to both shareholder and consumer. The split-off of Schweppes, factory closures, and job redundancies followed, though as Stitzer put it: "in a very Cadbury Schweppsian way— by being thoughtful and consultative and sensitive". New marketing strategies and a range of healthier products helped boost global confectionery sales, and Stitzer believes that the company is well on its way to achieving profit margins in the mid-teens by 2011.

Fred Green President & CEO, Canadian Pacific Railway

BIOGRAPHY
Born in Stephenville, Canada, in 1957. Green received a degree in commerce from Concordia University, Montreal.

BEST DECISION
Buying the biggest regional railway in the USA, which raised the pressure on his Canadian competitors and signaled his big ambitions.

LESSON IN BUSINESS
Take the long view—Green's long-term, step-by-step development process has made CPR a much stronger company.

EMERGING FROM the tough Canadian rail business as one of the top transport CEOs in the world, Green signalled his intentions to push Canadian Pacific Railway beyond national boundaries with acquisitions in the US and partnerships in Asia.

Green spent 25 years with Canadian Pacific Railway (CPR) before being elevated to CEO in 2006. He had long been a key part of the company's leadership team, and in 1996 ran the relocation of the head office from Montreal to Calgary, the biggest headquarters move ever undertaken in Canada. This was just the start of a ten-year program of transformation for CPR. The company rebuilt its track network, renewed its intermodal rail and truck fleet, modernized its information technology, and was spun off from its parent company, Canadian Pacific, to take its chances on its own. These changes set the background for Green, on becoming CEO, to increase scheduled service levels, create partnerships in Asia, and maintain strong competition with Canadian National Railway. A key component in growth plans was the $1.5 billion acquisition of Dakota, Minnesota & Eastern Railroad, the largest, and one of the most successful, regional rail companies in the US.

"I'm consultative, but not consensual. I don't believe in the tyranny of consensus." Todd Stitzer

Lou Jiwei Chairman & CEO, China Investment Corp. (CIC)

WITH AN UNUSUALLY WIDE experience of Chinese business and politics, Lou is a skilled financial operator. His first challenge as CEO of new sovereign wealth fund CIC was to steer it through the global financial crisis.

Lou left university in 1984, just as China was shifting toward aggressive economic expansion. He joined China's State Council Research Center, which advises the cabinet on policy, and rose through local and national executive positions, becoming vice-governor of Guizhou Province in 1995. In 1998 he became China's deputy finance minister, and in 2007 served briefly as deputy secretary-general of the State Council. Just prior to the 2008 global economic meltdown, he was appointed CEO of the newly created sovereign wealth fund, China Investment Corporation. Lou was tasked with generating returns on $200 billion, including $70 billion earmarked for foreign investment, but CIC lost billions. Nevertheless, *Time* magazine considers Lou one of China's most seasoned financial operators and named him one of "The 2008 Time 100", predicting he would become one of the world's most powerful fund managers. In early 2009, CIC domestic share purchases led an economic rebound.

Wang Jianzhou Chairman & CEO, China Mobile Ltd

A PROFESSOR-LEVEL senior engineer, with thirty years' experience in the telecommunications industry, English-speaking Wang became CEO of China Mobile, the largest mobile telecommunications provider in China, in 2004.

While serving concurrently in senior government positions at the Ministry of Posts and Telecommunications, and the Ministry of Information Industry, Wang became involved in the strategic decisions of China Unicom. He left his ministry positions in 1999, becoming president of the company in 2001, and in 2004 was offered the position of CEO of China Mobile. One of Wang's main initiatives has been to offer universal mobile access, particularly in rural China, home to two-thirds of the country's 1.3 billion population, and he joined forces with the government's agricultural bureaux to offer farmers technical telecoms advice. His role as CEO of the *Fortune* Global 500 company is complicated by the need to obey the wishes of the Chinese government, China Mobile's regulator and controlling shareholder, while also answering to investors and customers. In 2008, Wang announced the company had access to the personal data of its 420 million subscribers, which it passed over to Chinese security officials.

"On my way home… I'll sit in the back of the car and put my name into Baidu or Google to look for the daily news reports about myself." Wang Jianzhou

Vikram Pandit CEO, Citigroup

BIOGRAPHY
Born in Nagpur, India, in 1957. Pandit moved to the US when he was 16 to study at Columbia University, from which he gained a BS and an MS in electrical engineering and a PhD in finance.

BEST DECISION
Foregoing his bonus entitlement in the wake of the global financial crisis, a lesson that many other bankers could learn from.

LESSON IN BUSINESS
Be collegiate—in an industry better known for testosterone-filled Alpha males, Pandit stood out for his inclusive style.

WITH AN OUTSTANDING track record in investment banking, Pandit was recruited as Citigroup's saviour—the man to turn the company around, and banish memories of multibillion-dollar losses on the securitized debt market.

From economics professor at Indiana University, Pandit moved to Morgan Stanley, leaving the bank in 2005 after missing out on the top job. He started his own hedge fund, Old Lane, LP. This was purchased by Citigroup for $800 million in 2007, allegedly in the hope of acquiring its founder, and Pandit joined Citigroup as CEO. Widely regarded as one of the sharpest brains on Wall Street, he could, however, do little to stem the losses at Citigroup when the banking sector crashed in 2008. Write-offs mounted, the share price collapsed, and calls for the break up of what had been the world's largest financial services network grew. By the end of the year, Citigroup had lost a total of $28.5 billion, taken US Government handouts to the tune of an eye-watering $45 billion, and cut some 75,000 jobs, or 20 percent of its workforce. In early 2009, Pandit announced that Citi was to split into two firms: Citicorp to handle traditional banking business and Citi Holdings the rest, essentially an isolated receptacle for the firm's "toxic" assets.

H. Lawrence Culp, Jr. President & CEO, Danaher Corp.

BIOGRAPHY
Born c.1964. Culp gained a BA in economics from Washington College, and an MBA from Harvard Business School.

BEST DECISION
Walking away from the bidding for First Technology plc, a British technology company, when the price suddenly escalated, then posting a record profit.

LESSON IN BUSINESS
Know when to say no—steely discipline in pursuit of acquisitions earned Culp a ranking among the the UK's Cass Business School's Top 50 World CEOs Under 50.

HAVING MORE THAN TRIPLED Danaher's profits during his stint as CEO, Culp is leading the corporation's charge to the upper echelons of Standard & Poor's 500 stock index, through considered acquisitions and operational efficiency.

After joining Danaher in his mid-20s, Culp Jr progressed quickly through various divisional roles, before being nominated executive vice-president in 1999, and COO in 2000. In 2001, he was awarded the position of group CEO. He exemplifies the lean, intensely-focused, profit-driven management model Danaher took from Japanese corporate culture, which is imposed on all new company acqusitions. Danaher designs, makes, and markets consumer and professional tools, professional instruments and medical, dental, and industrial technologies, and Culp's strategic vision has helped transform it from a leveraged-buyout specialist into a high-cash-flow manufacturing firm, described as "the best run conglomerate in America." During his tenure, revenues have more than tripled to $13 billion. Market capitalization registered almost threefold growth, to $26 billion, and Culp has been able to set realistic revenue targets for the company of $25 billion by 2012

"I do consider the role of the CEO as that of a risk manager." Vikram Pandit

Wolfgang Mayrhuber Chairman & CEO, Deutsche Lufthansa

BIOGRAPHY
Born in Waizenkirchen, Austria, in 1947 Mayrhuber completed an executive management course at the Massachusetts Institute of Technology (MIT), Boston.

BEST DECISION
Having the long term vision and focused follow-through to target high-end, high-yield air travelers at a time when rivals were cutting back on service.

LESSON FOR BUSINESS
Be different—Mayrhuber's apparently contrarian approach to service gave Lufthansa first-mover advantage, and left its competitors struggling to catch up.

BEGINNING HIS CAREER at German airline Lufthansa as a humble engineer, Mayrhuber's ascension to leadership has seen him push the company to the next level by focusing on high-end service, and acquisitive expansion in Europe.

Mayrhuber held a variety of management roles before becoming executive vice-president and COO of the technical division in 1992. For the next two years he led a restructuring team, and was appointed chairman of Lufthansa Technik AG's board when the company became independent in 1994. In 2001, Mayrhuber was promoted to the airline's main executive board, and was nominated chairman and CEO in 2003. Lufthansa was already successful and profitable when Mayrhuber took charge, presenting the challenge of where to take it next. First, he oversaw the acquisition and turnaround of Swiss International Airlines, and launched the innovative Lufthansa Private Jet service. This marked the inception of a strategy of focusing on high-end customers, with the introduction of lie-flat seats, first-class terminals, and rewards for frequent flyers, whilst still continuing to offer competitive low-cost flights. Profits of more than €3 billion during Mayrhuber's tenure as CEO emphasize the success of his strategies.

Wulf H. Bernotat Chairman & CEO, E.ON

BIOGRAPHY
Born in Göttingen, West Germany, in 1948. Bernotat studied law at the University of Göttingen, before taking his bar exam and completing a doctorate in 1976.

BEST DECISION
Increasing investment in renewable energy sources such as wind turbines, hydro and tide power, and solar technology.

LESSON IN BUSINESS
Keep up to date—Bernotat's interest in law has enabled him to stay abreast of the legal complexities of the energy industry within Europe.

SPECIALIST LAYWER TURNED energy baron, Bernotat heads energy giant E.ON. One of Europe's most influential figures in the industry, he is part of a growing movement in the fight against climate change and global warming.

Bernotat joined Shell's legal department in Hamburg, Germany, before moving to London in 1981 as the company's business development manager for Eastern Europe. Joining energy company VEBA AG in 1996, he remained on the board while spending two years at Stinnes AG, a leading global provider of transportation and freight services. When VEBA merged with the recently privatized energy company, VIAG, in 2000, the resulting operation was named E. ON. By 2003, when Bernotat took over as CEO, E.ON already owned Powergen, a British energy provider, and Ruhrgas, Germany's premier supplier of gas. Bernotat concentrated on the core energy business, selling off shareholdings in Degussa chemicals and Bouyges Telecom. He launched a £49-billion investment program and acquired assets in Italy, Spain, and France. Bernotat has also led E.ON to invest in a £2-billion project to build the world's largest offshore wind farm in London's Thames Estuary.

"You cannot put all your eggs in one basket. You need to have the right blend of generation… coal, gas, nuclear, and renewables." Wulf Bernotat

Randy Eresman President & CEO, EnCana Corp.

PUBLICITY-SHY EXECUTIVE Eresman is not the most flamboyant or well known businessman, but he has displayed a steely determination in his ascent to CEO of EnCana, one of North America's largest natural gas and oil companies.

BIOGRAPHY
Born in Alberta, Canada, in 1958. Eresman attended the University of Wyoming, graduating with a BSc in petroleum engineering in 1984.

BEST DECISION
Purchasing new exploration rights in the belief that unconventional gas supplies were the future of the industry.

LESSON IN BUSINESS
Focus on your strengths— Eresman is not motivated by EnCana's size; he is willing to break up the company's considerable assets to make it more efficient.

Eresman joined Alberta Energy Company (AEC) in 1980. When AEC merged with PanCanadian Energy Corporation in 2002 to become EnCana, he was promoted to COO. In a strategy known as "resource play," EnCana subsequently sold off almost all foreign assets to acquire drilling rights for natural gas fields in western Canada and the US. Eresman faced criticism from some analysts who believed that the strategy was a euphemism for high costs and low returns. However, he continued to move the company's focus from large wells toward more unconventional sources. In 2005 Eresman was appointed CEO. He faced considerable challenges trying to drive growth at a time when production costs were spiralling upward, although soaring natural gas prices in North America worked in his favor. Eresman's plan to divide EnCana in two, increasing the company's worth by around a fifth, is seen by some as a stroke of genius—but this project has been put on hold by the global financial crisis.

C. Kevin McArthur President & CEO (2006–08), Goldcorp, Inc.

FROM MINING ENGINEER to head of Goldcorp, Inc., one of the top five gold mining companies in the world, McArthur knows the business inside out. He has held leadership roles in the industry through periods of unprecedented growth.

BIOGRAPHY
McArthur is a graduate of the Department of Mining Engineering at the Mackay School of Mines, the University of Nevada.

BEST DECISION
Merging with Goldcorp to create a major precious metals mining group.

LESSON IN BUSINESS
There's power in partnership —the merger of Glamis and Goldcorp created a global player in the gold industry.

McArthur began his career as a mining engineer at BP Minerals North America before moving on to Homestake Mining Company. In 1988, he joined mining company Glamis Gold, where he held a variety of positions including CEO and president. McArthur guided Glamis through a period of unprecedented growth, culminating, in 2006, in a merger with leading Canadian gold mining company Goldcorp, Inc., and McArthur was appointed president and CEO of the newly enlarged Goldcorp precious metals mining group. As group CEO, he continued with his policy of growth through acquisitions, notably the purchase of Gold Eagle Mines Ltd, and instigated efficiency initiatives to reinforce Goldcorp's status as one of the lowest cost producers. Goldcorp now controls about 45 million ounces of gold reserves. McArthur retired in 2008, remaining a director, and serving as an adviser through 2009 to the new CEO, Charles "Chuck" Jeannes.

> "[McArthur] left Goldcorp positioned as one of the finest companies in the world – that will be his legacy." Ian Telfer, chairman, Goldcorp, Inc.

Paul S. Otellini President & CEO, Intel Corp.

BIOGRAPHY
Born in 1959 in San Francisco, California. Otellini gained a degree in Economics from University of San Francisco.

BEST DECISION
Pursuing a relationship with Apple CEO Steve Jobs, which led Apple to switch to Intel processors in its Macs. The first generation of Intel-based Macs was released in January 2006.

LESSON IN BUSINESS
Look beyond present success—Otellini is pulling Intel away from computer chips and moving into mobile internet devices.

THE FIRST HEAD of Intel without an engineering background, Otellini has pushed many a boundary since he took the helm, spearheading strategic changes that have guided the chipmaker's entry into lucrative new areas.

Otellini joined Intel in 1974. When he moved from being COO to CEO in 2005, he had a clear vision for Intel's future, and it involved major changes. Stepping away from the chipmaker's PC-focused approach, Otellini announced a strategy of diversification. The company began to make a variety of chips, rather than just microprocessors, and moved into new areas such as consumer electronics and wireless communication, as well as software that could be linked to make platforms. Otellini restructured the firm, creating business units for each new product area, and hired 20,000 new staff. Just one month after his appointment, he announced a major coup: Apple was to use Intel processors in its Macs for the first time. More recently, Otellini has led the push for a more interactive, "personal internet" space. A big part of this strategy was the launch of the Atom processor in 2008, for use in mobile internet devices, and, in 2009, Intel announced a move into the smartphone chip market.

Olavo Egydio Setúbal CEO (1986–2008), Banco Itaú

BIOGRAPHY
1923–2008. Born in Brazil, Olavo was the son of the noted writer and lawyer Paulo Setúbal. He studied mechanical and electrical engineering at the Polytechnic School of the University of São Paulo.

BEST DECISION
Starting work for his uncle's bank, a decision that would lead to a great legacy over 50 years later.

LESSON IN BUSINESS
Build a future—Setúbal believed that it was important to contribute to the development of his country, whether as a banker or as a politician.

BANKER, POLITICIAN, and entrepreuneur, Setúbal was undoubtedly an inspired leader. He was responsible for transforming the Banco Itaú into one of the largest private sector banks in Brazil.

Setúbal started in business aged 24, creating Deca, a knob, key, and tap manufacturing firm, with a friend. In the 1950s he joined the family-owned Banco Federal de Crédito, becoming director-general in 1959. In 1965, Setúbal led the successful merger with the little-known Banco Itaú, to create Banco Federal Itaú de Investimentos SA. Over the next 10 years, Setúbal acquired other financial institutions, including Banco União Comercial and Português do Brasil. He entered politics twice, first in 1975 as mayor of São Paulo, and again in 1985 as Minister of Foreign Affairs, but quickly returned to banking on both occasions. As CEO, Setúbal renamed the bank Itaúsa-Investimentos Itaú in 1991, incorporating the "Itaúsa" brand name, and allowing centralized control of strategic and financial decisions. He became chairman of the Itaúsa holding company in 2001 and of Banco Itaú Holding Financeria SA in 2003, where he worked actively up until his death in 2008.

"We're investing in America to keep Intel and our nation at the forefront of innovation." Paul S. Otellini

THE POWER OF PERSUASION

"Power is the ability to convince people to accept your ideas," **Donald Trump** (p417), chairman and CEO of the Trump Organization, has pointed out, adding "you don't want people to accept your ideas because you've bulldozed them into accepting them. That's a recipe for disaster. Instead, let them think the decision is theirs—it will give them a sense of power and control as well." Trump puts a lot of effort into preparing for negotiation and in particular sounding out how the other party feels about it. When Trump set out to buy 40 Wall Street from the German Hinneberg family, he grew frustrated dealing with the US agent. So he did his research, found out about the Hinneberg's attitudes and hopes, and flew to Germany to talk with them in person. As a result 40 Wall Street is now commonly known as the Trump Building.

Chrysler's famously successful and persuasive CEO **Lee Iacocca** (p261), stressed the need for creativity, communication, character, courage, conviction, and charisma when it comes to persuasion—a combination of qualities he displayed in abundance when he fronted commercials for the company and, in the process, created his own persuasive catchphrase, "If you can find a better car, buy it" ●

> "I only have the power of persuasion; it's a very simple power, but sometimes it can be very strong."
> DONALD TRUMP

Follow the Leader

It's all very well persuading people from a position of financial power and market clout, but it can be even more challenging when you're just starting out in business. **Vail Horton**, co-founder and CEO of medical-device manufacturer Keen Mobility, has discovered this since forming the company in 2002. Horton has found that one of the more difficult challenges has been attracting and keeping the most talented people, especially with bigger, more established companies ready to pounce for the top performers. But Horton, known for his sales skills, pulled off a significant coup in 2006 when he convinced the experienced Brian Creadon to join the company as senior vice president. Creadon, who initially rejected the offer to join Keen, was the first full-time sales executive Horton had recruited. Creadon says that Horton persuaded him that taking the job was "the right thing to do for the good of our industry, [because] no one else innovates like Keen does." The move certainly paid off, with Keen securing more sales and attracting new customers as a result.

Like Horton, **Shai Agassi**, CEO of Better Place, the world's first electric-car grid operator, has persuaded others to sign up to his vision, no mean feat given that the car industry is often accused of being conservative and reluctant to embrace change. Better Place's innovative scheme aims to introduce fleets of electric cars, not by building the vehicles (that, it believes, is best left to the car industry) but by operating like a mobile phone provider with monthly fees for the electricity costs. Customers can pay for unlimited miles, a maximum number of miles driven each month, or use a pay as you go system. Agassi may have no background in the car industry, but his enthusiasm, sincerity, tireless campaigning, and his natural persuasive powers have seen him raise $200 million in one of the fastest seed rounds in history.

Presentation Skills

Persuasion technology is the armoury of tools used to sway opinion and, as such, covers anything from books and pamphlets to subliminal advertising. But in modern business the principal persuasion tool has become the PowerPoint presentation. Although undeniably effective, PowerPoint presentations can run the risk of diluting or distracting from the personal element, and, as such, some persuasive purists eschew them. **Lou Gerstner** (p266), the CEO who turned IBM around in the 1990s, insisted that all proposals be made with a single overhead slide and a single color marker pen. Taking away such distractions remains the acid test of a true persuader.

Persuasive Personalities

Persuasion is an essential skill in business, as these CEOs show:

Lucian Tarnowski, BRAVE NEW TALENT (Internet: UK)—*Aged 25, he was the youngest entrepreneur to win EU financial backing for his internet recruitment site, and the youngest to join the UK Trade and Investment Global Entrepreneur Program.*

—

John F. Brock, COCA-COLA ENTERPRISES (Beverages: UK)—*Persuaded the Coca-Cola company to expand its portfolio with Vitaminwater and ice tea Fuze.*

—

Tim Smit, EDEN PROJECT (Biodiversity: UK)—*Put his personal enthusiasm for the £80-million ecological initiative to work as the principal fundraiser for the entire project.*

—

Richard Brown, EUROSTAR (Railroads: UK)—*Not content with rebranding the international rail link as a green initiative, Brown is pushing to change government policies and redevelop the rail network.*

Bryan *and* **Jeffery Eisenberg**, FUTURENOWINC.COM (Marketing: US)—*Calling themselves "persuasion architects", the brothers' FutureNowInc monitors websites, uncovering the reasons why visitors fail to buy or register, and then provide companies with specific recommendations to address these points.*

—

Naveen Jain, INTELIUS *and* FREEI (Internet: US)—*Serial entrepreneur, talked his way back from the wilderness after the dotcom boom and went on to found both online directory Intelius and Freei, which offers free internet access funded by advertising.*

—

Michael McGrath, MUSCULAR HEALTH FOUNDATION (Charity: UK)—*A persuader by dint of walking the talk, literally. He visited both poles despite suffering from muscular dystrophy, and now promotes the charity through school talks and fundraising meetings.*

—

David Jones, RSCG (Advertising: France)—*Jones's claim to persuasive fame is negotiating the biggest contract of 2006 in the world of advertising.*

—

Thomas J. Falk Chairman, President & CEO, Kimberly-Clark

BIOGRAPHY
Born in 1958 in Waterloo, Iowa. Falk studied accounting at the University of Wisconsin and earned an MBA from Stanford.

BEST DECISION
Making product innovation a key part of strategy in an industry that might appear largely innovation-proof.

LESSON IN BUSINESS
There's always a new way to do things—by applying innovation to both products and processes, Falk gave Kimberly-Clark renewed purpose and drive.

SHREWD FINANCIAL SKILLS and a taste for innovation enabled Falk to turn around hygiene-goods giant Kimberly-Clark. Under his leadership, a sprawling business was turned into a lean machine, challenging its main competitor.

A one-company man since joining Kimberly-Clark in 1983, Falk was already an important part of the leadership before becoming CEO, having overseen the successful integration of US rival Scott Paper. This acquisition helped provide a solid platform for the company's growth. However, when Falk took charge in 2002, the group needed new direction. In order to match the huge marketing spend of Kimberly-Clark's main rival, Procter & Gamble, Falk freed up cash by taking steps to streamline the business, including outsourcing its IT, human resources, and financial functions. His insistence on sticking to well thought-out plans, and a strong emphasis on innovation, saw the company recover from its problems and expand into new product areas that took the fight for market share right to P&G—completing Kimberly-Clark's transformation from a sprawling paper and pulp-based company into a leading manufacturer of branded, paper-based hygiene products.

Wolfgang Reitzle CEO, Linde Group

BIOGRAPHY
Born near Neu-Ulm, Germany, in 1949. Reitzle received bachelor's degrees in engineering and economics, and a doctorate in engineering, from the Technical University of Munich.

BEST DECISION
Buying BOC, which gave Linde a huge international presence.

LESSON IN BUSINESS
Build transferable skills—despite being steeped in the motor industry, Reitzle showed that good leadership is the same everywhere.

LONG-REGARDED as a likely leader at car-maker BMW and then rival Ford, Reitzle's move to German industrial facilities company Linde surprised many, but demonstrated that clear leadership and strategic vision know no boundaries.

For most of his career, Wolfgang Reitzle was one of the rising stars of the motor industry. As number two at BMW he oversaw the design of the new Mini, which became a runaway sales success. In 1999, he left BMW for Ford, where he created and ran the Premier Automotive Group, comprising Jaguar, Land Rover, Aston Martin, and Volvo. In 2002, however, he surprised the industry by leaving Ford for the seemingly less glamorous job of running German industrial gases, forklifts, and refrigeration company Linde. One of Germany's great old industrial houses, Linde was regarded as old-fashioned and hidebound. Reitzle initiated a rapid modernization plan, selling the refrigeration operation and focusing the company on the gases business. His biggest and boldest step was the £8-billion acquisition of the British industrial gases company BOC in 2006. This secured Linde's global presence and positioned it as one of the likely industrial giants of coming decades.

"I don't sleep well at night unless I see the next three generations of our products." Thomas J. Falk

Mike Jatania CEO, Lornamead Group

BY REVIVING discarded cosmetics brands such as Yardley and Lypsyl, Jatania and his family have built a £1-billion fortune at Lornamead. Although he is the youngest of four shareholding brothers, Jatania has the leading role as CEO.

BIOGRAPHY
Born in Uganda in 1965, Jatania was raised in the UK. He studied accountancy at South Bank University in London before joining the family firm Lornamead.

BEST DECISION
Buying the Yardley cosmetics brand from Procter and Gamble for $100 million. Jatania has since revived the brand and turned it global.

LESSON IN BUSINESS
Exploit brand power—Jatania revitalized old, faded brands as bestsellers through introducing new ranges and improving distribution.

A failed venture has been identified by Jatania as the pivotal moment of his career. The company he runs with his three brothers had been doing reasonably well, representing the brands of major cosmetic multinationals, when it decided to launch its own brand. It began manufacturing Tura, a range of antiseptic soaps for the African market. The brand failed because Lornamead had not injected sufficient resources into its marketing. Instead of giving up and returning to selling other people's products, Jatania learned the lesson and persevered. The group began acquiring older, faded brands it believed could be revived. In 1998 Jatania bought Unilever's Harmony hairspray, followed by Gold Spot breath spray, Lypsyl lip balm, and Natural White teeth whitener. In 2005, he acquired Yardley from Procter & Gamble for $100 million and used the brand to build growth at Lornamead as well as his family's fortune, estimated at over £1 billion.

Clarence Cazalot President & CEO, Marathon Oil Corp.

A LONG AND IMPRESSIVE career with one of the oil majors gave Cazalot the insight and expertise he needed to turn Marathon into a genuine energy contender as soon as he was given the opportunity.

BIOGRAPHY
Born in New Orleans, Louisiana, 1951. Cazalot has a bachelor of science degree in geology from Louisiana State University.

BEST DECISION
Launching a bold acquisition program as soon as he could.

LESSON IN BUSINESS
Don't hang around—Cazalot moved fast to establish Marathon as a serious oil and gas player.

After nearly 30 years learning the oil trade with Texaco, Cazalot moved to Marathon Oil Corp. shortly before it was spun out of the giant steel conglomerate USX in 2001. As soon as the new company, based in Houston, was up and running on its own, the new CEO set out to expand its asset base through ambitious investments in worldwide exploration and production, aiming to establish it as quickly as possible as a player among the oil industry heavyweights. Over the next two years he sealed a number of substantial acquisitions and joint ventures across the world. These included the acquisition of a significant natural gas presence in Equatorial Guinea, buying upstream interests in Norway, and gaining methane reserves in the US. These steps resulted in high levels of profitability, and helped position Marathon as a rising star of the oil world. It also acquired assets in western Siberia, where, in just three years, it doubled production before selling to a subsidiary of Lukoil.

"When you're doing something entrepreneurial, you have to be ready to face challenges—we were fortunate and we got a few things right." Mike Jatania

David B. Snow Jr Chairman & CEO, Medco Health Solutions, Inc.

BIOGRAPHY
Born in the US in 1954. Snow received a bachelor's from Bates College, Maine, and a master's degree in health care administration from Duke University, North Carolina.

BEST DECISION
Investing $140 million in a "next-generation mail-order facility," allowing Medco to fulfill an additional million prescriptions per week.

LESSON IN BUSINESS
Change needn't be revolutionary—Snow still believes problems can be solved through continuous incremental change.

INDUSTRY VETERAN Snow has spent his career creating and implementing solutions to manage the rising costs of health care. His tenure at Medco has seen him globalize the company, and set industry practice standards.

As president and COO at health insurer Empire BlueCross BlueShield, Snow successfully transformed the organization, and was part of the team that took the company public as WellChoice in 2002. Highly respected within the industry, he was made CEO of Merck-Medco Managed Care in 2003, overseeing his second initial public offering within a year, and taking the company public as Medco Health Care five months later. 2004 saw Medco settle outstanding litigation from the 1990s, relating to undeclared incentives in twenty states. The company did not admit liability, but Snow has since instituted new business practices to improve accountability, now regarded as the "gold standard" for the industry, and has made a number of key acquisitions to strengthen Medco's domestic position, including Accredo Health in 2005 and Polymedica Corporation in 2007. In 2008, Snow oversaw the acquisition of a majority stake in Europa Apotheek Venlo, giving Medco a foothold in the profitable European pharmacy market.

Gerard Kleisterlee CEO, Philips

BIOGRAPHY
Born in Germany in 1946. Kleisterlee studied electronic engineering at Eindhoven University of Technology on a scholarship from Philips.

BEST DECISION
Selling off the semiconductor business in 2006 to private-equity buyers for more than $10 billion, and using the proceeds for a stock buyback.

LESSON IN BUSINESS
Keep your focus—Kleisterlee's restructuring of divisions transformed Philips from an unwieldy megalith, into a streamlined world-beater.

BY REFOCUSING PHILIPS into four core businesses, risk-taker Kleisterlee has transformed the company from an old-fashioned European conglomerate into a hi-tech, high-growth competitor in the global electronics market.

Following his scholarship-derived graduation in 1974, Kleisterlee joined the medical division of Philips, before working his way up through the professional audio and components divisions. After heading up operations in China and Taiwan, Kleisterlee returned to Holland, becoming COO in 2000. His appointment as CEO in 2001 coincided with the bursting of the dotcom bubble. He set about implementing a complete restructuring of the huge and unwieldy conglomerate, dividing it into four divisions: medical, lighting, consumer electronics, and domestic appliances. He oversaw the sale of a number of low-growth businesses, and the closure of over a hundred factories. He transformed the corporate structure at Philips, and brought in the company's first chief marketing officer. Perhaps his boldest move was selling off the profitable semiconductor division to raise $10 billion, earning him the title of *Fortune*'s 2006 European Businessman of the Year.

"My career commitment to innovation… and high quality services over the past 25 years fits well with the platform [at Medco Health]." David B. Snow Jr

Alan Joyce CEO, Qantas Airways Ltd

BIOGRAPHY
Born in Dublin, Ireland, in 1966. Joyce studied applied science at Trinity College, Dublin, where he also received an MSc in management science.

BEST DECISION
Going ahead, in the face of recession, with the launch of the new spacious and fuel-efficient Airbus A380 superjumbo service to London, to increase capacity.

LESSON IN BUSINESS
Solutions can always be found—Joyce uses the same analytical approach to solving business dilemmas that he once applied to math and physics.

CAREER AVIATION EXECUTIVE Joyce spent five years turning low-cost airline Jetstar into the fastest-growing division at Qantas, the world's second oldest airline, before being appointed to the top job in 2008.

Joyce spent eight years working at Irish carrier Aer Lingus before moving to Australia to work for now defunct Ansett. He joined Qantas in 2000 as head of network operations, rising to CEO of Jetstar, Qantas's low-cost airline, three years later. He raised revenue by charging for extra leg room and in-flight entertainment, snacks, and beverages, and within six months the business was profitable. After turning the short-haul domestic carrier, with its 14 single-aisle jets, into a fleet of 34 planes flying to long-haul destinations, Joyce's leadership skills were internationally recognized, and Jetstar won the Center for Asia Pacific's (CAPA) Low Cost Airline of the Year Award in 2005 and 2007. Despite being seen as an outsider for the job, Joyce was appointed CEO of Qantas in November 2008. Days after taking up the position, he was forced to deal with speculation following leaks about secret BA-Qantas merger talks. The venture was later abandoned when the two sides failed to reach a deal.

Dai Houliang Senior Vice-President & CFO, Sinopec Corp.

BIOGRAPHY
Born in 1963. Dai graduated from Jiangsu Chemical Institute, subsequently studying for an MBA and earning a PhD from Nanjing University.

BEST DECISION
Securing a stake in overseas oil supplies to drive China's 21st-century economic development.

LESSON IN BUSINESS
Understand your industry—the combination of Dai's scientific, engineering, and business backgrounds gave him the necessary focus for global strategy-making.

RISING LIKE A ROCKET in China's newly privatized energy industry, Dai became a key player in his country's global strategy for securing oil supplies when he became CFO of China Petroleum & Chemical Corporation (Sinopec Corp.).

Graduating in organic chemical engineering at 22, Dai honed management skills at university, published patent-winning scientific research, and became deputy manager at Sinopec Yangzi Petrochemical Co. Ltd, China's major chemical manufacturing company. Dai was general manager in his mid-30s and, by age 40, was president and chairman. In 2006, he joined the board of directors and became senior vice president and CFO of parent Sinopec Corp., China's biggest oil refiner. This came amid financial turmoil in China's petroleum industry, and signalled government plans to dramatically expand strategic ownership of shares in oil companies outside Asia. In late 2006, Sinopec announced government approval of plans to acquire a share of Canadian Tanganyika Oil, whose heavy oil reserves are mainly in the Middle East. Other share acquisitions and "understandings" mark China's plans to develop long-term supplies in Canada's oil sands, Indonesia, the Caspian Basin, and Russia.

"[Joyce's] experience and background with Qantas and Jetstar should help him steer the company in this current environment." Chong Phit Lian, CEO, Jetstar Asia

Christopher Dale Pratt Chairman & Director, Swire Pacific

BIOGRAPHY
Born in 1956, Pratt gained a bachelor's and an honors degree in modern history from Oxford University.

BEST DECISION
Buying rival Hong Kong-based airline Dragonair for just over $1 billion in 2007—this extended Cathay's reach into China, and lifted profits by 50 percent.

LESSON IN BUSINESS
Dominate your market—Cathay's unique selling point is connecting China to the rest of the world. Pratt's acquisitions made Cathay the leading East-West carrier.

ALTHOUGH HE HAS the reputation of a company man in charge of a long-established trading house, Pratt has had an extraordinary impact. Deals with Air China and Dragonair cleared the way for Cathay to exploit China's rapid growth.

When Pratt took over as chairman and director of Cathay Pacific and its parent Swire Pacific in 2006, the question he faced was how the group could earn more from China's exponential rate of growth. In Pratt's first year at the helm, shipping profits doubled, but it was clear that Hong Kong's flagship airline could have been earning more. China's demand for new routes between the mainland, Hong Kong, and the rest of the world was insatiable. However, Cathay was lagging well behind domestic Chinese carriers. Pratt decided to expand by acquisition. In 2007, he made his move in a $1-billion buy out of Chinese-owned Dragonair, which sent sales soaring. As part of the deal, Cathay announced a tie-up with Air China. This opened up more routes for the airline, and half-year profits jumped more than 50 percent to $330 million. However, fuel cost increases and weak demand from the US due to the global economic downturn, have since led to unexpected losses at Cathay.

Mário Cesar Pereira de Araújo CEO, TIM Participações

BIOGRAPHY
Born in Brazil in 1948. Pereira has a degree in chemical engineering from the Rio de Janeiro Federal University (UFRJ).

BEST DECISION
Launching a new advertising and marketing campaign to reposition the brand, centering on surfer Kelly Slater and footballing star Ronaldo.

LESSON IN BUSINESS
Build a network—Pereira's use of his extensive contacts across the industry has enabled him to keep abreast of innovations.

A SUBSTANTIAL TRACK RECORD led to Pereira's nomination for CEO of leading Brazilian cell phone operator TIM Participações in 2006. Since then he has focused both on innovation and on tactical partnerships.

Pereira began his career with Entel in 1967, subsequently working for Eletromar, Standard Elettrica, and Telerj. Joining Embratel in 1997, he spent 20 years working his way through the company before moving to Splice do Brasil, and then Tele Centro Oreste Celular, prior to becoming chairman of Norte Brasil Telecom in 1999. In 2003 Pereira transferred to TIM Brasil, also holding the post of chairman at TIM Celular. He was appointed CEO of TIM Participações in 2006. Following a slowdown in the growth of the cell phone market in Brazil, Pereira looked for new products. He was behind the release of the "TIM Casa Flex" in 2007. Covering 101 cities in ten different states, these hybrid handsets worked both as landlines and cell phones. Recently he has launched new services, including mobile broadband, video call, and 11 television channels through the TIM TV service—the fruit of new partnerships with HP, Microsoft, Nokia, Ericsson, Google, UOL, and Sky.

> "The recent and planned expansion… in sectors with foreseeable strong demand, provide good prospects for value-creating growth." Christopher Dale Pratt

Ann Moore Chairman & CEO, Time, Inc.

BIOGRAPHY
Born in the US in 1950. Moore graduated from Vanderbilt University in 1971. She received an MBA from Harvard Business School in 1978.

BEST DECISION
Taking *People* magazine to new heights by spinning off Australian *Who* weekly, *In Style* and its international franchise, *People en Español*, and *Real Simple*.

LESSON IN BUSINESS
Partnerships matter—in order to build as big an audience for Time Inc's online content as possible, Moore categorically refuses to sign exclusive partnerships.

FEARLESS, FOCUSED, and ambitious, Moore has reinvented media corporation Time, Inc. more than once, making it a force to be reckoned with in the women's magazine sector and, most recently, bringing it into the digital age.

Moore joined Time following her MBA. Her leadership potential showed early on in her career and she flew up the corporate ladder through a succession of key positions. In 1991, Moore became publisher, and later president, of *People*. Here she oversaw the launches of Australian *Who* weekly, *In Style*, *People en Español*, and *Real Simple*, giving Time a competitive edge in the women's magazine arena for the first time. Later, as executive vice-president, she ran the business and development operations for consumer magazines including *Time* and *People*, while managing the company's consumer marketing division. She was nominated CEO in 2002. A major mission then was to take Time into the digital age, a project which has enjoyed increasing success. In 2007, digital traffic growth hit 72 percent; in 2008, despite an economic downturn, revenue for *People.com* rose 51 percent; and Time, Inc.'s US website has grown to be among the 20 largest online media properties.

W. Edmund Clark President & CEO, TD Bank Financial Group

BIOGRAPHY
Born in 1947. Clark gained a bachelor's from the University of Toronto and a master's and PhD in economics from Harvard.

BEST DECISION
Adopting a low-risk strategy that avoided sub-prime mortgages, helping TD to avoid the worst of the global economic downturn.

LESSON IN BUSINESS
Understand your risk—Clark described as "frightening" the fact that his counterparts didn't understand the sub-prime products they were investing in, having delegated too far down.

ADROITLY AVOIDING direct or indirect exposure to the US sub-prime crisis, Clark, CEO of TD Bank Financial Group, was strongly commended and richly rewarded for his caution—a rare commodity among Canadian bankers.

Following his PhD, "Ed" Clark worked in the Canadian federal government for ten years before joining Merrill Lynch, where he specialized in underwriting mergers and acquisitions. In 1988, he was appointed chairman and CEO of Morgan Financial Corp., then joined Canada Trust Financial Services, Inc. in 1991. The latter was acquired by TD Bank Financial Group in 2000, and in December 2002, Clark took over as CEO. He proceeded to pursue a low-risk strategy, steering TD well clear of US sub-prime mortgages, unlike other major Canadian banks. Clark's caution saw his reward package rise to $14.2 million in 2007. His modest upbringing and early career have led Clark to recognize his good fortune, not only the "mental freedom" that it gives him, but also the pleasure he derives from sharing it. He is well known for an initiative that purchases land for charities to build homes for the poor, especially single mothers living in shelters.

"It is an enormous blessing... to do a job you like and be compensated well enough [to] give away money that actually transforms lives..." W. Edmund Clark

Patrick Cescau CEO (2005–08), Unilever

BIOGRAPHY
Born in Paris in 1948. Cescau attended ESSEC business school in Paris before gaining an MBA from the international business school INSEAD, Fontainebleau.

BEST DECISION
Launching a total overhaul of the company rather than trying a piecemeal approach to arresting a potentially precipitous slide.

LESSON IN BUSINESS
Nothing is taboo—Cescau looked at every Unilever business for possible closure or reduction.

THE FIRST CEO to combine leadership of both the British and Dutch sides of Unilever, Cescau conducted a radical restructuring of the sprawling consumer goods company, boosting its sales and producing a leaner organization.

A lifelong Unilever man, Cescau was appointed as the first sole leader of the Anglo-Dutch consumer product giant in 2005, just after the company had issued the first profits warning in its 75-year history. Cescau needed to act decisively to stifle the sense of crisis that was rising within the company, and to restore the faith of markets, customers, and employees. He began by swiftly selling a number of businesses and starting a thorough review of the company's operations. Then he launched an unprecedented restructuring program, involving the sale of up to €2 billion worth of businesses, the closure of 20 percent of the company's sites around the world, and the loss of 20,000 jobs. Cescau also hacked back tiers of middle management and injected fresh talent at all levels. Cescau's cost-cutting and improvements in efficiency resulted in strong sales rises and put the company back on the road to growth. With this achievement secure, Cescau stepped down at the end of 2008.

William R. Klesse Chairman & CEO, Valero Energy Corp.

BIOGRAPHY
Born in Chatham, New Jersey, in 1947. Klesse gained a BS in chemical engineering from the University of Dayton and an MBA in finance from West Texas A&M University.

BEST DECISION
Re-focusing the company on ensuring reliable, safe, and efficient operations.

LESSON IN BUSINESS
Set your goals—Klesse's focus on operational efficiency and quality enabled him to do better than expected in a difficult operating climate.

MORE THAN 35 YEARS in the energy industry, as well as a balanced approach to investment, have stood Klesse in good stead to steer San Antonio-based Valero Energy Corp. through difficult times, after assuming the role of CEO.

Klesse worked for oil-refinery and gas-station operator Ultramar Diamond Shamrock and its predecessors for 32 years until the company was acquired by Valero, the largest US oil refiner, in 2001. Klesse rose through senior positions at the new company, becoming executive vice-president and COO in 2003, CEO in 2006, and chairman in 2007. He instituted a strategic change of tack, moving away from acquisitions and toward operations. He aimed to improve safety, reliability, and efficiency, and to upgrade the company's refining portfolio, by investing in strategic growth projects at flagship refineries, to make them even more competitive. Klesse faced a number of challenges, including unplanned refinery stoppages and a period of record crude prices that led to a fall in profits. However, he has won praise for Valero by introducing openness in the company's dealings with the public, and has gained a reputation for plain-speaking, especially on government energy policy.

"We had to recognize that we were not as good as we thought. That makes you humble and, at the same time, is a motivation for change." Patrick Cescau

Ivan G. Seidenberg Chairman & CEO, Verizon Communications

BIOGRAPHY
Born in New York in 1946. Seidenberg received a bachelor's in mathematics from City University New York, and an MBA from Pace University, New York.

BEST DECISION
Sacrificing the top job of CEO in the short term at both Bell Atlantic and Verizon, thus avoiding any power struggles within the companies.

LESSON IN BUSINESS
Believe in yourself—Seidenberg didn't let a blue-collar background stand in the way of his ambitions, and has stayed in touch with his roots throughout his career.

ONE OF THE FEW *Fortune* 500 CEOs who have worked their way from the very bottom of the ladder all the way to the top, Seidenberg is well-known at telecommunications company Verizon as a man who is prepared to take risks.

A decorated Vietnam war veteran, Seidenberg was determined to improve himself. He attended night school for 14 consecutive years while working at New York Telephone, gaining a BA and MBA. In 1976, he joined AT&T and, following its break up in the 1980s, worked for NYNEX. He went on to lead two of the biggest communications mergers in history, firstly with Bell Atlantic in a $23-billion deal in 1997, then between Bell and GTE in a $50-million deal in 2000, creating Verizon. On the retirement of co-CEO Charles R. Lee of GTE in 2002, Seidenberg became sole CEO of Verizon. The company was facing increasing competition so Seidenberg displayed the steely side of his character, making major cuts to the New York workforce. His $8.44-billion acquisition of long-distance carrier MCI in 2006 positioned Verizon firmly in the 21st century, and he has continued to invest billions of dollars in wireless networks and the next-generation high-speed, fiber-optic broadband technology.

Vittorio Colao CEO, Vodafone Group plc

BIOGRAPHY
Born in Brescia, Italy, in 1961, Colao studied business at Bocconi University before attending Harvard Business School, from which he received an MBA.

BEST DECISION
Putting aside his pride to return to Vodafone as CEO, after losing out on the coveted role to a friend the first time around.

LESSON IN BUSINESS
Listen before making a decision—Colao believes in the importance of hearing what others have to say before drawing his own conclusions.

WELL-KNOWN for his analytical mind and discipline, leading Italian executive Colao made his name in the telecommunications industry. He took the helm of Vodafone at a time of stiff competition, declining prices, and economic downturn.

In 1996, Colao became COO of mobile phone company Omnitel Pronto Italia, which was taken over by Vodafone in 2000. An excellent grasp of corporate strategy led to his appointment as regional CEO for South Europe, Middle East, and Africa of Vodafone Group plc. Colao's area quickly became the group's most dynamic operation. Considered a candidate for CEO, in 2003 he lost out to colleague Arun Sarin, so left Vodafone to run RCS MediaGroup in 2004, returning in 2006 to head Vodafone's core operations in Europe. Cost-cutting measures resulted in around £550 million in savings and, on Sarin's departure in 2008, Colao became CEO. He tackled increased competition by driving the adoption of mobile internet access in Europe and expanding into the fast-growing emerging markets of Asia and Africa. However, the global economic downturn led to a focus on existing assets rather than new acquisitions, and a goal of cutting £1 billion a year from the group's operating costs of £22 billion by 2011.

"I feel an obligation to make sure this company is well positioned for the next 100 years." Ivan G. Seidenberg

Leif Johansson President, Director & CEO, Volvo

BIOGRAPHY
Born in Gothenberg, Sweden, in 1951. Johansson gained an MSc in engineering.

BEST DECISION
Controversially selling Volvo's car division to Ford for $6.5 billion in 1999. Johansson wanted to focus on heavy trucks.

LESSON IN BUSINESS
Do not baulk from making controversial decisions—Johansson defied a national outcry to sell Volvo cars, and then steered the group to large profits.

THINK OF SWEDEN, and the Volvo car comes to mind. Selling this symbol of national pride to the US giant Ford took both vision and nerves of steel. But it was Johansson's strategic decisions following the sale that made him a top CEO.

It was in Leif Johansson's genes to become a corporate master. His father, Lennart, was a senior executive for Sweden's corporate royalty, the Wallenberg family. Leif cut his teeth as a manager in one of their Electrolux factories, and later became chief executive. By the time he was appointed CEO at Volvo, the car company was in crisis. Its tiny production runs meant it could not achieve the economies of scale that gave its competitors the edge. Johansson believed Volvo was too small to compete as a top automobile manufacturer, but he had faith that it could become the world's top truck-maker. He sold the car division to Ford and invested profits in the truck business. He signed a deal with Renault to buy its truck division in 2002, and another to establish a Chinese production line the following year. By 2004 Volvo had supersized its 2000 sales from $13.8 billion to $25 billion. In 2008, Volvo recorded its highest ever quarterly sales of $11 billion.

Robert A. Iger President & CEO, Walt Disney

BIOGRAPHY
Born in New York in 1951. Iger earned a degree in Television-Radio at Ithaca College, and began his career in visual media working as a weatherman for a local TV station.

BEST DECISION
Buying Pixar Animation. The $7.4 billion acquisition in 2006 healed the rift with Roy Disney by returning groundbreaking animation to center stage.

LESSON IN BUSINESS
You can't make an omelette without breaking eggs—Iger had to dismantle his predecessor's empire to bring peace to Disney.

QUIET AND DECISIVE, Iger had long been underestimated at Disney but, when he replaced Eisner as president and CEO, he showed his true mettle. In his first year he completed a $7-billion takeover and returned it to the showbiz pages.

When Bob Iger was nominated Disney's CEO, there were roars of disapproval. Opponents cited poor ratings at ABC during his tenure as president; Disney shareholders expressed resentment at poor share price increases. The last surviving member of the dynasty dismissed Iger as a puppet of ousted CEO Michael Eisner. Roy Disney, the nephew of Walt, had fought a pitched battle with Eisner, accusing him of watering down the company's commitment to animation. The empire was divided and Iger had to exorcize Eisner's ghost to end the feuding. He removed one of Eisner's key aides, closed his strategic planning division, and returned creative decision-making to department heads. More importantly, he ended the damaging row with Pixar—which felt it had been cheated over *Toy Story 2*—in a $7.4-billion takeover that brought Apple's Steve Jobs, co-founder of Pixar and CEO since 1986, into the Disney fold as a member of the company's board of directors.

"The heart and soul of the company is creativity and innovation." Robert A. Iger

Richard Goyder CEO, Wesfarmers

BIOGRAPHY
Born in Western Australia in 1960 to farming parents. Goyder received a bachelor of commerce degree from the University of Western Australia.

BEST DECISION
Strengthening Wesfarmers' position with acquisitions, including the supermarket retail group Coles, and budget insurer Your Insurance Group.

LESSON IN BUSINESS
Be prudent in times of crisis—Goyder is taking action to reduce debt and cushion Wesfarmers' operations through tough times.

AS A SCHOOLBOY Goyder had toyed with the idea of entering politics, but instead he chose a commercial career that led him to the top job at Australia's largest private-sector employer, coal-to-groceries conglomerate Wesfarmers.

Goyder worked for construction supplies firm Tubemakers Australia before joining Wesfarmers as a business development manager in 1993. He rose to CEO of Wesfarmers Dalgety, overseeing the successful formation of Wesfarmers Landmark, then became CFO in 2004 and CEO in 2005. His predecessor had transformed the company from a $1-billion rural-dominated conglomerate into a $10-billion hardware, energy, chemical, and insurance giant. In 2007, Goyder oversaw the acquisition of supermarket retailer Coles Group for nearly AU$20 billion, one of the largest corporate takeovers in Australian history. However, by the end of 2008 he and his remuneration package were under scrutiny from shareholders as the Australian economy nosedived, Wesfarmer's share price continued to fall, and the company's debt faced refinancing by 2010. In early 2009, Goyder announced a cut in dividends and launched an AU$1.8-billion share sale to reduce debt.

Michael Luscombe CEO & MD, Woolworths Ltd

BIOGRAPHY
Born in 1954 in Melbourne, Australia. Luscombe grew up in a large family. He attended Monash University, Melbourne, where he graduated with a bachelor's degree in economics.

BEST DECISION
Standing by Woolworths' commitment to reduce carbon emissions by up to 40 percent by 2015, which won widespread support from consumers.

LESSON IN BUSINESS
Surround yourself with people of integrity—Luscombe credits much of his success to working with diligent colleagues.

WORKING FROM the bottom up, Luscombe spent nearly thirty years climbing through the ranks of Woolworths Limited, Australia's largest grocery chain. His success was rewarded with the CEO's job in 2006.

After leaving university, Luscombe traveled around Europe and the US, and worked for the Australian Bureau of Statistics, before accepting a job as a management trainee with Woolworths. His star began to rise after the merger of Woolworths and Safeway in Victoria in the 1980s, when he became the first "Woolies" man to be put in charge of a Safeway store. He moved to Sydney in 1998, and by 2004 was made director of supermarkets, leading the company's principal trading division. Luscombe was appointed CEO in 2006, and has continued to oversee Woolworths' growth, both organically and through acquisitions. Despite coming under fire from Australia's trade practices organization, the ACCC, over the practice of using planning laws to object to the construction of competing supermarkets, Woolworth's became the first Australian retailer to appear in the top 25 global retailers list published in the Deloitte *2008 Global Powers of Retailing* report.

"Instead of thinking: how do we stop spending, how do we stop hiring, how do we shed people, we are actually thinking and have a plan." Michael Luscombe

PASSING ON THE TORCH

Changing CEOs is one of the most important tasks a company faces. Some aim for continuity but end up stagnating, while others try to break with tradition and take a wrong turn. Succession is a huge challenge, both for the outgoing leader who may be tasked with selecting an heir and for the incoming CEO who has to build on success or turn around failure.

Following a company patriarch could be one of the hardest feats of all, although **Ray R. Irani** (p187) managed it at Occidental Petroleum when he replaced the imposing **Armand Hammer** following his death. Irani took a very different tack from his predecessor, but it was just what "Oxy" needed.

As the door closes for one CEO, it opens for another, though they may be stepping into a firefight. When **Gunter Thielen** (p265) took at Bertelesmann, he had to pour oil on troubled waters following differences between his predecessor, **Thomas Middelhoff**, and the controlling Mohn family over a mooted flotation. Skillfully, Thielen deferred the initial public offering and adopted a "back to basics" strategy that united the firm going forward ●

Prepare for Change

When **Edouard Michelin**, CEO of the eponymous French tire group, died unexpectedly in a boating accident in 2006, the company was shocked but prepared. Within days, CFO **Michel Rollier** took the helm as part of a carefully calculated succession plan. A year later, the group moved to its current three-CEO system with Rollier, **Didier Miraton**, and **Jean-Dominque Senard** acting as managing partners.

The pressure on high-profile CEOs to deliver impressive results can lead to unexpected departures too. **Carly Fiorina**'s turbulent reign at Hewlett-Packard ended when she was ousted by the board in 2005. As HP executives filled the CEO seat, boardroom rifts became public and confidence dwindled. Nine months later, HP finally found a successor in **Mark Hurd** (p314).

If they do plan ahead, firms naturally look within their walls to find a successor, and the current CEO is likely to play a key role in this. **Ellen Kullman**, who became CEO of US chemical company DuPont in early 2009, had been groomed for the role for two years as **Charles O. Holliday, Jr.** (p474) headed for retirement.

While some CEOs hang on to power, others see choosing a successor as key to their role. That was the view of Coca-Cola CEO **Roberto Goizueta** (p351), whose mantle passed to **Douglas Ivester** without fuss following Goizueta's death in 1997; Goizueta had been developing Ivester's potential since 1983.

Planning for Succession

Consider every scenario— There are many situations in which it may become appropriate to have a succession strategy in place, not just predictable, timed outcomes like retirement.

Don't just talk about it— Define responsibilities for making concrete succession plans, and follow these up.

Leave no stone unturned— Potential leaders can be found at every level of the organization, not just the highest. Seek them out and ensure that you encourage their development.

Grass is not always greener— Beware of the mindset that external candidates are always better. Don't underestimate the value of insiders' company knowledge and proven ability.

Successful Successors

Whether planned over years or instated suddenly, a change of CEO marks the start of a new era:

Joseph M. Hogan, ABB (Engineering: Switzerland)— *Hogan joined from GE Healthcare following a six-month search process.*

—

Mark Zesbaugh, ALLIANZ LIFE (Insurance: US)— *Zesbaugh's predecessor,* **Robert MacDonald**, *resisted naming his successor too early. Instead, he announced his retirement and chose CFO Zesbaugh a few weeks later. Retiring himself in 2007, Zesbaugh was succeeded by* **Gary Bhojwani**.

—

Craig Dunn, AMP LTD (Finance: Australia)— *Dunn was chosen as CEO having previously run AMP's superannuation business, where he caught the eye of former leader* **Andrew Mohl**. *Dunn continues his "boring but beautiful" growth strategy.*

—

Kevin Rollins, DELL, INC. (IT: US)— *Rollins spent several years as COO and president at Dell before becoming founder* **Michael Dell**'s *co-CEO and finally sole CEO in 2004. On Rollins' resignation in 2007, Dell resumed the role.*

—

Rodney O'Neal, DELPHI (Automotive parts: US)— *O'Neal regards board succession as being just as important as executive succession.*

—

Alan Mulally, FORD MOTOR COMPANY (Automotive: US)— *Joining from Boeing, he replaced* **Bill Ford** *in 2006. Although not a "car guy", Mulally has since proven himself.*

—

Myron E. Ullman III, J.C. PENNEY (Retail: US)— *Previous CEO* **Allen Questrom** *had chosen his number two to succeed him, but Penney's board recruited Ullman on the strength of his CEO experience at Macy's instead.*

—

James A. Skinner, McDONALD'S (Restaurants: US)— *McDonald's saw the importance of a succession plan two years in a row: Skinner became CEO when his predecessor* **Charlie Bell** *died of cancer in 2005. Bell had only just taken over from* **Jim Cantalupo**, *who died of a heart attack in 2004.*

—

Ian Smith, REED ELSEVIER (Publishing: UK)— *Smith took the reins in March 2009, following a three-month transition period as CEO-designate.*

—

Jonathan Schwartz, SUN MICROSYSTEMS (IT: US)— *Schwartz was carefully groomed by* **Scott McNealy** *to take over as Sun's CEO following his own 22-year tenure.*

—

"Develop a cadre of outstanding people who can do a really good job. You can't develop great CEOs overnight. It takes a lot of time." JOSEPH L. BOWER, HARVARD BUSINES SCHOOL

6

The Rebuilders

Herbert Hainer CEO, Adidas AG

AN ALL OR NOTHING character, Hainer worked in his family's butcher's shop when he first left university, and then launched his own bar while he chased his dream of becoming a professional footballer. When he realized he would not be able to follow his brother's success in the sport, he joined Procter & Gamble and threw his competitive spirit into raising their sales, before being headhunted to join Adidas. In Germany, where consensual, collaborative management is common, Hainer stood out as a decisive leader giving clear direction to staff and short shrift to "time-wasters."

BIOGRAPHY
Born in Dingolfing, Germany, in 1954. Hainer took a degree in business studies.

LEADERSHIP STYLE
Aggressive, focused, and demanding. Hainer's commitment to the cause is such that he switched his allegiance from 1860 Munich, the soccer team he supported as a boy, to their rivals Bayern, the team his company sponsors.

KEY STRENGTH
His head for marketing. Hainer understands the importance of tying in the Adidas brand to major sporting events, and has exploited industry sales opportunities to great effect.

BEST DECISION
The 2005 takeover of Reebok, which allowed Adidas to challenge Nike for market leadership.

LEARNING THE GAME Hainer is known for his sportsman's competitive instinct, and his devotion to the badge. When he joined the company in the late 1980s, Adidas was a struggling team that had lost the drive and direction of the founding Dassler family. Hainer could see that it had lost its luster. As a sales director, he was selling its sports bags, balls, tracksuits, and footwear before being given responsibility for national sales performance in 1991. He was appointed CEO ten years later.

BIGGER IS BETTER Adidas had been routed in the United States, where Nike and Reebok dominated. Olympic legend Jesse Owens and boxing hero Muhammad Ali both wore Adidas and the company's famous three stripes logo had retained its iconic status, but in the popular market, it was being lapped. Hainer demanded better quality products, and cut production lead times to major sporting events. He made sure Adidas could cope with the surge in shirt demand that followed a series of wins by the German soccer team, and used offical tournament draws to heighten the promotion of match-specific balls. In 2005, he completed the purchase of Reebok, taking Adidas onto the same playing field as Nike for the first time. The gap in sales between the giants narrowed, but Hainer's inroads into the Chinese market look set to give Adidas the edge. His sponsorship of the successful 2008 Olympics gave Adidas maximum brand exposure as it opened its largest-ever sports store in Beijing. If his projections are correct, sales from China alone will allow Adidas to defeat the old enemy and establish itself as world champion in sporting goods.

LESSONS IN BUSINESS: LIVING THE MOTTO

Hainer never misses an opportunity to promote Adidas and doesn't allow excuses. "I am very direct. I tell people what I think, good or bad. I am aggressive in getting things done. I don't want bullshitters around."
→ Dedicate yourself to your company. Identify with and demonstrate the brand at all times.
→ Avoid behavior that runs against the mission statement or motto of your company.
→ Make heavy demands on your people; they will give of their best working hard and playing hard to meet your expectations.

"I am a passionate leader who motivates people with my own—impatient!—style." Herbert Hainer

Gail J. McGovern President & CEO, American Red Cross

IMPECCABLE CREDENTIALS in both the business and academic worlds were the driving factors behind McGovern's appointment as president and CEO of American Red Cross in April 2008. A veteran of some of the leading US corporations and a respected Harvard Business School professor, she offered just the kind of blue-chip corporate know-how required to turn around the fortunes of the ailing humanitarian organization, at a time when it was suffering setbacks in both its public perception and its finances.

BIOGRAPHY
Born in 1952 in Springfield, New Jersey. McGovern earned a bachelor's degree in quantitative sciences from Johns Hopkins University, Baltimore, and an MBA from Columbia Business School, New York.

LEADERSHIP STYLE
Building the right team quickly and effectively is central to McGovern's approach both in business and philanthropy.

KEY STRENGTH
Promoting the brand that is at the heart of the Red Cross, which donors, governments, and community groups respond to.

BEST DECISION
Making an urgent priority of repairing the organization's relations with key groups.

CORPORATE STAR McGovern began her career as a programmer at telecoms giant AT&T, rising to become executive vice-president of its largest business unit, the consumer markets division. She moved to Fidelity Investments in 1998, as president of its distribution and services wings, dealing with four million customers with assets of $500 billion. As a result, she was recognized by *Fortune* as one of the 50 most powerful women in corporate America in 2000 and 2001. In 2002, she began teaching marketing at Harvard Business School.

CHARITY IN CRISIS When McGovern took over at the American Red Cross in 2008, the 127-year-old organization faced serious challenges. Its hallowed reputation had taken a beating from a fumbled response to Hurricane Katrina in 2005, poor fundraising efforts, a leadership crisis that made McGovern the seventh chief in as many years, and rising debts. Just as she took the job, the charity was fined for failing to manage its blood supply properly, its disaster fund was depleted by floods in the US Midwest, and the earthquake in China's Sichuan province presented another urgent crisis.

Recognizing that the American Red Cross was "a brand to die for", McGovern quickly turned her well honed marketing skills to restoring it to its former glory. She began a campaign to raise $100 million to replenish the disaster fund, and also to deal with the problems of low morale and the need for restructuring within the group. McGovern was quick to smooth relations with government officials, business sponsors, and community-based groups, who were all central to the charity's effective operation.

LESSONS IN BUSINESS: PROTECTING THE BRAND

It seems inconceivable that the Red Cross "brand" could ever become tarnished; but repairing its image and putting in place processes to prevent disillusionment with the organization became McGovern's top priority.
- → Remember that brands take a long time to establish and exploit, but almost no time at all to destroy.
- → Make sure people understand that whatever their job, from research and development to distribution, they can enhance or damage the brand.
- → Define your corporate vision in line with your brand, and communicate this both internally and externally.

"Our mission is to be there for the American people every day." Gail J. McGovern

Cynthia Carroll CEO, Anglo American

THE CHOICE of Carroll to be CEO of global mining group Anglo American in 2007 came as a big surprise to those familiar with the company. Traditionally, Anglo American's executives had been life-long insiders, South Africans, and men. Carroll was none of these. Her appointment signalled an intention to provide an outsider's fresh perspective on the company, and she immediately set in train a range of new initiatives and, most importantly, shook up the company's tired corporate culture, fostering responsibility, risk-taking, and action.

BIOGRAPHY
Born in Philadelphia, Pennsylvania, in 1956. Carroll received a BSc in geology from Skidmore College in Saratoga Springs, New York, an MSc from the University of Kansas, and an MBA from Harvard.

LEADERSHIP STYLE
Warm, friendly, and easy-going, Carroll believes in inspiring others to lead.

KEY STRENGTH
Not afraid to make changes, no matter how unpopular.

BEST DECISION
Changing the culture at Anglo American, realizing that it was holding everything back.

THE OUTSIDER Carroll worked her way up through the tough world of the mining industry and by 2006 she was running a large part of the aluminum maker Alcan when she met Anglo American's chairman at Davos. At the time, Anglo had lost its title as the world's largest mining group, the performance of its shares had fallen behind that of its major rivals during the biggest resources boom of all time, and the company was in need of a serious dose of rejuvenation.

CULTURE SHIFT Carroll injected a sense of urgency and pace into a company that was renowned for its conservative, old-school ways. While Anglo's biggest competitors focused on a takeover mania that was running through the industry, she concerned herself instead with implementing a far-reaching internal shake-up aimed at revitalizing the group. Anglo had traditionally been run as a disparate conglomerate, resulting in little interaction between the different business units, and Carroll set out to change that, integrating its various operations and slimming down its myriad layers of management. She altered the company's values, demanding that executives show initiative after years of receiving instructions from above. She launched the long-awaited sale of the UK-based building materials business Tarmac, the final step in a restructuring aimed at focusing the group on its mining operations, and made a number of key acquisitions, buying big stakes in an iron-ore mine in Brazil and copper projects in Peru and Alaska. Carroll has made significant strides toward her goal of turning Anglo American into the world's leading mining company.

LESSONS IN BUSINESS: THINKING AFRESH

Big is not necessarily beautiful. The biggest, best-established businesses can be the most moribund, and all businesses can benefit from an outsider's viewpoint and a revitalizing gust of fresh thinking.
➔ Appoint staff with particular expertise that you lack.
➔ Use consultants only for their expertise in planning processes. Get them to help you or your people come up with the new ideas.
➔ When fresh thinking makes change necessary, use enthusiastic "agents of change" to help sell the idea.

"I'm looking for people to act as leaders." Cynthia Carroll

Randall L. Stephenson Chairman, President & CEO, AT&T, Inc.

THE LEADING telephone services provider in the US was facing the twin challenges of intense competition and rapidly changing technology, when Stephenson stepped up to the role of CEO in 2007. He responded to the situation by accelerating the transformation of AT&T from a largely landline-based company into a multiplatform telecoms provider, developing new technology, acquiring companies to complement AT&T's services, and forming alliances with a variety of partners ranging from individuals to major players.

BIOGRAPHY
Born in Oklahoma City in 1960. Stephenson received a BSc in accounting from the University of Central Oklahoma and a master of accountaning degree from the University of Oklahoma.

LEADERSHIP STYLE
Blunt, charismatic, and easy-going, Stephenson is particularly hands-on.

KEY STRENGTH
An ability to see through the tangle of competing issues and identify the key challenges facing a huge, sprawling, and complex organization.

BEST DECISION
Focusing on the wireless world as the key to the future.

DEBT-BUSTER Stephenson spent more than 20 years at Southwestern Bell Corp. (SBC), which merged to form AT&T, Inc. in 2005, before being named CEO. During his tenure as CFO of SBC, from 2001 to 2004, the company reduced its net debt from $30 billion to almost zero, giving it the financial muscle to make the key strategic acquisitions of AT&T Wireless, AT&T Corp., and Bell South that allowed it to position itself for the new telecoms world. Assuming the CEO role in 2007, his challenge was to use the newly acquired assets to grow the company in a fiercely competitive market.

FROM COST-CUTTING TO GROWTH
Stephenson's attention had to shift sharply from cutting costs to focusing on growth. AT&T was America's largest provider of landline, with more than 64 million phone lines, and it was earning healthy profits, but to prosper in the new telecoms world the company needed to make an impact in the areas of wireless, broadband, and television. From the outset, Stephenson set out his clear intention to place wireless services at the core of AT&T's activities and to develop multiplatform services, and he immediately took key steps in the new fast-moving areas. Central among these was the company's roll-out of the Video Share platform, a rival to YouTube, and U-verse, an IP-based television system that put AT&T into direct competition with cable companies. Stephenson also entered into partnerships with such big names as IBM and Mexico's América Móvil, as well as becoming the exclusive carrier of Apple's iPhone, an important step in establishing AT&T's position in the wireless world.

LESSONS IN BUSINESS: MONITORING THE CHANGES

However big you are and however secure, your industry is changing daily, especially if the word "digital" can be applied to any part of it. The days are gone when a market leader could rely on directing the market.
→ Keep a close eye on changes in the industry and reshape your business to be ready for the next stage.
→ Be prepared to move fast. If a competitor has made your new product irrelevant, change it.
→ Keep everyone aware that if their strategies do not include contingency plans for the unexpected, then they are being arrogant.

"If you're not pushing forward hard, nothing happens." Randall L. Stephenson

Andrea Jung CEO, Avon

PERSONIFYING A NEW openness to non-white CEOs in the US establishment, Jung is the highest-ranking Chinese-American CEO of a *Fortune* 500 company. She used her marketing experience to relaunch cosmetics giant Avon, revitalizing the brand by growing both her consumer and sales-force base, and recapturing its position as the leading seller of beauty products worldwide. As the daughter of first-generation Chinese immigrants, perhaps one of Jung's greatest achievements to date has been turning Avon China into a $600-million company.

BIOGRAPHY

Born in Toronto, Canada, in 1959, Jung grew up in Wellesley, Massachusetts. She graduated *magna cum laude* from Princeton University in 1979, with a degree in English literature.

LEADERSHIP STYLE

Decisive, driven, understanding. She has always encouraged flexible work schedules, recognizing that family sometimes takes precedence over work: "Eliminate 10 out of 20 things you don't have to do, and pick the 10 most important things for your family. Some days the company loses."

KEY STRENGTH

Understanding direct-selling strategies and adapting to the buying habits of women, for whom a professional career meant that when Avon called, there was nobody home.

BEST DECISION

Enabling sales reps to become self-sufficient, which released their potential to help grow the business and reform it as "The Company for Women".

TRANSFORMING THE BRAND

Jung went to Avon in 1994 after an early career with department stores Bloomingdale's and Neiman Marcus. It became obvious she had joined a company whose brand was old-fashioned and dated, compared to its far slicker French rival, L'Oréal. Enhancing the company's image was of paramount importance. One of Jung's first steps was to upgrade the packaging and unify Avon's various regional brands into global lines, such as Avon Color.

EXPLOITING GROWTH OPPORTUNITIES

Despite her lack of experience in operations and overseas business, Jung's decisive approach impressed the board and she quickly rose through the ranks, becoming the company's first female CEO in 1999. She has been committed to the task of turning a tired brand

into one of the world's top cosmetic companies and the leading direct-sales brand. Jung's vision was for Avon to become "The Company for Women," allowing the sales reps to achieve self-sufficiency by offering them loans to buy start-up stock. She has retained core customers and attracted a new generation of younger buyers and sellers, by offering products such as vitamins and weight-control programs. Jung has seized opportunities for growth, creating a special line of products for the retailer Wal-Mart and also exploiting the internet as an area of key expansion. When profits dipped in 2005, Jung faced the biggest challenge of her career. Criticized by industry analysts, she immediately responded by restructuring the company, eliminating eight levels of management, shifting production offshore and cutting costs by around $300 million.

LESSONS IN BUSINESS: KNOWING YOUR LIMITS

Aware that knowledge of operations wasn't her strong suit, Jung used Avon's reputation and her experience in marketing to develop new products and to woo new consumers, big retailers—and the sales force.

→ As a manager, you may come from a background in sales, production, or finance. Use that knowledge when in post and do not pretend to understand other areas deeply.

→ When talking to people in unfamiliar functions, agree a summary with them to ensure you have understood.

→ Encourage your people in areas where your skills are less strong—but lead where your talents lie.

"Women like myself, CEOs, can pave the way for more women to get to the top." Andrea Jung

Gunter Thielen CEO (2002–07), Bertelsmann AG

A TRAINED ENGINEER, Thielen impressed the board at publishing and media group Bertelsmann by turning around its printing division in the 1980s. He repeated the trick with the entire group after becoming CEO in 2002, placating the firm's owners and founders with a strategy of streamlining operations and ruthless achievement of financial targets that saw the company move back into profitability and focus. After just two years at the helm, Thielen steered the group to a 20 percent increase in profits.

BIOGRAPHY
Thielen was born in Quierschied, in Germany's Saarland region, in 1942. He studied mechanical engineering and economics at Aachen Technical University in western Germany.

LEADERSHIP STYLE
Diplomatic, decisive, visionary. Thielen's success at Bertelsmann was founded on decentralization, entrepreneurship, and leadership based on partnership. He smoothed over past conflicts, while mapping out an inspiring new vision for the group.

KEY STRENGTH
The ability to balance traditional family-business values and decisive strategic thinking.

BEST DECISION
Decentralizing the sprawling Bertelsmann business portfolio, which allowed the disparate divisions to perform.

TROUBLED WATERS From 1970, Thielen held a range of leadership positions at German chemicals group BASF, before becoming technical director of the Wintershall oil and gas refinery in Kassel in 1976. He joined media and publishing giant Bertelsmann in 1980, taking charge of its printing and manufacturing division from 1985, which he turned into Arvato, a cutting-edge communications and media service provider. Rising to the executive board in 1985, Thielen became CEO in 2002. He inherited a difficult situation, with debts of $3.5 billion and dubious recent acquisitions, such as Napster, the controversial online file-sharing site. Moreover, 82-year-old patriarch Reinhard Mohn, a member of the group's founding family, reasserted control after differences with the previous CEO. Thielen moved quickly to calm the situation with a "back to basics" strategy, returning the firm to its traditional decentralized management structure, a refocus on paper publishing, and astute divestments to cut back on debt.

NEW SUCCESS AND A NEW ROLE Thielen followed his reconciliatory start with a number of streamlining measures: deep cost cuts at BMG, the group's music division, the sale of websites Napster and BarnesandNoble.com, and a renewed emphasis on Europe rather than the US. TV station RTL made a major contribution to profit, and, by 2004, Bertelsmann had built cash reserves of €2 billion. Thielen retired in 2007 but remains an influential figure, becoming chairman and CEO in 2008 of the Bertelsmann Foundation, a private not-for-profit organization that pursues a range of social-reform goals, funded by a majority share in Bertelsmann.

LESSONS IN BUSINESS: STEERING LIGHTER

Realizing that central control was not the best way to manage Bertelsmann's broad portfolio of divisions, Thielen abolished the post of Chief Operating Officer and returned authority to divisional managers.
→ Make managers accountable for strategic outcomes in their divisions first, and group financial objectives second, but be careful to avoid a blame culture when these two do not coincide.
→ Identify performance bottlenecks created by joining unrelated divisions, and loosen the ties between them.
→ Find areas in which divisional managers know far more than central directors, and increase their control.

"The Bertelsmann businesses are all so different and require such different management skills that one person can't run them all." Gunter Thielen

John Chidsey Chairman & CEO, Burger King

BURGER KING was struggling to survive following years of indifferent management when Chidsey joined the company. Falling sales and unhappy franchisees were the clearest signs of the malaise at the restaurant chain, but Chidsey recognized that the underlying problem was a decline in the brand itself. His turnaround plan focused on a wholesale revitalization with a cutting-edge marketing campaign, and within a short period he had turned a dowdy name into a cool one, laying the basis for a sharp improvement in financial performance.

BIOGRAPHY
Born in 1963. Chidsey received a bachelor's degree from Davidson College, North Carolina, and both an MBA in finance and accounting and a law degree from Emory University in Atlanta, Georgia.

LEADERSHIP STYLE
Informal. Chidsey prefers casual one-to-ones to large meetings, and aims to create an environment in which people want to be part of the direction.

KEY STRENGTH
A holistic view of the business, recognizing that everything from the advertising to the style of the store and the size of the burger forms part of the consumer's experience.

BEST DECISION
Making the revitalization of the brand, through innovative marketing, the centerpiece of his turnaround plan.

HEAVYWEIGHT EXPERIENCE Chidsey developed his experience of big brands while working at PepsiCo. He then moved to the hotel, car rentals, and real estate group Cendant, where he became chairman and CEO of the $6-billion vehicle service division, which included Avis and Budget, and of the financial services division.

CRITICAL MOMENT When Chidsey joined Burger King as CFO in 2004, things were looking bad for the fast-food chain. A third of its restaurants were in financial distress, sales were stuck in a seven-year slide, franchisees were on the brink of revolt, and stores were closing. When, in 2006, he became the company's 12th CEO in 20 years, Chidsey began a turnaround that built on the initial work done over the previous couple of years

by the private-equity leadership group of which he had been a part. His strategy involved a two-pronged approach, introducing new upscale products and new menu options for cash-strapped customers, while also inventing new types of outlet designed to promote the company's offerings. Most crucially, he paid close attention to the Burger King brand, putting in place a long-range, cutting-edge marketing campaign aimed at boosting the brand's image and appealing to younger consumers in a way that had not been seriously tried for years. Within a year, Burger King was showing a sales increase for the first time and there was a net growth in the number of stores after two years of decline. Sales continued to grow in the following years, and Chidsey's plans for international expansion offer the promise of further improvement.

LESSONS IN BUSINESS: REVAMPING A BRAND

Chidsey showed that, with the right vision and strategy, even a brand that appears to be in terminal decline can be turned around. He had faith in the basic product, the brand and its international fame.
→ Measure the success of a brand by its longevity as well as its market share. A well-established brand should never die.
→ Take an old brand to a new market; it should be easier than taking the time to create a new brand.
→ Realize that with a little innovation and a new presentation an old brand could be given new life.

"The CEO job is the most overrated position in the world. It's the quality of the team." John Chidsey

Lee Iacocca President, Chairman & CEO (1978–92), Chrysler

SAVING CHRYSLER from oblivion in the 1980s, Iacocca's success as a CEO is one of the 20th century's classic corporate turnaround stories. His remarkable achievement in restoring the apparently doomed carmaker back to health has made Iacocca a highly revered figure both for his business acumen and his overall leadership skills. It has become a textbook example of how one person's vision, insight, and persistence can transform even the most troubled company from a basket case to a thriving concern.

BIOGRAPHY
Born in Pennsylvania in 1924. The son of Italian immigrants, Iacocca studied industrial engineering. In the 80s he was described by *Reader's Digest* as "the living embodiment of the American dream".

LEADERSHIP STYLE
Bold and prepared to take risks Iacocca was always ready to try radical solutions. If that meant coming across as dictatorial, so be it. He was also happy to take the spotlight.

KEY STRENGTH
Being creative when everyone else was panicking.

BEST DECISION
Having the strength to swallow the company's pride and go to the US government to ask for support to avoid bankruptcy.

AGAINST THE WALL Iacocca's 32-year career with Ford Motor Company came to a dramatic end when he was fired in 1978 by Henry Ford II, despite the company having produced a $2-billion profit in his last year as president. Iacocca was immediately snapped up to take over at Chrysler, where the impact of oil prices, competition from Japan, high manufacturing costs, vehicle recalls, and some poor strategic decisions had pushed the 50-year-old company to the brink of bankruptcy.

DOING THE UNTHINKABLE To deal with the immediate threat, Iacocca took the audacious step of petitioning the US government to guarantee $1.5 billion of loans. This was a controversial move for both the company and the government, but Iacocca argued that the number of jobs it would save would make it worthwhile. With the immediate threat removed, Iacocca then reshaped the company. He hired the best managers he could find, closed plants, and laid off workers. He streamlined factories and equipped them with the latest machinery. He stopped production of unprofitable big cars and began work on smaller ones, in line with the post-oil-shock demand for more fuel-efficient vehicles. As his changes began to bite and the company's health improved, Iacocca entered into joint ventures and made acquisitions that suited the new shape of the organization. He also became the public face of Chrysler, making frequent appearances, fronting TV commercials, and challenging consumers with the line, "If you find a better car, buy it." In his last year at the helm, Chrysler was the only American automaker to turn a profit.

LESSONS IN BUSINESS: TAKING DRASTIC ACTION

Being prepared to take big, bold steps was the key to Iacocca's success in saving Chrysler. His insight was one that few people accept: in drastic situations, sometimes only the most drastic solutions will do.
→ If a key customer is unprofitable and will not accept poorer terms, stop doing business with them.
→ Consider pulling out of less profitable markets if you are making 80 percent of your profit from 20 percent of your customers.
→ Swiftly move out a team member who is underperforming; it's in their interests as well as the company's.

"Motivation is everything." Lee Iacocca

Sergio Marchionne CEO, Fiat

THE RAPID TURNAROUND of the ailing car maker Fiat has assured Marchionne's place alongside Chrysler's Lee Iacocca in the list of great car industry saviors. Within just two years of his arrival, Marchionne's powerful instinct for how to generate change, together with his readiness to make the necessary cuts and his vision for the company's future, not only saved the venerable Italian giant from collapse but also put it comfortably on the road to aggressive expansion around the world.

BIOGRAPHY
Born in Chieti, Italy, in 1952. His father was a former member of the Italian police force. When Marchionne was 14, his parents moved to Toronto, Canada. He studied at the University of Toronto before earning an MBA from the University of Windsor, Ontario, and a bachelor of laws from Osgoode Hall Law School of York University, Toronto.

LEADERSHIP STYLE
Responsible. He makes accountability the cornerstone of his leadership.

KEY STRENGTH
The ability to find the very best people and let them get on with the job required.

BEST DECISION
Slashing the over-inflated bureaucracy that prevented Fiat from achieving its potential.

RESCUE EXPERT Two years before Marchionne was called in to try and save Fiat in 2004, the company was almost wiped out after reporting losses of nearly €3 billion at its car-making division. It somehow limped on, through four CEOs in the intervening two years and despite General Motors' refusal to buy the car-making arm as laid down in an option agreed in 2000. Marchionne, who had already performed a dramatic turnaround at Swiss-based SGS, was the perfect choice.

REINVENTING THE OLD FIAT Marchionne's success at SGS was founded largely on his willingness to cut jobs and expenses across the company and slash the number of bloated management layers. He immediately applied the same medicine to Fiat, cutting through the company's weighty bureaucracy, unraveling its antiquated organizational structure, and forming a can-do culture. He jettisoned non-core businesses, negotiated Fiat out of the alliance with GM, and set out an ambitious program of new car releases. To take the company forward he brought in a talented young team and gave them the power they needed. The medicine worked. A year after Marchionne took over, the company had returned to profitability for the first time in five years and was beginning to claw back market share in Europe, with the new models from the leaner, keener Fiat proving hugely successful. At the same time, Marchionne formed joint manufacturing ventures in India and China and began courting carmakers in the US. Fiat also re-entered markets that it had left years before, and plans a return to the US market after an absence of more than 25 years.

LESSONS IN BUSINESS: EXAMINING THE FUNDAMENTALS

A crisis in business may be caused by high costs or dwindling sales, but the root problem is usually deeper and a thorough overhaul could be the only solution. Getting to the heart of the matter involves examining every aspect of the company.
→ Come out of a crisis by examining divisional structure and their business processes, particularly sales.
→ Now review your systems, products and markets, working out which to grow, leave the same, or shrink.
→ Finally review your relationships with other companies to check that you are in win/win positions.

"The struggle for survival never stops." Sergio Marchionne

G. Richard Wagoner, Jr. Chairman & CEO (2000–09), GM

TRYING TO RESTORE General Motors to health after decades of poor management was Wagoner's overriding challenge even before he became CEO in 2000. GM's chronic problems of a slow-moving, bureaucratic culture, a history of questionable product releases, pension-fund deficits, enormous health-care costs, and recurring labor problems may take years to put right. Wagoner had deployed an entire toolbox of strategies to turn the company around but, as the economy worsened, he was forced to stand down in 2009.

BIOGRAPHY
Born in Richmond, Virginia, in 1953. Wagoner received a bachelor's degree in economics from Duke University in North Carolina, and an MBA from Harvard Business School.

LEADERSHIP STYLE
Low-key, easy-going, and self-effacing. Wagoner picks the right people and lets them get on with their jobs.

KEY STRENGTH
Being prepared to challenge a deep-seated corporate culture.

BEST DECISION
Appointing outsiders to key positions, thereby demonstrating that he would not let the company be held back by tradition.

COMPANY INSIDER A company man for three decades, "Rick" Wagoner knows the ins and outs of GM's problems better than anybody. He had his first major success when he updated the company's operations in the Brazilian market. Later, as president of GM's North American operations, he engineered a major turnaround, producing a profit in his first year, after three consecutive years of losses. His success made him the logical choice for the top job.

FACING THE CHALLENGE Made CFO in 1992, Wagoner was a key part of former CEO Jack Smith's efforts to bring GM back to health. When the company lost $30 billion during a three-year period in the early 1990s, Wagoner and Smith set out to force it back to basics. They began a bold program of cost-cutting, payroll reduction, and revamping aging plants. When Wagoner took over as CEO, he ramped up the efficiency drive. Within three years, his tough approach was showing results, putting GM close to industry leaders Honda and Toyota in productivity and quality. However, he still had the legacy of a bloated bureaucracy and lavish employee benefits to deal with. Wagoner made further progress by breaking with company tradition in appointing outsiders to the key positions of head of product development and CFO, and then giving them exceptional powers to try and solve the company's problems. GM has suffered in the global downturn, seeing its worst performances in its 100-year history. Despite this, Wagoner was confident of a rebound, and was focusing on cutbacks, restructuring product portfolios, and increasing federal bailout packages, when the American government cut him short and he stood down in 2009.

LESSONS IN BUSINESS: CHANGING THE CULTURE

Even a company insider can change a culture that's holding a business back. Wagoner has broken up previously warring factions within the company, and streamlined decision-making on new products, enabling the company to reduce development time for new models.

→ Rethink the ways things have always been done: there's a good chance they're being done wrongly.
→ Put top management in the spotlight by imposing strict and detailed performance targets.
→ Before an emergency happens, clear out the "old guard" who will at best hold you back, at worst kill you.

"Gains in quality and productivity come from years of hard work." G. Richard Wagoner, Jr.

LEADING TURNAROUNDS

Turning a failing company into a successful one is one of the greatest achievements for a CEO. When the going is tough, a company is facing the crunch, profits are falling or losses rising, and the share price is on the slide, it takes an outstanding degree of leadership to set things right. Great turnaround CEOs are able to act quickly and decisively to stop a company's decline and chart a new course. The stakes and the pressures are high, but so are the rewards, and CEOs with a proven record of turnarounds can name their price. **Lee Iacocca** (p261) made corporate history with Chrysler, taking the unprecedented step of asking the US government to guarantee the failing company's loans and then, with this protection in place, setting about streamlining the company to provide it with a future. In the same industry, **Sergio Marchionne** (p262) took a different but equally effective approach at Fiat, smashing its antiquated organization and creating a can-do culture that brought the company back to health ●

Change Masters

Leaders who have engineered turnarounds include:

Michael Sabia, BCE, Inc. (Telecommunications: Canada)— *When he left in 2008, Sabia had shifted BCE back to its phone company roots by selling off many of its various media holdings.*

Robert P. May, Calpine (Energy: US)—*By selling off plants and reducing the workforce, May saved Calpine from Chapter 11 bankruptcy.*
—

Restored to Health

Reversing the fortunes of an ailing company requires special qualities. Many leaders have tried to pull organizations back from the brink, but few have successfully accomplished one of the toughest tasks any CEO can face.

When **Fred Hassan** arrived as CEO of US pharmaceutical company Schering Plough in spring 2003, he was fresh from overseeing the recovery and sale of another drugs company, Pharmacia. Schering Plough was in a bad way: there were problems with the drug pipeline; its main money spinner, Claritin, was out of patent protection; and the stock was down by 75 percent. Hassan froze salary increases and bonuses, cut costs, hired new managers, changed the corporate mindset—telling the sales force if they

had to choose between doing what was right and making a sale, then to walk away from the sale—increased R&D spend, and licensed new drugs. Through a combination of cost-cutting, communication, building trust, and revitalizing R&D, Hassan nursed Schering Plough back to health and set the stock price on an upwards trajectory.

Nolan Archibald stepped up to the position of CEO at Black and Decker in the US in 1985 and proceeded to revive the faltering business. Armed with a three-step strategy—create a plan, build a new executive team, and make some tough decisions—he implemented a new global product strategy. The company's

engineers adopted a Japanese approach to manufacturing, stripping down tools made by other firms to analyze them and adopting just-in-time, continuous-flow supply chain methods for inventory management.

Eiji Hosoya became chairman of Japan's Resona Bank in 2003, following the company's bailout and effective nationalization. By reducing non-performing loans the company was turning a profit again by 2004 and starting to pay back its debts. The company even managed to avoid getting heavily involved in the sub-prime markets that created trouble for so many other banks worldwide.

Michael Laphen, Computer Sciences Corp. (IT: US)—*Used a five-point strategic plan to get CSC back on the information highway.*

—

Gary Convis, Dana Holding Corp. (Automotive parts: US)—*Arrived as CEO at Dana after it had filed for Chapter 11 bankruptcy, and helped get the company firing on all cylinders.*

—

Richard Dreiling, Dollar General: (Retail: US)—*By increasing private-label goods and adding other higher margin products, among other things, Dreiling was able to increase net income at the discount store by 48 percent.*

—

Benjamin Lipps, Fresnius Medical Care (Health sector: Germany)— *Led the group's expansion into services by acquiring the National Medical Care, and merging it with Fresenius's dialysis business.*

—

Michael I. Roth, Interpublic Group (Advertising: US)—*Brought in to deal with accounting anomalies, Roth shored up the company's financial standing.*

—

Masahiro Sakane, Komatsu Ltd (Manufacturing Japan)—*When he left in 2008, Sakane had turned around the failing heavy equipment manufacturer by concentrating on emerging markets.*

—

John Rishton, Koninklijke Ahold N.V. (Retail: Netherlands)—*Reversed the grocery chain's fortunes in the US by rebranding and repositioning stores.*

—

Trevor Fetter, Tenet Healthcare (Health sector: US)—*Launched a commitment-to-quality initiative to stem the flight of customers.*

—

Peter Lynch, Winn-Dixie Stores (Retail: US)—*By closing stores and formulating a long term plan to comprehensively remodel the ones left open, Lynch pulled Winn-Dixie out of Chapter 11 bankruptcy.*

—

"You develop a plan to leverage the strengths and correct the weaknesses, and you communicate that plan and get everybody to believe in it."
NOLAN ARCHIBALD

Building the Recovery

Pick the low-hanging fruit— Look for some quick successes for motivation, and to lay the groundwork for the tougher challenges to come.

Stop the bleeding—Identify and target the areas where the company is leaking money.

Take risks—Nobody ever turned a company around by being timid.

Change the culture—Find out how the company thinks and operates; reverse the mindsets that have led to failure.

Lou Gerstner Chairman & CEO (1993–2002), IBM

IN HIS NINE YEARS at the helm of IBM, Gerstner masterminded one of the greatest turnarounds in corporate history. Faced with a large, complicated organization that was cash-strapped and on the verge of disintegration, Gerstner took the hard decisions and the big steps required to turn things around. The key to his success was his transformation of a corporate culture that was destroying the company. He introduced rewards for teamwork and was prepared to ditch some products, a move that lifelong employees had resisted.

BIOGRAPHY
Born in Mineola, New York, in 1942. Gerstner received a bachelor's degree in engineering from Dartmouth College, New Hampshire, and an MBA from Harvard Business School.

LEADERSHIP STYLE
Direct, visible, and tough. Gerstner kept a sign in his office with a quotation from John le Carré: "A desk is a dangerous place from which to view the world."

KEY STRENGTH
Perceiving that the heart of a business is its culture, and being able to focus on this as the engine of change.

BEST DECISION
Keeping IBM united rather than allowing it to be broken up into separate divisions.

INTO THE BLUE After a glittering career at financial services giant American Express, during which its membership rose from 8.6 million to 30.7 million, followed by a stint as chairman and CEO of food and tobacco conglomerate RJR Nabisco, in 1993 Gerstner was named chairman and CEO of IBM, providing him with the toughest challenge of his business life. The "big blue" elephant that had practically run the computer industry for decades was fast becoming a dinosaur and was on the verge of extinction.

HARNESSING THE DINOSAUR When Gerstner arrived at IBM, a plan was in place to separate the company's divisions and allow them to brand and manage themselves. Gerstner took the view that IBM was worth more than the sum of its parts and stopped the plan. He took the hard decision to cut out billions of dollars in costs, mainly through layoffs, and to raise money by assets sales. He then created an entirely new focus for IBM, concentrating on IT services (which rapidly grew to represent half of the company's turnover) and emphasizing the future of the internet as a key business tool.

Perhaps the most distinctive feature of Gerstner's tenure was the way in which he approached IBM as an outsider, a viewpoint that he maintained throughout his tenure. Management, he believed, had become preoccupied with itself rather than with customers, with rivalry between departments. Introducing rewards for teamwork and getting rid of old products that others had found difficult to shed, making way for the new, he effectively gave IBM a new lease on life.

LESSONS IN BUSINESS: LOOKING IN FROM THE OUTSIDE

Gerstner's crucial insight was that insiders are the worst people to judge what's happening to a business. However long they've been there, the best CEOs always remain outsiders.

→ Take stock. Ask yourself what an outsider would make of your strengths and weaknesses.

→ Use third parties, such as market-research companies, to check that your opinion of how customers perceive you is correct.

→ Ask new recruits what they thought about you before they joined. They can give you vital observations.

"Transformation of an enterprise begins with a sense of crisis." Lou Gerstner

Samuel Palmisano President & CEO, IBM

APPOINTED CEO in 2002, Palmisano is the man who saved IBM for a second time, and took it on to unprecedented glory. Throughout more than 25 years with the company, he has displayed an extraordinary drive to succeed, and at key stages in IBM's development it was Palmisano who made the decisions that raised sales and kept it ahead of its rivals. Since his appointment, revenues have hit over $100 billion, the company has reached record pre-tax income levels, and IBM's profit margins have grown successfully year by year.

BIOGRAPHY
Born in Baltimore, Maryland, in 1951. Palmisano studied history at Johns Hopkins University, Baltimore.

LEADERSHIP STYLE
Intense, demanding, and loyal. Palmisano runs "the Big Blue" fervently, leading by example with a punishing workload and demanding the same from his fellow "IBMers".

KEY STRENGTH
Getting personally involved with the company and refusing to keep managerial distance, as seen through his personal business campaigns and attitude to micro-managing.

BEST DECISION
Launching "Project Pain" in 1999 when, in the face of a downturn, he sold IBM servers at a 70 percent discount to boost sales, keeping the company ahead of the competition.

GOING THE EXTRA MILE It wasn't just Palmisano's drive that drew attention to him at IBM, it was also his initiative. When the company launched its AS 400 computer in 1988, Palmisano mounted his own personal campaign to make sure it was a success. He toured software companies and met designers to persuade them to devise new applications that would give it a competitive edge. This caught the eye of the CEO, who appointed him as an executive assistant and later described him as the best he'd ever had. Palmisano was rewarded in 1991 when he was appointed senior managing director of operations for IBM Japan.

THE MIDAS TOUCH In 1993 the company faced calls for it to be broken up after revealing a loss of $5 billion. Palmisano was put in charge of Integrated Systems Solutions, selling service contracts. Within three years he had raised income from sales from $15 billion to $23 billion. The calls to break IBM into a collection of "small blues" faded away.

He is admired for his micro-managing style when under pressure. In December 1997, his Personal Systems division was about to miss its quarter sales target, so Palmisano had his reps on conference calls at 7am and 9pm over the holidays to push them harder, with success.

His appointment as CEO in 2002 coincided with one of the worst tech downturns in history. But, determined to return the company to a dominant industry position, Palmisano pushed for a 5 per cent annual growth and has remade IBM once again, this time as a globally integrated company selling technology and communication solutions. This has created record earnings under his leadership.

LESSONS IN BUSINESS: SHARING THE REWARDS

Palmisano succeeds by working harder than colleagues and rivals. He leads by example and rewards his team lavishly when they respond. He shared a bonus of up to $5 million with 20 of his top fellow "IBMers".
→ Dedicate yourself to the success of your business and others will follow your example.
→ Avoid "capping" bonuses. If people have over-performed and earned more than the reward plan expected, the reward plan has done its job—bonuses should reflect success and not become a "right."
→ To attract the best people, you sometimes have to pay the highest salaries.

"The digital and physical infrastructure of the world are converging." Samuel Palmisano

Dominique Strauss-Kahn Managing Director, IMF

GLOBAL ECONOMIC TURMOIL has served Strauss-Kahn well. After being pushed forward for the top job at the International Monetary Fund (IMF), partly, some believed, to prevent him from taking an opposition role in French politics, Strauss-Kahn has managed to cast himself as a white knight to the world's poor, while placing the IMF center stage in the fight to rescue the world economy. It's a fitting role for a heavyweight policy maker whose reformist career in French politics culminated in the successful launch of the euro in 1999.

BIOGRAPHY
Born in 1949 in the suburbs of Paris to Jewish parents, Strauss-Kahn spent his childhood in Morocco and Monaco. He gained a degree in public law and a doctorate in economics.

LEADERSHIP STYLE
Suave and charismatic, Strauss-Kahn's reputation as "un grand séducteur" has allowed him to steer a tricky course between ideology and pragmatism.

KEY STRENGTH
His art of persuasion has allowed him to sell a pro-business, reforming agenda in the teeth of French opposition to change, promising to revamp the IMF.

BEST DECISION
Campaigning for the IMF's top job on a platform of wholesale change, a pledge that has proven to be very timely.

POLITICAL MOVER Education and politics have been the twin drivers of Strauss-Kahn's life, his academic career acting as a springboard for his political ambitions. He met future French prime minister Lionel Jospin at a socialist education organization in the 1970s and entered parliament while an economics professor. After gaining government experience in the early 1990s in an industry post, he came into his own as finance minister in 1997. He pushed through deregulation and privatization policies popular with business, and successfully cut the French budget deficit to pave the way for the single European currency.

AN ILL WIND Political scandal interrupted his career in 1999—though he was exonerated—while his bid for the socialist presidential nomination was thwarted by Ségolène Royal in

2006. However, his popularity in Europe, enhanced by his performance during the euro negotiations, made him a front-runner for the top IMF job in 2007. It turned out to be a lucky appointment for both the man and the organization. Prior to the global economic downturn, the IMF had been written off as irrelevant; its resources were dwarfed by easily available private capital and it was shunned because of its stringent lending requirements. The situation was reversed as the crisis worsened, and the G20 nations soon rallied behind the IMF. Strauss-Kahn seized the opportunity to push his reforming agenda, giving developing nations greater influence, easing restrictions on loans, protecting the poor, and bolstering the organization's reserves with new donations. Under his leadership, the IMF is sure to regain something of its former global prestige.

LESSONS IN BUSINESS: SEIZING THE DAY

Strauss-Kahn has the presence and clout to have an impact on the international stage. But luck has played its part in his rise and part of his skill lies in knowing what to do with opportunities as they arise.
- → Consider the suddenness of economic decline, such as the global financial downturn, as a fantastic opportunity. Remember that chutzpah—gutsy audacity—can pay off in hard times.
- → Choose your own terms and negotiate hard when others are reeling.
- → Setbacks are certain, whether organizational or personal. Maintain a high level of stamina and resilience

"More than ever, we need the IMF to help us face the challenges of our times." Dominique Strauss-Kahn

Carlos Ghosn President & CEO, Nissan & Renault

THE DRAMATIC REVIVAL of ailing carmaker Nissan after 1999 established Ghosn as one of the great turnaround masters. His achievement has been compared to Lee Iacocca's turnaround of Chrysler 20 years earlier, making him not only a towering figure in the car industry but also a household superstar in Japan. His success was rewarded in 2005 when he was given the leadership of Renault to add to that of Nissan; he became the first executive to run two carmakers at the same time—and on opposite sides of the world.

BIOGRAPHY
Born in Pôrto Velho, Brazil, in 1954. Ghosn graduated with degrees in engineering from the Ecole Polytechnique and the Ecole des Mines in Paris. He has become such a celebrity in Japan that there is even a manga character based on him.

LEADERSHIP STYLE
Approachable and direct. Ghosn is noted for his ability to translate highly complex problems into terms easy for everyone to understand and act upon. Hence in France he was nicknamed "Le Costkiller" for his productivity drives, in Japan as "Mr 7/11" for his long hours.

KEY STRENGTH
Organization: only an exceptionally disciplined individual could run two successful car makers based across the world.

BEST DECISION
Resisting pressure for a full-blown merger between Renault and Nissan, on the grounds that the firms' cultural differences are too great to be overcome.

TURNAROUND TRAINING Ghosn's turnaround abilities were proven long before he worked his magic at Nissan. First he revived Michelin's failing operations in Brazil and restructured its troubled US business. Then Louis Schweitzer recruited him to Renault, where he drafted a restructuring plan that brought the French carmaker back into the black. When Renault injected $5.4 billion to try to save Nissan, Ghosn was the immediate choice for CEO at the Japanese company.

TAKING RESPONSIBILITY When Ghosn took over at Nissan, the company had just made a loss of more than $6 billion, it had debts of $20 billion and only three of its 48 models were showing a profit. Ghosn's solution was the classic cost-cutter's treatment: he closed five plants, laid off 21,000 workers, and shed the company's stakes in 1,400 suppliers and affiliated firms. These drastic steps were shocking in Japan, where lifetime employment was the norm. But the key to the process wasn't so much these steps themselves as the way Ghosn put himself on the line when he took them. Presenting his revival plan, he pledged that if he missed any of its targets, he would resign. This was the first time anyone had taken personal responsibility for Nissan, and the Japanese managers, markets, and public were impressed. Ghosn's fresh, outsider's perspective and his ability to focus on the key issues enabled him to drive his plan through to its targets ahead of schedule, and by 2001 the company was back in the black. Promoted to CEO, Ghosn then poured investment into new vehicles. Sales of these products in the crucial US market led Nissan back to robust health.

LESSONS IN BUSINESS: THINKING AHEAD

By combining strength in implementing processes—as typified by his cost-reduction drives—with a focus on new ideas like pure electric vehicles, Ghosn maximizes productivity today while planning innovation for tomorrow. This ability to think tactically and strategically is vital for any senior executive.
➔ If you are continuously in fire-fighting mode, break out of it by putting time aside for planning.
➔ Leave time in team meetings to discuss the way ahead for the team rather than just operational issues.
➔ Go off-site regularly to get away from the day-to-day issues and work on your strategic plan.

"Motivation is the ultimate weapon." Carlos Ghosn

Rochelle B. Lazarus Chairman & CEO, Ogilvy & Mather

WHEN OGILVY & MATHER was facing some of the most challenging times in the history of advertising, it was Lazarus who steered it through. Her arrival as CEO in 1996 coincided with the explosion of internet use that radically transformed the way consumers approach brands and products, presenting advertising agencies with a whole new set of problems and opportunities for getting their messages across. Lazarus led the way in creating a new model that turned the online world into a source of dramatic commercial success.

BIOGRAPHY
Born in Brooklyn, New York, in 1947, the daughter of Lewis Braff, an accountant. Lazarus studied psychology at Smith College, Massachusetts, before earning an MBA in marketing from Columbia University, where she was one of only four women in her graduating class.

LEADERSHIP STYLE
Dynamic and approachable. Lazarus inspires those around her through her passion for her work and her industry.

KEY STRENGTH
Being able to see that a changing environment required a new shape for her business.

BEST DECISION
Integrating Ogilvy's print, TV, and online creative arms into one flexible team.

NATURAL CHOICE "Shelly" Lazarus joined Ogilvy & Mather (O&M) in 1971 and by 1989, the year the company was bought by WPP, she was head of direct marketing, followed two years later by a shift to president of the New York branch. In that role she managed two coups that made her a star in the industry: helping to lure former long-time client American Express back, and persuading Lou Gerstner to sack IBM's various ad agencies in favor of O&M. When the CEO's job became vacant, these triumphs made Lazarus a natural choice.

NEW MEDIA TRANSFORMATION Lazarus's time in charge of O&M's direct marketing confirmed her commitment to integrated marketing, which turned out to be the ideal approach for coping with the dramatic growth of the internet and new media. The company adapted well to the new conditions, mainly as a result of Lazarus's decision to merge its print, television, and online creative departments into one large team, giving Ogilvy & Mather an industry-leading ability to deliver integrated marketing services. The agency's surge of success attracted clients such as Morgan Stanley, DuPont, Kodak, and Johnson & Johnson to add to a list that already included American Express, IBM, Nestlé, Ford, Cisco, Motorola, and Mattel. Lazarus's approach became the model for the industry, combining old and new media, involving user-generated content, and engaging the consumer rather than simply pushing a product. Less than 50 percent of Ogilvy & Mather's revenue now comes from traditional advertising, a clear indication of Lazarus's success in leading the company into the brave new online world.

LESSONS IN BUSINESS: CHANGING SHAPE

The structure that made your company a storming success yesterday might be a downright disadvantage today. Be prepared to completely reshape your business to suit changing conditions, however much it goes against the way things have always been done.
- → Look for signs that the organization is creaking, such as a rise in staff turnover or customer complaints.
- → Concentrate peoples' minds on reviewing structure by taking them off site to a planning session.
- → Get feedback from people who have moved into a new job. They will recognize where change is needed.

"Every point of contact should reflect the brand."
Rochelle Lazarus

Mary Sammons CEO, Rite Aid

ORIGINALLY PLANNING to be a teacher, a rethink led Sammons to a position with Fred Meyer Stores, part of a career with the company that spanned 26 years. In 1999, Sammons quit her position as president and CEO of Fred Meyer Stores to join Rite Aid as president and COO. At the time, the drugstore chain was reeling from an accounting scandal and suffering from years of financial mismanagement. With penetrating insight, Sammons tackled every aspect of Rite Aid's interface with the consumer. The results were dramatic.

BIOGRAPHY
Born in 1946 in Portland, Oregon. Sammons (née Jackson) was educated at Marylhurst College (now University), Oregon.

LEADERSHIP STYLE
Hands-on. In her words, she "spends a lot of time in the field."

KEY STRENGTH
Recognizing the need to build a relationship of trust between company and employee, vendor, and customer.

BEST DECISION
Leaving a safe and lucrative career with Fred Meyer Stores for the more risky challenge of salvaging an ailing drug company.

BUILDING RELATIONSHIPS With more than half of Rite Aid's revenue originating from its pharmacies, Sammons and her co-executives worked to fulfil Rite Aid's mission to be "a friendly neighborhood drug store". Sammons placed the relationship between pharmacist and patient at the forefront of boosting sales, and a series of ads featuring the slogan, "With us, it's personal" helped to hammer home Rite Aid's renewed commitment to customer satisfaction. Sammons also implemented in-store health clinics and information seminars, and an extended immunization service. A seniors' loyalty program offered discounts and customer benefits, teenagers were targeted via a "Glam Camp" website, and the inclusion of GNC stores within many of Rite Aid's stores attracted health supplement aficionados. Sammons worked hard, too, on improving staff morale, recognizing that Rite Aid employees needed to be knowledgeable and appreciated to deliver good customer care. To this end, Rite Aid introduced staff recognition programs and positive changes to working hours and conditions. Within a few years Sammons had turned the company round, and in June 2003 her achievements were rewarded with promotion to CEO.

LOOKING TO THE FUTURE In 2007, Sammons engineered the purchase of more than 1,800 Brooks and Eckerd stores from the Quebec-based Jean Coutu Group. The acquisition made Rite Aid the dominant drug retailer in the eastern US, gave it a wider geographical range, and helped to close the gap on CVS Caremark Corp. and Walgreen Co., the two leading US drug chains.

LESSONS IN BUSINESS: DEALING WITH TROUBLE

When a company is in trouble it must do first things first. Before Sammons could consider how best to take the brand and its products forward she needed to ensure a strong background of product sales. This allowed her to reorganize and produce her vision for the way ahead.
→ In a turnaround situation, concentrate first on how your consumers view the people who deal with them.
→ Having worked out the current interface between consumer and sales, identify how it needs to develop.
→ Train your people and create a culture that gives the customer a good feeling when they think about you.

"I would encourage everyone to get out of your comfort zone and be willing to take risks." Mary Sammons

John Rose CEO, Rolls-Royce plc

ROLL'S-ROYCE LOOKED ripe for takeover when Rose became CEO, but under his leadership it has expanded into the world's largest engine maker, investing billions in developing the next generation of engines, and boasting an order book worth more than £50 billion. Since taking over in 1996, Rose has carried the fight for market share directly to the American competition, steered the company through the post-9/11 crisis in the aviation industry, and placed it on the path to growth, becoming one of Britain's most respected businessmen.

BIOGRAPHY
Born in Blantyre, Nyasaland (Malawi), in 1952. Rose earned a master's degree in psychology at St. Andrew's University in Scotland in 1975.

LEADERSHIP STYLE
Confident, acerbic, and demanding, Rose is renowned for his fiercely sharp mind and has a reputation for not suffering fools. He rarely gives interviews.

KEY STRENGTH
A tough-minded approach to competitors, the market, and his investors.

BEST DECISION
Pushing ahead with costly investment in the fuel-efficient Trent engine, which has become the driver of Rolls's revival.

WARNING BELL Rose joined the company in 1984 and was rising through its ranks when, in 1991, it suffered a near-fatal shock—British Airways, its largest customer, decided to buy its engines from General Electric. Rolls's shares tumbled and many commentators believed the company would soon be taken over by GE. Rose realized that the company's polite British approach was not going to be good enough to take on the Americans.

WORLD'S BEST ENGINES Even before taking over as CEO, Rose took a key step in confronting GE by spearheading Rolls's acquisition of the Allison Engine Company in 1994, right in GE's own backyard. Returning to the UK as CEO two years later, he made a series of key decisions. His first big move was to insist on continued heavy investment in the Trent engine series initiated by his predecessor, an expensive development but one that created what are regarded as the best engines in the industry. They formed the basis for dramatic growth, enabling Rolls first to overtake Pratt & Whitney as the world's second-largest aero engine maker and then to leave it far behind. Rose then scored a big hit against GE by making the US Department of Defense Rolls's biggest client, with Rolls becoming the main engine supplier for the next-generation Joint Strike Fighter. Rose also launched the £576-million takeover of Vickers, to strengthen its position in power generation, and expanded the company's after-sales business.

The first CEO of Rolls-Royce not to have an engineering background, Rose was knighted in 2003 for his services to the defense and aerospace industries.

LESSONS IN BUSINESS: TURNING UP THE PRESSURE

Whatever your corporate or cultural traditions, there's no future in being polite to your rivals. Rose realized an introverted plan that concentrated on the product and ignored the competition would continue to fail.
→ Plan as though your competitors are trying to get you out of business, because, in the end, they are.
→ Take big, bold steps, attack competitors whenever you get the chance, and never stop pushing.
→ Take the competition into account when forming your strategy—they are just as important as your customers.

"Innovation and creativity don't exist in a vacuum."
John Rose

Jeroen van der Veer CEO, Royal Dutch Shell

A PROVEN COMPANY MAN with years of loyal service behind him—he joined straight after graduating—van der Veer was thrown into the top job at Royal Dutch Shell at the worst possible time. However, his rapid, decisive response to a serious crisis at the company stabilized what could have become a very damaging situation. His actions were so successful that the board took the extraordinary decision to make him the first executive director to have his contract extended beyond the usual retirement date.

INTO THE HOT SEAT After working his way through the Shell hierarchy all over the world for three decades, van der Veer found himself pitched into the hot seat in 2004 in the middle of a serious crisis. The company had admitted that it had been overstating its oil reserves by more than 20 percent, a scandal that had cost his predecessor his post. The markets and the press needed no excuse to look for more bad news from the Anglo-Dutch oil giant.

DECISIVE ACTION Realizing that the crisis could destabilize the company long term, van der Veer immediately began a radical overhaul of Shell's management and governance structure. After discussions with regulators and institutional investors that lasted months, he fully merged the two parts of the company, the Dutch and the British, into one with a single board and CEO. The company still faced fines from regulators and various lawsuits, but even its harshest critics were impressed by the way van der Veer had dealt with the situation. Instead of going into freefall, the share price rebounded, and only a few months after van der Veer's appointment it was well above where it had been before the crisis erupted.

To meet the challenge of climate change, van der Veer has steered Shell toward green technologies, although the company has been lambasted by regulators for overstating its green credentials. Profits have grown as demand for energy increased around the world, although the global economic downturn saw a sudden drop in demand. Even so, Shell's sheer size and resilience have allowed van der Veer to continue to invest in new energy sources, and the company is well positioned for future growth.

LESSONS IN BUSINESS: ACTING FAST IN A CRISIS

The situation facing Shell in 2004 could have caused the company long-term damage. Van der Veer's quick and decisive steps restored market confidence and turned a destabilizing crisis into a temporary glitch.
→ Loss of confidence from investors, employees, and customers is a big problem. Act quickly to restore it.
→ Don't be tempted to wait for more information before making decisions. Avoid analysis paralysis.
→ Solve a short-term problem quickly to preserve your vision of a long-term way forward for your company—and do not compromise.

"You have got to communicate from your heart."
Jeroen van der Veer

Yun Jong-yong CEO (1996–2008), Samsung Electronics Company

SOFTLY SPOKEN Yun joined Samsung straight from college in 1966, rising through the ranks to become CEO 30 years later. Since then he has led his division of the South Korean conglomerate (or "chaebol"), to the forefront of the keenly competitive consumer electronics industry, overtaking key rivals Sony. Only Nokia and Motorola are bigger in the cell phone market. In the process Samsung Electronics has surprised many people with its mix of design and technological innovation.

BIOGRAPHY
Born in Yonchun, Korea, in 1944. He was forced to give up his first love, philosophy, in favor of electrical engineering, and he graduated from Seoul National University in 1966.

LEADERSHIP STYLE
Persuasive, thoughtful, and consensual. He invites discussion and is always trying to remove layers of hierarchy.

KEY STRENGTH
He has rare people skills in a culture where authoritarianism can predominate. His gift for diplomacy and persuasion has protected his position inside the complex politics of the bigger Samsung conglomerate.

BEST DECISION
Focusing his firm on the "digital convergence revolution," transforming Samsung Electronics from a local copycat manufacturer into a global technology giant.

THE REVOLUTION STARTS HERE When Yun took over in 1996, Samsung Electronics was in trouble because of a sharp decline in chip prices. Top management authorized the new CEO to take drastic action. Yun moved quickly to restore the electronics company to financial health, slashing its payrolls by a third, selling off almost $2-billion-worth of corporate assets, and replacing about half of the company's division managers. As other South Korean chaebols were foundering in the Asian collapse of 1997, Yun oversaw a 100 percent increase in productivity at Samsung Electronics in his first year as CEO.

BACK FROM THE DEAD Backed by Samsung chairman Lee Kun-hee, Yun deployed a ruthlessness rarely seen in ultra-conservative South Korean business. At the heart of Yun's strategic plan for Samsung Electronics was innovation in product, process, and personnel. Yun moved quickly to extract Samsung from those businesses that were no longer producing an acceptable rate of return. The company reduced its television output and stopped producing dishwashers, electronic pagers, and juicers. These were replaced with high-tech, high-margin goods such as flat-panel displays, MP3 music players, and advanced mobile phones. He introduced performance-related pay and what he terms a "digital corporate culture," whereby the company's entire supply chain was controlled by an internet-based system.

Fortune magazine selected Yun as Asia's Businessman of the Year in 2000. He resigned in May 2008 during a dramatic corporate shake-up, saying, "It was the right time."

LESSONS IN BUSINESS: SUCCEEDING THROUGH CRISIS

"At times of crisis you have to change," says Yun. "And in order to keep on succeeding, you need to change even without crisis." That, say insiders, has become one of Yun's watchwords for management. He also believes in consultative decision making, unusual in his country.

➜ Run your company as if it is in perpetual crisis—practice revolution as a daily exercise.

➜ Get your people to approach every day at work as a challenge that could go badly as well as brilliantly.

➜ Remember: people enjoy helping their team through the threats of competitive life in a lively market.

"To have speed, bureaucracy and hierarchy have to go." Yun Jong-yong

Mervyn Davies Chairman & CEO (2001–06), Standard Chartered

THE DYNAMIC LEADERSHIP of Davies turned round ailing international bank Standard Chartered. In 2001, the company was in trouble after a series of ill-advised acquisitions had left its share price languishing and its reputation shattered. The bank's board turned to Davies to revive its fortunes. With his talent for finding and exploiting new business areas, Davies doubled Standard Chartered's market capitalization during his five years as CEO. He has since been appointed a trade minister to Gordon Brown's UK government.

BIOGRAPHY
Born in 1952 in North Wales, UK. Davies completed the Program for Management at Harvard Business School and is a Fellow at the Institute of Bankers.

LEADERSHIP STYLE
Forceful, garrulous, and straightforward. His infectious enthusiasm and short stature earned him the nickname "pocket dynamite."

KEY STRENGTH
Davies has comprehensively demonstrated a talent for finding and exploiting the business and geographical areas that will deliver most value.

BEST DECISION
Taking the risk of hiring Peter Sands, who had no accountancy training, in 2002. He and Davies worked closely and successfully as finance director and CEO, and the partnership continued in their revised roles of CEO and Chairman.

ALL CHANGE AT THE TOP Davies began his banking career at Citibank, joining in 1983 and working as a senior credit officer and managing director of UK banking. He moved on to Standard Chartered, the emerging markets bank, in 1993, working in Hong Kong and Singapore, and became group executive director in 1997. His appointment as CEO represented a complete change in leadership style from the studious and detached air of his predecessor, Rana Talwar. With his customary enthusiasm, Davies moved to reinvigorate the ailing bank, successfully integrating its acquisitions, scaling back Latin American operations, and making new deals in Asia, Africa, and the Middle East. Silencing critics who claimed that the bank was overpaying for its acquisitions, Davies' five years as CEO saw Standard Chartered's market capitalization more than double as it positioned itself to take advantage of trends, such as growing trade between China and Africa, and increasing consumer lending in India. Davies also avoided the temptation to move into the crowded and less profitable European marketplace.

TRIUMPH IN TAIWAN One of his final acts as CEO was to finalize the acquisition of Taiwanese bank Hsinchu, an unprecedented achievement in a country that traditionally shuns outside investment. In 2006, Davies stepped down as CEO and took on the chairman's role, but maintained a close working relationship with his successor Peter Sands, whom he brought into the bank as finance director. This partnership is seen as key to Standard Chartered's improved position following the 2008 banking crisis.

LESSONS IN BUSINESS: AVOIDING OVERREACH

Davies' realistic focus on the countries where Standard Chartered was most likely to prosper helped turn the bank around. His example extends to many businesses that are tempted to overreach geographically.
→ Identify the things your company does best. Focus on these, and don't take your eye off the ball.
→ Following the Pareto principle, direct your efforts toward the 20 percent of your business that produces 80 percent of the benefits.
→ Once you are satisfied the risks do not outweigh the potential, invest with total conviction.

"Leadership gives the scope to challenge and re-evaluate." Mervyn Davies

COOL HEADS
IN A CRISIS

Crises are an unfortunate yet inevitable part of corporate life. Disruption to organizational operations can come from alarmingly diverse circumstances: natural disasters, economic meltdowns, terrorism, lawsuits, product defects and subsequent recalls, scandals, and poor management. Regardless of whether the cause is externally- or internally-derived, how CEOs deal with a crisis has a huge impact on the future of their businesses.

After seven people died from taking cyanide-laced Tylenol capsules in 1982, **Jim Burke** (p159), CEO of Johnson & Johnson, took decisive immediate action and recalled all 31 million bottles of the painkiller, costing the company $100 million. He suspended production and cancelled advertising until a tamper-resistant bottle was created to stop future sabotage, and he offered to exchange capsules for tablets. Burke's proactive customer-oriented handling of a monumental crisis saved the brand.

Self-inflicted crises require the same decisive action. **Frank Appel** (p199) of logistics group Deutsche Post World Net, outsourced air express services and reduced costs, in an attempt to reassure shareholders in the wake of the personal tax fraud crisis of his predecessor ●

"Prepare for and then manage a crisis well, and you may even enhance the reputation of the business."
STEPHEN CARVER, CRISIS MANAGEMENT CONSULTANT

Troubled Water

In 1990, traces of the chemical benzene were found in Perrier mineral water in the US. Unlike Johnson & Johnson, however, Perrier's initial handling of the crisis was muddled. CEO **Ronald V. Davis** released a vague statement saying there was no significant health risk to the public, blamed an isolated error at a bottling plant that supplied North America, and recalled bottles from that market. However, benzene was then discovered in Perrier water in Holland and Belgium. It transpired that Perrier, which advertised its water as "Naturally Sparkling", had

failed to change some filters that removed benzene during the artificial carbonation process. Consequently, Davis had to issue a much wider product recall. Contradiction instead of coordination exacerbated the issue. While Perrier made mistakes when the crisis broke, its long-term recovery strategy, under CEO **Kim Jeffreys**, was professional and effective. Jeffreys spent money on PR and advertising, relaunched the product, and, by the end of the 1990s, had regained market share.

CEOs need advance strategies in place to maintain operations under adverse conditions. Take the assured

way that **Robert J. Keegan**, CEO of Goodyear Tire & Rubber, weathered hurricane Ike in the US in 2008. He had business continuity plans in place for such an eventuality. These preparations included closing three production plants in advance of the hurricane arriving, and pulling forward a limited amount of previously announced reductions in tire manufacture to ease the pressure on its raw-materials supply chain, while continuing to produce tires that were in demand by consumers. "We see the management of this process as a real competitive advantage in these types of circumstances," said Keegan.

Leading in a Crisis

Don't wait for a crisis to hit— Start planning a coherent crisis management strategy now.

Act fast— In the Exxon Valdez oil spill in 1989 it took CEO **Lawrence Rawl** over a week to visit the scene of the accident, giving the impression it was not a top priority.

Practice conveying your point— If the public and media view you as a villain, your reputation will suffer regardless of who's to blame.

Follow a three-point strategy of communication— "Regret, Reason, Remedy": show humanity and regret; explain the situation; give forward positive traction to prove you are dealing with it.

Be conspicuous— As head of the company, you must take the lead to indicate the importance managment places on the problem.

*based on advice formulated by Stephen Carver, crisis management consultant at Cranfield University School of Management in the UK.

Crisis-crunching CEOs

Some CEOs seem to have a talent for keeping their head in a crisis:

David R. Anderson, AMERICAN FAMILY INSURANCE GROUP (Insurance: US)—*Despite "dealing with weather-related factors considerably outside of the historical norm" in the US midwest in 2006 and 2007, the company's policy of diversifying its risk base helped to minimize the losses.*

Francisco González Rodríguez, BBVA (Finance: Spain)— *Diversified out of domestic property before the onset of the Spanish property slump in the late 2000s.*

Neville Isdell, COCA-COLA (Beverages: US)—*Isdell was brought out of retirement in 2004 at a time when Coca-Cola was losing out to its rival Pepsi. By restoring discipline, and launching new, healthier products, Isdell was able to restore confidence and get Coca-Cola back on track.*

David Neelman, JETBLUE (Aviation: US)—*After hundreds of passengers were left on a runway for up to six hours because of bad weather, Neelman acted swiftly offering millions of dollars in compensation and profuse apologies. His handling of the crisis meant that the JetBlue brand emerged stronger than ever.*

Michael McCain, MAPLE LEAF FOODS (Foodstuffs: Canada)— *When a listeriosis outbreak that killed four people and left dozens of others seriously ill was traced back to Maple Leaf Foods products, McCain's swift, sincere, and compassionate handling of the crisis meant that the company did not completely lose public sympathy. In fact, so impressive was his performance that the Canadian press voted him CEO of the year in 2008.*

Chen Tianqiao, SHANDA ENTERTAINMENT (Internet: China)—*The online gaming company continued to grow and outperform most of its rivals, despite having to suspend operations for three days after the Sichuan earthquake in 2008.*

Harold Kvisle President & CEO, TransCanada Corp.

VETERAN OILMAN Kvisle had the vision and drive to transform a regional gas company into a diversified continental energy player, tripling cash flow and boosting investment more than twelve-fold. Thanks to his eye for key deals, TransCanada has successfully expanded into oil pipelines and power generation, growing assets from $12.5 billion to $20 billion. Kvisle's efforts have been rewarded with positions on the board of Bank of Montreal and the Nature Conservancy of Canada, and the title of Canada's outstanding CEO of the year in 2008.

BIOGRAPHY
Born in 1952 in the small town of Innisfail, Alberta, Canada. Kvisle gained an engineering BSc from the University of Alberta, and received an MBA from the University of Calgary.

LEADERSHIP STYLE
Affable, steady, and determined. Kvisle's success is partly due to his ability to assemble a strong executive team, and he has always been ready to give them due credit for their achievements.

KEY STRENGTH
Clearly understanding the need for TransCanada to expand and diversify far beyond its core business in western Canada.

BEST DECISION
The $3.4-billion acquisition of US pipeline operation ANR in 2007, opening up a vast energy market in the US heartland.

NORTHERN EXPOSURE A consummate engineer who had worked in the Albertan oil and gas fields since 1970, "Hal" Kvisle gained a taste for deal-making after working his way up to the finance department of Dome Petroleum, where he handled the company's sale to Amoco in 1988. It was there that he developed his core leadership philosophy: that organizing people properly and giving them the right focus is the key to success. In 1999, after becoming president of the new Canadian operation of New Zealand holdings company Fletcher Challenge, Kvisle looked like an ideal fit for TransCanada, which had merged with Nova the year before.

THE CONTINENTAL OP It took Kvisle just two years to step up to CEO at TransCanada, the start of a truly remarkable turnaround process that has utterly tranformed the company. He embarked on a number of large-scale projects: the purchase and integration of US company ANR, with its extensive network of gas pipelines; construction of the $12-billion Keystone pipeline carrying shale oil from the Alberta oil sands to the US; the acquisition and rebuilding of the Bruce Power nuclear plant in Ontario; the purchase of the Ravenwood oil and gas power station in New York; and the $13-billion Mackenzie Valley arctic gas pipeline. Kvisle's aquisitions have defined his time at the helm, and constituted a reinvention of what had been a cosy, if over-regulated, west Canadian player into a continental powerhouse. But his real skill has been in developing his executive team and giving each of them the authority to take his vision forward. He even sought a replacement for CFO Russ Girling so that Girling could run his own business unit.

LESSONS IN BUSINESS: PLANNING SUCCESSION

Safe in the knowledge that the talent is in place for his succession to be orderly, Kvisle also knows when to let go. He is already planning his departure once TransCanada has hit certain key milestones in its Alaska gas pipeline and Keystone oil pipeline, and the two power generation plants it has acquired.
➔ In any business, including those that are ruthless and technology-based, focus on the importance of people.
➔ Create a culture where managers believe it to be a career advantage to recognize particularly talented staff.
➔ Add succession planning into the appraisal and personal development processes of all your key people.

"What I did foresee was that we could no longer be a one-trick pony." Harold Kvisle

Anne Mulcahy Chairman & CEO, Xerox Corp.

AFTER TAKING OVER from a beleaguered predecessor in 2001, Mulcahy was labelled "the accidental CEO" by *Fortune* magazine. In 2007 she ranked number two on *Fortune's* list of the 50 most powerful women. That personal reversal of fortune mirrors the remarkable turnaround she engineered at Xerox. The firm that was once synonymous with photocopying hovered near bankruptcy in 2001. Mulcahy cut the dividend, reduced the workforce, and then led Xerox in a new direction. Revenues rose, the stock price went up, and the company thrived.

BIOGRAPHY
Born in Rockville Center, New York, in 1952. Mulcahy (née Dolan) was the only girl among five siblings. She studied English literature and journalism at Marymount College in New York.

LEADERSHIP STYLE
Energetic, brutally honest, and an excellent communicator. Mulcahy is committed to listening to both customers and staff.

KEY STRENGTH
She is able to identify the best ideas from a range of sources and implement a clear strategy.

BEST DECISION
Traveling huge distances to meet with staff, customers, and bankers early in her tenure.

INSIDE UP Whatever else may be said about her, Mulcahy certainly knew the company when she was named CEO in August 2001. Starting as a field service representative in 1976, she made her way up through a variety of sales and management positions including corporate senior vice president, president, and COO. She served as temporary CFO at one point, and in the early 1990s she was vice president for Human Resources—a career path not many CEOs can claim to have trodden.

NO ACCIDENT When Mulcahy was tapped as CEO, the company was beset by problems: disorganization, low morale, unhappy customers, serious debt, a budding accounting scandal, and over two years of financial losses. Mulcahy had never aspired to be CEO, but almost immediately she set out to regain market share and boost the bottom line. She moved much of Xerox's production to outside vendors and concentrated on service and innovation. To improve morale, she logged 100,000 miles in her first year, visiting company locations and getting to know staff. She solicited ideas from client CEOs and even managed to placate the bankers that were holding her corporation's debt.

Xerox began to overhaul its product line and branch out into new markets. Under Mulcahy, for example, it launched Xerox Global Services, which provides document imaging and consulting services. Xerox now allocates roughly $1 billion annually for research and development. Xerox's "green" agenda includes reducing paper consumption. Anne Mulcahy continues to travel and build relationships with customers and staff.

LESSONS IN BUSINESS: PEOPLE WORK FOR PEOPLE

Hold onto your humanity as a CEO. Xerox UK's managing director Alan Charnley explains it this way: "Anne Mulcahy is the mother of the company, in the nicest way. She has a unique ability to touch people."
- → Tell people how lucky it feels to have them on board and how much you want them to succeed.
- → The key attribute of a loving and motivating mother is listening. Do it actively all the time.
- → Avoid being remote from anyone in your organization, even if it involves traveling to multiple locations to meet with staff. Plan your communication to show people that you care.

"I tell our teams, make timely decisions, not perfect decisions. In our business late and perfect is not a great solution." Anne Mulcahy

Miles D. White Chairman & CEO, Abbott Laboratories

BIOGRAPHY
Born in Minneapolis, Minnesota, in 1955. White attended Culver Military Academy in Indiana. He also gained a BSc and MBA from Stanford.

BEST DECISION
Withdrawing from the production of poor-performing drugs. Abbott had spent vast sums in the field without gaining a competitive advantage.

LESSON IN BUSINESS
Focus on winners—by withdrawing from uncompetitive drugs, White freed resources to focus on more successful drugs, and to grow the firm.

INSIDERS WERE SURPRISED when White won the race to lead ailing Abbott Laboratories, but he confounded critics by turning it into the world's tenth largest pharmaceutical company, with sales of more than $25 billion.

As a military academy student, White learned both how to lead and to serve. He has an informal style, and has set an example in encouraging women and minorities into senior positions. When he took over at pharmaceuticals firm Abbott in 1999, the company was seen as too small to compete in an industry where research-spend is crucial. Many questioned his appointment, believing Abbott had become a likely takeover target. White quickly centralized his research team, promised dramatic increases in research investment, and halted work on poorly performing renal, cardiac, and HIV drugs. He warned scientists that they needed to come up with better new products, not "me-too" drugs with existing equivalents. White also launched an aggressive campaign of acquisitions, including Knoll Pharmaceuticals, whose Humira therapy for rheumatoid arthritis was about to be launched. This was an inspired move, as the drug is predicted to rake in more than $650 million in sales.

William P. Sullivan President & CEO, Agilent Technologies

BIOGRAPHY
Born in Washington in 1949. Sullivan received a BSc in environmental science from the University of California, Davis.

BEST DECISION
Selling off Agilent's semiconductor business to a private equity partnership for $2.6 billion in 2005, thus reducing the company's operating costs by $450 million a year.

LESSON IN BUSINESS
Companies need innovation to grow—Sullivan has maintained Agilent's position as an industry leader by refocusing and diversifying its arena for growth.

CEO OF AGILENT since 2005, Sullivan has overhauled the technology firm—once part of Hewlett-Packard—and in particular its Electronic Management Group, turning it into a more diversified measurement company.

Sullivan joined Hewlett-Packard (HP) in 1976, and when Agilent was spun off from HP in 1999, he was named head of its Semiconductor Products Group. Rising to COO in 2002, Sullivan had responsibility for Agilent's largest business division, renamed the Electronic Measurement Group (EMG). Agilent suffered huge financial losses and massive job cuts during the economic downturn of the early 2000s, so Sullivan played an instrumental role in restoring the financial equilibrium of the EMG, while helping Agilent's CEO Ned Barnolt to transform overall operations. In 2005, on Barnolt's retirement, Sullivan took over as CEO. He continued the company's restructuring process by making two major sales, of its semiconductor business, which had been a drain on the company's growth, and its 47-percent stake in Lumileds Lighting. In his first few years as CEO, Sullivan diversified the company by spending over $700 million on 17 acquisitions in the life science, aerospace, and defense sectors.

"I used to be a workaholic and never took vacations. Now, I have no problem taking a Friday afternoon off."
William P. Sullivan

Patricia Russo CEO (2006–08), Alcatel-Lucent

BIOGRAPHY
Born in Trenton, New Jersey, in 1953. Russo studied at Georgetown University, Washington, DC.

BEST DECISION
Rejecting advice to put ailing Lucent into bankruptcy. Russo believed the company would bounce back as a market leader—and she was right.

LESSON IN BUSINESS
Hard work pays off—Lucent was dragged back to health and profit by Russo's ferociously competitive nature. She constantly slashed costs until she had achieved her targeted results.

PROVING THEM ALL WRONG, Russo fought not only sexual discrimination from men who thought women had no place in sales, but also those who believed veterans of AT&T had no future in its communications services spin-off, Lucent.

Russo is said to be so competitive that she had to be discouraged from playing in staff golf and tennis tournaments—she always won. Her reputation was sealed not only on the fairway, but also in the boardroom, where she built a track record for saving failing companies. In 1992, Russo resurrected AT&T's Global Business Communications Systems by slashing costs, improving core products, and raising revenues by $2 billion to put the division back in the black. In 1997, she helped launch the AT&T spin-off Lucent Technologies. However, being sidelined as the company declined, she left briefly to join Eastman Kodak. Russo returned to Lucent in 2001 as CEO to save the firm from losses of $16 billion. Again she cut costs, axed thousands of jobs, improved products, and boosted sales. By 2004, the company was in the black. She engineered the $10 billion merger with French telecom giant Alcatel in 2006, and was nominated CEO of Alcatel-Lucent, but she stepped down in 2008 amid losses.

Gregory Case President & CEO, Aon

BIOGRAPHY
Born in the US in 1963. Case gained a BA from Kansas State University and an MBA from Harvard.

BEST DECISION
The wholesale restructuring of Aon. His drastic action managed to heal the rot.

LESSON IN BUSINESS
Quick action can fix the biggest problems—Aon was on the brink of decline, but swift, decisive action from Case shocked it back to health.

CONFRONTED WITH just about all that can go wrong for an insurance company when he became CEO, Case showed how strong leadership can rapidly turn things around. His rescue plan startled industry observers, but worked.

In 2005, the future looked shaky for the world's second-largest insurance group. Growth was weak, profit margins were down, and both Aon's reputation and its share price had suffered heavily from a regulatory action led by New York attorney general Eliot Spitzer. This alleged that Aon and other brokers had engaged in fraud and anti-competitive practices. Case used the experience gained from many years at McKinsey to reshape the company. He initiated a much-needed integration and streamlining of disparate operations that had been gathered through more than 400 acquisitions made over the previous 20 years. He sold off the company's capital-intensive underwriting operation, focusing instead on its core brokerage and consulting businesses. He used his marketing skills to repair the damage done to Aon's image. Within two years, the company's net income had risen by more than 60 percent and its share price had doubled.

"Fundamentally, leadership is about helping other people succeed." Gregory Case

Rahul K. Bajaj Chairman & CEO (1968–2005), Bajaj Auto

BEFORE CEDING power to his son, Bajaj spent the latter years of his tenure as CEO at Bajaj Auto, one of the world's largest makers of motorcycles and scooters, turning the company around after the 2001 Indian economic slowdown.

Bajaj was a boxer in his youth, and the outspoken industrialist has been fighting ever since. After joining Bajaj Group in 1965, originally a steel and sugar mill company owned by his grandfather, he became CEO of Bajaj Auto in 1968. The Pune-based group, one of India's biggest companies, was the country's foremost scooter manufacturer by 1981. When the economy stalled in 2001, Bajaj Group faltered. Helped by his son Rajiv, he invested in R&D to create new product lines, reduced suppliers from 900 to 200, and developed markets across Asia, Africa, South America, and Europe. As Bajaj Auto grew, Bajaj overcame the businessman's greatest challenge: trusting his sons' expertise and judgment. He handed over leadership, remaining chairman. Rajiv is now CEO of Bajaj Auto, and his brother Sanjiv heads Bajaj Auto Finance. In 2006, meanwhile, Bajaj was elected MP for Maharashtra to fight new battles within India's parliament.

James M. Cornelius Chairman & CEO, Bristol-Myers Squibb

2006 WAS A TOUGH year for the pharmaceutical industry, and Bristol-Myers Squibb in particular. Since then, Cornelius has implemented a radical restructuring plan to put the company in pole position for the challenges ahead.

Before joining Bristol, Cornelius had an impressive record in the pharmaceutical industry, serving as CFO at Eli Lilly for 12 years, and as chairman and CEO of Guidant during its merger into Boston Scientific. He took over at Bristol in 2006 after CEO Peter Dolan was ousted under pressure from a federal monitor, and following criticism over his handling of a generic challenge to the company's leading drug, Plavix. Bristol's shares had more than halved in the course of the previous five years, reflecting the company's specific problems and concerns about the prospects for major pharmaceutical groups faced with the challenge of generic competitors. Cornelius began to rebuild Bristol's position, cutting ten percent of the staff and closing more than half of its manufacturing facilities, while making both major sell-offs and major acquisitions to focus the group on its core strengths in the oncology field. In 2008, Cornelius was elected chairman of the board.

"Dreaming is a fundamental human right and the starting point of all change." Rahul K. Bajaj

Willie Walsh CEO, British Airways

BIOGRAPHY
Born in Dublin, Ireland, in 1961. Walsh was the second of four children born to a Dublin glazier. He has an MBA from Trinity College Dublin.

BEST DECISION
Giving up the pilot's seat for a position in management, which led to his rise to the top of two of the world's biggest airlines.

LESSON IN BUSINESS
Know your opponents—Walsh's experience as a union representative at Aer Lingus put him in a good position to negotiate with disgruntled workers at BA.

NEVER ONE TO SHIRK a challenge, Walsh took two top jobs that nobody else wanted: CEO at Aer Lingus and then British Airways. He showed he has the determination to overhaul ailing airlines facing considerable external turbulence.

A trainee pilot for Aer Lingus at age 17, Walsh knew how to fly a plane before he could drive. He rose rapidly through the ranks at Aer Lingus, becoming CEO days before his 40th birthday. Following 9/11, Aer Lingus was losing $2 million a day, and radical solutions were needed. Walsh cut 33 percent of the workforce, sold non-essential assets, and cut costs by a third. Although he successfully moved Aer Lingus into profit, Walsh resigned after failing to persuade the Irish government to accept privatization plans.

He became CEO of British Airways (BA) in 2005 during unprecedented turmoil and industrial disputes. His initial success in sorting out BA's pension plan was followed by baggage and security crises, a fuel-price surcharge scandal involving senior executives and, perhaps most damaging of all, the chaotic opening of Heathrow's Terminal 5 in 2008. Record financial results and the waiving of his bonus that year helped Walsh to keep his job, but BA remained vulnerable to global economic slowdown.

Douglas R. Conant President & CEO, Campbell Soup Company

BIOGRAPHY
Born in New Jersey in 1952. Conant grew up in Chicago and was awarded a scholarship to Northwestern University, where he earned a bachelor of arts degree and an MBA.

BEST DECISION
Focusing on the image of Campbell Soup as key to the company's turnaround.

LESSON IN BUSINESS
It's all about what's in the customer's head—changing consumers' perception of a company's brands is what makes all the difference.

CAMPBELL SOUP'S iconic status failed to protect it from precipitous decline in the 1990s. By the turn of the millennium, the company was in real trouble, but the arrival of food industry expert Conant changed all that.

When Conant arrived at Campbell Soup at the beginning of 2001, its sales had been shrinking and its share price had gone with them, falling by nearly 40 percent in the two previous years. Conant brought with him a well-deserved reputation as a specialist in turning around troubled food companies. As president of Nabisco since 1995, he had engineered a remarkable transformation, picking up a troubled business and delivering five consecutive years of double-digit earnings

growth. His main challenge at Campbell Soup was to refresh the company's jaded image and, as a seasoned marketing man, he focused on this crucial area. However, he recognized that the quality of the company's products was equally important. He invested heavily in improving product quality and packaging, strengthened the marketing operation, and made innovation a key part of the business culture. The result was a revival of one of America's most familiar corporate names.

"A reasonable man gets nowhere in negotiations."
Willie Walsh

Wendell P. Weeks Chairman & CEO, Corning Incorporated

BIOGRAPHY
Born in Reno, Nevada, in 1960. Weeks grew up in Pennsylvania. He studied finance and accounting at Lehigh University, Pennsylvania, and gained an MBA from Harvard Business School.

BEST DECISION
Leading a program of diversification, which has opened up new markets for Corning.

LESSON IN BUSINESS
Never rely on just one product—Weeks learned this valuable lesson after watching the huge drop in share value from $113 to $1 following the collapse of the fiber-optic market.

APPOINTED CEO IN 2005, Weeks's succession marked the end of an era at specialty glass and ceramics manufacturer Corning Incorporated, which had been headed by a member of the Houghton family for most of its 154-year history.

After 25 years at Corning Incorporated in a variety of financial and business development roles, Weeks was appointed CEO in 2005. This had seemed unlikely just three years earlier, when the bottom fell out of the telecoms market while Weeks was head of optical communications, whose revenue plummeted from $5 billion in 2000 to $1.6 billion in 2002, and sent shares crashing. Jamie Houghton, CEO from 1983 to 1996, came out of retirement and, to the surprise of some, promoted Weeks to president and COO. Repaying Houghton's faith, Weeks helped to restructure the company and return it to profitability, turning a $5 billion loss to nearly $2 billion in profit by 2006. Weeks learned a valuable lesson from this experience, and has since diversified Corning's investments. Benefiting from demand for the thin, flat glass used to make liquid-crystal displays, Weeks has also invested in emerging technology, such as green lasers and diesel-engine filters, which may hold the key to the future of the company.

Oswald J. Grübel Co-CEO (2003–07), Credit Suisse

BIOGRAPHY
Born in Germany in 1943. Grübel attended the Geneva International Institute for Management Development and served as an apprentice in banking and securities trading at Deutsches Bank.

BEST DECISION
Coming out of retirement to resurrect the fortunes of the Credit Suisse Group.

LESSON IN BUSINESS
Know when you are wrong—Grübel always accepted as much criticism as he voiced, and was willing to change his decisions if he was mistaken.

MAKING ONE OF THE MOST successful comebacks in banking history, Grübel came out of early retirement in 2002 to rescue the Credit Suisse Group from financial crisis. He has turned Credit Suisse into a global, integrated bank.

Grübel joined White Weld Securities in 1970 as a floor trader. In less than eight years, he rose to become the CEO of the London- and Zürich-based eurobond house. During his tenure, the company was taken over by Credit Suisse and, after working in several divisions in Europe and Asia, Grübel was groomed for the group's elite management team. He took responsibility for global foreign exchange and money markets and, by the late 1990s, was in charge of the company's private banking business. He found himself isolated in opposing the acquisition policies of the then CEO, Lukas Muhlemann—particularly the €5 billion purchase of Winterthur Insurance. In 2002, when Winterthur incurred losses of over €1 billion, Grübel took early retirement. He returned as co-CEO alongside John Mack. By selling off non-critical businesses such as Churchill Insurance, Grübel raised badly needed capital. He successfully restructured the business until his final retirement in 2007.

"I'm a person who isn't afraid of choosing the fast track." Oswald J. Grübel

René Obermann CEO, Deutsche Telekom

BIOGRAPHY
Born in Düsseldorf, Germany, in 1963. Obermann studied economics at the University of Münster, graduating in 1986.

BEST DECISION
Dragging Deutsche Telekom into the twenty-first century by forging ahead with cost cuts and judicious overseas investment.

LESSON IN BUSINESS
Do what you have to—faced with several weeks of industrial action, Obermann stuck to his plan for changes to workers' pay and conditions, and eventually a compromise was reached that enabled him to cut costs.

KNOWN AS "DOBERMANN" and the "bulldozer" for his pursuit of often-controversial policies, Obermann rescued ailing German telecoms giant Deutsche Telekom, pushing through cost cuts and making strategic investments overseas.

In 2002, Obermann joined former state-owned telecoms monopoly Deutsche Telekom, acting as CEO of its subsidiary T-Mobile International and board member for Mobile Communications. In November 2006, he was appointed overall CEO, becoming the youngest leader of a German top-30 company. He inherited the same problems as his predecessor: defecting customers, a bloated workforce, and an uncompetitive cost structure. Flying in the face of powerful unions and the German government (still a major shareholder), he pushed through cost-cutting measures with the threat that the only alternative was a break-up of the group. He expanded into Eastern Europe and took a stake in Greek telecoms group OTE, but reduced risky investments in Asia and Africa. Although the share price declined amid the global financial downturn, Obermann's stability strategy seemed to be paying off, with Deutsche Telekom's performance relative to the market remaining strong.

David N. Farr Chairman, President & CEO, Emerson Electric

BIOGRAPHY
Born in the US in 1955. Farr received a degree in chemistry from Wake Forest University and an MBA from Vanderbilt University.

BEST DECISION
Continuing to invest in new technology throughout the dotcom downturn.

LESSON IN BUSINESS
Always be prepared—by being ready for the boom times that he knew would eventually return, Farr positioned Emerson strongly for the future.

AFTER TAKING OVER as CEO of industrial and domestic engineering group Emerson Electric at the worst possible time, Farr initiated a broad-ranging process of change that put the company back on the path of strong growth.

Emerson Electric had registered 43 successive years of earnings increases when Farr succeeded long-standing CEO Charles Knight in late 2000. However, this impressive record came to an end very soon after Farr's arrival, when the company suffered from the twin blows of the post-9/11 downturn and the bursting of the dotcom bubble, both of which hit demand for Emerson's products hard. Farr's response was a mixture of deep cost cuts and major restructuring, including the closure of production and office sites all over the world, along with acquisitions and strong investment in developing new technology. Some of these moves, particularly investing in technology research and development throughout the dotcom bust, were highly contentious. However, Farr pushed ahead to prepare the business for when the good times returned. Return they did, and Emerson reaped the rewards of strong earnings growth and renewed share price strength.

"The changes created a lot of tension, a lot of challenges in the company. But now those investments make sense." David N. Farr

Shigetaka Komori President & CEO, FUJIFILM Holdings Corp.

IN A CAREER dedicated to Fujifilm, Komori has seen more change than most. Originally a cinematic-film producer, he has transformed a once niche photographic company into a leading chemicals, health, and electronics business.

BIOGRAPHY
Born in China in 1939, Komori grew up in Nagasaki, Japan. He graduated with a BA in economics from the University of Tokyo.

BEST DECISION
Dropping "photo" from FUJIFILM's title in 2007, emphasizing the new direction in which he was taking the company.

LESSON IN BUSINESS
Move with the times—Komoro has demonstrated the need for flexibility, using his experience to steer FUJIFILM into a new, more profitable direction.

Komori joined Fuji Photo Film Company in 1963. He was appointed president in 2000 and CEO in 2003. He immediately aimed to double profits by 2007, cutting costs by $1.9 billion—a seemingly unrealistic target when the market for colour film began to shrink with the rise of digital imaging. Undertaking a radical restructuring of the company, Komori cut 5,000 jobs worldwide, shutting unprofitable factories and transferring camera production from Japan to China. He continued to spend on capital investments and acquisitions in the fields of medical equipment, commercial printing, and LCD screens. By late 2006 the company's financial position looked more secure and Komori created new core businesses within the cosmetics and nutritional supplement markets. In 2008, he spent $1.3 billion on a major stake in Toyama Chemical Co., a loss-making pharmaceuticals company, with which he aims to allow the restructured FUJIFILM to offer comprehensive health care.

Nicholas D. Chabraja Chairman & CEO, General Dynamics

WITH LONG-TERM VISION and an emphasis on good management to solve problems, Chabraja returned General Dynamics to a global defense-industry leader, specializing in aerospace, combat and marine systems, communications, and IT.

BIOGRAPHY
Born in Gary, Indiana, in 1942. Chabraja studied political science and law at Northwestern University, Illinois.

BEST DECISION
Shifting General Dynamics' corporate strategy from retrenchment to expansion, which yielded a return on equity that averaged twice that of other defense contractors between 1997 and 2001.

LESSON IN BUSINESS
Take calculated risks—Chabraja acquired companies in different sectors to hedge against potential losses in individual industries.

"Nick" Chabraja worked as a lawyer on General Dynamics cases for some 20 years, gaining an in-depth knowledge of the company and the challenges it faced. He finally joined the company in 1993 as general counsel and vice-president, and was nominated CEO in 1997. Chabraja reversed a policy of divestment that had been adopted in the early 1990s to offset losses at failing divisions, and instead launched an ambitious series of acquisitions in diverse industries. He aimed to expand from the company's core activities of combat vehicles and systems, armaments and munitions, shipbuilding and marine systems, into business aviation and mission-critical information systems and technologies. Purchases included fiber-optic specialist Advanced Technology Systems, Bath Iron Works shipyard, jet manufacturer Gulfstream Aerospace, and the defense units of Motorola and General Motors. By 2008, Chabraja had driven General Dynamics to become the world's fifth-largest defense firm.

"Generally, we bought businesses at reasonable prices and improved them." Nicholas D. Chabraja

James L. Ziemer President & CEO, Harley-Davidson, Inc.

BIOGRAPHY
Born in 1951, Ziemer grew up in Milwaukee. He served in the army, then studied at the University of Wisconsin-Milwaukee.

BEST DECISION
Commuting to a second high school for enriched math courses that weren't provided at his own school, giving him skills that helped launch his career.

LESSON IN BUSINESS
Study your business—Ziemer spent 30 years understudying in all areas, from parts to finance, before emerging as CEO of a company marketing self-image as much as motorcycles.

RISING FROM lift operator to the executive suite at heavyweight motorcycle firm Harley-Davidson, Ziemer personifies both the American dream and the resurgence of US manufacturing in the face of stiff foreign competition.

Growing up in a working-class neighborhood, "Jim" Ziemer dreamed of road-testing motorcycles from the nearby Harley-Davidson factory. But Ziemer was not one of the brawny, rebel bikers portrayed as the company's main customers, and his first motorcycle wasn't even a Harley. Nevertheless, he joined the company in 1969 as a freight elevator operator and rose through positions in manufacturing, engineering, accounting, and finance before becoming CEO in 2005. The company was losing market share to British and Asian competitors, so Ziemer redefined a corporate growth strategy based on selling expensive motorcycles to well-off baby boomers by appealing to iconic American values of patriotism, freedom, and maverick ideals. By 2007, Harley-Davidson had almost half the heavy motorcycle sales in the US, and 30 percent worldwide. Ziemer announced plans to retire in 2009, by which time he had identified the company's next growth market as women; female customers have increased five-fold.

Jack Bovender Chairman & CEO, HCA

BIOGRAPHY
Born in the US in 1945. His mother was a nurse, and Bovender studied psychology and later gained a master's in healthcare administration from Duke University, North Carolina.

BEST DECISION
Disposing of HCA's non-core operations.

LESSON IN BUSINESS
Trust your strengths—the attempt to turn HCA into a conglomerate nearly destroyed the company. Bovender took it back to basics.

A DEEP KNOWLEDGE of the healthcare sector has helped Bovender lead HCA, the biggest healthcare company in the US, from a critical situation back to strong commercial health. He also guided them through its leveraged buy-out.

After leaving HCA as COO in 1994, following the company's merger with Columbia Hospital Corporation, Bovender was called back in 1997 to help deal with a string of problems confronting the merged group. This included a federal investigation over Medicare and Medicaid fraud, and severe structural problems stemming from a failed attempt to turn the company into a health services conglomerate. Elevated to CEO in 2001, Bovender turned the hospital giant around by refocusing on its core strengths. He spun off or sold off about a third of the company, instituted a thorough programme of service-sharing in order to maximize efficiencies, and stopped providing services at less than cost to big health-insurance groups, a strategy the company had been pursuing to try to win new business. The result was a strong turnaround of the company, enabling Bovender to put together a $31.6-billion deal to take the company private at the height of the private-equity boom in 2006.

"The greatest dream I had was to be paid to ride motorcycles." James L. Ziemer

MAKING THE NUMBERS

Delivering the financial numbers is critical for any company and any CEO, but whether those numbers are good or bad, communication with the shareholders is of vital importance. In 2006, when Nissan CEO **Carlos Ghosn** (p269) had taken on the leadership of Renault as well, he was invited by **Kerkor Kerkorian** (p416), General Motor's largest shareholder at the time, to enter talks about a potential alliance with GM. Kerkorian was motivated by the Brazilian's reputation for being open about profits and sales targets, which he felt would be good for investors. Honesty and reputation count for a great deal, too. Under the leadership of **Terry Leahy** (p327), UK-based supermarket chain Tesco predicted in an annual report that the growth of UK grocery sales would decrease over subsequent years. One might have expected Tesco's share price to fall on such news, but actually it rose. Investors felt that, since Tesco was perceived as having an exceptional understanding of the market, if it thought that sales growth would decline, the company was probably right and would manage the business better to take account ●

Investor Relations

Investors don't like surprises, so if the figures are going to be disappointing, you can reduce the damage by communicating constantly and effectively with the market, making sure that investors understand your performance and you are aware of their expectations.

Communication can also involve sending out suitable signals at the right time. In October 2008, **Paul H. Stebbins**, CEO of World Fuel Services, announced that its board had authorized a $50-million share repurchase scheme. The move reassured shareholders, demonstrated the firm's market strength, and showed its commitment to long-term growth. Consequently it pushed up the share price by almost 25 percent. Investors' worries also need to be taken into account.

"Shareholders don't care where you are spending your time. What matters to them is results."
CARLOS GHOSN

In early 2009, **Jon Fredrik Baksaas**, CEO of Norwegian telecommunications company Telenor, listened to concerns from shareholders about the economic climate and the company's low valuation, and scrapped plans for a $1.78-billion rights issue that had been intended for expansion into India. Instead he looked at cutting dividends, selling assets, and reducing capital spending.

Not everyone plays by the rules. **Pär Boman**, CEO of Stockholm-based Svenska Handelsbanken, avoids making predictions about results. Rather than basing strategy around internal goals and targets, he looks outside and aims for a greater return on equity than the other listed Nordic banks. Svenska Handelsbanken has been one of Europe's top performing banks over many years.

Getting the Numbers Right

Don't conceal bad news—If the figures are poor, come clean. Investors must be told eventually.

Respect investor intelligence— Shareholders don't expect a company to perform regardless of negative business circumstances.

Accentuate the positive—Focus on the best performing areas, and the potential of weaker sectors.

Have a plan ready—Before releasing disappointing numbers, formulate a detailed and realistic plan for improvement.

Top Number Crunchers

These CEOs know how to improve the numbers in tough times, with asset sales and cost-cutting:

Manfred Wennemer, CONTINENTAL (Automotive parts: Germany)—*Tackled the numbers from every direction, expanding into innovative auto electronics, streamlining production, cutting debt, negotiating flexibility with the unions, delivering growth and profits, and raising the share value more than 500 percent in seven years.*

Joe Maria Alapont, FEDERAL-MOGUL (Automotive: US)—*Places the emphasis on acquisition to further environmental goals, and focuses on streamlining and management improvements to lower operating costs.*

Robert C. Henrikson, METLIFE, INC. (Insurance: US) *—Announced a plan to counter investment losses and lower investment income by selling 75 million shares, strengthening its capital position and reassuring customers.*

Jeffrey S. Lorberbaum, MOHAWK INDUSTRIES (Manufacturing: US) *—As one of the world's largest carpet manufacturers, coped with a downturn in the housing market by aggressively reducing staff in manufacturing, administration, and sales, while pushing to fill the order books.*

Glenn M. Renwick, THE PROGRESSIVE CORP. (Insurance: US)—*Boosted growth by the controversial strategy of reducing premiums, sacrificing some profit margin, and targeting customers looking for new policies and renewals.*

Frank O'Halloran, QBE INSURANCE GROUP (Insurance: Australia)— *Using acquisition as a key tool for growth and expanding the company overseas, O'Halloran only looks to buy companies that will increase QBE's earnings in the first year.*

Ronald Defeo, TEREX (Manufacturing: US)—*Responded to the global economic downturn by cutting production, reducing workforce and overheads, and targeting the most active markets for its mining and construction equipment.*

Glenn F. Tilton, UNITED AIRLINES (Aviation: US)—*Prepared to meet volatile fuel prices by announcing plans to raise cash and credit, and reduce flights and jobs. The news pushed the share price up 45 percent.*

Daniel Fulton, WEYERHAEUSER (Manufacturing: US)—*In the light of lower demand for wood products, sold the packaging business to International Paper in order to keep the company afloat.*

John B. Hess CEO, Hess Corp.

BIOGRAPHY
Born in the US in 1954, Hess is the grandson of a Lithuanian immigrant. He completed his MBA at Harvard in 1977.

BEST DECISION
Forming a strategic partnership with Dunkin' Donuts, offering a new range of coffee and food products in Hess outlets throughout America.

LESSON IN BUSINESS
Adhere to your objectives— Hess has never deviated from his plans to invest in oil exploration, a strategy that continues to drive his company's growth.

EXCEPTIONALLY PRIVATE, but with a competitive spirit and strong work ethic, Hess has rebuilt his father's firm into a leading oil company, exploring for oil and gas resources, and retailing them on America's east coast.

After spending ten years working his way through the company his father Leon had started in 1933, Hess became senior vice-president in 1986, and CEO in 1995. In 1999, when the change-resistant Leon died, and with the company facing massive losses, Hess knew he had to alter his management and move away from refining, marketing, and retail gas station sales into the more profitable field of oil production. After a failed bid for UK-based independent oil company Lasmo in 2000, he purchased the exploration and production company Triton Energy the followng year, for $2.7 billion in cash and $500 million in assumed debt. In 2006, Hess changed the company's name from Amerada Hess to Hess Corporation. With oil prices rising, he sold almost $115 million in company shares in 2008 and exercised substantial and lucrative share options. Envisioning shortfalls in oil production Hess remains committed to exploration, most recently with a large offshore field in Brazil.

Corrado Passera CEO, Intesa Sanpaolo

BIOGRAPHY
Born in Como, Italy, in 1954. Passera gained a first-class honors degree in business administration from Milan's Bocconi University, before gaining an MBA from Wharton School, University of Pennsylvania.

BEST DECISION
Increasing investment in training in spite of losses. Passera felt it was important that employees see a return for their efforts.

LESSON IN BUSINESS
Look for challenges—Passera has a reputation for turning around companies that are on the verge of collapse.

ONE OF ITALY'S best-known and most successful executives, Passera's name is synonymous with turning failing companies into profitable, efficient organizations His most notable triumph has been at leading European bank Intesa Sanpaolo.

Starting his career with McKinsey & Co. in 1980, Passera gained a reputation for salvaging ailing companies. He returned Olivetti, Italy's leading IT company, and the beleaguered Poste Italiane to profit. In 2003, Passera was nominated CEO of Banca Intesa, Italy's largest bank. Formed from three culturally diverse banks (Banco Ambrosiano Veneto, Cariplo Savings Bank, and Banca Commerciale Italiane), Passera inherited an organization with no clear strategic direction and losing $1 billion a year. He shed underperforming top and middle managers and brought in outsiders cutting 4,600 jobs in total. Meanwhile, Passera increased training and technology budgets and sold off the bank's Latin American assets, using the revenue to develop new products, such as life insurance. Branches were set up in post offices, improving customer convenience and boosting market share. In 2007, Banca Intesa merged with Sanpaolo Imi., and Passera became CEO of the newly formed Intesa Sanpaolo.

"Like his father, John is tireless. They're the same in their preoccupation with business. It's a way of life for John." Nicholas Brady, former US treasury secretary, on John B. Hess

Yogesh Chander Deveshwar Chairman & CEO, ITC

BIOGRAPHY
Born in 1947. Deveshwar graduated in mechanical engineering from the Indian Institute of Technology, Delhi, in 1968.

BEST DECISION
Giving greater autonomy to ITC's business units, allowing them to drive the company's growth in diversified areas.

LESSON IN BUSINESS
Corporate social responsibility pays dividends—Deveshwar has bound ITC's environmental and social strategy tightly to its business plan, winning plaudits and boosting the bottom line.

IT HAS TAKEN a delicate balancing act to turn floundering ITC into the diversified multibusiness player it is today, but Deveshwar has used vision and diplomacy to fend off critics and inspire outstanding corporate performance.

On taking the top job in 1996, "Yogi" Deveshwar inherited a series of financial scandals and a rudderless business that desperately needed direction. He moved quickly to remake ITC, taking it out of finanical services, fending off a takeover bid from part-owner British American Tobacco, and settling legal tax dispute problems with a mix of tenacity and charm. He then set about reducing the board's executive power and handing responsibility to business units, turning ITC into "a holding company with a venture capitalist mindset", and working to develop the company's interests in hotels, paper, and print. He has overseen sweeping vertical integration, as ITC hooked up rural farmers to a web-based marketplace to streamline its supply chain, and then used its distribution clout to gain a purchase in markets from packaged food to clothing and gifts. All this has seen an almost five-fold increase in ITC's pre-tax profit over the decade, and a market capitalization of $19 billion.

Nam Joong-soo CEO, KT Corp.

BIOGRAPHY
Born in 1955 in South Korea. Nam has a bachelor's degree in business administration from Seoul National University, an MBA from Duke University, North Carolina, and a PhD in business administration from the University of Massachusetts.

BEST DECISION
Beating rivals to roll out wireless broadband, creating a new revenue stream.

LESSON IN BUSINESS
The early bird catches the worm—being first to commercialize wireless broadband gave KT a local market.

OTHER HEAVYWEIGHT candidates pulled out when Nam decided to stand for CEO at KT, thanks to his 20 years of experience and political connections. His clear vision for re-energizing KT yielded large gains in earnings and profits.

The former South Korean state telephone monopoly company, Korea Telecom (renamed KT), had run out of steam when Nam took charge in 2005. Korean telephone, broadband, and mobile markets had reached saturation point, and operators could grow only by taking over rivals or developing new products. Nam saw the latter as the only real option KT would have to make substantial investments in developing new products and marketing them. His solution was to aggregate cellular, broadband, and wireless services to enable customers to play film clips, download music, make calls, and access the internet on a single device, at superfast broadband speeds. Nam invested heavily in internet TV and wireless broadband (WiBro), acquired the first Korean WiBro license, and made KT the first company to offer this as a commercial service. He has struck deals to offer the service in five US cities, and is expanding the company through acquisitions in Asia.

"Either we become world-class or we leave the business." Yogesh Chander Deveshwar

James Tisch President & CEO, Loews Corp.

BIOGRAPHY
Born in Atlantic City, New Jersey, in 1952. James Tisch gained a bachelor's in economics from Cornell, New York, in 1975 and an MBA from Wharton, University of Pennsylvania, in 1976.

BEST DECISION
Holding on to Diamond Offshore Drilling, Inc., a deepwater drilling contractor acquired in 1989, which now operates one of the largest offshore drilling fleets.

LESSON IN BUSINESS
Fish from the bottom and be patient—Tisch's bargain-basement buys have little risk, but can take years to mature.

HAVING INHERITED his father's keen eye for a bargain, Tisch was never going to work anywhere but in the family business. He has had his hands full turning around a firm whose cluttered holdings had become deeply unfashionable.

Bombed-out companies and assets have been the mainstay of Loews since 1947. Moving into tobacco, oil, insurance, and hotels when they were out of favor, and then milking the businesses for cash for years has been the hallmark of the group's success. Tisch was a chip off the family block, snapping up oil tankers at a price close to scrap and waiting patiently for their value to rise. By the time he made CEO in 1999, Loews was being hammered by tobacco litigation, asbestos claims, and a rock-bottom oil price, as well as ill-advised short bets on the market. Tisch used his executive muscle to restructure the failing insurance business and refocused Loews on its core strength of value investing with minimal downside risk. He has also spun off Loews's tobacco holdings to protect it from reputational damage, and whittled down the company's holdings in other sectors. In the process, he has boosted the firm's share price more than six-fold during his years at the top.

Stuart Rose CEO, Marks & Spencer plc

BIOGRAPHY
Born in Gosport, UK, in 1949. Rose is the grandson of White Russian émigrés who fled the revolution (his original family name was Bryantzeff).

BEST DECISION
Recruiting celebrities like Twiggy to front ad campaigns, which helped to re-establish M&S's credentials as an upmarket women's fashion retailer.

LESSON IN BUSINESS
Don't be afraid of a complete makeover—Rose quickly realized that M&S's tired image needed an overhaul, and pulled out the stops to achieve it.

WHEN MARKS & SPENCER hit a rocky patch, it chose former trainee Rose as the man to woo back customers. He had a track record for turning round troubled retailers and soon rose to the challenge of saving the British high street favourite.

At the time of Rose's appointment in 2004, Marks & Spencer (M&S) was in a sorry state. Rival fashion stores, offering trendier and cheaper clothes, had poached many of M&S's once loyal customers, and the company was facing a hostile takeover bid from Arcadia's new owner, the retail tycoon Philip Green. Selling off the company's financial services allowed Rose to concentrate on the company's core business of women's fashion. To get the cash registers ringing again, Rose recognized that M&S's image needed a major overhaul. To bring back the glamour, he implemented a series of advertising campaigns featuring celebrities, including 1960s supermodel Twiggy. He also bought the classy Per Una label outright from co-founder George Davies, and expanded M&S's upmarket, and highly profitable, food lines. Rose's pledge to make M&S carbon neutral, and the introduction of ethical clothing helped to boost sales, though profits dipped once again in the wake of the economic downturn.

"I want to please every woman, every time." Stuart Rose

Brian Duperreault President & CEO, Marsh & McLennan (MMC)

BIOGRAPHY
Born in Bermuda 1947. Duperreault received a bachelor of science degree in mathematics from Saint Joseph's University, Philadelphia.

BEST DECISION
Leading ACE's $3.45 billion acquisition of CIGNA's property and casualty insurance businesses in 1999, catapulting ACE into a global position.

LESSON IN BUSINESS
Think big—as Duperreault demonstrated with ACE, in a fairly short time the right moves can turn a small company into a big one.

HAVING LED A RAPID transformation of ACE from a small boutique insurance specialist into a global presence, Duperreault was called upon in early 2008 to take over at Marsh & McLennan in the midst of a serious crisis.

In his ten years running ACE, Duperreault used a combination of consistent organic growth and targeted acquisition to turn a small Bermuda-based specialist insurer into a well-positioned, multi-line international insurance business, with a market capitalization that grew from $1.1 billion when he took over to around $19 billion when he departed. This impressive track record made him an ideal candidate to take on the problems at MMC, which was suffering heavy outflows stemming from a bid-rigging scandal in 2004 that cost an initial $850 million settlement, plus further substantial ongoing costs year after year. Duperreault immediately put into action an emergency turnaround program, announcing plans to divest underperforming assets and lay off hundreds of employees in an effort to restore profitability. He still has a long way to go and the problems affecting MMC run deep, but Duperreault's track record leaves him better placed than most to solve them.

James A. Skinner Chairman & CEO, McDonald's Corp.

BIOGRAPHY
Born in Illinois in 1944. Skinner served in the United States Navy for ten years. He graduated second in his class from McDonald's Hamburger University.

BEST DECISION
Abandoning McDonald's strategy of opening new restaurants on a daily basis, which cut costs and led to a focus on existing outlets.

LESSON IN BUSINESS
Listen to your clients—Skinner addressed the need for a more health-conscious menu.

FROM RESTAURANT TRAINEE to CEO, Skinner has been with McDonald's, the world's leading hamburger chain, for more than 30 years. Company stock has doubled, and his changes have seen customers returning to the "Golden Arches".

Skinner's appointment as McDonald's CEO in November 2004 was the culmination of a long and successful career that began in 1971, when he became restaurant manager trainee in Carpentersville, Illinois. Prior to becoming CEO, Skinner held a number of key executive posts, including vice chairman, president, and COO. Once in charge, he dramatically restructured McDonald's. To counter charges that McDonald's was largely responsible for the unhealthy eating habits of a generation, Skinner introduced a new menu that included a range of "healthy" options. He scrapped the company's policy of opening four new stores a day, and moved instead to extend company franchises. This strategy reduced costs and improved the quality and service in existing restaurants, allowing some to remain open 24/7. Sales of Big Mac and other McDonald's classics continued to rise despite the global economic downturn. Skinner stated that the company was "recession resistant".

"I didn't take the job to be a caretaker or oversee incremental improvement." Brian Duperreault

John H. Hammergren Chairman & CEO, McKesson Corp.

BIOGRAPHY
Born in St Paul, Minnesota, in 1959, Hammergren is the son of a traveling salesman in the health-care business. He studied at the University of Minnesota and Xavier University, Ohio.

BEST DECISION
Introducing the ICARE (integrity, customer-first, accountability, respect, excellence) principles, which led to improved service.

LESSON IN BUSINESS
Focus on the customer—despite facing a disastrous situation, Hammergren's dedication to rebuilding customer confidence saved McKesson.

HEALTH-CARE GIANT McKesson was in the midst of an accounting scandal when Hammergren took over. His commitment to rebuilding customer confidence was central to one of the most remarkable turnarounds in recent corporate history.

Hammergren joined McKesson in 1996, making a huge success of his role as president of McKesson Health Systems. When it emerged that the earnings of newly acquired healthcare software company HBOC had been inflated, the share price halved, HBOC executives were dismissed and prosecuted, and key McKesson people resigned. Hammergren was chosen to address the emergency, becoming co-CEO in 1999, then CEO. He had demonstrated strong ethics and leadership as part of a rescue team at Kendall Healthcare Products in the early 1990s, and now he set about restoring the shaken confidence of McKesson's workforce, customers, and investors. Becoming the visible face of the company, he hosted customer meetings, demanded absolute integrity throughout the organization, instituted measures of financial success, and implemented customer and employee surveys. His strategy, which restored confidence, not only saved the business, but brought several years of record profits.

Eckhard Cordes Chairman & CEO, Metro AG

BIOGRAPHY
Born in Neumünster, Germany, in 1950. Cordes studied economics and gained a PhD in business administration at the University of Hamburg.

BEST DECISION
Bravely leaving Daimler, his *alma mater* for 30 years, to carve out a new career in retail.

LESSON IN BUSINESS
Move sideways to move upward—Cordes's resignation from Daimler in protest at failing to land the CEO job looked petty at the time, but paid off when he took control of a leader in another industry.

A PROVEN TURNAROUND expert, Cordes made his name at car maker Daimler by rejuvenating struggling divisions and brokering the merger with Chrysler, before switching industries to lead major retailer Metro AG.

Cordes joined Daimler-Benz in 1976, assuming a range of financial positions. In 1989, he moved to the firm's troubled AEG appliance subsidiary to prepare it for sale. He did the same for the group's Fokker aircraft unit. Cordes joined Daimler's management board in 1996, and acted as lead negotiator in the merger between Daimler and US automotive giant Chrysler. He negotiated in the enlarged group's acquisition of a stake in Mitsubishi in 2000. As the head of DaimlerChrysler's commercial vehicles division from 2000, he cut jobs and costs to lead the unit back to profit. In 2004 he led the Mercedes division, but resigned abruptly in 2006 when he failed to become CEO. The following year he was appointed chairman and CEO of Franz Haniel and he then moved to Germany's leading retailer, Metro AG, in which Haniel held a majority stake. He has focused on staying competitive and expanding into Eastern European and Asian markets.

"In risk, if you perform, it produces great opportunities." John H. Hammergren

Gregory Brown President & CEO, Motorola

BIOGRAPHY
Born in New Jersey in 1960. Brown is the brother of Dick Brown, former CEO of EDS and Cable & Wireless. He received a bachelor's degree in economics from Rutgers University, New Jersey.

BEST DECISION
Separating Motorola's handset business to maximize focus on its problems.

LESSON IN BUSINESS
Give good value—Brown's controlled product rollout was the key to success when he started at Motorola.

A GLITTERING CAREER in software earned Brown the CEO role at one of the biggest companies in the technology world. He took his experience to Motorola just as cell-phone failures presented a major crisis.

After a successful stint at Ameritech in Chicago, Brown became CEO of San Francisco software firm Micromuse in 1999. Within four years he had boosted its revenues from $22 million to more than $200 million. This impressive record led to him being hired by Motorola in 2003. Brown once again showed his ability to get results. As head of Motorola's $6.7 billion government and corporate communications equipment business, he instituted a disciplined rollout of new products, tight management of R&D spending, while also laying off three percent of the staff. The result was a ten percent increase in the size of his division, and a doubling of its productivity. He was appointed CEO in 2008. The company was suffering a serious battering in the handset market. He announced the separation of Motorola's Mobile Devices Business and Broadband & Mobility Solutions Business, and the appointment of Sanjay Jha as CEO of the handset division.

Bart Becht CEO, Reckitt Benckiser

BIOGRAPHY
Born in Rotterdam, Netherlands, in 1956. Becht grew up in Alkmaar and studied economics at the University of Groningen, graduating in 1977. He later obtained an MBA from the University of Chicago.

BEST DECISION
Concentrating on what the customers want and consumer habits, and focusing on core power brands".

LESSON IN BUSINESS
Keep things speedy—Becht prefers brief meetings, rapid decision-making, and quick turnaround of products.

WITH A REPUTATION for testing the products himself, Becht has turned Reckitt Benckiser into one of the world's most successful manufacturers and marketers of cleaning products. The company has also branched into health care.

Becht started his career as a brand manager with Procter & Gamble in 1982, joining Benckiser in 1988, and taking the helm in 1995. When the British firm Reckitt & Coleman merged with Benckiser in 1999, he was appointed CEO of Reckitt Benckiser. Becht has been credited with reviving a company that used to rank well below Unilever and Henkel. He implemented cost-cutting, disposed of unprofitable, non-core businesses, and concentrated on 18 "power brands," including Vanish and Finish, aiming to turn them into global household names. His "innovation marketing" has led to the constant introduction of new improved variations on these existing brands, with heavy investment in advertising and promotions. In addition to organic growth, Becht gave Reckitt Benckiser a stake in the growing over-the-counter health care market, through the purchase of Boots Healthcare for £1.9 billion and Adams Respiratory Therapeutics for £1.1 billion.

"At the end of the day, innovation is generated by new ideas, not messing around in the lab." Bart Becht

Antonio Brufau Chairman & CEO, Repsol YPF

BIOGRAPHY
Born in Lerida, Spain, in 1948. Brufau graduated in economics at the University of Barcelona and has a master's degree from the IESE Business School at the University of Navarra.

BEST DECISION
Reducing Repsol's exposure to South America.

LESSON IN BUSINESS
Find your core strength—by ensuring that Repsol's reliable core assets were in good health, Brufau laid the foundation for sustainable growth.

THE DEBRIS from a Latin American venture was just one of the problems facing Brufau when he became CEO of Spanish oil and gas company Repsol YPF in 2004. His strategic vision and rescue plan turned the company around.

Brufau was a partner at Arthur Andersen and then managing director of Spain's best-known mutual savings bank—an unusual route to the top of an oil company. However, Repsol YPF was no ordinary oil company when Brufau took over. Negligible oil and gas reserves and heavy debt from an ill-advised Argentine acquisition appeared to offer little prospect of growth. Brufau took up the challenge and implemented a restructuring program that turned the company around. He sold off a substantial part of Repsol's investments in Argentina and other Latin American countries, to focus primarily on core assets in OECD countries. He tripled investment with ten big projects in these countries, and his strategy bore fruit. Four years after Brufau took over, the company's debt had been reduced to a manageable level, sales were at $70 billion, margins were healthy, the share price had doubled, and Repsol had become one of the world's leading oil companies.

Alan J. Lacy Chairman & CEO (2000–06), Sears, Roebuck & Co.

BIOGRAPHY
Born in 1953 in Cleveland, Tennessee. Lacy studied industrial management before gaining an MBA from Emory University, Atlanta.

BEST DECISION
Disposing of non-core businesses, such as National Tire and Battery stores, leading to cut costs and increased profits.

LESSON IN BUSINESS
Fewer but better—Lacy transformed his department stores' image by replacing unpopular clothing lines with upmarket styles, and scrapping hovering attendants.

SEARS' STORES and business rose from crisis to profit under Lacy's leadership. Despite having no retail experience, he traded up his customer profile, improved the shopping experience, and disposed of non-core activities to boost sales.

When Lacy took over in 2000, the company was in the doldrums. Its stores looked tired and its reputation had taken a battering from a financial scandal—Sears had forced bankrupt customers to repay debts they had already discharged. Lacy cleaned up the mess, transforming Sears' credit card operations into one of the company's most profitable divisions. As CEO, he moved quickly to cut costs and improve sales. He discarded eight clothing lines, closed cosmetics counters, and fired 20 percent of the workforce. This saved the company $600 million. Lacy gave the stores a makeover and introduced a line of upmarket "yuppie weekend clothes," attracting wealthier customers. He also acquired the popular, middle-class online retailer Land's End for $1.9 billion in 2002, resulting in a significant rise in share price. In 2004, Lacy negotiated the $11-billion merger of Sears with Kmart, creating the US's third largest retail group. Lacy resigned in 2006.

"[Lacy] is a man of high integrity and business acumen" James M. Cornelius, CEO, Bristol-Myers Squibb

Toshifumi Suzuki Chairman & CEO, Seven & I Holdings Co. Ltd

BIOGRAPHY
Born in Nagano, Japan, in 1932. Suzuki gained a degree in economics and commerce from Chuo University, Tokyo, in 1956.

BEST DECISION
Quitting publishing sales for retail after meeting retailing pioneer Masatoshi Ito in 1963, Suzuki now heads the fifth largest retail group in the world.

LESSON IN BUSINESS
Never stand still—constantly improving products and the consumer experience has made 7-Eleven Japan's largest convenience-store chain.

INNOVATION AND DISCIPLINE are the hallmarks of Suzuki's management style. Driven by a dogged desire to meet customer needs, he has revolutionized retail distribution with 7-Eleven in Japan, and also rescued the brand in the US.

Soon after moving from publishing to the Ito-Yokado retailing chain, a chance visit to a 7-Eleven store on a trip to the US convinced Suzuki of its potential in Japan. His visionary zeal overcame opposition from the Ito-Yokado board and 7-Eleven's US owner, and he sold the franchising concept to a notoriously hidebound small retailing sector. Constant product and process improvements have kept 7-Eleven at the top of the sector in Japan, eclipsing the chain's US parent to the point at which Ito-Yokado, its major franchisee, led by Suzuki, rescued it from bankruptcy by buying a controlling share. In 2005, Seven & I Holdings was established, with Suzuki as chairman and CEO. Further acquisitions have made it the largest distribution and retailing business in Japan. Suzuki never stops innovating, using the 7-Eleven empire as a springboard for ventures into banking, e-commerce, and electronic cash. In 2007, he announced a $22.4-billion plan to expand 7-Eleven to over 7,000 stores in the US.

Peter Löscher CEO, Siemens AG

BIOGRAPHY
Born in 1957 in Villach, Austria. Löscher studied economics in Vienna, Hong Kong, and at Harvard Business School.

BEST DECISION
Making the restoration of Siemens' ethical credibility his first priority.

LESSON IN BUSINESS
Ethics can't be optional—Löscher's determination to clean up Siemens includes compliance training programs for managers worldwide.

THE FIRST CEO of Siemens AG not to be promoted from within the organization, Löscher was wooed from Merck in 2007 and given the task of establishing a new management culture in the scandal-tainted company.

Previously president of Global Human Health at Merck & Co., Löscher joined electronics and electrical engineering giant Siemens in July 2007. At the time of his arrival, the 160-year-old company was being shaken by a corruption scandal over alleged bribes to win contracts, illegal price fixing, and pressure on unions, as well as investigations by the German and US authorities. Löscher moved quickly to shore up the company's reputation and morale. With an outsider's perspective, and experience gained at companies such as Hoescht, Aventis, and General Electric, he immediately instigated a dramatic reorganization of the company's management structure, replacing personnel, and creating clear lines of authority and responsibility. Building on Siemens' global reputation for technical excellence and innovation, Löscher took steps to enforce ethical behavior in global operations, and demonstrated his faith in the company by buying several million euros' worth of shares.

> "We all support an absolutely clean business in the future. Anyone who doesn't accept this can't work for Siemens." Peter Löscher

Daniel R. Hesse CEO, Sprint Nextel

BIOGRAPHY
Born in 1954. Hesse studied at Notre Dame University, Indiana, Cornell University, and Massachusetts Institute of Technology.

BEST DECISION
Starring in Sprint Nextel's TV ads, pleading with disaffected customers to give the company another chance.

LESSON IN BUSINESS
Lead from the front—Sprint's customers were leaving because of poor service and Hesse's TV appearance presented a face saying "the buck stops here".

SPRINT'S CELL PHONE BUSINESS was a flop when Hesse arrived. In the first quarter of 2008 over a million subscribers, tired of poor service, walked away. Hesse took the flak, put service center stage, and gave the operator a new buzz.

Hesse was a mobile telecommunications veteran when he joined Sprint. He had spent 23 years with AT&T, including three years as president and CEO of AT&T Wireless. The company's reputation was so bad that few expected him to stay. He found a moribund business where no-one took responsibility and young talent was overlooked. Hesse made customer service the responsibility of every senior executive. He launched a new $99 unlimited voice and data package, clinched a $12-billion deal with Clearwire to provide a fourth generation network and marketed the Instinct handset, co-developed with Samsung, as the company's answer to Apple's iPhone. More importantly, Hesse has given the company a clear vision of what it should be offering its customers. Not "walled garden" service, but "everything now"—facilitating mobile internet, gaming, sending pictures, and downloading music at fast speeds easier, while turning Sprint into the favorite of third-party applications developers.

Ekkehard D. Schulz Chairman, ThyssenKrupp AG

BIOGRAPHY
Born in 1941 in what is now Poland. Schulz earned his PhD in metallurgy at Clausthal Technical University, Germany.

BEST DECISION
Focusing on the future. Schulz has reoriented the company's investment toward new technology and transport, energy, and infrastructure, deliberately targeting areas of future growth.

LESSON IN BUSINESS
Know what you're doing and do it better—Schulz achieved record profits by identifying core activities, making them competitive, and investing heavily in research.

AFTER STEERING the merger of Thyssen and Krupp, two of Europe's biggest steelmaking rivals, Schulz led the conglomerate to world dominance in steel fabrication, specialized equipment, new technologies, and capital services.

Schulz was a professor at Clausthal Technical University before joining Thyssen Group in 1972. In 1991, he was made chairman of the board of Thyssen Stahl AG. Following the merger of the flat-steel operations of Thyssen Stahl AG and Krupp Stahl AG in 1997, the two companies achieved further strategic development and operating synergies in a full merger in 1999, with the creation of Thyssen Krupp AG. Schulz became co-chairman, then chairman in 2001, overseeing the consolidation of an industrial colossus with more than 800 subsidiaries, almost 200,000 employees, no debt, and record annual profits topping $60 billion. The company has emerged as a world-leader in new technologies, investing heavily in research in climate, environment, infrastructure, and mobility. Technological innovations include combining different metals to produce lightweight cars, tripling the life of fuel cells, and a compact elevator that maximizes potential for designing efficient buildings.

"Our innovation competency determines our market success, and with it, the future of the company."
Ekkehard D. Schulz

John Murphy CEO, Visy

BIOGRAPHY
Born in Queensland, Australia, in 1963. Murphy started work in the post room of Carlton & United Breweries as a teenager.

BEST DECISION
Walking away from a company where he had spent 26 years, which led to new successes in a very different market.

LESSON IN BUSINESS
Trust is essential—joining Visy after a price-fixing scandal, Murphy had to use all his talents to restore trust in the company.

AFTER BREATHING NEW LIFE into Australian brewer Foster's, Murphy appeared to have the Midas touch, but he accepted a significant challenge when he became CEO of scandal-hit paper, packaging, and recycling firm Visy in 2007.

Murphy worked his way up through a series of positions at Foster's subsidiary Carlton & United Breweries (CUB), before becoming managing director of Brisbane CUB in 2004. One of the masterminds behind turning Foster's into a multi-beverage company, he was unexpectedly omitted from a management restructure in 2006. Murphy resigned despite the offer of a job elsewhere in the company and, in 2007, began consulting for paper, packaging, and recycling firm Visy. Six months later, he took the top job after the CEO resigned over price-fixing with rival Amcor, which resulted in a $36-million fine, the largest in Australian corporate history. Renowned for his customer-relations skills, Murphy focused on winning back aggrieved customers. He also improved accountability, efficiency, and control, and introduced plans to minimize the impact of climate change. In 2008, Murphy oversaw a strategic partnership to recycle waste from Spotlight, Australia's largest fabric, craft, and home-decorating retailer.

Alan Parker CEO, Whitbread

BIOGRAPHY
Born in the UK in 1946, Parker grew up in North London, where his parents ran a café. He studied hotel and catering management at the University of Surrey.

BEST DECISION
Walking away from a £900-million deal to buy Travelodge in 2008, which Parker believed would make Whitbread less vulnerable to recession.

LESSON IN BUSINESS
Concentrate on the detail—Parker's attention to customer satisfaction and providing value for money has ensured a high level of repeat business.

HAVING SPENT HIS ENTIRE career in the hospitality trade, Parker has transformed Whitbread, the UK-based leisure group whose history dates back to the 18th century, into a successful 21st-century global conglomerate.

Parker worked for both Thistle and Holiday Inn hotels before joining Whitbread in 1992 as manager of its ailing hotel division. He turned the £2-million operation into the UK's largest and fastest-growing hotel chain, and by 2003 Whitbread had shed the breweries, pubs, and bar businesses synonymous with its name. In 2004, Parker was appointed CEO and moved to focus the organization's growth into three core brands: Premier Inn hotels, Costa Coffee, and its pub restaurant business, which included the Beefeater and Brewers Fayre brands. He dissolved Whitbread's agreements with Marriott hotels, Pizza Hut, and TGI Fridays and, in 2007, sold off David Lloyd fitness clubs. In the long term, Parker plans to double the size of Costa Coffee and Premier Inn. Much of this growth will come from abroad, as Parker has targeted central Europe, the Middle East, and Asia for the expansion of Costa Coffee. Following the opening of the first Premier Inn in Dubai in 2008, he plans to open 80 more hotels in India.

"A lot of this will be about... showing [customers] that I am a fresh face and saying, 'You are dealing with someone who is... providing solutions.'" John Murphy

THE BUSINESS OF ETHICS

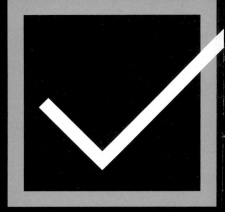

A CEO's role is to make money for the shareholders: some are successful, and others less so. But the truly successful CEOs are the ones who manage to make money while doing good, and it is heartening to see how many CEOs take their ethical responsibilities seriously. One of these is **Dominic D'Alessandro** (p319) who, when he took over at the Canadian life insurance company Manulife in 1994, established the company's values under the acronym PRIDE: Professionalism, Real Value to Customers, Integrity, Demonstrated Financial Strength, and Employer of Choice. Manulife is widely recognized as putting these values into practice, and this, together with its commitment to donating generously to the communities it serves, has made it one of the most admired and respected businesses in Canada. Another company strongly associated with promoting ethical business practice is Motorola. In the 1930s, founder and CEO **Paul Galvin** (p72) refusing to massage the details of a shareholders' report to show the company in a more favorable light, noted: "Tell them the truth, first because it is the right thing to do, and second because they'll find out anyway. If they don't find it out from us we will be the ones to suffer." Paul Galvin's lead was followed by successive Motorola CEOs, from **Bob Galvin** right up to recent co-CEOs **Greg Brown** (p295) and **Sanjay Jha** ●

"If you don't have integrity, you have nothing. You can't buy it ...if you are not a moral and ethical person, you really have nothing."
HENRY R. KRAVIS, co-founder, KKR

An Argument for Ethics

Between the WorldCom and Enron scandals that shook the corporate world at the beginning of the new millennium, and the later furore over bankers' bonuses after the credit crunch, it can be forgotten that most CEOs follow strict codes of ethics, and that some argue passionately that business leaders have a responsibility to set a moral example.

The argument for sound business ethics has been championed by a number of top executives, prominent among them **Dan Vasella**, CEO and chairman of Novartis, the Swiss

pharmaceutical giant. Vasella, a former doctor, has made a number of public statements asserting his emphasis on ethics. "If you look at the medical profession as an analogy we have the Hippocratic Oath, this is something that guides our actions and values. Boards and execs need something similar, a kind of code of ethics," he has said.

Aaron Feuerstein, boss of US textiles business Malden Mills Industries, demonstrated how corporate business ethics can have a positive impact on both company-employee relationships and the bottom line. After a major fire ripped through the company's factory buildings in 1995, the 3,000-strong workforce thought they were out of a job.

But despite the company having no immediate means of production, and hence no income, Feuerstein pledged to pay the employees' salaries and healthcare insurance out of his own pocket. Ninety days later, Malden Mills was back to almost 100 percent capacity, Feuerstein had no need to hire new, or rehire existing, employees, and his grateful workforce pulled out all the stops to enhance productivity and quality.

Bucking the Compensation Trend

Reacting to public indignation during the credit crunch at the compensation packages of disgraced bankers like RBS ex-CEO **Fred Goodwin**, and **Richard Fuld**, the Lehman Brothers CEO who took home $300 million over eight years before the bank went bankrupt, American Express signaled a welcome break from the usual stories of excess. The incentive plan it agreed with CEO **Kenneth Chenault** (p192) in 2008 was based on performance over six years—a long-term view by corporate standards—with tough targets: Amex must outperform the S&P 500 by an average 2.5 percent per annum. A less impressive performance will lead to reduced or no options for Chenault, and there is no provision for restricted stock, hence no reward simply for marking time.

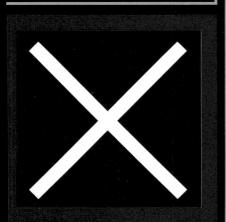

Ethical Role Models

There are many highly principled people running businesses today. Among those CEOs recognized for their outstanding ethics are:

Jim Koch, Boston Beer (Beverages: US)—*When a shortage of hops and rising prices threatened small breweries, Koch sold at cost so they could stay in business.*

Yoshihiro Yasui, Brother Industries Ltd (Manufacturing: Japan)—*To improve safety levels in manufacturing facilities outside Japan, and notably in China, Yasui operates strengthened safety patrols, danger prediction activities, and health and safety education.*

Peter Webster, EIRIS (Business information: UK)—*Researches the social, environmental, and ethical performance of over 2,800 companies, including all those on the FTSE All World Developed Index, on behalf of UK, US, and Asian investors.*

Penny Newman, Fifteen Foundation (Restaurants: UK) – *After driving impressive growth at Fairtrade food company Cafédirect, Newman moved to head up celebrity chef and founder* **Jamie Oliver**'s *restaurant chain in 2008. The charity helps disadvantaged young people build careers in the restaurant trade.*

Anders Dahlvig, IKEA (Retail: Sweden)—*To combat child labor, Dahlvig imposes and, through unannounced visits by third-party auditors, monitors a code of conduct at 1,300 suppliers in 53 countries.*

Haruka Nishimatsu, Japan Airlines (Aviation: Japan)—*Faced with having to cut budgets and encourage older employees to retire to ensure the airline's financial stability, Nishimatsu also reduced his own salary.*

Eve Jursch, Patagonia (Retail: US)—*Introduced a raft of anti-sweatshop initiatives to promote fair labor conditions and improve the quality of life of the company's outsourced garment workers.*

Joseph Keefe, PAX World Mutual Funds (Finance: US) – *Pursues sustainable investment, integrating environmental, social, and governance factors into investment analysis and decision-making.*

Peter Blom, Triodos Bank (Finance: Netherlands)—*Triodos finances enterprises that add social, environmental, and cultural value, including fairtrade and micro-credit organizations in developing countries.*

Danny Wegman, Wegmans Food Markets, Inc. (Retail: US)—*Banned the sale of cigarettes from his stores in 2008. Wegman was listed fifth on* Fortune *magazine's "100 Best Companies to Work for" in 2009.*

7

The Value Squeezers

Michael Diekmann Chairman & CEO, Allianz

THE POST OF CEO at German-based Allianz appeared a poisoned chalice when Diekmann took over in 2003. For Europe's biggest insurance company, a recent acquisition was proving to be a giant albatross around its neck. There had been a spate of major claims, and Allianz was hemorrhaging cash. Facing up to the challenge, Diekmann brought an aggressive and wholehearted approach to the task of sorting out the mess. Within a year Allianz was back on track and Diekmann was setting his sights on overseas markets.

BIOGRAPHY
Born in 1954 in Bielefeld, Germany, where his family owned a construction business. Diekmann studied law and philosophy at Göttingen University, graduating in 1982.

LEADERSHIP STYLE
Charming but tough. Diekmann has an open and direct management style that Allianz employees admire and respect, but equally he is known for taking action if people don't deliver.

KEY STRENGTH
Ruthlessness and an unbending, uncompromising bloody-mindedness.

BEST DECISION
Taking drastic cost-cutting action at Dresdner Bank to stem money losses.

PICKING UP THE PIECES Leaving the publishing company that he had founded, Michael Diekmann joined Allianz in 1988 and advanced steadily through the ranks. By 1996 he was heading up the Asia-Pacific and North America division, and in 2003 he was given the top job. Two years earlier the German company had bought Dresdner Bank for $22.5 billion. The intention had been to transform Allianz into a powerhouse that would produce big revenues by selling insurance and banking products to the same customers. Instead, it was a money-losing nightmare, and Allianz' share price fell by almost 75 percent.

CHALLENGING TIMES The company suffered huge claims as a result of the 9/11 terrorist attacks. The previous CEO, Henning Schulte-Noelle, had resigned unexpectedly,

and Diekmann came in to fix the mess. His appointment was a surprise to many, but he was already known for his problem-solving abilities and had the advantage of not having been involved in the purchase of Dresdner.

Diekmann quickly lived up to his reputation as a cost cutter, introducing radical changes to bring his company back. He axed more than 15,000 jobs at Dresdner Bank, got rid of non-core businesses, increased capital through a $5-billion rights issue, and established tough profit targets throughout the group. In under a year, Allianz was reaping the rewards of his drastic action. Its share price improved and profits for 2003 were almost $2 billion. In 2008, Allianz sold Dresdner to Commerzbank, ending its foray into "bankassurance." Allianz now has a presence in more than 70 countries with over 180,000 employees worldwide.

LESSONS IN BUSINESS: ACCEPTING THE CHALLENGE

As Diekmann discovered, life was a lot easier as a number two or three, but he felt honor-bound to accept the top job when it was offered to him.
→ Look for jobs in parts of the business that are struggling. You will learn more and enhance your reputation if you get them right.
→ Welcome accountability and take responsibility for achieving objectives in order to develop.
→ If, for any reason, you shirk a challenge, don't expect a more acceptable one to turn up later.

> "You can't stay all your life as a number two or number three." Michael Diekmann

Kenneth D. Lewis CEO, Bank of America

MORE THAN ANY OTHER figure, Lewis is responsible for transforming Bank of America into America's largest bank and the world's largest financial services group. By 2009 its assets totalled around $3 trillion, and its net income stood at over $14 billion. Lewis's story mirrors that of the bank itself, a rising star with ambitions to become America's number one. His innovations in retail banking, his judicious cost-cutting, and his judgement calls on when to expand and when to reward shareholders have underpinned the Bank of America's rise to the top.

BIOGRAPHY
Born in Meridian, Mississippi, in 1947. Lewis took a business degree from the state university.

LEADERSHIP STYLE
Prudent, creative, and ruthless. Lewis has proved himself to be a cost-cutter and an innovator in transforming the company into America's best retail bank.

KEY STRENGTH
Balancing the needs of shareholders with his own plans for growth, by launching an audacious takeover bid and impressing a market that previously thought of him as merely a cost-cutter dedicated to improving company value.

BEST DECISION
Launching Vision 95, a program of cost-cutting and process-implification measures that saved vast sums of money, improved the bank's reputation, and sealed his position as a CEO-in-waiting.

LEARNING THE ROPES Lewis learned valuable business lessons packing groceries, delivering newspapers, and selling shoes as a schoolboy. He joined the North Carolina National Bank as a credit analyst in 1969, worked in its international department, and moved to its US division before being appointed president of the bank's consumer and commercial division in 1990.

EFFICIENCY AND GROWTH While the CEO focused on expansion, Lewis was left to merge new acquisitions into a single, efficient bank with high standards of customer service. He found his answer in Texas, where lunchtime and payday lines left customers dissatisfied. Lewis increased the number of part-time tellers to cut lines and, because part-timers receive fewer benefits, Lewis saved 15 percent on staff costs.

The approach was rolled out at branches nationwide and was one of the many innovations that helped to make Lewis's name. In 1993, he became president of what had by then been renamed NationsBank.

Lewis simplified procedures and upgraded technology, but because the bank kept making new acquisitions (it joined with Bank of America in 1998) it was permanently in transition. By the time Lewis was made CEO in 2001, shareholders were disgruntled. Lewis promised two "no-excuse" years in which dividends would come first. He then launched his own series of takeovers, acquiring the MBNA credit card giant for $35 billion in 2005, and ABN AMRO's US operations for $21 billion in 2007. With the acquisition of Merrill Lynch for $50 billion in 2008, prudence had won out over the greedy, profligate former giant of Wall Street.

LESSONS IN BUSINESS: BUILDING A SOLID BASE

Lewis made his name as a creative cost-cutter, but he took Bank of America to the top with ambitious takeovers that left his bank standing tall while more flamboyant rivals collapsed on every side.
→ Check the basics: ensure you have good customer service, simple procedures, and happy shareholders.
→ Create a solid foundation of goodwill and liquidity by getting the basics right. Impress the market with your long-term future.
→ Avoid fads if they appear to break any basic rules of best practice, even if they offer short-term profits.

"It's not necessarily a contradiction to be both more efficient and more effective." Kenneth D. Lewis

Fujio Mitarai President & CEO, Canon Inc.

WITH A UNIQUE BLEND of Western and Japanese approaches to management, Canon has reached great heights. Mitarai transformed the company in the US into a profit-focused organization. When he returned to Japan 23 years later, he rescued the company's domestic base. He launched new cameras, staying in budget hotels while he toured the country to promote them. He also expanded the company's printer and copier operations through a joint venture with Hewlett-Packard, eventually winning 70 percent of the market.

BIOGRAPHY
Born in Kamae, Japan, in 1935. Unlike his three brothers, Mitarai decided not to follow his father into medicine. After graduating from Chuo University in 1961, he joined Canon.

LEADERSHIP STYLE
Collaborative, team-focused, but decisive. Mitarai is known for taking advice from fellow CEOs, lunching and persuading his managers, but leading from the front on costs and profits.

KEY STRENGTH
Unusually for a Japanese business leader, Mitarai is an exceptional communicator who gets more from his staff by explaining his vision to them and asking for their criticism.

BEST DECISION
Persuading his uncle to give him a chance to overhaul Canon's poorly performing US division—he transformed it and the whole company's fortunes, too.

THE CHALLENGE In 1961, Mitarai joined Canon, the company founded by his uncle, Takeshi Mitarai. After five years' training as an accountant, Mitarai was dispatched to the US to help Canon develop in the camera market. He discovered a financial mess, and his report showed a profit of just $6,000 on sales of $3 million. Auditors told him the company should close the US operation as it would earn more by banking the money and taking the interest. The challenge was daunting, but Mitarai decided to stand and fight.

DOING IT THE "MITARAI WAY" He launched cutbacks and production streamlining that later became his trademark, known as the "Mitarai Way", and restructured the division to focus on profit. He launched a series of new cameras, notably the Canon AE-1, which enabled amateurs to take professional quality photographs and took the company to the top of the SLR market. In 1984 he sealed a joint venture deal with Hewlett-Packard (HP) to produce photocopiers and printers using HP software and marketing, and Canon laser printing. In 1989 Mitarai returned to Japan where he discovered all was not well. Several of the company's divisions were in the red. It wasn't until 1995, when he was eventually made CEO, that he could take the action he knew was necessary. He shut unprofitable divisions, switched the focus from sales to profits, and rewarded the brightest staff. In the drive for profit, Mitarai introduced incentives into the traditional Japanese business model and created a winning combination. His devoted managers gave even more, to the great benefit of the company.

LESSONS IN BUSINESS: MIXING EAST AND WEST

In the drive for profit, Mitarai brought American management techniques to the Japanese model, which was based on devotion, loyalty, and jobs for life. He introduced incentives into this traditional model and created a winning combination.
→ Instil in managers the notion that the best expression of loyalty to the company is securing profits.
→ Learn from different cultures as well as your own. Bring in best practice from wherever you find it.
→ In a global market, look for success by combining the best from one territory with the best from another.

"I changed the mindset at Canon by getting people to realize that profits come first." Fujio Mitarai

José Luis Durán Chairman & CEO (2005–08), Carrefour SA

APPOINTED IN 2005 as CEO of Carrefour, Europe's largest retailer and the world's second largest, Durán was the youngest CEO on the CAC 40, the index of leading French companies listed on the Paris stock exchange. Tasked with fighting off competition from discounters in Europe, he was ideally qualified for the job as he already had 14 years' experience with the company, and a notable track record in financial management. However, in late 2008, despite reasonable sales growth, Durán fell victim to shareholder pressure and was ousted.

BIOGRAPHY
Born c.1964 in Spain. Durán gained a bachelor's degree in economics from the Catholic Institute of Business Administration (ICADE), Madrid.

LEADERSHIP STYLE
Meticulous, determined, calm under pressure. Even when a significant group of shareholders were opposing him, he maintained a steady, business-as-usual approach.

KEY STRENGTH
Understanding the need to think local and act global.

BEST DECISION
Tailoring Carrefour store formats to the countries and communities they serve, employing local staff and stocking local product ranges.

RISING THROUGH THE RANKS Following his degree in 1987, Durán started his career at audit firm Arthur Andersen. Four years later he joined Spanish grocery retailer Pryca, a subsidiary of Carrefour, and began a steady rise up through the ranks. He held various financial posts, culminating in chief financial officer at Pryca and then, in 1999, CFO for Carrefour Spain. Two years later he joined the group's executive committee. In 2005, Durán took the reins as group managing director, and later chairman.

CARREFOUR AT THE CROSSROADS While Carrefour has retained its position as Europe's largest retailer and the world's second largest after Wal-Mart, in recent years domestic sales have faced pressure from discount retailers. Durán's turnaround strategy involved

rationalizing the group's portfolio to pursue growth both organically and through acquisitions in major markets such as China, Brazil, Indonesia, Poland, and Turkey. As CEO, Durán designated 2008 as a breakthrough year, when profitability would exceed the group's projected sales growth of 6–8 percent. In the event sales rose 6.3 percent to €97.6 billion. The speed of the hoped-for turnaround was deemed insufficient by major shareholder Blue Capital, a consortium controlled by US company Colony Capital and Bernard Arnault, CEO of LVMH. Pressure from these shareholders, who hold a 9.1 percent stake, led to Durán's departure. Observers were unsurprised, but warned that Carrefour, and other hypermarket operators, would continue to face the problem of low or no growth in a highly competitive, price-driven market.

LESSONS IN BUSINESS: FOCUSING ON THE CUSTOMERS

Durán emphasized the need for companies, no matter how big, to focus on the core proposition for customers with different requirements. For Carrefour this meant providing the most price-competitive stores in each catchment area, as well as taking into account local demands.

➔ Do not assume that what worked in one environment will work unchanged in another.
➔ Adapt your core business to new markets. Use what you have learnt to find new ways to reach customers.
➔ When you do change products or markets, hang on to the original idea that made you successful.

> "...today it is more important to be quick than big."
> José Luis Durán

Ralph Norris MD & CEO, Commonwealth Bank of Australia

STRONG LEADERSHIP and a passionate commitment to customer service have been the hallmarks of Norris's varied and successful career. He created a virtual banking arm at ASB Bank that helped grow its market share by 60 percent, and developed a world-class e-commerce capability at Air New Zealand that pulled the airline up from its near death-dive in the early 2000s. His IT service improvements at Commonwealth Bank of Australia helped boost profits more than 23 percent in his first 18 months at the helm.

BIOGRAPHY
Born in 1949 of Maori descent, Norris was raised in Auckland, New Zealand, by a single mother. He was educated at Lynfield College, Auckland.

LEADERSHIP STYLE
Described even by competitors as "an exceptionally nice guy", Norris is a people person. Known for pitching in with galley crew on Air New Zealand flights when he was CEO, his commitment to his staff has seen him through tough restructuring and acted as a talent magnet.

KEY STRENGTH
Translating his considerable enthusiasm for IT and technology into customer-focused success. Leveraging the interactive possibilities of the web was key to the turnaround he wrought at Air New Zealand.

BEST DECISION
Coming out of health-related retirement and throwing his hat into the ring when the top job at Air New Zealand came up.

SATISFIED CUSTOMERS Norris's focus on technology-enabled customer service has allowed him to enjoy a career at the top levels of management in both banking and aviation. He may be unusual among business leaders in knowing how to code software, but he understands that technology is nothing if it doesn't engage people. His appreciation of the power of the internet led to a six-fold rise in profits and consistently high customer satisfaction ratings at New Zealand's ASB Bank. After 22 years with the bank, he gained the top job in 1991 and stayed at the helm for ten years, but diabetes forced him to retire in 2001.

COMEBACK KID After making a solid recovery, Norris embraced a new challenge by becoming CEO and managing director of the near-bankrupt Air New Zealand, of which he had been a board member for three years, in 2002. He focused on the airline's website as a vital tool to cut costs and win more business, pushing up online sales of domestic flights to 44 percent from just 4 percent. Meanwhile, the implementation of computerized self-check-in boosted efficiency at airports, and a strategic shift to a no-frills model for domestic flights hiked profitability.

His success paved the way for his appointment to the ailing Commonwealth Bank of Australia in 2005, which was suffering dire customer satisfaction ratings. Norris's turnaround strategy was a radical overhaul of the bank's computer systems, with a focus on customer-relationship management, leading to an 80 percent drop in complaints in two years. Norris has also engineered the bank's expansion into growing markets, such as India, China, and Vietnam.

LESSONS IN BUSINESS: UNDERSTANDING THE CUSTOMER

Norris's people-centerd approach infuses everything he does in management. At Air New Zealand, his core challenge was to change the organization's focus from flying aircraft to flying people from one place to another.
→ Understand how your organization interacts with customers in order to improve the customer experience.
→ Reward regular and dedicated customers with discounts and other extra benefits.
→ Recognize the fact that a company's internet web portal is its main interface with the public in today's business world. First impressions mean a lot, and nowadays that usually means your website.

> "It's usually the things that go wrong that teach you the most." Ralph Norris

James Sinegal Founder & CEO, Costco

THE PIONEER of the no-frills, bulk-buy and sell-at-a-discount method, Sinegal caught the retail bug with a job unloading mattresses at Fed-Mart while he was still a student. He learned the business from the ground up as the protégé of discount warehouse inventor Sol Price, Fed-Mart's chairman. The experience helped him develop a set of business beliefs that he applied when he opened his first Costco warehouse in Seattle in 1983. He now presides over the world's most profitable discount warehouse chain.

WORLD-BEATING PRINCIPLES Considered by many to be one of the most outstanding retailers of the 20th century, Sinegal has built a worldwide base of over 50 million customers with the help of these golden rules: buy in bulk, keep prices rock bottom, and sell fast. Costco never marks up more than 14 percent, whereas a department store will very often pass on 50 percent to customers. Sinegal also rewards good staff. Costco workers can earn almost double that paid elsewhere. "It's simple," he says. "If you hire good people, give them good jobs and pay them good wages, generally something good is going to happen."

PRINCIPLED GROWTH One customer Sinegal finds hard to please is Wall Street, where analysts think he should be more profit- and shareholder-focused. Sinegal frequently shrugs off calls from shareholders to raise prices in order to turn a quick profit. The temptation to "get a little more, a little more," he believes, "is the heroin that's killed many a retailer." Holding down prices, he says, "is part of the faith our customers have in us." Certainly, the formula seems to work. Costco has seen great profits, and in fiscal year 2007 the company's store sales totaled $64.4 billion.

The epitome of the "retail is detail" approach, Sinegal still, at the age of 72, regularly walks the aisles to find out what's selling. While the no-frills approach even extends to himself—he draws a modest salary and works at a Formica desk—he understands that to attract higher-spending customers he needs to offer premium items. Many customers are delighted to find diamond rings and designer clothes set tactically amongst the toilet rolls and cleaning products, giving a trip to his stores a "treasure hunt" element.

LESSONS IN BUSINESS: DOING THE RIGHT THING

Doing the right thing can make the best business sense. Refusing to bow to pressure and go for quick profits, Sinegal has stuck to old-fashioned principles. Costco is an empire built on trust.

→ Do not go for loans if they require you compromising the principles that underlie your business.
→ Financiers like businesses that regularly pay large fees for services they render. Do not worry about being criticised by financial analysts.
→ Be aware that banks prefer the hare to the tortoise. Do what you think is best for your business.

"You just can't get too focused on… what's going to happen in the next quarter. You have to worry about where the business is headed long-term." James Sinegal

Louis Gallois CEO & Co-CEO, Airbus & EADS

IN JULY 2006, when Gallois became CEO of Airbus and co-CEO of its parent company, EADS (formerly European Aeronautic Defense and Space Company), the pan-European company was in turmoil. Stocks had plummeted thanks to delays in launching Airbus's new A380 superjumbo airplane, and it was up to Gallois, with a reputation for discipline, cost cutting, and development, to get the company airborne again. Despite setbacks, Airbus recovered from a net loss at the end of 2006 to return to profitability.

BIOGRAPHY
Born in 1944 in Montauban, France. Gallois graduated from the French economic sciences school HEC, and France's Ecole Nationale d'Administration.

LEADERSHIP STYLE
Considered and decisive. Gallois believes in teamwork and listens carefully to his advisors, but ultimately he relies on his own judgement when it comes to making key decisions.

KEY STRENGTH
Being able to communicate effectively to everyone from the factory floor to the boardroom.

BEST DECISION
Streamlining production at European factories, and outsourcing components and jobs to other manufacturers, which drastically reduced costs.

AN EXPERIENCED PILOT Having been chairman and CEO of Aérospatiale, and head of SNCF, France's national railway, Gallois knew what it was to work with a large, pan-European company. While critics point out that Gallois failed to make Aérospatiale a profitable company, and that SNCF's freight business never developed the steam he had promised, he is praised for expanding the railway networks, succeeding with SNCF's joint-venture Eurostar, and cutting costs. All this while still managing to maintain a good working relationship with the company's employees despite heavy layoffs.

A STEADY HAND When Gallois stepped into the cockpit at Airbus, the company was described by one industry insider as being in "absolute crisis." Its new commercial aircraft had been delayed by two years due to faulty wiring, and the strong euro made the company less competitive than Boeing, its principal rival. Production costs were abnormally high because the airplanes were manufactured at different plants throughout Europe. Applying many of the strategies that he used at SNCF, Gallois began looking for ways to cut costs without losing competitiveness. In March 2007, Gallois launched Airbus's controversial restructuring proposal "Power8". The plan called for the elimination of 10,000 Airbus jobs over four years, the streamlining of pan-European operations, selling two of its factories in France and Germany, and the outsourcing of work to new suppliers. While the announcements prompted anger from both workers and politicians, Gallois remained calm and resolute throughout the furore.

LESSONS IN BUSINESS: LISTENING AND COMMUNICATION

Gallois makes a point of walking through the German EADS headquarters to demonstrate that he is as attentive to what German employees have to tell him as he is to his employees in France.
→ Remain calm at all times, listen to others, and always explain the reasons for your actions to those affected.
→ Take responsibility for the mistakes or shortcomings of your organization. Demonstrate this by announcing any problems personally to staff and press.
→ Deliver bad news with calm, quiet optimism. Ensure that people follow your lead and find a solution.

"...I had the capacity to explain to the people that they had to change." Louis Gallois

Jack Welch Chairman & CEO (1981–2001), General Electric

THE BEST-KNOWN corporate boss of the late 20th century, Welch was the son of a Boston train conductor and rose to become head of US industrial powerhouse General Electric (GE). Through aggressive restructuring he turned it into what was at the time the world's most valuable company. Under his regime—which pivoted on a series of tough-talking, sometimes brutal, and widely copied dictums—GE's market capitalization grew by an astonishing $387 billion to peak at $410 billion, earning him an almost god-like reputation for creating shareholder value.

BIOGRAPHY
Born in Peabody, Massachusetts, in 1935. Welch graduated in chemical engineering from the University of Massachusetts, Amherst, in 1957. He also gained a master's in 1958 and a doctorate in 1960, both from the University of Illinois, Champaign.

LEADERSHIP STYLE
Frank, focused, and fast, employing a ruthless combination of carrot and stick. He could be dogmatic, and blunt to the point of rudeness when confronted by inefficiency or inertia.

KEY STRENGTH
A born winner. Welch was so dedicated to besting rivals at every turn that he once listed his hobby as "competing".

BEST DECISION
Ruthlessly setting about the turnaround of GE with job cuts and divestments after becoming the company's youngest ever chairman and CEO in 1981, which set the tone for his 20 years at the helm.

"UP OR OUT" STRATEGY Impatient with bureaucracy, on landing the top job at GE in 1981 he commenced stripping out no fewer than nine layers of middle management and divesting underperforming businesses. By 1985, GE's headcount had been cut by almost a third to 299,000. The speed and zeal that he brought to this task stunned fellow managers, who dubbed him "Neutron Jack," because of the way he eliminated people while leaving buildings standing.

His chief tenet was that GE must be either the number one or two player in each of its markets, or get out. A forceful personality, he claimed to have been often rebuked for "excessive candor." He believed that staff deserved to know what was thought of them, both good and ill. Each year Welch would reward handsomely the top performing 20 percent of GE managers, while simultaneously firing the bottom performing 10 percent. In the 1990s he began modernizing the firm's operations, moving away from GE's manufacturing roots and into lucrative new markets such as financial services and healthcare, and emerging territories such as China and India. "If I'm wrong about China," he once said, "it'll cost a couple of billion dollars. If I'm right, it's the future of the company for the next 100 years."

POST-EMPLOYMENT PERKS His retirement in 2001 was mired in controversy. Alongside his multi-million-dollar pension, Welch enjoyed use of a smart New York apartment and private jet, and season tickets for the Boston Red Sox. Apparently surprised by the storm of protest, Welch agreed to pay for their continued use.

LESSONS IN BUSINESS: LEARNING TO LEAD

Welch was a perfect example of the 20th-century cult of the iconic, charismatic business leader. This counted for as much of his success as any explicit business strategy. However, it is important for all stakeholders in a business to realize that no one is indispensable.
→ Be a great leader. Companies need team leaders who make teams greater than the sum of their parts.
→ Praise your team when they have been successful.
→ Present your team with challenges and they will thrive. Do their jobs for them and they will wither.

"If you don't have a competitive advantage, don't compete." Jack Welch

DRIVING EFFICIENCY

Better Together

A popular buzzword when times are good, in a downturn operational efficiency becomes a matter of corporate life or death. CEOs who are unable to cut costs to the bone, reduce headcount, or achieve massive savings through mergers, divestments, or other economies, are likely to come under pressure from their shareholders. Those CEOs most able to thrive are those who have always based their business model on low prices and streamlined operations, such as **Stelios Haji-Ioannou** (p404) of easyGroup. His no-frills businesses have prospered while more traditional rivals have perished.

One of the best ways to keep costs low is to outsource. By moving elements of the business to a third-party that takes on similar work for a number of companies, greater economies of scale can be achieved. Under the leadership of **Nishida Atsutoshi** (p222), Toshiba has outsourced an increasing percentage of its electronics manufacturing to foreign companies. In 2008, Toshiba announced that the production of 1.5 million LCD television sets would be outsourced to the Taiwanese company Compal Electronics, under the leadership of CEO **Ray Chen**, bringing the total share of Toshiba televisions manufactured abroad to around 20 percent. This trend, which can be identified throughout the electronics industry, allows the production of low-cost models that are particularly popular in emerging economies such as China and India ●

"The cheaper you can make something, the more people there are who can afford it,"
STELIOS HAJI-IOANNOU

Often, companies are able to achieve greater levels of efficiency together than they can alone, which is why mergers and acquisitions are such common occurrences in the business world. By joining forces, businesses are able to exploit something called the "synergic effect", which means that they are both economically and operationally stronger as a single entity.

Jan Carlson, Swedish CEO of car safety manufacturer Autoliv, carried out the $42m 2008 acquisition of Tyco Electronics to enhance his company's position and become one of the world's largest suppliers of automotive radar products. Other CEOs have completed vertical acquisitions (where both companies are in the same industry, but involved in different parts of the production process), allowing them to benefit from reduced sourcing costs. Under **Susumu Kato**, Sumitomo Corp. acquired US company Apex Silver Mines for $27.5 million, giving it a majority share in the world's third-largest silver mine. This cut the cost of its metal products business dramatically. Likewise, **Merril Miller** of National Oilwell Varco acquired Grant Prideco, consolidating its grip on the oil-drilling industry.

Some mergers are intended to produce vast savings, such as that between Sears Roebuck and Kmart, overseen by **Bruce Johnson**. Others, such as the merger of Nokia's Networks Business Group and Siemens' carrier-related operations, overseen by **Olli-Pekka Kallasvuo** (p217) at Nokia and **Klaus Kleinfeld** (p191) at Siemens, aim to deploy technological innovation to improve efficiency.

Making the Right Cuts

Do your analysis first— Successful efficiency strategies are those that come about through a nuanced process of cost-benefit analysis.

Look carefully at outsourcing— Weigh up the cost savings against the extended supply chain, the potential lack of transparency and accountability, and the disruption to customer service.

Think before you buy— Consider whether the cost of an acquisition in a new business sector will be greater than the benefits. Is a strategy of diversification the best option over the longer-term?

Identify overlap— Assess whether departments or positions can be merged without losing essential skills and expertise.

Root out poor business— Evaluate whether underperforming products or services should be dropped, allowing resources to be focused on the successful areas.

Experts in Efficiency

CEOs noted for running their companies efficiently include:

Hariolf Kottman, CLARIANT (Chemicals: Switzerland)— *Announced a range of efficiency measures, including restructuring, and streamlining its supply chain and purchasing processes.*

Brian McNamee, CSL (Health sector: Australia)— *Oversaw the purchase of rival firm Talecris, thereby increasing profitability and diversifying CSL's product range.*

Howard Levine, FAMILY DOLLAR STORES (Retail: US)— *Follows his father's policy of laying out all stores identically, for efficient use of resources.*

Gérard Mestrallet, GDF SUEZ (Utilities: France)— *It took years to overcome French bureaucracy and union resistance in order to merge his water and energy business Suez with Gaz de France (GDF) in 2008, creating one of the biggest utility companies in the world.*

Michael Strianese, L-3 COMMUNICATIONS (Aerospace and defense: US)— *Strianese introduced an "integrity" plan to the company, developed a collaborative R&D program, and oversaw multiple acquisitions.*

Philip Bowman, SMITHS GROUP (Diversified: UK)— *Carried out a merger in 2007 to increase the company's diversification. Now encompasses security, medical, oil and gas, and cell phones, in addition to the core aerospace business.*

Mark Hurd CEO, Hewlett-Packard

WHEN HE WAS appointed to replace the controversial Carly Fiorina, analysts wondered whether Hurd could repeat the success he had at technology company NCR at a firm more than ten times its size. They soon discovered that Hurd was an exceptional learner who absorbed lessons from colleagues and clients, and turned them into an effective style of forensic management. At NCR he quadrupled share price in just two years as CEO. It took him 18 months to transform Hewlett-Packard from troubled giant to the world's biggest technology firm by revenue.

BIOGRAPHY
Born in 1957 in New York but raised in Florida. Hurd graduated on a tennis scholarship to Baylor University, Texas.

LEADERSHIP STYLE
Low-key and team-focused with a relentless and obsessive drive for clarity and brevity from his managers. Hurd is also famously publicity-shy, described as a "blue-collar boss" who prefers to roll up his sleeves and get stuck in rather than court the spotlight.

KEY STRENGTH
Hurd has a hard-drive memory for figures and a prosecutor's talent for forensic questioning—he gets to the heart of the matter quickly and holds executives to their promises.

BEST DECISION
Growing NCR's Teradata data storage division to cut costs and drive the company to soaring profits. It made his name as a rising CEO and crystallized his approach to running large corporations.

KNOWLEDGE IS POWER Hurd began as a salesman with NCR, but quickly acquired experience throughout the company before being appointed head of its Teradata data storage division. He saw how the data warehousing unit could drive the whole company, and realized that the data itself was the key to management success. With detailed performance indicators at his fingertips, he could act fast to either cut costs or push sales. When he became NCR's CEO in 2003, he used this knowledge to accelerate growth. By the time he left for Hewlett-Packard (HP), share prices had risen from $9 to $39.

SIMPLY SIMPLIFY When Hurd took the helm at Hewlett-Packard in 2005 it was suffering from its controversial $19-billion takeover of Compaq, which had been opposed by a number of major HP shareholders, and had a waning reputation for innovation. He found a company drained of morale, where a blame culture thrived. He quickly mastered the figures and showed his executives how he expected them to work. He brought in new systems to track every piece of HP equipment and procurement, flagging up duplication and areas where suppliers were over-charging; over-spending even on stationery can waste billions at a company the size of HP. Hiring consultants to simplify company procedures, he announced thousands of redundancies and transferred responsibilities for earnings and costs to division heads. By the end of his first year, he had chalked up $92 billion in sales and ended 40 years of IBM domination. Analysts say he will now be judged on whether he can restore HP's reputation for innovation.

LESSONS IN BUSINESS: USING INFORMATION

Hurd's career has several recurring themes. One is his commitment to, and insistence upon, teamwork. He also has high expectations of his executives and demands accountability, but above all he has an unrelenting quest for information on his operation.
→ Make use of data systems to track expenses and monitor costs across the business.
→ Ask penetrating questions, and listen hard to the answers, to understand how the business is running.
→ Use that information to make decisions on how to simplify operations, cut costs, and raise sales.

"My principles: do it simple, and have accountability and responsibility." Mark Hurd

Frank Blake CEO, Home Depot

INDUSTRY INSIDERS and analysts were shocked in January 2007 when Home Depot, the second-largest retailer in the US after Wal-Mart, announced Blake as its new CEO. Doubters felt the former lawyer and Department of Energy official was ill-equipped to handle one of the biggest jobs in corporate America. When he took over, Home Depot was in the worst shape in its 30-year history, but the mild-mannered Blake was quietly confident of his plan to restore profits in the world's number one DIY chain.

BIOGRAPHY
Born in Boston, Massachusetts, in 1949. Blake received his bachelor's degree in 1971 from Harvard and juris doctor in 1976 from the Columbia School of Law.

LEADERSHIP STYLE
Genuine, principled, and a brilliant strategist. Blake is a good listener and a consensual leader.

KEY STRENGTH
Recognizing that raising staff morale is the key to bringing consumers back to Home Depot when the economy improves.

BEST DECISION
Calling Home Depot's founder on his first day put the company back in touch with its retail roots.

BACK TO BASICS An ambitious expansion plan by predecessor Bob Nardelli had left the company reeling. Nardelli had spent billions of dollars building up a wholesale supply business while neglecting stores, and a top-down management style had demoralized the staff. Blake's first step was to reconnect with the company's retail roots. He called Bernard Marcus who, with Arthur Blank, grew Home Depot from a single store in Atlanta in 1978. Marcus told Blake he had to reconnect with staff: "Get the associates to talk to you, to trust you," he said. "Get them to understand that if you see something wrong in the store, you're not going to have them fired." Blake understood the deep malaise that had set in on the shop floor and moved quickly to boost confidence. He also had to rebuild the company's image in the middle of the worst housing market in decades. Rather than embarking on a huge cost-cutting drive, as might be expected after three years of decline, Blake is looking forward and concentrating on a long-term strategy to boost service and morale, reviving the sense of pride that employees had in the store's heyday.

POSITIVE START Wall Street analysts have been supportive, despite the company's poor figures and dwindling reputation. "A lot of what he's doing is very textbook," says Citigroup analyst Deborah Weinswig. "Invest in a down market when you've got time. That makes sense to me." Blake's strategy is focused on regaining trust and building the brand: engaging employees; making products readily available and exciting to customers; and improving the store environment.

LESSONS IN BUSINESS: TREATING STAFF WELL

Treat your staff right and they'll treat your customers right. Blake's "inverted pyramid" principle has the CEO on the bottom of the hierarchy and customers and employees on the top.
- → Banish "executive" dining rooms or exclusive facilities. Eat with your people and find out how they feel.
- → Avoid a "blame" culture. Make sure your people are confident in giving you feedback and explaining their problems and mistakes.
- → Convince everyone their main role is to support and encourage the people with direct customer contact.

"...part of your experience of our company is determined by whether an associate feels valued."
Frank Blake

Ingvar Kamprad Founder & CEO (1943–86), IKEA

THE HEROICALLY THRIFTY Swedish founder of global furniture retailer IKEA, Kamprad is a man with a $30 billion fortune who drives an ancient Volvo, dresses like an impecunious retiree, and encourages his staff always to write on both sides of a piece of paper. But the firm he founded in 1943 to sell cheap pens, wallets, watches, and nylons now sells tens of billions of dollars worth of kitchens, flat-pack chairs, tables, and bookcases annually, from its 278 stores in 36 countries. Although no longer CEO, Kamprad is still running the show.

BIOGRAPHY
Born in Ljungby, Sweden, in 1926.

LEADERSHIP STYLE
By example. He has a Calvinist work ethic and set standards of organizational and personal behavior that IKEA executives still adhere to—no flashy job titles, no complicated hierarchy, and strictly economy class flights and hotels on business.

KEY STRENGTH
Turning his natural frugality into a designer concept that people buy into. IKEA's designs are cheap to make and buy, while possessing a classless utilitarian style.

BEST DECISION
Sourcing his manufacturing partners in Eastern Europe and Asia decades before it became popular to do so.

LOOK AFTER THE PENNIES As a schoolboy in the remote Swedish countryside, Kamprad had his first taste of the economies of scale when he discovered that, by buying matches in bulk he could sell them on to his neighbors at a modest profit. IKEA itself started trading by mail order in 1943, but his eureka moment came in 1955 with the invention of flat-pack furniture. By shipping products in pieces, Kamprad realized that he could save postage and pass the assembly process to the customer. It was a revolutionary idea, allowing furniture to be sold so cheaply that chairs and tables became items that could be updated regularly.

PERSONAL IMPRINT IKEA's distinctive brand of cheap chic has struck a chord with customers the world over, and the huge stores have spread across Europe and into North America, Asia and beyond. The outlets and stock have Kamprad's character stamped right through them, from the bargain basement breakfast served in many stores to the quirky product names like BILLY—a result of Kamprad's dyslexia, finding names easier to remember than product numbers.

Kamprad retired as CEO in 1986, but is still an influential company figure, largely because of IKEA's Byzantine ownership structure. The firm's holding company, Ingka Holding, is owned by a charitable foundation that appoints the company board and is run by a five-strong committee chaired by Kamprad.

Over the years, Kamprad has battled alcoholism (a result of compulsory drinking with suppliers in Poland, he says) and apologized publicly for "the worst mistake of my life"—attending Nazi meetings in his youth.

LESSONS IN BUSINESS: EXERCISING POWER

You don't have to be CEO to be in control. It's over 20 years since Kamprad officially relinquished the reins of IKEA, but he is still running the business, largely because of the ownership structure he put in place.
- → Get to know the official and unofficial "networks" that have power and influence in your organization.
- → Start a social club, a lunch club, or an investment club, for example, to improve your knowledge of and influence over other parts of the business.
- → Work out the power structure of your key customers by studying top executives' background and careers.

"Time is your most important asset." Ingvar Kamprad

James Dimon Chairman & CEO, J.P. Morgan Chase & Co.

OFTEN REFERRED to simply as "Jamie," Dimon is a rock star of the banking world and his story is part of banking folklore—the "whiz kid" from Queens who became a banking aristocrat. A man with finely tuned financial skills, an outspoken manner, and exceptional attention to detail, he has moved through a series of major positions, cutting costs and improving operational efficiency, to become CEO of the largest US bank. In 2006 Dimon appeared in *Time* magazine's list of the world's 100 most influential people.

BIOGRAPHY
Born in 1956 in New York, the son of a broker. Dimon has a degree from Tufts University, Boston, and an MBA from Harvard Business School.

LEADERSHIP STYLE
A hard-hitting, ruthless workaholic. Dimon is a darling of the media, who love his fast-talking, direct approach. He can be brutally honest in meetings but expects colleagues to stand up for themselves: "If not, he won't respect you," says one.

KEY STRENGTH
Building financial empires from scratch: "I love the idea of being in on the ground floor."

BEST DECISION
Merging Bank One with J.P. Morgan Chase, allowing him to build one of the most powerful financial institutions in the world.

MAKING HIS MARK On graduation in 1982, Dimon was persuaded by his future mentor, Sandy Weill, to join him at American Express, despite other more lucrative offers. When Weill left American Express, Dimon went with him and became his number two at Commercial Credit. His numeracy skills complemented Weill's people skills to transform the company into the largest financial services conglomerate the world had ever seen—Citigroup. Dimon's first major setback came in 1998 when, after a series of disagreements, he was fired by Weill. As he left the building for the last time, he was given a standing ovation by the company's 1,000 traders.

BEING THE BEST After an 18-month break, Dimon re-emerged as CEO of Bank One. At the time, the company was facing losses of $511 million, but through a series of drastic cost-cutting measures Dimon was able to turn it around. In his first year, he saved the company $1 billion. In 2004, Dimon brokered the ultimate deal: a merger with J.P. Morgan Chase, of which he became COO, resulting in the creation of the third-largest financial corporation in the US, behind Citigroup and Bank of America. Never known for his subtlety, he vocally attacked disproportionate senior salaries and implemented a two-year program to cut the compensation for some staff positions by up to 50 percent.

At the end of 2005 he became CEO, and a year later he was made chairman of the board. Since then Dimon has steered his company through turbulent times more successfully than many. "It's all about having the best systems, the best people, the best products, and the best risk controls," he says.

LESSONS IN BUSINESS: LOOKING AFTER THE CENTS

Dimon has a formidable reputation as a cost-cutter, right down to closing company gyms and removing staff perks. "We all know that corporations can waste a tremendous amount of money," he says. "It's destructive. It's wrong."
→ View the company as your own and run it as though you owned it and were spending your money.
→ Pay attention to even the smallest details of waste. Build cost awareness into the culture.
→ Stay as focused on the nuts and bolts of business as on strategy; don't leave operational issues to others.

> "[Dimon's] strength is that he's a leader, not a classic manager." Charlie Scharf, CEO of Retail Financial Services, J.P. Morgan Chase & Co

Ray Kroc Founder & CEO, McDonald's

NEITHER THE INVENTOR of the hamburger, nor the first person to open a McDonald's restaurant, Kroc nonetheless deserves to be remembered as the father of the modern fast food industry. By the time of his death in 1984, at the age of 81, he had amassed a $500 million fortune and sold 50 billion hamburgers—that's ten for every person living at the time. Today, McDonald's is the biggest fast food chain in the world, with more than 30,000 restaurants in over 100 countries, and annual turnovers of tens of billions of dollars.

BIOGRAPHY
1902–1984. Born in Chicago, Illinois, to Czech immigrant parents.

LEADERSHIP STYLE
Technocratic. Kroc was a hamburger geek who lived and loved his work, and probably knew more about burgers than anyone else alive. From the precise dimensions and fat content of the patties, to the exact composition of the bun, no detail was too small to escape his close attention.

KEY STRENGTH
Branding the service in the same way as the product. His insistence on the consistency of both made the McDonald's experience what it is today.

BEST DECISION
To standardize the product and the process. The uniformity of McDonald's food not only appealed to customers the world over, but brought with it huge economies of scale as the firm grew to span the globe.

PATIENCE REWARDED In contrast to the classic American story of youthful energy and vision rewarded, Kroc had to wait a long time for success. He spent 30 years as a salesman before his fateful 1954 visit to the McDonald brothers' restaurant in San Bernardino, California. The 52-year-old Kroc was selling blenders, but ended up cutting a deal with reluctant owners Maurice and Richard McDonald to sell franchises on their behalf for $950 apiece and 1.4 percent of sales. "I felt like some latter-day Newton, who'd just had an Idaho potato caromed off his head," he later said. What Kroc saw was that the McDonalds had created a template for a chain of burger bars that could be easily, inexpensively, and profitably rolled out across the US. He quickly got to work signing up franchisees as well as opening his own restaurants.

The tough-minded Kroc could be ruthless. He notoriously drove the McDonald brothers out of business shortly after buying them out for $2.7 million in 1961 because he felt they misled him over the terms of the deal. However, he was also capable of great generosity—Fred Turner, a dollar-an-hour burger flipper rose to be Kroc's right-hand man, regarded by him as the son he never had.

GLOBAL DOMINATION By the mid 1970s, Kroc's relentless quest to export his personal "hamburger-ology" saw McDonald's opening up across Asia and Europe, hitting 5,000 outlets in 1978. His famous staff training Hamburger Universities also spread across the globe. Before the decade was over, Kroc had one of his last great marketing ideas—the Happy Meal, targeted directly at children.

LESSONS IN BUSINESS: USING FINANCIAL REFERENCES

The best ad for a franchise business is an army of prosperous franchisees. At first Kroc made more money for others than for himself, until he bought up sites and leased them to his franchisees at a profit.
→ Make colleagues rich and you will become rich yourself; this is the principle of scalability.
→ Customer references work just as well as franchisees; make sure you record satisfied customers who have made money with your products.
→ Where possible make extra profits out of customers by doing more than just supplying products.

"...salesmanship is the gentle art of letting the customer have it your way." Ray Kroc

Dominic D'Alessandro President & CEO, Manulife Financial

MOVING FROM his position as CEO of the Laurentian Bank of Canada, D'Alessandro became CEO of Manulife in 1994. Through aggressive expansion at home and abroad, he led it to become one of the most profitable life insurance companies in North America. He raised Manulife's value from $2 billion to a high of $60 billion, making it the second largest company in Canada by market capitalization (only Royal Bank of Canada, D'Alessandro's employer in the early 1980s, is larger), and putting it firmly in the top 100 of the *Forbes* Global 2000.

BIOGRAPHY

Born in Italy in 1947. His family emigrated to Canada, and he graduated from Loyola College, Montreal, with a degree in physics and mathematics. He qualified as a chartered accountant in 1971. In 2005 D'Alessandro was awarded the International Horatio Alger Award for rising from humble beginnings to achieve success.

LEADERSHIP STYLE

Ambitious, tough-minded, and uncompromising. Sticks closely to the core company values, summed up as "PRIDE": Professionalism, Real Value to Customers, Integrity, Demonstrated Financial Strength, and Employer of Choice.

KEY STRENGTH

D'Alessandro is ruthlessly focused on the bottom line, and his main ambition has been to make Manulife bigger, faster.

BEST DECISION

Leading the demutualization and conversion of Manulife to public company status in September 1999, helping it become a world leader in financial services.

MAKING BIG MOVES D'Alessandro has spent most of his working life in the financial services sector. His wide-ranging experience and in-depth knowledge of the business made him the right man to put Manulife on the global financial services map. Always ambitious in the scale of his transactions, he steered the company through the demutualization and conversion process, and in 2004 he created North America's second largest life insurance company with the merger with John Hancock Financial Services.

DON'T GET MAD, GET EVEN D'Alessandro faced possibly the biggest challenge of his career in 2008 as he attempted to steer his company through market turbulence. Manulife, however, found itself in a better position than most due to a combination of modest leverage and a stable deposit base. At a time when many financial institutions were fighting for survival, there was even speculation that it might bid for some assets of AIG, the giant US insurer that was bailed out with an $85-billion Federal Reserve loan in September of that year.

D'Alessandro does not shy away from confrontation. In 2002, when a commercial court in Jakarta declared Manulife's Indonesian subsidiary bankrupt and shut the operation down, D'Alessandro went public, saying his company had been treated unjustly by corrupt judges. Within weeks, the Supreme Court of Indonesia had reviewed the judgement and responded by overturning the decision.

D'Alessandro is very active in community affairs, and in recognition of his achievements he was was voted Canada's Most Respected CEO in 2004 by his peers.

LESSONS IN BUSINESS: KEEPING BUSINESS AND EMOTION APART

You have to be tough to survive in insurance. "I've dismissed people that I wish I hadn't needed to, because I liked them personally," D'Alessandro says. "But professionally, you have to make that separation."
- → Try not to appoint people who are "your sort of person". You need people who are going to challenge your way of thinking.
- → Leaders help people to achieve their potential through their talent and by driving them to succeed.
- → Avoid letting fondness for anything—products, customers, staff—blind you to the need for change.

> "I wish I was not as competitive as I am, and maybe a little less combative."
>
> Dominic D'Alessandro

Jeffrey B. Kindler Chairman & CEO, Pfizer, Inc.

SINCE BECOMING CEO of Pfizer, the world's largest research-based pharmaceutical company, Kindler's strategic vision has involved downsizing and reorganizing the company's operations. His objectivity stems from his legal background and previous business experience. Kindler faced a difficult job when he took over the leadership, as shareholders were impatient at the dearth of new drugs and slow recovery of stock, but Kindler remained calm and continued with his restructuring program despite the criticism.

BIOGRAPHY
Born in Florida in 1955. The son of a doctor, Kindler gained his bachelor's from Tufts University, Massachusetts, and juris doctorate from Harvard. He started out as a lawyer, and is a former editor of *Harvard Law Review.*

LEADERSHIP STYLE
Charismatic, open, and tactical. Kindler aims to give investors a deeper understanding of Pfizer's strategy going forward.

KEY STRENGTH
Underpinning decision-making with detailed, considered research, as was evident in the important Lipitor patent case, when Kindler consulted widely prior to choosing a law firm.

BEST DECISION
Selecting Connolly Bove, a relatively small firm, to represent it in the 2006 Lipitor patent case, rather than a large, high profile legal company. Locally based, Connolly Bove knew the distinctive Delaware court system, and also the presiding judge, giving it a decisive advantage.

AN INDUSTRY OUTSIDER Kindler joined Pfizer Inc. in 2002 as general counsel, having previously been chairman and CEO of Boston Market Corp., and president of Partner Brands. His new ideas were welcome at a time when the company faced a number of financial, structural, and product problems, including the halting of trials of a drug intended to replace its bestselling cholesterol drug, Lipitor. In 2003, Kindler gained a ruling in the company's favor in the most significant patent case in its history, a challenge to Lipitor patents by generics manufacturer Ranbaxy Laboratories. In 2006, Kindler was nominated CEO.

Among the challenges faced by Kindler was the determination of the Bush administration to make cuts in health spending. Having announced a program to transform almost every aspect of the business, his emphasis at Pfizer has been firmly on workplace and manufacturing cost cuts. Kindler has overseen the development of the painkiller Lyrica, and the smoking-cessation product Chantix. The company has benefited from an increase in joint ventures, with its sheer size and massive distribution making it an attractive partner.

MEETING CHALLENGES WITH CHANGE Kindler must now deal with the challenge of Lipitor coming off patent in late 2011. The resultant massive loss of income (it provides over 25 percent of the company's revenue) has been highlighted by some observers who note that there is nothing of its stature planned to replace this revenue stream. However, Kindler's restructuring has given the company a healthy cash flow that could enable it to buy out competitors.

LESSONS IN BUSINESS: REASSURING INVESTORS

Investors are hard to please—and not always realistic. Pfizer's lack of a drug to replace Lipitor has rebounded on Kindler, who has a tough job convincing the markets of the success of his transformation.
→ Be open in your dealings with investors to foster trust, even though information itself can fuel criticism.
→ Communication is key: encourage a culture of increased transparency at all levels.
→ Make sure you communicate a detailed management strategy from the outset to encourage an understanding of operational issues.

"Incremental evolution is not enough. Fundamental change is imperative, and it must start happening now." Jeffrey B. Kindler

Gordon M. Nixon President & CEO, Royal Bank of Canada

CURRENTLY THE MOST powerful man in Canadian finance, Nixon has built his banking empire by bold acquisition. Under his direction, Royal Bank of Canada has become the country's largest financial services group, with 70,000 staff and over 15 million personal, business, and corporate customers in Canada, the US, and over 40 countries worldwide. Nixon has long advocated a policy of mergers to protect his country's banks from foreign takeover, all the more important in the light of the global financial crisis.

BIOGRAPHY
Born in Montreal, Quebec, in 1957. His grandfather was a director at Royal Bank of Canada. He took a degree in Commerce from Queen's University, Ontario.

LEADERSHIP STYLE
Tough, forward-thinking, a team player who believes his staff are his most important asset.

KEY STRENGTH
Being unafraid to tackle thorny issues head on, he is a formidable strategist and spokesperson for his company and industry.

BEST DECISION
Pursuing a strategy of global expansion that has put Royal Bank of Canada securely on the world financial services map.

BANKING ON SUCCESS Following in family footsteps, Nixon's banking career began in 1979 in the Global Markets division of Dominion Securities in Toronto. In 1986, he was sent to Japan to head up Dominion's interests there, returning to Toronto when Dominion was bought out by Royal Bank of Canada (RBC) in 1987. From 1995, he was the head of global investment banking at a time when the bank was beginning to meet the challenges of global banking, and in 1999 was appointed CEO of RBC Capital Markets. He became president and CEO of RBC in 2001.

BANKING FOR TOMORROW Aged 44, Nixon was Canada's youngest ever CEO of a financial institution when he accepted the position. He embarked on an ambitious growth plan to take Royal Bank of Canada, firstly into the US, and ultimately onto the world stage. In just two years, he pulled off ten major acquisitions. Initially, shareholders recoiled as the share price fell, but Nixon was only just starting. In 2004, he launched the Client First initiative, restructuring and refocusing the bank. He slashed 2,000 jobs, waged war on needless bureaucracy, and made sure his organization was customer-centered.

With major assets in the US, RBC was inevitably exposed to the sub-prime mortgage crisis, but found itself in relatively good shape to face the subsequent downturn. And his organization seems in no hurry to dispense with Canada's longest-serving banking services CEO. While earnings went down as a result of the crisis, RBC is one of the banks that, as one analyst puts it, yields the least concern in terms of "negative surprises."

LESSONS IN BUSINESS: GOING FOR GROWTH

Nixon has made growth, both operational and performance-related, the priority. He believes it is important to respect the legacy you inherit as a CEO but, at the same time, to make sure the company moves forward.

➔ Look for the strengths that have made your organization successful and adapt these to new situations.

➔ Part of the success of any organization is the image of it that customers hold. Beware changing that image too rapidly.

➔ People in your organization have all the experience needed to suggest improvements and the way ahead.

"You are as good as the people who work with and for you." Gordon M. Nixon

FROM VALUES TO VALUE

If creating value is the day-to-day work of a business, then values are its dreams. They shape choices about what a business will do and how it will do it, giving a principled twist to corporate self-interest.

Values may be intangible, but they can still make a difference. **Mukesh Ambani** (p101), CEO of Reliance Industries, which has interests ranging from petroleum to textiles, is one of the world's richest men, but sees the Hindu principles of *dharma*, *moksha*, and *karma* (righteousness, salvation, and duty) as central to leadership. "The world is becoming apprehensive of all businesses that did not have their foundations in moral and human values," he says.

Values can drive the bottom line too. One study revealed that firms with a culture based on values outperformed their rivals, growing revenues four times as fast and delivering 750 percent as much profit. **Henning Kagermann** (p220), of German software company SAP AG, sees values and strategy as inextricably linked. "You can talk a lot about values, but if you have strategy and you link objectives, you can measure it… with just values alone, you cannot," he reasons ●

Values into Action

The most effective values are rooted in what a company does. For example, the UK property company Land Securities, led by CEO **Francis Salway**, demonstrates how its values of customer service, respect, integrity, and innovation translate into everyday business practice through its quarterly Values into Action awards, for which any employee can nominate or be nominated.

Shoei Utsuda, CEO of Japanese general trading giant Mitsui, sees values as the driver of success. "I am constantly telling people within Mitsui that they must undertake work that feels worthwhile, is valued by society, and creates outcomes of value," he says. "I believe that if we all act in this manner, profits will follow."

The values of jeans brand Levi's sound too big to be true: empathy, integrity, originality, and courage. Yet the firm has lived up to them. In the aftermath of the San Francisco earthquake in 1906, then-owners the **Stern brothers**, nephews of founder **Levi Strauss**, helped customers by offering credit, even though the firm's own premises lay in ruins. In the 1960s, CEO **Walter Haas** ensured that Levi's plants rejected racial segregation. More recently, under CEO **John Anderson**, its Terms of Engagement protect employees'

"Values are the essential and enduring tenets of an organization— the very small set of guiding principles that have a profound impact on how everyone in the organization thinks and acts."
JIM COLLINS, BUSINESS CONSULTANT

working conditions worldwide. Perhaps more than any other business leader, **Anita Roddick** embodied the idea that values can drive business. She made social responsibility and sustainability the *raison d'être* of cosmetics retailer Body Shop, and the core of its customer appeal.

How Merck Acted on Its Values

In 1988, US pharma giant Merck & Co., Inc., under CEO **P. Roy Vagelos**, developed Mectizan, a treatment for Onchocerciasis or "river blindness", a waterborne disease that blights the lives of millions in the developing world. Realizing that its target market couldn't afford Mectizan, Merck tried and failed to sell it to government agencies, but instead of shelving the drug opted to distribute it for free. The decision saved the sight of thousands and boosted the company's public image. Improving access to medicine remains a core value for Merck today.

Leaders of Integrity

Many CEOs are driven by their values as much as they are by the bottom line:

Donald J. Tomnitz, D.R. Horton (Construction: US)—*Eschewing corporate perks, Tomnitz pays for his own company cell phone and has no company car or jet.*

William Hewlett *and* **David Packard**, Hewlett-Packard (IT: US)—*The co-founders set out "The HP Way" in 1957, enshrining values of customer care, trust, teamwork, and innovation.*

Kazuo Furukawa, Hitachi (Electronics: Japan)—*Furukawa, sees the Hitachi Values as a key enabler of company unity, the most important being "trust" and taking the "initiative to challenge and reform".*

Robert Wood Johnson II, Johnson & Johnson (Health sector: US)—*Founding family member Robert Wood Johnson II crafted the firm's Credo in 1943, setting out its responsibilities to healthcare professionals, employees, communities, and shareholders.*

Keiji Kimura, Mitsubishi Estate Co. Ltd (Real estate: Japan)—*A 20-year urban redevelopment project to transform Tokyo's Marunouchi district goes beyond property developing into shaping the urban culture.*

Claiborne P. Deming, Murphy Oil (Oil and gas: US)—*Deming preserved Murphy's commitment to its hometown, El Dorado, instead of following other oil majors to Houston.*

Charles W. Moorman IV, Norfolk Southern (Railroads: US)—*Moorman emphasizes consensus and a hands-off leadership style. "The one thing you don't want to do is take the ball out of people's hands," he says.*

Thomas J. Quinlan III, R.R. Donnelley & Sons (Printing: US)—*Quinlan upholds Donnelley's reputation for integrity, but shuns the spotlight. "We live on behalf of our customers," he explains.*

Bruce Nicholson, Thrivent Financial for Lutherans (Finance: US)—*Drawing on his Christian values, Nicholson stands by stewardship, integrity, leadership, and philanthropy.*

Steve Burd Chairman, President & CEO, Safeway, Inc.

WHEN HE TOOK CONTROL of Safeway in 1992, Burd had already earned a reputation for fixing broken companies, and this one needed fixing. Sales were down, operating costs were at a premium, and employee morale was at an all-time low. Burd relished the challenge, calling it "a lot of fun," and within two years Safeway's stock had more than tripled. Now, after many years in the hot seat, Burd is spearheading Safeway's expansion into new growth sectors as the company adapts to shifting consumer preferences in the food retail market.

BIOGRAPHY
Born in Minot, North Dakota, in 1949. Burd has a bachelor's degree from Carroll College Waukesha, Wisconsin, and a master's degree in economics from the University of Wisconsin.

LEADERSHIP STYLE
Decisive and tough but open to discussion. When he first took up the CEO's post, Burd had his office door removed so that employees could approach him without knocking first.

KEY STRENGTH
Finding endless ways to reduce costs and overheads.

BEST DECISION
Joining Safeway at the right time—the company's poor performance gave him the ideal opportunity to showcase his renowned turnaround skills.

FROM CONSULTANT TO CEO Burd first came to know Safeway through his role as management consultant to New York financiers Kohlberg Kravis Roberts & Co., who negotiated Safeway's leveraged buyout in 1986 in response to a hostile takeover bid. Between 1986 and 1988, Burd played a key role in developing a managerial strategy for Safeway. From 1988 to 1991 he worked, again for KKR, with other retail clients, including Fred Meyer and Stop & Shop. In 1992, Burd became president of Safeway, and a year later succeeded Peter Mogowan as company CEO.

IN SAFE HANDS His first move was to examine systematically all aspects of Safeway's infrastructure. Recognizing that the company was losing revenue to low-cost stores, his priority was to make the store competitive on pricing. He implemented a series of cost-cutting exercises, including downsizing offices, centralizing buying, and eliminating unnecessary and costly practices. He also renegotiated employee contracts, particularly in Safeway's Canadian operations, after lower-cost competitors had, as Burd said, "redefined the market wage." Faced with action from members of the United Food and Commercial Workers Union, Burd opened the corporate books to union accountants to prove that operations were unprofitable and facing liquidation. Within a couple of years, revenue and stock prices had improved dramatically, and in 2004 *Fortune* magazine ranked Safeway as one of the "most admired" companies in its sector. Burd's strategy for Safeway now includes expansion into prescriptions, gas stations, and online home delivery services.

LESSONS IN BUSINESS: DEALING WITH UNIONS

Change can lead to conflicts between management and unions; handle these frankly and openly. Burd said, "As in any important journey, the first step requires courage. Business leaders who take it must be prepared to be demonized as heartless profiteers."
➔ Meet regularly with your employees and union leaders, and listen to them.
➔ Be open with union leaders—if cuts are needed, explain why; they don't want the firm to fail either.
➔ If you are unable to reach a compromise, be prepared to take decisive action, however painful.

"I'm good at cutting costs." Steve Burd

Andrew Gould Chairman & CEO, Schlumberger Ltd

WITH OPERATIONS across a range of industries, Schlumberger, which had begun life as an oilfield services firm, was fast turning into an amorphous, multifaceted technology services group when Gould took control. Recognizing the potential risks of this strategy, he took immediate steps to focus the business strongly on the oilfield services operations that had provided the basis of its success. This change of direction quickly began to produce impressive results, generating healthy returns, and earning Gould industry accolades in the process.

BIOGRAPHY
Born in the UK in 1946. Gould received a degree in economic history from the University of Wales, Cardiff.

LEADERSHIP STYLE
Gould takes a traditional, conservative approach to management, which has restored cohesion to Schlumberger's corporate culture.

KEY STRENGTH
An unerring sense of direction. Gould quickly expounded a clear vision of where the company should be heading, set out the goals, and took the steps to achieve them.

BEST DECISION
Selling off non-core businesses, sharpening the company's focus and reducing debt.

NUMBER CRUNCHER Fresh from accounting firm Ernst & Young, Gould brought his number-crunching skills to Schlumberger in 1975 when he joined the company's internal audit department. After a series of roles in different divisions he became executive vice-president of Schlumberger Oilfield Services, then corporate president and COO. He then led the company's core oilfield services operation for four years, finally becoming CEO of the group in 2003.

BACK TO THE CORE When Gould took over as CEO, Schlumberger was developing into a global technology services company with operations in a wide range of industries. He quickly asserted that such a wide spread of activities was not in the best interests of the business, and began to move the group back to focus on energy industry services. Gould sold some of the non-core technology parts of the business, raising more than $2 billion. He also outlined a range of ambitious goals: increasing return on capital to double digits; substantially reducing net debt; increasing after-tax margins of core operations; and raising earnings per share faster than revenue. Within two years most of these goals had been achieved. Return on capital had nearly doubled, net debt had been more than halved, and oilfield revenue increased by 9 percent and earnings per share by 28 percent. Gould also overhauled the company's pricing strategy and drove a cultural change that tied management incentives to margin expansion. The results were widely applauded by analysts and industry observers, and soundly endorsed Gould's approach of focusing the company on its strengths.

LESSONS IN BUSINESS: KNOWING YOUR STRENGTHS

Gould knew that a company builds up its ability to exploit sets of products and markets over the life of the business, so concentrated on doing what his people did best, rather than trying to crack new industries.
→ Remember that diversifying carries much more risk than focusing on your core businesses.
→ Concentrate on getting the most out of the current skills and knowledge of your people, rather than asking them to go into new areas.
→ Avoid owning a business that you or your team do not really understand; it will put you in a weak position.

"We need to rapidly adapt to more volatile times."
Andrew Gould

Osamu Suzuki President, COO & CEO, Suzuki Motor Corp.

HE MAY HAVE ENTERED Suzuki Motors after marrying into the family, but Suzuki can take full credit for building the company into the global powerhouse that it is now. Under his leadership, Suzuki has expanded into new markets to become the tenth largest car maker in the world, and has reached a strong position from which to ride out downturn in the automobile business. Despite being in his late 70s, Suzuki shows no signs of easing up; he returned to the position of president in late 2008, a post that he vacated in 2000.

BIOGRAPHY
Born in Gero, Japan, in 1930, Suzuki (né Matsuda) entered an arranged marriage with the granddaughter of the founder of Suzuki. As there were no male Suzuki heirs, he took his wife's family name, following Japanese custom. He was educated at Chuo University in Japan, graduating in 1953.

LEADERSHIP STYLE
Fiscally conservative, hands-on, involved. Regarded by his employees as a father figure more than a CEO.

KEY STRENGTH
The vision to apprehend new opportunities in emerging markets and a talent for striking up partnerships as a way of entering these markets.

BEST DECISION
Entering the developing Indian market, where Suzuki remains the number one car maker.

EXPANDING THE FAMILY BUSINESS

Suzuki joined the family company in 1958, becoming its fourth president and CEO in 1978. He traveled extensively to build up the company, forging partnerships with developing nations and setting up satellite plants in countries such as Thailand, Indonesia, and the Philippines, and later in Australia and Pakistan. In 1981, Suzuki formed an alliance with General Motors, which helped the company gain access to the lucrative European and North American markets. One of Suzuki's most successful and lasting alliances came in 1982, when he reached an agreement with Indian car manufacturer Maruti Udyog to produce low-cost cars. Now known as Maruti Suzuki India Ltd, the company was the first to mass produce and sell more than a million cars on the subcontinent. With over 50 percent of the market, the company is still the leading car manufacturer in India. Building on his success there, Suzuki expanded the company into Korea, Egypt, Hungary, and Vietnam during the 1990s.

SMALL CARS FOR BIG MARKETS
Suzuki avoided direct competition with rival Japanese car manufacturers by targeting an altogether different market. By focusing on relatively poor and densely populated areas of the world, Suzuki tapped into a whole new group of buyers, achieving a dominant market share in India, Pakistan, and China. His small, unostentatious vehicles sold well in developing countries because they were affordable and energy efficient. Suzuki was instrumental in pushing these qualities, and they have stood the company in good stead against less lean manufacturers in tough economic times.

LESSONS IN BUSINESS: MAINTAINING A TIGHT BUDGET

The Suzuki empire may have been built by selling low-end cars at nominal cost, but the company still makes a healthy profit, thanks to Suzuki's fiscal conservatism.
➔ Ask yourself if you really need receptionists and the other support people that make life a bit easier. Get rid of unnecessary luxuries.
➔ Don't rely on your accountant to flag up problems and areas for savings. Check on spending for yourself.
➔ Insist that employees use the cheapest method of transport, and justify any travel and subsistence expenses.

"I want to die in battle." Osamu Suzuki

Terry Leahy CEO, Tesco

BORN RETAILERS are hardly ever outstanding managers, but Leahy is one of those greatest of rarities who combines both skills to winning effect. His sureness of touch with employees, coupled with an unfailing nose for what customers want, have helped him turn Tesco from a "pile 'em high, sell 'em cheap" grocery store founded in London's East End into one of the world's top retailers. In the course of his years at the top, Leahy has brought Tesco from the 18th to the 4th biggest retailer in the world, behind only Wal-Mart, Carrefour, and Home Depot.

BIOGRAPHY
Born in Liverpool, UK, in 1956. Leahy graduated from UMIST, Manchester, in 1977 with a BSc in management sciences.

LEADERSHIP STYLE
Meritocratic. In Leahy's Tesco, talent, hard work, and results matter more than class, background, or polish.

KEY STRENGTH
Identifying with the customer. Leahy's famous "ordinariness" lends him a natural empathy with shoppers that is probably unique among supermarket CEOs.

BEST DECISION
Extending the Tesco "brand promise" of low prices and high quality to a whole range of offerings from electronics to insurance, and not just food.

LOCAL STORES, GLOBAL FOOTPRINT

Leahy can truly claim to know Tesco from the ground up, having worked there as a shelf-stacker during school breaks. He joined Tesco as a marketing executive in 1979 at the age of 23, was marketing director by the age of 30, and became CEO ten years after that.

Tesco's dominance of the UK retail market in particular, one of the most competitive in the world, is impressive and controversial. Leahy has forged it into such an intrinsic part of its customers' lives that sales now account for one pound in every seven spent in all British shops. Long before he runs out of room to grow in one market he is moving into new ones; witness Tesco's success in non-food retailing and in new formats—both smaller, city-center Metro and Express stores and huge out-of-town Extra hypermarkets. And yet he's kept the business growing at a heady pace abroad too—the firm now has some 1,800 stores, operates successfully across Asia and Eastern Europe, and has more floor space overseas than it does at home.

EXTRAORDINARY SUCCESS Self-styled as a regular guy from a humble background, Leahy eschews the trappings of his success, claiming to be happier talking shop with staff and customers than doing the cocktail circuit. He and his close-knit group of senior colleagues are obsessed with growing Tesco, and are one of the most competitive management teams in business. Leahy's hard-nosed approach has drawn criticism for driving suppliers into the ground on price, but has meant Tesco has reached operational efficiency in it's battle with large competitors and smaller local businesses.

LESSONS IN BUSINESS: TEACHING PEOPLE

Leahy knows how to turn microeconomic changes to macroeconomic advantage, and believes that getting bigger is always better for Tesco. This growth allows people to develop skills and make career progress.
→ Detail is key; make sure staff learn the miniscule details that make a good business exceptional.
→ Motivate staff by putting in place extensive staff development schemes. Make people thirsty to learn.
→ Keep learning; encourage people to go on training courses or temporary assignments, and seek out similar opportunities for yourself.

"The only personality I believe in is Tesco." Terry Leahy

Katsuaki Watanabe President & CEO (2005–09), Toyota Motor Corp.

THE EPITOME of the quiet company man, Watanabe joined Toyota in 1964 after graduation. He's been there ever since, progressing through roles in strategy, procurement, and general management before being named president and CEO in 2005. He knows the organization intimately, and his tenure has been marked by continued, brisk growth. With annual sales of over nine million units, Toyota now threatens to overtake General Motors as the world's largest car manufacturer, an achievement the austere, bespectacled Watanabe claims to care little about.

BIOGRAPHY
Born in 1942 in Mie Prefecture, Japan, Watanabe is the son of wealthy local landowners in Toyota City. He graduated in economics from Tokyo's Keio University.

LEADERSHIP STYLE
Rigorous, analytical, and pragmatic. One eye on the detail, the other on the horizon.

KEY STRENGTH
Finding endless incremental improvements in an already efficient process.

BEST DECISION
Building a strategy on quality as much as on expansion and cost reduction. He knows that cheap growth at the expense of quality could kill Toyota.

IMPROVING ON PERFECTION When he assumed control, Watanabe took the wheel of a very smoothly running machine. Toyota's focus on lean, just-in-time manufacturing techniques had made it one of the most productive car makers in the world. It was going to be very hard to improve, and very easy to screw up. Yet improve it he has, with a three-way focus on growth, quality, and costs. Watanabe's outstanding achievement though is cost control. The ease with which he found $8 billion of fat to trim from the industry's leanest supply chain left analysts scratching their heads and rivals worried.

GOING GLOBAL Watanabe took an important step when he considered other territories for manufacturing and services, as well as sales. Recognizing that, as the world's greatest car market, it made sense to make cars in the US as well as sell them there, Toyota set a threshold for manufacturing abroad and opened a new factory in the States when sales there topped one million a year. Watanabe knows that local acceptance precedes commercial success, and has striven to make Toyota a good neighbour. Investment in local communities has enabled the company to become part of the American fabric, outpacing home-grown competitors Ford and Dodge. Success has come thanks to old favourites like the Corolla and new models like the Prius hybrid. Fifteen per cent of US car buyers now choose a Toyota.

Along with other car makers, the economic downturn caused sales of Toyota cars to suffer, and, following the firm's first ever loss-making year, Watanabe ceded the CEO role to Akio Toyoda, grandson of the company founder, becoming vice-president.

LESSONS IN BUSINESS: USING *KAIZEN*

Watanabe's success is an example of Toyota's employment of *kaizen* (the Japanese concept of "continuous improvement"), achieving large productivity gains through small, continuous improvements in all areas of business, then the standardization of those improvements across the company.
→ Consider process and results (not results only), so that actions that achieve results come to the surface.
→ Think about the whole process, so that changes to part of the system avoid problems elsewhere.
→ Adopt a learning, non-blaming approach to change, so that problems can surface without fear of reprisal.

"Being satisfied with the status quo means you are not making progress." Katsuaki Watanabe

Koichiro Matsuura Director-general, UNESCO

AT THE TIME Matsuura was appointed to lead the United Nations Educational, Scientific and Cultural Organization (UNESCO) in 1999, the agency for international cultural cooperation had become renowned for its ineffectiveness, bloated bureaucracy, and poor management practices. Within three years of taking over, a mix of cool-headed rationality and drive had enabled Matsuura to carry through a reform that many had thought impossible, restoring the impact of an organization that is now more necessary than ever.

BIOGRAPHY
Born in Tokyo, Japan, in 1937. His father, who came from a small town about 60 miles (100 km) from Hiroshima, worked in the insurance industry. Matsuura studied law at the University of Tokyo and economics at Haverford College in Pennsylvania. He was Japan's ambassador to France from 1994 to 1999.

LEADERSHIP STYLE
Clear and direct. Matsuura's insistence on accountability and measurable results, plus his dialog with staff, provided refreshing motivation after years of weighty bureaucracy.

KEY STRENGTH
Having a rational and circumspect approach to reform that tackled all the organization's faults with an integrated program of change.

BEST DECISION
Dismissing unscreened political appointments as soon as he arrived, giving his reform program immediate momentum and sending an unmistakeable message.

DIPLOMATIC SKILLS Matsuura took the helm at UNESCO after 40 years as a career diplomat, during which time he had represented Japan's interests in countries that include Ghana, France, the US, and Hong Kong. Matsuura's breadth of global experience in dealing with diplomacy and foreign policy gave him the skills and understanding to tackle even the chronic problems of an organization of UNESCO's size, power, and complexity.

INSTANT IMPACT As soon as he arrived, Matsuura sent a clear signal about how he intended to approach the countless layers of lumbering management, the shadowy committees, and the runaway financial waste that had made UNESCO the least effective of all the UN organizations. He immediately dismissed 20 politically appointed advisers from his own office, who had been hired without professional screening, and he suspended more than 100 promotions and appointments that his predecessor had put in place just before leaving. His moves provoked staff protests and even hunger strikes, but this was just the first stage of his sweeping plan to return UNESCO to health. He pressed ahead, cutting more high-level posts, halving the number of divisions and the number of directors, strengthening resources in the field, and reshaping the organization's activities to focus on key program priorities. Matsuura's reforms rapidly improved UNESCO's impact.

In 2003, the US passed its judgement on Matsuura's reforms by officially re-engaging with UNESCO after an absence of nearly 20 years, and in 2005 he was re-appointed for a further four-year term.

LESSONS IN BUSINESS: COMMITTING TO CHANGE

Change works most smoothly when everyone agrees with what you're doing, but popularity doesn't necessarily make a good leader. Administer the medicine, however bad it tastes.
➔ Stick to the course of action that is right for the team or organization, and everyone will benefit.
➔ Sell the need for change by publicizing the benefits to the individual and teams, as well as the company.
➔ Look out for entrenched positions. Even when change is unnecessary, remind people that nothing remains the same for ever.

"[UNESCO] is shouldering increased responsibilities as the world community seeks to come to terms with the effects of globalization." Koichiro Matsuura

Sam Walton Founder, Wal-Mart

IN THE EARLY 1960s, Walton was the owner of a moderate-sized chain of variety stores dotted around a small cluster of US states. Just 20 years later, his Wal-Mart stores could be found in every corner of the country and he had become the richest man in America, almost without anyone noticing. Behind this remarkable expansion was a formula based on a rigorous commitment to cutting costs, even when it seemed there were no further costs to cut. Walton's approach has since formed the model for retail chains all over the world.

BIOGRAPHY
1918–1992. Born near Kingfisher, Oklahoma. He majored in economics at the University of Missouri.

LEADERSHIP STYLE
Charismatic and inspiring, Walton believed making your staff feel you were on a journey together was one of the keys to business success.

KEY STRENGTH
Cutting costs across the board, time and again, which has allowed Wal-Mart to remain competitive with rival discount retailers and extend its reach around the globe.

BEST DECISION
Joining the out-of-town discount store pioneers as soon as he saw them coming, even though he had existing interests in small town-center stores.

SMALL-TOWN STOREKEEPER Walton began his career as a retailer with a store in Newport, Arkansas, just after World War II, and he soon had a chain of 16 small-town stores in Arkansas, Oklahoma, and Missouri. When he noticed a rival setting up discount stores just outside the towns where his own stores were located, he studied the new developments and decided that this was the future of retail. In 1962, Walton opened his own discount store in Rogers, Arkansas, and then just kept on going.

THE COST-CRUSHER Walton's goal as a discounter was simple: to drive prices down as far as possible, and then down some more. He did everything he could to slice costs out of the merchandizing system at every possible point, which included manufacturers, middlemen, and the stores themselves. Just when it looked as though no further costs could be driven out of the system, he would come at it again and find some more. The only way to do this and survive was to grow, and grow fast. He traveled the country looking for locations, buying up land, throwing up a store, then setting off to look for the next one. Walton also invested in technology, introducing computerized merchandise controls in the 1960s, long before his competitors. Wal-Mart became renowned for its take-up of just-in-time inventory control and new logistics systems. Walton's charisma, and the company's innovative stock incentive programs for employees, kept the Wal-Mart machine moving forward. Today, Walton's little chain of stores has become the world's largest public corporation by revenue.

LESSONS IN BUSINESS: MAKING CUT AFTER CUT

Walton's success was due almost entirely to his unswerving dedication to finding and reducing costs in places where others would never think to look. That is how to pass on the most competitive price to customers.
→ Even if you think your business is lean, take the Walton view and find costs to cut somewhere.
→ Cut out any middleman who does not add value to a product but charges fees for business transactions.
→ Add parsimony into your company's culture and reward people who find a cheaper way of doing things or who cut the time from make to sell.

"Capital isn't scarce; vision is." Sam Walton

Nils Smedegaard Andersen CEO, A.P. Møller-Mærsk Group

BIOGRAPHY
Born in 1958 in Denmark, Andersen graduated with a master's degree in economics from Aarhus University in 1982.

BEST DECISION
Introducing an ambitious restructuring plan at Møller-Mærsk that gave more decision-making power to the company's "teams" in local regions.

LESSON IN BUSINESS
Maximize potential—figure out how all aspects of your company's operations work, no matter how minor, and how they can be made more efficient to boost profits.

HAVING INCREASED the share price by 240 percent when CEO of Carlsberg, Andersen left to take the helm at A.P. Møller-Mærsk Group, Denmark's largest company, and one the world's leading shipping companies and oil producers.

When it was announced that Andersen would be leaving Carlsberg to captain Møller-Mærsk, shares in both companies dropped. Carlsberg shareholders were nervous because Andersen had done more to make the company profitable than anyone could have imagined; Møller-Mærsk investors questioned his ability to transfer from retail to transportation, oil, and gas. None of this perturbed the indomitable Andersen. Two months after he took the helm in 2007, he announced radical changes to improve profitability: cutting the global workforce by 8 to 12 percent, decentralizing management into smaller regional teams, and splitting container operations into three divisions. Anyone familiar with Andersen's method of doing business could have seen this coming. As CEO of Carlsberg, Andersen shut down the 159-year-old brewery in the company's hometown of Valby to improve the company's bottom line. His changes at Møller-Mærsk meant that shareholders soon saw company revenues soar.

Alain J. P. Belda Chairman & CEO, Alcoa

BIOGRAPHY
Born in Meknes, Morocco, in 1943. Belda graduated in business administration from Universidad MacKenzie, São Paulo. He took Brazilian citizenship in 1982.

BEST DECISION
Focusing on cost-cutting measures. Belda saved the company over $2 billion, enabling it to remain competitive.

LESSON IN BUSINESS
Practice what you preach—by twice taking a reduction in his own compensation package, Belda demonstrated his commitment to cost control.

TALENTED, MULTILINGUAL and financially focused, Belda spent 30 years climbing the ladder at aluminum giant Alcoa, before taking over as CEO. He has since streamlined production and expanded the company to keep it on top.

Starting his career as an accountant with German chemical company BASF, Belda left to work in the financial planning department at Alcoa Alumínio in 1969. Moving up the company, he became the first non-US citizen to hold the post of president. Declaring American business to be a "meritocracy," Belda believes that the US is the only place where he could have risen to such a high level in a corporation. He launched a series of changes, the most significant of which was the introduction of the Alcoa Business System (ABS), based on the Toyota Production System (TPS). Belda focused the company on producing only what customers wanted. Nominated CEO in 1999, he kept the company financially viable in the face of global competition by investing heavily in acquisitions and manufacturing. One of his first tasks was to oversee a hostile takeover of Reynolds Metals Company, thereby ensuring Alcoa's position as the world's leading producer of aluminum products.

"What we have to do is focus on holistic solutions."
Nils Smedegaard Andersen

Matthew K. Rose Chairman, President & CEO, BNSF Corp.

BIOGRAPHY
Born in Salina, Kansas, in 1960. Rose studied marketing and statistics at the University of Missouri. While at college he spent his summers working as a brakeman and switchman on the Missouri Pacific Railroad.

BEST DECISION
Using the internet to maximize revenue by matching supply and demand for rail services.

LESSON IN BUSINESS
Focus on customer service—Rose's emphasis on the customer was a refreshing change in an industry with a reputation for unreliability.

FROM RAIL WORKER to CEO, Rose is one of the youngest executives in the railway industry. His appointment to the top job at Burlington Northern Santa Fe Corporation in 2000 was seen as a symbol of change.

After spells with Missouri Pacific Railroad, the trucking conglomerate International Utilities, and truckload carrier Schneider National, Rose joined door-to-door trucking business Triple Crown Services, where he became vice- president of transportation. He moved to Burlington Northern Railroad in 1994 and, following the merger with Santa Fe Railway in 1995, moved quickly through the ranks, being appointed president and COO in 1999, and CEO in 2000. Rose increased revenues to meet capital needs, while investing in new facilities and more efficient locomotives and freight cars to win back market share from truckers. By 2005, Rose reported record shipments and profits of $1.5 billion. Faced with rising energy prices, he imposed a surcharge on customers to keep costs under control. However, at the end of 2008, Rose announced that in order to offset a decline in shipping demand, the company would be forced to reduce costs by cutting the workforce by around 5 percent.

Gregg Engles Chairman & CEO, Dean Foods Company

BIOGRAPHY
Born in 1957 in Oklahoma, Engles grew up in Denver, Colorado. He graduated from Dartmouth College in 1979, before obtaining a law degree at Yale University in 1982.

BEST DECISION
Giving up a career in law to pursue his entrepreneurial ambitions.

LESSON IN BUSINESS
With hard work you can accomplish anything—Engles's grandmother instilled in him a work ethic and self-belief that he has carried through into his business life.

LITTLE KNOWN beyond the dairy business, Engles is credited with revitalizing the industry virtually single-handedly in the 1990s. He has been CEO of Dean Foods, the largest processor and distributor of milk products in the US, since 2001.

Engles cut his teeth on two unsuccessful ventures: a time-share business for corporate aircraft, and a property-investment venture launched just as prices began to crash. However, in 1988 he and a partner borrowed nearly $26 million to buy Reddy Ice Group. By 1990 they had acquired a further 15 ice factories. Advised to move into the dairy industry, in 1993 Engles acquired Suiza Dairy in San Juan, Puerto Rico. His legal training stood him in good stead as he personally negotiated the takeover of further dairy producers, then consolidated operations, merging his dairy acquisitions with Reddy Ice to become Suiza Foods Corporation in 1995. In 1996, he took the company public, after selling off Reddy Ice to concentrate on the dairy side of the operation. When Suiza Foods took over Dean Foods Company in 2001, Engles retained the Dean brand name for the new company, which had a 30 percent share of the US milk market. Engles then concentrated on raising profit margins and increasing branded products.

"I never wanted to be a lawyer, but I thought it was good general training for the business world."
Gregg Engles

John Donahoe President & CEO, eBay

BIOGRAPHY
Born in 1960. Donahoe received a BA in economics from Dartmouth College and an MBA from the Stanford Graduate School of Business.

BEST DECISION
Beginning a campaign of acquisitions to transform eBay from a single marketplace into a portfolio of retail sites.

LESSON IN BUSINESS
Nothing lasts forever—eBay's business model had been spectacularly successful but was showing diminishing returns in a mature market, meaning it was time to change shape.

A MATURING INTERNET marketplace and chillier economic conditions greeted Donahoe when he took over at eBay in early 2008. Immediate action was required to prepare the online auction group for a very different world.

Donahoe was lured from Bain & Company in 2005 to head eBay's marketplaces division, which is responsible for 70 percent of the company's revenues and even more of its profits. He began with an overhaul of the way things were done to suit a rapidly changing environment. The explosion of buying opportunities elsewhere on the web was the key problem facing the company, and Donahoe began acquiring suitable businesses and setting up new sites, with the aim of developing a set of platforms more tailored to different customers' needs. He also helped create a worldwide network of classified advertising sites and brokered revenue-sharing deals with Yahoo and Google to bring advertisements to eBay on a large scale for the first time. On becoming CEO, he cut 10 percent of the workforce and announced further acquisitions, continuing his shift of the business away from the shrinking growth of the core market toward more promising areas.

William P. Lauder President & CEO, Estée Lauder Companies

BIOGRAPHY
Born in 1960, Lauder was the grandson of Estée Lauder, founder of the eponymous cosmetics firm. He graduated from the Wharton School of the University of Pennsylvania, and joined the family firm in 1986.

BEST DECISION
Launching the "Dramatically Different Moisturizing Lotion," which became the best-selling skincare product in the US.

LESSON IN BUSINESS
Get organized—Lauder is a master scheduler, who manages by calendar, ensuring he has time for all key staff.

BORN WITH a silver spoon, Lauder has nonetheless proved himself a very modern executive. He has created new brands and retail concepts at the cosmetics giant, driving sales to new heights of around $8 billion.

Born into a successful family business, Lauder had a lot to live up to. As the grandson of a cosmetics and retail legend, he had to prove that his drive and talent justified the head start he'd enjoyed. He gave his first hint of what was to follow in the mid-1990s, when he developed a lifestyle brand, "Origins," and pioneered the idea of selling its products from small "stores within stores." The brand chalked up the highest growth rate of any upmarket cosmetics product in the US. In 1998, Lauder took over as president of Clinique Laboratories, where he repeated the trick. He launched Clinique's "Dramatically Different Moisturizing Lotion," and "Stop Signs Visible Anti-Aging Serum," which took the high street by storm. He also raised Clinique's profile and strengthened customer loyalty through its website. As COO and then CEO from 2004, he presided over the rapid growth of Clinique retail stores, which helped raise Estée Lauder earnings per share by over one-third.

"When I see people waste time, I call them on it immediately. Time is their greatest resource, and when it's gone, it's lost forever." William P. Lauder

THE ADVANTAGES OF POWER SHARING

In today's fast changing and demanding corporate environment, the CEO has to contend with a bewildering array of issues. Whether it is dealing with the relentless demand for greater efficiency or getting to grips with the latest ethical challenge, today's CEO is expected to have a broad range of expertise. It's perhaps not surprising that some organizations have decided to look beyond the lone CEO, and have split the role. Research in Motion, the company behind the BlackBerry mobile phone, drafted Silicon Valley veteran **Jim Balsillie** (p38) in 1992. His focus on commercial and marketing issues has allowed his co-CEO **Mike Lazaridis** (p62) to concentrate on technological innovation. For IT company SAP, the appointment of **Leo Apotheker** as co-CEO alongside **Henning Kagermann** (p200) was part of a planned succession that provided the company with a period of stability until he took sole control in May 2009 ●

Power Sharing in Action

Having scrambled to the top of the corporate ladder, one might assume that the ambitious CEO wouldn't want to cede any of his newly acquired power. In fact, many CEOs are happy to do so, acknowledging that power sharing can be a sensible approach to dealing with a testing business environment.

In some cases, the job simply proves too big for one person. When India's third largest software services firm, Wipro, lost its CEO **Vivek Paul** in 2005, chairman **Azim Premji** (p462) sought to take over his duties. However, it became apparent that the two roles were too much for one man, and that a more imaginative solution was required. Since 2008, the business has been run by co-CEOs **Girish Paranjpe** and **Suresh Vaswani**. Wipro's structure is complex, running across multiple territories and sectors, and therefore by appointing two experienced leaders,

Wipro believes it has improved its chances of hitting growth targets, without imperilling day-to-day operations.

New skill sets are required as a business evolves. The individual whose vision creates a company may not be best placed to realize its potential. Google co-founders **Sergey Brin** and **Larry Page** recognized that they needed some "gray hair" in their team when they recruited **Eric Schmidt** (p443) as CEO. The three run Google as a triumvarate, with Schmidt's experience reassuring institutions that the Google's fundamentals are moving in the right direction, allowing Brin and Page to operate as presidents of technology and products respectively.

A co-CEO arrangement may also be a strategic response to circumstances. Motorola in the US brought in **Sanjay Jha** from Qualcomm as co-CEO in 2008 to prepare the mobile phone division to be spun off as a separate company, which would have been a big ask for CEO **Gregory Brown** (p295) on top of his group-wide executive responsibilities.

"Given the enormity of the opportunity and the task at hand, we felt it was worthwhile to have two of us trying to drive this rather than leave it to one individual to try and do everything."
GIRISH PARANJPE

Creating a Partnership

While sharing power can sound like a good idea, it is far from the business norm. A business school study* has identified the following steps to improving the chances of successful power sharing:

Share expertise—Each CEO should specialize in different areas of the business.

Maintain compatibility—Friendship isn't necessary, but a good working relationship is.

Co-envision—A shared vision for the future and direction of the company is essential.

Define roles—Be clear about who is in charge of what.

Report back—Co-CEOs should communicate so they always know what the other is doing.

* study by Professor Álvarez, Instituto de Empresa, Madrid

Joint Leaders

A number of companies have shown that appointing two CEOs can yield results:

Monty Moran *and* **Steve Ellis**, CHIPOTLE MEXICAN GRILL (Restaurants: US)—*Moran was promoted to co-CEO in January 2009 alongside the founder, as the fast food player looked to expand into Europe.*

Gidon Novick *and* **Erik Venter**, COMAIR (Aviation: South Africa)—*Since replacing CEO* **Piet van Hoven**, *who served as CEO for 27 years, in 2006, they have continued a dual growth strategy of expanding Comair's British Airways franchise and its Kulula low-cost operation.*

Larry Reimert, Gary Smith, *and* **J. Mike Walker**, DRIL-QUIP (Engineering: US)—*The drilling manufacturer's three CEOs each has responsibility for distinct areas of operations.*

Peter Scott *and* **Debbie Klein**, ENGINE GROUP (Marketing: UK)—*Since its buy-out from Havas, the group has grown to employ 600 people. Duties are split so Scott deals with investors while Klein oversees day-to-day operations.*

Richard Gelfond *and* **Bradley Wechsler**, IMAX CORP. (Media: US)—*The company behind the big screen cinema experience operated with joint CEOs and chairmen from 1994 until 2009.*

Malcolm Streatfield *and* **Allan Rosengren**, LIGHTHOUSE GROUP (Finance: UK)—*The merger of Lighthouse with Sumus in 2008 saw a new structure emerge with joint CEOs drawn from the previously separate companies.*

Simon Denyer *and* **Oliver Slipper**, PERFORM (Media: UK)—*Assumed joint control of Perform after it was formed by the merger of sports rights business Inform Group and web firm, Premium TV.*

Heath Davies *and* **Jacques Mottard**, SWORD GROUP (IT: France)—*The former CEO of the UK arm of the business took a position alongside founder Mottard in 2007, before assuming sole control.*

Paul Freedman *and* **Reuben Isbitsky**, TIMESTRIP (Packaging: UK)—*Combining product development and banking backgrounds, the joint CEOs of the smart label company are able to focus their abilities where they are best suited.*

Kendall J. Powell Chairman & CEO, General Mills

BIOGRAPHY
Born in 1954. Powell gained a bachelor's in biology from Harvard University and an MBA from Stanford University.

BEST DECISION
Introducing a raft of cost-cutting measures, starting by reducing the number of pasta shapes in Hamburger Helper products, which saved the company millions of dollars.

LESSON IN BUSINESS
Build on a good legacy—Powell didn't hesitate to develop on the cost-saving ideas initiated by colleagues.

GENERAL MILLS has outperformed its rivals in the food sector under Powell, growing globally and constantly beating inflation. He has built on its financial strength by developing strategies for cost-cutting, productivity, and innovation.

Powell has been with General Mills since joining as a marketing assistant in 1979, rising through various roles before being nominated CEO in September 2007, then chairman in May 2008. Powell expanded the company's cost-cutting program, termed "holistic margin management," by offsetting higher commodity and transportation prices by trimming non-essentials and dropping less-popular products. Hamburger Helper was the first product to be targeted, and manufacturing costs were trimmed by ten percent. Dropping a number of pretzel shapes saved $1 million per annum, while jettisoning multi-colored Yoplait lids saved $2 million. Consolidating the purchasing of ingredients brought even larger savings. A strong stable of brands, product innovation—especially in the popular health and wellness and convenience categories—and Powell's focus on productivity and margins led to an increase in General Mills' market share, while its stock has outpaced other food manufacturers.

John Rishton President & CEO, Koninklijke Ahold N.V.

BIOGRAPHY
Born in 1958 in the UK. Rishton studied economics at Nottingham University, UK.

BEST DECISION
Implementing British Airways's Future Size and Shape strategy, which returned the airline to strength in the downturn following 9/11.

LESSON IN BUSINESS
Count your change—Rishton kept his focus firmly on the money at BA and has done the same at Ahold. His comprehensive cost-cutting exercises have seen finances improve as a result.

A KEY FIGURE in more than one company's turnaround, Rishton saved the day at British Airways with his financial astuteness and, in his role as CEO, is now helping fortunes rise at Dutch food retailer Koninklijke Ahold.

Rishton had a reputation for good money management before he came on board at Dutch food retailer and foodservice operator Ahold. Prior to joining the firm in 2006 as CFO, Rishton had spent most of his career in finance, at Ford Europe until 1994, and then at British Airways (BA), where he was chief finance officer from 2001 to 2005. Rishton built a name for financial acuity and is credited as one of the brains behind BA's cost-cutting Future Size and Shape initiative, which turned the airline's fortunes around after September 11. Measures included cutting 13,000 jobs, and the sale of its discount airline Go. As CFO of Ahold, he launched a strategic review in 2006, focusing on its core retail businesses in the US and Europe, and aimed at reducing operating costs by €500 million by the end of 2009. As CEO since 2007, it has fallen to him to see the plan through, orchestrating a process of divestment and rationalization that has seen sales halve while profits doubled.

"First, you have to protect your margins." Kendall J. Powell

Robert J. Stevens Chairman, President & CEO, Lockheed Martin

BIOGRAPHY
Born in Pennsylvania in 1952. Stevens studied at the Department of Defense Systems Management College, Slippery Rock University of Pennsylvania, the Polytechnic University of New York, and Columbia University.

BEST DECISION
Looking to international customers to fill the order books, which has paid dividends in times of domestic belt tightening.

LESSON IN BUSINESS
Understand customers' needs—much of Stevens' success has come through his ability to build special relationships.

FORMER US MARINE Stevens took over as CEO of Lockheed Martin, the world's largest defense contractor, in 2004. He is eager to diversify the company by expanding into new areas, while strengthening core aerospace and defense activities.

Joining Lockheed Martin in 1996, Stevens worked his way through various management roles, including head of strategic planning, CFO, and COO. Following reorganization in 1999, Stevens is credited with centralizing Lockheed's operations, cutting 2,800 jobs, and saving the company some $200 million a year. He took over as CEO in 2004 and has been committed to making Lockheed "a global security company that can help governments solve a range of problems, not just military ones." International sales have played an important part in Lockheed Martin's growth, and Stevens is keen to expand into healthcare, data processing and telecommunications services, and cyber security. Despite drawing the unwelcome attention of US Congress in 2007 over delays and overspend on the Lockheed-Northrop Grumman $24-billion modernization of the US Coast Guard, "Deepwater," the company's profit margins have more than doubled under Stevens.

Akimitsu Ashida President & CEO, Mitsui O.S.K. Lines

BIOGRAPHY
Born in Japan, c.1944. Ashida studied at Kyoto University, graduating in 1967.

BEST DECISION
Transforming the established Japanese shipping company into a global player, setting them clear targets to increase overseas revenue.

LESSON IN BUSINESS
Plan for growth—Ashida made global growth Mitsui's core aim and then worked to ensure the business could do this quickly.

BOLD, BENEVOLENT, and transparent in his dealings, Ashida played a key role in transforming Mitsui from a parochial Japanese giant into a lean company that set new earnings records year-on-year. Today it is a shipping industry leader.

Ashida has worked at Mitsui since leaving university. He first served in the company's San Francisco office, becoming general manager in 1993. When Ashida took the helm at Mitsui, the company was just emerging from stormy waters. Its costs were too high, and too much of its income came from short-term contracts with Japanese clients. Within days of taking over in 2004, Ashida unveiled a 20-year, fixed-price contract with Shanghai Baosteel to ship Brazilian iron ore to China. Within his first year, Ashida cut costs by more than $80 million, and he ordered his directors to chase long-term contracts overseas so that the company would be less vulnerable to local economic instability and price fluctuations. Under Ashida, Mitsui O.S.K. underwent a rapid expansion of its fleet and operations, with large bulk carriers commissioned specifically for long-term contracts. His first year yielded net earnings of $275 million. By 2007, Ashida had increased this to $1.7 billion.

"The industry is cyclical, but our business doesn't have to be that way." Akimitsu Ashida.

John J. Mack Chairman & CEO, Morgan Stanley

BIOGRAPHY
Born John Makhoul in 1944 in Mooresville, North Carolina. In 1968 he graduated from Duke University, North Carolina.

BEST DECISION
Walking away from Morgan Stanley in 2001 to make his name all over again by turning round ailing Credit Suisse within a four-year period.

LESSON IN BUSINESS
Be bold—Mack slashed costs at Credit Suisse by doing the unthinkable: persuading (and bullying) ambitious bankers to give up individual compensation packages for the greater good.

FROM STAR TRADER TO CEO, Mack's career shows what can be gained via aggressive re-engineering. He returned to the global financial services firm Morgan Stanley as CEO, fresh from having reshaped loss-making Credit Suisse.

Mack joined Morgan Stanley in 1972 and rose up the corporate ladder to president in 1993. In 1997, when Morgan Stanley joined with Dean Witter in a $10-billion merger, Mack struck a handshake deal with incoming CEO Phil Purcell to succeed him after five years. When Purcell refused to step down in 2001, Mack left to become CEO of Credit Suisse, the Swiss financial services company, where he launched a major cost-cutting drive. As part of this he persuaded bankers to return over $400 million from their compensation packages. In 2005, Purcell was forced out of Morgan Stanley and Mack returned. He subsequently steered Morgan Stanley through the global credit crisis by securing a $9-billion investment from Japan. "Mack the Knife" is renowned for his uncompromising approach to management and to cost-cutting. However, he claims to have softened his approach in recent years, and stresses the importance of putting team and company goals ahead of personal gain.

Steve Odland Chairman & CEO, Office Depot, Inc.

BIOGRAPHY
Born in 1958. Odland gained a bachelor's degree from the University of Notre Dame, Indiana, and a master's in management from the Kellogg Graduate School of Management, Northwestern University.

BEST DECISION
Cutting costs aggressively when he took over at Office Depot, which immediately revitalized sales and the stock price.

LESSON IN BUSINESS
Build your reputation—Odland's profile and track record as a bottom-line focused leader has consistently impressed analysts.

AN UNPARALLELED RECORD creating shareholder value, and a marketing background, made Odland the ideal candidate as CEO at office-supply firm Office Depot. A focus on efficiency and productivity saw sales rise and stock prices double

Efficiency and productivity are Odland's hallmarks. He made his mark at Quaker Oats, Sara Lee, Ahold, and AutoZone before joining Office Depot, the world's leading office supply company, as CEO in 2005. He gained a reputation for improving performance in challenging market conditions and, in his first year, sales rose and the stock price doubled thanks to his aggressive cost-cutting measures. This cemented Odland's reputation as a customer- and shareholder-focused leader.

However, sales weakened in 2007, and the global economic downturn led to losses in 2008. Primary customers—small and medium-sized businesses—were economizing. When rebel shareholders tried to oust the board, Odland responded with significant cuts, including store closures, cancellation of store remodeling, and reductions in staffing levels and new product lines. While overall company sales reflected the downturn, international sales rose as a result of targeted growth in China and Europe.

"There's been a sea change in our focus on corporate ethics. We've made more progress in the last three years than the previous thirty." Steve Odland

Marco Tronchetti Provera Chairman & CEO, Pirelli Group

BIOGRAPHY
Born in Milan, Italy, in 1948 to a wealthy entrepreneurial family. Tronchetti Provera gained a BA and MBA from Milan's Bocconi University. He married Cecilia Pirelli in 1978, daughter of Leopoldo, chairman of Pirelli.

BEST DECISION
Competing with other leading tire makers by concentrating on high-performance tires.

LESSON IN BUSINESS
Know your strengths and weaknesses—Tronchetti Provera recognized that to survive, Pirelli needed to focus on its core products while cutting costs.

AS CEO OF TIRE-MAKER Pirelli, Tronchetti Provera is one of the most powerful men in Italian business. Family connections may have helped him join Pirelli, but his aggressive, competitive management style won him the top job, and kept him there.

Tronchetti Provera joined Pirelli in 1986, working his way up through various managerial positions before becoming CEO in 1992. The company was heavily in debt so he aggressively cut costs and, rather than compete directly with larger tire companies, cleverly created a niche for Pirelli by concentrating on high performance tires, which offered higher profit margins. Astute marketing and advertising helped the company regain its edge and by 1996 finances were healthy. In 2001, Tronchetti Provera helped broker the deal that saw Pirelli and Benetton join forces to buy out the ailing Telecom Italia for $6.1 billion. Within a year he had transformed the company by selling assets, reducing debt, and appointing new managers, posting a profit of $1.7 billion. In 2006, Tronchetti Provera resigned as chairman of Telecom Italia because of government opposition to his plans to split up or sell the company's wireless operations. He remains chairman and CEO of Pirelli.

Harry Roels CEO (2003–07), RWE AG

BIOGRAPHY
Born in the Netherlands in 1948. Roels received a degree in physical chemistry from the University of Leiden.

BEST DECISION
Disposing of UK utility Thames Water, enabling RWE to focus purely on energy.

LESSON IN BUSINESS
Get the basics right—Roels demonstrated that expansion is only possible if building on firm foundations.

IN HIS FOUR YEARS at the helm of German utility company RWE, Roels pursued a bold, sometimes controversial cost-cutting and asset-disposal program that left the company leaner, and better prepared to face a fast-changing market.

After 30 years with Royal Dutch Shell, Roels was appointed CEO of RWE in 2003, at a time when the company was struggling with a mountain of debt following a period of acquisitions. He initiated a wide-ranging program of cost-cutting and asset sales that encountered opposition from some of the company's shareholders, but was a necessary step in getting the group back onto a firm footing. Among his key disposals was the £4.8-billion sale in 2006 of the UK utility Thames Water, which RWE had acquired only five years earlier. Roels's asset policy of sales and cost-cutting solved the company's debt problem, strongly boosted the share price, and turned its focus back toward its core area of energy. Meanwhile, however, other European utilities had been engaged in big takeover battles to expand their reach, and Roels's failure to make any large acquisitions is thought to have been the reason behind his departure at the end of 2007.

"Sometimes size is an asset. Sometimes, it's a liability." Marco Tronchetti Provera

Paula Rosput Reynolds CEO (2006–08), Safeco

BIOGRAPHY
Born in Newport, Rhode Island, in 1956. Reynolds graduated with the highest honors in economics from the prestigious Wellesley College in Massachusetts.

BEST DECISION
Embarking on a cost-reduction scheme at Safeco. Her cuts saved the company $75 million.

LESSON IN BUSINESS
Don't feel restricted to one industry—Reynolds switched horses from energy to insurance after 27 years, but proved every bit a winner in her new field.

ONE OF ONLY A HANDFUL of female executives to head a *Fortune* 500 company, Reynolds took the top job at Seattle-based insurance firm Safeco in 2006 and repeated the success she enjoyed in the energy industry, quickly boosting profits.

Reynolds joined the energy industry in 1979 and held a number of executive roles during her 27 years in the sector. She was president and CEO of Duke Energy North America and senior vice-president of Pacific Gas Transmission Company. Prior to joining Safeco in 2006, Reynolds was chairman, president, and CEO of AGL Resources, an energy services holding company. During her five years at AGL, the company evolved from a regional gas utility to a multi-state, integrated energy company, doubling its share price and market capitalization in the process. At Safeco Reynolds embarked on a cost-cutting exercise, reducing the workforce by several hundred, and selling the company's headquarters to relocate to a cheaper address. During her first year, Safeco reported a profit of $880 million, nearly $200 million more than the previous year. In 2008, Liberty Mutual Group acquired Safeco for $6.2 billion, and Reynolds announced that she would be stepping down as CEO.

Mats Jansson CEO, SAS

BIOGRAPHY
Born in Kolsva, Sweden, in 1951. Jansson studied economics and sociology at the University of Örebro.

BEST DECISION
Cutting costs in response to record fuel prices and over-capacity by cutting routes and shedding staff, which was essential to ensure SAS's survival.

LESSON IN BUSINESS
Think the unthinkable—as well as being essential for the company's survival, Jansson's cost-cutting program showed a strong hand at the tiller, generating market confidence.

AN EXCEPTIONAL LEADER and a firm decision-maker, Jansson's experience of change in consumer and business-to-business sectors made him the ideal choice to steer Scandinavian airline SAS through a time of turmoil in the aviation industry.

Jansson joined SAS as CEO in January 2007, having served as president and CEO of a number of major companies, including Axfood, Catena/Bilia, and Fazer. Hired to lead SAS at a time of increasingly tough competition, Jansson was soon faced with strikes over pay and working conditions, and the grounding of the fleet of Q400 planes following a series of crashes. To avert new strikes, Jansson introduced initiatives such as profit-sharing and share-ownership. A cost-cutting program saw SAS put up for sale its holdings in Air Greenland, Spanair, and BMI, the UK's second largest airline. Jansson stated that remaining independent was not the only option for the airline, and should be decided not only by management, but also by the Swedish, Danish, and Norwegian governments, which owned half the company. Jansson has stengthened SAS's position by drumming up support and fostering loyalty for the company among its major corporate clients, especially in Sweden.

"Of all the things I've done in my career, the turnarounds have been the most rewarding."
Paula Rosput Reynolds

Gregg W. Steinhafel President & CEO, Target Corporation

BIOGRAPHY
Born in Milwaukee in 1955. Steinhafel received a BA in business administration from Carroll College, Wisconsin, and an MBA from Northwestern University's Kellogg School of Management.

BEST DECISION
Filling Target's stores with stylish, high-quality, exclusive-brand merchandise, which differentiated it from other discount retailers.

LESSON IN BUSINESS
Loyalty pays off—despite the lure of his family's business, Steinhafel has remained committed to Target Corp.

KNOWN AS "TOP STYLE COP" at discount retailer Target Corporation, Steinhafel landed the role of CEO in 2008, capping a distinguished career with the company that has spanned nearly 30 successful years.

Steinhafel could easily have chosen to go into the family business, Steinhafels Furniture, but instead chose to join Minneapolis-based Target, starting as an assistant buyer in the paint department in 1979. By 1994, he was executive vice-president in charge of merchandising, bringing in signature labels, such as sportswear brand Merona, and other exclusive lines. Steinhafel became president in 1999, giving him considerably more power within the company, and enabling him to oversee Target's merchandise and the design of new stores. By 2004, annual sales had increased 74 percent, and in 2007 Steinhafel joined the board, becoming CEO in 2008 following the retirement of his mentor, Bob Ulrich. Under Ulrich's leadership, Target had managed to stand up to retail giant Wal-Mart but, with falling sales and an economic downturn, Steinhafel focused on value, realigning Target's marketing to emphasize the "pay less" side of its "Expect more. Pay Less" slogan.

John E. Potter Postmaster General & CEO, US Postal Service

BIOGRAPHY
Born in New York in 1956. Potter earned a bachelor's degree from Fordham University in the Bronx, New York, and a master's degree from the Sloan Fellows Program, Massachusetts Institute of Technology.

BEST DECISION
Cutting costs to keep the postal service in the black as the internet hit postal mail volumes.

LESSON IN BUSINESS
Be brutal on costs—faced with declining first-class mail revenues, Potter kept profits up by improving service and stripping costs.

COMPETITION FROM the internet was the biggest when Potter became postmaster general in 2001. Two more crises arose within his first four months: the attack on the World Trade Center, and anthrax sent through the mail.

The 9/11 Al-Qaeda attack on the US threw the US Postal Service into chaos. "Jack" Potter ordered his staff to join the rescue efforts, dispatching his fleet of vans to transport medical supplies, while the service introduced emergency measures to keep mail moving throughout the country. The suspension of passenger flights led Potter to re-route mail through cargo flights and commercial courier services. Once normal services resumed, two postal workers were killed and several others harmed when terrorists posted anthrax-contaminated packages by mail. Potter put the cost at $5 billion in damage to facilities, increased security needs, medical treatment, and lost postal volumes. Against this background, he outlined a survival strategy based on substantial cost savings and improved customer service. Potter saved $1.4 billion in cuts and oversaw record improvements in customer service and satisfaction, efficiency, and financial performance.

"As we look to the future, we remain confident in the relevance of our strategy, the strength of our brand, and the dedication of our talented team." Gregg W. Steinhafel

GIVING A LITTLE BACK

There comes a point in a chief executive's life when the horizon of mortality looms larger than the next set of final year figures. Microsoft founder **Bill Gates** (p36) clearly now believes that eradicating malaria is more important than including voice-recognition in Windows Vista. But it is often easier to make money than to give it away. One solution is to get someone else to do it. Investment legend **Warren Buffett** (p194) admitted philanthropy wasn't his strongest suit, so when he gave away $37 billion in 2006—the biggest ever US charity donation—he nominated Gates to spend the money for him via the Bill and Melinda Gates Foundation ●

Philosophy of Philanthropy

It's hardly surprising that some captains of industry want their legacy to be more than a smoother-shaving razor, and charitable deeds are a way for posterity to smile on a CEO's reputation. But the desire to give may be fired by less individualistic motives. Chinese executives, for example, often grew up in poverty, and see a direct link between their roots and their philanthropy. In addition, many are influenced by Confucian teaching, which demands that successful people should give as a matter of principle.

Born into a poor Chinese farming family, real estate entrepreneur **Huang Rulun**, chairman and founder of Century Golden Resources, says he is deeply influenced by Confucius, and he has topped philanthropy lists in China by giving away some 20 percent of his net wealth a year to causes such as poverty relief,

"When I was little, I had a dream that I would one day be able to repay my parents and all the people that helped me."
HUANG RULUN

education, and battling the respiratory disease SARS. Dubbed "China's Carnegie", Huang has, however, resisted setting up a foundation in his own name. Seemingly uninterested in posterity, he says "I donate because I like giving", reportedly often on the spur of the moment.

For some, their motivations are more ideological. Koch Industries US CEO, **Charles G. Koch**, became interested in libertarian ideas in 1963. "Market principles have changed my life and guide everything I do", he says. Building on this philosophy, in 1980 he created the Charles G. Koch Charitable Foundation, intended to advance social wellbeing by promoting libertarian principles of limited government, free market economics, and individual liberty. Such a stance is not without its hazards. Koch Industries has been put under the microscope by political critics who want to dish the dirt on the CEO who, they believe, is part of the US's "vast right wing conspiracy".

Enterprise as Philanthropy

It is good to give back, but sometimes it is better not to take in the first place. Classified advertising website Craigslist has a global reach and is in the top 20 most visited sites in the US. Wall Street analysts think it could easily make $500 million or more by charging for its advertising—but founder **Craig Newmark** sees money as a burden to the rich and calls the site "a community service" that just happens to have a business structure. "Groups like the Gates Foundation have lots of money to donate," he says, "but it's more effective to let people keep the cash."

Other CEOs like to make a game of it and turn philanthropy into a kind of financial engine, appealing to the competitive streak of beneficent billionaires to create a virtuous multiplier effect on the money, and thereby drive forward social or technological progress. When X-Prize Foundation US CEO, **Peter Diamondis**, offered an award of $10 million for the first privately-funded, repeatable sub-orbital space flight, Microsoft co-founder **Paul Allen** (p178) stumped up a further $25 million to develop the winning craft, SpaceShipOne, and help secure his own place in history.

Givers and Shakers

Other CEOs known for their generosity include:

Dan Amos, AFLAC (Insurance: US)—*Has given $44 million to the Aflac Cancer Center in Atlanta, which helps children with the disease.*

James L. Dolan, CABLEVISION SYSTEMS (Media: US)—*A former musician who has struggled with alcohol and drug addiction, Dolan set up the Lustgarten Foundation for Pancreatic Cancer Research and organized a benefit concert for victims of Hurricane Katrina.*

Frédéric de Narp, CARTIER (Retail: US)—*The Cartier Love Charity bracelet was launched by de Narp in 2006 and has become an annual event. Each year a new limited edition bracelet is designed, with all proceeds going to charity.*

Michael J. Ward, CSX (Chemicals: US)—*Made a personal donation of $1 million to the Wounded Warrior Project for the rehabilitation of wounded US armed forces personnel.*

Shin Chang-jae, KYOBO LIFE (Insurance: South Korea)—*Inherited the Daesan Foundation from his father, company founder **Shin Yong-ho**, with a brief to promote Korean culture and globalize Korean literature.*

Niu Gensheng, MENGNIU DAIRY (Foodstuffs: China)—*Has put more than $600 million of his assets into a foundation to donate to education, health, and agriculture improvement, and has so far disbursed around $85 million.*

Yorihiko Kojima, MITSUBISHI CORP. (Diversified: Japan)—*The Mitsubishi Art Gate Program aims to foster young artists by buying their work for auction, the proceeds of which fund art scholarships.*

Mark E. Ketchum, NEWELL RUBBERMAID (Consumer products: US)—*The company's Investing in Community scheme pumps $3.5 million a year into local communities, with a focus on in-classroom programs.*

Björn Wahlroos, SAMPO (Finance: Finland)—*Established a foundation in 2002 to support research and debate on market-based solutions to social and economic problems.*

Don Stewart, SUN LIFE FINANCIAL (Insurance: Canada)—*Under Stewart, Sun Life has donated millions of dollars to social, health, educational, and environmental initiatives.*

Gerald L. Storch, Toys 'R' Us (Retail: US)—*The Toys 'R' Us Children's Fund contributes millions of dollars in grants to organizations such as Safe Kids Worldwide, Autism Speaks, and Save the Children, as well as donating for disaster relief.*

8

The Visionaries

Irene Khan Secretary General, Amnesty International

AS THE SEVENTH secretary general in Amnesty International's history, Khan has the triple distinction of being the first woman, the first Asian, and the first Muslim to hold the top position, qualities that have brought a fresh perspective to the world's largest human rights organization. Since her appointment in 2001, Khan has traveled the globe to meet numerous world leaders in the fight for justice for the poor and the marginalized, and drawn attention to some of the less obvious violations of human rights.

BIOGRAPHY
Born in Dhaka, East Pakistan (now Bangladesh), in 1956. Khan studied law at Manchester University, UK, and at Harvard Law School.

LEADERSHIP STYLE
Softly spoken, gentle, yet dynamic. Khan is equally at ease talking to world leaders and the dispossessed.

KEY STRENGTH
A genuine commitment to speaking up on behalf of people without a voice.

BEST DECISION
Instigating an international campaign against violence toward women.

CHILD OF WAR TO WARRIOR OF PEACE

Human rights abuses committed during Bangladesh's fight for independence left a lasting impression on Khan as a teenager. She studied law, specializing in human rights, and in 1977 helped to set up Concern Universal, an international development and emergency relief organization. Khan joined the United Nations High Commission for Refugees (UNHCR) in 1980, becoming chief of mission in India in 1995, and leading the UNHCR team in Kosovo during the 1999 crisis. She joined Amnesty International as secretary general in 2001.

EXTENDING AI'S ROLE
While still upholding Amnesty's role in the fight against torture, miscarriages of justice, and illegal detention, Khan has extended its jurisdiction to cover issues such as discrimination, hunger, and illiteracy. In her first year, the challenge was to reformulate policy in response to crises such as the 9/11 Al-Qaeda attacks. She subsequently railed against the resumption of illegal practices justified in the name of national security, such as torture and detainment without trial, as part of the so-called "War on Terror." Never afraid to put herself in the line of fire, both metaphorically and physically, Khan has led missions to Pakistan during the US-led campaign against the Taliban in Afghanistan, and to Israel and the Occupied Territories. She has won international praise for her campaign against violence toward women, and has also drawn attention to less obvious human rights violations, including discrimination against the mentally ill in Bulgaria and asylum seekers in Australia. Enthusiastic and dynamic, Khan always puts people at the heart of policy making.

LESSONS IN BUSINESS: PUTTING PEOPLE FIRST

Khan's experiences as a child living in a war zone left her determined to dedicate her life to fighting injustice in any form. She took that experience directly into her work.
- ➜ Use the law to protect peoples' rights rather than using it to protect powerful interests. That's a long-term strategy.
- ➜ Use your life experiences in a positive way for your organization. They are part of your unique qualities.
- ➜ Put people at the core of your strategy; you need to convince them that what you are doing is right.

"Our challenge is to stand in solidarity with the victims, to know their names, their faces, their identities, their stories." Irene Khan

Frank Chapman CEO, BG Group

IN THE MACHO WORLD of oil and gas, where bigger is almost always better, Frank Chapman has outsmarted the industry Goliaths and carved out a lucrative niche for BG in the fast-growing liquified natural gas (LNG) market. The firm may be small compared to Exxon, Shell, or BP but, thanks to Chapman, it's a very profitable and fast-growing company. His success has been due largely to a succession of astute acquisitions around the globe, productive exploration for new resources, and the development of a highly motivated management team.

BIOGRAPHY
Born in the East End of London in 1953. He gained a first-class degree in mechanical engineering from Queen Mary's College, London.

LEADERSHIP STYLE
Performance driven. He sets stiff targets and rewards achievement generously, but doesn't give second chances to those who don't measure up.

KEY STRENGTH
Focus. Chapman is a pragmatist who eschews complex business philosophies in favor of focusing on the core business of getting oil and natural gas out of the ground and transporting it.

BEST DECISION
Spotting a gap in the LNG market and positioning the company to exploit this.

INTERNATIONAL EXPERIENCE Born on the edge of London's now-redeveloped docklands, Chapman ascribes his lifelong self-confidence to gregarious parents and a strong family background. An oil industry veteran, he joined BG (then British Gas plc) in 1996 after 22 years spent criss-crossing the globe with Shell and BP. He is a vocal advocate of the benefits of living and working in many different countries. Chapman's influence has turned BG—once the moribund rump of the state-owned British Gas utility's pipeline business—into a modern, meritocratic, and multicultural organization.

SPOTTING A NICHE When he took over the helm in 2000, Chapman spotted that the relatively immature LNG market presented a great opportunity for BG to grow quickly and punch above its weight. A series of acquisitions and agreements, including an Au$5.6-billion alliance with leading coal seam gas explorer, Queensland Gas Company, have enabled Chapman to increase the company's global presence. Championed by Chapman, BG's exploration business has prospered—big finds, particularly in Brazil, added 60 percent to the firm reserves in early 2008. BG operates in many countries around the world, and the firm is unrivaled as a producer and shipper of LNG, which is cleaner burning and requires less processing than oil.

Chapman has also worked hard to assemble a good management team and create a high-performance culture. Saying, "It is impossible to mind every single nut and bolt yourself," he is a believer in the importance of delegation, recruiting people to whom he can pass authority with confidence.

LESSONS IN BUSINESS: PACING YOURSELF

It's a marathon not a sprint. Despite his impressive productivity—a colleague described him as "absolutely tireless"—Chapman actively discourages a long-hours culture at BG. He prefers to leave at 5.30 sharp.
→ Balance your work and personal life to maintain formidable performance levels over many years.
→ Make a plan for work/life balance by listing work and home activities and putting percentages of a week against each area.
→ Set a work ethic with your team and lead by example.

"People who worry about what is round the corner don't tend to succeed." Frank Chapman

Bill Allen President (1945–68) & Chairman (1968–78), Boeing Company

BOEING COMPANY appointed Allen as president at a critical time, when the end of World War II had brought production to a standstill. Allen guided Boeing back to success, from the era of propeller-driven aircraft into the age of jets, intercontinental missiles, and spacecraft. The first successful jet airliner, the 707, was developed under him, despite safety and cost concerns from Boeing executives and airline companies. Allen also oversaw the early development of the 747, and established Boeing's place at the heart of the US space program.

BIOGRAPHY
1900–1985. Born in Lolo, Montana. He attended the University of Montana and Harvard Law School.

LEADERSHIP STYLE
Innovative, reserved, and impressive. Allen was an arch-conservative Republican, but also someone who encouraged innovation. Although his reserve reinforced a tough, unfeeling image, his honesty and integrity, as well as his commitment to the community, inspired those who worked under him.

KEY STRENGTH
His willingness to invest in new technologies, even in the face of opposition from within Boeing.

BEST DECISION
Investing in the 707 jet transport prototype, which ultimately led to Boeing's leadership in the commercial aircraft business.

HARD TIMES After graduating from Harvard Law School, Allen became a staff lawyer at Donworth, Todd, & Higgins in Seattle. He was assigned to handle the legal affairs of the Boeing Airplane Co., and in 1930 he joined the Boeing board. In September 1944, Boeing president Philip Johnson died suddenly and the board turned to Allen. He accepted the presidency in March 1945, at a critical time for the company. The war was drawing to a close, contracts for bombers (of which Boeing had built literally thousands) were being cancelled, and assembly lines were grinding to a halt. The company was almost out of business.

Boeing forged ahead with the development of jet-powered military aircraft, such as the B-52, but to Allen the future lay in civilian aviation. In the early 1950s, he sought funding from airline companies for developing a jet airliner, but the industry had concerns about safety. Even some Boeing executives were lukewarm about the prospects for jet-powered commercial aircraft.

BOLD DECISION Allen felt differently and, despite the lack of a buyer, he invested $16 million in the jet airliner project. When the 707 prototype took its maiden flight in July 1954, Allen appeared on the cover of *Time* magazine. Heralding a new era in passenger air travel, the 707 became one of Boeing's most enduring legacies, with almost 2,000 produced for civilian and military use over the next 40 years. Throughout his career, Allen was open to new possibilities, taking Boeing into helicopter manufacture in 1960, setting up collaboration between Boeing and NASA, and gaining a key role for the company in the Apollo mission.

LESSONS IN BUSINESS: TAKING A GIANT LEAP

Some CEOs change not only the business they are running but the way people live their lives. Allen's vision that what was good for military aircraft would eventually be good commercially ranks as one of the most far-sighted decisions in a complex industry, and revolutionized global travel.

➜ Explore how new innovations, from inside and outside of your industry, could be applied to your business.

➜ Listen carefully when people say "that cannot be done" but if you are sure you are right, then go ahead.

➜ Create a culture that encourages people to think up big, unconventional ideas.

"[Allen] knew when to gamble. He trusted his designers. He knew how to forge a team."

Time magazine, July 1954

Angela Ahrendts CEO, Burberry

WOULD-BE DESIGNER turned businesswoman, Ahrendts proves that it is possible to turn a small-town dream into a high-flying career. She spent years climbing the corporate ladder at DKNY, Henri Bendel, and Liz Claiborne, honing her merchandising skills, before landing the ultimate prize as CEO of Burberry in 2006. Identified by *Time* magazine as one of the most influential women in American fashion, she has returned Burberry to its status as a desirable luxury brand, after a period when it had drifted down market.

BIOGRAPHY
Born in New Palestine, in the farmland of Indiana, in 1960. Ahrendts graduated from Ball State University, Muncie, Indiana, in 1981 with a degree in marketing and merchandising. She is famous for never having taken a day off sick in over 25 years in the business.

LEADERSHIP STYLE
Collaborative, entrepreneurial, visionary, and popular with those who work with her.

KEY STRENGTH
Combining business and financial savvy with a flair for design.

BEST DECISION
Launching a $2,000 luxury handbag as part of the company's 150th anniversary, successfully placing Burberry back among the must-have, designer labels.

FORMULATING A STRATEGY Fellow American Rose Marie Bravo had reinvented Burberry during her tenure as CEO, but saw Ahrendts as her natural successor to take the brand forward globally. Ahrendts spent her first six months at Burberry formulating the next stage of the company's strategy, and when she formally succeeded Bravo in July 2006, she immediately unveiled five key strategic themes for the company under the title "Operation Excellence." Ahrendts initially focused on making the historic company more innovative and restoring the luxury brand name.

LOOKING FURTHER AFIELD Working closely with creative director Christopher Bailey, she planned the global expansion of the company by increasing top-end merchandise and developing more efficient product delivery.

Her financial awareness was critical in the implementation of her initial plans—on only her second day in the job she ordered all divisions to cut the number of items they produced by 30 percent.

Combining commercial strength with creative flair, Ahrendts has shown that she can balance the business side of Burberry while concentrating on her first passion, design. She has expanded the brand into luxury handbags, shoes, small leather goods, sunglasses, and accessories, while staying true to the heritage as an outerwear brand, best known for its signature "Burberry classic check" pattern.

Ahrendts has continued Burberry's growth in Brazil, Russia, India, China, Vietnam, and Malaysia. She can also make tough decisions: she closed the company's shirt factory in South Wales and moved production to China.

LESSONS IN BUSINESS: RECOGNIZING TALENT

It is possible to create a global fashion brand without being a superstar designer yourself. Ahrendts has always recognized talent in others and has used this ability to establish herself as a businesswoman with massive influence over the fashion industry.

→ Recognize the key part of a manager's job—to get the best possible performance out of your people.
→ Avoid looking as though you can do people's jobs better than them—it stifles development and morale.
→ Hire the best people, even if they want your job. They don't threaten your career, they make it flourish.

"I'm still as passionate about what I do as the day I started." Angela Ahrendts

Lew Frankfort Chairman & CEO, Coach, Inc.

AN UNCONVENTIONAL background has proved no deterrent to Frankfort in developing Coach into the premier American accessories brand, with sales of over $1 billion. As chairman and CEO since 1995, before Coach split from the Sara Lee Corp., he has developed it from a cottage-industry manufacturer of leather goods into a leading designer of fine accessories. A *Women's Wear Daily* survey of upper-income American women ranked Coach products ahead of megabrands Ralph Lauren, Hermès, and Prada.

BIOGRAPHY
Born in 1947. Frankfort studied in New York, gaining a bachelor's degree from Hunter College and an MBA in Marketing from Columbia University.

LEADERSHIP STYLE
Meticulous, driven, design-orientated. "The tremendous amount of testing they do differentiates them from a lot of other fashion companies," says Robert Ohmes, a retail analyst at Morgan Stanley.

KEY STRENGTH
Introducing and adapting some of the operational techniques learned in a government job to Coach's business procedures and planning.

BEST DECISION
Hiring Tommy Hilfiger designer Reed Krakoff as creative director in late 1996.

UNUSUAL BEGINNINGS Frankfort has one of the most unusual CVs in the fashion business. Before joining Coach in 1979, he worked in local government for ten years and served as commissioner of the New York City Agency for Child Development. He brought a unique, novel approach to selling to the company, encouraging his staff to develop what he termed as "a blend of logic and magic." This involved developing an instinct for the touch and feel of good products, and using logic to understand what customers want, both now and in the future.

TRANSFORMING THE COMPANY Frankfort became president of Coach in 1985, ending up as senior vice-president of Sara Lee Corp. in 1994. He has been chairman and CEO of Coach since late 1995. His task has been to

transform the original business—founded in 1941 in New York by Miles Cahn, an artisan leatherworker—into a modern marketing and manufacturing powerhouse. During his reign, Frankfort has broadened the product range, modernized stores, introduced e-commerce, and expanded internationally. Frankfort crossed swords with French luxury goods company LVMH in 2005 over alleged anti-competitive behavior in Japan. Coach's complaint to the Japanese Fair Trade Commission was rejected, but Frankfort maintained that his objective of demonstrating that he would not tolerate actions that limit consumer choice, was achieved. Determination, meticulous research into what consumers want, and an instinct for good, well-designed products, mean Frankfort has succeeded in making Coach a luxury brand.

LESSONS IN BUSINESS: REACTING TO FEEDBACK

Coach's top executives chart sales for every store and every type of merchandise every day, enabling them to drastically ramp up production of anything that's selling fast—and so satisfy more customers.

→ Make sure that management information systems have complete credibility so that people can confidently base decisions on them.

→ Give managers the information they need to do their jobs. Don't clutter them up with other data.

→ Make sure the IT department gets the right information to the right people at the right time.

"Coach is... run as a blend of logic and magic."
Lew Frankfort

Roberto Goizueta Chairman & CEO (1981–97), Coca-Cola

AS A BRAND, Coca-Cola belongs to the US, but the man who drove their business further than any other CEO was a Cuban by birth. Goizueta rose through the ranks to become the youngest vice-president in the history of the company, at the age of 35. He created more shareholder wealth than any other CEO in history and made himself a billionaire in the process. Famous for his business rivalry with Roger Enrico, CEO of PepsiCo, Goizueta remained passionate about his job right up until his untimely death at the age of 65.

BIOGRAPHY
1931–1997. Born in Havana, Cuba. He completed a degree in chemical engineering at Yale.

LEADERSHIP STYLE
Forthright, innovative, and meticulous. Goizueta was well-known for clearing his desk every night, and was a great believer in delegation.

KEY STRENGTH
His focus on improving relationships with his workers, furthering their training in risk taking and innovation in order to help the company.

BEST DECISION
Acknowledging his mistake in trying to replace the traditional Coca-Cola, and rebranding it as Coca-Cola Classic.

LOOKING FOR A NEW CHALLENGE A year after returning to Cuba in 1953 to join the family sugar business, and looking for a new challenge, Goizueta responded to an advertisement in a Havana newspaper and started working as a Coca-Cola bottler in Cuba. His managerial skills were soon noticed, and he was promoted to Chief Technical Director of five plants. After moving to Miami in 1960, Goizueta relocated to the company headquarters in Atlanta in 1964.

After gaining experience in both the technical and legal divisions of Coca-Cola, Goizueta became CEO in 1981, when the company was on the point of becoming unprofitable for the first time. Initially, his key challenge was to modernize the culture of the company and improve relationships with the Coke bottlers. Then, he could increase domestic sales, while continuing to penetrate international markets.

SHAKING UP THE BUSINESS By the mid-1980s sales began to fall and Coca-Cola's market share fell below that of archrival Pepsi. A changed formula and rebranding was an attempt to turn this around, but the US market rejected this "New Coke". Never afraid to admit a mistake, Goizueta reverted to the original taste, changed the packaging, and renamed it Coca-Cola Classic. Throughout his long tenure, he remained fully focused on the need to create value for his "shareowners", divesting the company of its non-core businesses, and putting all his efforts—save for the purchase of Columbia Pictures in 1982, which netted $800-million when it was sold seven years later—into the growth of Coke, as well as actively expanding global sales in Europe, Japan, Russia, China, and India. By the time of his death in 1997, only a fifth of Coca-Cola's business was from the US.

LESSONS IN BUSINESS: TAKING CALCULATED RISKS

Goizueta once said, "The curse of all curses is the revenue line." He understood his duty to shareholders and the need to be profitable, but equally showed it was okay to take risks and to make mistakes.
→ If your current way of assessing management performance is dominated by this year's targets, review the whole scheme.
→ Very few companies train their people in innovation and risk taking. Do that and gain competitive edge.
→ Give new ideas time to bed in; don't pull the carrots up to look at the roots.

"Communication is the only task you cannot delegate." Roberto Goizueta

Kushal Pal Singh CEO, DLF

USUALLY KNOWN AS "K.P.", Singh is the man who had the vision to take India's real estate sector into the modern era. DLF, owned by Singh and his family, builds state of the art corporate headquarters, malls, and luxury apartment blocks. In the process, he has become the world's richest real estate developer. When DLF was floated on the Bombay Stock Exchange in 2006, the Singhs became $5 billion richer and one of the wealthiest families in the world, with a fortune of some $30 billion.

BIOGRAPHY
Born in Uttar Pradesh, India, in 1931. Singh studied engineering at Meerut College and then went to the UK to study aeronautical engineering, returning to a career in the Indian Army as an officer in the prestigious Deccan Horse cavalry regiment.

LEADERSHIP STYLE
Perfectionist, ambitious, and driven. "He will move heaven and hell if he wants something," says his daughter Pia.

KEY STRENGTH
Knowing what his country needs and building a business empire in his bid to supply it.

BEST DECISION
Buying up an unpromising stretch of farmland outside Delhi and transforming it into a gleaming modern district.

FROM THE GROUND UP Following a stint in the army, Singh went to work for American Universal Electric Company, which merged with DLF Universal. DLF (formerly Delhi Land and Finance) was set up by Singh's father-in-law in 1946 to build housing for the refugees from Indian partition. When Singh joined, the housing market was in the doldrums and the company had branched out into car batteries. Singh became CEO of the new company in 1979 and within a year he had a plan to turn the business around.

BUILDING INDIA'S FUTURE Singh's big idea was to start buying up cheap farmland outside the capital, Delhi. Over the next two decades, DLF bought over 34,000 acres in the area and began a building program. The company put up ultra-modern corporate headquarters for companies such as Ericsson, Nestlé, and General Electric, as well as developing luxury apartment blocks and shopping malls. Today Gurgaon is a gleaming satellite town—the capital of corporate India's call center industry.

Through a succession of building projects, Singh has played a vital role in the ongoing process of turning India's urban sprawl into modern cosmopolitan cities. Even faced with a global downturn, Singh believes there is still potential in Indian real estate as young, increasingly prosperous, Indians flock to the cities for jobs and housing. "Urban development in India… will be the biggest sunrise industry that any country has seen in any part of the world," he has said. Singh hopes DLF will become synonymous with the infrastructure revolution in India.

LESSONS IN BUSINESS: TARGETING DEVELOPING MARKETS

In a developing economy such as India, it pays to think big. Why build one office block when the country is crying out for a whole new approach to urban living? Singh recognized the opportunity of urban growth.
→ Give the people what they want—even before they themselves know exactly what that is.
→ Where there is a large mass market, predict its needs and invest to meet them when the time comes.
→ The cliché "they are not making any more land, so invest in it" still holds true, particularly in fast-developing countries.

"You will need 100 DLFs there will be so much work." Kushal Pal Singh

Andrew N. Liveris Chairman & CEO, Dow Chemical Company

A NO-NONSENSE AUSSIE, Liveris appeared to have his work cut out when he took over as CEO of Dow Chemicals, one of the world's largest chemicals manufacturers, in 2004. Ninety-two factories around the world had been closed after losses of more than $700 million in the space of two years, and sceptics were openly saying that the days of the giant US industrial conglomerate were over. By early 2008, it was beginning to look as though Liveris might have pulled it off, but then he was hit by a triple whammy of events going against him.

SMART THINKER, TOUGH NEGOTIATOR
Liveris joined Dow in 1976 and worked his way up through stints in Australia, Asia, and the US, becoming CEO in 2004. His remedy for the company's ailing performance was to move away from commodity chemicals, which had always been its stock in trade, toward less-cyclical, higher margin speciality chemicals. It was a well-thought-out and executed move, and Liveris did not, as many others have done, baulk at playing hardball with powerful US labor unions. He negotiated productivity improvements and wage cuts that raised Dow's efficiency by 25 percent.

THE DOMINO EFFECT When the global economic downturn began in 2008, the effects were dramatic for Dow. The government of Kuwait pulled out of a planned $17.4-billion deal to buy half of Dow's commodity chemicals business in December 2008, days before finalization, and Liveris' strategy started to unravel. This, in turn, had a knock-on effect: the collapse jeopardized Liveris' other key deal, the $15-billion acquisition of US speciality chemicals business Rohm & Haas, and shares in both companies suffered. Lacking the funds that it would have received from the first deal, and despite Liveris' tough cost-cutting measures, Dow repealed the merger in 2009. Yet despite the economic crisis, as an instinctive seer of the big picture, Liveris has remained outspoken on the need for globally applicable solutions to the problems of energy shortages and prices. He has positioned the company to meet the challenge of falling demand for products by announcing an acceleration of Dow's ongoing "transformational strategy", cutting over ten percent of its workforce and mothballing some 180 plants.

LESSONS IN BUSINESS: EXPECTING THE WORST

Liveris and his strategies were widely respected before the sudden and swingeing onset of the global economic downturn, but the deals he had assembled were particularly susceptible to economic crisis.
→ Always look at the worst downside of a plan, and mitigate risks or change the plan where impossible.
→ Take calculated risks and consider expert opinions, particularly those of your experienced people.
→ Be prepared to make decisions that carry risks that your experts tell you are too high, if all your business instincts and experience tell you it's worth it—that is why you are an executive and they are not.

"Water is this century's oil." Andrew N. Liveris

THE VISION THING

The "vision" needed by the CEO of a large, well-established multinational is radically different from that needed by the head of a new start-up company. Equally, it takes a different sort of vision to steer a business through rapid geographical and operational expansion, to that required in a severe downturn. Even so, there are themes: aligning the interests of customers, employees, and investors demands a certain kind of vision. Pre-empting the direction of the market is another. **Bill Allen** (p348), president and chairman of Boeing from the 1940s to 1970s, made one of the greatest second-guesses of the 20th century when he committed the company to the development of a jet passenger aircraft. His vision was at odds with many in the industry, but his drive to see it through saw huge rewards.

Vision isn't always about future-sensing. Indeed, on a day-to-day level, the most important goal is to define an overall sense of purpose, a strategy that inspires the company to work as a team toward a common goal. At American Express, CEO **Kenneth Chenault** (p192) has fostered a culture of openness and good customer relations. His vision, like many CEOs, is to maintain his company's reputation, rather than to break radical new ground ●

Different Visions

Since a company "vision statement" has to satisfy the needs of corporate reporting, PR, and customer and employee relations, not to mention the legal department, it can end up sounding a little blandly rhetorical. However sincere, "We aim to be a world class company, excelling in innovation and putting the customer first" could apply to almost any large company. But there are rare exceptions. People like Semco CEO **Ricardo Semler** (p103), who cut against the grain of corporate-speak and created a company based on his employee's own ambitions and happiness. Semco's vision of company democracy, where employees choose their own hours, offices, and bosses, makes for a more entertaining read on the company website. Refreshing highlights listed under "Principles and Values" include: "Value honesty and transparency over and above all temporary interests", "Encourage everyone's participation and question decisions that are imposed from the top down", and "Have the humility to recognize our errors".

Outside mavericks like Semler, convincing statements often come from environmentally-active corporations, such

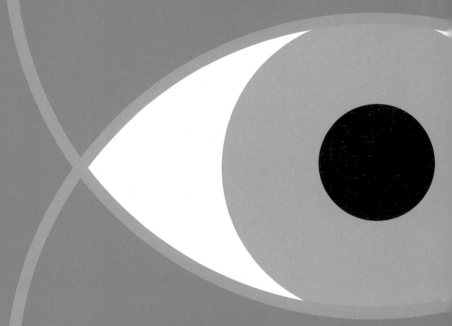

"If we do not let people do things the way they do, we will never know what they are really capable of and they will just follow our boarding school rules." RICARDO SEMLER

as energy companies striving to remodel themselves. These make a strong case for ecological protection through intelligent use of technology, while also building a sustainable business. **Ralph Izzo** (p392) of Public Service Enterprise Group argues that, "a clean energy transformation can be the equivalent of the New Deal" in its impact on society.

By contrast, **Shoji Muneoka** of Nippon Steel Corp. concentrates his gaze mainly on greater output volume, but also has strong views on the dangers of emission caps, which he has even conveyed to Japan's prime minister.

Stating Your Vision

Avoid rhetoric—Try not to use corporate jargon and cliché.

Be distinct—Concentrate on how the company can offer a true alternative to the competition.

Raise expectations—Aim for a higher company goal than mere profits, such as environmental improvement, company diversity, or community wellbeing.

DIY—For a personal touch, write the vision statement yourself. Don't leave it to the corporate communications department.

Visionaries

Other notably far-sighted executives include:

Francisco González Rodríguez, BBVA (Finance: Spain)—*Banking leader who had the vision to exit the domestic housing market, positioning his company to capitalize on low values.*

—

Fumio Kawaguchi, CHUBU ELECTRIC POWER COMPANY, INC. (Energy: Japan)—*Harnessed the power of liquid natural gas to create electricity and has acted on solid CSR principles to engage customers, employees, and investors.*

—

Takashi Shoda, DAIICHI SANKYO (Pharmaceuticals: Japan)—*Globally ambitious head of leading Japanese drugs company whose vision of his company's future led to the audacious acquisition of India's Ranbaxy Laboratories in 2008.*

Satoshi Seino, EAST JAPAN RAILWAY COMPANY (Railroads: Japan)—*Modernizing, farsighted head of Japan's largest rail operator, who has reduced emissions and raised speeds on his trains.*

—

David Philbrick Conner, OVERSEA-CHINESE BANKING CORP. (Finance: Singapore)—*Took over in 2002 and built on the Lee family vision by expanding overseas and improving its performance.*

—

Dhirajlal Ambani, RELIANCE INDUSTRIES (Materials and energy: India)—*Expanded his company from a textile business to a $40-billion global materials and energy group, with five million shareholders.*

—

Susumu Kato, SUMITOMO CORP. (Diversified: Japan) —*Has had the vision to move his company into socially and environmentally responsible areas such as recycling technology.*

Pierre Gadonneix CEO, EDF

AN EXPERIENCED businessman, Gadonneix has spent most of his career in industry, and has gained a reputation for running state industry like a commercial enterprise. He took the top job at Electricité de France (EDF) at a time when profits were slim and investors were few. He has since put the group on a sound footing and begun an ambitious expansion plan. Under Gadonneix's leadership, EDF took joint control of Edison and purchased the British Energy Group. The group now operates 58 reactors in France and generates 80 percent of the country's power.

BIOGRAPHY
Born in New York in 1943. He studied in Paris at the elite Ecole Polytechnique, graduating in 1962, and the Ecole Nationale Supérieure du Pétrole et des Moteurs. He has a doctorate in business economics from the Harvard Business School.

LEADERSHIP STYLE
Considered, ambitious, and forward-thinking. "Gado," as he is known to colleagues, is a mild-mannered engineer with a paternalistic attitude to business.

KEY STRENGTH
Carefully assessing the situation before instigating change.

BEST DECISION
The acquisition of British Energy Group, which silenced detractors and put EDF on the world map.

ENERGY AND METALS Gadonneix began his career when he joined the French oil company Elf Aquitaine in 1966 as an engineer in the Computing Department. From 1978 to 1987, he was Director of Metallurgical, Engineering, and Electrical Industries at the Ministry of Industry, where he played a key role in restructuring the French steel industry. He joined Gaz de France in 1987, taking the job of CEO in 1996 and fulfilling his ambition to be a captain of industry. After introducing a restructuring program and running the organization like a private company, he left to head up its sister company EDF.

NUCLEAR FUSION Gadonneix was appointed CEO in 2004 partly to repair the damage caused by a reckless expansion spree under his predecessor, and in his first year he succeeded in doubling the company's net income. He was initially accused of a parochial approach and a reluctance to play on the international stage. He soon silenced doubters by broadening EDF's interests in Europe, taking co-control Edison SpA, Italy's second-largest producer of electricity, in 2005, and then, in 2008, paying £12.5 billion for British Energy Group. The purchase of a company that owns eight of Britain's ten nuclear power reactors gave Gadonneix's nuclear ambitions a significant boost, and he has since said that EDF plans to build a further four nuclear power stations in Britain. He is also targeting China, the US, and South Africa as markets for EDF's expanding nuclear business. At home, Gadonneix has taken EDF into a partnership with Renault to build a nationwide electric car recharging network in France.

LESSONS IN BUSINESS: MAKING THE STATE COMMERCIAL

Gadonneix, a firm believer in the American "can do" approach to business, says running a state enterprise successfully offers a unique range of challenges, balancing the market economy with the role of the state.
- → In a state enterprise quantify your outputs in financial, as well as social and political terms, and carry out cost/benefit analysis.
- → Don't let targets set by government make you lose focus on the real social changes you want to achieve.
- → Emphasize the social and political benefits when you propose a solution to a government department.

"The important thing is not to have a theory that you are proud of. It is to have something that works."
Pierre Gadonneix

Alexei Borisovich Miller Deputy Chairman & CEO, Gazprom

THE "TSAR" OF RUSSIAN GAS, Miller has transformed the state-controlled gas company Gazprom from a sleeping giant into a powerful energy venture with a 20-percent share of global production. A former deputy energy minister and a close ally of former Russian president Vladimir Putin, he took control of Gazprom in 2001 and began ruthlessly cutting away the dead wood. In just three years, he gave it new direction and positioned it as an arm of foreign policy in support of Russia's global political ambitions.

BIOGRAPHY
Born in 1962 to Jewish parents in Leningrad (St. Petersburg), Soviet Union. Miller studied economics at the Leningrad Finance and Economics Institute, receiving a PhD in economics in 1989. He became the Russian Federation's deputy minister of energy in 2000.

LEADERSHIP STYLE
Highly personal, demanding commitment and loyalty from his co-workers and giving respect and praise in return. A dedicated state capitalist, he has proved himself willing to take controversial decisions.

KEY STRENGTH
Focus. He has identified three measurable targets for growth: regaining lost assets, increasing gas production, and eliminating theft.

BEST DECISION
Tackling the crooked culture within Gazprom head on by replacing a huge tranche of senior management.

HUMAN FACTORS When Miller was appointed CEO of Gazprom, he found a mismanaged and derelict enterprise, inefficient and riddled with corruption. He embarked on an ambitious program of renewal based primarily on simple human factors. He demanded dedication and absolute personal loyalty of the sort that he himself gave his protector Vladimir Putin. Within 12 months, 90 percent of the management had been replaced. New employees were chosen with care and treated with respect, and Miller later gave them much of the credit for ending the crisis in which Gazprom had been mired.

STEP BY FEARLESS STEP Crucial to Miller's Gazprom strategy was a disciplined program of development, first addressing internal issues and then moving on to expansion from a well-secured base. After firing managers who were stealing from the company, he cut ties to so-called "be-friended" companies that were buying gas cheaply and selling it on at a better price, and started buying back assets that Gazprom had lost over the years. He then turned his attention to the outside world, embarking on an ambitious plan to conquer new markets, diversify business activities, and to ensure security of supply. Emblematic of his no-compromise approach was his willingness to exercise the political muscle his role gave him, controversially cutting off supplies to neighbours such as Ukraine and infuriating the West by predicting that the price of oil could rise as far as $250 a barrel. Such brashness was seen as characteristic of Miller's, and the new Gazprom's, fearless West-baiting stance.

LESSONS IN BUSINESS: CONSOLIDATING FIRST

Consolidate your company first, and provide a secure base from which to operate. Significant external growth is only possible with a good internal set-up. Growth in a chaotic organization will produce more chaos.
- → Hire a strong and loyal team, picking people who share the same vision as their CEO.
- → Retain people who are prepared to work hard to deliver that vision.
- → Make sure effective marketing and selling processes are in place and working before you move into new markets or new products.

> "I think my work to be the most interesting in the world." Alexei Borisovich Miller

Roberto Civita Chairman & CEO (1990–2000, 2005–07), Abril Group

UNDER THE LEADERSHIP of Italian-born Civita, the São Paulo-based Abril Group started by his father grew to become one of the largest and most influential media groups in Latin America. Civita took over as CEO of Abril in 1990 and has built a varied and widespread media empire, providing information, culture, education, and entertainment to the population of Brazil. He has also cut partnership deals with various international media players. In 2007, Civita passed the title of CEO to his son Giancarlo, but remains chairman.

BIOGRAPHY
Born in Milan, Italy, in 1936. Roberto Civita is the son of Victor Civita, who established the international communications group Abril in 1950. Roberto has a degree in journalism and economics from the University of Pennsylvania's Wharton School, and took postgraduate studies in sociology at Columbia University.

LEADERSHIP STYLE
Passionate, innovative, and controlling, he has an enthusiasm for education and reading that he believes his staff should share.

KEY STRENGTH
A visionary and a pioneer, Civita recognized the opportunity beyond printed titles, and was among the first to bring pay TV, CDs, and CD-ROMs to South American markets.

BEST DECISION
Establishing a magazine 40 years ago when the literacy rate in Brazil was rising rapidly.

LAUNCHING *VEJA* In a bid to remove himself from his father's shadow in the late 1960s, Roberto Civita saw an opportunity to launch a serious news magazine in Brazil at a time when the literacy rate was growing rapidly. Despite the military government's opposition to dissenting voices, Civita managed to create and edit a hard-hitting magazine, *Veja*, that was to become Abril's flagship title, and that has endured for over 40 years. Its color layouts and hard-hitting news articles, which frequently target government corruption, set *Veja* apart from other Brazilian titles.

EXPANDING THE EMPIRE Even in times of economic downturn, Brazil's most influential periodical has retained its readership, and it now has one of the world's largest news weekly circulation at over one million copies. Civita

has continued to expand the group's publishing empire, using aggressive marketing tactics, and Abril now publishes seven of Brazil's ten best-selling magazines, selling a total of more than 170 million copies a year.

In a country where the majority of the population still chooses not to read, Civita recognized that Abril's future lay beyond print media. In 1991 he pioneered pay TV in Brazil, and offered digital TV, broadband internet, and internet telephone. In 2004, Civita acquired publishing houses Ática and Scipione.

In an effort to reach the country's 35 million schoolchildren, Civita launched SER, producing and distributing atlases, dictionaries, educational videos, and CD-ROMs. The strategic international partnerships that he has forged give him access to a wide range of content in many different media.

LESSONS IN BUSINESS: DOING YOUR RESEARCH

Civita believes journalists should read more books, study philosophy, and understand economics, to be able to explain the news that they are reporting from an intelligent and ethical base. This can go for everyone.
→ Read as though you were already in an executive position—widely and outside your own industry.
→ Be aware of Politics with a capital P. When you are the CEO you will inevitably be involved with it.
→ Research your business proposals thoroughly and make sure you have the hard evidence to back them up. Doing so may be time-consuming, but will soon give your company a reputation of accountability.

"We must defend all our freedoms to help our readers live better lives…" Roberto Civita

Chung Mong-koo Chairman, Hyundai-Kia

HYUNDAI WAS IN TROUBLE when Chung took over as chairman of the automotive business. Its products were cheap, but consumers, the media, and industry analysts knew why: Hyundai vehicles had a deserved reputation for poor quality. Within five years, Chung's obsession with improving the manufacturing process led to the start of a turnaround that has transformed Hyundai into one of the world's leading car makers. More recently, Chung has even bounced back from a conviction for embezzlement.

BIOGRAPHY
Born in Seoul, South Korea, in 1938, Chung is the son of Hyundai's founder, Chung Ju-yung. He graduated from Hanyang University, Seoul.

LEADERSHIP STYLE
Hard-nosed, detail-oriented, with a taste for micro-management. Chung gathers information quickly and has the charisma and reputation to impose his will on the company.

KEY STRENGTH
Recognizing that quality could be as strong a driver of growth as quantity or price.

BEST DECISION
To heighten attention to detail in Hyundai's manufacturing and improve its products' poor reputation.

LOW EXPECTATIONS Few commentators expected much from Chung when his father, Hyundai's founder Chung Ju-yung, named him his successor as head of the automotive arm of the immense family-run conglomerate. He had drawn little attention in his 24 years running Hyundai's after-sales service unit, and he was not expected to deliver the turnaround the company badly needed.

FROM JOKE TO POWERHOUSE Even company insiders admit that, when Chung took over, the Hyundai brand was worthless. It had become connected with poor quality; Hyundai vehicles ranked among the worst in the world in terms of initial defects, and they were unlikely to be seen anywhere outside South Korea. Chung announced his intention to employ the same intense focus on quality that Toyota had used decades before to overcome the cheap-import stigma. Styling was upgraded and the company's research and development budget was doubled, but the highest priority of all was given to faultless manufacturing. Chung transformed Hyundai, turning the company and its affiliate, Kia Motors, into major global competitors. Within five years, Hyundai had become the world's fastest-growing car maker and was ranked second in a leading survey of quality. Its stylish, well-priced, and reliable vehicles were closing in on the best-known brands in prime markets around the world, including China. In 2007, Chung was convicted of embezzlement, taking money from Hyundai to run slush funds. His initial sentence of three years in jail was reduced to community service and a $1-billion donation to charity. He has remained in the driving seat at Hyundai.

LESSONS IN BUSINESS: PUTTING QUALITY FIRST

Sometimes companies overlook the simplest things. Hyundai had expanded rapidly by turning out cars quickly and cheaply; quality had never before been considered an issue. By making it the only issue, Chung turned a target of derision into a serious global force.

➔ Make people proud of what they do by rewarding excellence and challenging mediocrity

➔ Set out up to five "principles" for people to work within; put quality at the top of the list.

➔ Implement a quality improvement program; get everyone analyzing problems and finding solutions.

"Quality is crucial to our survival." Chung Mong-koo

Kundapur Vaman Kamath CEO, ICICI Bank

BANKING IN INDIA has been revolutionized by Kamath. During his tenure as CEO of ICICI (formerly Industrial Credit and Investment Corporation of India), the bank's market capitalization has increased almost 20-fold, making it the largest bank on the subcontinent. It has expanded into Europe, Asia, the Middle East, and North America, and has assets of around $100 billion, over 1,300 branches, almost 4,000 ATMs, and 24 million customers. In short, Kamath has made ICICI a world-beating champion.

BIOGRAPHY
Born in Mangalore, India, in 1947. Kamath is an alumnus of the prestigious Indian Institute of Management in Ahmedabad, where he gained a reputation as having one of the best minds of his generation.

LEADERSHIP STYLE
Decisive, visionary, and quick-thinking.

KEY STRENGTH
His vision and drive have enabled him to transform India's old-fashioned banking sector into a huge, global force.

BEST DECISION
Leaving ICICI to gain wider experience of emerging markets by taking a job with the Asian Development Bank.

GAINING A GLOBAL VIEW Kamath joined the project finance division of ICICI as a management trainee in 1971, before working his way through the leasing and venture capital departments. His entrepreneurial skills caught the attention of chairman Narayanan Vaghul, but in 1988 Kamath left ICICI and joined the Asian Development Bank. His work there took him to China, Thailand, and Indonesia. When he returned to ICICI as CEO in 1996, he was ready to take on the world.

TEAMWORK AND TECHNOLOGY Kamath could see the huge banking potential in India's booming middle class, and was undaunted by the task of creating a modern banking system. As a priority, he began to recruit international quality managers to take forward his vision of a 21st-century banking system. Keenly aware of the key role of technology, Kamath moved quickly to digitize ICICI and install a nationwide network of ATMs, and in 1997 ICICI was the first Indian financial institution to go online. In 1999, ICICI Ltd. was listed on the New York Stock Exchange, followed by ICICI Bank a year later. In 2002, Kamath brought the group's entire banking and financial operations under one roof

These successes were somewhat tarnished by controversy about the bank's alleged use of over-zealous "goonda" thugs to collect overdue loan payments from poor farmers. Critics have alleged the practice led to a number of farmers taking their own lives, and one family even claimed a man was beaten to death by agents acting for the bank. Despite these problems, Kamath has been justly lauded for creating India's first truly universal bank.

LESSONS IN BUSINESS: ADAPTING BOLDLY TO CHANGE

To stay ahead of the game in financial services, banks such as ICICI need to be flexible and quick to adapt both the organization and its range of products to changing demands and new technological possibilities.
➔ Realize that welcoming and managing change is essential—not only to success but also to survive.
➔ Start by creating the team and structure of the organization imaginatively, overturning old methods where appropriate.
➔ In all you do, from getting ideas to executing them, one element is crucial: be bold.

"The key today is really technology productivity not employee productivity." Kundapur Vaman Kamath

Sarthak Behuria Chairman & Managing Director, Indian Oil Corp.

HAMPERED BY the price-fixing policies of the Indian government, IOC boss Behuria faces an uphill struggle to transform the state-owned company into a fully integrated global energy player. But if anyone can succeed, it is this mild-mannered, religious man. He has gained a reputation as a transformational and visionary manager, who successfully restructured the business of Bharat Petroleum, the company he previously led, and has overseen IOC's rapid revenue growth from $29.6 billion in 2005 to more than $60 billion.

BIOGRAPHY
Born in 1952, Behuria gained an economics degree from St. Stephen's College in Delhi and a post-graduate qualification in business administration.

LEADERSHIP STYLE
Avuncular, quietly spoken, and affable, Behuria is known as a "people man" whose skills include networking and strategic problem solving.

KEY STRENGTH
Understanding the importance of brand marketing and diversification to a sector facing deregulation.

BEST DECISION
Shaking up the oil market in India with the "Pure for Sure" campaign in 2002 that introduced the idea of oil product quality to consumers for the first time.

AGENT FOR CHANGE Behuria worked his way up in Burmah-Shell until he was made chairman in 2002 of the renamed Bharat Petroleum Corporation. On the way he revamped the company's entire retail operation and transformed its branding by focusing on customer expectations. Crucially, Behuria also served on the government's Oil Coordination Committee and helped formulate its regulatory regime, giving him an insider's knowledge. His expertise pushed him to global prominence, leading to his election as president of the World LP Gas Association, and he is cited as one of India's top ten most influential oilmen.

GROWING PAINS During Behuria's time in charge, Indian Oil Corp. has risen steadily up the rankings of the *Fortune 500*, and at the same time its revenues have seen around 25 percent annual growth. Profitability is an issue, however, as the Indian government forces state-owned oil firms to subsidize the pump price, causing IOC to lose some $50 million a day in 2007. Behuria's strategy therefore relies on growth through diversification. He is capitalizing on his long marketing career to drive expansion in non-fuel retail, moving the company further into pharmaceuticals at one end of the value chain and into oil exploration at the other.

Behuria is open to making acquisitions to give the company the expertise it needs to exploit the oilfield stakes it has taken in Libya, Iran, Gabon, and Nigeria. He also sees biofuels as another area of potential growth. A measure of his success is that the company easily exceeded its 2011 target of $60 billion in revenues three years early.

LESSONS IN BUSINESS: DIVERSIFYING TO PROSPER

Behuria's skills cover everything from marketing to supply and distribution, downstream infrastructure to industrial relations. Flexibility is crucial in an industry hemmed in by regulation and beset by volatility.
- → In a regulated industry look for diversification into new, unregulated revenue streams.
- → Try to influence industry regulations by demonstrating your vision of the future to the regulator and to the government.
- → Make sure that diversification is based on an understanding of how things will be in the long term.

"Governments cannot borrow from future generations to pay for today's inefficiencies."
Sarthak Behuria

Irene Rosenfeld Chairman & CEO, Kraft Foods, Inc.

THE FIRST FEMALE to be appointed to the top job at Kraft, Rosenfeld is one of the highest-ranking female CEOs in the US. When she accepted the post, she already knew the set-up at Kraft, having worked there for 22 years before leaving for PepsiCo's Frito-Lay division. Since her return to the world's second largest food company in 2006, bringing with her the vision that has been the key to her success throughout her career, Rosenfeld has steered Kraft toward growth through new acquisitions, innovative products, and emerging markets.

BIOGRAPHY
Born *c.*1953 in New York. Rosenfeld (née Blecker) holds a bachelor's degree in psychology, a master of science in business, and a doctorate in marketing and statistics, all from Cornell.

LEADERSHIP STYLE
Creative and direct. She is also able to empathize with her workforce.

KEY STRENGTH
Detecting trends in the food market before her rivals.

BEST DECISION
Leaving Kraft and proving her leadership qualities elsewhere.

IN TUNE Many believe that Rosenfeld should have been given the position of CEO back in 2001, when the board appointed Betsy Holden and Roger Deromedi as co-CEOs. During her first stint with Kraft, Rosenfeld had proved that she was in tune with what customers wanted. She was instrumental in instigating the purchase of the California-based fruit-drink company Capri Sun. With Rosenfeld's help, Kraft turned this brand into a national winner. A successful spell as president of Kraft's Canada arm during the mid-1990s proved Rosenfeld's worth, and in 2002 she was appointed president of Kraft Foods North America.

MOVING QUICKLY In her short, two-year stay with PepsiCo's Frito-Lay, Rosenfeld oversaw the development of a new line of healthier, low-calorie snack options, helping to make it the most profitable division in the PepsiCo company. In 2005, she took home a hefty $2.2-million paycheck, including a $1.4 million-bonus. Her performance made Kraft executives recognize that they had been wrong to let Rosenfeld go in 2003. Charged with pushing the company faster and further, she implemented a bold three-year plan that included new products, investment in brand building, and giving more control to managers in developing markets. The plan led to a healthy growth in profits, despite rising commodity costs, and in 2008 Rosenfeld made number two in the *Fortune* 50 Most Powerful Women. As Jean Spence, Kraft's executive vice-president of Global Technology and Quality, said, "Things move very quickly with Irene. She is really courageous and willing to speak up for what needs to be done."

LESSONS IN BUSINESS: SPOTTING MARKET TRENDS

Rosenfeld has the knack of seeing opportunities for new product lines, as success stories such as Capri Sun's foil fruit drinks or Frito-Lay's 100-calorie mini Cheetos snacks show. This is behind her success during three decades in the food manufacturing business.
→ Know your customers inside out. Talk to them, watch them shopping and predict what they want next.
→ Pay attention to "flavor of the month." Look for products that reflect the aspirations of the consumer.
→ Do not ignore downturns. If a product is going out of fashion, work out how to replace it.

"[Rosenfeld] understands the consumer. She has the ability to translate that into an appropriate business strategy." John Bowlin, Rosenfeld's former boss at General Foods

Allan Moss CEO (1993–2008), Macquarie Bank

THE "SAGE OF SYDNEY", Moss transformed Macquarie Bank from being a small subsidiary of the British merchant bank Hill Samuel into an investment powerhouse with 11,000 staff and a presence in 24 countries. His pioneering strategy, which focused on bundling infrastructure assets into funds and selling on, brought about a thirty-fold increase in profits at the bank over 15 years. His success made him the highest-paid executive in Australia and, when he retired in 2008, he had a personal fortune of AU$200 million.

BIOGRAPHY
Born in 1949 in Sydney. His father, Alfred, ran his own finance company. Moss received a bachelor's in economics and law from the University of Sydney, and an MBA from Harvard.

LEADERSHIP STYLE
Cool, calm, and collected, despite the adrenaline-fuelled teams that surround him. He is said to have ice in his veins and an incisive intellect.

KEY STRENGTH
The ability to assess investment potential rationally, without being distracted by trivia.

BEST DECISION
Targeting investment in infrastructure at a time when it was not considered glamorous or profitable.

SETTLING SCORES While a student, Moss wrote a paper railing against Australian subservience to foreign business. His success has been based on reversing this phenomenon, making a business out of buying crucial pieces of infrastructure all over the globe—toll roads, airports, and energy assets among others—and bundling them together into funds for sale to investors. It is a well-constructed strategy for these globalized times.

Moss was able to succeed because his nationalistic ambition was supported by a keen ability to process a vast amount of detailed and complicated information, a talent that set him above his competitors. He is said to pride himself on being able to answer any obscure question about the assets he controls, from pay scales on Britain's Isle of Wight ferry to runway lengths at Tokyo's Haneda airport.

UNIQUE INVESTMENT MODEL The ambitious young Moss was impatient with the existing business models. He wanted to create something more profitable, and came up with an idea that allowed for the taking of profits at various stages throughout the deal.

According to Moss's new model, bought assets are sold at a profit to the fund; the bank takes a fee for managing this fund (in which it also retains a stake), and then the bank takes profits again when selling the fund to the public. Employing this model, a typical transaction can be several times as profitable as a traditional deal, prompting one commentator to borrow a phrase from Louis XIV's finance minister, Jean-Baptiste Colbert, commenting on his ability to "pluck the goose as to obtain the largest amount of feathers with the least amount of hissing."

LESSONS IN BUSINESS: COMPETING FOR SUCCESS

Macquarie is successful partly because employees' pay is based on the profit they produce. Teams in the bank compete among themselves to buy target assets. It is a model that has given the bank the nickname "The Millionaires Factory", and it produces very motivated staff.

→ Prize an entrepreneurial culture above all else. Use the reward system to encourage everyone to innovate.

→ Do not, however, give teams complete freedom—handle key issues such as brand management centrally.

→ Make people rich if their performance merits it. This attracts talent like pollen does hard-working bees.

"Globalization is inevitable and pervasive." Allan Moss

J. Willard Marriott, Sr. Founder & CEO (1927–72), Marriott

THE FOUNDER and former CEO of Marriott Corporation, Marriott built a business empire from scratch. When he died at the age of 84, his original $6,000 investment had grown into a $3-billion enterprise, employing over 140,000 people in 143 hotels and resorts, 1,400 restaurants, as well as 90 flight kitchens for airline catering. With his achievements based on hard work, sound thinking, and strong principles, he was, as former US president Ronald Reagan said, "A living example of the American dream".

BIOGRAPHY
1900–1985. Born in Marriott, Utah, the town established by his great-grandfather. He was educated at Weber State College in Ogden, Utah, and the University of Utah. He taught English at Weber State College.

LEADERSHIP STYLE
Rock solid and systematic. A perfectionist, Marriott wrote detailed procedural manuals for every aspect of the business.

KEY STRENGTH
Exploring all the avenues for expansion in a changing world.

BEST DECISION
Establishing the In-Flite airline catering business.

THE BEGINNING OF AN EMPIRE The entrepreneurial career of "Bill" Marriott began in 1927 with a shrewd investment in an A&W root beer franchise in Washington, DC. To boost sales in the winter months, Marriott began to offer Mexican-style food cooked by his wife Alice. Marketing tactics such as free root beer coupons attracted custom to his Hot Shoppe restaurant, and by 1932 there were seven Hot Shoppes in the Washington area. In 1939, Marriott began providing food services to the US Treasury and other governmental departments. Hot Shoppe went public in 1953.

SPREADING HIS WINGS Having already diversified the company's interests with his earlier invention of an airline catering service, known as In-Flite, Marriott added the hotel business to his portfolio with the opening of the Twin Bridges Marriott Motor Hotel in Arlington, Virginia, in 1957. Looking for ways of making his hotel pay year-round, he hit upon a marketing plan that targeted businessmen and convention organizers, who until now had to stay in city hotels or family motels that lacked business facilities. A second hotel opened within two years, and many more in the years that followed. In 1964, Marriott Sr. turned over the presidency to his son, Bill Jr, though he continued in his role as CEO. Marriott went international in 1966 with the purchase of an airline-catering kitchen in Caracas, Venezuela. Other acquisitions included the Big Boy restaurant chain in 1967, and the following year he started the Roy Rogers fast-food chain. In 1972, Marriott relinquished the CEO post to Bill Jr., but was involved in the running of the business up to his death.

LESSONS IN BUSINESS: BRANCHING OUT SIDEWAYS

The only way a business can expand indefinitely is through continued diversification. As one Marriott director put it, "No tree grows to the sky". By continually adding new business branches to the corporation, Marriott was able to ensure that company growth never stood still.
➜ Make sure any new directions you take make use of the skills and knowledge your people already have.
➜ Bring in new people with appropriate skills rather than risk losses and slow growth in the learning curve.
➜ Notice how Marriott's diversifications were never a leap too far from the company's core business.

"If the employees are happy, they are going to make the customers happy." J. Willard Marriott, Sr.

Satoshi Miura President & CEO, NTT Corp.

WHEN APPOINTED CEO in 2007, Miura knew the difference between success and failure. His predecessor and former boss had just been ousted after Nippon Telegraph & Telephone Corp. announced lower than expected profits. The message could not have been more clear—the company needed not just a visionary who could redraw the roadmap but one who could make sure the journey was profitable. Miura did not disappoint. Within a year of his elevation the story was all about NTT's changing fortunes.

BIOGRAPHY
Born in Japan in 1944. Miura graduated in law before joining NTT Corp. straight from Tokyo University.

LEADERSHIP STYLE
Visionary, strategic, and urgent. Miura started by explaining to staff where the company was headed, and then made sure it was profitable on the way there.

KEY STRENGTH
His lawyer's grasp of both fine detail and the big picture have enabled him to outline his direction while micro-managing costs and revenues to improve the financials.

BEST DECISION
Cutting handset subsidies for its cell users and persuading them to pay more in an instalment plan—it transformed a fall in sales into a major increase in income.

KNOWLEDGE IS STRENGTH By the time Miura took over from Norio Wada, he already had 30 years of NTT experience under his belt. He could see that the industry was going through a period of rapid change—mobile handset sales were declining in Japan's mature market, landline subscriptions were under threat, and the company had failed to capitalize in developing markets. It was Miura's ability to exploit the commercial potential of the Web 2.0 revolution, and a short term plan to cut costs and maximize profits, that secured him the top job.

PROFITS TODAY AND TOMORROW Miura's first target was the declining revenues and fortunes of DoCoMo, which was responsible for 70 percent of NTT's income. The company had been paying large commissions to agents and huge subsidies on handset sales to new customers, clawing back the money through higher call plan charges. Miura changed tack, charging customers the full cost of handsets in instalments, with the incentive of lower monthly charges. It saved $50 million in commission payments, and more than $1.5 billion in subsidies, more than doubling half year operating income to $4.2 billion despite a fall in sales.

He also looked to emerging economies such as India, where he invested $2.7 billion in India's Tata Teleservices. It was DoCoMo's largest acquisition in eight years and it brought rapid subscriber growth. He invested in commercial property to develop new revenue streams, and in research and development to benefit from the rise of internet-based televison (IPTV) and internet telephony.

LESSONS IN BUSINESS: BUYING TIME FOR SUCCESS

Miura has shown himself to be a master politician as well as a business manager. By delivering a short-term increase in profits, he showed NTT's shareholders that he could deliver immediate results while developing new sources of revenue for the future.

→ Remember that time is money: a successful future is based on a solid short-term profitable platform.

→ Educate shareholders in your long-term strategy so that they give you enough time to achieve your goal.

→ Do not compromise your long-term strategy by putting too heavy a focus on today's results.

"NTT Group belongs to the service industry, and our priority is to satisfy our customers' needs." Satoshi Miura

DECIDING FACTORS

Make or Break

What makes a great decision? The answer is often obvious in retrospect. **Bill Allen**'s (p348) belief that Boeing's future lay in commercial not military jets was clearly a great decision, as was **Howard Schultz**'s (p456) conviction that Americans were ready for good coffee, which led him to buy up the small Starbucks chain. By contrast, the decision by RBS boss **Fred Goodwin** to buy up ABN Amro proved to be the bank's—and his own—undoing. Paying way over the odds for the Dutch bank left RBS financially exposed at precisely the moment when the US sub-prime crisis hit. Yet had events taken a different turn, Goodwin's call might not have turned out so badly. The fact is every decision a CEO makes is, to some extent, made on imperfect information and his or her judgement. Most will turn out to be of relatively minor consequence and be quickly forgotten. But some will be enough to change a company's destiny—or bring it to its knees. ●

Making life-changing decisions has always been a factor in business success. Around the turn of the 20th century **William Hoover** was a successful businessman making leather accessories for the horse-drawn carriage market. Yet, with remarkable prescience, he decided that the automobile, although a novelty, would soon kill off his company. So, he concentrated on other ideas and eventually came up with the mass market vacuum cleaner. Nearly a century later, this market was revolutionized, to Hoover's disadvantage, when **James Dyson** designed a vacuum cleaner that did not need bags, and founded the Dyson company to produce and sell his invention.

A later example is that of **Thomas Watson, Jr.**, son of the IBM founder of the same name. In the 1960s, computers were still largely the preserve of the military but, in 1962, he essentially staked the business, and around $5 billion, on developing the System/360 family of computers. IBM went on to produce the first commercial mainframe and enjoy decades of industry dominance that would only be ended by Bill Gates: the man who decided that the software was more important than the hardware.

Most CEOs develop a philosophy of decision-making, ranging from a rational assessment of the available facts to placing faith in gut instinct, though most settle for a healthy mix of the two. **Neil Berkett**, CEO of the UK's Virgin Media, says he solves problems by KISSing them better, with KISS standing for Keep It Simple, Stupid. This philosophy is used to good effect in the company's no-nonsense ads fronted by the famously straight-talking Hollywood actor, Samuel L. Jackson.

Making the Right Decisions

Make decisions based on what you understand—In the late 1990s, **Warren Buffett** (p194) was famously derided for not buying internet stocks, because, as he said, he didn't understand them. In a few months this looked very smart when the dotcom bubble burst.

Seek wise counsel wherever you find it—Walt Disney (p21) was convinced that Mortimer was the right name for his mouse. Luckily he asked his wife for a second opinion and she suggested Mickey.

Don't be afraid to build on others' decisions—The iPod wasn't the first MP3 player, but the decision to focus on user-friendliness led to success.

Don't rest on your laurels—The bold and radical decisions of corporate youth can become the millstones of corporate middle age; keep rethinking your decisions and taking bold new ones, or hand over to someone who can.

Great Deciders

CEOs who have made significant decisions include:

Alberto Weisser, BUNGE LTD (Consumer products: US)—*Weisser abandoned a deal to buy Corn Products in 2008. At the time, the deal seemed good, but plunging grain prices meant the decision to drop it was the right one.*

—

Dwight C. Minton, CHURCH & DWIGHT (Consumer products: US)—*In the early 1970s, the decision to market Arm & Hammer baking soda's deodorizing qualities led to a 72 percent increase in profits in three years, and doubled the size of the business overnight.*

—

Henry Heinz, H.J. HEINZ COMPANY (Foodstuffs: US)—*Looking for a snappy slogan, Heinz eventually decided on "57 varieties". In fact, Heinz produced 60 products at the time, but the 57 tag stuck for over a century.*

—

Fumio Sudo, JFE HOLDINGS, INC. (Metals: Japan)—*Sudo is a believer in bold decision-making, declaring "...the company begins to weaken when the cautious are in the majority."*

—

Paul Julius Reuter, REUTERS (Media: UK)—*In the mid-1800s, with no continuous telegraph line between Germany and Belgium, Reuter decided to use carrier pigeons, marking the beginning of the famous news and information business, now headed by* **Tom Glocer**.

—

Robert E. Wood, SEARS (Retail: US)—*In the 1920s, Wood worked at the mail order business Montgomery Ward and wanted to develop a high-street presence. Management were not interested so he decided to leave and take his ideas to rival Sears Roebuck. That company went on to become the world's biggest general retailer.*

—

Sandy Weill, TRAVELERS GROUP (Insurance: US)—*Weill took the decision to quit American Express after disagreements with the chairman made him realize he would never make CEO. This decision led him to create the Travelers Group insurance giant, and eventually to become CEO of Citigroup when the two companies combined in a $76-billion merger.*

—

"I decided long ago that in an investment lifetime it's too hard to make hundreds of smart decisions... Therefore, we adopted a strategy that required our being smart—and not too smart at that—only a very few times. Indeed, we'll now settle for one good idea a year."
WARREN BUFFETT

Indra Nooyi President, Chairman & CEO, PepsiCo, Inc.

PEPSICO WAS doing fine when the board appointed Nooyi as the new CEO, but she thought it could be even more successful. Implementing a strategy of building markets overseas and promoting social and environmental responsibility, she has been proven right. Only the 11th woman to hold the CEO position at a *Fortune* 500 company, she was number one on *Fortune*'s list of the most powerful businesswomen in the world in 2006 and 2007, and was among *Time* magazine's 100 most influential people in the world in 2007 and 2008.

WHATEVER IT TAKES When she came to America in 1978, Nooyi recalled in an interview, "At the end of the month I would have $2 left over and if I had $5 I thought I had died and gone to heaven." But she hung on, earning a master's degree in 1980 and moving on to Boston Consulting Group, Motorola, and ABB. Joining PepsiCo in 1994, she was involved from the start in strategic planning and development. She became president and CFO in 2001, CEO in 2006, and added the chairman's title in 2007.

A PERSONAL APPROACH When Nooyi learned she had been selected as CEO, she flew to Cape Cod to talk to her chief competitor for the job. Mike White was PepsiCo's foremost operations person and Nooyi wanted him to stay on. "Tell me whatever I need to do to keep you, and I will do it," she told her colleague. She enlisted three former CEOs to help convince him and asked the board to increase his compensation to a level close to hers. White was persuaded to stay. It was an unusual first step by Nooyi, but it speaks much about her approach, which is very personal and direct, and open to the opinions of others. As CEO she has played a lead role in introducing new —often healthier—products, and has made several key acquisitions. Internally, she has overseen a restructuring of the business and its top leadership team, emphasizing the role of the International division. The issues of PepsiCo's social and environmental impact have also been brought to the fore. What's more, from the time she became CFO, the company's revenues, profits, and earnings per share have risen strongly.

LESSONS IN BUSINESS: FINDING ROOM FOR IMPROVEMENT

Nooyi was not appointed CEO to turn PepsiCo around. It was doing just fine when she took over and would probably have continued to hold its own, whoever held the position. But she thought the company could be made even more successful by expanding still further.
➜ Look beyond profit and loss, and improve the working conditions of your people to the highest level.
➜ Search for growth. Any market where a very successful brand is not present is an opportunity.
➜ Pursue a socially and environmentally responsible agenda to add to your reputation.

"Companies today are bigger than many economies …If companies don't do [responsible] things, who is going to?" Indra Nooyi

Roberto Marinho Chairman (1931–2003), Globo

FROM JOURNALIST to radio broadcaster, to media tycoon, Brazilian-born Marinho became one of the most powerful business figures in Latin America. As head of the Globo empire, Marinho wielded enormous power over the hearts and minds of the Brazilian people, shaping the country's political and cultural life to such an extent that he has been criticized for overtly using his business to further political ends. At the time of his death in 2003, Marinho was one of the richest men in Latin America.

BIOGRAPHY
1904–2003. Born in Rio de Janeiro, Brazil, Marinho was the son of journalist and newspaper founder Irineu Marinho.

LEADERSHIP STYLE
Patriotic, bold, and hands-on. Marinho would spend his mornings at the Globo newspaper and afternoons at the television station.

KEY STRENGTH
An astute player, Marinho built his wealth and power by using political connections to help his business, and his business to influence politics.

BEST DECISION
Moving into television, and striking a deal with local transmission stations, helped him to build TV Globo into a station so far-reaching that it became a force for national unity.

FROM JOURNALIST TO MEDIA BARON

Initially trained as a joiner and mechanic, Marinho became a cub reporter for his father's fledgling newspaper *O Globo* in 1925. Marinho senior, however, died within a few weeks of the paper's founding, and Roberto inherited control. He spent the next few years learning as much as he could about the business before becoming managing editor in 1931, at just 26. Marinho built up the paper's circulation, preserving its political independence and securing it financially by reprinting US comics in Portuguese. In 1944, he made his first moves into broadcasting with the purchase of a radio station. Radio Globo played a key role in the 1964 military coup, and Marinho was rewarded with his first TV license. He set up TV Globo in 1965 through a controversial deal with Time Life (the Brazilian constitution

banned foreign shareholdings in media firms). TV Globo offered a menu of soap operas and populist news bulletins, and became the most wide-reaching channel in Brazil with 77 percent of advertising revenues and a 54 percent share of the audience.

PLEASING THE GENERALS
Despite its professionalism in many areas, TV Globo was accused of interference in the political arena. News bulletins proclaiming Brazil's "economic miracle" during the times of the generals, who held power between 1964 and 1985, reflected Marinho's ties to the dictatorship. During the 1989 election there was a broadcasting bias against the left-wing candidate, who was defeated. But when Marinho died, president Luis Inácio Lula da Silva (the former defeated candidate) announced three days of mourning.

LESSONS IN BUSINESS: LEARNING FROM THE BOTTOM UP

Marinho was an inexperienced reporter when he inherited his father's newspaper at the age of 21. Instead of taking over responsibility immediately, Marinho chose to spend several years as a trainee reporter.

→ Get involved at the sharp end. In most industries a grounding in what goes on there proves invaluable.
→ Familiarize new people with the organization by getting them to be, for example, check-out operator for a day in a supermarket.
→ Learn from those with more experience: 20 years facing the customers can give you valuable insights.

> "Brazil lost a man who spent his life believing in Brazil." Luis Inácio Lula da Silva, president of Brazil, on the death of Roberto Marinho

Anil Ambani CEO, Reliance ADA

THE FINANCIAL "WHIZZ KID" of the company, Ambani is the chairman of Reliance Capital and Reliance Communications, chairman and managing director of Reliance Energy, and was formerly vice chairman and MD of Reliance Industries Ltd. He and his estranged brother Mukesh enjoy wealth that places them among the top ten richest people in the world, and their rival Reliance empires dominate the Indian economy. Anil Ambani holds one of the world's fastest-growing dollar fortunes.

BIOGRAPHY
Born in Bombay (Mumbai), India, in 1959. The son of entrepreneur Dhirubhai Ambani. He spent his early years in a Bombay slum where seven members of the family lived in one room, while his father strove to build his business interests. Ambani holds a BSc from the University of Bombay and an MBA from The Wharton School at the University of Pennsylvania.

LEADERSHIP STYLE
Driven, focused, and willing to listen to criticism. Ambani once embarked on a fitness regimen when a colleague pointed out that if he was out of shape, his company was also likely to be out of shape.

KEY STRENGTH
An extremely competitive streak and a keen eye for investment. Described as having a killer instinct, he has been referred to as the Indian Warren Buffett.

BEST DECISION
Taking full responsibility for his role in the family business after his father suffered a stroke.

LEARNING CURVE From an early age, the Ambani brothers were given ambitious goals. When Anil returned from Wharton Business School in 1982, the day after completing his masters degree in 14 months instead of 24, he thought he was due a break. His father had other ideas: that evening he was dispatched to the company's textile plant in Ahmedabad, where he spent the next five years learning the business from the ground up.

Within Reliance, Anil is the Ambani with the head for figures. As co-CEO in the 80s, he was credited with many financial innovations in the Indian capital markets.

A BOLLYWOOD ENDING? The Ambanis were only in their twenties when their father had a stroke, forcing them to take control of the company. Anil says this time was the toughest but most valuable period of his life. The brothers agreed on a process of backward integration from the manufacture of polyester cloth to petrochemicals and oil refining.

Following the death of their father, tensions between the brothers came to a head in late 2005, when a long-simmering disagreement over company strategy erupted into a highly publicized feud. In the end, a truce was brokered by their mother, Kokilaben, and the Reliance empire was broken up in 2006 with Anil controlling the telecommunications, energy, and capital finance interests.

Since 2005, when he took over Indian film production and distribution company Adlabs, Ambani has had interests in the entertainment industry. His current projects include the creation of one of the world's largest entertainment conglomerates.

LESSONS IN BUSINESS: EARNING RESPECT

Many of Ambani's business principles were learned at his father's knee. One of the key lessons was the importance of earning the respect of the people who work for him.

→ Talk to every person you come across in your organization, from a cleaner to your main shareholder.
→ Gain trust from your stakeholders by never letting anyone down—avoid defaulting on any promise.
→ Make sure all your people understand that they all have an important role in your organization. By creating an atmosphere of respect for each other's contributions, you will gain respect in turn.

"My father's core values: being down to earth, being humble, and being simple." Anil Ambani

Edward Rogers, Jr. President & CEO (1962–2008), RCI

RISK-TAKER extraordinaire, "Ted" Rogers was the founder of Rogers Communications, Inc. (RCI), one of Canada's largest cable, wireless, and media companies. Rogers' willingness to put everything on the line—he faced bankruptcy many times throughout his career—enabled him to create a media empire from what started as a small radio station business. At the time of his death in 2008, he was the richest person in Canada. Roger's empire is an apt tribute to his famous father, Ted Rogers, Sr., who inspired his ambition.

BIOGRAPHY
1933–2008. Born in Toronto, Ontario, the son of radio pioneer Edward Rogers Sr. Ted Jr. was educated at the prestigious Upper Canada College and the University of Toronto. He also attended the Osgoode Hall Law School, before training at a Toronto law firm.

LEADERSHIP STYLE
Intense, driven, workaholic. Known for speaking his mind, though good-natured and polite in company.

KEY STRENGTH
Recognizing the next big trend well ahead of his rivals. "He has an incredible ability to look into the future and see what people need before they know they need it," said John Tory, leader of the Ontario Progressive Conservative Party.

BEST DECISION
Investing in mobile communication through a private company.

FOLLOWING IN HIS FATHER'S FOOTSTEPS
The untimely death at 38 of Ted Rogers, Sr., the inventor of the batteryless radio and founder of the CFRB Toronto radio station, left his five-year-old son with a burning ambition to follow in his father's professional footsteps. Although most of the family's business, including the radio station, was sold off, Ted Jr's interest continued. In 1960, Rogers bought CHFI, Canada's first FM radio station, ignoring the fact that few Canadians had FM access at the time. He later acquired an AM station, revamped it as a rock station, and took it to the top of the ratings. In 1967, Rogers spotted the niche for cable television, acquiring Bramalea Telecable (renamed Rogers Cable TV). After a chance discussion with a cable engineer, Rogers became convinced that mobile communication was the next big thing.

However, his enthusiasm was not shared by other members of the board, so Rogers, undeterred, made the initial investment into wireless through a private company.

BRANCHING OUT
Throughout the 1980s and 1990s, Rogers risked millions (money that he often did not have) in his drive to expand the company. As well as acquiring his first television station—CFMT—and buying more radio stations, Rogers invested heavily in the internet and home phone service, opened video and DVD rental outlets, and bought an interest in some 70-odd magazines. In 1994, in what was then the largest buyout in Canadian history, he acquired communications company Maclean-Hunter. In the last decade, RCI has gone from strength to strength, and Rogers has become a telecommunications legend.

LESSONS IN BUSINESS: BEING PREPARED TO TAKE RISKS

Rogers was an insatiable risk taker, risking his neck to see his vision through. Going millions into personal debt may not be ideal, but he proved that if the stakes are high, then the rewards may be worth the risk.
→ Make sure you really believe in your product. Change it until you do, then take the promotion and marketing risks to grow dramatically.
→ How much risk are you willing to take? If you won't bet your house, don't expect major rewards.
→ Remember that staying small but safe is a viable business strategy but a limited one in terms of success.

"[Rogers] was a very fierce competitor. He believed in momentum. Getting it. Building it. Keeping it."
Alek Krstajic, former RCI executive

Abdullah S. Jum'ah President & CEO (1995–2008), Saudi Aramco

WHEN THE United States-led coalition invaded Saddam Hussein's Iraq in 2003, its key ally was Jum'ah—the CEO of Saudi Aramco and the only man who could keep the world's oil flowing while Iraq's infrastructure was being destroyed in the crossfire. His assurance that the world's largest oil company would fill the gap made the invasion of Iraq a viable option. By investing in exploration and processing, and entering into various joint ventures, he has moved the state-owned company into a seemingly unassailable position.

BIOGRAPHY
Born in Al Khoba, Saudi Arabia, in 1941. Jum'ah studied political science at Cairo and Beirut Universities before joining Saudi Aramco. He completed Harvard Business School's Program for Management Development.

LEADERSHIP STYLE
Urbane, strategic, and eclectic. Jum'ah has used his political and business leadership skills to consolidate the company's position as the world's largest oil producer and most important petro-chemical firm.

KEY STRENGTH
His ability to assess his own company's weaknesses and strengths, and to harness them to maximum advantage.

BEST DECISION
Diversifying the company from oil extraction into refining, petro-chemicals, marketing, and distribution.

A BROAD KNOWLEDGE Jum'ah joined Aramco's government affairs department in 1968 as the first step in a tour of duty that took him through almost all the company's key departments before his appointment as CEO. He oversaw its publications, managed a department in its power systems division, and was in charge of its industrial relations before being made head of its international operations. By the time he took the big chair in 1995, he had a complete grounding in almost every aspect of the company's business.

UPSTREAM AND DOWNSTREAM Not content with controlling 25 percent of the world's oil reserves, Jum'ah strove to maximize Aramco's potential by doing more to exploit refined products and petrochemicals. Drawing on his experience in employee relations, he set up a training institute to reduce the company's dependence on foreign engineers. In 1998, Shell and Aramco (by then called the Saudi Arabian Oil Company, or Saudi Aramco) signed a 50:50 joint venture deal in Motiva, a refinery and distribution company to supply diesel, gas, LPG, aviation fuel, and lubricants throughout the southern states of America. In 2004, it earned $24 billion in revenues. In 2001 and 2003, Jum'ah opened two new gas plants to exploit Saudi Arabia's vast and under-exploited gas reserves, and in May 2004 he signed a $4-billion deal with Japan's Sumimoto Corporation to develop a major petrochemical plant. At every step he maximized the company's resources.

After 40 years with the company, Abdullah Jum'ah retired as president and CEO of Saudi Aramco at the end of 2008.

LESSONS IN BUSINESS: EXPLOITING KNOWLEDGE

With a solid grounding in every aspect of Aramco's business, Jum'ah knew where the company needed to be. He realized that by raising skills and making acquisitions, Aramco could take a larger slice of the cake.
- → Consider areas of business where you and your company have knowledge. Work out what other activities that knowledge makes possible.
- → Use SWOT analysis, identifying strengths, weaknesses, opportunities and threats, at the start of planning.
- → Remember that studying your industry, the economy, and business generally will always pay dividends.

"Energy is the prime mover of world economies, and indeed of our civilization." Abdullah S. Jum'ah

Ratan Tata Chairman & CEO, Tata Group

THE COMPANY headed by Tata has almost single-handedly built Indian industry. Initially mill owners, the group now includes India's largest software house and one of its most prestigious hotel chains (the Taj), as well as steel and car production. The success of the Tata Group, India's largest conglomerate, is largely down to Tata's courageous and principled management strategies, and yet Ratan himself does not appear on any rich list; the Tata family owns just one percent of the holding company.

BIOGRAPHY
Born in Bombay (Mumbai), India, in 1937. Tata trained as an architect at Cornell University, New York State, and took a management course at Harvard.

LEADERSHIP STYLE
Audacious, dignified, and philanthropic. One of Tata's first principles in business is to be bold but to "do no harm."

KEY STRENGTH
The ability to think globally. Tata has transformed a lumbering, bureaucratic, Empire-era conglomerate into a dynamic world player.

BEST DECISION
Deciding that Tata Group should make its own cars. Critics said it was a vanity project, but Tata Motors is now India's second biggest car maker.

A SLOW STARTER Early business failures in the Tata Group's electronics and mill interests did not mark Ratan out for a starring role. Indeed, when he succeeded his uncle, J. R. D. Tata, as chairman in 1991, few expected the group to survive the challenges of liberalization. By trimming the group's 300 "fiefdoms" and removing managers who didn't share his "global not local" vision, Tata reinvented the company.

GLOBAL PLAYER Today, the Tata Group has the largest market capitalization of any business house on the Indian Stock Market. His ambitious global acquisition spree began in 2000 with the takeover of Tetley Tea. The 2007 purchase of Anglo-Dutch steel giant Corus for $13 billion was the biggest takeover of a foreign company by an Indian corporate,

marking his arrival as a truly global player. It is often said that Tata's heart is in the motor industry. Famously media shy, Tata was propelled into the spotlight in 2008 with his bold takeover of prestige British brands Jaguar and Rover, a move that was branded as "reverse colonialism." In 1998 he launched the Indica, the first totally Indian car. With typically unwavering belief in his project to create a people's car, Tata proved sceptics wrong in 2008 with the launch of the "one lakh" (about $2,150) car, the Tata Nano.

Under Tata's leadership, the group has set a standard for corporate responsibility. As well as providing housing, education, and medical care to employees, the company plows over two thirds of profits into trusts that finance good causes. Unusually in India, the company is known to be incorruptible.

LESSONS IN BUSINESS: PUTTING SOMETHING BACK

Tata believes passionately in using his company's growth for the betterment of his employees' lives and the community at large. He believes the company's long-term position and influence depend on this approach, and that shareholders will prosper in such a regime.

→ Avoid all corrupt activities even when times are difficult and temptation is high.

→ Obey your instincts when they tell you that what you are being offered is too good to be true.

→ Make sure your company listens to the community around it and contributes to its well-being.

"Mr. Tata encourages us to take big, calculated risk." Ravi Kant, managing director, Tata Motors

Ruben K. Vardanyan President & CEO, Troika Dialog

AT THE TENDER AGE OF 29, it is a remarkable achievement to be nominated CEO of the largest private investment bank in Russia, and tasked with managing some $3 billion in assets. Yet Troika Dialog's new CEO, Vardanyan, already had a track record. Since his appointment to the post in 1992, his performance and reputation have made him one of the leading figures in Russia's capital markets, and one of the first Russians to have joined the global rich lists, with a fortune estimated at more than $1 billion.

BIOGRAPHY
Born in Yerevan, the capital of Armenia, in the then Soviet Union, in 1968. Vardanyan graduated from Moscow State University with a degree in economics. He subsequently took courses at the University of Harvard, and INSEAD (the European Institute for Business Administration), Paris.

LEADERSHIP STYLE
Visionary, principled, people-focused. Vardanyan has said that Russia's future lies in its people, not its oil and gas.

KEY STRENGTH
What sets Vardanyan apart from his contemporaries is his vision that Russia will become part of the global world. He believes that foreign companies will invest in Russia, which will create business opportunities for Russians to provide services for them.

BEST DECISION
Applying international banking standards in Russia, with the emphasis on transparency.

AN OUTSTANDING STUDENT In early 1991, US businessman Peter Derby founded Troika Dialog, and set out to recruit staff from Russian universities. Moscow State University sent him just one candidate, but tipped off Derby that their student was outstanding. That was 22-year-old Vardanyan, a man with exceptionally high ethical standards that matched those of Derby and his then-partner, Bernard Sucher. This quality enabled Troika Dialog to set an example as a notably transparent and ethical business, at a time when this was not the norm.

EXPLOSIVE GROWTH After being made CEO in 1992, Vardanyan supported numerous business start-ups to great effect. Growth over the next decade was explosive: from an initial investment of just $35,000, Troika Dialog grew to more than $36 million in assets by 2002. That

year, Vardanyan expanded into Russia's growing insurance markets with the acquisition of Rosgosstrakh, the Soviet-era monopoly provider of insurance; he grew premiums from $200 million to $1.3 billion by 2005. Vardanyan's unrelenting insistence on the highest ethical standards led to his nomination to numerous significant positions, including director with the Bank of Moscow, board member of the National Association of Stock Market Participants (NAUFOR), which controls the development of Russia's capital markets' infrastructure, and director of the Russian Trading System (RTS stock exchange). A raft of awards includes a nomination from the World Economic Forum as one of the "100 Global Leaders for Tomorrow." Troika Dialog continues to thrive and Vardanyan predicts that business will grow by an average of 35 percent in revenues per annum.

LESSONS IN BUSINESS: BEING OPEN AND HONEST

To differentiate his firm from the competition, Vardanyan has stuck to his core principles, and his long-term focus on client services is underpinned by the highest standards of ethical, responsible business.
→ Respect yourself, your people, your country, competitors and clients. In return you will earn their respect.
→ Build a culture where your people are open and honest by being open and honest yourself.
→ Bear in mind that the financial downturn, prompted by the sub-prime crisis, emphasized yet again that maintaining high ethical standards pays off in the long term.

"In the 20th century, it was about industrial assets and natural resources. In the 21st century, the main fight will be for the best people." Ruben K. Vardanyan

Steven Roth CEO, Vornado Realty Trust

ONCE DUBBED the "strip mall king of New Jersey", Roth is now a major property owner in New York's midtown Manhattan. Self-styled "greedy man" Roth took control of Vornado Realty Trust in 1980 and has turned it into the second largest real estate investment trust in the US. With more than a billion dollars safely in the bank, Roth doesn't need to worry about money any more, but that hasn't stopped him from looking for the next great property deal as he continues to acquire prime real estate in the US.

BIOGRAPHY
Born in 1941. Roth gained his AB degree at Dartmouth College, New Hampshire, and his MBA at Dartmouth's Amos Tuck School of Business Administration, passing with the highest distinction in 1963.

LEADERSHIP STYLE
Bullish, energetic, and inspirational, Roth is both feared and admired.

KEY STRENGTH
Spotting the potential in property deals, and thinking big.

BEST DECISION
Changing retail company Vornado into a property real estate developer by shutting Two Guys.

SEEING THE POTENTIAL Roth's road to real estate domination began in 1968 when he founded Interstate Properties with partner David Mandelbaum. The company bought New Jersey retail chain Two Guys in the 1970s and later also acquired its parent company Vornado. Roth saw more potential in developing the properties occupied by the Two Guys stores than in keeping the struggling chain in operation, and when he took control of Vornado in 1980 he closed down the stores and converted the space into strip malls.

BUILDING UP Roth repeated this process in 1995 after acquiring Alexander's, another floundering retail company. Among its many real estate holdings, Alexander's included one of the most sought-after parcels of land in Manhattan. Roth erected a $630-million,

56-story building on the site, complete with 100 luxury condos, and space for Bloomberg LP and H&M. Off-record, Roth is said to have announced his intention "to become the largest owner of commercial real estate in New York." With this in mind, Vornado spent more than $2 billion in the late 1990s on properties in Manhattan's West 30s. The company also purchased Manhattan Mall on Sixth Avenue for $689 million in 2006.

Roth's shrewd and bullish behavior in New York real estate has increased Vornado's market capitalization from $100 million in 1980 to over $14 billion. The company now controls over 18 square feet of retail, office, and public space in US cities, including the $7-billion redevelopment of Madison Square Graden and Penn Station, a collaboration with Related's Steve Ross.

LESSONS IN BUSINESS: IF THE TIME IS RIGHT, KEEP EXPANDING

Not content with owning a whole host of lucrative shopping centers, Roth's shrewd and bullish behavior pushed Vornado to buy into Manhattan's commercial market.
→ Take advantage of bull markets but take care that when asset prices decline you have enough reserves to wait for the uptick.
→ Use gearing or borrowing to buy assets, but don't let it get out of control. Increase share capital too.
→ Make sure you know what business you are in. If you have become a property company, tell the world.

"Steve Roth is an exceptional industry leader."
Steven A. Wechsler, president and CEO, NAREIT

TURNING THE COMPANY GREEN

In recent years, the environment has been making business headlines and, increasingly, companies from all industries are recognizing that pursuing green policies makes sound financial sense as well as good PR. The varying costs of energy and materials are encouraging many companies to aggressively pursue supply reduction policies, or to embrace sustainable power supplies such as wind, wave, and biofuels. Similarly, the increasing cost of dealing with waste has led to some surprising zero-waste targets.

CEOs like **Takeo Fukui** (p157) at Honda have demonstrated to the world the importance of taking risks and investigating new technological avenues, as people turn to energy-efficient vehicles. Fukui has been a key developer in the field since designing the first automobile to meet the US Clean Air Act without an expensive catalytic converter, proving that environmentalism could also have a notable economic competitive advantage. Meanwhile, in the even more emissions-heavy aviation industry, **Lawrence Kellner** (p86), CEO of Continental Airlines, has stressed his desire to see the company cut its carbon footprint and switch to sustainable fuels to keep us all flying ethically. Under Kellner, the company was the first to complete a US demonstration flight of an aircraft powered by jatropha-based biofuel. Green strategies are not and never have been, simply a luxury. They may well mean survival ●

Green to the Core

Turning an established company green is about making a coherent argument for change within the business. Many CEOs are seeing the sense, both financial and social, in moving toward ethical, ecological, and sustainable business practices. While greenwashing, the spinning of company practice into appearing to have ethical integrity, is prevalent, an ever-increasing number of executives are taking the lead and making genuinely ground-breaking efforts to green their businesses; discovering in the process that, far from being incompatible, environmentalism and conventional business models can strike up a profitable partnership.

Companies relying on exhaustible and depleting resources have extra incentives for adopting an ecological standpoint. **Jan Johansson**, CEO of Swedish wood and paper products company SCA, knows the importance of sustainability for long-term survival in big business. Under his leadership, SCA uses a greater recycled content in its paper products than any other producer in Europe, and has invested heavily in sustainable forestry. As Johansson has pointed out, the world's substantial CO_2 problems could be solved if all countries adopted Sweden's model of productive forestry; SCA's forests have an annual growth that exceeds rates of felling.

Retail businesses engaged in the burgeoning fairtrade market also need to maintain impeccable green standards to keep their ethically-minded customers on board. Working to alleviate poverty in developing nations, they need to demonstrate that what is sustainable economically can also be sustainable environmentally. **Annie MacCaig**'s ethical credentials were notable enough to bring her to the attention of Fairtrade company Cafédirect, now the sixth largest consumer brand in the UK, when they were seeking a new CEO. As marketing director at beverages company Ribena, she was instrumental in arguing for green initiatives and successfully pushed for a change to 100 percent recycled bottles, an important factor in the company's decision to give her the job. MacCaig has applied her green business brain at Cafédirect by deepening the company's commitment to promoting organic methods of production, and has worked to lower carbon emissions across the business.

"We'd like to have the brand image as the world's biggest contributor to the environment." TAKEO FUKUI

Going Green

Argue the economic case— Sell greening your company to the board by proposing it as a long-term investment that reduces risk.

Avoid "greenwashing"— Token green gestures are not enough. Embed environmental values prominently in your core long-term strategy.

Communicate the strategy to staff—A firm's green approach often improves employee morale.

Measure your efforts—Employ professionals to audit and evaluate activities across the business for their green credentials.

Green Activists

The following CEOs have sought significant green development within their companies:

José Manuel Entrecanales, Acciona SA (Construction and energy: Spain)—*His leadership has transformed a construction company into a world leader in renewable energy and other environmental solutions.*

Dirk Meyer, Advanced Micro Devices (IT: US) – *The Silicon Valley chipmaker has achieved colossal reductions in their greenhouse gas emissions.*

Frank Chapman, BG Group (Energy: UK)—*Firm commitment to sustainability and ethical behavior at this natural gas company.*

Ian Livingston, BT Group (Telecommunications: UK)—*Livingston is committed to his predecessor* **Ben Verwaayen**'s *(p124) aim to dramatically reduce the company's carbon footprint.*

James H. Quigley, Deloitte (Finance: US)—*Quigley has insisted on greater use of teleconferencing instead of air travel.*

Satoshi Seino, East Japan Railway Company (Railroads: Japan)—*Seino has set a company target to reduce CO_2 emissions by 50 percent by 2030.*

Greg Clarke, Lend Lease (Construction: Australia)—*Clarke has committed the company to targets of zero net carbon, water, and waste.*

Mark Constantine, Lush (Retail: UK)—*Has significantly reduced packaging on its cosmetic products with a range of innovative approaches.*

Herbert Fisk Johnson III, S. C. Johnson (Consumer products: US)—*This family firm, headed by the founder's great-great-grandson, now sources 40 percent of its global electricity from renewable sources.*

Jouko Karvinen, Stora Enso (Paper products: Finland)—*Karvinen has committed the company to a rigorous environmental strategy, including a 20 percent reduction in CO_2 emissions by 2020.*

Tim Mead, Yeo Valley (Foodstuffs: UK)—*Intelligent and thoughtful approach to sustainability in the dairy business is reflected in its green waste policies at every stage of the business process.*

John Mackey Chairman & CEO, Whole Foods Market

BY TAKING a niche activity and transforming it into a rapidly expanding business with global possibilities, Mackey turned conventional business thinking upside down. The organic food company that he began in Austin, Texas, has become the food retailing phenomenon of the US, breaking the rules of retailing not only in the kind of products it sells but also in the business model it adopts and in its approach to employee involvement and motivation. Whole Foods Market has extended both the range and the availability of organic food.

BIOGRAPHY
Born in Houston, Texas, in 1953. While studying philosophy and religion at the University of Texas at Austin, Mackey joined a vegetarian co-op where he met Renee Lawson Hardy, with whom he opened the first Texan organic supermarket.

LEADERSHIP STYLE
Down-to-earth and accessible. Mackey made employee input a key part of his approach to business from the outset. A sign of his style is that he reduced his own salary to $1 a year in 2006.

KEY STRENGTH
Reconciling a moral perspective with commercial imperatives.

BEST DECISION
Broadening his range beyond vegetarian products, providing much greater scope for growth while still ensuring quality and ethical sourcing.

ORGANIC ENTREPRENEUR The organic supermarket that Mackey opened with his girlfriend in 1978 could easily have been ill-fated. No matter how good the intention, counter-cultural idealism rarely extends to good business management. However, Mackey's rare combination of dedication to an alternative sector and commercial expertise, saw Whole Foods Market emerge from its difficult early years, assuming an ideal position to profit from a dramatic change in consumer tastes.

PRINCIPLES PLUS GROWTH From the beginning, Mackey ensured the survival of his business by combining his commitment to organic principles with flexibility and ruthless control of production and costs. He widened the range of products available to include meat and alcohol, but retained an emphasis on ethical and organic sourcing, supporting small-scale suppliers. Staff were motivated by egalitarian pay structures and a say in the business. Expanding by buying smaller, rival operations and incorporating them, he achieved the kind of growth sought by more conventional retailers. He held out against the bigger-means-cheaper model of conventional retailers and emphasized quality, being prepared to charge the higher prices that excellence and sound sourcing demanded. It was a radical business model, but it succeeded, playing a key part in putting organic food on the mainstream menu. Whole Foods was well placed to benefit from the consumer backlash against "big food" in the 1990s, when the percentage of organic food consumers in the US doubled; Whole Foods Market's sales rose by an average 32 percent a year.

LESSONS IN BUSINESS: PRIORITIZING ETHICS

Cutting prices isn't the only way to pull in customers. If people really care about the moral aspects of a product and you can offer them the kind of quality they're looking for, they will be prepared to pay for it.
→ Pay close attention to the energy efficiency of your operation and publicize what your divisions are doing to help the planet.
→ Source your materials locally when possible; the local market will repay your thoughtfulness.
→ Make sure you understand the situation of the people who make your products in foreign countries.

"There's a movement in our society toward higher quality." John Mackey

Nancy McKinstry CEO, Wolters Kluwer

WHEN SHE BECAME CEO of Dutch publisher Wolters Kluwer—a specialist in accounting, legal, and health products, McKinstry inherited a company in seriously bad shape. It had just turned in the worst year's figures in its history, and some analysts regarded its chances of recovery as minimal. But within three years of moving to Amsterdam from New York, McKinstry had knocked the jaded company back into shape, restored growth to all of its various divisions, and doubled its share price.

BIOGRAPHY
Born in Middleton, Connecticut, in 1959. Her mother was a schoolteacher and her father a banker. She received a bachelor's degree in economics from the University of Rhode Island and an MBA from Columbia University.

LEADERSHIP STYLE
Informal analytical, and communicative. McKinstry believes in constant contact with staff and customers. She holds regular town-hall meetings with rank-and-file employees.

KEY STRENGTH
Being innovative at the same time as being a hard cost-cutter.

BEST DECISION
Focusing on the core strengths of the business and getting rid of everything else.

THE INSIDER McKinstry came to the top job at Wolters Kluwer as the classic company insider. Apart from a brief stint at a different business in the late 90s, she had spent more than a decade working for the company and its subsidiaries in North America. Although taking over as CEO in 2003 meant moving her base to The Netherlands, she already knew the company from the bottom up.

CUTS PLUS INNOVATION Despite her experience, McKinstry faced a formidable task when she moved into the hot seat. The heart of her plan was a wide-ranging restructuring program that focused on what the company was best at. That meant the laying off of 2,000 staff and the divestment of unrelated non-core businesses, such as management services provider ISBW. Going sharply against the trend in the publishing industry, which was all for consolidation, McKinstry made it clear that she intended to keep Wolters Kluwer independent and to strengthen the company by focusing on building its brands with its core customers, such as doctors, lawyers, and accountants. Within that focus, she then began expanding the reach of the company's portfolio of print and internet publishing properties. She introduced innovative electronic products and made a series of well-judged acquisitions, some in key markets such as Russia and Germany.

McKinstry also restructured the company's operations, turning what had been a very decentralized set of businesses into a more centralized group integrated in line with the different markets they served. The result was a highly successful turnaround, returning growth and profitability to Wolters Kluwer.

LESSONS IN BUSINESS: CONFRONTING THE IMPOSSIBLE

No matter how gloomy the situation may look, there will be a solution. It may need some fresh thinking and hard decisions, but finding the right elements and bringing them together can crack even the toughest nuts.
- ➔ Going through the situation in a step-by-step process often uncovers at least the start of the solution.
- ➔ Realize that a combination of old-fashioned cost cutting, enterprising innovation, and strong market knowledge can work wonders.
- ➔ Promote from within to keep a comprehensive body of market knowledge at the top of the company.

"There aren't any unsolvable problems." Nancy McKinstry

Anna Christina Ramos Saicali President & CEO, B2W

BIOGRAPHY
Born in São Paulo, Brazil, in 1963. Saicali studied at Mackenzie Presbyterian Univeristy, São Paulo, and the Univeristy of São Paulo.

BEST DECISION
Seeing through the merger of retailers Americanos.com and Submarino to create B2W— profits have been increasing ever since.

LESSON IN BUSINESS
Fight your corner—Saicali defended her company from the incoming threat of competition from multinational retailers by instigating a merger to create a super-retail presence in Brazil.

STRONG-MINDED and gutsy, Saicali, CEO of Brazilian retailers B2W, has consistently developed successful strategies to fight off the threat of competition from global rivals, while building up a national force to be reckoned with.

Following a period as director of HR at discount retailers Lojas Americanas, Saicali became CEO of Americanos.com, the company's e-commerce subsidiary, in 2004. In 2006, she oversaw its merger with internet store Submarino, creating B2W Companhia Global do Varejo, where she became co-CEO with since-departed Submarino co-founder and CEO, Flavio Jansen. The merger paid off—in 2007 B2W, which sells books, toys, mobile phones, and hardware, saw a 46 percent increase in gross revenues to R$3.6 billion. Since then, Saicali's strategy has been to improve B2W's position in the Brazilian retail market, fighting off growing competition from multinationals. She has invested heavily, and 2007 saw R$140 million plowed into growing the company, including the acquisition of the Blockbuster licence for internet rental and sales operations in Brazil, and the development of a DVD and film rental download service. Saicali has since seen gross profits reach R$672 million, rising by more than third since she took over.

Werner Wenning Chairman & CEO, Bayer

BIOGRAPHY
Born in Leverkusen-Opladen, Germany, in 1946. Wenning opted to join a Bayer commercial training program in 1966, rather than go to college.

BEST DECISION
Splitting Bayer in half in 2003, allowing the company to refocus on its core values, a bold move rewarded by an immediate increase in Bayer's share value.

LESSON IN BUSINESS
Concentrate on the task in hand—Wenning has always devoted his full attention to his current job, believing that everything else will follow on

WIDELY ADMIRED for his decisive leadership style since taking over as CEO of German pharmaceutical company Bayer in 2002, Wenning is perceived to be reinventing the company at which he has spent more than 40 years.

Wenning started his career with Bayer in 1966 before working for the company in Lima, Peru, in 1970 where he successfully set up and ran the finance and accounting department of Bayer Industrial SA. After further spells in Germany, Spain, and Peru, he was made CFO in 1997. Wenning introduced a strategy of "value management", squeezing maximum value from spending, but by 2001 Bayer was suffering huge losses, largely due to legal problems over a drug, Baycol. Impressed by his decision-making abilities and perseverance as CFO, the board made Wenning CEO in 2002. He implemented a number of new measures, including a restructure that split the pharmaceutical and chemical divisions. This enabled Bayer to focus on health care, agrochemicals, and material sciences, while the lower-earning chemical unit became a new company. In 2006, Wenning acquired pharmaceuticals firm Schering for nearly €17 billion. He is approachable, and appears to enjoy being the public face of Bayer.

> "Innovation and growth are the keys to success in a globalized world." Werner Wenning

Laurent Beaudoin CEO (1979–99, 2004–08), Bombardier Inc.

BIOGRAPHY
Born in Laurier Station, Canada, in 1938. Beaudoin received a master's in commerce at the University of Sherbrooke, Québec.

BEST DECISION
Transforming Bombardier from a snow machine company to a transportation company that builds snowmobiles, boats, trains, and airplanes.

LESSON IN BUSINESS
Work as a team—Beaudoin demonstrated the importance of developing a good team, motivating and listening to colleagues, and making things happen in business.

THE SON-IN-LAW of Joseph Armand Bombardier, who founded a company making snow-going machinery for rural Québec, Beaudoin expanded Bombardier beyond all expectations, transforming it into a global train and plane manufacturer.

Beaudoin joined Bombardier as a comptroller when he was 25 years old, and was promoted to president three years later in 1966. He foresaw the popularity of snowmobiles, and expanded the company's small manufacturing operation to fit his vision. Immediately after becoming CEO and chairman in 1979, Beaudoin diversified the company further by building trains for Montreal's new subway. In 1986, he spearheaded the company's entry into aeronautics, acquiring Canadair in Québec, Learjet in the United States, De Havilland in Ontario, and Shorts in Northern Ireland. Bombardier became the third-largest producer of civil aircraft, after Boeing and Airbus. In 1999 Beaudoin stepped down as CEO, but returned five years later to help the company through the downturn in the airline industry following the events of 9/11. Bombardier went from strength to strength, with strong demand for its fuel-efficient turboprops. In 2008, Beaudoin stepped down a second time.

Cem Boyner Chairman & CEO, Boyner Holdings AS

BIOGRAPHY
Born in the Black Sea town of Tosya, Turkey, in 1955. Boyner is the son of a textiles magnate. He studied business administration at Bosphorus University.

BEST DECISION
Moving his family firm into a new market with the launch of T-box in 2004, providing affordable, humorous clothing and accessories in a box.

LESSON IN BUSINESS
Maximize your assets—Boyner cemented a 20-year-old license agreement with Benetton into a true partnership in 2005, to the benefit of both companies.

EITHER SIDE of a brief spell in politics, the fluent English- and German-speaking Boyner has served as CEO of his family's firm, Boyner Holdings AS, Turkey's leading textile retail group.

In 1978, Boyner joined the family business, a traditional textile operation more than 200 years old, initially working at the firm's manufacturing business, Altinyildiz. In 1982, he was appointed CEO of Boyner Holdings, which, in addition to Altinyildiz, encompassed luxury retailer Beymen, sole distributor in Turkey of brands such as Prada, D&G, and Fendi; Boyner department stores; and Benetton Turkey, a joint venture with Benetton International. In 1994, Boyner's political ambitions led him to chair The New Democracy Movement, a reformist political party that he had co-founded in 1993. Three years later he left politics and returned to Boyner Holdings AS as vice-chairman and CEO. Over the next decade, Boyner exploited the favorable economic climate in Turkey to build upon the Boyner brand name. Since 2003, this has included expanding Boyner Stores through a franchise system, and the launch of the T-box product range.

"I can't tell you what the worst day in my life taught me. I don't live in the past... I look forward. If I look too far back, who knows what I'll see." Laurent Beaudoin

Mark P. Mays President & CEO, Clear Channel Communications, Inc.

BIOGRAPHY
Born in 1964. Mays holds a bachelor's in mathematics and economics from Vanderbilt University, Tennesee, and an MBA from Columbia Business School, New York.

BEST DECISION
Realizing that radio giant Clear Channel had to change both its image, and its approach, to thrive in the digital age.

LESSON IN BUSINESS
Change when you have to—Clear Channel had a winning way with acquisitions, but it had its limits. Mays found a new way forward.

TO COMPETE in the new digital age, Mays knew his father's global media and entertainment company, Clear Channel Communications, was in need of a serious overhaul. As CEO, he set about the task in earnest.

After graduation, Mays worked for an investment bank and for broadcaster CapCities, before joining Clear Channel in 1989. Founded in 1972 by L. Lowry Mays, Mark's father, Clear Channel began as a radio group, and expanded by acquiring stations before moving into TV, billboards, and live shows. By 1997, when Mays became a director, the company had become a major force in US radio and entertainment. However, when he took over as president and CEO in 2004, Clear Channel faced new challenges: listeners were switching to MP3 players and advertisers to the internet. Spinning off the entertainment and billboard businesses, Mays focused on new media content (digital radio and podcasts) and licensing deals with Yahoo!, Apple, and Microsoft. He also cut down on ads as a proportion of airtime, hoping to hold the grasshopper-like attention of modern listeners more effectively. Mays' role oversees company operations in over 65 countries.

Antonio M. Perez Chairman & CEO, Eastman Kodak Company

BIOGRAPHY
Born in the fishing village of Vi_o, Spain. Perez studied electronic engineering at Madrid University but left before graduating.

BEST DECISION
Making the Kodak name synonymous with easily accessible digital images.

LESSON IN BUSINESS
Get your best people on board—Perez gained leadership credibility throughout his organization by assembling a committee of sceptics, and listening to their criticisms.

ONE OF A GROWING number of leading Hispanic CEOs, risk-taker Perez spearheaded a transformation of photographic film company Eastman Kodak, moving the business from paper to digital, and from film to pixels.

When Perez joined Eastman Kodak as president and COO in 2003, he built on a 25-year career at Hewlett-Packard. A digital revolution was taking place, but the company's management had failed to capitalize on it. Consequently Perez was forced to close film factories and cut around 28,000 jobs worldwide. Promoted to CEO in 2005, he set about making the existing, innovative Kodak technology more accessible, introducing a new range of digital services for customers. Just as Apple had revolutionized the music business, Perez aimed to provide services, such as online photo sharing and rapid scanning, to help consumers organize and arrange their image libraries. Perez has had to overcome resistance to his changes from within the company, which has led him to replace the majority of top management with executives from outside the company. The transformation has seen the introduction of new products, including inkjet printers, sensors for cell phones, and retail printing kiosks.

"When the electricity didn't work, when television didn't work, when the Internet didn't work, when pay radio didn't work, free radio worked." Mark P. Mays

Dale Vince Founder & MD, Ecotricity

BIOGRAPHY
Born in Great Yarmouth, UK, in 1961. Vince left school at the age of 15 and claims never to have had a "proper job".

BEST DECISION
Persisting with his scheme to supply wind power to the national grid, which eventually proved that renewable energy could be a viable business.

LESSON IN BUSINESS
Maintain integrity—Vince has emphasized and demonstrated time and again that you don't have to betray your beliefs to succeed in business.

A FORMER PEACE ACTIVIST, Vince is the founder and owner of renewable energy company Ecotricity. One of a new generation of green entrepreneurs, Vince is boss of the seventh-largest retail supplier of electricity in the UK.

Leading a simple, vegan lifestyle and with a background as a new-age traveler, Vince isn't a typical executive. He made the transformation from hippy drop-out to boss of a £100-million utility company in double quick time. Vince built his first wind turbine when living rough in the back of a truck, and had his first brush with entrepreneurship when he offered to sell wind power to his electricity supplier. Undeterred by their amusement, Vince persisted and began supplying the grid. He set up the Renewable Energy Company in 1995 (now renamed Ecotricity), expanding the company's wind turbine capacity with money borrowed from Dutch-based ethical bank Triodos. Despite continual confrontation with planners and grid companies, Vince has constructed 12 percent of Britain's wind turbines, and Ecotricity became Britain's seventh-biggest retail electricity company, supplying 50 percent green electricity to 35,000 customers, and promising to reinvest all profits in new wind schemes.

Juliet Davenport CEO, Good Energy

BIOGRAPHY
Born in the UK in 1968. Davenport has a degree in physics from Oxford University. She studied environmental economics at Birkbeck College, London.

BEST DECISION
Founding Good Energy in 2002, anticipating the explosion of interest in alternative energy sources that was to follow.

LESSON IN BUSINESS
Green is good—the success of Good Energy has proven that "alternative" energy has the potential to go mainstream, make a difference, and make a profit.

A PHYSICIST CONCERNED by climate change, Davenport turned a personal commitment to climate issues into a thriving business when she founded Good Energy, the UK renewable energy provider.

Davenport tuned in to the importance of climate change as an undergraduate, and focused her studies on atmospheric physics. She worked for the European Commission in Brussels, concentrating on energy policy and became convinced of the need for western economies to lead the way on climate change. Davenport returned to the UK to consult for the British government on renewables. In 1997 she helped set up Good Energy to offer "alternative" energy to consumers willing to pay a little more for their ethics. She became CEO in 2002. Good Energy derives most of its power from wind, plus some small-scale hydroelectric and solar sources. It is the only company in the UK to get 100 percent of its electrical energy from renewable sources. Ranked as the UK's greenest electricity supplier by the National Consumer Council, Good Energy also encourages people to generate their own electricity. By 2008 the company had over 25,000 customers.

"[Vince] is not a hippy when it comes to a deal. He's as hard-nosed as any businessman."

Paul Monaghan, head of ethics and sustainable development, The Co-operative Bank

Daniel Servitje CEO, Grupo Bimbo

BIOGRAPHY
Born in 1959 in Mexico. Servitje received a BA in business administration from Ibero-American University, Mexico, and an MBA from Stanford University.

BEST DECISION
Breaking away from tradition and transforming the secretive image of the company by hiring a public relations firm for the first time in its history.

LESSON IN BUSINESS
Expand your horizons—Servitje has positioned a family-run Mexican company firmly into the 21st century by looking beyond the domestic arena.

THROUGH A SERIES of major expansions and shrewd acquisitions, Servitje, CEO of Mexican-based Grupo Bimbo, has turned a national bakery outfit into one of the world's largest baked goods companies.

The youngest son of a founder of Grupo Bimbo, Servitje joined the bakery company in 1978 and gradually worked his way through the ranks. Prior to taking over as CEO from his uncle in 1997, he was responsible for Latin American operations and president of the Marinela baked goods division. Keen to expand into the US Hispanic market, Servitje bought Texas-based Mrs. Baird's Bakeries, Inc. for $250 million in 1998, taking the company's annual sales in the US to some $600 million, virtually overnight.

Further acquisitions included Brazilian firm Plus Vita for $65 million, and the US subsidiary of Canada's George Weston Ltd for $2.4 billion, making Grupo Bimbo one of the world's largest baked food companies. Servitje also expanded into Europe with chocolate factories in Austria and the Czech Republic. By 2002, he had more than tripled sales, particularly through increased exports. With the objective of making Grupo Bimbo the world's largest bread manufacturing company, Servitje plans to expand into China.

Luis Frias Chairman & CEO, Grupo Folha UOL

BIOGRAPHY
Born in 1964. Frias was one of four children of publishing magnate Octavio Frias de Oliveira. He studied at the University of São Paulo, Cambridge University, UK, and the Sorbonne, France.

BEST DECISION
Catching the crest of the internet wave in the early 1990s, enabling Grupo Folha to launch early and carve out massive market share.

LESSON IN BUSINESS
Embrace new business models —Frias was undeterred by the technical complexities of the internet, and set out to conquer the Latin American market.

AGED JUST 25, Frias became CEO of the family-run Brazilian media giant Grupo Folha in 1989. Pioneering internet access in Brazil, in 1996 he founded Universo Online (UOL), which became the market leader in Latin America.

Frias started work at his family's newspaper, *Folha de São Paulo*, in 1981 at the age of 17 as a classified ads salesman. Sales stood at some $30 million, and *Folha*'s paid circulation was less than 150,000 copies. Frias became CEO in 1989 and chairman in 1991, and laid plans to set up internet service provider UOL. In 2005 Frias reorganized the group as Grupo Folha UOL. *Folha*'s circulation has since topped 1.5 million, and UOL has become the biggest paid internet service provider in Latin America,

with 1.2 million subscribers in Brazil and Argentina. UOL Brazil is the most visited Portuguese-language site in the world, regularly attracting 75 percent of Brazil's web users. UOL International operates in Portugal, offers Spanish-language portals in Spain and Latin America, and is developing the US Hispanic market. Since its reorganization UOL has seen steady growth, in profits. Unusually, Frias pays no dividends to family shareholders —everything is reinvested.

"In 1991, I got a feeling that the internet was going to be huge... Being the first mover in this market is more than half the battle." Luis Frias

Emilio Botín President, Santander Group

BIOGRAPHY
Born in Cantabria, Spain, in 1934. Botín's father was president of Banco Santander. Botín studied law and economics at Bilbao University.

BEST DECISION
Merging Santander with Banco Central Hispano, creating Spain's largest bank and providing a solid base for global acquisitions.

LESSON IN BUSINESS
Add value—Botín has created added value for each of his acquisitions by improving customer service, cutting costs, and minimizing risk.

ONE OF BANKING'S most charismatic leaders, Botín has transformed Banco de Santander into the world's seventh largest bank. He is a master deal-maker and a hands-on executive—an unrivaled builder of market share.

When Emilio Botín took over from his father as president of Banco Santander in 1986, the company was Spain's eighth largest bank. He launched a banking revolution, introducing new low-rate mortgages and high-rate deposit accounts. He also began a series of mergers and acquisitions that catapulted Santander to the top of the banking sector, first in 1993 when he took over Banesto Bank and, more significantly, in 1999 when he led the merger with Banco Central Hispano. Since then Botín has actively pursued takeover opportunities in Latin America. Santander is the only European bank to command a 10 percent market share in the BRIC (Brazil, Russia, India, and China) countries. In the UK in 2004 he bought Abbey National for £9.5 billion before smartly selling off its life business for £3.5 billion. In 2008, Botín took Santander's UK market share to more than 10 percent when he bought the Alliance and Leicester building society for a little over £1 billion.

David J. Lesar Chairman, President & CEO, Halliburton

BIOGRAPHY
Born in Madison, Wisconsin, in 1954. Lesar gained a BSc and an MBA from the University of Wisconsin-Madison.

BEST DECISION
Preparing Halliburton to exploit the trend toward oil services outsourcing. By 2001, this was generating 20 percent of Halliburton's revenue.

LESSON IN BUSINESS
Invest for the future—Lesar studied industry trends and invested more than $1 billion to capitalize on them.

TRANSFORMING the erstwhile mining company into an oil services giant earned Lesar more than $40 million and helped secure Halliburton a key, if controversial, role in the rebuilding of Iraq after the US-led invasion of 2003.

Although formally appointed CEO in 2000, Lesar had already been running the company for three years, while his boss, Dick Cheney, focused on courting customers and pursuing a political career that would see him elected US vice-president in 2001. Lesar identified Halliburton's biggest challenge as being the need to diversify into every area of the oil and gas industry. He predicted oil- and gas-servicing work would be increasingly outsourced, and launched a series of acquisitions and investments to ensure Halliburton was in pole position to win such business. Lesar invested more than $1 billion in new products to exploit this new market. When the US intervened militarily in Afghanistan and then Iraq, Halliburton was perfectly placed to win huge new contracts to provide troop-support logistics and reinstate oil production infrastructure, though it has faced criticism for the efficiency of its efforts. Lesar is now leading the relocation of the company's headquarters to Dubai.

"If you don't know very well your customers, don't lend them any money..." Emilio Botín

FOCUSING ON THE FUTURE

Everything changes in business. You have to stay ahead of the game, so those at the top of their field are future-focused. At the core of every good future plan, and firmly within the mind's eye of every successful CEO, is a clear vision of what the future looks like and how the company they are leading will get there. To forecast and deliver future plans, CEOs figure out which goals should be pursued and which strategies should be used with a blend of knowledge (research, trend-spotting, analysis, testing, their own experience within the market) and intuition. But it all starts with a vision.

One of the most famous and transformative visions of any CEO was that of **Henry Ford** (p23), who dreamed of creating a "car for the masses". The resulting Model T, built inexpensively using Ford's revolutionary assembly line, made personal mobility a reality for millions of people.

In 1994, **Jeff Bezos** (p48), founder and CEO of Amazon.com, saw that web usage was growing at 2,300 percent a year, which inspired his vision of the future for e-commerce. So convinced was he by this vision that he quit his well-paid job to start Amazon.com, now one of the most successful e-retailers in the world ●

Forward-thinking Strategies

Strategy is derived from the Greek word for leadership. No surprise then that CEOs excel at strategizing their future plans.

Severin Schwan, CEO of leading Swiss pharmaceutical and healthcare company Roche, uses innovation and collaboration strategies to realize his future vision of changing the direction of healthcare toward "personalized medicine" that will be tailored to the individual needs of patients.

"We see a day when treatment choices will be based on a patient's genetic makeup, not trial and error, and when treatments will be tailored to the biology of patients' diseases, not symptoms. This is our vision of personalized medicine", explains Schwan. His vision of developing personalized medicine is based on research and knowledge, and these strong foundations have informed Roche's strategy of boosting R&D spending, increasing collaboration between pharmaceuticals researchers and diagnostic teams, and targeting acquisitions to companies that produce diagnostic tools, such as genetic tests.

Schwan and Roche may be on the beginning of their journey into the future, but for **Ian Marchant**, CEO of UK firm Scottish and Southern Energy (SSE), the future has already arrived. Marchant's vision for the future is to change the face of energy supply by moving away from traditional power generation toward cleaner, greener renewable energy. This may sound like an obvious strategy, but

"Proud as we are of our past and present achievements, however, what really excites us is the future."
SEVERIN SCHWAN

Marchant spotted this key trend of alternative and renewable energy long before it even became a trend. And, crucially, Marchant has backed this vision with decisive action. Unlike his competitors, Marchant has acquired power stations, wind farms, and gas-storage facilities instead of companies. Marchant confirmed the future direction he was headed in by acquiring Irish windfarm Airtricity in 2008 for £1 billion, making SSE the UK's biggest renewable energy organization.

His future-focused drive has resulted in SSE becoming the largest company in Scotland since he became CEO with revenues of over £15 billion, while his environmental planning has saved SSE £10 million per annum in waste reduction.

"The future isn't what it used to be. A lower carbon economy is a once-in-a-generation opportunity."
IAN MARCHANT

Planning for the Future

Visualize the future—Create a mental picture of your company's destination. Where are you going and why are you heading there?

Gather knowledge—Learn from research, talking to people on the frontline, using your own and your team's combined expertise, market testing and analysis, and intuition.

Create an action plan—Detail exactly what actions need to be taken, by whom and by when in order to deliver future-focused vision-realizing results.

Leaders Leading the Way

Other CEOs known for their excellence at planning for the future and delivering their vision:

James J. O'Brien, Jr., ASHLAND (Chemicals: US)—*Built a positive future for the group by acquiring Hercules Incorporated to create a leading specialty chemicals company.*
—

Gunnar Brock, ATLAS COPCO (Manufacturing: Sweden)—*He has targeted future growth by refurbishing factories and making acquisitions in India.*
—

Zuo Xunsheng, CHINA NETCOM GROUP (Telecommunications: China)—*Zuo aims to turn China Netcom into the largest third-generation mobile telecoms operator in China.*
—

Pierre-Olivier Beckers, DELHAIZE GROUP (Foodstuffs: Belgium)—*Governs The Food Business Forum's "Future Association", which seeks to improve the way the consumer goods industry meets consumers' needs.*
—

Johannes Sittard, EURASIAN NATURAL RRESOURCES CORP. (Commodities: Netherlands / Kazakhstan)—*As CEO of the sixth largest exporter of iron ore, Sittard is constantly focusing on future trends*

and sees a "bright future ahead for commodities", with demand for natural resources higher than supply.
—

Thomas Watson, Jr., IBM (Electronics: US)—*The son of the company's founder pioneered a new system: System/360 made IBM so successful that its rivals became known as the Seven Dwarves.*
—

Ma Mingzhe, PING AN INSURANCE GROUP (Insurance: China)—*Opened the doors to foreign investors making his company one of the earliest to float successfully in Hong Kong.*
—

Katherine J. Harless President & CEO (2006–08), Idearc, Inc.

BIOGRAPHY
Born in San Angelo, Texas, in 1952. Harless has an accounting degree from the University of Texas in Austin.

BEST DECISION
Taking an all-women executive team on the road in 2006 and successfully persuading investors around the country to finance Idearc's debts of more than $9 billion.

LESSON IN BUSINESS
Don't disregard the traditional—the company's Superpages.com service continues to grow, but it is the *Yellow Pages* that still bring in the money.

PERHAPS THE BIGGEST challenges for chief executives are to be found in less dynamic, more mature business sectors. Harless is credited with successfully reinvigorating the staid directory-publishing business of Dallas-based Idearc.

Harless began her career in telecoms in 1973, later becoming president of GTE Airfone. From 2000 she was president of Verizon Information Services, from which Idearc was spun off in 2006. Harless faced the challenge of re-launching the company at a time when it was saddled with debt and facing significant competition from new internet-based services. In order to convince a sceptical investment community that the future of the company was bright, Harless mounted a four-week roadshow where she impressed with the business's evident ability to adapt and survive amidst cutbacks, competition, and involuntary separation. Idearc now thrives, publishing 1,200 directories in 34 states, and offering internet and mobile-based directory services. Harless is one of the most highly paid women in US business, according to *Forbes* magazine. Harless left Idearc in 2008, and is now a director of the Minnesota-based lawnmower manufacturer, the Toro Company.

John V. Faraci Chairman & CEO, International Paper

BIOGRAPHY
Born in 1950. Faraci received a bachelor's degree in history and economics from Denison University in Ohio, and an MBA from the University of Michigan.

BEST DECISION
Shaking up a stale organization with a thorough restructuring program, marking a new chapter in company history.

LESSON IN BUSINESS
Take a fresh view—by looking at his company's entire business model, Faraci was able to think the unthinkable and come up with a bold plan for long-term improvement.

BY SETTING OUT to transform International Paper's business model, Faraci initiated the boldest restructuring program in the history of the paper industry. The courageous move earned him accolades from industry analysts.

Soon after becoming CEO in 2003, Faraci stated that the business model of the world's biggest pulp and paper company was not working, and set about transforming it. He began the sale of nearly $10-billion worth of International Paper's assets. He used the proceeds to strengthen the company's balance sheet and buy back billions of dollars' worth of stock, but primarily to enable the company to focus on two key platforms: uncoated paper, and consumer and industrial packaging—two of the industry's most competitive markets. As part of this strategy, Faraci has expanded IP into countries with fast-growing demands for these products, such as China, Eastern Europe, and Brazil. He has also bought a 50 percent stake in Ilim Pulp, Russia's biggest pulp and paper company, which exports primarily to Eastern Europe, the Middle East, and China. In this way IP hopes to compensate for a slowing domestic market, although it may take some time for the strategy to pay off.

"Reputations take a long time to earn and not very long to lose." John V. Faraci

Yang Yuanqing Chairman, Lenovo Group Ltd

BIOGRAPHY
Born in Hefei, China, in 1964.
Yang gained a bachelor's degree
from Jiaotong University in
Shanghai, and a master's degree
from Science & Technology
University of China in Hefei.

BEST DECISION
Acquiring IBM PC, a household-
name US company three times
Lenovo's size. Turning it to profit,
Yang also acquired new markets.

LESSON IN BUSINESS
Going for gold doesn't guarantee
a win—Yang secured Lenovo as
a technical sponsor of the Turin
and Beijing Olympics but results
were disappointing.

TAKING OVER IBM's PC business in 2005, computer company Lenovo became the first Chinese firm to buy an iconic western company, making Yang's name. *Business Week* named him a Star of Asia, and China's first truly global capitalist.

In 1988, Yang joined the small Beijing company Legend as a salesman. His blunt honesty impressed his superior, who made him a manager. Yang worked hard and imaginatively to grow the company; by 1997, Legend was China's biggest computer supplier, and eight years later it was third-largest in the world. Yang became CEO in 2001 and in 2003 renamed the company Lenovo. In 2005, he steered the $3-billion company through acquisition of $10-billion global player IBM PC, halting the latter's cash haemorrhage, turning a profit, and acquiring a sales presence in more than 100 countries. In a setback in 2006, US officials cited a potential security threat to block a $13-million sale of US-made Lenovo computers to the state department. Yang failed to change their minds. Lenovo annual revenue to March 2008 was a healthy $16.4 billion but the financial crisis later that year damaged sales. To weather the downturn Yang laid off workers, merged subsidiaries, and slashed executive pay.

Håkan Samuelsson Chairman & CEO, MAN AG

BIOGRAPHY
Born in Motala, Sweden,
in 1951. Samuelsson studied
mechanical engineering
at Stockholm's Royal
Institute of Technology.

BEST DECISION
Implementing an innovative labor
policy that retained key workers
across the peaks and troughs of
the economic cycle.

LESSON IN BUSINESS
Treat staff with respect—
Samuelsson recognized that
when management and workers
find ways to cooperate,
everybody prospers, even
in difficult times.

THINKING BIG and acting decisively have been Samuelsson's characteristics as he drives one of Europe's most distinguished, historic manufacturing firms to its goal of being the world's leading manufacturer of trucks and commercial vehicles.

From its 1758 origins as a humble Swedish ironworks, MAN AG is now one of Europe's leading manufacturers of commercial vehicles, engines, and mechanical engineering equipment, with annual sales of more than $20 billion. After almost 20 years at truck and bus manufacturer Scania, Samuelsson joined MAN AG in 2000 and became chairman of the executive board in 2005. He swiftly identified the company's principal strengths—transportation, energy-efficient engines, and green alternative fuel technologies—and divested other sectors that were peripheral to core operations. He also took the company global, establishing strategic production platforms in South America, China and India. While competitors downsized in the slump following the global financial crisis, Samuelsson added 2,261 new employees to a MAN AG payroll of 52,660. Manufacturing volume actually grew as the transport technology firm dealt with a three-year backlog in demand for diesel engines.

"We can't have this system of hiring people in good times and firing them in bad times." Håkan Samuelsson

Stanley Fink CEO (2000–07), Man Group

KNOWN AS THE "GODFATHER" of hedge funds, Fink transformed ED&F Man into a hedge fund pioneer, and in the process became one of Britain's wealthiest executives, with a personal fortune of more than $240 million.

Fink joined ED&F Man brokers at a time when industry analysts had raised doubts about the company, expecially over the role of Man's agriculture business and how it contributed to group earnings. This suspicion was an obstacle and Fink realized that transparency was the answer. He decided to separate the business and focus on the growing hedge fund and alternative investment markets. When he took over as CEO of the demerged Man Group in 2000, the firm had $4.7 billion under management and shares stood at 60 pence. Fink decided to retire in 2007 following a health scare, but he managed a smooth succession and left the company in good health. When he stepped down, Man was managing $74 billion with shares at 620 pence. In 2008, the group posted a 60 percent increase in pre-tax profits to $2.07 billion, a 20 percent increase in funds under management, and a 5 percent rise in share price. Fink later returned to work, heading a smaller firm.

Judith McGrath Chairman & CEO, MTV Networks Company

TV EXECUTIVE McGrath instinctively knows what young people want to see on their screens. As head of MTV Networks, McGrath is responsible for the operation of some 136 channels including MTV, VH1, Comedy Central, and Nickelodeon.

McGrath began her career as a writer for *Mademoiselle* magazine. In 1981, Warner Amex Satellite Entertainment executive Bob Pitman was on the lookout for bright new talent to help him put music on cable TV. His then-wife suggested her *Mademoiselle* colleague McGrath. Initially working as a promo-writer for MTV, McGrath quickly worked her way to the top. She brought passion, creativity, and originality to the network, helping to turn the fledgling operation into a $7-billion-a-year global enterprise with programmes and events that have become cultural landmarks. McGrath and her team have developed some of the most watched channels on cable TV, seen in 169 countries and in 28 languages, including *The Hills*, *The Real World*, *South Park*, and the *MTV Video and Movie Awards*. Appointed chairman and CEO of MTV Networks in 2004, and group president in 2006, McGrath's biggest challenge now is maintaining MTV's position as a trendsetter in the iPod era.

"The smartest thing we can do when confronted by something truly creative is to get out of the way."
Judith McGrath

Miuccia Prada Chief Designer, Prada

BIOGRAPHY
Born in 1949 in Milan, Italy. Prada is the youngest granddaughter of company founder Mario Prada. She has a PhD from Milan University.

BEST DECISION
Teaming up in business with (and also marrying) Patrizio Bertelli, enhancing the potential of their outstanding creative and commercial talents.

LESSON IN BUSINESS
Take the spotlight—sometimes it pays to be the public face of the company, particularly in creative industries. Prada has built up a devoted personal following.

COMBINING FANTASTIC creative talent with strong commercial nous, Prada turned her grandfather's small leather-goods business into a global fashion phenomenon. Prada is a fashion icon, yet eschews the fashion "world".

Prada is a maverick. Her partnership with CEO Patrizio Bertelli has led her to the pinnacle of the global fashion world, but it is a world that she largely derides. She first put her stamp on the family leather-goods company in 1985 by designing a simple but expensive black, woven-nylon bag that became a must-have accessory. In the late 1980s, Prada launched her first ready-to-wear collection to huge critical acclaim. In 1992 she introduced the less expensive, yet no less desirable, Miu Miu brand (named after her nickname). In the late 1990s, Prada spent €700 million to acquire or buy into top labels including Azzedine Alaia, Fendi, Helmut Lang, Jil Sander, and Church's shoes. Funding problems later led to the sale of most of these and a return to core ranges, such as shoes, perfume, and, following a tie-in with LG in 2007, designer cell phones. In a fiercely competitive field, Prada's unerring eye for the unconventional yet irresistibly aspirational, maintains her brand's extraordinary success.

Patrizio Bertelli CEO, Prada

BIOGRAPHY
Born in Tuscany, Italy, in 1946. Bertorelli's father died when he was a boy, and his mother ran a shoe store. He studied engineering at the University of Bologna before setting up his own leather goods company.

BEST DECISION
Expanding Prada beyond its comfort zone, in the belief that its creative resources were good enough to fuel global growth.

LESSON IN BUSINESS
Be both businesslike and creative—as Bertelli recognized, creative flair can be a huge asset to a business.

SUCCESS IN THE FASHION industry depends on a rare mixture of hard-headed business instinct and creative flair. At fashion house Prada, Bertelli's strong ideas have turned a minor company into a world fashion power.

Bertelli's involvement with Prada began when he met Miuccia Prada, who had recently taken over her family-owned luxury goods company. Their meeting resulted in a marriage and a highly productive business partnership. While his wife focused on the creative side, producing a style that influenced designers all over the world and made Prada one of the hottest properties in fashion, Bertelli set out to build the business. In the 1980s, the company opened new stores and branched out of bags into shoes and clothing. In 1998, an audacious purchase of nearly ten percent of Gucci, which was then sold on to LVMH, left Bertelli with a war chest with which to help fund further purchases. The addition of top-level brands such as Fendi, Helmut Lang, Jil Sander, and Azzedine Alaia turned Prada into an international fashion conglomerate. Bertelli's famously tempestuous management style and strategic business vision have combined to consolidate Prada's identity as the coolest thing in town.

"My only fear in life is that I might start to behave like a fashion designer." Miuccia Prada

Jeffrey H. Schwartz Chairman & CEO (2005–08), ProLogis

BIOGRAPHY
Born c1959 in Philadelphia. Schwartz grew up in New Jersey and completed a BS at Emory University in Atlanta and an MBA at Harvard in 1985.

BEST DECISION
Selling the company that he co-founded, which had grown into the largest industrial developer in Florida, to ProLogis.

LESSON IN BUSINESS
Ensure economic viability—Schwartz' vision of eco-friendly properties won acclaim, but rapid expansion and high levels of borrowing have their downside when the economy contracts.

A GREEN FUTURE of energy-efficient buildings was planned by Schwartz, head of the world's largest warehousing and distribution owner and developer, ProLogis. However, the green agenda was disrupted when he stepped down in late 2008.

Schwartz qualified as an accountant in 1981 and soon joined industrial developers Anderson McDonald & Senkbeil as a junior partner. He co-founded The Krauss/Schwartz Company in 1987, which he sold to ProLogis in 1994. He then joined ProLogis and held senior positions in global development and overseas operations in Amsterdam, Mexico, and Denver, becoming CEO in 2005 and chairman in 2007. Under his guidance, ProLogis developed big-box warehouses that used green technology, such as passive solar heating and wind power. ProLogis earned several major awards, including *Fortune*'s Most Admired Company in 2006 and 2007, and Schwartz was lauded as a visionary. By September 2008 ProLogis owned 2,898 facilities in 136 markets across North America, Europe, and Asia and held assets worth $40.8 billion. However, shares plummeted 73 percent in late 2008 due to the global financial crisis, and the company was forced to cut costs and liquidate assets. In November 2008, Schwartz resigned.

Ralph Izzo Chairman, President & CEO, Public Service Enterprise Group

BIOGRAPHY
Born in 1957. Izzo received a bachelor's, a master's, and a PhD from Columbia University. In 2002 he completed an MBA at Rutgers Graduate School of Management.

BEST DECISION
Selling off a number of PSEG's international assets, raising $1.6 billion, reducing debts and risk, and enabling Izzo to concentrate on the core US market.

LESSON IN BUSINESS
Invest to be the best—Izzo has spearheaded an investment program in new technologies and projects, including solar and wind energy, and nuclear power.

VISIONARY, PRAGMATIC, and inspirational, Izzo, CEO of energy company PSEG, is a keen advocate of green energy, with a roadmap for the future of electricity supply that paints a positive picture for suppliers and consumers.

Since Izzo became CEO in 2007, PSEG's nuclear and fossil-fuel power stations have all produced record or near-record outputs, while in 2007 the company gained a valuable strategic asset when it resumed independent operation of its nuclear plants. Izzo has also taken up the environmental gauntlet. He is a frequent speaker on the future of renewable energy sources, while also promoting the potential of nuclear power. He has driven PSEG to embrace new technologies, such as a $100-million solar program aimed at making solar power more affordable for customers, and exploring the potential of compressed air storage to store wind energy for release during peak electricity usage. In 2008, PSEG scored a coup when it won a bid to provide New Jersey's first offshore wind farm. PSEG's net income almost doubled from 2006 to 2007 to $1,335 million, with stock prices rising nearly 50 percent. Another feather in Izzo's cap is the company's consistent rating as the US's most reliable electricity provider.

"Nuclear power is green power." Ralph Izzo

Pierre-André de Chalendar CEO, Saint-Gobain

BIOGRAPHY
Born in France in 1958. De Chalendar is a graduate of ESSEC Business School and the Ecole Nationale d'Administration (ENA).

BEST DECISION
Increasing investment in energy-saving and renewable products, which has placed Saint-Gobain in pole position to capitalize on growing demand in these areas.

LESSON IN BUSINESS
Adapt or die—Saint-Gobain started out producing glass for mirrors in 1665, but de Chalendar has guaranteed its future by moving into new markets and product lines.

SHREWD AND ENTERPRISING, de Chalendar keeps his eye firmly on the future. As CEO, he took up the environmental gauntlet, cementing Saint-Gobain's position as a leading player in the global construction and glass-making industries.

With 15 years in senior roles, from vice-president of corporate planning in 1989 to senior vice-president in 2003, de Chalendar was in prime position to become CEO of Saint-Gobain in 2007. Since then he has led the company through a series of astute acquisitions and changes. De Chalendar reinforced Saint-Gobain's position as a key player in the Japanese construction industry through the 2008 acquisition of Nippon Sheet Glass's 43.6-percent stake in glass wool manufacturer MAG. He also expanded operations in India, building a third flat glass plant. De Chalendar led the company into the energy-saving and renewables market, to which 40 percent of its business is linked, and steered more than half of the company's total sales to the construction industry into the renovations market. De Chalendar oversees Saint-Gobain's presence in 57 countries, employing more than 200,000 people. Profits run into the billions, with 2007 figures topping €2.1 billion.

Galina Ilyashenko General Director & CEO, Seventh Continent

BIOGRAPHY
No information available.

BEST DECISION
Expanding on all fronts while the time was right, including purchasing the Citimarket store group and launching the Nash chain of hypermarkets.

LESSON IN BUSINESS
Seek opportunities in emerging markets —a CEO who can successfully yoke the business to consumers' changing needs will be rewarded with strong growth.

AS CHIEF EXECUTIVE of Russian retailer Seventh Continent, Ilyashenko has successfully ridden the wave of the country's modernization by introducing western-style grocery stores to cater to the growing, affluent middle class.

Before most others in the sector, Ilyashenko foresaw the impending land grab that would occur in the Russian retail industry as consumers' tastes became more sophisticated, evolving beyond small grocers and outdoor markets. Accordingly, she has driven an ambitious growth program at the Moscow-based retailer, diversifying from supermarkets into huge hypermarkets and small convenience stores. Expansion is set to continue, with plans to acquire 50 more hypermarkets and more than 100 new supermarkets. Ilyashenko has also introduced product improvements that have helped the group, which is Russia's only listed grocery chain, to increase the average consumer spend per visit by nearly 20 percent. This has taken place at a time when Russia's ten-year period of economic growth continues, which augurs well for the future. Seventh Continent's rapid expansion policy has brought strong overall growth, with a 47 percent rise in net profits in 2007.

"...I did not take on this responsibility thinking that it would be an easy ride." Pierre-André de Chalendar

Gérard Mestrallet Chairman & CEO, GDF Suez

BIOGRAPHY
Born in Paris in 1949. Mestrallet studied at the elite Ecole Nationale d'Administration (ENA).

BEST DECISION
Selling off Suez's finance and banking holdings to focus on utilities. This wiped out growing debts and gave the company a clear focus.

LESSON IN BUSINESS
Be objective—Mestrallet decided Suez could not prosper in banking and finance, so he sold up and bought into utilities.

A MERGER MAESTRO who has pulled down a crumbling empire and created a new one through carefully-negotiated alliances. Mestrallet's empire, GDF Suez, is now one of the world's leading energy suppliers, with revenues of €74 billion.

When Mestrallet, an eleven-year veteran of Suez, became chairman and CEO in 1995, the company was a sprawling, debt-ridden multinational. It owned banks and financial institutions, but was going nowhere. Mestrallet was charged with restructuring to reduce debt. Deciding the future lay in power and water, he sold the company's finance and banking assets and bought out the Belgian energy company Tractebel. He then merged Suez with the French water giant Lyonnaise des Eaux, instantly creating a global utilities company. The move began Suez's transformation into one of the world's biggest power, water, and waste treatment companies. Mestrallet made a series of shrewd acquisitions, spending $6 billion on Calgon, United Water Resources, and Nalco in the USA, and power plants in North America, Asia, and South America. In 2008, Mestrallet pulled off the coup of his career when, after two years of negotiations, he merged Suez with Gaz de France to create GDF Suez.

Jonathan Schwartz President & CEO, Sun Microsystems

BIOGRAPHY
Born in 1965 in the US. Schwartz studied at Wesleyan University, Connecticut. His father came from a poor background in the Bronx, but rose to become a professor at the University of California.

BEST DECISION
Maintaining a blog (http://blogs.sun.com/jonathan/), which won him a reputation as a great communicator.

LESSON IN BUSINESS
Be prepared to adapt—Schwartz has stayed ahead of the game by steering Sun to take advantage of developments in internet and computer use.

WITH HIS UNCONVENTIONAL approach to business and marketing, pony-tailed Schwartz is restoring Sun Microsystems as a force to be reckoned with. Since taking over as CEO in 2006, Schwartz has shown he is not afraid to take a chance.

Schwartz began his career in 1987 as a consultant at McKinsey & Co., but left in 1989 to move to Maryland. Together with college friends, he co-founded software company Lighthouse Design, then relocated the company to San Mateo, California, where it caught the eye of Sun Microsystems. Sun acquired the company in 1996, along with its then-CEO Schwartz, who subsequently held a number of executive positions at Sun, including chief strategy officer and executive vice-president for software. Schwartz became Sun's president and chief operating officer in 2004, overseeing all operational functions, before succeeding Sun's co-founder Scott McNealy as CEO in 2006. Schwartz took the company in a new direction, believing that giving away open-source software would not only raise the global profile of Sun, but generate sales of paid-for products and IT support. He acquired the open-source MySQL database management system, used by Google, Wikipedia, and Flickr, for $1 billion in 2008.

"I belong to a club that exists around the world that says progress is made by the unconventional."
Jonathan Schwartz

Tom Carroll President & CEO, TBWA Worldwide, Inc.

BIOGRAPHY
Born c.1956, in Schenectady, New York.

BEST DECISION
Pulling out all the stops to win the estimated $600-million Visa account, which doubled revenues overnight.

LESSON IN BUSINESS
Drive hard but keep a sense of humor—Carroll has been described as one of the few advertising executives who visibly enjoys the high-stress business.

WINNING PRAISE for growing TBWA globally without compromising its reputation, Carroll has consolidated the company's position as one of the world's top ad agencies and is reshaping the way corporations think about advertising.

Carroll began his career at advertising agency Mathieu, Gerfen & Bresner in 1978. In 1983, he joined Chiat\Day, leading the GE, Pizza Hut, and Miller Brewing accounts. Carroll then set up his own agency in 1989, with clients that included Citibank and Guinness Import. Following a spell as a partner with MVBMS, Carroll joined the newly merged TBWA\Chiat\Day as president of the LA office, moving up the hierarchy until, in 2007, he was made CEO of TBWA Worldwide, Inc. Carroll has recruited visionary talent from competitors and launched a creative revolution around a proprietary process that he calls "disruptive ideas,", which aims to challenge clients' conventional views. He has also succeeded in knitting TBWA offices around the world into a genuinely collaborative network, a feat that helped him win the lucrative Visa account in 2008. In that year, *Advertising Age*, one of the industry's leading magazines, chose the company as Global Agency of the year, and honored Carroll as Executive of the Year.

Catherine Elizabeth Hughes CEO, Radio One

BIOGRAPHY
Born in Omaha, Nebraska, in 1947. Hughes (née Woods) became fascinated by the radio when young. At 22, without completing her university studies, she entered the radio industry.

BEST DECISION
Going all out to find a bank willing to fund the purchase of her own station. She contacted 32 banks before eventually finding a sponsor.

LESSON IN BUSINESS
Embed the cultural values of your target audience in your product—Hughes implemented this in her focus on black communities.

A PIONEERING BLACK female entrepreneur and media personality, Hughes was the first African-American woman to head a US public company. Radio One floated in 1999 with a value of $924 million.

An unmarried teenage mother and college drop-out with, it seemed, few prospects, Hughes had ambition. While selling advertising at a small black radio station in Omaha, and later as general manager of WHUR-FM, the station of Howard University in Washington, Hughes observed that black audiences were inadequately served. Spotting an opportunity, in 1979 she and her first husband, Dewey Hughes, borrowed the money to buy WOL, a struggling radio station for black audiences in Washington, and revamped it as Radio One. When her marriage ended, Cathy bought her husband out, and kept costs down by doing the talk shows herself and living on-site. Her Radio One network now has over 60 stations, and in 2004 the company expanded into cable TV. Hughes' successful approach to business aims at reflecting the values of the community she serves: staunch black pride, and a midwestern work ethic. She has been outspoken on black issues, and honoured with many awards.

"Where information is power." Radio One slogan

EXECUTIVE EDUCATION

There are no rules about the level of education required to be a good CEO. Some argue that a postgraduate degree is important, while others stress the value of experience. There are famous bosses who dropped out of college, and there are CEOs with MBAs and PhDs. **Michael Dell** (p50) set out to follow a traditional academic route at the University of Texas, but his idea of putting together PCs and selling them proved such a success that he dropped out to concentrate on his business and never looked back. At the other end of the formal educational scale, **Thomas Krens** (p444) director of the Guggenheim Foundation, took a long road through the institutions before becoming an executive. He gained a bachelor's in political economy and a master's in art, followed those with an MBA from Yale and then, as if that wasn't enough academic experience, spent 17 years as an art history professor ●

Drop-outs and Doctorates

The range of educational experience among top executives is immense. Research by *BusinessWeek* magazine showed that around one in three high-level executives in the US had MBAs, while at the World Economic Forum Annual Meeting in 2006, **Eric Hippeau**, managing partner of the US independent venture capital firm SoftBank Capital, noted that about a quarter of the top 100 *Fortune* companies are run by people who dropped out of school.

Examples from the more academic end of the spectrum include **Henning Kreke** of German retailer Douglas Holding AG, who alongside his MBA holds a doctorate in political science.

Then there's **William Mitchell** of Arrow Electronics in the US, who has master's degree in engineering from the University of Michigan, and was named a National Science Foundation Fellow. A qualification in the professions is often a starting point for senior business leaders, particularly beginning in accountancy and law. **Michael Morris** of American Electric Power began his studies in science, earning both a bachelor's and a master's degree, but then added a law degree and remains a member of the Michigan Bar Association.

Others regard post-school education as more of a hindrance to their business ambitions. **Tom Watson Sr.** tried teaching for one day, then took a one-year course in accounting and, for a short time, worked as a bookkeeper. He finally became a salesman, which

eventually brought him to the leadership of a company he renamed IBM and turned into a global powerhouse.

Whatever their qualifications, CEOs of all stripes emphasize the importance of continuous learning. Some organizations, including McDonald's, Motorola, Boeing, Walt Disney, and Ford, have operated their own universities or equivalent institutions, while many CEOs have attended the advanced management executive education programs at places like Harvard Business School, the London Business School, and INSEAD in Paris. For example, **Manoj Kholi** of Bharti Airtel, the Indian telecoms company, who has a law degree and an MBA, attended both the Executive Business Program at Michigan Business School and the Advanced Management Program at Wharton Business School, Pennsylvania.

"I got rich without the benefit of a college education or a penny of capital."
FELIX DENNIS, founder and chairman, Dennis Publishing Ltd

Dyslexics Welcome

What do **Henry Ford** (p23), **F. W. Woolworth**, **William Hewlett** of Hewlett-Packard, **Richard Branson** (p421), **John Chambers** of Cisco (p20), **Charles Schwab** (p65), **O. D. McKee** of McKee Foods, **Paul J. Orfalea** of Kinko's, and media tycoon **Ted Turner** have in common? Besides being great business leaders, they were or are all dyslexics. Not only does dyslexia appear to offer no barrier to corporate advancement, but both sufferers and experts argue that it could be an advantage. To overcome their difficulties, dyslexics are forced to create simpler ways of doing things, and learn to rely on the abilities of others. In other words delegating and not getting bogged down in details, both essential skills that go to the heart of good management and business leadership.

Learned CEOs

Some of the qualifications that have taken executives to the top:

Kalle Hvidt Nielsen, Bang & Olufson AV (Electronics: Denmark)— *An engineering degree from the Technical University of Denmark, and a bachelor's in marketing made Nielsen perfect for the top job at technology firm Bang & Olufson.*

—

David M. McClanahan, CenterPoint Energy (Energy: US)—*A certified public accountant, McClanahan has a mathematics degree from the University of Texas and an MBA from the University of Houston.*

—

Dennis J. Manning, Guardian Life Insurance Company of America (Insurance: US)— *A graduate of Notre Dame University, where he received his degree in business administration.*

—

William Utt, KBR (Engineering and construction: US)—*Holds bachelor's and master's degrees in mechanical engineering from the University of Virginia and an MBA from The Colgate Darden School of Business at the University of Virginia.*

Henry L. Meyer III, KeyCorp (Finance: US)—*Received a bachelor's degree in econometrics from Colgate University, New York State, and an MBA from Harvard.*

—

Gregory Maffei, Liberty Media (Media: US)—*Has an MBA from Harvard Business School, where he was a Baker Scholar, and a BA degree from Dartmouth College.*

—

Choi Tae-won, SK Holdings (Diversified: South Korea)—*Holds a doctorate in economics from the University of Chicago.*

—

Thomas R. Watjen, Unum Group (Insurance: US)—*Earned a bachelor's in economics from the Virginia Military Institute and an MBA from the Darden School at the University of Virginia.*

—

9

The Controversialists

Michael Szymanczyk Chairman & CEO, Altria Group, Inc.

LITIGATION, PUBLIC ABUSE, and legislative pressure were just some of the challenges facing Philip Morris, one of the biggest tobacco companies in the US, when Szymanczyk joined the firm in 1990. By the time he took over as CEO of the group in 1997, his main task, like that of any other tobacco company boss, was less running the business and more working out a survival strategy. Making clear his intention to take Philip Morris in a new direction, he renamed the company, moved its headquarters, and took the group into wine production.

BIOGRAPHY
Born in Washington, DC, in 1949. Szymanczyk earned a BSc degree in finance from the Kelley School of Business at Indiana University.

LEADERSHIP STYLE
Szymanczyk has a campaigning style of leadership, and pushes hard for his far-sighted vision of what the tobacco industry needs.

KEY STRENGTH
A willingness to face, and respond to, opposition, rather than ignoring it.

BEST DECISION
To spin off Altria's international tobacco business, opening the way for broader acquisitions outside the tobacco industry.

TOUGH JOB Szymanczyk spent nearly 20 years learning the ropes of consumer products at Procter & Gamble and Kraft before joining Philip Morris USA as senior vice-president of sales in 1990. Seven years later he became the fifth CEO of its US operation in ten years, at a time when litigation and growing public opposition made it one of the toughest posts in corporate America. In 2002, with the pressure rising all the time, he became CEO of the entire Philip Morris group.

INTO THE STORM The tobacco industry was facing lawsuits, ever-growing support for tighter legislative restrictions on smoking and the sale of tobacco, and a groundswell of public disapproval. Szymanczyk's predecessors had largely adopted a stonewalling attitude, but as sales slid and court cases multiplied, the industry's image grew uglier. Szymanczyk adopted a new approach, reinventing Philip Morris as a new type of company and distancing it from the popular image of a rapacious corporate monster. A year after he took over, the group was renamed Altria, providing an immediate move away from its former identity, and Szymanczyk made it clear that he intended to turn the company into a more broadly-based consumer products group, with an eye on acquisitions. Selling off the group's non-US tobacco operation, Philip Morris International, he added US wine producer Ste. Michelle Wine Estates to Altria's substantial existing interest in international brewer SABMiller. However, Szymanczyk has remained true to the group's core strengths by acquiring UST, Inc., the world's leading smokeless tobacco manufacturer.

LESSONS IN BUSINESS: FACING THE PROBLEM

Ignoring your problems is no way to solve them. Szmanczyk realized that ignoring the company's public-relations problem was not going to mitigate it, so he bent to the common will and planned for change.
- → The "elephant in the room" can be anything from poor industrial relations to out-dated products. Put it at the top of everyone's agenda and ensure energies are focused on resolving it.
- → Recognize that although the best form of defense may not be attack, it is also not just lying down.
- → Communicate with your detractors and ensure they cannot demonize you and your people.

"You can't remove all the risks in life." Michael Szymanczyk

August A. Busch IV President & CEO (2006–08), Anheuser-Busch

THE KING OF BEERS until he was dethroned by InBev's $52-billion take over of Anheuser-Busch in 2008, Busch IV is a controversial business leader who worked hard to prove that, despite his party-boy image and four generations of nepotism at the American beer giant, he was a confident and capable leader who could add fizz to an ageing brewing company. He succeeded in updating the company's image and traditional consumer base, modernizing its product range, and putting A-B on the lips of a younger demographic.

BIOGRAPHY
Born in St. Louis, Missouri, in 1964. Busch IV was heir-apparent to the Anheuser-Busch beer-manufacturing dynasty, founded by his great-great-grandfather Adolphus Busch, and grown by successive Busch patriarchs. He received an MBA from St. Louis University, and a brewmaster's degree from the International Brewing Institute in Berlin.

LEADERSHIP STYLE
Innovative team player. Through working his way from the bottom to the top of his company, Busch gained comprehensive, hands-on experience of his business.

KEY STRENGTH
Figuring out how to market Anheuser-Busch products to a new generation of drinkers.

BEST DECISION
Focusing on new products that appealed to young adults.

THE GENUINE ARTICLE When Busch became Anheuser-Busch's president and CEO in December 2006, he was the target of significant scepticism. Not only because some felt he had inherited his position more than he had earned it, but because of his wild past, which included two serious brushes with the law. In fact, Busch had spent 22 years working his way up from an intern on the malt house floor to the company's top job.

A BIG HIT Busch moved into marketing in 1989. His first trial product, Bud Dry, was a complete failure, but all this changed when he took over the marketing of Budweiser. The beer was the main source of A-B's profits, but it had topped at 22 percent of industry sales in 1990, and hadn't grown since. Realizing the younger generation viewed Budweiser as the beer their parents drank, and that they were switching to imports and microbrews, Busch looked for new ways to appeal to a more youthful market. He oversaw the advertising campaign of frogs croaking "Bud-Weis-Er". Busch also launched hard liquors, microbrews, and other speciality drinks. When he assumed leadership in 2006, the business was finding it hard to keep pace with inflation in barley prices. Eighteen months later, Belgium-based brewer InBev offered Anheuser-Busch shareholders an intoxicating $52-billion merger deal few could refuse, with prospective annual sales of $36.4 billion. Busch had once vowed the company would never be sold "on my watch", but with less than four percent of the company under family control there was little he could do about it. Busch held onto a position on the company's board of directors, and is, publicly at least, a fan of the merger.

LESSONS IN BUSINESS: RENEWING CONSTANTLY

A company that relies heavily on the purchasing decisions of young adults must regularly re-brand itself. Following the success of the "frogs" campaign, Budweiser commercials have grown with the times.
→ Realize that targeting a younger market involves developing a totally different image that is flexible enough to move with the times.
→ Recognize that young people are fickle: don't get left behind as fashions change.
→ If the adult content of your advertisements precludes them from television, use the internet instead.

> "Together, we will achieve our goals far more effectively than either company could on its own."
> August A. Busch IV

Philip Green CEO, Arcadia Group

A SWASHBUCKLING retail entrepreneur who has made a personal fortune of some £3.6 billion from his Bhs and Arcadia businesses, Green is probably best known for his two failed attempts to acquire British retail giant Marks & Spencer. His companies make him the second largest player in the UK clothing retail market, with over 2,000 shops. With minute attention to detail and an acute understanding of the retail industry, he revolutionized Top Shop, Top Man, and Bhs, turning them into impressive profit-making machines.

BIOGRAPHY
Born in Croydon, London, in 1952. His father, an electrical retailer, died when Green was aged 12 and he helped his mother to run her laundromat and gas station business. He then took a job selling shoes before setting up on his own, selling damaged stock, in 1973.

LEADERSHIP STYLE
Brash, straight-talking, funny, and shrewd. Green works his favored employees hard but treats them well.

KEY STRENGTH
A born trader, Green has such an incredible nose for a bargain it sometimes seems that he can't help making money.

BEST DECISION
Keeping his business empire private, getting support from like-minded entrepreneurs rather than traditional financial institutions.

BORN TO TRADE After setting up on his own in 1973, Green made his first big money in 1985, selling the Jean Jeanie fashion chain for £3 million only a year after buying it for a mere £65,000. It was the first public sign of his remarkable nose for a winning deal. Green's earliest attempt at running a public company, Amber Day, was treated with scorn by the City of London, and he was forced to resign by institutional shareholders in 1992. Since then he has been driven by an intense desire to prove that his instinct is a better judge of potential than the best brains in the City.

M&S BRUSH-OFF His Marks & Spencer bids have made Green a household name in the UK and worldwide. His first crack at buying the retail chain came in 1999. The M&S board rejected his £7 billion hostile offer, but simply being able to raise that kind of cash proved Green's mettle. He tried again in 2005, with the same result. On both occasions he stuck to his guns and refused to raise his offer. It's impossible to rule out his making another attempt at M&S, especially if the financial climate drives share prices down.

Bhs was an unloved wreck when he bought it for £200 million in 2000. It's worth has increased more than five-fold since. He defied the experts by repaying the £800 million he borrowed in 2002 to buy Arcadia—owner of Top Shop and Top Man—in an amazingly rapid two years. He also believes in rewarding himself well—in 2005 he and his wife (between them they own 92 percent of Bhs) took a £1.17-billion dividend, the largest ever in the UK. In 2006, he received a knighthood for services to the retail industry.

LESSONS IN BUSINESS: BUCKING THE MARKET

Green's first quoted company was derided by the City of London, and the shareholders insisted that he resign. Now his driving force is to prove that his instinct can outwit the best brains in the City.
- → Whatever your motivation, drive yourself hard toward a goal that you feel passionate about.
- → Don't accept the opinions of people who say it can't be done if your instincts tell you that with great effort it can.
- → Believe in yourself and pursue your goals in a single-minded way. Never take no for an answer.

"No deal is worth going bankrupt for." Philip Green

François Pinault Founder, PPR & Artemis Group

SELF-MADE BILLIONAIRE Pinault has enjoyed one of the most spectacular careers in modern French business, rising from obscurity as a regional timber merchant to national prominence as a leading French industrialist. According to *Forbes*, Pinault is among the top 40 richest people in the world, with an estimated personal fortune of almost $17 billion. He is the founder and former president of PPR and holding company Artemis Group, which is owned entirely by his family, and includes brands well known in France and across the world.

BIOGRAPHY
Born in Champs-Géraux, France, in 1936, Pinault was a high-school drop out.

LEADERSHIP STYLE
Instinctive, visionary, trusting. Publicity-shy Pinault has never run operating company PPR himself, preferring to delegate authority and hire strong managers.

KEY STRENGTH
Having the confidence to invest in new businesses and allowing other people to run them for him.

BEST DECISION
Taking control of Gucci, the biggest-selling Italian fashion label in the world, which cemented PPR's position in the luxury goods market and complemented its existing strength in mainstream department stores.

TURNING WOOD INTO MONEY Pinault began his working life as a timber merchant in Brittany. He formed Pinault-Printemps-Redoute (PPR) in 1963 and during the 1970s and 1980s bought and transformed struggling businesses. Starting with timber companies, he soon moved into retailing and luxury goods. As well as his business acumen, his political connections have helped. In the 1980s and 1990s he received backing from Crédit Lyonnais, a then government-owned bank keen to promote French business, and bought a state-owned wood business for one symbolic French franc while friend Jacques Chirac was prime minister.

BUILDING AN EMPIRE His business includes some of the best-known names in France, including the Printemps department store, the Fnac bookstore chain, and Chateau Latour vineyard. Although his brands are known worldwide (including Samsonite and Vail Ski Resorts in the US), Pinault prefers to remain out of the limelight and delegate authority. He has continued to drive the business forward internationally with two particular acquisitions. In 1998, through holding company Artemis Group, he acquired a majority share in Christie's auction house and in 2001, after a long and bitter battle with business rival Bernard Arnault, Pinault took control of Gucci, the Italian fashion house. His business tactics have not been without their controversy, and he has had brushes with French tax authorities that led to a reform of French company law. In 2001, he announced he was splitting ownership of the company between his three children, and designated François-Henri, his eldest son, as his successor.

LESSONS IN BUSINESS: REMAINING FLEXIBLE

Don't be afraid to diversify and move on. Pinault has always followed this policy throughout his business career, using his entrepreneurial skills to build up a strong and varied retail empire—at the same time selling off anything that wasn't profitable.

→ Most entrepreneurial problems are concerned with selling late rather than buying at the wrong time.
→ Never get so fond of a business or a product line that you can't make an objective decision to sell.
→ Nothing lasts forever. Review your strategy frequently and take radical decisions when the time is ripe.

"Monsieur Pinault is one of Europe's most successful entrepreneurs..." Lakshmi Mittal, chairman & CEO, Arcelor Mittal

Stelios Haji-Ioannou CEO, easyGroup

A FAMILIAR FACE to consumers across a whole range of markets in the UK and Europe, "Stelios" is the epitome of the bold entrepreneur prepared to take on established interests and bring services to consumers who would never have been able to afford them before. With its rigorously no-frills approach and distinctive bright orange color scheme, his easyJet airline has become a dominant presence in European airspace, and he continues to apply his bare-bones approach to an ever-growing list of diverse ventures, including car rental and internet cafés.

BIOGRAPHY
Born in Cyprus in 1967. Haji-Ioannou went to school in Athens, then to the London School of Economics and Cass Business School. He began his career working in his father's shipping business.

LEADERSHIP STYLE
Direct and highly focused. Haji-Ioannou's meetings with his managers last just ten minutes.

KEY STRENGTH
Bringing a whole new approach to a range of industries, and recognizing that media coverage is great advertising.

BEST DECISION
Starting to sell airline tickets on the internet in 1998, allowing low-paying customers to bypass travel agents.

BREAKING THE MOLD At the age of just 28, Haji-Ioannou set up easyJet in 1995, a bold experiment in low-cost aviation based on the model of Southwest Airlines in the US. EasyJet has since become a solidly established player in the intensely competitive European aviation market, with numerous other easyGroup ventures up and running, all following the same business model of super-tight cost controls and optimum use of assets.

SWEATING THE ASSETS A natural performer, Haji-Ioannou employed a rare mix of crowd-pleasing showmanship and almost fanatical bean-counting in getting easyJet off the ground. He took the same approach when finding markets for his various other low-cost ventures, including car rental, hotels, internet cafés, and cruises. Some projects have proven over-ambitious, but overall the easyGroup has been a triumph of branding and timing. Cutting costs to the bone, maximizing publicity, and sweating the assets are key. Haji-Ioannou's innovations are clever. The then-radical step of making easyJet passengers buy their own drinks not only generated cash but also reduced the demand for bathrooms, allowing more space for seats. When British Airways launched an easyJet clone called Go, Haji-Ioannou and nine colleagues went on the inaugural flight and handed out free easyJet tickets, with great publicity. Four years later, easyJet bought Go. And, behind all the showbiz, Haji-Ioannou's assiduous use of sophisticated yield management techniques has allowed him to maximize profits from assets most people wouldn't have thought possible.

LESSONS IN BUSINESS: TARGETING THE MASS MARKET

You might think your customers want a full-service product. But they might just want the core product as cheap as possible. Haji-Ioannou asked what customers wanted and gave it to them.
➔ Understand that business is about meeting customer's needs, not about producing products and services that you would like for yourself.
➔ Look to expand from niche top-of-the range products and services into mass markets.
➔ Beware of market research on customers who don't pay for your products out of their own pocket.

"The cheaper you can make something, the more people there are who can afford it." Stelios Haji-Ioannou

Gianni Agnelli President (1966–2003, honorary from 1996), Fiat

A STYLISH PATRIARCH, Agnelli became one of the most widely recognized and influential figures on the European business, political, and social scenes of the second half of the 20th century. As president and principal shareholder of Fiat, he turned his grandfather's modest domestic car company into the country's largest industrial conglomerate, a proud symbol of the Italian post-war economic miracle. At its height, Fiat employed some three percent of Italy's industrial workforce, producing almost five percent of its GNP.

BIOGRAPHY
1921–2003. Born in Turin, Italy. Agnelli was the son of an industrialist father and the Princess of San Faustino. In his 20s and 30s he was a playboy whose name was linked to film stars, princesses, and socialites. After taking over at Fiat aged 45, he settled down to preserve his family's patrimony.

LEADERSHIP STYLE
Regal. He kept an aristocratic distance not only from his vast frontline workforce but also from local management. Agnelli believed in maintaining close control only of a small group, most of them relatives, who then did his bidding.

KEY STRENGTH
A born seducer. Formidably persuasive, he used a combination of charm, personal impact, and ruthless negotiating to broker a series of remarkably favorable deals for Fiat.

BEST DECISION
Persuading GM to buy a 20 percent stake in Fiat in return for a 6 percent stake in GM itself, to keep Fiat in the Agnelli family.

REFORMED PLAYBOY When style icon Agnelli acceded to control in 1966 he was already wealthy, and Fiat was doing well at home thanks to its famous Nuova 500 model. Domestic success, however, was not enough for Agnelli, who possessed an ancestral drive to put himself and his family back on the international commercial map. He reorganized, diversified, bought up rivals, and pursued a series of novel international partnerships, gaining new markets in Russia, Eastern Europe, and Brazil. By the mid-1980s Fiat was Europe's largest carmaker.

CONSUMMATE POLITICIAN Cultured and suave, Agnelli used his huge personal charisma to great effect when negotiating the shark-pool of Italian domestic politics and the legal system. Under him, Fiat had reinforced Italy as an industry powerhouse, and it had become a company for whom it was said that the government was always ready to turn a blind eye to any inconvenient legislation. When the firm hit trouble in the slump of the 1990s, he made his last and most extraordinary deal, persuading GM to buy a 20 percent stake in Fiat in return for 6 percent of GM itself. Its purpose was to help keep FIAT in the Agnelli family.

His later life was marked by tragedy. His chosen heir, Alberto Agnelli, died of cancer aged only 33. Then in 2000, his only son Edoardo committed suicide. Agnelli himself, popularly dubbed "Il Re", the uncrowned King of Italy, died of prostate cancer in 2003. At his funeral, over 100,000 mourners, including prime minister Silvio Berlusconi, lined up for hours to pay their respects.

LESSONS IN BUSINESS: WORKING WITH GOVERNMENT

Agnelli was an industrial aristocrat who knew that the prosperity of his dynasty was best served by making it as large as possible and binding it tightly to the state. He built wide political and economic relationships.
→ Form close relationships with government customers. They, like you, are in it for the long term.
→ Consider the benefits of linking your business plan to the government of the day's economic strategies.
→ You cannot motivate government customers by an appeal to make profits, so listen hard to what they are trying to achieve.

"I like the wind, because you cannot buy it." Gianni Agnelli

Carlos Slim Helú Founder & Chairman, Grupo Carso

NOW ONE OF the world's richest men, with huge influence over the Latin American telecommunications industry, Slim Helú has never forgotten his roots. His years spent learning the family grocery business as a child at his father's side ignited in him a passion for commerce, and his father's tragic death when Carlos was only 13 inspired him to build the foundations of what would later become known as Grupo Carso. After running the company for 28 years, he became the honorary lifetime chairman of the business.

BIOGRAPHY
Born in Mexico City in 1940. Slim Helú studied civil engineering at the National Autonomous University of Mexico (UNAM), where he taught algebra and linear programming to help fund his studies.

LEADERSHIP STYLE
Optimistic, practical, balanced. He has created an organization with simple hierarchies and no corporate staff, enabling greater efficiency and flexibility.

KEY STRENGTH
Maintaining austerity in prosperous times, avoiding the need for drastic change in times of crisis.

BEST DECISION
Buying cigarette manufacturing company Cigatam, which boosted the group's cash flow.

BUILDING THE EMPIRE Slim Helú learned his first business lessons as a child from his father. He began investing in properties and industrial companies throughout the 1960s and 1970s, and incorporated his interests as Grupo Galas in 1980, which later became Grupo Carso. When the Mexican economy crashed in 1982, Slim Helú picked up assets on the cheap, ruthlessly cutting costs, jetissoning unprofitable products, and boosting the productivity of his acquisitions. As his father had done, he tested the business knowledge of his own sons, even asking his 12-year-old if he should acquire cigarette maker Cigatam. This turned out to be an important acquisition: its cash flow allowed him to invest in other opportunities.

Bearing in mind his father's maxim, "Though Mexico will have its ups and downs, don't ever count the country out", Slim Helú acquired a number of Mexican interests in US-based brands. His empire continued to grow, with the average Mexican encountering one of his businesses whenever they used an ATM, drove a car, bought insurance, or stopped for coffee.

MOVE INTO TELECOMS Slim Helú seized the "home-grown" opportunity to expand into new markets in the 1990s, turning his attention to telecoms, which has made him a billionaire many times over. His acquisition of the state-owned Teléfonos de México (Telmex), Telcel, and América Móvil gave Grupo Carso almost total domination over the telecommunications industry in Latin America and the Caribbean, and it continues to finance overseas expansion. Slim Helú has now withdrawn from the day-to-day running of Grupo Carso, placing his remarkable legacy in the hands of his sons.

LESSONS IN BUSINESS: LOOKING AFTER THE PENNIES

Slim Helú understood that many successful companies that build impressive head offices, with helicopter pads and a member of a royal family to open them, do not survive. A prudent board of directors has to plan for the business cycle of growth and no growth.
→ Spend company money as though it were your own: when you are CEO it will be your own.
→ If an asset you own has made you a good profit, objectively consider selling it to lock in that profit.
→ Remember that a small increase in costs often causes a large decrease in profits.

"When you live for others' opinions, you are dead. I don't want to live thinking about how I'll be remembered." Carlos Slim Helú

José Ignacio Sánchez Galán CEO, Iberdrola

NOTORIOUS FOR CLASHES with investors, journalists, and competitors alike, Sánchez Galán is one of Spain's leading industrialists. Despite having no previous links with the utility sector, he has driven the Spanish electric utility Iberdrola—a 100-year-old company—into the 21st century, making it the world's largest renewable energy operator, and expanding his business across the globe. Much of his success derives from his setting of targets and his unwavering adherence to a well-defined plan for achieving them.

BIOGRAPHY
Born in Salamanca, Spain, in 1950 Sánchez Galán studied industrial engineering at Comillas Pontifical University, Madrid, and completed a diploma in business management and another in business administration and foreign trade at Spain's EOI business school.

LEADERSHIP STYLE
Passionate, competitive, and creative. His style leaves little room for doubt. He sets very specific and measurable objectives and communicates these clearly to employees.

KEY STRENGTH
Recognizing that utility companies can operate outside the domestic environment and that a Spanish company can sell gas or electricity to anyone.

BEST DECISION
Pushing hard for the development of renewable energy sources.

DEFINING A STRATEGIC PLAN Multilingual Sánchez Galán brought an impeccable business pedigree to Iberdrola. Years spent honing his skills at Spanish aero-engine giant Industria de Turbo Propulsores and Airtel Móvil (now Vodafone España) highlighted his abilities as a strategist. With no prior links to the industry, Sánchez Galán has shown that he can put together top-class teams of professionals to tackle the challenges facing utility company Iberdrola. On becoming CEO in 2001, one of Sánchez Galán's first moves was to put in place an ambitious five year plan to double Iberdrola's size through investment in core power and gas activities.

Sánchez Galán has continued to drive the recovery of the business, enabling Iberdrola to consolidate its position as the leading utility company in Spain and transforming it into one of the world's top five multinational utilities in the world, with particular growth in Mexico and Brazil. An important part of his strategic plan involves the productivity of his workers, and to this end he has implemented a work/life balance that gives employees a certain degree of flexibility in their working hours.

GOING "GREEN" Sánchez Galán has pushed Iberdrola's international growth program, acquiring Scottish Power, the UK's leading wind power company and one of the country's top five electricity distributors, and the US company Energy East. He remains convinced that the future of Iberdrola lies in the field of clean energy, including hydroelectricity and wind power, and the company is now the world's largest renewable energy operator, with one of the lowest CO_2 emission levels in the sector.

LESSONS IN BUSINESS: LEADING WITH CLARITY

Sánchez Galán gets the best out of people by leaving them in no doubt what their job is and how their performance will be measured. Knowing exactly where you are aiming is essential for you—and your team.
→ Set "Smart" objectives: Specific, Measurable, Achievable, Relevant, and Time-bound. Review regularly.
→ Reward people for achieving their objectives. Avoid lowering the motivation of good performers by occasionally rewarding poor performance.
→ Work out when to direct your team, and when to consult them and involve them in planning.

"[Sánchez Galán is] a professional willing to break molds…" Rafael Orbegozo, head of chairman's office, Iberdrola

THE ART OF CONFIDENCE

Not all successful CEOs are extroverts, but even those without bold confident personalities have an inner confidence.

Take **Terry Leahy** (p327) CEO of UK-based retail giant Tesco. "The only personality I believe in is Tesco," says notoriously shy Leahy. Yet, when it comes to running his company, Leahy has inner confidence by the shopping basketful. This innate self-belief is based on his knowledge (he joined Tesco as a graduate trainee, so he knows the business inside out) his vision, experience, team, and own abilities.

Walt Disney (p21) had unswerving confidence in his vision. He knew exactly what he was going to accomplish. When Disneyland first opened, a reporter commented, "Isn't it a shame that Walt isn't here to see this?" A Disneyland executive replied, "Walt has seen all this; he saw it before anyone else… he created it in his mind before he had it built." ●

He Who Dares Wins

Confidence and self-belief, like uncertainty and self-doubt, become a self-fulfilling prophecy. It's not surprising that leading CEOs tend to possess a firm belief that they will achieve, as these positive expectations drive accomplishment. CEOs require confidence in their decisions, the risks they take, their team, their vision, their abilities, and their instinct.

With an estimated net worth of $7 billion, **Masayoshi Son**, CEO of Japanese media company Softbank Corp., has an innate confidence that has made him Japan's richest man. In 2006, he made the bold decision to trigger a price war in the

Confident CEOs

Other CEOs known for their self-belief and confidence include:

Martin H. Richenhagen, AGCO CORP. (Engineering: US)—*Has an in-depth understanding of the agricultural equipment industry, and this knowledge gives him the confidence to act decisively.*

—

Micky Arison, CARNIVAL (Travel: Panama)—*Despite industry-wide trepidation, Arison, known for his drive and confidence, has commissioned the construction of more cruise ships.*

—

Theodore M. Solso, CUMMINS (Energy: US)—*Has confidence in his vision to lead the way in diesel emissions standards.*

—

Shi Yuzhu, GIANT INTERACTIVE (Internet: China)—*Following bankruptcy, Shi had the confidence to start over, rising to 14th position on Forbes Richest Chinese List by 2008.*

—

Yoshinori Ida, ISUZU MOTORS LTD (Automotive: Japan)—*Has confidently taken the company from huge losses to record operating profit and sales.*

—

Marc Bolland, MORRISON SUPERMARKETS (Retail: UK) – *Bolland needed confidence when sceptics questioned his abilities. He has delivered with consistent growth.*

—

Donald E. Washkewicz, PARKER HANNIFIN (Engineering: US)—*Steered the company from falling profits to become the world's leader in motion and control technologies.*

—

François-Henri Pinault, *PPR* (Retail: France)—*Bold enough to challenge the fashion industry by focusing on brands over designers, a strategy that has helped the company succeed even in difficult economic operating conditions.*

—

Alexey Mordashov, SEVERSTAL OAO (Metals: Russia)—*Had the inner confidence to embrace a new culture and merge with European giant Arcelor. Now controls 32 percent of the world's largest steel company*

—

Katsuhiko Machida, SHARP CORP. (Electronics: Japan)— *His unshakeable belief in focusing production on solar panels and LCD TV screens has resulted in record earnings and made Sharp Solar the top solar manufacturer worldwide.*

—

saturated cell phone market and focus on gaining market share. Ever since, Softbank has chipped away at leaders DoCoMo's market share. By 2009, it had almost 20 percent of Japan's 93 million cell phone users, up from 16 percent in 2007.

Son has had the confidence to invest in web start-ups when nobody else would (investing in any start-up was previously unheard of in Japan). This has paved the way for a new generation of risk-taking entrepreneurs.

"I was the last believer of the internet," says Son. "Many people became very sceptical. But I did not lose confidence. So we kept on investing."

For others, confidence gives them the courage and self-assurance to be able to handle a crisis.

Faced with the recall of over 21 million Chinese-made toys due to lead paint levels, Mattel CEO, **Robert Eckert**, confidently tackled the issue by moving quickly and decisively, halting Far East deliveries and ordering the inspection of each toy. He intrepidly hit the front line himself to get the message out personally on television programs, online webcast apologies, and via a *Wall Street Journal* opinion piece.

"Deep down I'm a shy introverted type person", says Eckert, "so I don't get up in the morning looking forward to getting grilled by news anchors. But the company needed that at the time. People want to hear from the leader of the company. We needed to tell people what we were doing to fix these issues."

"You have to think and act as you think."
MASAYOSHI SON

Acting with Assurance

Don't be afraid of failure—Why are CEOs confident? They know that mistakes provide valuable lessons for the future. That realization empowers confidence.

Be open to learning—There's a fine line between pleasant self-confidence and complacent over-confidence. The best CEOs remain open to new information.

Have a clear vision and action plan—If leaders don't believe in their ideas, in what they are doing, or where they are heading, they will struggle to convince other people to believe them.

Bernard Arnault Chairman & CEO, LVMH & Christian Dior

A TROPHY HUNTER, interested only in the top-end brands, Arnault is the richest man in France and one of the richest in the world, with a fortune in excess of $25 billion. Owner of Louis Vuitton, Marc Jacobs, TAG Heuer, Dom Pérignon, Moët Hennessy, and more through the LVMH group, which he controls, Arnault is also an art patron and newspaper proprietor, and a major shareholder in French supermarket group Carrefour. He is globally influential and politically well connected, counting Nicolas Sarkozy among his friends.

A CHANGE OF FOCUS In 1976, Arnault convinced his father to change the focus of the family firm from construction to real estate, and in 1979 he took over the helm. In 1981, following the election of socialist president François Mitterand, Arnault emigrated to the US and created Ferinel Inc., developing condominiums in Palm Beach, Florida. In 1984 he returned to France and acquired Boussac, a textile company. He sold nearly all the company's assets, keeping only Christian Dior and Le Bon Marché department store.

BOARDROOM DRAMA In 1987 Arnault started a hard-fought battle to take over LVMH, the vehicle that merged drinks brands Moët et Chandon and Hennessy with fashion house Louis Vuitton. The group had rights to Dior perfumes, which Arnault wanted for Dior Couture. Exploiting a conflict between Alain Chevalier, Moët Hennessy's CEO, and Henry Recamier, president of Louis Vuitton, he finally won control of LVMH in 1989 and then consolidated his power by purging executives.

Under Arnault's direction, the company is expanding into China, Russia, and India. He has shown a keen eye for talent, employing John Galliano in 1996 to design Dior, and Marc Jacobs in 1997 as artistic director of Luis Vuitton. In 2003 Jacobs brought in the then virtually unknown Takashi Murakami, initially to redesign the iconic Louis Vuitton monogram and then to produce a very successful range of handbags. Arnault also befriended Nicolas Sarkozy at an early stage, attending his first wedding, and has kept up the connection: Carla Bruni made headlines on her first state visits abroad by wearing nothing but Dior.

LESSONS IN BUSINESS: PROTECTING YOUR INTERESTS

Arnault is no stranger to the courts. He has used his legendary wealth to maintain an American-style litigious approach. He took on eBay for failing to do enough to block sales of counterfeit goods in a case designed to send a clear warning to others.
→ Nip problems in the bud. If someone is acting against your interests, take action now.
→ Get rid of poor performers. Keeping them on is usually worse than being sued in an industrial tribunal.
→ Use court action to get invoices paid. Being kind to a debtor may be intuitive but it's not good business.

"Luxury goods are the only area in which it is possible to make luxury margins." Bernard Arnault

Maurice Saatchi Co-founder, Saatchi & Saatchi & M&C Saatchi

SAID TO BE the business brains behind Saatchi & Saatchi, the hugely successful advertising agency, Saatchi's rise to the top was meteoric. Within a few years of founding the agency in 1970, he had landed some of the most sought-after accounts in advertising. By 1979, the agency had grown into the UK's largest, and by 1986 it was the largest in the world. When it all came tumbling down in the mid-90s, Saatchi and his brother Charles simply founded another company, M&C Saatchi, which has met with equal acclaim.

BIOGRAPHY
Born in 1946 in Baghdad, Iraq. Saatchi graduated from the London School of Economics with a first-class honors degree in economics.

LEADERSHIP STYLE
Charming and courteous but ruthless. He goes for the jugular.

KEY STRENGTH
The ability to combine creativity with decisive business leadership.

BEST DECISION
Refusing a purely honorary position with Saatchi & Saatchi in 1995 and leaving the agency to set up a new business.

SELF PROMOTION Saatchi has never been one to lack confidence. When the 21-year old Saatchi went for his first job at the Haymarket publishing empire, he demanded that Michael Heseltine, company owner and future deputy prime minister, pay him double the usual graduate starting salary. Recognizing his exceptional talent, Heseltine conceded. In 1970, he and his brother Charles set up Saatchi & Saatchi. They were 24 and 27 respectively.

NOTHING IS IMPOSSIBLE Highly creative as well as brainy, Saatchi did not take long to make his mark in the world of advertising. Following the Saatchi & Saatchi credo that "Nothing Is Impossible," the persuasive Saatchi went after the most lucrative and high-profile contracts in advertising, securing, among others, the Conservative Party account. The

Saatchi & Saatchi poster campaign for the Conservatives in 1979, featuring the "Labour Isn't Working" slogan, played a significant part in the outcome of the general election. With clients including Silk Cut and British Airways, the agency expanded rapidly, gaining a stock market listing through a reverse takeover of a rival. Not all went Saatchi's way, though. In 1995, a shareholder revolt saw the brothers thrown off the board of their own company. Undeterred, they set up M&C Saatchi, taking the British Airways account. Others followed, and the new agency has flourished.

In the advertising industry, Maurice Saatchi clearly found his métier. In politics he found an outlet for his philosophy and his desire for power and influence. He was made a life peer in 1996 and later served as shadow Treasury spokesman in the House of Lords.

LESSONS IN BUSINESS: PLAYING TO YOUR STRENGTHS

Being talented is just the start. Maurice Saatchi found his calling in the advertising industry, which demands hard-nosed business analysis, psychological insight, and creative flair.
- → Know what your talents are, understand their value, and then find or create the context that best suits them.
- → Use a mentor to check that your assessment of your talents bears the scrutiny of another person.
- → Understand what drives you and use your business life to advance whatever you aspire to be or do.

"If you can't reduce your argument to a few crisp words or phrases it probably means there's something wrong with your argument." Maurice Saatchi

Rupert Murdoch Chairman & CEO, News Corp.

FROM LITTLE KNOWN Australian newspaper proprietor to one of the world's most powerful media moguls, the rise of Murdoch is a tale of huge riches and high drama. In the 20 years or so from 1968, through a series of audacious takeovers, he established his News Corp. dynasty as the major player in the UK, the US, and Asian media markets. Murdoch's approach was resolutely commercial rather than political, and yet in consequence he came to enjoy an unprecedented degree of power in both fields, particularly in the UK and the US.

BIOGRAPHY
Born in 1931 in Melbourne, Australia. His father, Sir Keith, owned the *Adelaide News* and several other newspapers. His mother, Dame Elisabeth, came from wealthy Irish stock. Murdoch has been married three times and his six children range in age from 5 to 50.

LEADERSHIP STYLE
Ambitious, engaged, decisive. Murdoch is fiercely loyal to a small number of long-serving lieutenants in his organization.

KEY STRENGTH
Cracking open markets using a potent combination of money, contacts, and determination.

BEST DECISION
Retaining effective control of the NYSE-listed News Corp. through a series of family trusts. The corporate governance types don't like it, but the arrangement allows Murdoch to run his huge public company more like a dynamic family business.

FROM OZ TO THE OLD COUNTRY Born into a wealthy Australian newspaper family, Murdoch enjoyed a privileged upbringing. After the death of his father in 1952, he rescued the debt-ridden family business, which had considerable shareholdings in Australian newspaper publishers. By 1968, he had turned his attention to the British market, beating Robert Maxwell to acquire first *The News of the World* and then the recently-launched tabloid daily *The Sun*, both of which he made into huge sellers, with a mix of right-of-center politics, plenty of scandal, sex, and sports

DEEP SELF-BELIEF A pragmatist, Murdoch made his name in Britain as a Thatcherite union buster in the 1980s thanks to his introduction of new production technology and working practices, but he switched allegiance to support

Tony Blair ahead of the 1997 New Labor landslide. Murdoch is a gutsy and self-assured decision-maker, even under huge pressure. When News Corp. was in serious financial trouble in the recession of the early 1990s, Murdoch saved the day by betting everything on his latest purchase, Sky TV. It worked and BSkyB is now the number one pay-TV channel in the UK.

Murdoch's main interests now lie in the US, where he launched the controversial Fox News TV channel in 1996 and bought Dow Jones & Company (publishers of the *Wall Street Journal*) for $5 billion in 2007; and in China, where his Star TV and Phoenix TV are now key players. In addition to his broadcasting interests, he now owns more than 100 newspapers across the world, as well as the pioneering social networking website MySpace, which he bought for $580 million in 2005.

LESSONS IN BUSINESS: GOING FOR IT

When Murdoch sees something he wants, he moves fast and with total commitment. He usually gets the prize, as with his most recent trophy purchase, America's *Wall Street Journal* (part of the Dow Jones group), overcoming the objections of the family owners.
→ Strike quickly. Don't take no for an answer. Wrongfoot the competition by getting your bid in first.
→ Offer enough money to overcome resistance to a take over but give assurances you will protect quality.
→ Put processes in place to demonstrate that your buying a company will not affect its integrity.

> "When you're a catalyst for change you make enemies—and I'm proud of the ones I've made."
> Rupert Murdoch

Michael O'Leary CEO, Ryanair

A FOUL-MOUTHED controversialist, O'Leary is the man who has revolutionized European air travel. By offering fares as low as a few euros to destinations all over the continent, he has persuaded millions of budget-conscious consumers to use no-frills Ryanair where they would previously have taken a train or bus. Since being made CEO in 1994, he has transformed the airline from basket-case local outfit into Europe's fastest-growing and largest budget carrier, with profits nearing £300 million.

BIOGRAPHY
Born in 1961 in Mullingar, Ireland. Attended a Jesuit boarding school, and studied business at Trinity College, Dublin.

LEADERSHIP STYLE
Belligerent. O'Leary does not seem to care whom he offends, and has picked fights with just about everyone who is anyone in the airline world, from British Airways to the Irish Government.

KEY STRENGTH
Cost control. Notorious for excising every last ounce of fat from his own processes, and those of his suppliers.

BEST DECISION
That "no frills" should really mean "no frills", not even an allocated seat. It made Ryanair into something genuinely original—essentially a flying bus service.

OUTSPOKEN PUBLICITY-SEEKER O'Leary worked as an accountant before founding a newsagent's business in 1985. He so impressed Ryanair founder Tony Ryan with his financial skills that the Irish tycoon decided to give the entrepreneurial youngster a chance at saving his ailing airline. Basing his ideas on a personal study of US low-cost pioneer Southwest Airlines, he soon had Ryanair back in the black and it quickly became Europe's fastest growing airline.

Along the road to success he has cheerfully poured vitriol on competitors, industry bodies, —indeed, on anyone he perceives as getting in his way. He states explicitly his desire to beat British Airways, derides conventional polite etiquette toward industry rivals, and gives short shrift to travel agents, on the grounds that they do nothing for customers. Even passengers don't escape his tirades—quizzed about his firm's much-criticized complaints procedure, he once responded, "What part of 'no refund' don't you understand?"

A SHARP OPERATOR O'Leary is an extremely astute and canny executive who achieves higher loadings and operating margins than just about anybody else in the airline business. He believes the cost base of many full-service rivals is unsustainable, and that the industry is peopled by enthusiasts rather than commercial brains. He has been criticized for a "take it or leave it" attitude to both suppliers and his own staff, and for constantly pushing the boundaries of what is legally acceptable in the advertising campaigns that Ryanair runs, none of which seems to have persuaded him to change his tactics or belligerent stance.

LESSONS IN BUSINESS: KEEPING A FIRM GRIP ON COSTS

O'Leary's approach may be uncompromising but it is extremely effective. Ryanair is in a better position than practically all its rivals to survive changing oil prices and diminishing consumer demand.
→ Watch out for losing control of costs when things are going very well. Impress on people the importance of building reserves.
→ Show leadership by avoiding conspicuous spending on your office or on traveling.
→ Expect the unexpected and build the financial strength to withstand risks with a very low probability.

"Now anyone can afford to fly." Micheal O'Leary

Subroto Roy Chairman & CEO, Sahara Group

DESCRIBED VARIOUSLY as a genius, maverick, visionary, crook, and money launderer, sometimes all in the same breath, Roy is an enigma at the head of a mystery. It is difficult to reach the truth about the charismatic leader of Sahara Group and the company he calls his "family", but he is undeniably an influential and fascinating business leader in modern India. Having started with virtually nothing, he is now believed to have assets of around $11 billion from a portfolio that spans financial services, media, and property.

THE RUPEE KING In 1978, with 2,000 rupees (about $40), two colleagues, and an old Lambretta scooter, Roy launched himself into business with a savings scheme for farmers in the state of Bihar in northeast India. Based on deposits as low as a few rupees, which he initially collected personally on his scooter, the business that he built now has an estimated six million investors.

ANGELS AND DEMONS This "parabanking" or "savings scheme for the poor", has made Roy one of India's richest tycoons with an impressive range of business interests. He now owns a 24-hour TV entertainment channel, newspapers, and a production company that has up to 50 films in production at any one time. He builds shopping malls, housing developments, and new towns. He sold his airline, Air Sahara, for $560 million to Jet Airways in 2006. He attributes his success to nurturing talent and building strong teams, but to many outsiders his business methods seem unconventional. Critics say he is running a cult in which employees have to greet each other with their right arm over their chest and say "Sahara Pranam" ("Good Sahara"). The organization is intensely private, and figures are difficult to come by. Sahara says the group's profits are either plowed back into the business or into good causes.

Roy enjoys an extravagant lifestyle and is rarely out of the gossip columns. When his sons were married, it was described as the "Indian Wedding of the Century". He enjoys all the trappings of success, with houses that include replicas of the White House and Buckingham Palace.

LESSONS IN BUSINESS: GETTING EMOTIONAL

Roy has a unique style of management that he describes as "collective materialism". He defines the concept as giving the first priority to the emotional aspect and blending it with materialism. This results in continuous collective growth.
→ Make sure every employee has a reason for going to work in the morning that makes them feel good.
→ Nurture a culture where teams respect each other, work supportively, and feel connected to success.
→ Instil pride in people. Pride in the organization motivates people to take pride in their own contribution.

"I'm very proud to be the guardian of the world's largest family." Subroto Roy

Christophe de Margerie CEO, Total SA

A DISTINCTIVE MUSTACHE gives de Margerie a jovial, military bearing, and as leader of Total SA, he commands the most valuable company in the eurozone and the world's fourth largest publicly traded oil and gas company. Unusually for a French CEO, de Margerie has spent his entire working life in business. As well as being a no-holds-barred spokesman for the oil industry, he has proved himself adept at striking up profitable relationships with oil-rich nations. He believes, however, that the future of energy is nuclear.

BIOGRAPHY
Born in the Vendée region of France in 1951. De Margerie is a member of the family that makes Taittinger champagne. He is a graduate of the Ecole Supérieure de Commerce in Paris.

LEADERSHIP STYLE
Outspoken, bold, and tough. De Margerie's pragmatism gives him a no-nonsense approach to leadership.

KEY STRENGTH
Telling it how it is. Whether discussing gas prices, oil reserves, or the future of the industry, de Margerie prefers to be realistic rather than diplomatic.

BEST DECISION
Signing a deal with Gazprom to develop the Shtokman gas field in the Barents Sea.

BLUNT SPEECH Most French oil leaders learn their business at the elite and rarefied Ecole des Mines. De Margerie is proud to have learned the business out in the field, as *un homme du terrain*. Since becoming CEO in early 2007, de Margerie, who is never afraid to speak his mind, has happily broken ranks with the rest of the oil industry. For example, he has declared that the world will never be able to produce more than 85 million barrels of oil per day, let alone increase its output to the 120 million barrels that energy analysts predict will be needed by 2030.

A PRAGMATIC OUTLOOK De Margerie is aware that, with the difficult technological and political challenges of oil extraction, oil companies are going to have to work a lot harder to meet the global demand for fuel.

A process of "resource nationalization" is under way, as developing oil-rich countries seek to control resources and renegotiate old deals.

A large proportion of Total's output is from dangerous or politically sensitive areas, but de Margerie sees these challenges as an opportunity for growth. As part of his strategy for the company's future, de Margerie has negotiated important relationships in difficult parts of the world, though it has led to accusations of cozying up to questionable regimes. Total recently won a contract to help Gazprom, Russia's state-controlled gas giant, develop Shtokman, a massive offshore gas field. The company is also involved in projects in Iran, Kazakhstan, and Venezuela. Meanwhile, de Margerie is already looking at the possibility of helping to build a civil nuclear energy plant in the Middle East.

LESSONS IN BUSINESS: OILING THE WHEELS

De Margerie believes the technical ability to pump oil is no longer enough. To be successful, today's oil companies have to recognize that they are using up finite resources and need to develop accordingly, moving with environmental legislation and other changes in the long term. This has lessons for all companies.
➔ Ask yourself and your team how your customers will meet their needs and wants in a few years' time.
➔ Today's global issues will impact the future. Make sure your business plan is realistic for the long term.
➔ Where your customer is a state owned business, include action steps on global environmental issues.

"In 20 years I don't see how we could be absent from the fields of clean fuel and nuclear power."
Christophe de Margerie

Kerkor Kerkorian President & CEO, Tracinda Corp.

DAREDEVIL PILOT, amateur boxing champion, and Las Vegas high roller: Kerkorian's life is the stuff of movie legend. Yet beyond his vast wealth—he sits at number seven in the pantheon of living billionaires, with a fortune of $18 billion—he maintains a remarkably low public profile, despite marriages to a former showgirl and to a tennis star, and a wheeler-dealing business career that has seen him buy and sell airlines, film studios, and casinos, and make three abortive attempts to gain a foothold in the automotive industry.

BIOGRAPHY
Born in 1917 in Fresno, California, to immigrant Armenian parents. Kerkorian dropped out of school.

LEADERSHIP STYLE
A risk-taker, Kerkorian has made and lost fortunes on, effectively, a roll of the dice. He is always ready to bounce back with a new deal.

KEY STRENGTH
Buying assets with excess value that can be stripped and sold back. Kerkorian managed to finance his purchase of war-surplus bombers by selling off the aviation fuel in the tanks.

BEST DECISION
Purchasing 80 acres of low-priced land for $960,000 near the Las Vegas Strip in 1962. He parlayed it into $9 million and set himself up for his Vegas career.

RISKY BUSINESS Following the bankruptcy of his parents' watermelon farm in 1921, "Kirk" Kerkorian had to hustle to make a living, selling newspapers and doing odd jobs. He claims it shaped his outlook, giving him the drive that would shape his business life. Risk-taking was a key component, as was serendipity. Sent to reform school as a teenager, he developed a fearsome reputation as a welterweight boxer. Kerkorian also fixed water heaters for a pilot acquaintance and became hooked on flying. Gaining a pilot's licence in 1940, he delivered aircraft to the UK in World War II, building up capital to start a small airline in the 1950s.

THE ART OF THE DEAL From there, Kerkorian's career has been one deal after another. After taking Trans International Airlines public, he sold out to Transamerica in 1968 for $85 million. Meanwhile, after developing a love of the Las Vegas gaming tables, he made money in land deals on the Strip, buying the legendary Mafia-owned Flamingo Hotel in 1967, before re-imagining the Nevada playground as a family-friendly resort and pioneering the multimillion-dollar mega-resort. Kerkorian is not a turnaround artist, however. His repeated purchase and sale of MGM since 1969 boosted his bottom line, but never revived the film studio's fortunes. Later, he became involved with the car industry, buying and selling stakes in GM, Chrysler, and Ford, but failing to gain control of any of them. As the global economy contracted in the late 2000s, Kerkorian retrenched to his hospitality stronghold, clearly believing in the power of the Las Vegas dream to see him through recession and beyond.

LESSONS IN BUSINESS: EMBRACING RISK

Kerkorian's business approach was exemplified by a night's gambling in the Las Vegas casinos. After losing all but $5 at the craps table, he decided to risk the last of his money rather than buy breakfast—and won $700.
→ Recognize that successful entrepreneurs risk losing vast sums in deals that go wrong, but continue to invest.
→ Always bounce back. No plan is implemented without mistakes and problems, but encourage resilience.
→ Have at least some "high risk, high return" businesses in your portfolio to improve your peoples' ability to adapt quickly to new circumstances..

"When you're a self-made man you start very early in life. In my case, it was at nine years old."
Kerkor Kerkorian

Donald Trump Chairman & CEO, Trump Organization

"THE DONALD", as his first wife Ivana called him, is the one CEO everyone recognizes. Hardly a day goes by when property mogul Trump is not in the news. As head of Trump Organization, he owns more than 18 million square feet of Manhattan and he is one of the world's highest-paid TV stars. He also operates casinos and hotels across the world. His deal-making, glamorous lifestyle, and outspoken manner had made him a household name even before NBC asked him to host US primetime reality show *The Apprentice*.

BIOGRAPHY
Born in Queens, New York, in 1946. Son of wealthy property developer and founder of the Trump Organization, Frederick Trump. He attended New York Military Academy, Fordham University, and University of Pennsylvania.

LEADERSHIP STYLE
Flamboyant, audacious, and egocentric. He has been called a "21st-century reincarnation of PT Barnum." Employees say he operates an open-door policy, but many believe it is mainly so he can shout at them through it.

KEY STRENGTH
Recognizing opportunity where others don't. He is the master of creating a buzz and sweeping investors along in his enthusiasm for ambitious new projects.

BEST DECISION
Using his own name to build a multibillion-dollar brand. Trump Towers, Trump Palaces, Trump Plazas, Trump Hotels, Trump Golf Clubs: naming properties after himself is ingenious, subliminally suggesting a building belongs to him long after it has been sold.

TRUMP TOWN Trump learned his deal-making and entrepreneurial skills from his father, Frederick. From the early age of 11 he helped out at the family firm, and was soon impatient to forge his own business career. To everybody except Trump, the redevelopment of the Commodore Hotel seemed impossible. Nevertheless, in 1974, he purchased the hotel for $10 million and began negotiating his first big deal. He completely renovated the exterior of the Grand Central Station and the entire hotel. The Commodore, renamed the Grand Hyatt Hotel, opened in 1980, by which time Trump was regarded as the city's best-known developer. But Trump was far from satisfied. He wanted to create unique buildings that people would talk about and admire, making them eponymous to advertise the family business brand. In 1982 the world-renowned 58-story skyscraper, Trump Tower, was opened, attracting well-known retail stores and celebrity renters. However, rapid early expansion led to mounting debt, and during the 1990s Trump faced financial problems.

THE COMEBACK KID He carried out a dramatic turnaround with the financial help of his three siblings, and the late 1990s saw him amass another fortune. According to *Forbes* magazine he is worth $2.7 billion; Trump insists one should "Double that" to be accurate.

Golf is one of Trump's secret weapons, and he claims to have made a lot of money socializing on the links. He has had planning approved to construct the "greatest golf course in the world" in the northeast of Scotland, cited to be the prospective financial saviour of the region when North Sea oil supplies run dry.

LESSONS IN BUSINESS: HAVING CONFIDENCE

Trump's motto is undoubtedly "think big"—don't build 20 floors if you can build 120, and never stop believing in yourself. Leadership often means doing more than others would advise.
- → Use your self-confidence to rebound from financial calamity or setbacks however often they happen.
- → Be passionate about the business—without passion it can be impossible to build confidence.
- → When people urge caution listen to them, but trust your own judgement as well. If you still believe something will work to the benefit of the business, do it.

"I don't make deals for the money. I've got enough, much more than I'll ever need. I do it to do it."
Donald Trump

POLISHED PUBLIC RELATIONS

The image of a company in the public eye is a vitally important component of its success or failure. However well a business is run, if it has a bad public image it will struggle to survive, and CEOs neglect public relations at their peril. There are two broad approaches. Some company chiefs are tempted to make as much noise as they can, dressing up in bizarre outfits, jumping out of balloons, and going to other headline-inducing extremes in the quest for publicity. Others take a defensive tack, staying as quiet as possible until a threat arises and only then fronting up to the public. The usually reserved and analytical **Jeroen van der Veer** (p273) took over as CEO at the energy and petrochemicals company Royal Dutch Shell in the middle of a crisis, after it was revealed that the company had overstated its oil reserves by more than 20 percent. The controversy threatened to cause lasting damage, and his response included a textbook case of swift and effective defensive PR. At the other extreme, **Larry Ellison** (p59) has made himself the public face of US software company Oracle at every opportunity, singing the praises of his company and putting the public boot into his rivals whenever possible ●

"I've worn almost every costume there is to wear. It makes a back page photo into a front page one. And they come back for more."
RICHARD BRANSON

The Impact of Good Publicity

Many CEOs would prefer to focus on the big strategic issues, but it's impossible to avoid the connection between what the CEO does and how the entire company is perceived; they are widely regarded as the embodiment of their company and its values. The wise executive recognizes this and acts accordingly, realizing that every word and action can have an impact on public perceptions.

Apart from those few, such as **Richard Branson** (p421) and **Steve Jobs** (p17) for example, who are natural showmen and have an instinctive grasp of handling the media, most CEOs take a great deal of considered professional advice before making public gestures of any kind. Failing to think through the implications of any move or statement on different markets, customers, or interest groups can be expensive, and failing to see how the company's fortunes can be boosted with a few well-chosen words or acts can result in the loss of cheap opportunities.

Gestures can have a big effect. With sales at clothing retailer Gap slumping, CEO **Glenn Murphy** volunteered to earn a salary of just $1 while he worked to turn the ailing company around. It made a great headline and showed him to be committed to the company and its fortunes. The fact that he was still in receipt of other forms of remuneration that totaled a good deal more than $1 was secondary; the impact had been made.

Good PR can transform the toughest situations. Bridgestone could hardly have faced a worse outlook than when it had to recall 6.5 million tires produced by its subsidiary Firestone, which had been the cause of fatal accidents in the US. However, through his assiduous work across all areas of public contact, new CEO **Shigeo Watanabe** rebuilt the company's reputation and returned it to health and profitability.

Giving Out Good PR

Think before you act—Before making any public statement or move, ensure that you assess its possible impact on the widest range of audiences: customers, shareholders, employees, partners, competitors, and regulators.

Look after the media—You may not want to talk to journalists, but it is usually better than neglecting communication with them. Establishing open channels with the media means you're much less likely to be misunderstood.

Consider a makeover—In our media-saturated age, all firms should consider employing PR professionals to assess their company's image and manage its presentation.

Media-wise Bosses

There are many ways to generate good PR, as these CEOs show:

Tony Fernandes, AirAsia (Aviation: Malaysia)—*Renowned for his media savvy, he actively used publicity to develop a significant regional airline.*

Noel Bartram, Bernard Matthews (Foodstuffs: UK)—*Bartram's rebranding and vigorous PR helped turn the tide of negative publicity at the poultry company, following a dip in sales after a bird-flu scare.*

Michael Bishop, BMI (Aviation: UK) - *When a BMI aircraft crashed in Britain, Bishop's response, which involved going straight to the scene and answering media questions immediately, was regarded as textbook.*

Wayne Smith, Community Health Solutions (Health sector: US)—*Believes the CEO should keep out of the limelight and let the collective efforts of staff at his hospitals provide all the good PR.*

Richard Rowe, Goldenpalace.com (Internet: Canada)—*Used brash publicity stunts, including streakers at sports events emblazoned with the company name, to create a global brand.*

Francis Salway, Land Securities Group (Real estate: UK)—*Added the presidency of his industry's body to his role as CEO in order to raise the profile of both and lobby government more effectively.*

Robert Eckert, Mattel (Consumer products: US)—*When it was discovered that millions of Chinese-made toys breached safety standards, he earned admiration from both consumers and retailers for his speed in getting the message out, turning a potential disaster into a success.*

Mark Pigott, Paccar (Automotive: US)—*Maintains a low public profile but gains attention and plaudits for his work and results.*

Evan Williams, Twitter (Internet: US)—*Regular media interviews ensured that his emerging company became a familiar name.*

Vijay Mallya CEO, United Breweries

THE MOST FLAMBOYANT of the new generation of superstar Indian CEOs, Mallya is worth in excess of $1 billion. He is rarely out of a press captivated by his lavish lifestyle, which includes owning one of the world's largest luxury yachts, 250 vintage cars, and a stud farm. He presides over a multinational conglomerate involved in alcoholic beverages, engineering, chemicals, information technology, aviation, and leisure. His drinks empire is now the third largest spirits business in the world. Mallya is also a member of the upper house of the Indian parliament.

BIOGRAPHY
Born in Bantwal, India, in 1955. Vijay is the son of industrialist Vittal Mallya. He holds a bachelor's degree in commerce from the University of Calcutta.

LEADERSHIP STYLE
Charismatic, energetic, and ostentatious. Mallya is a hands-on leader who believes firmly in taking full responsibility for all of his decisions.

KEY STRENGTH
Glamourizing his brands by making them reflect his lavish personal life, while still maintaining the ability to focus on the nitty-gritty of company structure and strategy.

BEST DECISION
Asking his father to back his plan to promote Kingfisher beer, which was to become his flagship lifestyle brand.

THE INDIAN RICHARD BRANSON Mallya initially had no intention of going into business—he wanted to be a doctor—but his father wanted him to join the family firm. Mallya inherited United Breweries from his father in 1983, at the age of 27, and is sensitive to criticism that his mega-wealth came easily. He points out that it is his vision that has seen the group grow into a conglomerate of over 60 companies, which by 1998 had an annual turnover of $1.2 billion. His eye-catching brand of self-promotion has certainly helped, earning him the nickname of the Indian Richard Branson.

SPEED KING When Mallya inherited United Breweries, he restructured it, selling off 22 divisions, including petrochemicals, plastics, foods, and car batteries. The core business became spirits, beer, fertilizers, engineering, and IT. "That," he says with satisfaction, "is a far tighter ship than I inherited."

Believing in the huge potential for aviation in India, Mallya launched Kingfisher Airlines in 2005, named after the group's popular beer brand. With its fleet of new Airbus A-380s and glamourous flight attendants, Kingfisher now connects over 30 cities and Mallya believes he is still only scratching the surface.

In 2007, Mallya spread United's wings beyond India when he bought Scotch whisky maker Whyte & Mackay for £595 million. In the process, he became chairman and CEO of the historic Scottish company. Mallya is keenly competitive when it comes to sports as well. He has his own racehorse stud farm and is the co-owner of the Force India Formula 1 race team (formerly the Spyker F1 team).

LESSONS IN BUSINESS: MAKING AN IMPRESSION

Mallya believes business should never stand still: "You need to be gutsy, you need to have fire in your belly, and there's no point in being scared of the system or of people who are against you."
→ Mold the system to your own ends if you can't work within its existing conventions.
→ Use your own personality to gain publicity. The tactic will be criticized but if you have charisma the public will love it.
→ Be your own person. You are responsible for your success; take the decisions you think are correct.

"I love what I do. To me, work is not stress. It's just non-stop excitement." Vijay Mallya

Richard Branson Founder, Chairman & CEO, Virgin Group

THE DEFINITIVE brand entrepreneur, Branson's unrelenting drive and flair for marketing have enabled him to amass a fortune of over £3 billion, seemingly out of little more than the Virgin name. His relaxed style and penchant for thrill-seeking have made him an international celebrity, but beneath the glossy façade lies an astute and passionate businessman, whom rivals underestimate at their peril. His Virgin empire now numbers over 350 businesses in markets as diverse as travel, health care, media, and financial services.

BIOGRAPHY
Born in 1950 in Surrey, UK. By the age of 15, while attending Stowe School in the UK, Branson had started two business ventures.

LEADERSHIP STYLE
Open and informal. Famous for his lavish staff parties and generous rewards for high achievers, he also drives the team extremely hard. Virgin staff have to give unstinting effort and keep on the top of their game.

KEY STRENGTH
Instinctive marketer with a talent for spotting opportunities. Makes lots of small wins, a few big ones, and very few mistakes.

BEST DECISION
Making the classic Virgin business a model—buying or leasing services from existing operators to minimize risk.

FROM RETAILER TO AIRLINE BOSS

Branson struggled with dyslexia at school and left at age 16; by the time he was 20, Virgin Records was well established as a retailer and record label. When he launched Virgin Atlantic Airlines in 1982, his reputation was already sufficiently fearsome to goad arch-rival British Airways into an ill-advised "dirty tricks" campaign. Branson made hay with the "David and Goliath" publicity, the value of which far exceeded the £500,000 settlement he eventually received from BA.

MARKETING MAGIC

His daredevil exploits—setting a new record for the fastest transatlantic boat crossing and making several attempts to circumnavigate the globe by hot air balloon—helped make Virgin one of the most glamorous brands of the 1980s and 1990s, but his crucial insight was that his high-profile name would work equally well in essentially pedestrian sectors. This opened up huge opportunities in everything from credit cards and gyms to beauty products, cell phones, and cable TV. He's also a talented dealmaker—the reverse takeover of struggling cable operator NTL to form Virgin Media in 2006 created, at a stroke, a quad-play (landline and cell phone, TV, and internet) media business big enough to worry Rupert Murdoch's Sky.

Rare mis-steps include a high-profile losing bid for the UK's National Lottery and a stillborn attempt to take over ailing UK bank Northern Rock in 2007. The group's most intriguing and exciting current project is Virgin Galactic, the company's move into space-tourism, the pioneering of which has been a long-held ambition of Branson's.

LESSONS IN BUSINESS: MINIMIZING THE RISK

Branson's methods are surprisingly cautious. He targets a range of established markets where brands are weak, applying the Virgin brand magic, and selling it on.

→ Avoid high profile *grands projets*. The publicity may be good at the beginning but poor if they prove difficult to implement.

→ Go for projects where you can "suck it and see"—where investment to discover their potential is low.

→ Don't take risks with an established brand—every new venture should exploit it and build it further.

"I never dress up to go and see my bankers. They might think I was in trouble." Richard Branson

Fu Chengyu CEO, China National Offshore Oil Corp.

BIOGRAPHY
Born in China in 1951. Fu studied geology at the Northeast Petroleum Institute, and later gained a master's in petroleum management from the University of Southern California.

BEST DECISION
Acquiring stakes in oil fields in Africa and Asia, contributing to an overall strategy to feed China's growing energy needs..

LESSON IN BUSINESS
Play by the rules—Fu learned the importance of following protocol and operating within a company structure from his failed takeover attempt of Unocal.

WITH OVER 30 YEARS of experience working within the oil industry in China, fluent English-speaker Fu is CEO of China's biggest offshore energy producer, commonly known by its acronym, CNOOC.

Fu first joined CNOOC in 1982, but left to become vice president of Phillips Petroleum International Corporation (Asia) in 1995. He was the first Chinese person to hold such a senior position in the international oil industry. Fu returned to CNOOC Nanhai East Corporation as general manager in 1999. Following the successful restructure and overseas public flotation of CNOOC Ltd and COSL, the two major subsidiaries of CNOOC, he became CEO of CNOOC in 2003. Since then he has expanded the company's overseas presence, notably in Asia and Africa. In 2005, Fu caused controversy in Washington, DC when he offered $18.5 billion for US oil and gas giant Unocal, in the largest takeover ever attempted by a Chinese company. However, the bid failed as Fu had not managed to gain the backing of his board of directors in time. Since then, he has announced a long-term plan to invest $29 billion in oil and gas exploration in the South China Sea.

Brian L. Roberts Chairman & CEO, Comcast Corp.

BIOGRAPHY
Born in Philadelphia in 1959. Roberts graduated with a BS from Wharton School of the University of Pennsylvania. He is also a talented squash player.

BEST DECISION
Buying AT&T's broadband division in 2002. This catapulted Comcast from a regional player to the largest cable company in the whole of the US.

LESSON IN BUSINESS
Seize the moment—buying AT&T Broadband was a gamble, but Roberts recognized it as a one-off opportunity to redefine his business.

A BID TO BUY AT&T's broadband division marked Roberts as a top deal maker, but turning Comcast's cable communications business around made his reputation as a talented CEO. Roberts calmly invested in a downturn, and reaped the rewards.

From his earliest days in the business world, Roberts earned a reputation as a swashbuckling deal maker. He hijacked CBS's deal to buy the shopping channel QVC in 1994, greeting the owner from his private plane at New Jersey with a $2.5 billion offer. At that time he was working with his father, Ralph J. Roberts, Comcast's founder. However, a deal to acquire AT&T Broadband was of a different order altogether, and it was all of Brian's own making. There had been opposition to it as the $29-billion takeover left Comcast vulnerable at a time when other cable firms were going bust, and shares in the survivors were tumbling. Roberts invested $2 billion to upgrade the old AT&T cable network. However, the real gamble lay in predicting how many subscribers would sign up for high-speed broadband. Luckily for him, Roberts had made the right call. Profits rose, and Comcast has grown to more than 24 million cable customers and 14 million broadband subscribers.

"The computer has crashed into the television set."
Brian L. Roberts

John W. Rowe Chairman, President & CEO, Exelon Corp.

BIOGRAPHY
Born in Wisconsin in 1945. Rowe was educated at the University of Wisconsin and Wisconsin Law School.

BEST DECISION
Publicly apologizing for Exelon's service after a blackout paralyzed central Chicago. He went on to fire senior executives and invest heavily in new infrastructure.

LESSON IN BUSINESS
Court your customers—Rowe bought nuclear plants when they were unpopular, and won public support by opposing new reactors until the country's spent-fuel disposal problem was solved.

CHALLENGING the industry orthodoxy on human contribution to climate change, maverick energy tycoon Rowe sought mandatory carbon-emission targets, while aggressively placing Exelon as the largest power company in the US.

Rowe practiced briefly as a lawyer but, aged 38, quit for a 25-year career leading successively larger electricity utilities. He served as CEO of Central Maine Power Company, the New England Electric System, and Unicom Corp. In 1998 Unicom merged with PECO Energy Company, creating Exelon. Rowe became a director in 2000, chairman and CEO in 2002, and also president in 2004. As CEO he launched an aggressive campaign to acquire and improve nuclear capacity to complement fossil and hydro generation. A drive for efficiency created the US's biggest and most profitable electrical utility (annual revenues topped $19 billion). Rowe has attempted to lead a sometimes recalcitrant energy industry toward green responsibility. He advocates legislative limits to carbon emissions and has pledged to chop 15 million tonnes from Exelon's greenhouse gas emissions by 2020—equal to the company's annual carbon footprint, and equivalent to removing three million cars from the road.

Andrew Forrest CEO, Fortescue Metals Group Ltd

BIOGRAPHY
Born c.1962, Forrest grew up at Minderoo, his family's sheep station in the Pilbara region of Western Australia. He worked for a while as a "jackeroo," or apprentice, on the station, and attended college for only a short period.

BEST DECISION
Going after the red-hot Chinese market for iron ore.

LESSON IN BUSINESS
Bounce back—public disapproval and investor distrust over his Anaconda Nickel losses didn't stop Forrest from convincing new investors to back his Fortescue iron ore venture.

BATTLING IT OUT at the mineshafts and in the stock market, through his iron ore business Fortescue Metals Group, maverick entrepreneur Forrest has become Australia's richest citizen with an estimated fortune of AU$13 billion.

"Twiggy" Forrest overcame a childhood stutter to pursue success as a mining entrepreneur after early careers as a stockbroker and alpaca farmer. In 1994, he founded Anaconda Nickel, but the company fell short of its promise with investors losing heavily, and the stock was dismissed as a "penny dreadful." In 2003, "silver-tongued" Forrest again charmed international investors into putting up vast sums to create Fortescue Metals Group to mine iron ore in the metal-rich Pilbara for Chinese markets. The mega-project involved building a 100-mile rail line and the construction of an Indian Ocean port. As ore prices soared in early 2008, investors scrambled aboard. Initially, Chinese buyers held back, restricted by government regulations and cautious about Fortescue control. In early 2009, despite falling ore prices and plummeting share value, the company made a modest recovery. Forrest, who sees little good in wealth, is renowned for giving away much of his fortune.

"Forrest is the quintessential Aussie bloke, just as happy to say g'day to the garbage man as the prime minister." Tim Treadgold, mining commentator

Ren Zhengfei President & CEO, Huawei Technologies Company Ltd

BIOGRAPHY
Born in Guizhou Province, China, in 1944. Ren studied at Chongqing University of Posts and Telecommunications.

BEST DECISION
Winning the contract, in 1996, to provide network products to Hutchison Whampoa Ltd in Hong Kong, which began Huawei's expansion into overseas markets.

LESSON IN BUSINESS
Hunt like a wolf—Ren has said that Huawei can only compete with multinationals by developing the spirit of a wolf.

SUSPICIONS ABOUT Ren's long-standing military connections have cost telecom group Huawei foreign contracts, but have not deterred its rapid growth and rise to become a leading global player. Ren has also become one of China's richest men.

After being forced out of the downsizing Chinese army in 1982, Ren worked for an oil firm prior to founding Huawei Technologies in Shenzhen in 1988. Specializing in telecoms equipment, the company built communications networks for the Chinese government and army. In 1996, Ren began a policy of expanding, first into Hong Kong and then internationally, marketing lower-cost alternatives to western products. He struck up strategic partnerships with companies such as Siemens in Germany, 3Com and Symantec in the US, and Optus in Australia. Ren's aggressive pursuit of partners and technological advantage soon led to rapid growth. However, Huawei has been accused of industrial espionage and poor working conditions for employees, and its ex-military CEO and closed ledgers have led to criticism. US fears that Huawei products could siphon sensitive information to China, although since downplayed by security experts, led Huawei to pull out of buying ailing Canadian telecom company Nortel.

Gareth Davies CEO, Imperial Tobacco

BIOGRAPHY
Born in Bolton, England, in 1950. Davies graduated from Sheffield University with a degree in geography and economics.

BEST DECISION
Purchasing the German Reemtsma Cigarettenfabriken, with its Davidoff and West brands of cigarettes, thus ensuring Imperial's position as a global tobacco company.

LESSON IN BUSINESS
Follow your own path—Davies is one of the most maligned CEOs in Europe because of antipathy to the cigarette industry, but he has stood by his company.

CITY FAVORITE Davies has over 35 years' experience of the tobacco industry and has played a significant role in turning Imperial Tobacco into one of the world's leading multinational tobacco businesses.

Joining Imperial Tobacco in 1972 as a management trainee, Davies worked his way through the ranks. His appointment as CEO followed his successful handling of a demerger in 1996, and his overseeing of Imperial's subsequent listing on the London and New York stock exchanges. Davies has streamlined operations and transformed the group from the world's thirteenth biggest tobacco company to one of the top four. Imperial's Lambert & Butler and Richmond remain two of the most popular brands in the UK. Responding to declining domestic sales, Davies promoted the budget brand Regal, Golden Virginia (a roll-your-own tobacco), and Rizla papers. Davies has faced criticism for his failure to clamp down on wholesaler cigarette smuggling, and for targeting young smokers. The company has also faced allegations of price fixing. With plans to retire in 2010, Davies's legacy will be to have shaped one of the most efficient cigarette manufacturers in the world.

"Our business fundamentals are excellent and our resilience in times of turbulent economic conditions is well known." Gareth Davies

Koo Bon-moo Chairman & CEO, LG Group

BIOGRAPHY
Born in South Korea in 1945, the grandson of Koo In Hwoi, founder of Lucky Goldstar. Koo was educated at Ashland University, Ohio.

BEST DECISION
Introducing the "Right Way" ethics code and a new corporate governance structure to overhaul the company's image.

LESSON IN BUSINESS
Image is crucial—Koo realized that a company's image must appeal to investors as much as to customers. His implementation of major changes reassured both.

SUCCEEDING HIS FATHER at a time when the electricals and chemicals giant was in decline and the ethics of Korea's family firms under scrutiny, Koo changed the name from Lucky Goldstar to LG and introduced a new code of conduct.

No-one doubted LG's capacity for innovation, but investors were alarmed that the company was bailing out loss-making parts of its empire with transfers from profit-making divisions. To succeed in global markets, LG needed to build Chinese walls between its divisions. To this end, Koo introduced a new ethics code called "Jeong Do," or "the Right Way." He also managed to allay the fears of investors when more than $144 million was transferred to the ailing LG Card Company from the LG Electrical Company. He achieved this through the introduction of a new corporate structure and implementation of fundamental management changes, which clearly showed that sound leadership overrode family ties; Koo sacked his own brother when his LCD screen joint venture with Phillips ran into trouble in 2007. Overall, LG is thriving under Koo's control: sales are up, transparency has improved, and Koo's personal fortune has more than doubled.

Vagit Alekperov Founder & President, LUKOIL

BIOGRAPHY
Born in Baku, Azerbaijan, in 1950. Alekperov's father, an oil worker, died when Vagit was a boy. At 18, Alekperov combined work on an oil rig with study for his PhD at Azerbaijan's Oil & Chemistry Institute.

BEST DECISION
Creating LUKOIL, when he was the deputy oil minister of the USSR, and becoming president and a ten percent shareholder.

LESSON IN BUSINESS
Work within the system—adapt to the rules of governments and befriend those in power.

WITH A NET WORTH of $13 billion, Alekperov is one of the wealthiest men in the world. He worked his way from rig work in the Caspian Sea to be head of LUKOIL, an oil company with reserves second only to ExxonMobil.

In 1991, as the USSR's deputy minister of oil, Alekperov combined three state-run oil fields and several refineries to create LUKOIL. Two years later, new privatization laws enabled him to step down from his government post to become president of LUKOIL. He courted foreign investors by promoting LUKOIL— and himself—as a dependable source of oil. Reportedly, whenever a foreign company was having a tough time starting up an oil-development project in Russia, Alekperov would make the oil flow in exchange for a share in the project. Alekperov made LUKOIL truly global by tapping into reserves in Colombia, Libya, and Iraq. Following deals with Getty Oil in 2000 and ConocoPhillips in 2006, LUKOIL operates gas stations across Europe and the US. Alekperov has also moved into the banking sector and the media, where his shareholder power has reportedly led to the firing of editorial staff who criticize either LUKOIL or Vladimir Putin.

"It is impossible to divide the interest of a country and a company that works on its soil." Vagit Alekperov

Nabeel Gareeb CEO (2002–08), MEMC Electronic Materials, Inc.

BIOGRAPHY
Born in Pakistan in 1965. Gareeb completed a BSc in electrical engineering, followed by a master's in engineering management.

BEST DECISION
Focusing MEMC on supplying polysilicon wafers to the rapidly growing solar energy industry, a long-term strategy worth billions of dollars to the company.

LESSON FOR BUSINESS
Find a company's USP—in the case of MEMC it was the ability to manufacture its own wafers, giving Gareeb the chance to revive a flagging industry pioneer.

THE HIGHEST PAID CEO under the age of 45 in 2007, according to *Forbes*, Gareeb has been credited with resurrecting MEMC and turning it into one of the world's leading, and most profitable, suppliers of polysilicon wafers.

When MEMC, purchased by Texas Pacific Group from Germany's E.ON AG in 2001, began looking for a new CEO, they were drawn to Gareeb. The highly paid COO of Rectifier Corporation had a comprehensive understanding of the market and its customers, making him the ideal candidate. Gareeb took up the post in 2002 on an initial four-year contract. One of his first challenges was to produce raw polysilicon profitably. In 2002, although the company's sales had increased by 11 percent from the previous year, it had still posted a loss of $22 million. Gareeb drew up a strategy that included cutting costs, upgrading production facilities to increase efficiency, and gaining MEMC a unique position as both a producer of raw polysilicon and a maker of polysilicon wafers (for computer chips and semiconductors). By 2006, profits and sales had increased by 40 percent over the previous year. In 2008, having turned MEMC into a major player, Gareeb announced his departure.

Hugh Grant Chairman, President & CEO, Monsanto

BIOGRAPHY
Born in Scotland, UK, in 1958. Grant studied at Glasgow University, Edinburgh University, and the International Management Center, Buckingham, UK.

BEST DECISION
Moving the company's focus to developing seeds with improved yield potential, which has led to increased market share and profit.

LESSON IN BUSINESS
Focus on sustainability—under Grant, Monsanto is working toward a sustainable agricultural model that will enable it to increase production while using fewer resources.

THE TRADITIONAL characteristics of prudence and thrift displayed by Scottish CEO Grant have paid dividends for food biotechnology company Monsanto's bottom-line, as well as helping the global farming community at large.

Grant joined Monsanto in 1981 as a product development representative. In 1991, he relocated to the US as global strategy director of the agriculture division. Since Grant became CEO in 2003, Monsanto has evolved, growing as a business and focusing on corporate and social responsibility. Grant has refocused Monsanto on increasing yield, reducing use of natural resources, limiting its impact on the environment, and sharing developments with farmers, particularly in developing countries.

Grant's primary objective has been to develop drought-tolerant seed, with the first drought-tolerant corn expected to be available by 2012. Monsanto's goal is to double yields of its corn, soybean, and cotton by 2030, using a third less fertilizer, water, and energy per unit of output. To achieve this, Monsanto spends $2 million a day on research. Grant has already proved his approach is good for business, with recorded sales topping $11 billion, despite vocal criticism from opponents of genetically modified crops.

"I believe that Monsanto... [has] a responsibility, as we make these advancements in science, to... share them worldwide..." Hugh Grant

Christian Streiff Chairman & CEO (2006–09), PSA Peugeot Citroën

BIOGRAPHY
Born in Sarrebourg, France, in 1954, the multilingual Streiff studied civil engineering at ENSMP in Paris.

BEST DECISION
Accepting that it would take time to get to know the company before making changes, and inviting insiders to advise him.

LESSON IN BUSINESS
Diplomacy is key—Streiff learned the hard way, both at Saint Gobain and Airbus, that the need for tact must sometimes come before results.

IN A CAREER characterized by boldness and an impatience to get things done, outspoken Frenchman Streiff faced new challenges in his role as CEO of PSA Peugeot Citroën, but lost his job in the global economic downturn.

During a 26-year career at building-materials firm Saint-Gobain, Streiff restored ailing divisions in Germany and Italy, becoming CFO in 2004. Unexpectedly, Streiff left within a year, citing strategic differences. He became CEO of troubled aircraft manufacturer Airbus in 2006, but again left after just three months, unable to pacify the interests of the French, German, and Spanish governments. A month later he became CEO of PSA Peugeot Citroën, a company that had enjoyed a decade of considerable success, but had begun to lose its way. Streiff realized he would need time to get to know the company before making changes. After giving ten teams of ten people 100 days to identify key problems and solutions, he drew up a recovery strategy focused on four key areas: quality, cost reduction, product strategy, and international operations. In 2007, he unveiled plans to boost sales and restore margins with 29 new car models by 2010, but the global financial crisis led to falling sales and he was forced to resign in 2009.

Sergey Bogdanchikov President, Rosneft

BIOGRAPHY
Born in Orenburg Oblast in the Soviet Union in 1957. Bogdanchikov earned a doctorate in engineering from the Ufa Petroleum Institute in the Urals.

BEST DECISION
Driving through Rosneft's IPO in 2006. This provided closer connections with the international oil industry, and funds expansion.

LESSON IN BUSINESS
Think big—from small beginnings, Rosneft has become a world player in the industry.

THE RISE OF ROSNEFT, the Russian state petroleum company, into the ranks of the large oil companies has been dogged by controversy. It has also reflected the skill and determination of Bogdanchikov, a lifelong oil professional.

When the Russian government appointed Sergey Bogdanchikov president of Rosneft in 1998, the company was little more than a cluster of obsolete and poorly producing assets. He has devoted himself to building the company up from unpromising beginnings. These were left over from the reshaping of the country's oil industry after the demise of the Soviet Union. Eight years later, Bogdanchikov had built the company to the point at which it could successfully launch one of the largest initial public offerings in history, raising more than $10 billion on the London and Moscow stock markets for 15 percent of the company. The growth of Rosneft into a large, integrated energy group was in large part due to the controversial acquisition of assets belonging to the former oil giant Yukos by Rosneft in 2004, amid allegations of political chicanery. The acquisition gave Rosneft huge reserves and turned it into one of the world's biggest oil extraction and refining companies.

> "I do have a certain reputation for turnarounds."
>
> Christian Streiff

OLDER AND WISER?

Does age matter? In an increasingly youth-obsessed world, the business world is still pondering trade-offs such as energy versus experience, and there is no doubt that older CEOs can contribute not only longer experience, but also a certain serenity and immunity from the stresses that afflict younger execs. **Muriel Siebert** (*b. 1932*; p104) was the first woman to gain a seat on the New York Stock Exchange and the first to head one of its member firms. She founded her own firm in 1967, Muriel Siebert & Co., undertaking research for firms, and buying and selling analysis. To her, age and experience are a huge advantage and she worries that young traders are disadvantaged by inexperience: "They made money so quickly and in such vast quantities, they didn't realize they could lose it twice as fast."

For **Li Ka-shing** (*b.1928*; p68), founder of Cheung Kong Ltd, the hard lessons he learned as a penniless refugee in 1940s Hong Kong have stood him in good stead. "I never forget to maintain stability while advancing, and I never forget to advance while maintaining stability." His experiences over the years have made him into one of the most astute investors today ●

Growing Old Successfully

The incredible **Jack Weil** currently holds the world record for oldest CEO. Described as being to Western shirts what **Henry Ford** (p23) was to cars, Weil is credited with being the first to put snaps on cowboy shirts. He remained a fully involved CEO of his company, Rockmount, until his death in 2008 at the tender age of 107. One of the advantages of being an older CEO is that you have seen it all before.

Milton Pierce was a teenager during the Great Depression of the 1930s. The odds of finding a job or starting a business successfully in those days were pretty slim, but Milton beat those odds. After his father's tailor's shop was broken into, Milton designed and installed a burglar alarm. This experience was enough to get him a job with an "alarm man" and he started his own company, Guardian Alarms, in 1930 when he was just 15. He remains CEO and Guardian Security Services has more than 80,000 clients across four US states and Canada.

Rising Stars

In the global business world, there is plenty of room for CEOs of all ages. The average age of a CEO worldwide is around 55 and in China it is as low as 47. There are some exceptional individuals, however, whose drive and ambition get them to the top even earlier. **Suhas Gopinath** set up his web solutions company Globals, Inc. in 2000 when he was just 14; he was officially recognized as the world's youngest CEO three years later. Other notable success stories include **Adam Stewart**, who was named CEO of Jamaican family firm Sandals Resorts International by his father and founder, **Gordon Stewart**, at the age of 25, while **Harry Vafias** was appointed CEO of Greek shipping firm StealthGas when he was 27. In 2007, **Yolanda Cuba** was slightly older when she reached the top of South African investment firm Mvelaphanda, at age 29. CEOs in their 30s are a little more common, but still a breed apart. **Matt Williams** became CEO of Topps Tiles, a UK flooring specialist, when he was 34, while **Sahba Abedian**, a qualified lawyer, became CEO of Australian property development company Sunland when he was 31.

"Anyone who stops learning is old, whether at 20 or 80. Anyone who keeps learning stays young. The greatest thing in life is to keep your mind young." HENRY FORD

Wise Old Men

Proving age no barrier to success, these CEOs have kept working long after most of us retire:

Edward C. Johnson III *(b. 1931)* FIDELITY INVESTMENTS (Finance: US)—*Johnson's tenure running the largest mutual fund company in the US has spanned three decades. The only other change of leadership in 61 years at Fidelity was when Johnson took over from his father.*

—

Albert Frère *(b. 1926)* THE FRÈRE GROUP (Investments: Belgium)—*Frère made his money in scrap metal and steel, before selling the business and starting an investment company.*

—

Robert Lutz *(b. 1932)* GENERAL MOTORS (Automotive: US)—*Currently vice-chairman of product development at GM, Lutz has worked at four of the world's premier automotive companies, on both sides of the Atlantic, holding CEO or senior executive roles for several decades.*

—

Frank Bennack *(b. 1933)* HEARST ARGYLE TELEVISION LTD (Media: US)—*Having been chairman and CEO of Hearst Corp. between 1979 and 2002, Bennack returned to his former job in 2008.*

—

Gerard Roche *(b. 1927)* HEIDRICK & STRUGGLES (Recruitment: US)—*For over 40 years, Roche has helped to place dozens of the world's most senior executives at top companies including Home Depot, Nike, Alcoa, IBM, Coca-Cola, the Walt Disney Company, and AT&T. He specializes in recruiting other older executives.*

—

Sumner Redstone *(b. 1923)* NATIONAL AMUSEMENTS (Media: US)—*Now chairman of National Amusements, Redstone was CEO of Viacom from 1987 to 2006. He and his family are still majority shareholders of Viacom and a variety of other media companies, including CBS and MTV.*

—

Hugh Hefner *(b. 1926)* PLAYBOY ENTERPRISES (Publishing: US)—*Hefner started Playboy magazine, of which he is chief creative officer, in 1953, and developed it into the bestselling male lifestyle magazine.*

—

O. Bruton Smith *(b. 1927)* SONIC AUTOMOTIVE, INC. (Retail: US)—*Smith began his career as an automobile salesman while promoting local motor races. Now in his 80s, chairman and CEO Smith is reportedly grooming his son to take the wheel.*

—

10

The Globalists

Lakshmi Mittal Chairman & CEO, Arcelor Mittal

THE POSTER BOY for India Inc., Mittal was named, appropriately for one of the world's richest men, after the Hindu goddess of wealth. When his Dutch-based company Mittal Steel took over Arcelor of Luxembourg, he created a steel group three times larger than its nearest rival, with ten percent of the global market and some 330,000 employees. His flamboyant lifestyle, including a $55-million wedding for his daughter, has ensured plenty of international front page newspaper coverage.

BIOGRAPHY
Born in 1950 in Rajasthan, India. When his family moved to Calcutta (Kolkata), his father Mohan Lal Mittal set up a small steel mill, in which Mittal worked after classes. He graduated from St. Xavier's College, Calcutta, with a degree in business and accounting.

LEADERSHIP STYLE
Focused and ruthless, but willing to listen. He is a brilliant businessman and one who understands the nooks, crannies, and fluctuations of his industry.

KEY STRENGTH
His razor-sharp understanding of the steel market. He acquires companies, sometimes direct from national governments, and then makes them work better.

BEST DECISION
Leaving the family business in India in order to focus on global interests, after spotting the potential of an industry booming due to massive demand for steel in the new economies.

GLOBAL STEEL Mittal started in the family's small steelmaking business in India. In 1976 he set out to establish its international division, beginning with the buyout of a run-down plant in Indonesia. In 1994 he branched out on his own, taking over the international operations of the Mittal steel business. A series of shrewd takeovers has enabled Mittal to dominate an industry that is currently booming, thanks to enormous growth in countries like China.

MAKE WAY FOR THE NEW WORLD The real strength of Mittal's business lies in his talent for spotting under-utilized plants, often in low-cost corners of the world, and making them productive. His empire, employing more than 200,000 people, spans Romania, Bosnia, Algeria, Trinidad, Indonesia, Kazakhstan, China, the US, and continental Europe.

Never afraid to ruffle feathers, his takeover of Arcelor, one of the largest hostile bids in the history of European business, horrified the old guard who viewed it as a rough attempt by "new" India to take on "old" Europe.

Mittal's career has been associated with plenty of controversy. In 2002, he was accused of paying $250,000 to the UK government in return for help in acquiring Romania's state steel industry. There have been accusations of "slave labor" from employees following a row over deaths and injuries of workers at his Romanian site, numbering in the hundreds.

There should be plenty of lucrative deal-making to come. Even as the world's number one producer of steel, Arcelor Mittal only accounts for around one-tenth of a highly fragmented industry, leaving vast scope for further mergers and takeovers.

LESSONS IN BUSINESS: KNOWING YOUR MARKET INSIDE OUT

With understanding, you can venture boldly where others fear to tread. Mittal's bid for Arcelor, the second-biggest steel group in the world and his main rival, achieved a level of global domination that would not have come through steady, organic growth.

→ Keep studying your market like an outsider to gain a competitive edge in thinking about the way ahead.
→ Once your knowledge is far ranging, take risks that for you are calculated, for others a step in the dark.
→ Precis reports have their place but be prepared to get stuck into the detail if it seems important.

"In this new world, entrepreneurs such as Mittal... are making the rules." *Time* magazine

Alfredo Sáenz Abad CEO, Banco Santander

A KEY FIGURE in the transformation of the Spanish banking sector, Saenz has been instrumental in its metamorphosis from a regional banking system into one of the most dynamic, most competitive, best-capitalized, and fastest-growing in the world. Arriving at Santander with a proven track record of saving troubled banks, Sáenz turned his skills to a different goal—guiding Santander to become one of the world's biggest banking groups. His leadership gave the bank the stability it needed when the 2008 banking crisis shook many of its rivals.

BIOGRAPHY
Born in Vizcaya in Spain's Basque country in 1942, Sáenz studied law at the University of Valladolid, Castile-León, and economics at the Jesuit Deusto University in Bilbao.

LEADERSHIP STYLE
Renowned for his unwavering single-mindedness, Sáenz is a firm believer in leaders getting involved in the detail.

KEY STRENGTH
Focusing on the most fruitful path, to the exclusion of everything else.

BEST DECISION
Limiting Santander's Latin American exposure, thereby eliminating a problem that could have seriously hampered his bold expansion plans.

BANK SAVIOR Sáenz earned his reputation as a rescuer of banks during the 1980s, when he was placed in charge of the failing Banca Catalana by its new owner, Banco Vizcaya. He turned Catalana into one of the country's most profitable banks, and in 1994 his reputation led to his appointment as head of Banesto. By 1997 he had restored Banesto to health.

GLOBAL PLANS When Saenz became CEO at Banco Santander in 2002, the bank was facing a crisis in its substantial exposure to Latin America, particularly Argentina, which was going through serious economic problems and had placed restrictions on banking operations. Sáenz demonstrated his intention to cut out non-performing areas and focus on growth by refusing to provide any more capital to the Argentinian operation and lowering the bank's profile in Latin America overall. He then set out on an aggressive acquisition program in Europe and the US, with the aim of turning Santander into an international banking powerhouse and putting it among the world's top ten banks by market capitalization. The list of Sáenz's acquisitions was impressive. In 2004 Santander bought Abbey National, the UK's sixth-biggest bank; in 2005 it bought Sovereign Bancorp, the 18th-biggest bank in the US; in 2007 Santander made up 28 percent of the consortium that bought ABN AMRO, and in 2008 Sáenz announced his intention to take over the UK's Alliance & Leicester. He also agreed to buy the savings business of the UK's Bradford & Bingley, after it was nationalized by the British government. Sáenz had achieved his goal, with Santander ranked ninth largest in the world.

LESSONS IN BUSINESS: SETTING YOUR SIGHTS

Don't let any concern other than the strategy you have set to even enter your day. Sáenz not only has the visions necessary to give the organization an aiming point, but he also gets involved in implementation. He can see the broad picture and also take part in the operations.
→ Define your key objectives—four or five at most—and then concentrate only on them.
→ Shape every action to achieving the objectives you've set yourself; ensure others' objectives support you.
→ Ask yourself why you are continuing to do something that is not directed toward your goals.

"You cannot be a leader without rolling up your sleeves." Alfredo Sáenz Abad

Marius Kloppers CEO, BHP Billiton

EYEBROWS WERE RAISED when Chip Goodyear's replacement as CEO of the world's largest mining company was announced. At just 45, Kloppers was young with only 15 years experience under his belt, and his pushy and assertive leadership style contrasted greatly with that of his smooth, urbane predecessor. What's more, Goodyear had left on an all-time high achieving record profits of more than $13 billion. Critics predicted there could be trouble ahead. But Kloppers soon proved his worth with profit increases of $2 billion in his first year.

BIOGRAPHY
Born in Cape Town, South Africa, in 1962. Kloppers studied economics at the University of Pretoria before taking an MA in mining from Mintek mining research institute, a doctorate on iron chemical alloys, and an MBA from INSEAD.

LEADERSHIP STYLE
Aggressive, ambitious, and strategic. He is regarded as a youthful CEO with the energy BHP Billiton needs to consolidate its position in the mining industry.

KEY STRENGTH
An excellent educational background, which combined with his energy and ambition has enabled him to formulate effective strategies..

BEST DECISION
Leading the $9 billion acquisition of WMC in 2005—it set Kloppers up to be BHP Billiton's next CEO, and secured future income for the company.

SLOWLY BUT SURELY An enigma in the corporate world, Kloppers didn't get his foot on the first rung of the management ladder until he was 30, after serving two years in the South African Army, and studying at some of the world's best mining institutes and elite business schools. He later said his prolonged stay in academia revealed indecision about his career plans, but the courses and colleges he chose were perfect for a would-be mining conglomerate CEO. He joined Gencor, which became Billiton in 1996, and later led the 2001 merger talks that created BHP Billiton.

STRIKING GOLD Having played a key role in the merger, Kloppers was already set for great things. He worked closely on integrating the two companies after the takeover, and was given responsibility for the company's bid for Australian mining rival WMC, who owned the Olympic Dam copper and uranium mine in south Australia. Klopper's bid was successful, but the scale of his success emerged only later when it was discovered that it contained 7.7 billion tons of uranium, copper, and gold; almost double the anticipated reserves.

When his predecessor, Chip Goodyear, stepped down in 2007, after announcing record profits, he credited Kloppers with the lion's share of the success through his stewardship of BHP Billiton's non-ferrous metals division. It was Kloppers who rescued BHP's disastrous nickel mining project in Ravensthorpe by getting costs under control and speeding up construction. The plant is one of a number of projects expected to guarantee BHP strong earnings in the future. Kloppers was planning ahead even before he got the top job.

LESSONS IN BUSINESS: TRAINING FOR BATTLE

Kloppers established himself as a soldier, student, scientist, and acquisitions wizard. Within weeks of becoming CEO, he focused all these skills on a hostile takeover of Rio Tinto, which he later abandoned.
- → Demonstrate confidence in your new company by taking radical steps in mergers and acquisitions from the outset.
- → Take an aggressive approach to building your company, accepting difficult and hostile takeover battles.
- → You won't win every battle, but learn from the experience and hone your skills for future fights.

"The organizational structure is simple, there are no fancy charts. In the end, we dig stuff out of the ground." Marius Kloppers

Baudouin Prot CEO, BNP Paribas

IN MANY RESPECTS, Prot is a classic product of France's Ecole Nationale d'Administration—an efficient administrator and a consummate diplomat. But he has shown himself to be much more than just another civil servant thrust into the corporate battle zone. Prot has demonstrated a clear eye for a bargain, excellent judgement on acquisitions, and a clear commitment to organic growth in retail banking and asset management. Prot's judgement has been a key factor in BNP Paribas's rise to become Europe's largest bank by total assets.

BIOGRAPHY

Born in 1951. Prot studied at the Hautes Etudes Commerciales in Paris where he took a master's in business administration before switching to the Ecole Nationale d'Administration, France's elite college for civil servants. After graduating in public administration he served as an area administrator and in the Industry Ministry.

LEADERSHIP STYLE

Calm and cautious, but capable of opportunism. Prot has pursued a risk-averse strategy, but has moved fast when required for bargain acquisitions.

KEY STRENGTH

Understanding how important acquisitions can be not just to a bank's size and efficiency, but also for its own safety.

BEST DECISION

Acquiring Fortis, the ailing Low Countries bank, which made BNP Paribas the largest bank in the Eurozone.

MINION TO CONQUEROR Prot began his career as a district administrator in Franche-Comte, before being promoted to finance inspector in the French Treasury and then serving as deputy head of the energy and commodities department in the French Industry Ministry. He joined BNP in 1983 as deputy managing director of its Banque Nationale de Paris Intercontinentale. He was appointed COO in 1996 and three years later led the merger that created BNP Paribas, one of Europe's largest banks.

PATIENT RAIDER Appointed CEO in 2003, Prot's brief was to develop BNP Paribas as a retail brand, grow its asset management business, bolster its position within the Eurozone, and expand through organic growth and takeovers in the emerging economies. He launched a $30-billion spending spree by acquiring the US-based Community First Bankshares for $1.2 billion in 2004, followed by BNL, Italy's sixth largest bank, for $10.9 billion in 2006. The following year he acquired RBS International Securities Services, which had assets of just under $4 billion, and topped it with one of the biggest banking coups of 2008—the $19.6-billion takeover of Fortis Bank's Belgian and Luxembourg operations. The deal vaulted BNP Paribas from the Eurozone's seventh largest bank to number one, with $810 billion in deposits. What made the takeover extraordinary was the timing—it was finalized in October, just as the world's major banks were in turmoil over their exposure to the US sub-prime crisis. Prot's cautious approach to risk had paid off, and BNP Paribas was in a perfect position to capitalize.

LESSONS IN BUSINESS: PROCEEDING WITH CAUTION

Although conservative on risk, Prot made informed acquisitions that considerably increased BNP Paribas's size—cautious moves that made the bank strong when others were fighting to survive the sub-prime debacle.

➔ Always consider the contrary position. Avoid going with the crowd, particularly when risks are bringing spectacular returns.

➔ Get yourself in a position to "buy" when, generally speaking, assets are at a low valuation.

➔ Remember the old motto: "If it sounds too good to be true then it probably is."

"In terms of market share, deposits, and assets under management, bigger is better, especially if you do it at an attractive price." Baudouin Prot

Paul Adams CEO, British American Tobacco

AN IMPRESSIVE MARKETING pedigree, ranging from Beecham and Colgate-Palmolive to Pepsi and Shell, has no doubt prepared Adams for one of the toughest sales jobs in the world. His task, as CEO of the world's second largest producer of cigarettes, is to promote a product considered by most to cause an estimated 750,000 premature deaths a year. It is a task he faces with a degree of bullishness and brio that has won him some admirers, not least on the stock market. In the first three years of Adams' leadership, BAT's stock rose 130 percent.

BIOGRAPHY
Born in Manchester, UK in 1953. Adams studied business at Ealing College, London. He abandoned ambitions to become a lawyer and took a job at Shell.

LEADERSHIP STYLE
Straight-talking, bullish, and formidable; all essential qualities in an industry where nerves of steel are a prerequisite.

KEY STRENGTH
A seemingly limitless confidence in his ability to lead.

BEST DECISION
In 2004, British American Tobacco became the first foreign company to be granted approval to build a cigarette factory in China. Considered the "holy grail" of the tobacco industry, China is the world's biggest cigarette market.

TAKING RESPONSIBILITY Adams first joined BAT in 1991 as regional director, rising to CEO in 2004. Adams is no apologist for the industry. His view is simple, "We will sell where it's legal, where we can operate to our own international standards, and where we can make money." He is, however, committed to portraying the tobacco giant as socially responsible. BAT plows millions into researching "healthier" cigarettes and funds a substantial "harm reduction" program.

INDUSTRY SPOKESMAN A controversial figure in a vilified industry, Adams has been at the center of several tobacco industry scandals. His appointment as CEO was opposed by many after he was named in damning documents detailing how BAT exploited cigarette smuggling. He has been a spokesman for the industry at a

pivotal and controversial time in its history. Never have people in the developed world been more aware of the risks of smoking, and many governments have banned smoking in public spaces, resulting in a dramatic drop in sales. Nonetheless, BAT still sells 684 billion cigarettes annually, much of it in emerging economies. Adams believes the growing middle classes in Russia, India, and Brazil will lead to higher sales of key premium brands.

Judicious acquisitions have also been part of Adams' strategy, and in early 2008, BAT bought Tekel, Turkey's state-owned tobacco company, and the Danish tobacco company Skandinavisk Tobakskompagni. BAT is also working to develop new products, including replacements for tobacco, such as a substitute based on "Snus", a Swedish product that comes in sachets to be sucked.

LESSONS IN BUSINESS: THERE'S ALWAYS A WAY

When the world is against you... innovate. In the tobacco industry you have to find something to be passionate about or you'd lose hope. Where others would see a brick wall, Adams sees possibility. "Premium brands will grow if you innovate," he says.
→ Where social conditions dictate a decrease in the use of your product look for new markets.
→ Review how your products are packaged and adjust or radically change quantities or design.
→ Always have potential variations of, for example, flavor in the pipeline and react fast to market change.

"I'm running a business that sells risky products and I see myself running that in a responsible way."

Paul Adams

Gregory Page Chairman & CEO, Cargill

A WORTHY LEADER of Cargill, Page joined the Minnesota-based agricultural giant in 1974 as a trainee, when it was still an eponymous, family-owned company. He was posted to Singapore and Thailand before returning to Minneapolis. He became corporate vice-president in 1998 and executive vice-president in 1999. Since being named as Cargill's CEO in June 2007, Page has steered the company—one of the largest privately owned businesses in the US —toward greater openness, profitability, and environmental awareness.

BIOGRAPHY
Born in 1952, in the rural town of Bottineau, North Dakota. He has a degree in economics from the University of North Dakota.

LEADERSHIP STYLE
Plain-speaking and open, yet careful. Page balances the special requirements of managing a privately owned business with the realities of the modern business world.

KEY STRENGTH
Having the business scope and initiative to cope with market and financial turbulence, and further even his predecessor's stellar performance.

BEST DECISION
Pushing for greater transparency and openness in business practices, as part of a move toward creating greater trust in the company.

AT THE HEAD OF A GIANT Unlisted Cargill, founded in the 1860s, is a privately held, family- and staff-owned company, with some 160,000 employees and annual revenue in excess of $120 billion. It dominates global agriculture and consists of 78 operating units spread across 67 countries. Cargill has had a reputation for being insular and secretive; Page was only the fourth non-family member to lead the company. His predecessor, Warren Stanley, had delivered strong growth and overseen Cargill's repositioning as a partner to other businesses rather than a mere supplier of commodities.

STEERING A STEADY COURSE Page took control of Cargill at a time of major change in the global food industry, with impending shortages and strong interest in grain-based biofuels. His vision was for a larger, greener, and more visible enterprise, and he has expressed views on public policy, in contrast to Cargill's hitherto highly discreet approach. He has also continued the company's trend toward greater transparency—Cargill now publishes its headline numbers, even though, as a privately held firm, it is not obliged to do so. And it shows a willingness to discuss any issues raised by its large-scale crop production. Page emphasizes "trust-based trade," building up long-term relationships between the company and its growers, as the most effective way to prevent shortages. He has also sought to increase the "connectivity" between the business's various subsectors, vying for greater efficiency. Despite the euphoria surrounding biofuels, Page has remained cautious in this area, seeking to balance energy needs with human nutrition.

LESSONS IN BUSINESS: ENGENDERING TRUST

Page continued the work of his predecessor in making Cargill more accountable, both externally and internally, proving that openness needn't mean weakness.

➔ By sharing information with workers, industry partners, and customers, you create a trust that will enforce the company ethos and encourage people to give their best; staff work to fulfil a vision, not complete a task.

➔ Keep those who have a stake in your success in the loop—even if you're under no obligation.

➔ Stay within the spirit of the law and consider the value of trust in making deals work.

> "If you don't go out and explain yourself, you'll be defined by your mistakes." Gregory Page

James Mulva Chairman & CEO, ConocoPhillips

HAVING SPENT HIS ENTIRE working career with the company that he now heads, there is probably very little Mulva doesn't know about the highs and lows of the oil industry. He is widely respected for his astute judgment and ability to build a global business through a combination of cost-cutting and shrewd takeovers. When he took over as CEO in 1999, Phillips' assets were $15 billion; following the merger with Conoco they were more than $75 billion. The combined operation is now a global top ten energy group.

BIOGRAPHY
Mulva was born in Oshkosh, Wisconsin, in 1946. He took degrees in finance and business administration from the University of Texas. He joined the US Navy after graduating in 1969, serving as an officer until he joined Phillips in 1973.

LEADERSHIP STYLE
Capable and open to new ideas, with an extremely analytical mind.

KEY STRENGTH
Willing to gamble, Mulva is seen as a more ambitious risk-taker than other oil chiefs.

BEST DECISION
Judging the right time to grow and consequently setting his company on the road to global greatness.

FULL-STEAM AHEAD Mulva joined Phillips Petroleum in 1973, after a stint in the navy. He started as a management trainee in the treasury department and progressed through the organization. His term as vice-president and treasurer of the Europe/Africa division of Phillips from 1980 to 1984, when Mulva was responsible for refocusing the company, was a key time for him.

THE DEAL MAKER In the 1980s, when most oil companies were focusing on the Middle East, Mulva decided to look to the North Sea, Venezuela, Asia, North America, and Kazakhstan. When he took over as CEO in 1994, he developed the first offshore oil field in China. He also diversified with a range of joint ventures, including polyethylene plastic production in China.

In his early years at the helm, Mulva cut costs and built capital. In the early 2000s, he embarked on an ambitious mergers and acquisitions spree that included the takeover of Atlantic Richfield Company and a merger with Tosco Corporation. The merger with Conoco in 2002 took the company into a new league. ConocoPhillips became the largest refiner in the US and the sixth largest energy company worldwide.

One of his toughest challenges came in 2000, when a chemical tank exploded at a Phillips plant in Pasadena, killing one worker and injuring many others. The company was fined for safety violations and worked hard to improve safety. Mulva is emphatic that oil companies have a duty to put something back into the local communities, and offers internship and scholarship programs for staff.

LESSONS IN BUSINESS: ACCEPTING THE BUCK

Mulva believes that scrupulous transparency and taking responsibility when things go wrong —as he did in Pasadena—is essential in an industry where so much is at stake for both workers and the environment.
- ➔ Beware of creating a fear of failure in your people by taking responsibility yourself for their mistakes.
- ➔ Remember that when you admit a mistake, blaming your people for it is demeaning and looks petty.
- ➔ Avoid taking people to task in public; always show that your confidence in your people is irrevocable and complete.

"If you don't have your health and integrity, you don't have much to offer." James Mulva

Dieter Zetsche Chairman & CEO, Daimler AG

WITH HIS TRADEMARK walrus mustache, Zetsche is a recognizable personality in the global motor trade, credited with masterminding the controversial merger of Daimler and Chrysler. Since joining Daimler-Benz in 1976, he has held jobs in every department from trucks to luxury cars, and spent five years in Detroit trying to spearhead a turnaround at Chrysler. His "Ask Dr. Z." TV commercials made him a minor celebrity in America. In addition to his role as group Chairman and CEO, he is head of the Mercedes-Benz Cars division.

BIOGRAPHY
Born in Istanbul, Turkey, in 1953. His father was an engineer. Zetsche graduated in engineering from the University of Karlsruhe, Germany, in 1976 and completed a doctorate at the University of Paderborn, Germany, in 1982.

LEADERSHIP STYLE
Open and decisive.

KEY STRENGTH
Earning a reputation as "Mr Fix-it," Zetsche has proved he can move swiftly and decisively to lead his company through even the most difficult periods.

BEST DECISION
Shedding the Chrysler brand —a painful but career-defining decision for Zetsche.

THE DRIVE OF HIS LIFE In 1998 Zetsche was the force behind the merger between Chrysler and Daimler, creating a new company that had 442,000 employees and a market capitalization of nearly $100 billion. While the deal was touted as a "merger of equals", two years later Daimler installed a German management team. Within 12 months, the company's market capitalization had sunk to $44 billion. "My five years as CEO of Chrysler were personally among the very best of my life," he said, "but I still had to put my feelings aside and view the situation objectively from a business perspective."

DR. Z. TO THE RESCUE By 2007 it was clear the merger of Daimler and Chrysler had been a financial disaster. While both companies had made inroads with new products, they had overestimated the potential for passing leading-edge technology from Mercedes-Benz to Chrysler. The harsh reality was that Chrysler, a company to which Zetsche had a great attachment, was pulling Daimler under. Zetsche moved quickly to shed Chrysler and focus Daimler on the premium market it knew best. Zetsche lost credibility with the analysts for a while but, by continually explaining this strategy, the company recovered. Daimler's profit jumped from a net loss of €12 million in the last quarter of 2006, pre-breakup, to a profit of €1.7 billion a year later.

It was to be Zetsche's defining moment. "The toughest thing is to see your convictions fail," he said. "That's when you really have to deal with your personality and grow as a person. Those are the cases that are more important than the successes you have."

LESSONS IN BUSINESS: ACTING DECISIVELY

The Chrysler sale shows the importance of knowing what needs to be done and doing it—fast. "We have an obligation to make the right decision," Zetsche said. "Not the convenient one or the one we'd like to make."
→ Avoid "analysis paralysis"—inability to make a decision because it may have an unwanted outcome.
→ Understand that one of the differences between a CEO and other managers is that they go for it, rather than cover themselves against failure.
→ Build yourself as a decisive person. Use a process that you can go through quickly to come to a decision.

"Management has to be where the action is."
Dieter Zetsche

GLOBAL OPPORTUNITIES

Globalization signifies the emergence of a single and increasingly accessible world market, boosted by deregulation, growing political and economic interdependence, media exposure, and consumer demands and aspirations. The risks posed by differing economic and political situations, operating conditions, legislation, languages, currencies, tastes, traditions, and cultural norms are more than compensated for by the potential rewards of new markets, lower costs, and higher profits.

Luxottica, the world's leading manufacturer of sunglasses, was facing strong competition from low-cost production in China at the time when **Andrea Guerra** (p448) took over as CEO. Italian-made products inevitably cost more and consumers were voting with their feet. Guerra responded by opening two factories in China to reduce production costs. He then went a step further, pursuing growth for his luxury products in China's under-developed retail market. He did this by buying up three Chinese retail chains, giving Luxottica a tactical presence across the country.

Innovative market opportunities are also assiduously targeted by **Richard Branson**'s (p421) Virgin Group, a UK-based branded venture capital organization with a portfolio of businesses ranging from flights to financial services. Branson has taken advantage of the increasingly deregularized global economy by establishing more than 200 companies, many as joint ventures with other partners, in over two dozen countries worldwide. This strategy took Virgin from a small UK music retailing business in the 1970s to a diversified global empire with a total turnover in excess of £10 billion ●

"No new business is worth starting in these times unless it can go global."
RICHARD BRANSON

Local Support, Global Success

To minimize risk by tapping into local knowledge and support, many CEOs opt to work in partnership with companies on the ground. **Pablo Isla Álvarez de Tejera**, CEO of Spanish retailer Inditex, one of the world's largest fashion companies, entered a joint venture with Trent Ltd, led by managing director **N.N. Tata**, and part of the Indian Tata Group, to launch a chain of its flagship Zara stores into New Delhi, Mumbai, and other major Indian cities, starting in 2010. The sheer size of the market offers huge potential. Since 2005, expansion has been constant and Inditex is now present in over 70 countries around the world.

How and to what extent you approach global expansion varies, of course. Organic growth, acquisitions, mergers, franchising are all widespread. There is also sourcing of products or raw ingredients from abroad, outsourcing to

Going Global

Be prepared—Assess the risks before you move into a new market, and be prepared to adapt aspects of your operation.

Work out the logistics—Make sure you have fully assessed the political, legal, and regulatory environment of the country you will be operating in.

Get informed—Make sure you fully understand the differing needs of foreign markets, particularly if you

workforces abroad, selling abroad or, like Zara, expanding and setting up shop abroad.

Small family businesses, too, can thrive globally, especially when their products are niche. **Hanni Toosbuy Kasprzak**, owner and chairperson of ECCO, the Danish footwear company, continues to embrace a rather unusual solution to exploiting global potential—to ensure quality, ECCO controls its entire value chain "from cow to shoe". Claiming to be the only such company in the world to do so, it operates its own tanneries and production units in Europe, China, and South East Asia, and sells worldwide through five sales regions on three continents. This approach minimizes the risk not only of variations in raw and worked leather and craftsmanship, but also of potential supply and delivery disruption. Until the late 1970s, when pressure for deregulation began substantially to ease international barriers to trade and investment, such global operating would have been incredibly difficult.

are trying to sell in a developing economy. Assess whether your products or services are relevant.

Go local—Explore ways to tap local talent and knowledge, through joint ventures, mergers, and acquisitions, or franchising. Joining forces locally can give a competitive advantage.

Be conscientious—Ensure that every aspect of your business is sensitive to the culture it is operating within. Be particularly mindful of company branding and promotion.

Global Players

These CEOs are all tapping into the potential of the global market with operations across the world:

Gilles Pélisson, ACCOR (Hotels: France)—*A global group and European leader in hotels, and world leader in services to corporate clients and public institutions. Accor has some 150,000 employees in almost 100 countries.*

Jacquelyn Tran, BEAUTY ENCOUNTER (Retail: US)—*Recognizing the potential of the internet as a sales tool, in 1999 Tran created this leading online source to market a wide range of fragrances and beauty products. She exports to some 30 countries worldwide.*

David Childs, CLIFFORD CHANCE LLP (Legal: UK)—*One of the world's leading legal firms, with over 3,000 legal advisers in 30 offices in more than 20 centers around the world. It has been regularly nominated as Global Law Firm of the Year.*

Yoshihiko Miyauchi, ORIX CORP. (Finance: Japan)—*An integrated financial group that provides products and services to corporate and retail customers in over 20 countries and regions worldwide.*

Michel Landel, SODEXO SA (Facilities and hospitality: France)—*Though not a household name, Sodexo's work providing catering and facilities management is ubiquitous around the world. The company operates within over 30,000 sites in 80 different countries.*

Carlo Bozotti, STMICROELECTRONICS (Electronics: Switzerland)—*The world's fifth largest semiconductor company, with tens of thousands of employees working in advanced R&D units, design and application centers, manufacturing sites, and sales offices in over 30 countries.*

Fred DeLuca, SUBWAY (Restaurants: US)—*Founded in 1965, and with the first franchise granted in 1974, the sandwich chain now has over 28,000 franchisees in over 80 countries and territories worldwide.*

Jon Fredrik Baksaas, TELENOR (Telecommunications: Norway)—*The world's seventh largest provider of mobile communications in subscriptions, and with telecom operations employing over 30,000 employees, in countries across Europe and Asia.*

Larry Pillard, TETRA LAVAL INTERNATIONAL SA (Packaging: Switzerland)—*Includes the flagship Tetra Pak packaging company that operates in over 150 countries worldwide. In 2008, Pillard announced an $88-million investment in a state-of-the-art plant in India.*

Franck Riboud Chairman & CEO, Groupe Danone

THE YOUNGEST in a family of high-achievers, Riboud has always had a lot to prove. Since joining Danone in 1981, he has demonstrated the same determination that made him a French skiing champion. Succeeding his father, the legendary industrialist Antoine Riboud, as CEO of the company in 1996, Franck proved his critics wrong by successfully refocusing the company on its core products. His ability to think creatively and act strategically reversed the company's profit slide and led Groupe Danone into new global markets.

BIOGRAPHY
Born in Lyon, France, in 1955, the youngest of four children of leading industrialist Antoine Riboud. Franck Riboud holds a degree in engineering from the Ecole Polytechnique Fédérale de Lausanne in Switzerland.

LEADERSHIP STYLE
Instinctive, approachable, informal. He is known to make snap decisions and prefers one-to-one meetings to committees, but is not afraid to delegate authority. He has a reputation for a great sense of humor, as well as a fiery temper, and is respected for his knack of keeping ahead of the competition.

KEY STRENGTH
An obsessive belief in his own products. He never misses a marketing opportunity to be seen eating a Danone yogurt or drinking Evian water.

BEST DECISION
Concentrating on the three core brands of the company at a time of economic uncertainty.

SUPERMARKET "PROWLER" After joining Danone in 1981 as a sales manager, Riboud walked the aisles of French supermarkets, checking the competition and making sure that the Danone shelf placement was favorable. He became general manager of Evian in 1990 and helped to facilitate the $2.5-billion takeover of Nabisco's European biscuit operations in 1992. As general manager of corporate business development, he was responsible for the internationalization of Groupe Danone and more than tripled sales outside Western Europe.

A STRATEGIC OVERHAUL Despite 15 years of hard work with the company, Riboud's accession to CEO in 1996 was not easy. Many investors feared he would not be able to live up to the legacy of his father, and share prices plummeted. However, his iron will stood him in good stead. In 1997, he sold off half of the company's grocery product holdings and all of its confectionery business, and focused on the core business areas of dairy products, cookies, and beverages, representing 85 percent of sales. His strategy reversed a profit slide and doubled the share price within three years.

Riboud turned his attention to China, Indonesia, and Mexico as emerging markets for dairy products, while building the group's water business in Asia and its cookie brands in India. His astute marketing has kept the company one step ahead of the competition.

Riboud is committed to his belief in "positive globalization," convinced that following new business models can address the interests of a multinational company, as well as the need to behave in a socially responsible way.

LESSONS IN BUSINESS: THE BENEFITS OF GLOBALIZATION

Riboud believes in the benefits of "positive globalization": that multinational companies can develop practices and systems that are not only good for business, but enable them to act in a responsible and ethical way.
- → Go for affordability and offer a new range of products for low-income consumers in emerging countries.
- → Add "going international" into your business plan as soon as possible. The opportunities are huge, particularly compared to a saturated home market.
- → Move with the times and change your product mix to meet new international demands.

"He didn't try to become his father or part of the Establishment. He remained himself."
Christine Mital, sister of Franck Riboud

Eric Schmidt CEO, Google

WITH OVER 20 YEARS' experience as an internet strategist and software developer, Schmidt was an obvious candidate for the position of web browser Google's first CEO in 2001. By 2003, Schmidt had transformed Google into the world's leading dotcom company, helping to take its revenue past the $1 billion mark. Like company founders Brin and Page, Schmidt takes home a nominal $1 annual salary, but his holdings in company stock reveal a truer picture of his wealth, and Schmidt is now a multibillionaire.

BIOGRAPHY
Born in Washington, D.C., in 1955. Schmidt earned a bachelor's degree in electrical engineering from Princeton University and a master's and PhD in computer science from the University of California at Berkeley. Pursuing his childhood ambition to be a science professor, he teaches part-time at Stanford University.

LEADERSHIP STYLE
Communicative, fun, and informal. Schmidt fits in with Google's corporate philosophy that "work should be challenging and the challenge should be fun."

KEY STRENGTH
Schmidt has the vision and the ambition to see beyond the day-to-day running of the company and plan for the future.

BEST DECISION
Acquiring YouTube and DoubleClick, which enabled Google to diversify its interests.

A TECHIE START Schmidt's early career positions included technical posts at Bell Labs and Zilog. He worked in the research department at the Computer Science Lab at Xerox's famed Palo Alto Research Center. In 1983, he joined Sun Microsystems Inc., rising to chief technology officer and corporate executive officer. At Sun, Schmidt headed the development of Java, Sun's ubiquitous programming language, and was responsible for developing the company's internet software strategy. In 1997, he became chairman and CEO at Novell.

BUSINESS ACUMEN By 2001, Google founders Sergey Brin and Larry Page had realized that they needed someone with more business experience to lead the company through its next growth phase. They approached Schmidt at Novell and, liking what they saw, offered him the CEO's post. Faced with a relatively small and young company, Schmidt's immediate concern was to focus on building a corporate infrastructure capable of dealing with hoped-for rapid growth and diversification. He led the company in its initial public offering in August 2004, which raised $1.67 billion and gave Google a market capitalization of more than $23 billion. Schmidt then embarked upon a series of opportune acquisitions for the company, buying out small start-up companies such as Keyhole, Inc., the developer of Earth Viewer, which has morphed into Google Earth. Other purchases included the online video site YouTube, JotSpot, and DoubleClick. He has also struck up a number of partnerships with companies such as eBay, MySpace, and MTV.

LESSONS IN BUSINESS: MAKING THE RIGHT FRIENDS

Schmidt recognized that Google needed partnerships if it were to diversify further and reach more customers. By negotiating deals with companies such as Dell and MySpace, Schmidt tapped into established networks, reaping the benefit of the work that these companies had already put in.
→ Realize you can't do everything yourself. Choose partners to give you a shortcut to the skills you need.
→ List potential new partners, and work out when an approach to them will fit in with your plan.
→ Choose partners who take your company in new directions with a lot less risk than doing it yourself.

"Innovation comes from places that you don't expect." Eric Schmidt

Thomas Krens Director (1988–2008), Guggenheim Foundation

A CONTROVERSIAL FIGURE in gallery management, Krens completely reshaped the Guggenheim Foundation in his 20 years as director. His bold strategy of opening galleries and museums around the world and focusing on financial as much as artistic value made him plenty of enemies at all levels of the art world, but it also transformed the Guggenheim from a venerable New York institution into an international powerhouse. He was behind the iconic Guggenheim in Bilbao, and ventures in Las Vegas, Mexico, and Abu Dhabi.

ART PROFESSOR After 17 years as an art history professor at Williams College in Massachusetts, where he was also director of the college's museum of art, Krens was appointed director of the Guggenheim in 1988. At the time, the New York museum had a modest endowment, a varied exhibition history, a landmark building that needed repair, and not enough room for exhibits. It had also sold off a number of significant works. Armed with a bullish management style and a solidly populist agenda, Krens set out on a drastic program of transformation.

GOING GLOBAL Krens's crowd-pleasing, expansionist approach has become a model for institutions all over the world, including the Tate in Britain and the Louvre in France. His key initiatives in New York were two major overhauls of the Guggenheim's iconic Frank Lloyd Wright-designed Fifth Avenue headquarters, organizing trend-setting shows of contemporary artists, and initiating a style of high-profile themed exhibitions that had never been seen before.

Among his international projects, the opening of the titanium-clad Guggenheim Bilbao in 1997 was a bold step that drew criticism from spectators, yet the museum now attracts more than a million visitors a year. A partnership in Las Vegas with Russia's Hermitage Museum soon followed, and projects in Mexico and Abu Dhabi were begun. During his tenure Krens also increased the size of the Guggenheim's endowment from $20 million to $118 million. Krens's ambitious vision and bold approach changed the rules for how museums could operate in the 21st century.

LESSONS IN BUSINESS: IGNORING THE CRITICS

Forget about the detractors. Every industry, every activity has a plethora of vested interests who will try to stop you doing what you need to. Decide where you want to go, ignore negative criticism and go there.
→ Only argue publicly with a detractor if you are sure the debate will be fair and chaired by a neutral.
→ To win over support, work hard on selling the personal benefits of a proposal to a person whom you know is going to be resistant initially.
→ Use other people, perhaps someone who might not be expected to agree with you, to argue your case.

"Art is for the masses." Thomas Krens

Stefan Persson CEO, H&M

A SILVER-HAIRED SWEDE with Savile Row taste, Persson has his finger on the pulse of the clothing retail industry and knows more about female fashion than most. Since taking control of the company in 1982, he has turned it into one of the world's largest high street fashion chains, with over 1,300 stores in 24 countries, including the US, Hong Kong, China, and Dubai. According to *Forbes* magazine, Persson was worth $18.4 billion in 2007, making him the second richest man in Sweden and placing him in the top 20 worldwide.

BIOGRAPHY
Born in Sweden in 1947, Persson is the son of Erling Persson, who founded the Swedish fashion company Hennes & Mauritz (now H&M). Persson attended the University of Stockholm.

LEADERSHIP STYLE
Reserved, diligent, and modest. His leadership style can perhaps be summed up by his laid-back reaction to hordes of shoppers lining up in Manhattan for the opening of the first US H&M store: "As a newcomer to the US, we were pleasantly surprised by the positive reaction."

KEY STRENGTH
Keeping costs low and volume high, without jeopardizing H&M's upmarket image.

BEST DECISION
Breaking into the US market at the right time.

A NEW CONCEPT During a post-war trip to the US, Stefan's father, Erling, discovered a new retail clothing concept—high turnover and low prices—and decided to import the idea to Sweden. H&M was listed on the Stockholm stock exchange in 1974; the Persson family retained the largest share. In 1982, Erling turned over the role of managing director to son Stefan, who strengthened the brand and maintained a low-debt, cash-rich position, enabling H&M to respond quickly to trends. By introducing new lines on a near-daily, rather than seasonal, basis, Persson attracted repeat shoppers.

EXPANDING ABROAD To keep costs low, Persson employed around 50 designers in-house and moved manufacturing to Asia and Europe, particularly Bangladesh, China, and Turkey. When he was made CEO in 1990, he dramatically expanded the company, making H&M one of the largest retailers in Sweden. Spotting the emergence of "global fashion" —young consumers following trends set by Hollywood, MTV, and the internet—he drove the company into new markets, opening around 60 stores a year across Belgium, Luxembourg, Austria, and Germany. H&M even penetrated the notoriously snobbish French market with six stores in the Paris area in 1998, won a significant market share in the UK, and entered the lucrative accessories and cosmetics markets. In 2000, H&M opened its first store in the US—the country that had been its inspiration —in New York. Persson has guided H&M from strength to strength, opening its first stores in Asia in 2006 and the Far East in 2007, and scoring designer ranges from high-profile figures including Karl Lagerfeld and Madonna.

LESSONS IN BUSINESS: KEEPING STOCK MOVING

By keeping costs low, styles up-to-date, and stock moving, Persson has ensured H&M has one of the fastest turnarounds in the industry, moving merchandise from drawing board to stores in as little as three weeks.
→ Emphasize that the middle manager's job is to drive working capital around the business—fast.
→ Make sure your people realize that most businesses have to be quick on their feet.
→ Try to avoid letting goods that are not going to sell languish on shelves. Discount them or admit the problem and move on.

"We offer the best value for your money." Stefan Persson

Michael Geoghegan CEO, HSBC Group

JUST 20 YEARS OLD when he joined HSBC in 1973, Geoghegan rose steadily through the ranks. Throughout his many years with the company, in locations all over the globe, he has shown that he has a cool head, breadth of vision, and the management skills of a high flier. Nonetheless, he was not the obvious choice for the top job in 2006, when the bank was facing internal problems, and an external appointment was expected. His term has been a resounding success, rising to the challenge of dramatic changes in the banking world.

BIOGRAPHY
Born in Windsor, UK, in 1953. In the course of his career he has lived and worked in a dozen countries, including Brazil, where he established HSBC Group's operations.

LEADERSHIP STYLE
Cool-headed and driven. Viewed as a man who gets things done.

KEY STRENGTH
A global perspective, based largely on his extensive international experience, including 12 years working in North and South America.

BEST DECISION
Swiftly addressing HSBC's problems during the global financial crisis. Geoghegan even won praise from those who had opposed the company's decision to spend $14.5 billion on Household International, the lender at the center of the US sub-prime crisis.

SEEN FROM ALL SIDES In the course of his career, Geoghegan has viewed HSBC's operations from every direction. Since his first job as an international manager, he has held posts throughout the group, including 12 years in charge of business in North and South America, eight years in Asia, seven years in the Middle East, and three years in Europe. He has been chairman of HSBC America and group general manager of HSBC Holdings plc, the part of the company responsible for UK high street banking operations. In 2006, he replaced Stephen Green as CEO.

SUB-PRIME TIME Michael Geoghegan's calm but tough style was just what the bank group needed to deal with the problems in its American business. He had only been in the job a few months when the group's acquisition, three years earlier, of Household International, the US consumer finance business, started to look like a bad call. In 2007, HSBC was pulled into the sub-prime crisis when Household's customers started defaulting on loans and the bank had to increase its bad-debt provisions. Geoghegan issued HSBC's first profit warning. The beleaguered CEO knew he had to move fast—as he said, "the buck stops with me"—and he began by making changes to the American management team and taking charge of the American unit. Working with HSBC's finance director, he brought the company back on track but acknowledged that change would not be overnight, saying, "It will probably take two or three years to work this out." Geoghegan also faces the challenge of reassuring investors and focusing HBSC's efforts on emerging markets.

LESSONS IN BUSINESS: CHALLENGING POOR PERFORMANCE

When things start to go badly wrong, investors need to know that the situation is being dealt with firmly. Never be afraid to hold executives responsible and let "heads roll," as Geoghegan did at HSBC Finance to stem the damage caused by sub-prime debts. Work hard to keep investors looking toward better times.
→ Make sure an underperfomer understands and recognizes their mistakes before attempting to rectify.
→ Before letting go of employees, make sure there is no alternative solution to poor performance.
→ Communicate with stakeholders, particularly your employees, clearly and frequently in hard times..

"We must make decisions now, however difficult, to manage for the future." Michael Geoghegan

Nandan Nilekani Co-founder, Chairman & CEO (2002–07), Infosys

INDIA HAS BECOME the home of cutting-edge IT solutions and, as co-founder of Infosys Technologies Ltd and CEO for five years, extrovert businessman Nilekani is synonymous with that transformation. His company, known as the "Indian Microsoft", was launched from a small flat in Pune, southern India, in 1981, with a working capital of 10,000 rupees (about $250). Two years later, Infosys moved to a state-of-the-art site in Bangalore, India's Silicon Valley. It now provides software and support for many of the world's biggest companies.

BIOGRAPHY
Born in Karnataka, India, in 1955. At an early age Nilekani was sent to live with an uncle, an experience that taught him to be independent. He graduated from the prestigious Indian Institute of Technology, Bombay (Mumbai), in 1978.

LEADERSHIP STYLE
Innovative, thoughtful, pioneering. To Nilekani it's all about "outsmarting the other guy". He is a figurehead for the company.

KEY STRENGTH
Devising new business practices and being able to take the world with him.

BEST DECISION
Acting on his vision of the enormous, world-transforming potential of business outsourcing.

FROM THIRD WORLD TO FLAT WORLD

With Nilekani at the helm, Infosys urged the world to "think flat" with its pioneering Global Delivery Model, based on the principle of taking work to the location where the best talent is available and where it makes most economic sense. The boom that followed saw India emerge as the world leader in business process outsourcing and changed global business practice fundamentally.

Infosys now has development centers in India, China, Australia, Czech Republic, Poland, UK, Canada, and Japan, offering services to a vast and growing range of clients in areas including business and technology consulting, product engineering, custom software development, independent testing and validation, IT infrastructure services, and business process outsourcing.

THE GREAT EXPLAINER According to

trendspotter Thomas Friedman, Nilekani is respected both as a businessman and as a visionary thinker for not only his programming skills, but his unique ability to explain how each program fits a specific niche in the emerging trends in computing as well as how those trends will "transform the computing business, and how that transformation will affect global politics and economics."

Nilekani stepped down as CEO in 2007 but, as chairman, he continues to be the company's brand ambassador, much sought after as an adviser by Infosys clients, opinion-formers, and politicians. Nilekani has also turned his attention to wider problems such as climate change —he is passionately involved in reducing his own company's carbon footprint—and helping India's poor.

LESSONS IN BUSINESS: BEING AWARE OF THE BIGGER PICTURE

In the words of Infosys co-founder Narayana Murthy: "A good leader is one who can connect a bird's-eye view with a worm's-eye view of the world. Nandan is good with the bird's-eye view."

→ Once you have created a great product, study its impact on the market—who is buying and who is not—and react to what has changed.

→ Look for the trends in your market; use market research to find out what is likely to happen next.

→ Think globally. Anticipate where development is going to occur by thinking at a high level.

"Seattle has Bill. Bangalore has Nandan."
Thomas L. Friedman, Pulitzer Prize-winning author and journalist

Andrea Guerra CEO, Luxottica

LUXOTTICA'S POSITION as the world's largest manufacturer of sunglasses, owner of brands including Ray-Ban, Persol, and Oakley has been cemented by Guerra. Through a series of bold moves, he ensured that an Italian company rooted in manufacturing also became a significant global retail presence, acquiring outlets and rival brands and opening up in new territories previously ignored by the fashion industry. His firm, strategic direction and an easy-going, collegiate approach to management has brought success in a challenging field.

BIOGRAPHY
Born in Milan, Italy, in 1965, Guerra received a bachelor's degree in economics and commerce from La Sapienza University of Rome in 1989.

LEADERSHIP STYLE
Modest and low-profile, Guerra forms a close bond with his staff, playing soccer with them and encouraging a strong sense of a group mission.

KEY STRENGTH
His ability to find aggressive, growth-building solutions to different challenges.

BEST DECISION
To begin retailing in China, tapping into a huge new market.

ITALY'S YOUNGEST CEO Before he joined Luxottica, Guerra spent ten years at Merloni Elettrodomestici, one of the largest appliance makers in Europe. In 1999, at the age of 34, he was promoted to CEO, becoming the youngest person ever to hold the post at a public Italian company. This early experience of top leadership and dealing in foreign markets provided him with crucial skills with which to take on Luxottica's complex challenges when he took over at the sunglasses group in 2004.

CHINA SYNDROME One of the greatest challenges facing Luxottica when Guerra arrived was competition from China. Western businesses were increasingly unable to compete on price with China's low labor costs, and consumers were increasingly reluctant to pay a premium for the privilege of owning products made in Italy. In a drastic move, Guerra opened two factories in China. He then took an even bolder step by treating China as an undeveloped retail market for Luxottica's high-end products. The company bought three Chinese retail chains, spreading its presence across the country and opening up a new field of revenue and growth. Guerra also set out to deepen the company's strong position in the US. He bought Oakley, adding it to Ray-Ban and the company's other house brands, and boosted investment in all of them. The company's three US retail chains were updated to bring them into line with Luxottica's brands manufactured under licence, such as Donna Karan, Versace, Prada, and Dolce & Gabbana. Guerra's aggressive retail-focused business model left the company in a powerful position in an often-fickle industry.

LESSONS IN BUSINESS: CHALLENGING THE COMPETITION

Competition is always welcome because it shows that the market wants the products. In business, as in sports, playing catch-up is painful and rarely successful; so the key is to attack and innovate to stay ahead.
→ Know your competitors weaknesses, and exploit them. Know their strengths and match them.
→ Stay on the front foot and take the fight to the competition wherever you find it; add a competitive angle to every plan.
→ Make it everyone's aim to be better than the competition in their part of the business, whatever it is.

"One person is not responsible for the results of a company." Andrea Guerra

Steen Riisgaard President & CEO, Novozymes A/S

SINCE JOINING enzyme producer Novo as a microbiologist in 1979, Riisgaard has managed to combine successfully the roles of scientist and businessman. Currently the president and CEO, he has always recognized the importance of investment and profit, while never losing sight of the greater good. His belief in "green chemistry" extends from making the textile industry environmentally friendly through his enzyme-based genetically engineered "bugs", all the way to his membership on the board of the World Wide Fund for Nature, Denmark.

BIOGRAPHY
Born in Esbjerg, Denmark, in 1951. Riisgaard studied at the University of Copenhagen, where he received a master's degree in biology. Following his graduation he spent a few years as a research fellow at the Serum Institute of Denmark.

LEADERSHIP STYLE
Focused, inspirational, practical. Riisgaard has never lost sight of the bottom line and has not allowed his passionate belief in environmental issues to cloud his drive to keep Novozymes one step ahead of the competition.

KEY STRENGTH
A keen eye for business opportunities within previously underdeveloped scientific fields and markets.

BEST DECISION
Acquiring Earth Biosciences, Inc. in 2006, adding new alternative pesticide technologies to Novozyme's "green" plant care portfolio.

IN PURSUIT OF ENZYMES Riisgaard has spent almost his entire career with Novozymes. Joining in 1979 as a microbiologist in enzymes research and development, he rose through the ranks, heading the company's enzyme business in Denmark and overseeing Novo's activities in China. In 1999, the board split the company in two, with health care and industrial enzymes becoming separate businesses. Riisgaard was appointed president and CEO of Novozymes A/S and was finally able to focus on what he did best—enhancing the status of the overlooked industrial enzymes division.

EMERGING MARKETS Riisgaard has focused the company's Danish research capabilities on developing speciality bio-engineered enzymes, offering a sustainable solution to industrial and ecological problems, being biodegradable and more effective than synthetic chemicals. The company is now a leader in producing enzymes that extract alternative biofuels from plants. Intent on achieving competitive results, and focusing on accelerating sales, Riisgaard turned to the markets of China and India. One of the first Danish companies to look at the potential of Asia, Novozymes now has research, marketing, sales, and production facilities within China.

One of Riisgaard's greatest challenges has been working with Chinese industries to develop new business opportunities, including improving the texture and taste of noodles. Since 2006, Riisgaard has made acquisitions outside the existing core enzyme business, including Delta and GroPet, seeing the chemical industry as a future growth area. The acquisition of Biocon in 2007 marked a step in strengthening the company's position in India.

LESSONS IN BUSINESS: COLLABORATING WITH OVERSEAS INDUSTRIES

As well as expanding into emerging markets through acquisitions, Riisgaard has struck up collaborative ventures with existing industries in those markets, giving Novozymes the ability to target specific needs.

→ Going into new markets carries risk. Reduce this by working with companies already established there.

→ Use your research and development capabilities to attract overseas companies for joint ventures. Make money out of your intellectual property.

→ Cut the cost of competitive and industry research needed for a new market, by creating a joint venture.

"There are no doors closed to us. Everybody wants to work with us." Steen Riisgaard

INDIAN LEADERS

"The country is now universally recognized as a nation on the move and takes its place amongst the successful economies in the region."
RATAN TATA

India is now a key global player, with the second-fastest-growing economy in the world (after China) and the largest pool of skilled and professional manpower on Earth. India's economic growth is transforming the country and has created a number of high-profile business billionaires. One of the most well-known of those billionaires is Reliance ADA chairman **Anil Ambani** (p376). In 2005, as part of his strategy to become a player in the global entertainment industry, he acquired the Indian film production and multiplex cinema company Adlabs, where he increased profits through cost-cutting. In 2008, he signed a deal with film director Steven Spielberg's DreamWorks to create a new production company, bringing Reliance greater US exposure.

It's not just the super-rich Indians who have money to spend; while poverty is still rife, many more people now have disposable income, a fact that Indian business has been quick to exploit. **Ratan Tata** (p379), Tata Sons chairman, targeted both middle-class motorbike-riding youths and modest families with auto-rickshaws when he announced development of the four-door, "one-lakh" micro-car, the "Nano". Its extraordinarily low price and fuel-efficient design are also attracting western interest ●

The Power of Outsourcing

India's greatest resource is its huge, well-educated workforce. This, allied to the relentless pressure for western companies to cut costs, has given rise to the phenomenon of outsourcing, one of the most significant factors in India's economic transformation.

Ananda Mukerji, CEO of Firstsource, is just one of the many Indian business leaders to have made a success of outsourcing. Mukerji, who has worked as CEO of the company since its inception in 2002, has guided Firstsource to a strong position in business process outsourcing (BPO). Firstsource delivers a range of services, including telesales, direct marketing, call centers, online transaction support, and helpdesks. Under Mukerji's leadership, the company has grown to operate from over 30 differenrt centers across India and has secured contracts from more than 20 *Fortune* 500 and FTSE 100 companies. It has been ranked third in *BusinessWeek* magazine's list of "hot players" in the offshore outsourcing world.

Outsourcing generates over $30 billion a year in revenues for Indian companies. Of this total, BPO was responsible for around $11 billion, with IT outsourcing making up the rest. **Sudhakar Ram**, chairman and managing director of Mastek Ltd, has focused his company on providing IT solutions to insurance, financial service organizations, and government. Mastek has been ranked in the top 20 in the Global Outsourcing 100 list by the International Association of Outsourcing Professionals.

Return of the Entrepreneurs

India sends more of its students to study overseas than any other nation, and more than half to the US, where the rewards of a "developed world" economy tempt many to remain. However, India's burgeoning economy and domestic market are luring home a significant number of talented executives. **Sumir Chadha** and **K.P. Balaraj** of venture capital firm Sequoia, and **Anurag Dod**, CEO of search engine Guruji.com, are typical of these returnees. Others include **Vinod K. Dham** ("Father of the Pentium") who studied engineering at the University of Cincinnati and then joined Intel. He later met **Tushar A. Dave**, an engineer and expert in Indo-US start-ups. They returned to India to establish NewPath Ventures, the first Indo-US venture capital fund. Another IT entrepreneur, **K.B. Chandrasekhar**, returned from the US to found e4e, a global technology holding company, while **Rajesh Reddy**, founder of Unimobile, recently launched July Systems in Bangalore to build wireless infrastructure.

Drivers of Growth

India's expanding economy has provided a fertile ground for innovative executives:

V.G. Siddhartha Hegde, CAFÉ COFFEE DAY (Retail: Karnataka)—*Pioneered the café concept in India, creating the largest chain in the country, with plans to launch abroad.*

Karan Johar, DHARMA PRODUCTIONS (Media: Mumbai)—*Has produced a string of award-winning international blockbusters.*

—

O.P. Manchanda, DR LAL PATHLABS (Laboratories: Delhi)—*Has announced plans to build Asia's biggest laboratory.*

G.V. Sanjay Reddy, GVK BIOSCIENCES PRIVATE LTD (Biosciences: Hyderabad) – *Has developed the company into Asia's leading contract research organization.*

Sanjeev Aga, IDEA CELLULAR, (Telecoms: Delhi)—*Expanded customer base to 40 million. In 2008, launched services in Mumbai metro, the largest single metro launch ever*

—

Naresh Ponnapa, INDECOMM GLOBAL SERVICES (Consultancy and outsourcing: Bangalore)—*Aggressive organic growth reached 100 percent annually over the three years to 2008.*

Sabeer Bhatia, NAVIN COMMUNICATIONS (Telecoms: Mumbai)—*Co-founder of Hotmail, sold company to Microsoft in order to found Navin Communications, currently at the forefront of unified voice messaging communications.*

—

Anupam Mittal, PEOPLE INTERACTIVE PRIVATE LTD (Internet: Mumbai)—*His flagship brand, shaadi.com, is claimed to be the world's earliest and most successful online matrimonial service for Asians worldwide.*

—

Vikram Akula, SKS MICROFINANCE (Finance: Secunderabad)—*Founded one of the world's fastest growing microfinance organizations.*

—

S. Ramadorai, TATA CONSULTANCY SERVICES LIMITED (IT: Mumbai)—*Credited with building TCS into a $5.7 billion global company.*

—

Arun Natarajan, VENTURE INTELLIGENCE (Business information: Chennai)—*Founded this leading provider of information and networking services to the private equity and venture capital ecosystem in India.*

Wendelin Wiedeking CEO, Porsche AG

THE UNDISPUTED KING of the German automobile business, Wiedeking is responsible for the recent outstanding success of luxury carmaker Porsche, masterminding its transformation from a loss-making niche player into a global giant. With annual sales in excess of €6.5 billion, Porsche now enjoys worldwide representation; the Porsche and Piech families, who still own the company, are billionaires; and Wiedeking is the highest paid German boss of all time, receiving an estimated salary of around €44 million.

BIOGRAPHY
Born in Ahlen, Germany, in 1952. Wiedeking studied mechanical engineering at RWTH Aachen University, graduating in 1978. He earned a doctorate in engineering from the same university in 1983.

LEADERSHIP STYLE
Sharp-tongued and quick-tempered, but fair-minded. Deeply respected by his employees, so much so that the union leadership presented Wiedeking with an honorary membership. A great orator and admired by the general public; according to a poll, the majority of Germans think he would make an excellent chancellor.

KEY STRENGTH
Keeping the workforce on side, despite the often unpopular decisions he has had to make.

BEST DECISION
Producing an SUV, ensuring global success for Porsche and making the company less vulnerable to downturns.

THE NEW BROOM When Wiedeking joined Porsche in 1992 as head of production and materials, the company was in deep financial trouble. Sales of its flagship 911 model were dwindling and the company had lost money the previous year. Wiedeking, who had visited car plants in Japan, knew that Porsche work habits were outmoded and inefficient, and he drafted in a team of Japanese time-and-motion experts to restructure production.

BRINGING ON THE NEW Acting in accordance with the German proverb "you sweep the steps from the top down," Wiedeking cut the managerial workforce by 35 percent and made some 1,800 employees redundant. He also successfully negotiated lower prices with its suppliers. Within a year, the company was back in the black, and Wiedeking was given the post of CEO in 1993. He then turned his attention to the models themselves. Wiedeking vetoed plans to drop the 911, believing that Porsche customers saw the iconic model as a vital part of company heritage. Then, in keeping with Porsche's image as a maker of sporty cars, he cancelled a nascent family car project and brought in the Boxster. Realizing that Porsche could not afford a new factory to build the Boxster, Wiedeking took the unheard-of decision to build the car outside Germany, in a Finnish factory.

Wiedeking extended Porsche's range to include an SUV thereby opening up new markets, particularly in the Middle East, Asia, and South America. One of his rationales behind the decision to produce a bigger car was that it allowed customers to remain faithful to the brand after having a family.

LESSONS IN BUSINESS: THINKING BIG

In September 2008, Porsche gained control over Europe's largest car manufacturer when it raised its stake in Volkswagen AG to over 35 percent. With plans to increase this to 75 percent, Wiedeking will create one of the world's biggest car manufacturers.

→ If your company is small, don't let a sense of size inferiority hold you back.

→ Small companies should think big—is there a merger or acquisition that could give you a lift?

→ Look for a competitor with a poorer reputation who might benefit from your brand and know-how.

"If size did matter the dinosaurs would still be alive."
Wendelin Wiedeking

Leigh Clifford CEO (2000–07), Rio Tinto

IF ANYONE can claim credit for the emergence of Rio Tinto as one of the giants of the global commodities boom, it is probably Clifford. A mining engineer by training, he joined Rio Tinto Zinc (as it was then known) in 1970 and rose through the ranks to become CEO in 2000. Clifford's economic understanding and mining experience enabled Rio Tinto to make the most of the opportunity that globalization presented, tripling profits during his tenure, thereby securing the company's position for the future.

BIOGRAPHY
Born in 1947 in South Australia. Clifford has a first class honors degree in engineering (mining), and a master of engineering science degree from the University of Melbourne.

LEADERSHIP STYLE
Tough and uncompromising. Clifford knows his business from the bottom up. He is driven and ambitious, both for himself and for his company.

KEY STRENGTH
Running a tight ship. Just because your profits soar, that doesn't mean you can get sloopy. He has also stuck to the mining mantra: the most profitable operations come from the world's best sites. Control them, and you make money.

BEST DECISION
Plowing Rio Tinto's profits into acquisitions and exploration, strengthening the company for the future.

IN AT THE DEEP END Despite coming from a well-established Australian commercial family, Clifford knew that miners need to get their hands dirty to succeed. After leaving university, he spent six years working underground to get his mine manager's certificate. With that on his resumé, plus his academic qualifications, he was an obvious hire for one of the two natural resources giants, RTZ and BHP, that dominated Australia's vast mining industry.

TOUGH AND DRIVEN By reputation, Clifford is as hard as the ore his company deals in. Natural resources is a tough industry, full of tough men, and for much of Clifford's career, not an easy one to operate in. Through the 1980s and 1990s, the price of much of the stuff that RTZ digs out of the ground was falling rather than rising, but by the time Clifford took the helm of the business in 2000, commodities were just about to take off. Industrial revolutions in India and China were fueling a massive global boom in manufacturing, and all those new factories needed steel, copper, and iron going in one door before toys, televisions, and mobile phones could come out the other. Rio Tinto was perfectly placed to supply them.

By focusing obsessively on market shares and cost control, Clifford managed to triple profits during his tenure at the helm. He then used the benefits judiciously to expand through acquisitions and new exploration in readiness for a less bullish market. In 2007, Leigh Clifford passed the reins of the minerals and metals giant to Tom Albanese, before being made chairman of Qantas Airways Ltd.

LESSONS IN BUSINESS: WATCHING GLOBAL DEVELOPMENTS

With a weather eye on approaching market conditions, Clifford positioned the company to benefit and then took full advantage of the situation. In the end it is hard to beat being in the right place at the right time.
→ Study global cycles and prepare for the next swing while enjoying the "booms" or enduring the "busts".
→ When times are good do not compromise on any financial imperatives in the expectation that growth will prevent a problem occurring.
→ Never lose sight of cost control and keep your peoples' eye on it whatever the economic situation.

"Success is down to perseverance, ability, skills, and experience, but it is also about being given an opportunity." Leigh Clifford

Graham Mackay CEO, SABMiller

FROM EARLY JUNIOR ROLES setting up IT systems for South African Breweries and managing one of its domestic regions, Mackay has come a long way. As the company's CEO, he has shifted SAB's listing to London and transformed it, through a series of shrewd mergers and an aggressive policy of expansion into emerging markets, into the world's second largest brewer, behind InBev. Today, the company is well positioned to challenge for market leadership, following its tie-up with US brewer Coors.

BIOGRAPHY
Born in Johannesburg, South Africa, in 1949. He graduated with a BComm from the University of South Africa.

LEADERSHIP STYLE
Open, plain-speaking, and decisive. After the takeover of Miller, Mackay decided to take a chance on its CEO. Six months later he realized he'd made a mistake and replaced him.

KEY STRENGTH
Mackay's willingness to take risks has repeatedly given him the edge over rivals when it comes to making a quick deal.

BEST DECISION
The acquisition of Miller from Philip Morris, making the new SABMiller the world's second largest brewing group.

LEARNING THE HARD WAY Mackay describes himself as a graduate of the school of hard knocks, after an early career of major mistakes at the industrial conglomerate BTR (ex-British Tire & Rubber). He first joined SAB in the IT department. After designing and building SAB's information system, he was given one of the company's South African regions to run. His impressive showing saw him leapfrog more experienced internal rivals when he was appointed CEO in 1999.

GETTING STUCK IN When Mackay took over, SAB was the world's fourth largest brewing group, but it was still vulnerable to a weak Rand. Mackay's first challenge was to reduce the group's exposure to devaluation, and he shifted its main exchange listing to London. He saw the industry was in a consolidation phase, where, as he said, "There will be a lot of deals in this industry and we either have to take part or be a spectator." He began by out-maneuvering rivals Bass and Heineken to buy Czech brewer Urquell for $321 million. In 2002, he paid $5.6 billion for Miller, creating the world's second largest brewing group. As demand for beer dropped in most of Europe and North America, Mackay targeted brewers in growth markets: Italy's Peroni for $280 million in 2003 and the South American giant Bavaria for $5.6 billion in 2005. In 2007, he led the merger of SABMiller's North American operations with Molson Coors to steal a march on rivals Anheuser-Busch. Following criticism that he had paid over the odds, he said he had paid for their potential under SAB management. So far he has called it right.

LESSONS IN BUSINESS: SEEING IT YOUR WAY

The Miller brand may not have been worth $5.6 billion to market analysts, but Mackay knew what SAB's progressive management could do with it—how he could expand, and bring cost savings.
➔ When you understand the value of an asset, back your opinion with confidence whatever the pundits say.
➔ Aim high; the ultimate objective is market leadership and brand domination.
➔ Assess what your organization and people will bring to a new acquisition—and where you know it will add value, go for it.

> "I am more a manager of the head than the heart."
> Graham Mackay

Jacques Lamarre President & CEO, SNC-Lavalin Group, Inc.

VOTED CANADA'S CEO of the Year by *Canadian Business* magazine in 2003 and Canada's Outstanding CEO of the Year by Caldwell Partners International in 2004, Lamarre runs the engineering, construction, and manfacturing company SNC-Lavalin. Since his appointment in 1996, SNC-Lavalin has enjoyed continuous growth, with revenues increasing from CAN $1.4 billion to nearly $7 billion, and market capitalization growing from CAN $600 million to more than $7 billion, making it one of Canada's biggest international companies.

BIOGRAPHY
Born in Quebec, Canada, in 1943, the 8th of 11 children. Lamarre's father was a building contractor and often looked to Lamarre and his siblings as a source of cheap labour. Lamarre has a bachelor's in humanities and a BSc in civil engineering from Laval University, Quebec City He later completed an Executive Development Program at Harvard.

LEADERSHIP STYLE
Honest, open, and ethical, Lamarre is strong on people skills. In his own words: "I like human interaction, which is why I genuinely enjoy lunching with employees in the cafeteria."

KEY STRENGTH
Making sure that projects are financially sound before giving the go-ahead to proceed.

BEST DECISION
Pressing on with the program of expansion started by his predecessor, which has taken SNC-Lavalin into new markets and contributed increased revenues to the company.

STARTING OFF WITH BIG BROTHER
Lamarre's career in civil engineering began in 1968, when he joined Lavalin, Inc , the Montreal-based engineering and construction company later headed by his older brother, Bernard. He held a series of increasingly senior roles in the company, managing many high-profile projects. By 1991, a policy of over expansion had left Lavalin heavily in debt and the engineering giant was acquired by rival SNC, Inc. Lamarre stayed on after the merger, becoming executive vice-president in 1994 and president and CEO in 1996.

DISTRIBUTED LEADERSHIP As CEO,
Lamarre has strengthened SNC-Lavalin's position as a global competitor in engineering, construction, and infrastructure development, working in more than 100 countries. The expansion that was the hallmark of his predecessor's reign has continued under Lamarre, taking the company into overseas markets, petrochemicals, and the ownership and management of infrastructure. In 2003, SNC-Lavalin acquired the Houston-based oil and gas processing company GDS Engineers, Inc., and, in 2004, it bought out its partner in the Canatom NPM, Inc. venture, making SNC-Lavalin Nuclear the largest private sector nuclear engineering company in Canada.

Early in his career, Lamarre discovered the benefits of encouraging workers and managers to feel a degree of ownership for their work and of the company as a whole. Calling his style of management "distributed leadership," he trusts people to set their own, realistic targets. The sting in the tail is that they are then expected to meet those targets.

LESSONS IN BUSINESS: LEARNING FROM MISTAKES

Nowadays it seems that Lamarre can do little wrong. Nonetheless, he is the first to admit that he made blunders early on in his career. In 1979, for example, he faced the indignity of being hauled before a provincial inquiry to explain why costs on Montreal's Olympic Stadium had soared sky high.
→ Encourage people to take risks. In an established company people will make mistakes—even costly ones.
→ Give every employee the chance to learn from their mistakes.
→ Analyze mistakes. Make sure everyone learns from what has gone wrong, as well as what has gone well.

"If I could re-engineer myself, I'd make me calmer and less excitable." Jacques Lamarre

Howard Schultz Chairman & CEO, Starbucks

IN LESS THAN twenty years, Schultz took a chain of six coffee shops in the US Pacific Northwest and turned it into a runaway commercial success, with an unavoidable presence around the world. Through his combination of marketing insight and a relentless drive for expansion, Schultz created an entirely new market, set up thousands of branches in dozens of countries, and made Starbucks so ubiquitous that it threatened to dethrone McDonald's as shorthand for hugely successful branding and global dominance.

BIOGRAPHY
Born in 1953 in Brooklyn, New York. He gained a football scholarship to Northern Michigan University.

LEADERSHIP STYLE
Inspirational, tough-minded, self-assured. His enthusiasm and charisma play a big role in his ability to motivate. His experience, at the age of seven, of seeing his injured father out of work with no compensation and no health insurance, led Schultz to place a strong emphasis on benefits for his employees.

KEY STRENGTH
A talent for marketing and an insight into how new opportunities can work.

BEST DECISION
Ignoring conventional wisdom and setting out to find the American market for good coffee.

KITCHENWARE SALESMAN While working as a salesman for a Swedish kitchenware company, Schultz flew from New York to visit Starbucks, a Seattle coffee store that was buying a lot of his appliances. He joined the company, and, after a buying trip to Italy, proposed that the Italian style of coffee bar could succeed in the US. The company disagreed, so he set up on his own, and then had a chance to test his theory when he bought the six-store Starbucks chain in 1987.

WORLD DOMINATION Schultz promised his early investors that Starbucks would expand rapidly. Given that Seattle was already full of coffee houses and the rest of the US showed no apparent interest, that looked optimistic. But Schultz's great insight was that, even though the market didn't yet appear to exist, he had

seen how it could. The growth did come, and quickly: 15 additional stores in the first year and nearly 150 within five years. Schultz's confidence was combined with an instinct for the kinds of display and style that female consumers in particular wanted, creating a trademarked experience that people could trust. The recipe was so successful that the company expanded exponentially throughout the 1990s, opening branches all over the world. The importance of Schultz's presence was underscored when he stepped down as CEO in 2000, after which the chain began to encounter problems that prompted him to return in 2008. Nowadays Starbucks is no longer the fresh pioneer but finds itself to be the dominant presence, under attack from younger rivals and changing tastes, and unpopular with those who oppose the increase in globalization.

LESSONS IN BUSINESS: CREATING MARKETS

Schultz's achievement in the market isn't just a new kind of coffee, but an entire consumer experience, complete with an "emotional" connection. He sees Starbucks as being "not in the coffee business serving people, but in the people business serving coffee."

→ Remember, just because nobody else is doing it, doesn't mean there isn't a market out there.

→ If businesses only ever set out to capture shares of proven markets, nothing new would ever happen.

→ Drive your people to think about customers and markets, then make the products to meet their needs.

"Seek to renew yourself even when you are hitting home runs." Howard Schultz

César Alierta Chairman & CEO, Telefónica

THIS GLOBAL LEADER has shown an outstanding talent for international strategy and deal-making in his career, both in the tobacco industry and as CEO of Spanish-based Telefónica. His global vision has extended beyond Spain and Latin America to make acquisitions and develop new markets in Europe—a regional spread that increases growth potential and mitigates risk in turbulent economic climates. Under Alierta's leadership, Telefónica has developed into one of the leading global integrated telecommunications operators.

BIOGRAPHY
Born in Zaragoza, Spain, in 1945. Alierta has a law degree from the University of Zaragoza and an MBA from Columbia University, New York. Before studying law he considered an academic career in philosophy.

LEADERSHIP STYLE
Low-key, disciplined, and focused. Has a reputation as a team player with strong delegation skills. Some complain of his poor communication skills and a lack of charisma.

KEY STRENGTH
Strategic thinking has enabled Alierta to raise Telefónica's global profile through astute acquisitions.

BEST DECISION
Moving into Western and Central Europe in 2003, markets his predecessor had avoided.

GLOBAL VISION Alierta is a fast learner, with early careers as a financial analyst and in brokerage. In 1985, he founded a stockbroking firm, Beta Capital, and in the 1990s he was president of the Spanish Stock Market Association (AEMV). In 1996, he was appointed head of Tabacalera, the state-run tobacco company, and led its expansion into the US and Central America. Under his stewardship, Tabacalera became a leading global player and, in 1999, Alierta oversaw its merger with French tobacco company Seita.

AN EYE FOR ACQUISITION In 2000, Alierta was nominated CEO of Telefónica. His initial focus on stability met with approval However, critics complained that his attention to detail made him slow to act on opportunities. He was also dogged by an investigation into claims against him of insider trading while at Tabacalera. At the same time Telefónica was badly hit by a financial crisis in Latin America, which had been providing some 50 percent of revenue. However, Alierta had spread the risk, investing not only in Argentina, the worst affected market, but also in Brazil and Mexico. He demonstrated his confidence in the growth potential of the region by acquiring Bell South's Latin American operations. In 2005, Alierta extended operations into Western and Central Europe through the acquisition of O2, the UK cell phone company, and Çesky Telecom in the Czech Republic, giving the company a presence in the British, Irish, German, Czech, and Slovakian markets. It is now the market leader in Brazil, Argentina, Chile, and Peru, and has operations in Mexico, Colombia, Guatemala, and Venezuela.

LESSONS IN BUSINESS: HEDGING YOUR BETS

Alierta's expansion in Europe and Central America cushioned the impact of the financial crisis in Argentina. Risk analysis and hedging your bets can extend to different geographic areas and different products—Alierta saw more future growth potential in cell phones than landlines.
→ Ensure your business is not too regionally concentrated; look for territories with different business cycles.
→ Look for warning signs or helpful market trends so that you focus on growth markets for products.
→ Consider mergers and acquisitions in global markets, which bring "knowledge on the ground."

"Telefónica has a lot to thank Latin America for, and Latin America should be grateful to Telefónica."
César Alierta

Solomon Trujillo CEO (2005–09), Telstra

"WE LIVE TWO LIVES", Trujillo has said. "One, we are given upon birth. The second, we make." The Mexican-American son of a railroad employee who worked his way through college, he has made his mark by challenging the status quo. He believes that growing up without a lot means you have to be creative and work hard. From humble beginnings, the life Trujillo worked hard to create now rewards him to the tune of an estimated AU$11 million a year as CEO of Australia's largest telecommunications company, Telstra.

BIOGRAPHY
Born in Cheyenne, Wyoming, in 1951. He holds a bachelor of business degree and an MBA from the University of Wyoming.

LEADERSHIP STYLE
Humble, soft-spoken, and earnest, Trujillo is also determined and resolute when it comes to getting things done. Colleagues say his industry acumen is not always matched by a deft personal touch.

KEY STRENGTH
A lifetime in telecommunications has given Trujillo unparalleled expertise and understanding of his sector. He is also adaptable and ready to shift positions as the market dictates.

BEST DECISION
Insisting on dramatic change when he took over at Orange. Trujillo increased margins, dramatically raised revenue growth rate, cut costs by over $1 billion, and grew the group's customer base by more than ten percent in 15 months.

THE FUTURE'S ORANGE On graduating, Trujillo went to work for telecoms giant AT&T. Aged 32 he became the youngest executive in the company's history. In 1984, he joined US West where, over 15 years, he worked his way up to chairman, CEO, and president, becoming America's first native-born Hispanic to serve as CEO of a *Fortune* 200 company. Labeled "US Worst" before he arrived, Trujillo's leadership led the telecommunications company, and industry, in deploying high-speed data services and advanced wireless services, and introducing more customer-centric approaches to service delivery. In 2001, Trujillo joined the board of Orange, the Paris-based wireless giant with 50 million customers in 19 countries. When he became CEO two years later, he was the first American to lead a CAC-40 (French stock market index) company. Despite his successes with company restructuring and revenue increases, his position as a forward thinking "odd man out" within the management instigated a move to Telstra, in 2005.

IN THE PALM OF HIS HAND Trujillo is a proven innovator with a string of achievements in the highly competitive communications arena, skills that were implemented in his new position: he guided the company through key technological developments such as the company's Next G Mobile broadband network, as well as Telstra's full privatization in 2006. Despite this, his appointment as CEO has not been without controversy. Even Australian prime minister John Howard joined in the criticism of Trujillo's AU$11-million pay packet, calling it an abuse of the capitalist system. He announced his departure in early 2009.

LESSONS IN BUSINESS: TALKING TO THE CUSTOMER

Trujillo frequently talks of "customer intimacy" and "market-based management" in which a company's strategy and product development drive toward tailored solutions, based on "a deep customer understanding". He believes this is particularly true of telecommunications companies.
→ Recognize that a mass market is made up of individuals who each have their story to tell.
→ Encourage all your people to talk to and get close to customers, whatever their role in the business.
→ Deal with myriad "markets of one" rather than mass markets to avoid pricing products like commodities.

"One thing I've learned is that good leaders are unafraid to court controversy. They're not afraid to challenge the status quo." Solomon Trujillo

Frank P. Lowy Co-founder & Executive Chairman, Westfield Group

A BILLIONAIRE BUSINESS leader who ranks among the most influential people in Australia, Lowy is an outstanding example of determination, entrepreneurial flair, and achievement. He is distinguished for his pivotal role in Westfield, the world's largest listed retail property group, and for his wider community, intellectual, and sporting involvement. Lowy was on the board of the Reserve Bank of Australia and chairman of the Football Federation Australia. He was made a Companion of the Order of Australia (AC) in 1999.

BIOGRAPHY
Born in Fil'akavo, Slovakia, in 1930. Lowy survived the Holocaust and left Europe for Israel, where he fought for the Zionist cause. In 1952, he rejoined surviving members of his family in Australia. He has a degree in commerce from the University of New South Wales.

LEADERSHIP STYLE
A courteous, consultative team player. Lowy inspires strong loyalty and some staff members have remained with Westfield for decades. He also has a reputation for ruthlessness.

KEY STRENGTH
His trendspotting abilities and strong analytical skills.

BEST DECISION
Moving from retailing into property development. The creation of Westfield's first shopping center in the late 1950s drew the attention of both the public and investors.

BUILDING ON SUCCESS Lowy's tenacity and business acumen saw him progress from delivery van driver to co-founder and head of Westfield Group—today a global retail property giant. From the early days in their delicatessen and coffee shop in Blacktown, New South Wales, he and his partner John Saunders nurtured contacts and studied trends at home and in the US. Lowy studied the Australian banking and legal systems and established close relationships with banks. Their property business grew from buying re-zoned farmland for mobile homes to house newly arrived European workers, to acquiring land for retail development.

GOING GLOBAL Their first retail center, Westfield Place in Blacktown, opened to great public acclaim in July 1959 and led to a raft of offers of joint ventures and commissions.

The company floated on the Sydney Stock Exchange in 1960, when Lowy was just 30 years old. The first foray outside Australia came in 1977 with the purchase of a mall in Trumbull, Connecticut, the first of many in the US. Built up over time, Westfield shopping centers varied from modest to luxurious, but all aimed to offer a pleasing environment for socializing as well as shopping. The formula proved a huge success. Saunders sold his share of the business to Lowy and retired in 1987, by which time Lowy's three sons had joined the business. Today, Westfield owns and manages some 120 malls in Australia, New Zealand, the UK, and the US, working with over 20,000 retailers. Others are in the pipeline. Lowy's determination is also evident in his stance in the face of ongoing tax investigations, which he vehemently denies. He doesn't give in easily.

LESSONS IN BUSINESS: COMBINING STRENGTHS

Lowy and his partner pooled their talents to launch a suburban delicatessen, then a coffee lounge, and subsequently a property business that was to become the world's largest listed retail property group.
→ Recognize the power of partnership built on mutual trust, teamwork, and complementary skill sets.
→ Two minds, with one on operations and the other on the long-term, are greater than the sum of parts.
→ Listen and learn from others, in both social and business environments. Interesting nuggets of information can invaluably inform strategy.

"I would back [Lowy's] intuition against the most rigorous analysis any day." Tony Berg, Westfield director, 1985–93

THE CHINA GENERATION

On becoming de facto leader of the People's Republic of China in 1978, Deng Xiaoping moved away from Mao Zedong's strictly communist vision to launch a pragmatic program of economic reform and large-scale development to enable China to compete globally. His market liberalization unleashed a latent entrepreneurship that saw China emerge as the "workshop of the world" for products such as textiles and clothing.

Over the last 30 years, a new generation of Chinese business people has made its mark, reaping the rewards of Deng Xiaoping's free-market reforms. **Zhang Ruimin** (p129) is at the forefront of the economic revolution, becoming chairman and CEO of the Haier home appliance firm in 1984 and transforming it from a small, collectively-owned factory into a multibillion dollar global player with a reputation for quality and innovation. **Ma Huateng** (p74), chairman and CEO of internet business Tencent, has also capitalized on the economic reforms, tailoring his business to the interests and spending potential of Generation Y Chinese, the newly affluent, grown-up children of the one-child-per-family system ●

"Although we are a state-owned enterprise, ever since we were established we have run as a separate and independent commercial enterprise."
XIAO YAQING

State Enterprise

While China has emerged as a leading global player, many aspects of traditional Chinese culture remain. Chinese society continues to place great value on family relationships in business, principles encompassed in the term *guanxi*.

State-owned businesses certainly have an advantage when it comes to *guanxi*. One such company is the Aluminum Corp. of China (Chinalco), which is majority-controlled by the Chinese government. Growth through diversification was the strategy pursued by **Xiao Yaqing**, CEO until early 2009.

Xiao targeted acquisitions in other metals sectors, personally overseeing the purchase of Peru Copper, Inc., and raising Chinalco's profile at home and abroad. His ambitious global strategy led to an upsurge of profits. Exactly how much influence China's political leaders have in the day-to-day running of the company, however, is unclear, as evidenced by the decision in 2008 to spend $16.7 billion to acquire a 9-percent share in London-based mining company Rio Tinto, China's largest overseas investment. Despite Xiao's assertions that the company took the decision independently, many analysts believed the investment was part of a government strategy to block a takeover of Rio Tinto by Anglo-Australian giant BHP Billiton, which could have impacted negatively on the Chinese economy.

While old-fashioned state control may still be alive, the Chinese authorities have certainly embraced new technology. Accepting that their economy is over-reliant on fossil fuels, the government has invested heavily to ensure that ambitious targets for generating more renewable energy are met. With the aid of generous support from regional government, one company that has benefited from this investment is Suntech, now China's largest solar panel manufacturer. The company's success has made CEO, **Shi Zhengrong**, into the world's first solar billionaire.

The New Philanthropists

A growing number of dollar millionaires and billionaires demonstrates China's exciting new dynamism. Perhaps reflecting the Confucian tradition of charitable giving, or an awareness among the newly rich of what it is to be poor, many rich list names are also major philanthropists. **Yu Pengnian**, president of property group Pengnian Industries, has donated some 3 billion yuan ($439 million) to provide cataract operations, and further major sums to support other health initiatives, higher education, and rural communities. **Huang Rulun**, chairman of Jinyan Hotel Group, has given 850 million yuan ($124 million) to charitable causes, and **Chu Mang Yee**, chairman of property developer Hopson 1.1 billion yuan ($161 million). **Li Ka-shing**, chairman of conglomerate Hutchison Whampoa Ltd in Hong Kong, and the wealthiest person of Chinese descent in the world, has made donations exceeding HK$10.7 billion ($1.37 billion).

Leaders of Transformation

Innovation, whether in products or services, and globally-oriented growth strategies, are marked features of major Chinese CEOs:

Li Lihui, BANK OF CHINA LTD (Finance: Beijing)—*Founded in 1912, this is the oldest bank in China and the first Chinese bank to establish a presence on all major continents.*

Ma Weihua, CHINA MERCHANTS BANK (CMB) (Finance: Beijing)—*The first bank in China to launch systematic internet banking.*

Yang Huiyan, COUNTRY GARDEN HOLDINGS CO (Real estate: Guangdong Province)—*Reputed to be the richest person on mainland China, Yang runs this high-end residential property developer, the biggest in China, which was founded by her father.*

Guo Guangchang, FOSUN INTERNATIONAL LTD (Diversified: Hong Kong)—*From specializing in pharmaceuticals and property, has diversified into iron, steel, retail, and financial services.*

Liu Chuanzhi, LENOVO (IT: Beijing)—*Founded Lenovo and turned it into the world's fourth largest PC manufacturer.*

Liu Yonghao, NEW HOPE GROUP (NHG) (Agribusiness: Sichuan Province)—*Grown from a modest family fodder business into China's leading agribusiness operator.*

Zhang Yin, NINE DRAGON PAPER (HOLDINGS) LTD (ND PAPER) (Paper recycling: Guangdong Province)—*Now the largest producer of containerboard products in China.*

Ma Mingzhe, PING AN INSURANCE (Insurance: Guangdong Province)—*Developed the company into an independent insurer and welcomed foreign investors.*

Xu Rongmao, SHIMAO GROUP (Real estate: Shanghai)—*Develops large, luxury residential property projects in China's major cities.*

Zuo Zongshen, ZONGSHEN INDUSTRIAL GROUP (Manufacturing: Chongqing)—*Founded as a motorcycle repair shop, now a manufacturing giant with 18,000 employees across the globe.*

Azim Premji Chairman & CEO, Wipro

WITH THE STOCKS of his family's vegetable oil business, Premji created India's leading software company and a vast personal fortune. He inherited the Western India Vegetable Products Limited (Wipro) at 21 when his father died suddenly, and he spent the next decade proving to investors that he could fill his father's shoes. His eureka moment came in the late 1970s when he saw an opening for Indian companies to make mini-computers after the major firms such as IBM were thrown out of India by the government.

BIOGRAPHY
Born in Bombay (Mumbai) in 1945. Azim was about to complete his electrical engineering degree at Stanford University when the sudden death of his father, Hasham Premji, brought him home to run the family business.

LEADERSHIP STYLE
Team-focused, ethical, and down to earth. Premji travels economy class and drives a basic car.

KEY STRENGTH
Establishing a reputation for trustworthiness that has encouraged Western companies and governments to enter into partnerships with Wipro.

BEST DECISION
Creating a new software research and development laboratory in Bangalore with engineers he might otherwise have laid off.

GAINING A FORTUNE Unique among the entrepreneurs who led India's emergence as a global software and service center, Premji is a businessman, not a techie. When he saw the opportunity to fill the gap left by Western computer firms, all he had was warehouses full of vegetable oil. He acquired a troubled technology firm, Sentinel of Cincinnati, and built an Indian mini-computer, which he upgraded using talent from Bangalore's Indian Institute of Science. By investing heavily in research and development, his firm quickly developed a reputation for quality.

PROGRAMS FOR PEOPLE When the Indian government relaxed its ban on foreign technology companies, Premji found he no longer needed so many software developers to invent new programs and products. Instead of scaling back, however, he used the excess talent to create a new "research and development laboratory" as a service for hire to Western companies. With this decision he became one of the pioneers of India's business process outsourcing and IT-enabled services industries, which have transformed the country's fortunes and revolutionized the way Western firms run their businesses.

Today Wipro is the world's largest independent supplier of research and development, and the third largest process outsourcing company in the world. Its partners include Microsoft, IBM, and Sun Microsystems, and its clients include Nokia, Sanyo, Hewlett-Packard, Ericsson, and Toshiba. Wipro's services range from developing software for cell phones to managing payroll and customer support services through its many call centers across the Subcontinent.

LESSONS IN BUSINESS: NOT TRYING TO DO EVERYTHING

Take an objective look at how you get your products to market. Premji realized the potential of outsourcing when he "bought in" the technical skills and products he needed to build his mini-computers.

→ Distinguish between your company's strengths and weaker areas where others could do the job better.

→ Work out what you are really good at. If it is sales and marketing, consider getting rid of production.

→ Take no pride in being involved in the whole production chain from start to finish. Your job is to satisfy customers and make money.

"It is easier to teach bright people technology than technicians the fundamentals of business management." Azim Premji

Robert B. Zoellick President, World Bank Group

A VARIED CAREER in law, finance, and government led to Zoellick's 2007 presidency of the World Bank Group, which provides loans, grants, and advice for economic, social, and environmental projects in developing countries. Prior to his appointment, his flair for detail and negotiation made him a valued member of both Bush administrations in the US. A staunch supporter of free trade, he has championed US interests while warning of the need for globalization to be more inclusive, particularly of developing nations and China.

BIOGRAPHY

Born in Naperville, Illinois, in 1953, Zoellick's family derives from Germany and he speaks fluent German. He studied at Swarthmore College, Pennsylvania, and gained a master's in public policy from Harvard University.

LEADERSHIP STYLE

Diligent, committed, and occasionally outspoken. Coworkers have described him as an imposing intellect, frequently quoting facts and figures from memory.

KEY STRENGTH

Zoellick is regarded as a master of detail, able to comprehend the most convoluted of subjects, and translating his knowledge into policy.

BEST DECISION

Unequivocally backing China as a key economic ally of the US at a time when government hawks were questioning where the relationship might go in the future.

A GIFTED NEGOTIATOR Following a brief spell as a law clerk, Zoellick worked in the US Treasury from 1985 to 1988, and under secretary of state James Baker in 1989. In 1992, he became White House deputy chief of staff for George H.W. Bush, then served at the Federal National Mortgage Association ("Fannie Mae") as executive vice-president from 1993 to 1997. After several academic and advisory posts, Zoellick returned to government as George W. Bush's US trade representative, stoutly defending US economic interests, calling for lower trade barriers, and successfully negotiating the entry of China and Taiwan to the World Trade Organization. As deputy secretary of state in 2005, he shaped US policy toward China, before taking up a senior position at Goldman Sachs in 2006. His pre-World Bank career was not without controversy, notably due to his support for military action against Iraq, and his active role in Japanese prime minister Junichiro Koizumi's re-election campaign. However, he won praise for his response to the conflict in Darfur.

MEETING THE CHALLENGE In 2007, President George W. Bush nominated Zoellick as president of the World Bank, succeeding Paul Wolfowitz. He inherited an organization that some observers said had outlived its usefulness, arguing that it should focus on giving grants rather than making loans. His first priority was to rebuild trust and credibility, both with the Bank's member countries, and within its own walls. Zoellick has continued to emphasize the positive side of China's economic development, as well as pointing to the need to safeguard "fragile" states such as Afghanistan.

LESSONS IN BUSINESS: NEGOTIATING SMART

Zoellick's achievements as a negotiator illustrate the benefits of making a key discussion lead to the outcome you want. A detailed command of the facts was key to his success.

→ Have all the facts at your fingertips, so your counterparts can't outflank you with superior knowledge.

→ Determine your "top line" (best case) and "bottom line" (worst case) outcomes, so that you will know exactly when to be satisfied, and when to walk away from the negotiating table.

→ Understand and respect cultural differences, but watch out for their manipulation by your opponents.

"People everywhere want to build a better life for themselves... If given a chance, [that] can contribute to a healthy, prosperous global society." Robert B. Zoellick

Martin Sorrell CEO, WPP

TWENTY-TWO YEARS at the helm of WPP, one of the world's largest communications services groups, have given Sorrell an in-depth understanding of the industry and its challenges. In this highly competitive sector, he has been lauded and criticized in equal measure for his sheer passion for the business, persistence, and aggressive ambition. Described by one agency head as a master at "manipulating people," Sorrell is credited with playing a major role in changing the way advertising agencies are run.

BIOGRAPHY
Born in London in 1945. Sorrell gained a master's in economics from Cambridge and an MBA from Harvard. He received a knighthood in 2000, for services to the communications industry.

LEADERSHIP STYLE
Visionary, competitive, and driven. Sorrell strives ruthlessly to be first, but has considerable power to motivate.

KEY STRENGTH
His ability to retain major accounts by moving clients from one operating unit to another within the company if they express dissatisfaction.

BEST DECISION
Creating GroupM, WPP's combined media planning and buying operation, to maximize media resources.

BREAKING THE MOULD In his early days with Saatchi, Sorrell was less than impressed at the way the industry was run. In 1985, he branched out on his own, purchasing Wire and Plastic Products, a wire basket manufacturer —the precursor to WPP—with the intention of using this as a vehicle for advertising agency acquisitions. Two years later he launched a successful hostile bid for J. Walter Thompson, subsequently incorporating Ogilvy & Mather, Young & Rubicam, and Grey Global Group into a burgeoning empire. By 2005, WPP had an annual turnover of almost £20 billion.

THE IMPORTANCE OF WINNING WPP has some 110,000 employees in 2,000 offices across 106 countries. One of Sorrell's many skills has been in encouraging the group's units to cooperate as well as compete, important both to meet clients' varied demands and to enable the transfer of clients between agencies. Sorrell is a consummate networker, both with clients and media people, and he spends considerable time visiting WPP companies and clients overseas, sometimes even assisting in pitching for accounts. He is reputed to be excellent company, somewhat arrogant but no snob— the *Financial Times* described him as "not overly concerned with social niceties." Sorrell believes winning to be very important and has admitted he doesn't like to come second, which is a challenge in an extremely competitive industry. Curiously, he claims to be insecure and to be driven by a fear of failure. Sorrell was nominated best CEO in the media sector by *Institutional Investor* in 2007, a sign of the esteem in which he is held by the global business and investment community.

LESSONS IN BUSINESS: FOCUSING ON RELATIONSHIPS

Sorrell has been described as "an industry phenomenon." Certainly he is totally absorbed in WPP's growth, acquiring some of the biggest names in the business. At times, this has led him close to bankruptcy, which is when relationships with banks, shareholders, and clients really count.
→ Woo your banks. You might want them to take equity to offset debt so they need to believe in your vision.
→ Build relationships in your industry—their views could prove crucial to potential shareholders.
→ Cement client relationships and foster loyalty by finding benefits for them as you network.

"What we're seeking to do is capitalize on the benefits of scale, with the heart, mind, soul, and energy of a small company." Martin Sorrell

Michael Davis CEO, Xstrata plc

A NO-NONSENSE EXPANSIONIST, Davis transformed Xstrata from a bit-part player into a global leader with an aggressive sequence of acquisitions, becoming the UK's highest-paid executive in the process. He first worked as an accountant before joining Eskom, the South African utilities giant, where he slashed headcount and raised $1 billion for the previously undercapitalized firm. He became finance director at 29 but left when he failed to land the CEO role. Others saw his potential and he has made Xstrata a huge success.

BIOGRAPHY
Born in South Africa, in 1958. Davis attended Rhodes University.

LEADERSHIP STYLE
Punchy, decisive, and bold. Former Scotiabank CEO Peter Gocsoe describes him as "an acquisitions machine".

KEY STRENGTH
Locating acquisition targets and pushing through deals with accuracy and efficiency.

BEST DECISION
Floating minor player Xstrata on the stock exchange in the aftermath of 9/11, establishing the acquisitive momentum to propel the company ultimately into the FTSE 100.

AN AUDACIOUS COUP After leaving Eskom, Davis joined Billiton, the UK/South African mining giant, in 1997, becoming its finance director. He then became chief development officer in the newly enlarged organization after Billiton's 2001 merger with BHP. Davis moved to Xstrata, a diversified mining group based in Zug, Switzerland, in October 2001. When he took the reins, it seemed he'd opted to become a big fish in a small pond: the company was undoubtedly a minor player. However, that picture soon changed. Glencore, a major shareholder in Xstrata, was attempting to float its coal-mining businesses in Australia and South Africa, and Davis seized his opportunity. Engineering a £650 million flotation in London for Xstrata he used the proceeds to snap up Glencore's coal-mining assets, making Xstrata the world's largest exporter of thermal coal. Critics claimed that Glencore's 38 percent stake in the newly public Xstrata would curb its independence, but Davis didn't let it hold him back. He embarked on an ambitious string of acquisitions, beginning in 2003 with the takeover of Australian copper, zinc, and coal miner MIM Holdings, therby doubling Xstrata's size. It was followed by a two-stage deal for Falconbridge Ltd.

GLOBAL EXPANSION In just a few short years, Xstrata grew into a major multinational with assets around the world, becoming easily the fastest-growing firm on the London Stock Exchange with a minimum of one deal per year. Today, the group spans 18 countries with interests in five key commodities (alloys, coal, copper, nickel, and zinc), plus a technology services business.

LESSONS IN BUSINESS: PUSHING YOUR ADVANTAGE

As mining became a borderless industry and consolidation advanced apace, Davis had the vision to see that a smaller firm could achieve great things given sufficient drive and leverage.
→ Take an approach that embodies an unshakeable belief in your strategy and your own ability to drive through obstacles.
→ There is always another deal around the corner. Remember that if you miss out on one.
→ Go for an acquisition when others fear that the time is wrong—you can buy better value then.

"There is a window of opportunity to do things and if you don't move then you lose that." Michael Davis

Michael Smith CEO, ANZ

BIOGRAPHY
Born in the UK in 1956. Smith read economic sciences at London's City University.

BEST DECISION
Relocating to Hong Kong in 1984. This move signaled the first step of Smith's climb to the top of the career ladder, which has seen him work right across the globe.

LESSON IN BUSINESS
Be decisive—when Smith became CEO in 2007 he strengthened ANZ by setting some big changes in motion, including a restructuring.

OUTSPOKEN, AMBITIOUS, and wily, Australia and New Zealand Banking Group (ANZ) CEO Smith is a financial professional through and through, who is not afraid to make hard decisions to keep ahead of the game.

When Smith started out in banking 30 years ago, Asia was not the economic powerhouse it is today. With much of his career spent in the Asia-Pacific region, the ANZ CEO plays ahead of the game. Starting out at The Hongkong & Shanghai Banking Corporation (HSBC), Smith rose to head of the bank's Asian operations, working out of various locations from Asia-Pacific, to South America. His success saw him offered the CEO's position at ANZ, and his remuneration package made him the highest paid banking boss in the country, opening the door to a new project: turning ANZ into a super-bank. To achieve this, Smith has his eye firmly set on Asia, planning to increase the contribution Asia-Pacific makes to group profit from 7 to 20 percent within five years. In 2008, ANZ received the go ahead for its third branch in China. Smith has been quick to shore up the bank's defences at home, instigating a restructuring in 2008 aimed at cost-cutting by reducing staff numbers and moving back-office operations offshore.

Xu Lejiang Chairman, Baosteel Group

BIOGRAPHY
Born c.1959. Xu studied at Jiangxi Metallurgy Institute, West Virginia University, and gained an MBA from Fudan University/University of Hong Kong.

BEST DECISION
Contracting Siemens to build the world's largest Corex pig iron production plant in 2007, which cut costs and carbon emissions.

LESSON IN BUSINESS
Invest in research—Xu showed that technological innovation brings production efficiencies and new products, liberating even the heaviest industries from the constraints of orthodoxy.

A CHAMPION of scientific research, technological innovation, and new product development, Xu has transformed Baosteel Group, a once-moribund state-controlled entity, into China's biggest steel producer and an agile, global force.

Xu joined Baosteel in 1982 and, during his rise through management, the company won awards for scientific innovation and environmental protection practices, becoming China's largest and most advanced integrated steel company. His appointment as chairman in 2007 signalled a strategic shift for the *Fortune* Global 500 firm. Under his predecessor, "Iron Lady" Xie Qihua, Baosteel had aggressively pursued its ranking as the world's sixth-largest manufacturer of hi-tech steel products, gaining automobile, appliance, ship-building, energy, and container customers in more than 40 countries. Xu refocused the company on product development, production innovation, corporate organization, and growth through acquisition and alliances. He has been credited with corporate R&D initiatives that generated more than $160 million in net profits. Xu is a member of the Communist Party's Central Committee, and a committee member of the China Association for Science and Technology.

"Technological innovation is an important engine for growth. Chinese companies must have a global perspective." Xu Lejiang

John Varley CEO, Barclays Bank

BIOGRAPHY
Born in Warwick, UK, in 1956, the only son of a lawyer, Varley studied at Oriel College, Oxford, where he gained a first-class degree. He subsequently continued his studies at the London College of Law.

BEST DECISION
Taking time out from banking, which enabled him to recover his health and reignited his enthusiasm and ambition.

LESSON IN BUSINESS
Use your ambition for the good of your company—Varley puts the good of the organization ahead of personal gain.

AN AGGRESSIVE, RUTHLESS pursuit of growth since Varley was appointed CEO in 2004 has done much to fulfil his self-proclaimed ambition "to catapult Barclays to becoming one of the handful of global banks leading the industry".

Varley started work as a clerk in 1975. He gave up practicing law a few years later, and in 1982 joined BZW, the investment banking arm of Barclays. He was subsequently appointed BZW MD in southeast Asia. By 1994, Varley had been promoted to deputy head of global equities. However, ill-health led him to take a part-time job with leading hedge-fund manager Crispin Odey. After 18 months, Varley felt ready for a full-time position again and rejoined Barclays, taking charge of asset management.

He held a number of executive positions in the years that followed, including the post of CFO from 2000 to 2003. In 2004, he was appointed Barclays group CEO. Although disappointed by his failure to strike a merger with ABN AMRO in 2007, Varley has had the satisfaction of seeing the bank grow into a major force in global banking. Barclays successfully weathered the international credit storm of 2008, controversially spurning UK government support to take investment from Arab backers.

Martin Bouygues Chairman & CEO, Bouygues Group

BIOGRAPHY
Born in Suresnes, France, in 1952. The son of Francis Bouygues, founder of Bouygues Construction, Martin joined the family firm in 1974 after dropping out from the University of Paris.

BEST DECISION
Refusing to pay $4.5 billion for a government 3G license. He later bought one for just $550 million after ministers backed down.

LESSON IN BUSINESS
Focus on costs and deadlines—Bouygues has applied this to all his enterprises.

BY USING RUTHLESS project management, ambitious acquisitions, and meritocratic promotion policies, Bouygues was able to take his father's successful construction firm and turn it into a giant global conglomerate.

Bouygues learned the majority of his most important business lessons as a lowly supervisor on one of his father's sites; there he saw the importance of micro-managing projects in an industry renowned for narrow margins, and understood the do-or-die significance of meeting deadlines. He was appointed CEO in 1989, but it was following his successful bid for the leading French television channel, TF1, that he defined his unique approach to business: he sacked almost all the channel's top executives and replaced them with his top construction managers, in the belief that it is best to go into a new business with people who are extremely smart but don't know anything about it. The channel thrived. He again outsmarted telecommunications rivals over the price of 3G (third generation mobile network) licenses. Bouygues stood by his own judgment that the licences were too expensive to be viable—and won. He is a close friend of French President Nicolas Sarkozy.

"We start with a clean slate and build everything from the foundation. We're not pulling the past with us." Martin Bouygues

Alberto Weisser Chairman & CEO, Bunge Ltd

BIOGRAPHY
Born in 1956. Weisser earned a bachelor's degree in business administration from the University of São Paulo in Brazil, subsequently attending courses at Harvard Business School, and INSEAD business school, Fontainebleau, France.

BEST DECISION
Acquiring Cereol in 2002, making Bunge the world's largest soy processor.

LESSON IN BUSINESS
Bring in outsiders—Weisser illustrated the benefits of recruiting outsiders into a family-run business.

RECRUITED BY BUNGE as CEO in 1999 to take the company global, Weisser has transformed the family-run agribusiness, fertilizer, and food production company, through key acquisitions and the disposal of non-core assets.

Prior to joining Bunge as CFO in 1993, Weisser spent 15 years with German chemicals company BASF. Joining Bunge, he found a company beset by infighting and struggling to compete with multinational agribusinesses. Weisser set about consolidating the company into three sectors: agribusiness, food products, and fertilizers, selling all non-essential assets. He spearheaded a major expansion in South America and, within a few years, Weisser had turned Bunge into the largest fertilizer producer and soy processor in South America. He was made CEO in 1999 and moved the company headquarters to White Plains, New York. Two years later, Weisser listed Bunge on the New York stock exchange. With the acquisition of French company Cereol in 2002, Bunge became the world's largest soy processor and a market leader in Europe. Weisser's expansion plans continue, new plants are opened every year, and Bunge now has interests in numerous countries, including Russia, Turkey, Poland, and China.

John P. Wiehoff Chairman & CEO, C.H. Robinson Worldwide

BIOGRAPHY
Born in the US in 1962. Wiehoff graduated in accounting and political science from St. John's University, Minnesota.

BEST DECISION
Pushing forward with his expansion plans—in so doing, Wiehoff has built one of the largest third-party logistics providers in the world.

LESSON IN BUSINESS
Don't rest on your laurels—Wiehoff attributes the company's success to constantly diversifying its services.

THROUGH LAUNCHES and acquisitions that have seen it become a third-party logistics behemoth, providing truck, rail, ocean, and air freight services, Wiehoff has given C.H. Robinson Worldwide an almost unrivaled edge over competitors.

Wiehoff was appointed CEO at C.H. Robinson Worldwide (CHRW) in 2002. He had started his career with accountants Arthur Andersen, before joining CHRW in 1992, progressing through senior roles up to the position of president. Wiehoff played a key part in the company's first public offering and its transition to public company status. As CEO, Wiehoff has orchestrated a period of national and international expansion that has made the company one of the largest of its kind. In 2003, it moved into Germany with its acquisition of a Hamburg-based international freight forwarding and third-party logistics company, while 2004 saw it expand into China. The following year saw the acquisition of two European freight-forwarding companies based in Italy and Germany, and three produce sourcing and marketing companies. Wiehoff has since purchased companies in North America and India, and opened a new office in Singapore, seeing gross profits top $1.3 billion.

"We have two hundred years of history. We plan to be in business another two hundred years, at least."
Alberto Weisser

Bill Gammell CEO, Cairn Energy plc

BIOGRAPHY
Born in Edinburgh, UK, in 1952. The son of an investment banker, Gammel graduated from the University of Stirling, Scotland, in economics and accounting.

BEST DECISION
Drilling in the mature Pennsylvania field where his company made its first strike.

LESSON IN BUSINESS
Maintaining personal networks —Gammell attended school with future British prime minister Tony Blair and counts US presidents George H. W. Bush and George W. Bush as family friends.

GAMBLING ON REGIONS thought marginal by others, Gammell made aggressive plays in South Asia, North Africa, and the Arctic that put iron ore business Cairn and its subsidiaries in a position to fuel India's emerging growth.

Described as an old-style Texas wildcatter from Scotland, Gammell demonstrated his flair early as an international rugby player for Scotland against Ireland in 1977. Injury ended his career and in 1988 he set up Cairn Energy. Deftly employing knowledge and contacts gained from his father's work financing the Bush family in oil exploration, Gammell ventured into the US, where he made a modest discovery after several failures. In 1990, after a Cairn technician noticed previously overlooked evidence of oil in an apparently dry hole in India, Gammell restructured his company to launch explorations there. He took over an unsuccessful drilling program from Royal Dutch Shell, and made some dramatic discoveries. Cairn's Indian oil play accelerated the company's strategic plan for servicing future energy demand in the booming Asian economies. Gammell was named Entrepreneur of the Year for the UK in 2004, and received a knighthood in 2006.

James W. Owens Chairman & CEO, Caterpillar

BIOGRAPHY
Born in Elizabeth City, North Carolina, in 1946. Owens gained a BS and a MS in Textile Technology and a PhD in economics from North Carolina State University.

BEST DECISION
Focusing on overseas growth, particularly in China, helped Caterpillar continue to grow during the US downturn.

LESSON IN BUSINESS
Think global—as a barometer for the industry, Caterpillar is one of the first to feel a slump; Owens' solution was to grow globally to offset domestic recession.

A COMPANY MAN through and through, Owens became CEO of Caterpillar, the world's largest manufacturer of construction and mining equipment, in 2005. He set out a bold vision to raise earnings to $50 billion by 2010.

When Owens took over at Caterpillar after 22 years with the company, he was determined to change the corporate image. Caterpillar had a reputation for honesty, good governance, reliability, and steady earnings. However, it had always been regarded as a questionable investment; fine for the good times but, in a downturn when construction slows, Caterpillar is among the first to feel the pinch. Owens felt strongly that his company was undervalued and set out to tackle the root causes. While remaining focused on organic growth, he speeded up order-to-delivery times, increased cost flexibility, and targeted overseas expansion in emerging markets, such as China and India. As the global economic downturn and American sub-prime crisis cast a shadow over western economies, Owens' strategy paid off. Following record profits for five successive years, Caterpillar registered another record second quarter, with sales exceeding $13 billion, and demand soaring throughout a booming Asia.

> "I learned a lot about the oil business from George W. Bush." Bill Gammell

BRAZIL'S NEW BOSSES

In one of the most unforgiving geographical and economic territories in the world, aging entrepreneurs make their succession plans early, ensuring the younger generation is equipped to do the job.

CEO of Brazilian publishing giant Editora Abril since 1990, **Roberto Civita** (p358) has overseen the transformation of the company his father, **Victor Civita**, founded as a print-focused news publisher into the region's multimedia leader.

Similarly, innovation and development has been a hallmark of the rise of **Ricardo Semler** (p103), CEO of Brazil's Semco, a services and supply firm founded by his father, **Antonio Semler**, which operates in a wide range of fields. While Civita followed through with his father's belief in anticipating and adapting to trends in the field of communication, Semler fought the conservative position held by his father, prompting *TIME* magazine to name him one of the "Global 100" young leaders of the future at the age of just 25. Today, family businesses in Brazil are far from stagnating; they are pushing out of the traditional geographical and sector limitations at the hands of the dynamic third generation ●

"It's natural for later generations to carry a growing responsibility in looking to improve upon achieved results, on the other hand, there is the possibility of living with and learning from previous generations."
MARCELO ODEBRECHT

Family Matters

The economic growth of Brazil from the mid-20th century on was largely limited by the controlling hand of the dictatorship. A certain alignment of forces, however, saw the rise of the free market, the implementation of a stable currency, and the gradual transfer of control of some of the country's biggest family-run firms to a generation of young CEOs.

In South American aviation, the name of "Constantino" has long been the traditional driving force, but more recently has provided fresh impetus in helping to reinvent the structure of the sector. **Nenê Constantino**, the old patriarch of the Brazilian Áurea passenger transport group, passed control over to his son **Constantino de Oliveira Júnior** in 2004, following the founding of the Gol airline company in 2001. Pioneering the concept of "low costs, low tariffs" in the region, Constantino Jr. changed the domestic industry's ground rules by acquiring the traditional airline Varig in 2007.

Radical breaks with the past are now common, but some CEOs have remained loyal to old practices. **Marcelo Odebrecht** became CEO of Brazil's Odebrecht mining, construction, and petrochemicals empire at the age of just 40. In the tradition of his grandfather, **Norbeto Odebrecht**, the group's founder, Marcelo is committed to the group's central philosophy of delegation as a means of renewing ideas, strategies, and areas of activity.

Rebel in the Family

There are those who see the family business as a way in but not a way forward. As a member of the traditional Brazilian Ometto sugar family, **Rubens Ometto Silveira Mello** became CEO of Cosan, Brazil's largest cane sugar and ethanol-producing company, in 1986 at 36 years of age. He quickly established a reputation for aggressive purchases and disrespect for the family traditions; indeed, his most controversial acquisition was that of his own uncle's sugar mill in 2003. However, such moves have seen the company's cane production increase over ten-fold in volume, and the strategy continues as the world looks to ethanol as an eco-friendly alternative to gasoline.

World Leaders

Brazilian CEOs are among those setting the standard in many global industries:

Bernardo Vieira Hees, ALL (Logistics: Brazil)—*Due to the implementation of his massive expansion plans, is seen as one of the most influential and admired leaders in the sector.*

—

José Alberto Diniz, CAMARGO CORRÊA (Engineering: Brazil) —*After a career in financial management, Diniz is betting upon Brazil's competitive edge to win international engineering contracts.*

—

Michel Klein, CASAS BAHIA (Retail: Brazil)—*Continues to build and consolidate the company's globally recognized position as a retailer specifically to the low-income classes.*

—

Benjamin Steinbruch, CSN (Metals: Brazil)—*Led the consortia that bought the CSN and CVRD engineering and mining companies at the start of Brazil's industrial privatization program in the early 1990s.*

—

Frederico Fleury Curado, EMBRAER (Aerospace: Brazil) —*In 2007, he was chosen from the internal ranks to continue Embraer's consolidation as the world's third largest airplane manufacturing company.*

—

Joesley Batista, JBS-FRIBOI (Foodstuffs: Brazil)—*Within two years of taking over from his father,* **José Batista Sobrinho**, *he had structured the international acquisitions of four of the largest American and Australian beef-farming businesses, turning JBS into one of the largest companies in the sector.*

—

Alessandro Carlucci, NATURA (Retail: Brazil)—*Has built a successful natural cosmetics company, with many of the ingredients ethically sourced from the Amazon rainforest.*

—

Gilberto Tomazoni, SADIA (Foodstuffs: Brazil)—*With growing demand from Europe and Russia, São Paulo state is the world's largest frozen chicken exporter, and Sadia now supplies to 40 countries.*

—

Laércio José de Lucena Cosentino, TOTVS (IT: Brazil) —*One of TOTVS's founding directors, Cosentino has built the company into the world's ninth largest in the IT sector and second largest in the region in just 25 years.*

—

José Luciano Penido, VOTORANTIM CELULOSE E PAPEL (VCP) (Paper products: Brazil) —*Won industry analysts RISI's "Latin American CEO of the Year" award in both 2007 and 2008, as a result of focusing the company on joint ventures and expansion.*

—

Lorenzo H. Zambrano Chairman & CEO, Cemex

CEMENT MAY APPEAR a rather mundane product, but Zambrano's sound strategy, hi-tech approach, tolerance for risk, and grass-roots knowledge give Cemex a huge advantage in the traditionally conservative construction sector.

BIOGRAPHY
Born in Monterrey, Mexico, in 1945. Zambrano studied at the Institute of Technology, Monterrey, and Stanford School of Business.

BEST DECISION
Concentrating on sales in developing countries. Zambrano took great risks to position Cemex to outsell multinational competitors, and to provide better service at a local level.

LESSON IN BUSINESS
Develop distinctive methodology— "The Cemex Way" was evolved to manage companies worldwide, using technology and automation to boost productivity and cut costs.

Zambrano joined the family cement business in 1968, working in a variety of roles for Cementos Mexicanos, now Cemex, in the industrial city of Monterrey. He CEO and chairman in 1985 and, as multinationals moved in on Mexican markets, deployed new technology and reorganized the company to compete. Over the next 20 years he bought 16 cement firms, transforming Cemex from a regional to a global player. His management teams integrated newly acquired firms by introducing Cemex methods, encouraging employee ideas, and picking up good practices. Zambrano also succeeding in turning the formerly hostile US into Cemex's biggest market, accounting for more than 25 percent of sales, and expanded into more than 50 countries with bagged or ready-mix cement, building supplies, and design and financial services. Zambrano is also a philanthropist —Cemex lends building funds and delivers cement to poor families.

Roger Agnelli CEO, Vale

EMERGING AS one of the most dynamic players in 21st-century mining, Agnelli has been dubbed the "Iron Man," not only for forging Vale's domination of the industry but also for his cool approach to negotiations.

BIOGRAPHY
Born in Brazil in 1959. Agnelli graduated in economics in 1981, then specialized in mergers and acquisitions at Brandesco, the financial conglomerate.

BEST DECISION
Buying Canadian mining company Inco for $18 billion in 2006, which transformed Vale into the world's second largest mining company.

LESSON IN BUSINESS
First things first—companies in developing economies must consolidate their domestic markets before globalizing.

In 2000, shortly after Agnelli was appointed board chairman of Companhia Vale do Rio Doce, as Vale was then known, he told shareholders the iron ore behemoth should diversify into other metals and markets. They agreed, on condition that he implemented the plan himself as CEO. Agnelli accepted the challenge, and in 2001 he launched a plan to triple market capitalization to $25 billion by 2010. By 2008 it had already increased more than tenfold to $103 billion. Agnelli began looking for long-term iron ore supply contracts to hedge against price fluctuations, and he signed a 20-year deal worth $2 billion with China's largest steelmaker. He then moved to consolidate in Brazil's market, spending $1.4 billion buying out local rivals, and launching a major campaign to keep Anglo-Australian mining giant BHP Billiton out of Vale's backyard. He did this by winning a takeover battle, first for Ferteco, and then for Caemi, another iron ore mining company.

"[Agnelli] did a fantastic job taking advantage of the timing and realizing that a company like Vale had to expand abroad." Eike Batista, billionaire Brazilian mining entrepreneur

Muhtar Kent President & CEO, Coca-Cola

BIOGRAPHY
Born in New York City in 1952, the son of a celebrated Turkish diplomat. Kent studied in the UK, taking economics at Hull, and an MBA at Cass Business School, London.

BEST DECISION
Expanding Coca-Cola's European bottling operations throughout 12 countries. This led to a 50 percent increase in turnover.

LESSON IN BUSINESS
Know your business from the bottom up—Kent learned Coca-Cola's business as a junior salesman traveling the US in company trucks.

NO-ONE KNOWS Coca-Cola's business as well as Muhtar Kent. For more than 20 years, he has expanded the company's European and Asian operations, and penetrated new markets, earning him the promotion to CEO in 2008.

Starting his career as a traveling salesman, Kent's second appointment at Coca-Cola was not without controversy. He had left the company in 1999 after allegations of insider trading, which were later settled. However, Kent's reputation for boosting sales and market share was such that, when Neville Isdell was brought out of retirement to be CEO of Coca-Cola, he immediately asked Kent to return to the fold as head of international operations in North Asia, Eurasia and the Middle East.

Eighteen months later Kent was promoted to President. His vast international experience sealed his ultimate promotion to CEO in 2008. More than 80 percent of Coke sales are made outside of the US, and Kent had been responsible for pushing operations to that level. Next is the charge into China, where he is planning to increase sales of non-carbonated drinks with the $2.4 billion takeover of the China Huiyuan Juice Group, the country's largest foreign takeover.

Wei Jiafu President & CEO, China Ocean Shipping Co. (COSCO)

BIOGRAPHY
Born in 1950 in Jiangsu Province, China. Wei studied at Dalian Maritime University and Tianjin University.

BEST DECISION
Diversifying COSCO, Wei seized new market opportunities by branching out into areas such as air and land freight-hauling, ship building, and terminal operations.

LESSON IN BUSINESS
Seize your opportunity—seeing that shipping and logistics were being hit hard, Wei saw the global economic slowdown as a chance to restructure, streamline, and strengthen the business.

STEAMING AHEAD of the competition, COSCO, the world's largest shipping company, almost doubled in size in the five years since Wei became CEO. The $17-billion corporation is one of the world's top ten container liner operators.

In the late 1960s, Wei joined state-controlled COSCO as a ship's radio officer. He served as senior engineer and ship's master for more than ten years, before moving into executive positions in a range of company subsidiaries in China and abroad. Between 1992 and 1998 Wei rose to general manager of the Chinese-Tanzanian Joint Shipping Co., COSCO Tianjin, and COSCO Bulk Carrier Co. He oversaw the flotation of COSCO (Singapore) Ltd, COSCO's first venture in international capital markets,

while president from 1993 to 1995, and became president and CEO of the group in 1998. Wei has overseen COSCO's renewal into a comprehensive logistics provider—including land, sea, and air freight, terminal operations, and e-commerce—with hi-tech IT systems at the core of its operations. In 2000, COSCO became the first Chinese member of the World Economic Forum, and has grown to become the world's biggest bulk shipping company, serving 1,300 ports in 160 countries.

"Shipping is diving... but the diver has to come up eventually." Jiafu Wei

Brian A. McNamee CEO, CSL Ltd

BIOGRAPHY
Born in Australia. McNamee completed bachelor of medicine and surgery degrees at the University of Melbourne in 1979.

BEST DECISION
Co-developing the award-winning cervical cancer vaccine Gardasil, which became one of the most important drugs to be developed by Australian science.

LESSON IN BUSINESS
Success depends on technology and ability, not location—McNamee has taken a provincial pharmaceutical firm and turned it global, through shrewd acquisitions and innovation.

WITH OVER 25 YEARS' experience in the pharmaceutical industry, McNamee has grown the medical-products manufacturer CSL from a $23-million government-owned business into a multibillion-dollar global industry leader.

After leaving his job as a practicing doctor in 1982, McNamee worked his way up through a number of pharmaceutical firms, including Dr Madaus & Co., F. H. Faulding & Co. Ltd, and Pacific Biotechnology. In 1990, he became CEO of Melbourne-based Commonwealth Serum Laboratories (CSL). In 1994, McNamee oversaw the privatization of the Australian state-owned company, which soon became the country's largest pharmaceuticals firm, then steered it into global markets. Under McNamee, CSL spent some $180 million a year on R&D, and was bolstered by three major acquisitions: Swiss plasma firm ZLB Bioplasma AG in 2000, which doubled the company in size; German medical company Aventis Behring in 2004; and US firm Talecris Biotherapeutics in 2008. McNamee was the inaugural winner of the BioMelbourne Network Industry Award in 2007 for overseeing the testing development of Gardasil, a cervical cancer vaccine, with Merck & Co. Looking to the future, CSL turned to a vaccine for bird flu.

Charles O. Holliday, Jr. Chairman & CEO (1998–2008), DuPont

BIOGRAPHY
Born in Nashville, Tennessee, in 1948. Holliday holds a bachelor of science degree in industrial engineering from the University of Tennessee. He is a founding member of the International Business Council.

BEST DECISION
Selling DuPont's fibers business to Koch. This allowed the company to focus on cutting-edge materials and biotechnology.

LESSON IN BUSINESS
Be responsible—it is possible to be both profitable and environmentally sound.

DURING HIS TEN YEARS at the top, Holliday presided over DuPont's transformation from a traditional oil and chemicals company into a $30-billion-per-year, innovative science-based company operating in more than 70 countries.

A DuPont man through and through, after graduating from university in 1970, Holliday began work as an engineer at DuPont's Old Hickory site. In the 1970s and 1980s, he held various positions in different branches of the company, including the roles of business analyst for Fibers operations, director of marketing for Pigments & Chemicals, and global business director of Kevlar® and Nomex®. Between 1990 and 1997, Holliday worked in a number of managerial positions in Asia, reaching the position of chairman of Asia Pacific. He became president of DuPont in 1997, and CEO the following year. Holliday has been instrumental in efforts to reduce the company's carbon footprint and, during his tenure, the company achieved its goal of sustainable growth with minimal environmental impact. Holliday negotiated business deals worth more than $60 billion during that time, including the $4.4 billion sale of DuPont's substantial Invista fibers business to Koch Industries in 2004.

"...there is high global demand for Australian ideas, technology, and know-how..." Brian A. McNamee

Pier Francesco Guarguaglini CEO, Finmeccanica

BIOGRAPHY
Born in Tuscany, Italy, in 1937. Guarguaglini studied electronic engineering at the University of Pisa and gained a PhD from the University of Pennsylvania. His wife, Marina Grossi, is CEO of SELEX Sistemi Integrati.

BEST DECISION
Capitalizing on the perfect PR opportunity to supply the American presidential helicopter.

LESSON IN BUSINESS
Keep abreast of technology—Guarguaglini combines lecturing and business, keeping him ahead of his competitors.

USING HIS IN-DEPTH technological skills and managerial experience, Guarguaglini has steered Italian aerospace company Finmeccanica away from the brink of bankruptcy to becoming a major global competitor.

Guarguaglini began his professional career as an assistant lecturer in nuclear electronics at the University of Pisa. He was an assistant lecturer in radar systems at the University of Rome for fifteen years, also gaining managerial experience at electronics operation Selenia, where he worked for almost 20 years. He joined Finmeccanica in 1996 as head of its defense sector business. He left in 1999 to run Italy's main shipbuilding group, Fincantieri, returning to Finmeccanica as CEO in 2002.

He restructured the company, hand-picking a new managerial team and consolidating various divisions. His greatest success has been overcoming political obstacles to penetrate overseas markets. In 2005 Finmeccanica's helicopter unit, AgustaWestland, became the first foreign design to be chosen as the US President's Marine Corps One. The acquisition of the leading US defense electronics company, DRS Technologies, then gave Finmeccanica a direct entry into the US defense market.

Luis Alejandro Pagani President & CEO, Grupo Arcor

BIOGRAPHY
Born in Argentina, Pagani is the son of the founder of Grupo Arcor. He studied at the National University of Córdoba, Argentina, and New York University.

BEST DECISION
Launching Arcor's pioneering business-to-business website in 2001, enabling orders to be placed across time zones.

LESSON IN BUSINESS
Pay your debts—despite the peso's devaluation in Argentina in 2001, Pagani ensured Arcor maintained its interest payments to the banks, allowing it to ride out the country's economic crisis.

CEO OF HIS FAMILY'S business since 1993, Pagani has turned Grupo Arcor into South America's, and the world's, biggest confectionery manufacturer and the leading candy exporter in Argentina, Brazil, Chile, and Peru.

Pagani joined Grupo Arcor in 1983. After his father's death in 1990, Pagani studied business in the US, and in 1993 became CEO. He oversaw a number of critical acquisitions, including Águila Saint, a traditional chocolate company in Argentina. Overhauling Arcor's low-key marketing, Pagani instigated an advertising campaign that included commercials on CNN. Having already found a relatively cheap way to penetrate the US market, by producing private-label sweets for Wal-Mart

and Sara Lee, Pagani signed a multimillion dollar deal with Brach's Confections to produce 30,000 tons of Brach's-branded sweets a year. In 2005, Pagani joined forces with Mexican bakery and confectionery firm Grupo Bimbo, culminating in the opening of the huge Mundo Dulce ("Sweet World") plant in 2007 to produce chocolate, chewing gum, and lollipops for the US, Mexican, and Central American markets. Having established Arcor within Latin America, Pagani now looks set to take on the world.

"For us, international cooperation is one of the pillars of our company." Pier Francesco Guarguaglini

Joaquín Ayuso García Chairman & CEO, Grupo Ferrovial, SA

BIOGRAPHY
Born in Madrid in 1955.
Ayuso García graduated in
civil engineering from the
Madrid Polytechnic University.

BEST DECISION
Acquiring BAA, the British airport
management company, in 2006,
to diversify the business away
from construction.

LESSON IN BUSINESS
Learn the business from the
ground up—Ayuso García has
spent nearly three decades
working in every sector of
Ferrovial, and knows the
company inside-out.

BY DIVERSIFYING Grupo Ferrovial around the globe, CEO Ayuso García has led the Spanish engineering and building giant into projects involving airports, toll roads, parking lots, and municipal services in more than 40 countries.

Ayuso García's first job was as an on-site engineer for Madrid-based construction company Ferrovial, in 1982. He gained promotions throughout the company over the next decade, becoming general manager of construction in 1992 and, from 1999, when the company went public, to 2002, he was CEO of Ferrovial Agromán, the construction division. He was nominated as CEO of the group in 2002. During his tenure, he has overseen progressive changes such as environmental sustainability programs, flexible work hours, parental leave, and special support for disabled workers and their families. In 2006, Ayuso García was instrumental in the purchase of British airport management company BAA. As CEO, he enjoys the challenge of directing an ethnically diverse, far-flung workforce of over 100,000 people, with more than half of Ferrovial's employees working outside of Spain. In 2006, he received a medal of honor from the Madrid Institute of Civil Engineers.

Claus-Dietrich Lahrs CEO, Hugo Boss AG

BIOGRAPHY
Born in 1964. Lahrs is a
graduate of business schools
in Bochum and Cologne in
Germany, and Paris.

BEST DECISION
Taking European fashion further
afield by targeting the growing
markets in Asia and America,
resulting in growth for the group.

LESSON IN BUSINESS
Boost brand awareness—Lahrs'
marketing strategy focuses on
rapid growth, notably through
promoting brand awareness in
growing markets in Asia and
the Americas.

AN IMPRESSIVE track record in generating global brand awareness at luxury goods group LVMH, and numerous industry contacts, made Lahrs an ideal candidate to lead fashion house Hugo Boss in its ongoing pursuit of growth.

Following 12 successful years in Germany, the US, and Canada with Christian Dior/Louis Vuitton Moët Hennessy (LVMH), the world's leading luxury goods group, Lahrs was headhunted from his role as managing director of Christian Dior Couture to lead German fashion house Hugo Boss in 2008. Hugo Boss shares rose six percent when his nomination was announced. Lahrs has a notable track record in brand management in the premium and luxury segments of the fashion industry, having been responsible during his career for the sales and marketing of Cartier products in Northern Europe, for managing Louis Vuitton Deutschland, and for heading Louis Vuitton businesses in the US and Canada. At Hugo Boss, Lahrs is planning for rapid growth from an already strong market position. In the growing Asian and Americas' markets, where he sees huge potential in all product categories, he intends to open more stores and to generate even greater brand awareness.

"[Ayuso García is] a complex combination of future vision, ambitious goals, and confidence in his own possibilities." Juan Carlos Cubeiro, managing director, Eurotalent

Carlos Alves de Brito CEO, InBev

BIOGRAPHY
Born in 1960 in Brazil. De Brito studied mechanical engineering in Rio de Janeiro before gaining an MBA from Stanford University.

BEST DECISION
Leading AmBev into a merger with Interbrew, creating a global platform from which he created the world's leading brewer.

LESSON IN BUSINESS
Persevere—de Brito knows that it can be one step back to go two forward. The merging of AmBev and Interbrew made AmBev the junior partner—but now de Brito calls the shots.

A BUSINESS SURVIVOR, de Brito always ends up on top. Each time his company has merged or has been taken over, de Brito has thrived. In 2008, he became the brewery king when he formed the world's largest brewer, InBev.

When brewery firm Brahma merged with rival Antarctica in 1999 to create AmBev, the new firm was hailed as a Brazilian multinational ready to take on the world. De Brito had joined Brahma in 1989 and became COO of AmBev. Between 1999 and 2004, he led a takeover spree, spending millions on acquisitions and joint ventures to make AmBev the world's fifth largest brewer. With limited opportunities to expand into Europe and North America, de Brito led a $12.8-billion "merger" with Belgian giant Interbrew, creating InBev in 2004. This gave each access to the other's markets. The merger, however, was a takeover that left de Brito as CEO only of the new group's American operations. He mounted a ruthless wave of cutbacks and engineered a "palace coup" to replace Belgian board members with Brazilians. After consolidating his grip on the company in 2008, de Brito mounted the ultimate coup: a $52-billion takeover of Anheuser-Busch that made InBev the world's largest brewer.

Brad D. Smith President & CEO, Intuit

BIOGRAPHY
Born c.1965 in Kenova, West Virginia. Smith has a master's in management from Aquinas College, Michigan, and a bachelor's in business administration from Marshall University, West Virginia.

BEST DECISION
Launching Intuit's own low-cost web-hosted CRM applications to defend against the CRM giants targeting QuickBooks users.

LESSON IN BUSINESS
Capitalize on technology. Intuit has launched online communities for small businesses, and is developing mobile applications.

INNOVATIVE AND ON THE BALL, Smith has cornered new markets for Intuit during his tenure as CEO of the financial software firm, moving it into the online on-demand service space and defending its customers from fierce competition.

It was straight down to business when Smith became CEO of financial services software developer Intuit in January 2008. A five-year rise through the company gave Smith a clear vision for its future. He kick-started some major objectives, including a strong customer, technology, and market-driven focus on innovation, as well as both product and global expansion. Smith's strategy involves growing Intuit's connected services, which represent more than half its revenue. He has brought the company into the on-demand software market with a trio of web-hosted customer relationship management (CRM) applications to support its QuickBooks software, and expects its online services to be key growth drivers. To this end, 20 percent of revenue is spent on research and development, focusing on mobile applications and online communities devoted to tax and accounting for small businesses. Smith's first year in office saw 15-per-cent growth in total revenue, reaching $3.1 billion.

"Great people attract more great people. Mediocre people attract more of the same." Carlos Alves de Brito

TIGERS OF THE FAR EAST

In the 1950s, Japan's post-World War II recovery developed into high-speed growth as its anti-communist stance brought it crucial access to western markets. By the 1960s, the adoption of lean production and quality processes, combined with *Kaizen*, a continuous improvement concept, had given Japanese industry a competitive edge and an unrivalled reputation for quality. By then other export-oriented Asian economies were developing fast, notably South Korea, Hong Kong, Singapore, and Taiwan, earning themselves and, in their turn, countries such as Indonesia, Malaysia, the Philippines, Thailand, and Vietnam, the sobriquet "tiger economies".

An innovator since its foundation as a local spinning and weaving company in 1926, Toyota has become a leading global group. Most recently, **Katsuaki Watanabe** (p328), Toyota Motor Corp. president from 2005 until his promotion to vice-chairman in 2009, introduced a renewed emphasis on quality, a cost-cutting program resulting in savings of some $10 billion, and oversaw the increase of its hybrid car range, contributing to the company's rise in 2008 to the world's number one car manufacturer.

"High Tech, Low Tech, Make Money is Tech!" TERRY TAI-MING GOU

Meanwhile, countries such as South Korea and Taiwan have become particularly noted for their electronic expertise. **Terry Tai-ming Gou** (p54) founded Hon Hai Precision in Tapei in the 1970s, moving into PC parts in the 1980s, and subsequently building Hon Hai into the world's largest contract manufacturer of electronics. Gou's strategy was to manufacture in lower-cost China, enabling him to combine competitive pricing with quality control, successfully wooing the likes of Dell, Motorola, Nintendo, Apple, Nokia, and Sony ●

Technological Edge

One of the key reasons for the rapid economic rise of Japan and the tiger economies in the post-war period has been their ability to develop and exploit technological advances. In a range of industries, new technology is embraced with enthusiasm and the innovatory impulse is strong.

Yoshiyuki Kasai, chairman of the Central Japan Railway Company, a veteran of the state-owned Japanese National Railways that launched the revolutionary Bullet Train, confirmed, in 2008, plans to build the world's fastest "maglev" passenger train, between the cities of Tokyo and Nagoya. Maglev, or magnetically levitated, trains use electromagnetic technology to travel above the track, removing friction and allowing the trains to reach record speeds in excess of 500 kmph (300 mph). The project, which will cost over $50 billion, keeps Japan at the forefront of passenger train innovation.

The economies of the Far East are not only technologically innovative in themselves, they are also often the first to embrace advances developed elsewhere. **Chew Choon Seng**, CEO of Singapore Airlines, was one of the first aviation bosses to confirm an order for the double-decker A380 jetliner, produced by European firm Airbus (CEO **Tom Enders**). Covered in the Singapore Airlines livery, the world's largest passenger aircraft made its debut commercial flight in 2007, flying from Singapore to Sydney and giving the airline invaluable publicity right across the world.

Kaizen — Concerted Group Effort

Until the economic slump of the late 1990s, Japanese labor relations tended to be harmonious, based on a cultural value of the group rather than the individual. This focus favored ideas of communal striving for constant improvement formalized in the concept of *Kaizen*, which involves continuous cycles of assessment, standardization, and innovation. *Kaizen* applies as much to management as to manufacture, from top to bottom of the hierarchy. The constant checking and realigning includes the processes of lean manufacturing, just-in-time, and overall avoidance of waste, whether of resources or effort. These have lead not only to cost-savings but also to enhanced efficiency, and have proven to be both profitable and motivating.

Eastern Executives

Through innovation, acquisitions, and astute decision-making, the region's CEOs continue the successes of recent decades:

Kazunori Ueno, BANDAI (Consumer products: Japan) —*Created the hugely popular Tamagotchi digital pet that can be fed, cleaned, and cared for. More than 70 million have been sold across the world.*

Kunio Noji, KOMATSU GROUP (Mining and construction equipment: Japan) —*Through its subsidiary, Kelk Ltd, Komatsu has launched commercial production and sales of the world's most efficient thermoelectric generation modules.*

Chang Jae Shin, KYOBO LIFE INSURANCE COMPANY LTD (Insurance: South Korea) —*Launched a joint asset-management venture with UK's AXA Investment Managers to boost third party institutional and retail clients, and develop equity expertise.*

Shoji Muneoka, NIPPON STEEL CORP. (Metals: Japan) —*Tackling the slowing demand for steel by reducing output but continues to develop new technologies for future growth, such as high anti-rust steel products for use in wet climates.*

Satoshi Miura, NTT CORP. (Telecommunications: Japan) —*Announced accelerated development by 2011 of the next-generation IP network for landline and cell phones.*

Tsuyoshi Kikukawa, OLYMPUS CORP. (Optics and imaging: Japan)—*Bought UK-based Gyrus Group, strengthening its position in the medical devices sector.*

Cheong Choong Kong, OVERSEA-CHINESE BANKING CORP. LTD (OCBC) (Finance: Singapore) —*Responded to an uncertain economic climate by reintroducing cash draws as an incentive to continue saving.*

Kan Trakulhoon, SIAM CEMENT GROUP (Diversified: Thailand)—*Uses waste heat recycled from the production process at its cement plants to generate electricity.*

Morris Chang, TAIWAN SEMICONDUCTOR MANUFACTURING Co. (TSMC) (Electronics: Taiwan)—*Announced a strategic partnership with US company Tela Innovations to develop co-optimized design solutions using Tela's lithography-optimized design technology, and TSMC's derivative processes.*

Sadayuki Sakakibara, TORAY INDUSTRIES (Chemicals: Japan)—*Bought a 21 percent stake in Germany's Advanced Composite Engineering in a bid to expand in the automotive sector.*

Ian Cheshire CEO, Kingfisher plc

BIOGRAPHY
Born in the UK in 1959.
Cheshire graduated from the
University of Cambridge with a
degree in economics and law.

BEST DECISION
Selling Kingfisher's Italian DIY
retail chain Castorama to Leroy
Merlin in 2009 for €615 million,
thereby reducing the group debt.

LESSON IN BUSINESS
Change takes time—despite
pressure to deliver shareholder
value, Cheshire argued for time
for the new structures he put in
place to take effect.

WITH MANY YEARS of retail experience and extensive knowledge of the home improvement market, both domestically and internationally, Cheshire was perceived as the ideal candidate to drive forward home retail group Kingfisher.

After starting his career as a mangement consultant, Cheshire joined Kingfisher in 1998 as group strategy director, becoming CEO of its newly formed e-commerce division in 2000. After successfully developing the online business for B&Q, Comet, and Woolworths, Cheshire was promoted to CEO of International and Development, and was responsible for all retail operations outside the UK and France. He restructured the division and played a key role in the integration of Castorama and Brico Depot, following their acquisition in 2002. Such was his success, boosting profits to over £80 million by 2005, that he was nominated CEO of B&Q UK, modernizing the business to meet increasingly tough trading conditions. He was promoted to CEO of the Kingfisher group in 2008. To counteract a continued decline in global sales, and to improve shareholder value, Cheshire devised a three-year strategy to turn around B&Q China, roll out in Eastern Europe, and exploit UK trade opportunities.

Bruno Lafont Chairman & CEO, Lafarge

BIOGRAPHY
Born in 1956. Lafont graduated
from the French Ecole des Hautes
Etudes Commerciales and Ecole
Nationale d'Administration.

BEST DECISION
Buying the Egyptian cement
firm Orascom in 2007. The
acquisition helped Lafarge
leapfrog its rivals to win new
business in the Middle East.

LESSON IN BUSINESS
Target growing markets—by
targeting China, India and the
Middle East, Lafont minimized
Lafarge's exposure to a
downturn in the US and Europe.

THROUGH ACQUISTIONS and growth in China, Lafont has galvanized Lafarge. When he took over, the French cement company was already the world's largest, but it lagged behind its rivals in global markets. Lafont plugged the gaps.

By the time Lafont was made CEO, he already had a proven track record of boosting sales and market share in overseas markets. As executive vice-president in charge of Lafarge's Gypsum division, in 1998 he led the company's charge into Asia and North America, overseeing a doubling of sales and an increase in presence from 12 to 25 companies in just five years. As CEO, Lafont stepped up a gear, engineering the $15 billion purchase of Orascom to open up the growing oil boom markets of the Middle East. He invested $600 million in expanding Lafarge's China presence, and spent $349 million to take over Larsen & Toubro's concrete division in India. These developments, together with the $3 billion acquisition of Larson & Toubro's US subsidiary in 2006, greatly expanded the company's global reach, increasing its income from foreign markets by ten percent. By 2010, overseas business is predicted to account for 65 percent of Lafarge's income.

> "It is a three-year voyage to get value out of this business. There is no magic button you can press to get a return." Ian Cheshire

Paul Bulcke CEO, Nestlé

BIOGRAPHY
Born in Roeselare, Belgium, in 1954. Bulcke graduated in commercial engineering at the University of Louvain, and received a postgraduate degree in management from the University of Ghent.

BEST DECISION
Focusing on the quality of Nestlé's portfolio as the key to future growth.

LESSON IN BUSINESS
Strength lies in continuity—Bulcke's predecessor developed a highly successful formula, and Bulcke recognized the value of concentrating on what works.

WHEN HE TOOK OVER leadership of Nestlé, the Swiss-based global food giant was in very good health. Wisely, Bulcke chose not to fix what wasn't broken, and made continuity a key plank of his plan for future growth.

Nearly 30 years as a loyal company man paid off for Paul Bulcke when he became CEO of Nestlé in early 2008. His career had seen him running the company's operations in markets as far-flung as Peru, Portugal, and Germany. However, it was in his last regional post as head of Nestlé's Zone Americas—US, Canada, Latin America, and the Caribbean—that he really staked his claim to the top job. In his four years running the Americas, Bulcke's focus on driving forward the company's extensive portfolio of brands turned the region into the biggest and most profitable part of Nestlé's global empire. Once in the top job, Bulcke made it clear that he intended to continue focusing on the company's key strengths, just as he did in the Americas, in addition to investing strongly in research and development, and pushing for growth in Nestlé's "nutrition, health, and wellness" business. Bulcke has made it clear that he sees developing nations as markets for "targeted" products.

Zhou Jiping President & Vice-chairman, PetroChina Company Ltd

BIOGRAPHY
Born in 1952 in China. Zhou has a master's degree in marine geology from the South China Sea Institute of Oceanology at the Chinese Academy of Sciences, Guangzhou.

BEST DECISION
Clinching the strategically vital China-Kazakhstan oil pipeline deal, securing future supplies from the Kazakh oil fields.

LESSON IN BUSINESS
Aim to win—in the global game for oil and gas concessions, winning is everything, and those who close deals are the most highly valued.

BEING THE FASTEST growing economy on the planet makes China the thirstiest for oil. By securing concessions in Africa, Central Asia, and Russia, PetroChina chief Zhou has been instrumental in keeping China growing.

Zhou's career as an oil and gas exploration engineer ended in 1996, when he was appointed deputy director of the International Exploration and Development Co-operation Bureau of state-run China National Petroleum Corporation (CNPC), and deputy general manager of China National Oil & Gas Exploration and Development Corporation. The job he faced was as much political as commercial: to secure the oil reserves China needs to fuel its growth; it was a brief that pitted him against India and South Africa in the race for new energy sources. In more than a decade at CNPC and its publicly-listed arm PetroChina, Zhou oversaw key deals in 22 countries on four continents. In 2007, Zhou announced the largest oil-field discovery for a decade in China. PetroChina has become Asia's most profitable company and Zhou was promoted to president and vice-chairman in 2008, and is regarded as one of the continent's most successful CEOs.

"When you have a good vision, you don't change it dramatically each year." Paul Bulcke

Mohamed Hassan Marican President & CEO, Petronas

BIOGRAPHY
Born in 1952 in Sungai Petani, Malaysia. Marican left home in 1972 to train as an accountant with Touche Ross & Co. in London, and returned to Malaysia in 1980.

BEST DECISION
Taking Petronas global and ignoring international sanctions along the way in the pursuit of new areas of production.

LESSON IN BUSINESS
Seek new partnerships—Marican made deals in countries that other petroleum companies had previously avoided.

PURSUING A STRATEGY of expansion and diversification, former accountant Marican has transformed Malaysia's state-owned oil and gas company Petronas into a *Fortune* Global 500 company, operating in more than 30 countries.

Marican joined Petronas in 1989 as senior vice-president of finance, and became chairman and CEO in 1995. The state-owned company had until then been concerned with the development of domestic resources but, under Marican's leadership, Petronas began to expand outside Malaysia. It pursued a policy of diversification, investing in all aspects of the petroleum industry and seeking new partnerships in underdeveloped countries that had hitherto been largely ignored by the larger petroleum companies. In 1997, Petronas joined Chinese partners to work in Sudan, within a two-year period successfully turning the African country into an oil exporter. Disregarding a US embargo, Marican joined forces with a French company to begin oil production in Iran. Other partnerships soon followed, and Petronas now operates in more than 30 countries, and is the most profitable company in Asia, contributing significantly to the wealth and growth of Malaysia.

William J. Doyle President & CEO, PotashCorp

BIOGRAPHY
Born c.1951. Doyle graduated in 1972 with a major in government from Georgetown University in Washington, DC.

BEST DECISION
Expanding sales into growing overseas markets, such as China and Brazil, where farmers must produce larger crops on limited arable land.

LESSON IN BUSINESS
Control production—PotashCorp produces 22 percent of potash worldwide, and holds 75 percent of global potash capacity. Controlling production keeps demand steady and prices high.

IN A SECTOR that is increasingly important as farmers worldwide produce more food on limited arable land, Doyle has transformed PotashCorp, the world's largest producer of potash, into one of Canada's most valuable businesses.

Doyle joined PotashCorp as president of sales in 1987, becoming a director in 1989 and president and CEO in 1999. By controlling resources and targeting countries under pressure to grow more food, Doyle has led PotashCorp to become the world's largest producer of potash, a compound used mainly as an agricultural fertilizer. The company also supplies feed supplements, industrial chemicals, and agricultural nitrogen and phosphate, with operations across North America, in the Middle East, and Brazil. Although supportive of world agriculture and the environment, PotashCorp has drawn criticism for limiting production to maintain prices, damaging water resources near its plants, and a safety-related death. A large proportion of the company's shares are US-owned, and Doyle himself lives in Illinois, but he has nonetheless transformed PotashCorp into one of Canada's most valuable businesses, with a market capitalization of almost CAN $63 billion.

"We don't fly under the radar anymore." William J. Doyle

Paul Desmarais, Jr. Chairman & Co-CEO, Power Corp. of Canada

BIOGRAPHY
Born in Sudbury, Canada, in 1954. Desmarais is the son of billionaire entrepreneur Paul G. Desmarais. He graduated in commerce from McGill University and gained an MBA from the European Institute of Business Administration (INSEAD), France.

BEST DECISION
Orchestrating the $3.9 billion takeover of US-based Putnam Investments in 2007.

LESSON IN BUSINESS
Think globally and take the long-term view—Desmarais's success in doing so has led to strong growth and stability.

DRIVING GROWTH beyond traditional boundaries, Desmarais Jr. aggressively reshaped his father's company into a diversified global financial empire, expanding in less than a decade from 13th to 5th largest company in Canada.

As a child, Desmarais Jr. sat with his father as he conducted business, transforming the family's small bus company into one of Canada's most influential corporations. A share-exchange offer in 1968 with leading utilities, pulp, and paper company, Power Corporation of Canada, led to Desmarais Jr's father taking control of the latter company, as chairman and CEO. In 1990, Desmarais Jr became chairman, assuming the co-CEO role in 1996, with younger brother André taking charge of overseas operations.

The company has diversified under Desmarais Jr's leadership, providing investment products and financial services in life, health, speciality, and general insurance for individuals, businesses, and public and private organizations. Like his father, Desmarais Jr. has focused on ventures that provide secure long-term growth. In 2007, he added Putnam Investments to Power Corp's financial, publishing, and industrial interests, and its European arm incorporates media, energy, minerals, water, and waste services.

Prasert Bunsumpun President & CEO, PTT

BIOGRAPHY
Born in 1952 in Thailand. Bunsumpun received a bachelor of science degree in civil engineering from Chulalongkorn University, Thailand, and an MBA from Utah State University.

BEST DECISION
Building the exploration and production side, a key part of making PTT an integrated energy company that could compete on the global stage.

LESSON IN BUSINESS
Leave your comfort zone—Bunsumpun steered PTT away from the option of the easy life and toward much bigger things.

THAILAND'S PART-PRIVATIZED national oil and gas company, Petroleum Authority of Thailand (PTT), has developed rapidly under Bunsumpun's leadership, becoming a serious player in the international energy industry.

When Prasert Bunsumpun took over at PTT in 2003, the company was still dealing with the aftermath of part-privatization two years previously. Despite the sale of a minority stake to public investors, it would have been easy for the state-dominated company to sit on its assets and watch its guaranteed revenues flow in. Bunsumpun had bigger ambitions for the company. He set out to turn PTT into the leading energy group in the region. He re-organized and streamlined the company's

bureaucracy and finances, upgraded its technology and began increasing its stakes in refineries and involvement in joint ventures. During this time he showed the fine-tuned political skills needed to balance the interests of the majority and minority shareholders. He also developed the company's exploration and production operations across South-East Asia, and in the Middle East and North Africa, putting PTT, once a local refiner, on the road to becoming a global energy player.

"Being decisive is my key strength." Prasert Bunsumpun

Jean-Pascal Tricoire Chairman & CEO, Schneider Electric

BIOGRAPHY
Born in Beaupréau, France, in 1963. Tricoire studied electronic engineering before receiving an MBA from CESMA-Lyon business school. Tricoire is Chinese-speaking and has the Chinese name Zhao Guohua.

BEST DECISION
Making internal forecasts public for the first time in the company's history, demystifying its results and raising its profile.

LESSON IN BUSINESS
History counts—Tricoire has continued to expand Schneider in China, building on links dating back to the early 20th century.

ELECTRICAL ENGINEER Tricoire spent most of his career with automation giant Schneider Electric, becoming CEO in 2006. He has pushed the company's strategy of geographic transformation, notably in its long-standing Chinese market.

Tricoire joined Groupe Schneider in the 1980s, working on projects in Italy, China, and South Africa before returning to France and spending four years rising through the ranks. His success led to his appointment as COO in 2003, and he succeeded Henri Lachmann as CEO in 2006. Tricoire continued his predecessor's strategic and geographic transformation of Schneider, with key acquisitions aiming to turn the company into a global energy management specialist. Tricoire purchased Xantrex Technology for $412 million in 2008, giving Schneider a foothold in the renewable energy market. However, the economic downturn led to a slowdown in the company's growth, not least in China, which played an important role in the group's expansion, accounting for 40 percent of its business in the Asia Pacific region. With Schneider also affected by the collapsing housing market in North America, Tricoire introduced worldwide cost-cutting measures aimed at reducing operating costs.

Helge Lund President & CEO, StatoilHydro ASA

BIOGRAPHY
Born in 1962 in Norway. Lund has business degrees from the Norwegian School of Economics and Business Administration (NHH) and INSEAD, France.

BEST DECISION
Forging close relationships with national oil companies, such as Petrobras and Gazprom, which has helped with the development of new oilfields.

LESSON IN BUSINESS
Think "big but balanced"—Lund's corporate model is a successful balance between creating stability for investors and earning strong returns for the state.

AN EXPERIENCED international manager whose political nous stands him in good stead in the energy industry, Lund strives for strong governance and good resource management, while pushing StatoilHydro's international growth.

Lund assumed the role of president and CEO of Statoil in 2004, and when the company merged with NorskHydro's oil and gas activities in 2007, he took the same role at newly formed StatoilHydro. The biggest seller of oil products in Scandinavia, and a world leader in deepwater technology and the capture and storage of carbon, the company is majority-owned by the Norwegian government. While Lund's general focus has been on identifying projects with the highest returns, he has occasionally accepted reduced stakes, such as in Venezuela, where the state acted to reduce the influence of foreign companies. StatoilHydro competes strongly on the international stage, having business operations in 40 countries. Lund's current focus for growth is on operations in the Gulf of Mexico, Canada, West and North Africa, and Brazil, which, following the discovery of huge oil reserves, will be one of the most important areas for StatoilHydro. Lund is also investing in wind power, with a project planned in the UK.

"[Arctic oil reserves] will never replace the Middle East, but it has the potential to be a good supplement." Helge Lund

Kunio Takeda Chairman & CEO, Takeda Pharmaceuticals

BIOGRAPHY
Born in Kobe, Japan, in 1940. Takeda joined the family firm at 22 after gaining an economics degree at Konan University.

BEST DECISION
Embracing the global market, with a clear focus on development through R&D and overseas expansion.

LESSON IN BUSINESS
Tradition need not limit innovation—Takeda's willingness to innovate and expand his family's business has led it to thrive.

SCION OF A DYNASTY that established the family company in 1781, Takeda has succeeded in leading Japanese firm Takeda Pharmaceuticals into the modern business world, while preserving its core ethical values, dubbed "Takeda-ism".

Takeda took over the role of president and CEO in 1993, becoming chairman and CEO in 2003. Despite spending his entire career in a family business, he has never shied away from change. Under his stewardship, Takeda has enthusiastically embraced globalization by swallowing up giant foreign competitors, such as biotech firm Millennium Pharmaceuticals, which it acquired for $8.8 billion in 2008. Takeda also invested in R&D to help the company expand into new treatment areas and develop new markets in the US and Europe. He restructured the company in the early 1990s when faced with stagnation in the Japanese economy, shedding jobs to maximize shareholder returns and ensure the company's future. His efforts were rewarded with eight years of record earnings, bringing the company to the position of the world's fourteenth largest drug company. Takeda's outward-looking vision has even earned him the post of honorary chair of the Ireland-Japan Chamber of Commerce.

Masaaki Furukawa President, Toyota Tsusho Corp.

BIOGRAPHY
Born in Japan in 1940.

BEST DECISION
Launching two subsidiary companies in India to produce cars for Toyota Motors in 1998, marking a first step in TTC's expansion and diversification.

LESSON IN BUSINESS
Don't put all your eggs in one basket—Furukawa saw that Toyota Tsusho had the potential to develop far beyond its traditional markets, and boldly led the firm beyond the confines of its own conservatism.

DETERMINED TO TAKE his company forward, Furukawa has transformed Toyota Tsusho Corp. from a cautious trading company primarily serving Toyota Motors into Japan's sixth-largest trading firm with diverse global interests.

Toyota Tsusho Corp. (TTC) is a trading house that finds markets for other companies' products—principally those of its parent, the Toyota Motor Corp. When he became president of the company, Furukawa expressed an ambition to move out from under the wing of Toyota Motors and diversify. To this end, in 1998, TTC launched two Indian subsidiaries serving Toyota Motors, and followed up with a joint venture (with Mitsubishi and Chinese oil giant Sinopec) devoted to producing polypropylene for car interiors. However, Furukawa wanted to go further. Targeting information technology, food products, consumer goods, and environmental developments—particularly green fuels —the early 2000s saw him forge alliances with Environmental Systems Products, Nichimen, Tomen, Kobe Steel, and Mitsui and Zeon Corp., opening new plants in the US, South America, and China, and building a worldwide distribution network.

"TTC has had a reputation as a company that taps a stone bridge to confirm safety but does not cross it. From now on we will cross the bridge." Masaaki Furukawa

Alessandro Profumo CEO, UniCredit Group

BIOGRAPHY
Born in Genoa, Italy, in 1957.
Profumo studied business
administration at the SDA
Bocconi School of Management
in Milan, Italy.

BEST DECISION
Expanding UniCredit through
domestic and overseas mergers
and acquisitions, which won
the group more than 40 million
customers in 22 countries.

LESSON IN BUSINESS
Put your money where your
mouth is—Profumo bought
150,000 shares in UniCredit,
unequivocally demonstrating
his faith in the company.

HIS DETERMINED "value creation" and acquisitions skills have enabled Profumo to build UniCredit into one of the world's largest banking empires, with operations in over 20 countries, making him the star of the Italian banking sector.

In the mid-1990s, Profumo was nominated deputy general manager, and then chief general manager, of Credito Italiano. In 1997, with the formation of the UniCredit Group, he was named CEO. Since then, Profumo has focused on expansion through acquisitions and mergers. "Value creation" has been his mantra; seeking sustainable profit to meet the needs of clients, employees, and shareholders. Profumo's program of acquisitions, including Italian bank Capitalia, Germany's HVB, and majority holdings in institutions in Kazakhstan and the Ukraine, was considered a brilliant strategy. Despite this, he has admitted that UniCredit underestimated the impact of the global financial crisis, and critics suggested that the bank had over-extended itself and become a victim of its own success. However, Profumo responded confidently to the crisis, selling assets to boost the bank's capital while continuing with plans for aggressive organic growth in central and eastern Europe.

Arun Sarin CEO (2003–08), Vodafone

BIOGRAPHY
Born in 1954 in India. Sarin is a
graduate of the Indian Institute of
Technology, Kharagpur, the Haas
School of Business, Berkeley,
and the University of California,
where he gained his MBA.

BEST DECISION
Buying Hutch, the Indian mobile
operator, which added 23 million
subscribers and a large share in
a fast-growing market.

LESSON IN BUSINESS
Focus on emerging markets—
seeing that Western markets
were saturated, Sarin moved into
Asia, making Vodafone the
world's biggest mobile operator.

REPUTED TO HAVE one of the thickest hides in corporate Britain, Sarin survived a boardroom revolt and shareholder unrest to transform Vodafone into a world-beating telecommunications company, earning record profits.

In March 2006, barely three years after Sarin was appointed CEO, Vodafone UK was facing an asset write-down of £28 billion, record losses of £14 billion, and uproar among shareholders. Even the chairman who hired him appeared to have lost faith, but Sarin stood his ground. With Western markets saturated, he mounted a series of mergers and takeovers in developing economies in Africa, Latin America, and Asia, culminating in the purchase of Indian mobile operator Hutch for $11 billion. The purchase immediately added 23 million subscribers to Vodafone's international tally, bringing the company its third largest market after the US and Germany. By August 2008, this Indian subscriber base had risen to total more than 52 million. By the time Sarin stepped down to seek new challenges that year, the company had chalked up record net profits of £6.7 billion, and had added an extra 100 million subscribers worldwide to its customer base.

"I've always considered that the creation of a large international network is an important platform for our country." Alessandro Profumo

James T. Ryan President & CEO, W.W. Grainger, Inc.

BIOGRAPHY
Born in the US in 1958. Ryan studied business at the Miami University of Ohio, and received an MBA from Chicago's DePaul University.

BEST DECISION
Seeing the potential of expanding into India and China early on, and ensuring Grainger was quick off the mark in doing so.

LESSON IN BUSINESS
The customer is king—when customers demanded a broader product range, Ryan gave it to them, and as a result, sales rose to a record $6.9 billion.

A CANNY BUSINESSMAN and smart decision-maker, W.W. Grainger CEO Ryan knows when to listen and when to act, skills that have helped drive the industrial equipment company through a successful global expansion.

Ryan was no stranger to Grainger when he became CEO in 2008, having joined the company as a product manager in 1980. With 18 years at the firm under his belt, Ryan had earned himself a number of top roles, including group president in 2004, president in 2006, and president and COO in 2007. Under his leadership, Grainger has focused on expansion, with record results: Ryan's first year as CEO saw sales of $6.9 billion, up seven percent on 2007. Since taking over, Ryan has also overseen the completion of the firm's market expansion in the US, which contributed $476 million in incremental sales in 2008. He masterminded the firm's ongoing expansion overseas, including the purchase of a 49.9 percent stake in Asia Pacific Brands India, one of India's largest industrial and electrical wholesale distributors, and expansion in China. Closer to home, in 2008, some sharp decisions brought Grainger $9.7 million through property sales, and an extra 44,000 catalogue items.

Yin Yimin President & Executive Director, ZTE Corp.

BIOGRAPHY
Born c.1965. Yin earned an engineering MSc from Nanjing University of Posts and Telecommunications in 1988.

BEST DECISION
Moving aggressively into the developing world, Yin secured a $100-million cell phone order in Brazil, the largest ever for a Chinese vendor.

LESSON IN BUSINESS
Go where you can grow—operating in the shadow of giant rival Huawei Technologies, ZTE rocketed to prominence by shrewdly identifying demand in unexploited markets.

RAPID EXPANSION has seen ZTE Corp. claim second rank in China's booming telecommunications market, and executive director Yin has set his sights on the growth potential of the Middle East, Africa, and less-developed Asian countries.

A spectacular first year as president in 2004 saw Yin shake up global telecommunications, establishing him as one of the young tigers of Asia. Despite intense competition, ZTE rang up record profits, with sales of wireless and telecommunications systems and equipment increasing by more than 50 percent. Yin's strategy was for aggressive expansion into developing countries, where wireless and mobile telecoms enabled ZTE to leapfrog traditional infrastructure, reducing costs. He aimed to boost overseas sales from 20 to 50 percent of the revenue, which totaled $5 billion in 2007. Yin also planned to enter mature markets in North America and Europe. Yin allocated more than 30 percent of ZTE's 50,000-strong work force to R&D, and 10 percent of revenue to cover costs. By the end of 2007, Yin led ZTE to apply for almost 12,000 national and international patents, 90 percent of which were claimed to be innovative patents with associated intellectual property rights.

"Truthfully, every day what I think about isn't development—it's survival" Yin Yimin

ONES TO WATCH

Some are born CEOs, some achieve CEO-dom, and some have CEO-ship thrust upon them. In this feature we look at a selection of each, but they are all worth keeping an eye on, either because they are self-made captains of business, because they lead smaller companies that have remained largely below the radar, or because they have only recently taken up their positions, often under challenging circumstances, and in many cases replacing long established CEOs who can prove to be hard acts to follow ●

New Appointees

As the effects of the credit crunch reverberated through the world's economies, many companies saw the need for a change of leadership. In some cases, revenue had fallen dramatically and individual CEOs were held to blame. In others, although business was holding up, the rapidly changing economic landscape seemed to call for a new way forward. Either way, the newly appointed CEOs found themselves in a situation to test their mettle.

Edward Liddy, AMERICAN INTERNATIONAL GROUP (Insurance: US)—*Replaced* **Robert Willumstadt** *as part of an $85-billion government bailout in September 2008. After the bailout figure doubled, he came under fire for approving the payment of $165 million in bonuses to top AIG executives.*

—

Tim Cook, APPLE (IT: US)—*Picked up the reins of one of the world's most iconic brands while* **Steve Jobs** *(p17) took a leave of absence for health reasons. As Apple's COO, he had long been involved in the company's inner workings, and was regarded as a very capable pair of hands.*

—

Thomas Millner, CABELA (Retail: US)—*The former CEO of Freedom Group, Inc., parent company of arms manufacturer Remington, succeeded* **Dennis Highby**, *who oversaw the growth of Cabela to an annual income of more than $2.5 billion. Millner's experience made him ideally suited to lead the hunting, fishing, and outdoor gear retailer.*

—

Francois Perol, CAISSE D'EPARGNE (Finance: France)—*Named in 2009 as CEO of France's second-biggest bank, formed by the merger of rivals Banque Populaire and Caisse d'Epargne, which suffered a €2-billion loss in 2008. This high-handed political appointment of one of his senior aides by French President Nicolas Sarkozy, elicited cries of "Foul!" from businesses, political parties, and unions alike, complicating an already difficult job for Perol.*

—

Lars Olofsson, CARREFOUR SA (Retail: France)—*Installed at the start of 2009, at the behest of the dominant shareholders, replacing* **José Louis Durán** *(p307). Olofsson, formerly an executive with Nestlé SA, announced €600 million of investment in France to cut prices and increase advertising, vowing to make Europe's largest retailer "more agile and competitive".*

—

Pierre Mariani, DEXIA (Finance: Belgium/France)—*Taking over from* **Axel Miller** *in 2008 as part of a rescue deal by European governments, Mariani moved quickly to increase liquidity by selling assets, but faced a struggle to stem losses.*

—

Takanobu Ito, HONDA MOTOR COMPANY LTD (Automotive: Japan)—*Despite his success in keeping Japan's second-largest car maker in profit during troubled times,* **Takeo Fukui** *(p157), who had reached retirement age, was replaced as CEO in June 2009. A younger man, with an engineering background and experience in the US, Ito is expected to restructure to meet the dramatically altered market conditions.*

—

John Thain, MERRILL LYNCH (Finance: US)—*Brought in to guide the financial giant through the turmoil of a collapsing credit market, Thain is credited with limiting the damage to a loss of $27.61 billion in 2008. After a takeover by Bank of America, he left without his requested $10-million bonus.*

—

Philippe Varin, PEUGEOT CITROËN (Automotive: France)—*In March 2009, in the same week that saw* **"Rick" Wagoner** *(p263) removed from his post as CEO of General Motors, the board of PSA Peugeot Citroën ousted CEO* **Christian Streiff** *(p427). In his previous job, Varin returned Corus (formerly British Steel) to profitability and oversaw its merger with Tata Steel in 2007.*

—

Tidjane Thiam, PRUDENTIAL (Insurance: UK)—*Taking over from* **Mark Tucker**, *whose four-year tenure brought the firm some of the best figures in the industry, Thiam made history in 2009 as the first black CEO of a FTSE 100 company. Born in Côte d'Ivoire, where he was briefly in government as minister of planning and development, and educated in France, Thiam was managing director of Aviva International before joining Prudential in 2008 as CFO.*

—

Nadir Mohamed, ROGERS COMMUNICATIONS, INC. (Telecommunications: Canada)—*In 2009 he stepped into the role left empty by the death of* **Edward Rogers, Jr.** *(p371). His success as head of the wireless division suits him for the battle already underway for market share in that fast-moving sector of the industry.*

—

Stephen Hester, ROYAL BANK OF SCOTLAND (Finance: UK)—*Took over the RBS hot seat in October 2008 after the resignation of* **Fred Goodwin**, *whose drive for expansion took him an acquisition too far. Hester quickly announced plans for a return to profitability by selling overseas assets and retrenching the bank in its UK business.*

—

Peter Voser, ROYAL DUTCH SHELL (Petrochemicals: UK/Netherlands)—*Replaced CEO* **Jeroen van der Veer** *(p273) when he retired in July 2009. Inheriting a company with good reserves and high production, Voser, the company's experienced former CFO, was nonetheless expected to exercise some belt tightening to maintain a healthy balance sheet in financially troubled times.*

—

Lee Yoon-woo, SAMSUNG ELECTRONICS COMPANY (Electronics: South Korea) – *Replaced* **Yun Jong-yong** *(p274) who resigned in May 2008 after company chairman Lee Kun-hee was charged with tax evasion. Lee's immediate task was to see the company through a major reorganization and stabilize it after the scandal.*

—

Chris Viehbacher, SANOFI-AVENTIS (Pharmaceuticals: France)—*Took over at the end of 2008 from* **Gerard Le Fur**, *whose two-year tenure saw the share price fall by 30 percent. Viehbacher, former president for GlaxoSmithKline's North American operations, faced the daunting task of implementing a new strategy that refocuses R&D efforts, targets emerging markets, and expands medicine and health care activities.*

—

Akio Toyoda, TOYOTA MOTOR CORP. (Automotive: Japan)—*The grandson of company founder* **Kiichiro Toyoda** *took over as president in June 2009, replacing* **Katsuaki Watanabe** *(p328), who became vice-president. Following the company's first ever loss-making year, Toyoda was expected to appraise all aspects of the business, including the possibility of moving more production outside Japan.*

—

Marc Lefar, VONAGE (Telecommunications: US)—*Took over from founder* **Jeffrey Citron** *in 2008. Although Citron solved many of the company's immediate financial and legal problems, Lefar faces tough competition from other Voice Over Internet Protocol (VOIP) providers, and from a growing range of wireless services.*

—

Mike Duke, WAL-MART (Retail: US)—*Took over from* **H. Lee Scott, Jr.** *(p112) in early 2009 and is capitalizing on the expansion into overseas markets, such as Brazil and India, that he spearheaded as chief of the company's international division. Within weeks of his appointment, he awarded $2 billion in financial incentives to Wal-Mart's US hourly employees after good end of year figures.*

—

Dean Douglas, WESTCON (Information commerce: US)—*Former Motorola and IBM executive, and former CEO of wireless engineering firm LCC International, Inc., replaced co-founder* **Tom Dolan** *in 2009. His task is to expand the business internationally, on the basis of its strong relationships with vendors such as Nortel and Cisco.*

—

Execs On the Up

The CEOs featured here have one thing in common: they have picked up the ball and run with it. Some of them have been given responsibility for a newly merged entity or a newly created division, and have made it their own. Many have started from scratch and built up their own firms, learning the ropes of leadership as they go. All of them have lessons for current and aspiring CEOs.

Henry Engelhardt, ADMIRAL GROUP PLC (Insurance: UK)— *The Chicago-born inventor of the "niche" approach to insurance, with a clutch of brands aimed at different types of driver, has made his company the third biggest car insurer in the UK. Having expanded into Spain, Italy, and Germany, he is now launching in the US.*

—

Tim Anderson, AOL (Internet: US)—*The former Google sales chief became CEO of Time Warner's underperforming internet division in 2009, and took on the task of boosting audience and advertising figures, and optimizing company structure.*

—

Nicholas *and* **Christian Candy**, CANDY HOLDINGS (Real estate: UK)—*In less than ten years, the two young brothers have built up personal assets in excess of £100 million creating super-luxury London apartments for the super-wealthy. Clientele ranging from oil-rich Arabs to Russian oligarchs puts them in a good position to weather the downturn.*

—

Charles Dunstone, CARPHONE WAREHOUSE (Telecoms: UK) —*Since starting the business in 1989, selling cell phones from a rented apartment, Carphone Warehouse has grown through a successful flotation and the acquisition of several of its rivals, to become one of Europe's largest retailers of cell phones, as well as a provider of phone services and broadband.*

—

Strive Masiyiwa, ECONET WIRELESS (Telecoms: South Africa)—*Born in Rhodesia (Zimbabwe) in 1961, and educated in the UK, Masiyiwa has become a role model for young African entrepreneurs. Overcoming many difficulties, including government attempts to protect the state-owned telephone monopoly, he founded a cell phone network that now operates in 15 different countries.*

—

Charlene T. Begley, GE ENTERPRISE SOLUTIONS (Professional services: US) —*When, in 2007,* **Jeffrey Immelt** *(p92) announced the creation of a new technology-based unit to provide GE's customers with the means to increase their productivity, he named Begley as CEO. Now among* Fortune's *50 most powerful women in business, she has consistently provided impressive profit growth.*

Andrea Illy, ILLYCAFFÈ S.P.A. (Foodstuffs and retail: Italy) *The grandson of the inventor of the modern espresso machine, Illy has marketed the family name as a luxury coffee brand—the "Armani of coffee" —and now supplies some 50,000 restaurants and hotels. One of the top three coffee firms in the world, Illy has now taken on the likes of Starbucks by opening its own upmarket coffee bars, "espressamente illy".*

—

Heidi Miller, J.P. MORGAN CHASE & CO. (Finance: US)—*As head of the company's treasury and securities services since 2004, Miller has worked to streamline the business, introduced new products, and dramatically increased net profits year on year.*

—

Simon Calver, LOVEFiLM (Internet: UK)—*After holding executive positions with Dell, Pepsi, and Unilever, Calver became CEO of Video Island Entertainment Ltd and then of LOVEFiLM when the two merged in 2006. He has since grown the company to be Europe's leading online DVD rental service, topping the one million customer mark in early 2009, and attracting new investment to fund technological development.*

—

Chris DeWolfe, MYSPACE (Internet: US)—*A co-founder, with* **Tom Anderson**, *of what is now the most popular social networking website for US users, DeWolfe made advertising revenue an integral part of the business plan from the start, and the income keeps on growing. Actively courting cell phone users, he is now developing the software to "hypertarget" market sectors with tailored advertising.*

—

Natalie Massenet, NET-A-PORTER (Internet: UK)—*An experienced fashion magazine editor, Massenet developed an online designer-label retail website that rapidly attracted a large clientele. Combining sales and editorial in a chic and efficient package, netaporter.com featured in* Time *magazine's 50 Best Websites of 2008.*

—

Wale Tinubu, OANDO (Oil and gas: Nigeria)—*CEO since 2001, Tinubu has grown Oando into Nigeria's largest indigenous diversified oil and gas company. He studied law in the UK, and entered petrochemicals via his family's law firm.*

—

Tim Steiner, OCADO (Logistics: UK)—*With his two fellow founders, Steiner set up the first online grocery delivery service in the UK, effectively outsourced by the Waitrose supermarket chain. Steiner's alternative business model has produced four successive years of 100 percent compound annual growth.*

—

Garvis Snook, ROK (Construction: UK)—*With the aim of turning his company into the "nation's local builder", Snook, the son of a scaffolder, has extended the Rok "brand" throughout the UK with a series of major acquisitions.*

—

Evan Williams, TWITTER (Internet: US)—*Changing places with co-founder* **Jack Dorsey**, *who becomes chairman, Williams took over as CEO in October 2008. The move signaled a sea change in the business plan, as the company sought to turn its huge popularity and real-time polling possibilities into hard cash in a toughening economic climate.*

—

Chad Hurley, YOUTUBE (Internet: US)—*When eBay bought PayPal in 2002, Hurley and his colleagues,* **Steve Chen** *and* **Jawed Karim**, *left the company and discussed setting up a business together. The video-sharing website YouTube, which now serves up more than one third of all video on the web, was the outcome. In October 2006, they sold YouTube to Google for $1.65 billion, and all three continue to work there, with Hurley as CEO.*

—

Index

Page numbers in **bold type** indicate a main entry. Main entries may be for featured topics (e.g. innovation), or for individual CEOs.

Main entries for individual CEOs give their business biographies, with details of their leadership styles, key strengths, best decisions, and lessons in business. These details are not normally indexed separately.

Page numbers in *italics* indicate a quotation from that individual.

This index is arranged in letter-by-letter order, which normally ignores any punctuation or spaces between words. However, occasional exceptions have been made to this rule for additional clarity. Numbers that form part of a company name are treated as if they were spelled out in full.

A

The Contributors

Andrew Davidson is chief business interviewer for *The Sunday Times* of London where, for the last six years, he has conducted over 45 major interviews a year with global CEOs such as Jeff Bezos (Amazon), Arun Sarin (Vodafone), Yun Jong-yong (Samsung Electronics) and Jean-Bernard Lévy (Vivendi). In addition to his work with *The Sunday Times,* Andrew also conducts interviews for *Management Today* magazine.

Before moving to *The Sunday Times*, Andrew conducted similar interviews for the *Financial Times The Business* magazine. He was previously assistant business editor at *The Sunday Times* and editor of *Marketing* magazine.

He has published three books, the latest a collection of interviews with entrepreneurs entitled *Smart Luck.*

A previous winner of the PPA Business Writer of the Year, Andrew has also been Industrial Society Magazine Journalist of the Year. An archive of his recent interviews is available at www.andrewdavidson.biz.

Marshall Goldsmith is a world authority in business management, one of a select few advisors who have been asked to work with over 100 major CEOs and their management teams. The author of 24 books, *What Got You Here Won't Get You There* is a New York Times bestseller and has been translated into 23 languages. His new book *Succession: Are You Ready* has been ranked number 1 on Amazon.com.

The American Management Association has named Dr. Goldsmith as one of 50 great thinkers and leaders who have influenced the field of management.

Marjan Bolmeijer is one of an elite group of CEO coaches with over 15,000 hours coaching experience with CEOs of *Fortune* 500 companies. Marjan is the CEO of Change Leaders, Inc., an international leadership and senior team development company.

She is an expert in creating sustainable change for senior executives and their teams. She excels at demystifying persistent people patterns (structures, processes, skills, identities, values, practices, rituals, beliefs, etc.) and zooms to the core of what gets executives unstuck. During her work, she connects the dots between the way individuals and groups change, the way organizational systems work, and the executive's current business realities. Marjan can be reached at Marjan.Bolmeijer@Change-Leaders.com

Acknowledgments

Ken Langdon has a background in sales and marketing in the technology industry. As an independent consultant, he has trained salespeople and sales managers in the US, Europe, and Australia and has advised managers on the coaching and appraisal of their staff. He has also provided strategic guidance at board level. Ken is the author of many books, including several titles in the *Essential Managers* series for Dorling Kindersley. Ken wrote the "Lessons in Business" for the full-page CEO profiles.

Profile authors
Tom Albrighton, Richard Brass, Craig Carpenter, Simon Clarke, Matthew Lynn, Melanie May, Susan Mayse, Sharon McGowan, Dean Nelson, Clare Pearson, Nadine Pedersen, Sarah Powell, Andrew Saunders, Ed Shelton, Julie Whitaker, Richard Williams.

Feature authors
Tom Albrighton, Mike Bourne, Richard Brass, Claire Burdett, Simon Clarke, Steve Coomber, Stuart Derrick, Marshall Goldsmith, Melanie May, David Nicholson, Sarah Powell, Cheryl Rickman, Rhymer Rigby, Steve Shipside, Sarah Sutton, Ian Whitelaw, Stephen Wingrove, Bibi van der Zee.

Editors Becky Alexander, Sharon Amos, Richard Gilbert, Gillian Holmes, Tom Howells, Laura Palosuo, Sarah Powell, Jimmy Topham
Senior Editors Peter Jones, Alastair Laing
Editorial Manager Ian Whitelaw
Senior Art Editor Sara Robin
Features Designer Jason Godfrey
Picture Researcher Frances Vargo
Senior Production Editor Jenny Woodcock
Creative Technical Support Sonia Charbonnier
Senior Production Controller Wendy Penn
Managing Art Editor Kat Mead
Executive Managing Editor Adèle Hayward
Art Director Peter Luff
Category Publisher Stephanie Jackson

Publisher's acknowledgments
Dorling Kindersley would like to give special thanks to Aparna Sharma at DK Delhi and the team: Dheeraj Arora, Alicia Ingty, Alka Ranjan, Ankush Saikia, Sunil Sharma, Rohan Sinha, and Saloni Talwar. Thanks also to Susan Bosanko for indexing, Irene Lyford for proofreading, Charles Wills for co-ordinating Americanization, Saskia Janssen, Laura Mirgozzi, Andrew Pitchford, and Helen Spencer for design assistance, and Ashley McNeal, Director of Operations at Change Management Learning Center.

Picture credits

The publisher would like to thank the following for their kind permission to reproduce photographs:
(Key: a-above; b-below/bottom; c-centre; l-left; r-right; t-top)

16 3M United Kingdom plc. 17 Getty Images: AFP/Shaun Curry. 18 Getty Images: AFP/Rafa Rivas. 19 The Children's Investment Fund Foundation. 20 Getty Images: ChinaFotoPress/Cai Daizheng. 21 Getty Images: Hulton Archive. 22 PA Photos: Landov/Adam Berry. 23 Library Of Congress, Washington, D.C.. 26 Getty Images: AFP/Clemens Bilan. 27 Photoshot: Bloomberg News/Landov. 28 Getty Images: Time & Life Pictures/Alfred Eisenstaedt. 29 Grupo Inditex. 30 © Intel Corporation. 31 Getty Images: AFP/Berthold Stadler. 32 Getty Images: AFP/Torsten Blackwood. 33 Merck & Co., Inc.. 36 Microsoft. 37 Getty Images: AFP/Stan Honda. 38 Getty Images: Harry How. 48 Getty Images: Aurora/Randall Scott. 49 Getty Images: AFP/Raveendran. 50 Courtesy of Dell Inc.. 51 Discovery Holdings Limited. 52 Getty Images: Time & Life Pictures/Ray Ng. 53 Corbis: Bettmann. 54 PA Photos: Bloomberg News/Landov/Maurice TSAI. 55 Landmark Group. 58 Corbis: epa/Peter Foley. 59 Getty Images: Justin Sullivan. 60 Corbis: Bettmann. 61 Getty Images: AFP. 62 Getty Images: Dave M. Benett. 63 XTO Energy Inc.. 80 Getty Images: AFP. 81 Reuters: Paulo Whitaker. 82 Getty Images: Time & Life Pictures/Jon Brenneis. 83 (c) Bechtel Corporation. 84 Best Buy Co., Inc.. 85 Copyright The Boeing Company. 86 Getty Images: Stephen Lovekin. 87 J.C. Decaux. 90 PA Photos: Landov/Graham Barclay. 91 Expeditors International. 92 General Electric Company. 93 Getty Images: WireImage/George Pimentel. 94 Leo Burnett Co. UK. 95 Getty Images: AFP/Pierre Verdy. 96 Getty Images: Time & Life Pictures/Ralph Morse. 97 Getty Images: Mike Simons. 100 Getty Images: Paul McConnell. 101 Getty Images: AFP/Deshakalyan Chowdhury. 102 Reynolds American Inc.. 103 Corbis: James Leynse. 104 Getty Images: Gary Gershoff. 105 Getty Images: AFP/Noah Seelam. 106 PA Photos: Bloomberg News/Landov/Raul Vasquez. 107 Getty Images: AFP/Eric Feferberg. 110 Corbis: Reuters/Will Burges. 111 PA Photos: DPA/VW. 112 Corbis: epa/Matthew Cavanaugh. 113 Getty Images: Time & Life Pictures/Diana Walker. 114 Ricochet Public Relations. 115 Reuters: Robert Sullivan. 116 Getty Images: AFP/Torsten Blackwood. 117 World Food Programme: Rein Skullerud. 118 Getty Images: AFP/Fabrice Coffrini. 119 WWF International. 146 Affiliated Computer Services, Inc.. 147 Getty Images: AFP/Pierre Andrieu. 148 CARE International. 149 Deutsche Börse AG. 150 Getty Images: AFP/Stephane de Sakutin. 151 Getty Images: Hulton Archive/Pictorial Parade. 152 Corbis: Axel Koester. 153 PA Photos: Landov/Simon Dawson. 156 Rex Features. 157 Getty Images: Scott Barbour. 158 International Federation of Red Cross and Red Crescent Societies. 159 Johnson & Johnson. 160 Merck & Co., Inc.. 161 Oxfam. 162 Getty Images: AFP/Mehdi Fedouach. 163 Sony Corporation of America. 166 Rex Features: Tony Buckingham. 167 Getty Images: FilmMagic/Soul Brother. 168 UPS Corporate Public Relations. 169 Getty Images: Peter Kramer. 170 Vivendi: © Jean-François Deroubaix/Gamma. 171 Getty Images: AFP/Pierre Verdy. 190 Getty Images: AFP/Toru Yamanaka. 191 Getty Images: Stock 4B/Stefan Pielow. 192 Getty Images: Liaison/Amilcar. 193 Archer Daniels Midland Company. 194 Getty Images: David Silverman. 195 Getty Images: Mat Szwajkos. 196 BMW AG. 197 Getty Images: AFP/Image courtesy of APEC 2007 Taskforce. 198 Getty Images: AFP/Thomas Lohnes. 199 Deutsche Post AG. 202 Getty Images: Justin Sullivan. 203 Getty Images: AFP/Maurizio Riccardi. 204 PA Photos: AP Photo/Richard Drew. 205 Orange France Telecom: © Fabrice Bessière (Agence Reuters) for Orange France Telecom. 206 Goldman Sachs International. 207 (c) Greenpeace: Laura Lombardi. 208 Reuters: Susana Vera. 209 Heineken International. 210 Image courtesy of Kimberly-Clark Corporate Archives. 211 Corbis: Jurgen Frank. 214 Getty Images: John Stillwell. 215 Getty Images: Junko Kimura. 216 Getty Images: AFP/Toshifumi Kitamura. 217 Nokia. 218 Newscast: Pearson plc. 219 Newscast: Jason Alden. 220 Getty Images: AFP/Thomas Lohnes. 221 Supervalu Inc.. 222 Toshiba Corporation. 223 Getty Images: Andreas Rentz. 224 Reuters: Joshua Lott. 225 Corbis: Reuters/Lou Dematteis. 254 adidas Group. 255 American Red Cross. 256 Anglo American Services (UK) Ltd.. 257 PA Photos: AP Photo/Peter Dejong. 258 Getty Images: Brad Barket. 259 Bertelsmann Stiftung. 260 Photoshot: UPPA/Nelson Ching. 261 Getty Images: Hulton Archive/Bachrach. 262 Fiat Group: Daniele Badolato/LaPresse. 263 Getty Images: Bill Pugliano. 266 Courtesy of International Business Machines Corporation Unauthorised use not permitted. 267 Courtesy of International Business Machines Corporation Unauthorised use not permitted. 268 Corbis: AGP/Antoine Gyori. 269 Renault Communication: Jean-Brice Lemal. 270 Corbis: Deborah Feingold. 271 Rite Aid Corporation. 272 Rolls-Royce plc. 273 Newscast: Ashley Bingham. 274 Getty Images: AFP/Jung Yeon-Je. 275 Getty Images: Neilson Barnard. 278 Reuters: Todd Korol. 279 Courtesy of Xerox. Xerox is a Trademark of the Xerox Corporation.: William Taufic. 304 Getty Images: AFP/John MacDougall. 305 PA Photos: AP Photo/Victoria Arocho. 306 Getty Images: Junko Kimura. 307 Groupe Carrefour: Stephan Gladieu. 308 Getty Images: Ross Land. 309 courtesy Costco Wholesale: France Freeman. 310 © EADS : Marquardt. 311 General Electric Company. 314 Hewlett-Packard Development Company, L.P.. 315 PA Photos: Bloomberg News/Landov/Daniel Acker. 316 Ikea: Merlijn Doomernik. 317 PA Photos: AP Photo/Mark Lennihan. 318 Getty Images: Time & Life Pictures/Evelyn Hofer. 319 Manulife Financial Corporation. 320 PA Photos: Bloomberg News/Landov/Robert Caplin. 321 PA Photos: AP Photo/Adrian Wyld. 324 Getty Images: Alex Wong. 325 PA Photos: AP Photo/Carl Abrams. 326 Getty Images: AFP/Yoshikazu Tsuno. 327 Tesco Stores Ltd. 328 Getty Images: Junko Kimura. 329 © UNESCO: Michel Ravassard. 330 Getty Images: Time & Life Pictures/Rob Nelson. 346 Getty Images: AFP/Chris Young. 347 PA Photos: AP Photo/Rick Rycroft. 348 Copyright The Boeing Company. 349 Getty Images: WireImage/Nick Harvey. 350 Getty Images: AFP/Yoshikazu Tsuno. 351 Corbis: Louie Psihoyos. 352 DLF Ltd.. 353 PA Photos: AP Photo/Paul Sancya. 356 Getty Images: AFP/Bertrand Guay. 357 Getty Images: Sean Gallup. 358 Linhas & Laudas. 359 Getty Images: AFP/Jung Yeon-Je. 360 Reuters: Amit Dave. 361 Getty Images: AFP/Prakash Singh. 362 PA Photos: AP Photo/Kraft Foods Inc. HO. 363 Getty Images: AFP/David Hancock. 364 PA Photos: AP Photo/ John Rous. 365 Reuters: Toru Hanai. 368 Getty Images: AFP/Stan Honda. 369 Corbis: Sygma/Raymond Reuter. 370 Getty Images: AFP/Indranil Mukherjee. 371 PA Photos: The Canadian Press/Adrian Wyld. 372 PA Photos: AP Photo/Pat Sullivan. 373 courtesy Tata Sons. 374 PA Photos: Bloomberg News/Landov/Jamie Rector. 375 Vornado Realty Trust. 378 Whole Foods Market ®. 379 Photoshot: UPPA/Paul Dijkstra. 400 PA Photos: AP Photo/Amy E. Conn. 401 Corbis: Louie Psihoyos. 402 Getty Images: Dave M. Benett. 403 Getty Images: AFP/Stephane de Sakutin. 404 easyGroup. 405 Fiat Group. 406 Corbis: Keith Dannemiller. 407 Getty Images: AFP/Javier Soriano. 410 Corbis: WWD/Condé Nast//Dominique Maitre. 411 Getty Images: Dave Hogan. 412 Corbis: Reuters/Fred Prouser. 413 Getty Images: AFP/Fred Dufour. 414 Getty Images: AFP/Raveendran. 415 Getty Images: AFP/Eric Piermont. 416 Reuters: Mkhitar Khachatrian. 417 Getty Images: Evan Agostini. 420 Getty Images: AFP/Sajjad Hussain. 421 Getty Images: Michael Buckner. 432 ArcelorMittal: Himanshu Pahad. 433 Grupo Santander. 434 BHP Billiton. 435 BNP Paribas. 436 Newscast: British American Tobacco. 437 PA Photos: AP Photo/Susan Walsh. 438 Reuters: Lucy Nicholson. 439 Getty Images: Sean Gallup. 442 Getty Images: AFP/Stephane de Sakutin. 443 (c) Google Inc. Used with permission. 444 The Solomon R. Guggenheim Museum, New York: © SRGF, New York/David M. Heald. 445 H & M Hennes & Mauritz UK & Ireland. 446 Reuters: Paul Yeung. 447 Infosys Technologies. 448 Getty Images: AFP/Paco Serinelli. 449 Novozymes A/S. 452 Getty Images: Ralph Orlowski. 453 Rio Tinto. 454 SABMiller plc: Tom Stockill. 455 PA Photos: AP Photo/Kamran Jebreili. 456 Getty Images: Bill Pugliano. 457 Getty Images: AFP/Javier Soriano. 458 Getty Images: Ian Waldie. 459 Getty Images: Harold Cunningham. 462 Getty Images: AFP/Dibyangshu Sarkar. 463 Getty Images: AFP/Tim Sloan. 464 Getty Images: AFP/Pierre Verdy. 465 Xstrata

All other images © Dorling Kindersley. For further information see: www.dkimages.com
Every effort has been made to trace the copyright holders. The publisher apologizes for any unintentional omission and would be pleased, in such cases, to place an acknowledgment in future editions of this book.